AF473913

Dawn Ades

Writings on Art and Anti-Art

Dawn Ades

Writings on Art and Anti-Art

Edited by Doro Globus

Ridinghouse

Contents

Dawn Ades in conversation with Doro Globus

DORO GLOBUS This is a book of your collected writings, but it also represents a long curatorial career. Before we discuss some of the exhibitions specifically, I wondered if you could talk about how you view the relationship between curating and writing for yourself and for your progression?

DAWN ADES Yes, I think it goes back to the very beginning of my career as an art historian because my PhD dissertation was going to be on the relationship between word and image in the Surrealist magazines and Surrealist reviews. Before I could finish that, I was asked to be the primary person responsible for the catalogue of a really big exhibition at the Hayward Gallery, *Dada and Surrealism Reviewed*, that took place in 1978. The idea of the exhibition was to place Surrealism within the intellectual, political and historical contexts that its reviews, or magazines, provided. That was my first experience of curating and, perhaps, also one of the most important. I wasn't the only person involved in that exhibition. I was very much a junior member of a very impressive team.

DC When you were invited to be on the curatorial team, were you asked at the same time to write for the catalogue?

DA I was invited to join the curatorial team because of a little book I had published in the Thames & Hudson *Dolphin* series in 1974 on Dada and Surrealism – it originally cost 95 pence with 62 colour

illustrations! David Sylvester, who was one of the leaders of the team, had read and liked the book, and he asked me to join them. Then we discussed the structure of the exhibition and our idea was to use the reviews as the framework. The very clever title was found by Alan Bowness, then director of the Tate Gallery. I think the catalogue was discussed as the exhibition developed and it became clear that it should reflect the structure of the exhibition and that it should have a section on each major magazine or group of magazines.

DG What do you think you achieved through the writing that can't be achieved through curating in general? You often write very substantial texts that go along with exhibitions that you've helped curate.

DA I've been lucky in that I've had opportunities to curate exhibitions in my specialist fields and published much of my research in the accompanying catalogues. This may be one of the differences between the academy and museums, for art historians. If you are based in a museum or gallery, you probably have to be more of a generalist and work on exhibitions across a wide range of periods and subjects, as well as dealing with other issues such as acquisitions, conservation, loans, regular displays and so on. It is less likely that you can devote several years to research on one particular topic, as one can in a university. Teaching a course based on current research and sharing ideas in seminars can be tremendously fruitful. (The trend towards separating teaching from research in universities is disastrous, but that is a different subject.)

But then an exhibition – rather than just a monograph – is often an ideal way to realise, to test, if you like, one's research and ideas. It brings one into direct contact with the objects, something academic art historians sometimes lack. I am interested in making an argument work visually, bringing out some – not necessarily the only – aspect of an object by working with the specific spatial/visual character of an exhibition. It's also possible to test or to challenge exhibitions by asking them to translate one form of expression into another – a magazine into an exhibition, as we did with *Undercover Surrealism* for example.

Looking back I think some of the most interesting dialogues have been when the research and ideas have run in parallel with, and may amplify, but not just explain, the exhibition. Catalogues should have a life beyond the exhibition, present an argument and stand in their own right. I have in mind the essay for the Francis Bacon exhibition at the Tate (pp.213–42), in which I introduced the ideas of Georges Bataille as a way of understanding the violence of the paintings. Or the essays for the Hayward exhibition *Art and Power: Europe under the Dictators 1930–1945*: a huge and difficult subject, which had to be condensed and clarified for the exhibition (pp.89–106). I suppose many of the exhibitions I've curated or co-curated have been ideas-led, and come out of long-term research interests: *Dalí's Optical Illusions*, for instance, or *Dalí and Mythology*, which I curated with Fiona Bradley for Tate Liverpool, or *Undercover Surrealism: Georges Bataille and Documents*, with Simon Baker at the Hayward Gallery. In the case of *Dada and Surrealism Reviewed*, the catalogue devoured my PhD (which was therefore never completed as such). It's also worth noting the dramatic differences in exhibition catalogues over the last 50 years or so. They were quite modest and rarely had masses of full-page colour illustrations.

DG You mentioned the *Art and Power* exhibition as an example of bringing together research, curating and writing. How did you specifically approach this complicated topic?

DA In 1995 I was one of a team invited by the Council of Europe to address the still sensitive topic of art during the 1930s and through the Second World War, when much of the continent was under the control of totalitarian dictatorships: Hitler, Stalin, Mussolini and Franco. The essay 'Art as Monument' appeared in the catalogue for the resulting exhibition at the Hayward Gallery, *Art and Power: Europe Under the Dictators 1930–1945*. The Council of Europe had overseen other very inclusive exhibition projects, like *Tendenzen der zwanziger Jahre* (Trends of the 1920s, Berlin, 1977). For this subject it was felt that only the UK could generate the exhibition because of its historical position: it had not been subject to totalitarian rule during the 1930s nor to invasion during the war. The first iteration of the exhibition focused on modern art of the 1930s and the artists who mostly went into exile: it was to have started with Beckmann's triptych *Departure*, and ended with Picasso's *Charnel House*. But the Council of Europe wanted the exhibition to examine the role of art under the fascist and Nazi dictatorships, and in the Stalinist Soviet Union: not the modernist art that was censored but the art that was supported by the regimes. The title 'Art and Power' indicates both the power of the state that could command the service of artists, architects and sculptors, but also the perception of the power of art itself, distorted as this became.

DG How do you think the discipline of Art History has changed since you were a student?

DA It was a very interesting time to become an art historian, in the 1960s, as the way the subject could or should be studied was constantly questioned, and indeed what the subject itself was. For instance the social history of art, and feminist art history, were asking questions about methodology, theory and looking beyond the canon. But the biggest difference between then and now is the attitude to contemporary art. There seemed to be a gulf between the 'modern art' we were studying and what was happening in the studios and galleries – far fewer of the latter in those days. Not that we weren't interested in what was going on, but it seemed to be the domain of critics, not historians. I wanted originally to write my thesis on Jackson Pollock but was told that this was too recent a subject. It's totally different today – by far the most popular courses in History of Art departments are contemporary art or art since the 1960s. That's where students begin. There weren't courses on curating, gallery studies and so on either.

Very early on I was shocked by the narrowness of the subject as we studied it at the Courtauld – not a single artist from Latin America, for example. That was the beginning of a major strand in my research, which led to the exhibition at the Hayward Gallery in 1989, *Art in Latin America: The Modern Era, 1820–1980*.

DG What first drew you to Surrealism and what sustained your interest over time?

DA I read English at Oxford and was a rather literary person, in a way. Then I went to the Courtauld in London to work on the notion of satire from the visual and verbal point of view in the eighteenth century. There, I fell in with the modern world sort of suddenly, which was wonderful. I worked with the artist and art historian John Golding who was fabulous; everybody else was doing Renaissance in those days – this is 1965–67 – and he suggested that I work on Jean (Hans) Arp because he knew I was interested in Dada and Surrealism. I looked at Arp as a poet and as an artist for my MA thesis. I looked at Arp's work in the context of the Dada magazines where he is present as a poet and as a visual artist, and then I got interested in the magazines in their own right. I thought, 'Wow, these are extraordinary things!' That's where it really began – with Arp.

DG Throughout your career you have been trying to break down the specific discourse surround Surrealism. In your writings on the subject, how did you further open up the discussion?

DA As an art historian who is not really theory-led at all, I do care a great deal about various contextual issues as well as, in a sense, theoretical ones. Surrealism and Dada – they tend to be decoupled nowadays, but they were very much coupled in those days, at the time that I was working on the 1978 exhibition. Surrealism has been a primary focus for my research, and I always felt the need to look at it as a whole. In a way Surrealist painters had got detached from the ideas that were so important for Surrealism – so, for me, writing about the ideas and setting the painters in the context of the magazines was really important.

I was and am so interested in the way that the magazines actually do provide a collective voice – I should say, a collective with different voices – and those voices have different sorts of interests that sometimes conflict with each other. When you read the Surrealist journals like the first one, *La Révolution surréaliste*, you immediately

learn that they're fascinated by Freud, but that they're not really interested in psychoanalysis. That's immediately setting up an issue that one would want to look at. There's the whole question of visual expression in the first issue, somebody writes about how, actually, there's a problem with the visual in the context of Surrealism. Then you've got politics, which enters into it as well, and poetry. I really wanted to make all these different possibilities of interest to people.

DG You, of course, write on a wide range of subjects but Surrealism underlies a lot of your work; you always seem to find a new approach, what keeps you coming back?

DA Well, I'm glad if it seems that I do. Sometimes I worry that I'm circling round and round the same problems all the time, which, I think, I am in a way. But – I find Surrealism endlessly interesting. When I was an undergraduate at the Courtauld, Surrealism was quite marginalised. In the 1960s it was hardly even seen as part of modern art. It wasn't taken seriously or, at least, it didn't fit. When people started trying to fit it, it was with the mistaken idea that there was something called 'Surrealist art'. I became more and more convinced that one needed to persuade people that each artist has had to negotiate their own relationship with Surrealism because there's no set rule of how to be a Surrealist artist. It is not an 'ism' in that sense. There is no such thing as a 'Surrealist style', something I go on about quite a lot, most recently in the essay on Surrealism and dreams. It's ideas, and the artists found their own solutions to the problem of automatism; the problem of the dream and so on. I think the fact that there's not a stylistic continuity within Surrealism makes it an oddity in the context of the classic history of modern art.

DG You are still finding strands to explore within this rich topic. Two recent texts concern Surrealism and dreams ('Dreams in Surrealist Discourse') and Surrealist female photographers ('One Hundred Percent Photographic'). How do these work in the context of the older texts?

DA You could almost say that Surrealism's hybridity and the things that made it so uneasy a subject in modernism have turned out to be a strength today. Style, which there isn't in Surrealism, is no longer the way we approach art. The push to uncover overlooked female artists has been especially fruitful for Surrealism, and the LACMA (Los Angeles County Museum of Art) exhibition of women Surrealist photographers – *In Wonderland: The Surrealist Adventures of Women Artists in Mexico and the United States* in 2012 – was an eye-opener. And photography – only recently admitted into Tate's collection – was a major mode of expression for the Surrealists.

DC You also approach subjects through looking at different uses of media and unpacking categories like in 'Why Film?' (pp.475–96) and 'Camera Creation' (pp.543–69), and also general changes in photography from the beginning to the 1960s. Why do you view the introduction of new media as a good topic for artists and, later, art historians?

DA I think it's partly because of the way that the opening up of possibilities in terms of medium for artists seemed to me to go back to Dada and Surrealism. It wasn't restricted to painting; it wasn't restricted to working in bronze or iron or whatever it might be. It could really be anything. It seems that was one of the key things that contemporary artists – artists of my generation and subsequent ones – had found so interesting. Not that they necessarily felt themselves indebted to Surrealism otherwise, but it was the idea that pretty well anything can be used as a medium.

DC Art was changing and more possibilities were opening up for artists like Joseph Cornell and later John Stezaker, who are using ephemera, some of which is from that time period. Stezaker's postcards and film stills are relics of a peak time in cinema history and Cornell was selecting found objects and putting it all together.

DA That's right, the gradual dissolution of the notions that skill in one particular medium was the key criterion for becoming a great artist; that you had to master the difficult technique; that you had

to be able to use it to its utmost advantage. Then there were people who basically were working in a completely different way with a medium. Let's say that many weren't actually exploring the medium – for instance the medium of photography as such, but they were exploring one of its products, if you like – one of its by-products in the case of Stezaker. And, in the case of Cornell it was anything, really, from feathers to broken wine glasses, to old maps and photocopying.

DG You continue to write on photomontage past and present, and have recently co-curated an exhibition on Hannah Höch. Can you discuss how your early *Photomontage* publication for the *World of Art* series came about (pp.35–66)? What drew you to the topic and what resulted from the book?

DA The idea for a book on this topic came about in conversation with my editor at Thames & Hudson, Nikos Stangos. He was organising the *World of Art* series and had created a book I contributed to – *Concepts of Modern Art: From Fauvism to Postmodernism*. He had been poetry editor at Penguin, and was really a huge influence on writing about modern art. He was determined to make it accessible to a wide audience. Photomontage was a great subject as it cut across isms and it was also very timely. During a panel discussion recently at the Whitechapel Gallery in London (2014), the artist Linder told me how important the book was for her and other artists in the 1970s. Photomontage seems to be a practice that is constantly renewable.

DG On the topic of medium, I think that is also part of why the Francis Bacon and Richard Deacon (pp.173–79) texts are very interesting in the context of the book – not only because they're more contemporary artists, but because they're two artists who are very much associated with very traditional forms of art making – painting and sculpture. Did you find these texts more challenging or are they an extension of your territory?

DA I did find them more difficult than the other texts because I

wasn't sure where I stood in relation to each artist. They were artists whose work I really liked and with whom I'd spoken a lot. It wouldn't have been appropriate to situate them in relation to Surrealism in a straightforward way, which tended to be the road along which I travelled, so this was definitely a deviation, for me. It was more difficult and I really wasn't at all sure that I've managed anything in either case, but I was very pleased when Francis Bacon wrote me this lovely letter after he read the text, he said: 'I know how almost impossible it is to write about painting but you have conveyed so much I want and try to do in my work.' So that was nice. It is a text I would probably not write in the same way now.

DG Why not?

DA It seemed to me that what Bataille was doing in *Documents* was an extreme form of challenging a conventional idea of the human – what it is to be human. Apart from the basic argument about Bacon and Bataille that really chimed with Bacon's idea about being in the world, I think I possibly wrote more about paintings that had a kind of literary connection than might be healthy for the essay.

DG You worked on the Bacon exhibition at the Tate Gallery in 1985 as well, but you would not have been the obvious choice?

DA I wouldn't have been an obvious choice, no. Some of the exhibitions that I have most enjoyed and most benefited from, are where I have been allowed to both write in the catalogue and be involved in curating – in this case I worked very closely with curators Richard Francis and David Sylvester. David was very brilliant and very thoughtful in terms of how he put people – artists and curators – together and that was great for me.

DG You mentioned that with Bacon and Deacon you had the opportunity to meet them and to speak about the work. You actually met Dalí and Man Ray in a time when, perhaps, art historians were further distanced from artists.

DA I did meet with Dalí when I was a student. I just went down to Port Lligat in Spain and knocked on the door. I was given admittance and he said, 'Come and sit and talk to me while I paint.' So I said, 'Okay!' He was painting a very, very large picture called *The Hallucinogenic Toreador* (1968–70), which he was halfway through. I didn't really know a great deal about his work at the time. I didn't even know about the paranoiac critical double images, which he told me all about and he demonstrated how you can see this double image in that painting. I spent a whole day talking to him. We spoke in a mixture of French, Spanish and English and then he said that he really enjoyed the conversation which was basically a monologue. But he said, 'Well, come back tonight. Bring your husband', because we were staying nearby, 'Come and ask me intelligent questions. I will introduce you to my intellectual Catalan friends and we will have a soirée.' So we went back and there was indeed his circle of local friends, and he was completely different because he had put on his public persona. In the studio he was extremely straightforward and friendly and normal, but in the evening he had waxed his moustaches and got his cane and put on this show. It was very interesting to see the double image of Dalí.

DG Did you see him again?

DA Well, I didn't, I wish I had. He said, 'Will you come and see me in Paris?', but I never did. I got sort of sidetracked. And then I was asked to write the book about Dalí because, don't forget in those days he wasn't popular among the art historians because of his break with Surrealism, because of his apparent friendship with Franco, because he seemed to have these right-wing connections (which I wasn't fully aware of when I went to see him), and because his painting was seen as wholly regressive, trying to revive a dead tradition. I defended him against the common view that he was just a showman or that he was taking advantage of everyone or that he was imposing a fake image on his own artistic identity, and so on and so forth. So I agreed to do the book, but he didn't like the idea of a book in a series (the *World of Art* series) and he wasn't on very good terms with Thames & Hudson, and so I just didn't keep up the connection, which I regret, actually, very much now.

DC What other doors did you knock on?

DA I met Dorothea Tanning, but not Max Ernst, who was ill at the time. Man Ray was another knock on the door – oh no, I think I actually prepared that one a little bit better. He was living in Paris, he was quite the reverse of Dalí. It was curious given that Man Ray was so celebrated as a photographer, it is hard to imagine that he was really quite poverty-stricken in his latter years. Also, that he only wanted to be remembered as a painter and wasn't really so interested in photography. He didn't want to talk about photography. He wanted to talk about his recent paintings and we talked a bit about the old days.

DC Did you ever work full time in a museum?

DA No, I was always the outside art historian. Looking back, I've been really, really fortunate, I think, in having been allowed to work on some of these major exhibitions. The Cornell exhibition at MOMA (1980) was very much a museum show and it gave me access to the museum protocol – the museum habits, which have been very interesting.

DC Did you ever think, 'Oh, actually, I would like to work for a museum?'

DA Why, yes, I suppose I would have quite liked that... I would have liked to work with a permanent collection, but I've never done that. I got very close to the Art Institute of Chicago when I was invited to write the catalogue for the Bergmans' Surrealist gift (*Surrealist Art: The Lindy and Edwin Bergman Collection at the Art Institute of Chicago,* 1997). I was able to work closely with the conservators, which was fantastic because I have a very strong interest in materials, and in how things are made.

DG Your enthusiasm for materials comes out when you read these texts together – you look at magazines, posters, installations, film, photography in relation to art of a specific period as well as artists who use such materials.

DA Yes, and this points in so many different directions. Avant-garde artists started working in photography and film during the 1920s, though the relationship between these new modes of representation and art goes back a long way. Making them a new medium for experiment may seem so obvious now but was a challenge at the time, and also helped to break down the division between art and popular culture. The Dada and the Surrealist magazines included photographs of all kinds: scientific, sex, pin-ups, etc. Then there is the physical importance of medium for artists labelled as conceptual. Materials, for instance, are an important element for an artist that I really have thought about a lot, Marcel Duchamp: the other side of his activity is actually the making. He was fascinated by the ways materials can be worked with and what they can do, and by slightly old-fashioned processes, old-fashioned techniques like *pochoir* for making prints. He used this in his *La Boîte-en-valise* (Box in a Suitcase, 1935–41).

DG You have often approached themes or periods that have been under-researched, one crucial example was the exhibition *Art in Latin America* in 1989. At the time, this really wasn't an area that was being discussed. How did you become interested in art in Latin America?

DA It was entirely a function of the job at the University of Essex. It was a young university at the time, founded in 1964. I was part of the Department of Art but there was no making, no Fine Art. The art department was within the structure of our School of Comparative Studies so there were departments on the one hand, and then there were area studies – one of the areas was Latin American studies. Each department had to offer courses that would be relevant to the area of study – so, one day (this is shortly after I joined part-time in 1968) the question arose: who was going to

teach Latin American art? Well, I said I would. It was acknowledged from the beginning it was going to be a learning process; I was learning as I taught. That was very exciting. I took one or two major fieldwork trips to Latin America in the early 1970s with my camera because, in those days, there was very little published. So it began very specifically in the Essex context.

DC And so was it your idea to do that exhibition?

DA No; well, partly. A friend of mine at the Hayward Gallery, Andrew Dempsey, who was also very interested in Latin America, wanted the Hayward to do a Latin American show. He knew I was teaching Latin American art and we started talking about it and he said, 'There's a quincentenary – a five-hundredth anniversary – 1492, of Columbus. So there would be lots of exhibitions about Latin America. I want to get in ahead – so let's do it in 1989 before anybody else.' I wanted to call it *Art in Latin America since Independence*, but people said, 'Nobody in the UK has the faintest idea what independence means', despite being a great colonial power. I started travelling there in 1986 to various countries. My first trip was to Buenos Aires for an ICOM (International Council of Museums) meeting where I, luckily, met a lot of people who were going to be absolutely crucial to the development of that exhibition. Although it may look as if I was the sole curator, I had a tremendous amount of support and help from a lot of museum people and art historians within Latin America. I was looking at it from the outside, which is a reasonable criticism, but it really *had* to be somebody from the outside, not least if one was trying to cover the whole continent. Most of the countries in Latin America were quite nationalistic but not that interested, at least culturally, in the concept of Latin America – you could say that it was an outsider concept, but this is isn't wholly fair. Latin America as a term, a concept, originated, like 'nuestra America', our America, from within, in opposition to the United States of America.

DC How was the exhibition received?

DA **Not well at all; people couldn't get it. I remember one review in *The Guardian*, I think, said that there was only one interesting painter in the exhibition. It's a different approach; it is not art that all comes out of Cézanne, which is basically how we're trained to see things. I included a lot of popular art, which seemed to me very important, also prints and photography; I even included some pre-Columbian things because I wanted the importance of the rediscovery of pre-Columbian art in the nineteenth century, and especially after the Mexican Revolution, to be recognised. People came, to an extent. It had serious interest from art historians. I think it encouraged some people with their interest in Latin American art, but it wasn't a huge popular success – let's put it that way.**

DG It is amazing how much has changed since then; for instance, the Tate has a Latin American art curator and an acquisitions programme. You must be very happy with this new attitude?

DA **Oh yes. It's wonderful. I feel slightly antiquated – dinosaur-like. There has been a more general shift within art and the history of art towards the contemporary. People start there rather than starting in a former age; this has happened with Latin America. The region has benefited hugely from this because so many of the most impressive artists today are from Latin America. It has been a wonderful coincidence, which I'm fascinated by – although I didn't include those artists in that exhibition because I stopped in 1980!**

DG In one of your texts, 'Orbits of the Savage Moon' (pp.395–413), you look at identity while travelling from Mexico to Paris, you explore Surrealism and Dada as well as femininity and masculinity. It seems like this text represents your territory very well – it's not Latin American art here and so-called Western art *there* but you are bringing everything together in the work of a single artist.

DA **I hope that's the case. One is trying to point out the fact that it's a two-way route. It's not just Latin America in debt to Europe. There's a constant crossover and what's happening there is not completely**

detached from everything else. I find the Mexican painter María Izquierdo, who is the focus of that essay, completely fascinating – an extraordinary artist. I would like to do more on her and the whole question of women artists in Latin America and feminist movements, because there was a lot going on in the 1930s and 1940s. I mean, many of the things I've written about I would like to go further with but then get distracted and do some-thing else.

DG I was going to ask you about identity, feminism and gender roles, as these issues are often topics or underlying principles in your texts. I don't think you take a stereotypical feminist approach, but you do look at the territory.

DA **Yes, I think it's true; I probably should be a more precise feminist. But I also find myself constantly having to defend some of the victims, if you like, of feminist attitudes.**

DG It's such a good approach because you really look at the person.

DA **I'm glad you say that because it's becoming more and more of an issue, it seems to me, that, if you are looking at questions of identity and, through that, questions of gender – it's quite difficult to do so without actually becoming quite biographical as well. I suppose, on the one hand, I've always been resistant to the idea that there's such a thing as a 'woman artist'. I don't see why that should make the slightest difference. On the other hand... it does, or can do!**

DG You found questions surrounding biography to be a challenge when looking at Hannah Höch recently when you were curating the retrospective exhibition at the Whitechapel Gallery in 2014?

DA **Yes, very much so; there's a question on how relevant it is to talk about her bisexuality. I don't know; it's an open question. There are art historians who say, well, one should only address the work. Her sexuality has nothing to do with the nature of the artist. That's what I've been thinking about – how justified one would be in looking**

at some – particularly some of those Dada-period photomontages, and the later ones from the 1930s, in terms of her life and her partnerships, first with Raoul Hausmann then with the novelist and poet Til Brugman. I think her work is extremely important as a critique of gender stereotypes, from her personal experience.

DG From your point of view, do you think the art world has become any more equal?

DA Yes, the attitudes have changed and I've experienced this a lot. The identity question seemed to be quite an abstract question for a long time, in a sense, to do with race and gender and so on. For me it has become more and more a pressing personal question with the artists I have been working on and I'm not sure whether that's a good thing.

DG That's why the 'Surrealism, Male-Female' (pp.371–93) text is so interesting because you are turning it, in a way. You are taking the notion of being anti-female and looking at females who are actually part of the movement; you are not taking the straightforward or expected route. Was that approach controversial at the time?

DA Yes, I think it was. But I was also partly defending the Surrealists against the idea that they were just misogynists and a boys' club and trying to say, actually, it's more complicated than that. That's what I was doing.

DG Two of the texts in this volume show another side of your writing, they are in-depth historical approaches: 'Function and Abstraction in Poster Design' (pp.113–58) and 'Little Things: Close-Up in Photo and Film 1839–1963' (pp.511–41). Do you think that they say as much about history, urbanity and nationality as they do about visual culture? How do you balance this approach?

DA I do think I function more naturally as a historian, although I don't want to separate it. I'm very, very interested in certain

particular historical questions. I enjoy doing research of the kind that will, hopefully, uncover other things because I think it is important to understand the history of a given subject. But at the same time I think I do approach it as an art historian as opposed to a historian; I think there is a difference. What people nowadays call 'a pictorial turn in history' is historians looking to the visual and using it as part of their arguments; I think they do so in order to use the visual as evidence. I think art historians by contrast start with the image or the object or whatever it is, and then ask questions about it.

I suppose, for me, it is a matter of trying to understand what particular factors – what particular dynamics – affect the way something is produced and the way it is received and the way it is presented; what one can deduce about its public significance.

DC Your approach is also about how art is being used.

DA How art is being used – yes, that's right. Why, if you like, it's important to have the visual in these particular contexts. I mean, what does that add? What is it that art is able to do that other things can't do? What sort of function do they happen to have at this particular moment, and why, and what are the possibilities for it, and how is it being exploited and why? I approach it as an art historian and a historian and assume that there are always other ways of telling it. There are many different ways of telling. You can't say, 'Oh, this is the truth', but you can say, 'These are some of the things that you might consider when you think about that object.'

DC Reading the texts together for this book, six very strong themes arose for both of us: Art and Power, Abstraction, Surrealism, Gender and Identity, Dalí, and the Photographic Image. Was this unexpected for you?

DA Yes, it was – very unexpected. I really wasn't expecting abstraction to come out quite so much as an interest. It's not always just because it is apparently in opposition to Dada or Surrealism. I think I have an

interest in it partly through medium – I mean, that's one of the ways that it's come to the fore.

DG It is funny because that was our first organising principle for the book and then, when we read the texts again, even though there's one dominant topic – maybe two – per text, you do touch on almost all of them in each text and so it became a very interesting web.

DA **Well, that's right. Like cards – you can throw them up and they'll come down in different groupings.**

Art and Power

Grouped here are three essays concerned in different ways with the relationship between art and power. The title is from the exhibition *Art and Power: Europe Under the Dictators 1930–1945* which I helped to curate in 1995 at the Hayward Gallery in London; the text 'Art as Monument' was one of my contributions to the catalogue. It took as its starting point the 1937 Paris Exhibition at which the German and Russian Pavilions confronted each other symbolically. The pavilion of the Spanish Republic defied the looming Franco victory with spectacular modernist art by, among others, Joan Miró, Alexander Calder and Pablo Picasso with his giant painting *Guernica* (1937). 'Art and Power' indicates both the power of the state that could command the service of artists, architects and sculptors, but also the perception of the power of art itself, distorted as this became.

I have always found it interesting that there was no unity about this in the historic avant gardes. Both Dada and Constructivism, for example, argued the case from opposite positions. Under the same banner-name, Dada, there were at least two completely opposed responses to the First World War, the revolutions and the political turmoil that engulfed Europe. On the one hand, Dada in (neutral) Zurich and in occupied Cologne asserted its autonomy and its interest in aesthetics as a form of protest (even if in apparently non-art forms, experimenting with chance and abstraction and what is now known as assemblage). 'While the guns thundered in the distance, we pasted, we recited, we versified, we sang with all our soul. We searched for an elementary art...'[1] Dada in Berlin, however, engaged directly with the war, German militarism, the street and the media: 'The highest art will be that which in its conscious content presents the thousand-fold problems of the day, that art which has been visibly shattered by the explosions of the last week, which is forever trying to collect its limbs after yesterday's crash.'[2] What was being described here would not have qualified as 'art' in its conventional forms. Out of this idea in Berlin Dada emerged 'photomontage'.

1 Jean (Hans) Arp, 'Dadaland', *XXe Siècle*, no.1, 1938.

2 Richard Huelsenbeck, *En Avant Dada: A History of Dadaism* (1920) in Robert Motherwell (ed), *The Dada Painters and Poets*, Wittenborn, Schultz, New York, NY, 1951, p.40.

Whether art is, could or should be autonomous are age-old questions, long debated by critics and philosophers as well as artists. The ways art has been written about recently often give the impression that modern art mostly asserted its independence from and distaste for religion and politics, and has not been much interested in questions of social responsibility. This, though, is from a European perspective and is manifestly untrue of much of the art from Latin America in the twentieth century. For some, the power of art resides in its autonomy; for others, art can only have meaning when it is engaged directly with the world, with politics in a narrow sense or ideologies in a broader one.

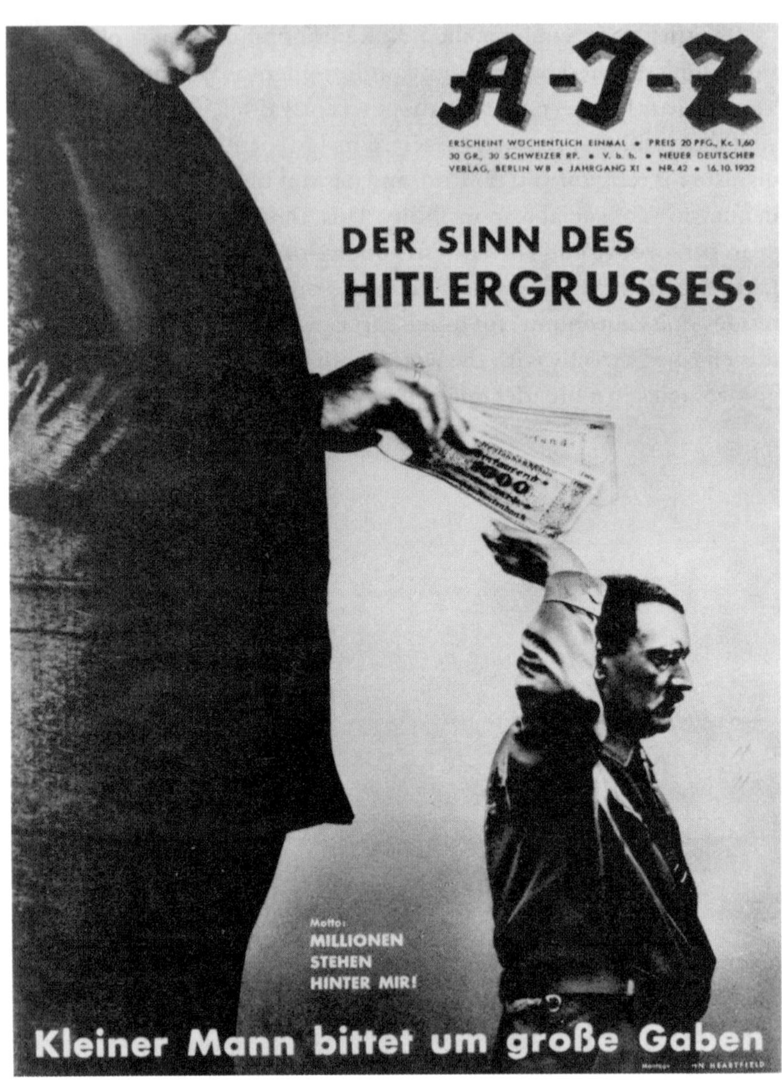

34 **John Heartfield**
Millionen stehen hinter mir! (Millions Stand Behind Me!)
Cover of *AIZ*, 16 October 1932

Photomontage

Introduction to *Photomontage*, Dawn Ades (ed), Thames & Hudson, London, 1976

Introduction

Manipulation of the photograph is as old as photography itself. Fox Talbot's 'photogenic drawing', one of the earliest photographic processes, developed during the 1830s, involved the direct contact printing of leaves, ferns, flowers, drawings, and was rediscovered and put to use with an almost infinite repertoire of objects by Man Ray, Christian Schad and László Moholy-Nagy in their 'photograms' of the 1920s. Double exposures, 'spirit photographs' (sometimes the outcome of an unexpected result when an old collodion plate was imperfectly cleaned and the previous image dimly appeared on the picture), double printing and composite photographs are all enthusiastically discussed in popular nineteenth-century books on 'photographic amusements' and trick photography. Cutting out and reassembling photographic images belonged on the whole to the realm of popular diversions – comic postcards, photograph albums, screens and military mementoes.

The term 'photomontage', however, was not invented until just after the First World War, when the Berlin Dadaists needed a name to describe their new technique of introducing photographs into their works. (The Futurist painter Carlo Carrà and the Suprematist Kasimir Malevich had already used photographs, but as isolated examples, not, as with the Dadaists, more than one photograph or parts of photographs combined.) The word gained currency, therefore, in the context of an art (or anti-art) movement. The name was chosen with rare unanimity by the Berlin Dadaists, although they were later to dispute its exact historical origins within their own group. 'Seized with an innovatory zeal', Raoul Hausmann wrote, 'I also needed a name for this technique, and in agreement with George Grosz, John Heartfield, Johannes Baader, and Hannah Höch, we decided to call these works *photomontages*. This term translates our aversion at playing the artist, and, thinking of ourselves as engineers (hence our preference for workmen's overalls) we meant to construct, to assemble [*montieren*] our works.'[1] *Montage* in German means 'fitting' or 'assembly line', and *monteur* 'mechanic', 'engineer' or fitter. John Heartfield, perhaps the best-known practitioner of photomontage, was known as the Monteur Heartfield by the Dadaists, not simply because of his photomontages, but in recognition of an attitude, which they all shared, towards their work and its relation to existing artistic hierarchies.

The Berlin Dadaists used the photograph as a readymade image, pasting it together with cuttings from newspapers and magazines, lettering and drawing to form a chaotic, explosive image, a provocative dismembering of reality. From being one element among several, the photograph became dominant in Dada pictures, for which it was peculiarly effective and appropriate material. Its use was part of the Dadaists' reaction against oil painting, which is essentially unrepeatable, private and exclusive. Photomontage belonged to the technological world, the world of mass communication and photomechanical reproduction. When Hannah Höch said of photomontage: 'Our whole purpose was to integrate objects from the world of machines and industry in the world of art',[2] I think she meant it in the sense that the materials of photomontage, particularly newspaper photographs and newsprint, were made by mechanical processes, as well as in the iconographical sense. The Russian Constructivists were to value photomontage for very similar reasons. There was also a close connection between Dada photomontage and the Dada poetry of, for instance, Jean (Hans) Arp, Tristan Tzara and Kurt Schwitters, which involved the random use of sentences from newspapers, scraps of conversation and clichés out of context, words wrenched from their normal associations.

When Dada photomontage was invented it was within the context of, although in opposition to, collage. The name was chosen, clearly, to

1 Raoul Hausmann, *Courrier Dada*, Le Terrain vague, Paris, 1958, author's translation, p.42.
2 Quoted in Van Deren Coke, *The Painter and the Photograph*, University of New Mexico Press, Albuquerque, NM, 1972, p.259.

distance the two activities, and Dada recognised a very different potential in the new technique. Louis Aragon, in his essay of 1923 on Max Ernst's collages and photomontages, sees a fundamental difference between Ernst's works and Cubist collage: 'For the Cubists, the postage stamp, the newspaper, the box of matches that the painter sticks on to his pictures, have the value of a test, an instrument of control of the reality itself of the picture... With Max Ernst it is quite different... collage with him becomes a poetic procedure, completely opposite in its ends to Cubist collage, whose intention is purely realist.'[3] In a later essay, 'La peinture au défi' (1930), Aragon distinguishes between the two quite distinct categories of collage: the first is that in which the stuck element is of value for its representational qualities, the second for its material qualities. In the second, he suggests, collage operates only as an enrichment of the palette, while the first is prophetic of the direction it is to take, 'where the thing expressed is more important than the manner of expressing it, where the object represented plays the role of a word'[4] – the direction taken by Ernst.

While Ernst, who explicitly distanced himself from Berlin Dada, moved in one direction, away from Cubist collage, Richard Huelsenbeck, who returned to Berlin from Zurich in 1917, had found that Dada in Zurich pushed collage further in the Cubist direction:

> With the new medium, the picture, which as such remains always the symbol of an unattainable reality, has literally taken a decisive step forward, that is, it has taken an enormous step from the horizon across the foreground; it participates in life itself. The sand, pieces of wood, hair that have been pasted on, give it the same kind of reality as a statue of the idol Moloch, in whose glowing arms child sacrifices are laid. The new medium is the road from yearning to the reality of little things, and this road is abstract.[5]

Huelsenbeck here criticises the Zurich Dadaists for not taking the logical step – which, in fact, Marcel Duchamp had already taken in his

3 Louis Aragon, 'Max Ernst, peintre des illusions', in *Les Collages*, Hermann, Paris, 1965, author's translation, p.29.

4 Aragon, 'La peinture au défi', *op. cit.*, p.44, author's translation.

5 Richard Huelsenbeck, 'En avant Dada', in Robert Motherwell (ed), *The Dada Painters and Poets*, Wittenborn, Schultz, New York, NY, 1951.

'readymades' – of advancing 'along the abstract road, which ultimately leads from the painted surface to the reality of the post-office form'. The Berlin Dadaists never took this step either; they were diverted from these predominantly aesthetic and philosophical questions by the desire for a more direct and political form of expression. Like Ernst, though with a different intention, they introduced photographs into collages to emphasise the signifying role of the found image; theirs was, perhaps, a shift, a choice in yet another direction, from Duchamp's readymade to the already seen.

There is little general agreement over the definition of photomontage among artists and historians; the word does not appear in the Oxford English Dictionary. The Penguin English Dictionary gives 'composite picture made from several photographs; art or process of making this'. The word has tended recently to be used more in connection with photographic processes, with darkroom techniques like printing from two or more different negatives (the 'combination printing' of the nineteenth century), than with cutting up and reassembling photographs, as in the original Dada photomontages. William Rubin, for example, in his catalogue to the 1968 exhibition *Dada, Surrealism and Their Heritage* at the Museum of Modern Art in New York, stated: 'The most significant contribution of the Berlin group was the elaboration of the so-called photomontage, actually a photo-collage, since the image was not montaged in the darkroom.'[6] Sergei Tretyakov, on the other hand, writing about John Heartfield in 1936, took a different position: 'It is important to note that a photomontage need not necessarily be a montage of photos. No: it can be photo and text, photo and colour, photo and drawing.'[7] And he quotes Heartfield himself in support: 'A photograph can, by the addition of an unimportant spot of colour, become a photomontage, a work of art of a special kind.' Although Heartfield is talking about additions to a single photograph and not of several photographs with additional elements, it is clear that it is not the technical process that

6 William Rubin, *Dada, Surrealism and their Heritage*, Museum of Modern Art, New York, NY, 1968, p.42.

7 Sergei Tretyakov, *John Heartfield*, OGIS State Publishing House, Moscow, 1936, quoted in Joanna Drew (ed), *John Heartfield, 1891–1968: Photomontages*, exhibition catalogue, Arts Council of Great Britain, London, 1969 p.15.

interests him, but the idea, the operation that transforms the meaning of the original photograph. The definitions of Rubin and Tretyakov are really different in kind, the first assuming that photomontage is a very specific technique, the second that it must signify in a particular way. Tretyakov goes on to say: 'If the photograph, under the influence of the text, expresses not simply the fact which it shows, but also the social tendency expressed by the fact, then this is already a photomontage.'[8]

Only in the 1930s did the different users of photomontage – on the one hand amateur and professional photographers experimenting in the darkroom, and on the other hand artists who turned to the photograph, for various reasons, as a readymade figurative element – become fully aware of each other. The 1931 edition of *Photographic Amusements*, first published in 1896, included an essay by Harry Potamkin mentioning and illustrating Moholy-Nagy, Man Ray and Francis Bruguière. Some of the illustrations in Marcel Natkin's *Fascinating Fakes in Photography* from 1939 show the unmistakable influence of Surrealist photomontage. Natkin describes in detail photomontage by cutout, by composition, by superposition (and superposition with mask), by superimpression, by combined superimpression and superposition, by repetition of a negative, by double printing and by combination, and also suggests, in a spirit belying the title of the book, that the ideal use of photomontage is dialectical and that above all the idea behind it must be clear.

My practice in compiling this book has been to include works 'when the imagery is predominantly photographic, whether collaged or rephotographed, rather than according to the technique'.[9] A few examples of photograms ('rayograms', 'schadographs') are also included, because, although not strictly photomontage, they can transform relationships between familiar objects, upset the scale, suggest strange spatial effects, in a way very similar to photomontage, although finally they have more to do with chance than has the latter.

8 *Ibid.*

9 Aaron Scharf, in a letter to the author. The book, *Photomontage*, was published by Thames & Hudson in large format in 1976, and a much expanded version in the Thames & Hudson *World of Art* series in 1986. This essay was the introduction to the original publication.

The Supremacy of the Message

1 DADA

The invention of photomontage among the Berlin Dadaists has been claimed on the one hand by Raoul Hausmann and Hannah Höch, and on the other by George Grosz and John Heartfield. Hausmann asserts that the germ of the idea was planted while he and Hannah Höch were on holiday in the summer of 1918 on the Baltic coast, where they saw in almost every house a framed coloured lithograph with the image of a soldier against a background of barracks. 'To make this military memento more personal, a photographic portrait had been stuck on in place of the head.' Hannah Höch has a more precise memory, recorded by Hans Richter in *Dada: Art and Anti-Art* (1965), of an 'oleograph of Kaiser Wilhelm II surrounded by ancestors, descendants, German oaks, medals and so on. Slightly higher up, but still in the middle, stood a young grenadier under whose helmet the face of their landlord, Herr Felten, was pasted in. There in the midst of his superiors stood the young soldier, erect and proud amid the pomp and splendour of this world. This paradoxical situation aroused Hausmann's perennial aggressive streak.'[10] Hausmann realised immediately that he could make pictures composed exclusively of cut-up photographs, and his excitement must have been due to the idea not just of a new technique, but of a technique in which the image would *tell* in a new way.

It was precisely this possibility that also interested Grosz. As he says in his rival statement, again quoted by Richter, about the origins of photomontage:

> In 1916, when Johnny Heartfield and I invented photomontage in my studio at the south end of the town at five o'clock one May morning, we had no idea of the immense possibilities, or of the thorny but successful career, that awaited the new invention. On a piece of cardboard we pasted a mishmash of advertisements for hernia belts, student song books and dog food, labels from schnapps and wine

10 Hans Richter, *Dada: Art and Anti-Art*, Thames & Hudson, London, 1965, p.117.

bottles, and photographs from picture papers, cut up at will in such a way as to say, in pictures, what would have been banned by the censors if we had said it in words. In this way we made postcards supposed to have been sent home from the Front, or from home to the Front. This led some of our friends, Tretyakov among them, to create the legend that photomontage was an invention of the 'anonymous masses'. What did happen was that Heartfield was moved to develop what started as an inflammatory political joke into a conscious artistic technique.[11]

Notwithstanding these interestingly different sources, the one in popular and comic arrangements of photographs, the other closer to collage, both Hausmann and Grosz seized on the possibilities of signification and on the subversive potential of the medium itself. This is how Hausmann was to describe it much later, in his lecture on the occasion of the first major exhibition of photomontage, in Berlin in 1931:

> People often assume that photomontage is only practicable in two forms: political propaganda and commercial publicity. The first photomonteurs, the Dadaists, started from the point of view, to them incontestable, that war-time painting, post-Futurist expressionism, had failed because of its non-objectivity and its absence of convictions, and that not only painting, but all the arts and their techniques needed a fundamental and revolutionary change, in order to remain in touch with the life of their epoch. The members of the Club Dada were naturally not interested in elaborating new aesthetic rules... But the idea of photomontage was as revolutionary as its content, its form as subversive as the application of the photograph and printed texts which, together, are transformed into a static film. Having invented the static, simultaneous and purely phonetic poem, the Dadaists applied the same principles to pictorial representation. They were the first to use photography as material to create, with the aid of structures that were very different, often anomalous and with antagonistic significance, a new entity which tore from the chaos of war and revolution an entirely new image; and they were aware that their

11 *Ibid.*

method possessed a propaganda power which their contemporaries had not the courage to exploit.[12]

Towards the end of the war Berlin was a half-starved nightmare city, and there was increasing social and political chaos; in 1918 Soviet Republics were briefly set up in several major German cities, including Berlin. Of the Berlin Dada Club, which included Huelsenbeck, Hausmann, Grosz, Wieland Herzfelde and his brother John Heartfield, Hannah Höch, Johannes Baader and, briefly, Franz Jung, only Herzfelde and Heartfield were founder members of the German Communist Party in 1918. But the group sided with the radical left wing against the middle-class republic of Friedrich Ebert and Philipp Scheidemann and, after the defeat of the November Revolution, through the early months of 1919, were vociferous in their opposition. They produced many periodicals, news-sheets and pamphlets, for which conventional layout was clearly inappropriate, and typographical anarchy began. Heartfield's collage advertisement in the periodical *Neue Jugend*, June 1917, combined letters, newsprint and pencil marks at all angles, like his later *Dada Photomontage* of 1919, though here additional photographic material is included. The catalogue of the 1969 photomontage exhibition at Kunstverein Ingolstadt states that Grosz and Heartfield first used photos in collage in 1919, and that the cover by Heartfield of the single issue of the illustrated paper *Jedermann sein eigner Fussball* (Every man his own football) – which is a brilliant parody of conservative layout – was the first dated Dada photomontage; the vignette at the top first juxtaposing two photographs to make a new whole.

In artistic terms, Dada's constant chosen enemy was Expressionism, and in singling out its inwardness and utopianism, and the emptiness of its rhetoric, Huelsenbeck, in the first *Dada Manifesto* of the Berlin group in 1918, called instead for an art 'which in its conscious content presents the thousandfold problems of the day, the art which has been visibly shattered by the explosions of last week, which is forever trying to collect its limbs after yesterday's crash. The best and most extraordinary artists will be those who every hour snatch the tatters of their bodies out of the frenzied cataract of life, who, with bleeding hands and hearts, hold fast

12 Hausmann, *op. cit.*, p.46, author's translation.

to the intelligence of their time.'[13] Photomontage perhaps comes closest to fulfilling Huelsenbeck's ideal. The visibly shattered surface of Grosz and Heartfield's *Dada-merika* (1919), or Heartfield's *Dada Photomontage*, is a truer image of a violent and chaotic society than, for example, *The Funeral of the Anarchist Galli* (1910–11), a painting by the Futurist Carrà. And in using the very stuff of today's and yesterday's news, Dada was beginning to subvert the voice of society itself. Grosz's montage *My Germany*, for the unpublished anthology *Dadaco* (1919), has some of the power of Heartfield's later work: Prussian soldiers are enthroned in the heart of a fat capitalist whose bland bald head sprouts snippets of the financial news. This is perhaps the first work to show the inglorious association of money and war, later to be a constant theme with Heartfield.

The *First International Dada Fair*, held in Berlin in 1920, included works by Arp, Francis Picabia and Ernst as well as by the Berlin group. The highlight of the fair, which led to prosecution, was the stuffed dummy dressed in a German officer's uniform with the head of a pig. But the stated theme was 'Art is dead! Long live the machine art of Tatlin!' The recurrent motif in the photomontages exhibited by Hausmann and Hannah Höch is the machine, yet their attitude to the machine is far from unambiguous. Beside Hausmann's *Dada Conquers* (1920), which proclaimed the world victory of Dada, hung *Tatlin at Home* (1920), demonstrating, apparently, the admiration and sympathy of the Berlin Dadaists for the new Production art in Russia. However, Hausmann stated in 1967 that this was an accidental, haphazard accumulation of images, rather than a planned affirmation of 'machine art' – of whose manifestations, if any, in Russia, they had only the haziest idea. Leafing through an American review, Hausmann had come across a photograph of a man, which, for no particular reason, 'automatically' reminded him of Tatlin. He was, however, more 'interested in showing the image of a man who only had machines in his head'. From this point, images were added to balance and expand this first idea: the dummy with soft, organic insides, the man turning out empty pockets ('Tatlin can't have been rich'), the boat's stern with screw propeller adding the final touch. As in *Dada Conquers,* the background is painted, a steeply receding, platform-like floor, which,

13 Huelsenbeck, in Motherwell, *op. cit.*, p.40.

together with other details and a certain oneiric quality, is reminiscent of the paintings of Giorgio de Chirico.

Hannah Höch's photomontage *Schnitt mit dem Küchenmesser Dada durch die letzte Weimarer Bierbauchkulturepoche Deutschlands* (Cut with the Dada Kitchen Knife through the last Weimar Beer Belly Cultural Epoch of Germany, 1919),[14] is considerably larger than those of Hausmann, Grosz or Heartfield. Cogs, wheels and other bits of machinery, street scenes and buildings are incorporated with heads and bodies, which are sometimes portraits of other Dadaists and are often grotesquely reassembled. Intricate details combine with dominant, startling images, all floating freely in space: another contrast with Hausmann's photomontages, where the preference is often for a distorted room-like pictorial space. Self-portraits are not uncommon with both Hausmann and Höch, whereas Heartfield rarely appears in his own works.

Raoul Hausmann's *ABCD (Self-portrait)* (1923–24) is like a swan song of Dada, a scrapbook of Dada activities. Hausmann himself, in a photograph that appears more than once in his photomontages, declaims one of his phonetic poems (*ABCD*), and has a wheel-like monocle drawn on his eye. Numbered tickets from the Kaiser's jubilee recall provocative interruptions of official ceremonies; the Merz ticket commemorates Hausmann's friendship with Schwitters; and the tiny scrap of map in the top right shows Harar, the town in Ethiopia where Arthur Rimbaud, Hausmann's favourite poet, acknowledged by Dada and Surrealism in general, lived after renouncing poetry. What is the birth to which Hausmann refers with the obstetric examination cut from the pages of a medical textbook – Dada itself?

Grosz and Herzfelde wrote in *Die Kunst ist in Gefahr* (Art is in Danger, 1925): 'Our mistake was to have concerned ourselves with art at all... We saw then the insane end-products of the prevailing social order, and burst out laughing... We did not yet see that a system underlay this insanity.'[15] It was precisely this system that Heartfield was to reveal and make comprehensible, the better to fight it.

14 See p.414 in this publication.

15 George Grosz and Wieland Herzfelde, *Die Kunst ist in Gefahr*, Malik Verlag, Berlin, 1925.

Photomontage was used increasingly by all political factions in Europe and Russia in the decades before the Second World War. During the Spanish Civil War montage posters were made for both Franco and the Republicans; the Italian Fascists under Mussolini also used it extensively. But it is not surprising that photomontage is associated particularly with the political Left, because it is ideally suited to the expression of the Marxist dialectic. It was undoubtedly used most brilliantly by John Heartfield, first against the Weimar Republic and then to chart the terrible rise of Fascism and the dictatorship of Hitler.

Disillusioned by art school in Munich, Heartfield had worked for a film company in Berlin from 1916. After Dada, he turned more or less exclusively to photomontage, working for the German Communist press and designing covers and illustrations for books published by Malik Verlag, a publishing house which he and his brother had founded during the First World War. Hounded out of Germany in 1933, he continued to work from Prague, and then in 1938 took refuge in London. He died in 1968 in East Berlin.

In the 1935 essay 'John Heartfield et la beauté révolutionnaire' from his book *Les Collages* (1965), Louis Aragon evokes the way Heartfield moved from chaotic Dada images to his unique kind of art: 'As he was playing with the fire of appearances, reality took fire around him... John Heartfield was no longer playing. The scraps of photographs that he formerly manoeuvred for the pleasure of stupefaction, under his fingers began to *signify*.'[16]

As images, Heartfield's photomontages are immediately clear and direct, however subtle the message may be. They were published most frequently in the *Arbeiter-Illustrierten Zeitung* (AIZ), later called the *Volks-Illustrierte*. When works done for *AIZ* were exhibited, Heartfield always insisted on having a copy of the paper on show beside the original to underline the fact that his works were political propaganda aimed at a wide public, not private works of art. He used to save pictures from books, magazines, photographic agencies and newspapers, or have photographs made for him, and always called his works photomontages, even when

16 Aragon, 'John Heartfield et la beauté révolutionnaire', *op. cit.*, p.78, author's translation.

using photographs unaltered or specially posed, on the basis of the caption. In the end, remarkably, whether montaged or not, many still *look* like newspaper photographs. The image fills up the whole page, and, however grotesque, remains curiously uncomposed, almost arbitrary; the immediate impression is almost that of an extraordinarily lucky piece of reporting. While the Dadaists, perhaps unconsciously, attempted to avoid the expression of an ideology – implicitly present in any image that is intended to represent reality – by breaking up images, Heartfield was able by juxtaposing them to reveal the ideology for exactly what it was, rendering visible the class structure of social relationships or laying bare the menace of Fascism.

In Heartfield's *The Finest Products of Capitalism* (1932) the unemployed man, with the degrading placard hung round his neck as though he were an object for sale, stands squarely on the priceless lace veil of the bride, who is raised on a slight platform – altar, or part of the window-dressing? At first she looks like a dummy, but it is a confrontation between two real people. We do not need the original caption, 'Wedding dress for 10,000 dollars, 20 million jobless', to see them also as symbols of the injustice of capitalism. They are both soiled by the inability of that system to treat anything as other than a financial counter.

The burning of the Reichstag in February 1933 and the subsequent trial at Leipzig where the Bulgarian Georgi Dimitroff, one of the four accused communists, so successfully defended himself that they were all acquitted amid massive publicity, while the guilt was fixed, though without positive proof, on the Nazi Party, gave Heartfield material for some of his most powerful photomontages. The Nazis themselves constantly and unwittingly supplied him with the captions. For instance, the caption which accompanied *Through Light to Night* (1933) when it appeared in AIZ read: 'Thus spake Dr Goebbels: "Let us start new fires so that those who are blinded shall not wake up."' A bonfire of books, representing the book burning in Berlin and in various German universities on 10 May 1933, melts into and becomes a part of the flaming Reichstag. The essential difference from caricature is that the artist has cut out and assembled real objects and events. As John Berger puts it in his brilliant essay 'The Political Uses of Photomontage': 'The peculiar advantage of photomontage lies in the fact that everything which has been cut out keeps its familiar photographic appearance. We are still looking first at *things* and only afterwards at symbols.'[17]

The photomontages, which are photographs of specially constructed objects, like the bayoneted dove or the Christmas tree with its branches bent into a swastika in *O Tannenbaum im deutschen Raum...* (O Christmas Tree in German Soil, 1934), are an odd extension of this quality, because, although clearly symbolic, their effect is all the more powerful because they *are* real objects.

Heartfield did not do his own photography, and W. Reissman, one of the photographers he employed, gives a fascinating account of working with him:

> The photographs which I made for Heartfield, in accordance with an exact pencil sketch and always under his personal supervision, often took hours, many hours. He insisted upon nuances which I could no longer perceive. In the darkroom he would stand by the enlarger until the prints were ready. I was generally so tired that I could no longer stand or think... but he hurried home with the photos still damp, dried them, cut them out, and assembled them under a heavy sheet of glass. Then he would sleep for one or two hours, and at eight in the morning he would be sitting with the retoucher. There he would stay for two, three, four or five hours, always fearing that the retouching would spoil it. Then the photomontage is finished, but there is not much relaxation: new tasks, new ideas. He burrows in the photo-libraries for hours, looking for a suitable photo of Hermann Müller, [Alfred] Hugenberg, [Ernst] Roehm, whoever is needed – or at least for a suitable head, for the rest can be managed. Then he turns again to the photographers, all of whom he hates, me included, because of the nuances we are unable to perceive.[18]

In *Adolf the Superman* (1932) the montage is so skilful, the airbrush so discreetly used, that the impression of a real figure, even down to the unnaturally puny shoulders, is perfect, and the more successfully punctures the illusion of Hitler's rhetoric. The speeches that were so

17 John Berger, *Selected Essays and Articles: The Look of Things*, Penguin, London, 1972, p.185.
18 Quoted in Drew (ed), *op. cit.*

essential a part of the Nazi programme are shown for what they really were, not just bombastic but money-fed and representing the interests of capital: he 'swallows gold and spouts junk'. This theme is continued in *Millionen stehen hinter mir!* (Millions Stand Behind Me!, 1932; p.34) in which Heartfield renders Hitler's salute ambiguous – from Nazi salute, intended to thrill and terrify millions, it becomes a deceitfully open, receiving hand. An opposition is set up between the apparent and the real nature of the salute, which is thus demystified and deprived of its rhetorical power. By contrast, the poster made by Xanti Schawinsky for Mussolini in 1934 is simple rhetoric, the visualisation of a political commonplace: the leader at, or as, the head of his people. But such is the capacity of photomontage to suggest the opposite of what it intends, so narrow the dividing line between thesis and antithesis, that I think it is possible, given an uncommitted spectator, to see Mussolini as a lowering tyrant, devourer of his people. It is Heartfield's genius almost never to let the significance of his work be confounded in this way. The significance does not depend upon the prejudice one way or the other of the spectator, with very occasional exceptions as pointed out by Berger in his essay. He suggests that the looming soldiers of the Red Army, towering over a tiny Hitler in *The Suicides' Wish-Fulfilment* (1935), are ambiguous, offering a threat or liberation according to one's prejudice. He instances as a different kind of failure the famous snarling tiger's head, which warned against the SPD (Social Democratic Party of Germany). Heartfield and the German communists, Berger suggests, accepted an ideological direction from Moscow condemning all social democrats, thereby losing any chance of influencing or collaborating with the nine million SPD voters, which might have blocked the Nazi advance. Though effective superficially as propaganda, *The Crisis Party Convention of the SPD* (1931) is weak in the kind of revealed internal evidence Heartfield's best photomontages contain. It also lacks the satirical force of, say, *Herr von Papen* (1934): as Georg Lukács said, a good photomontage has the effect of a good joke.

Anchored in history as it is, Heartfield's work is still strikingly alive today. This is not just because we see in it alarming parallels with the present. It is because it is both eternal and local, like all good art, and is no more or less dependent on historical facts, or the spectator's prejudice, than Goya's *Disasters of War* (1810–20).

Gustav Klutsis's statement 'Photomontage as a new kind of art of agitation', which appeared in Moscow in 1931 and was also printed in the catalogue of the photomontage exhibition in Berlin in the same year, was already in a sense retrospective. He emphasised the links between photomontage and both revolutionary politics and industrial and technological progress: 'Photomontage, as the newest method of plastic art, is closely linked to the development of industrial culture and of forms of mass cultural media... There arises a need for an art whose force would be a technique armed with apparatus and chemistry MEETING THE STANDARDS OF SOCIALIST INDUSTRY. Photomontage has turned out to be such an art.'[19] He also claimed priority in the field of political photomontage:

> There are two general tendencies in the development of photomontage: one comes from American publicity and is exploited by the Dadaists and Expressionists – the so-called photomontage of form; the second tendency, that of militant and political photomontage, was created on the soil of the Soviet Union. Photomontage appeared in the USSR under the banner of *LEF* when non-objective art was already finished... Photomontage in the USSR as a new method of art dates from 1919 to 1920.[20]

Hausmann later angrily repudiated this date, and said that his ideas had been stolen by other artists, adding at the same time an interesting light on his own early photomontages: 'The efficiency of the technique, once separated from its oneiric and automatic element, which was replaced by the propaganda element, answered exactly the USSR's need for public instruction.'[21] It is difficult to verify the date of Klutsis's first photomontage: the early photomontages were certainly based in their design on his abstract paintings and drawings of 1919 and 1920

19 Quoted in Szymon Bojko, *New Graphic Design in Revolutionary Russia*, Lund Humphries, London, 1972, p.21.

20 Quoted in Hausmann, *op. cit.*, p.49, author's translation.

21 *Ibid.*, p.49.

(like *Dynamic City*, 1919) which would tend to confirm the early date. Photographic elements were incorporated into a geometric structure influenced by Suprematism and by Lissitzky's 'proun' compositions – and Klutsis suggested, in one case, that the photomontage could be looked at either way up, which could also be true of his 1922 photomontage *Sport*. On the other hand Lissitzky, who left Moscow for Germany late in 1921, apparently saw photomontages for the first time in Hausmann's studio in Berlin.

Whatever the truth of the priority question, Klutsis is certainly right in saying that photomontage gathered momentum with *LEF* (Journal of the Left Front of the Arts, published between 1923–25), whose founders included Vladimir Mayakovsky, Osip Brik, Tretyakov and Alexander Rodchenko. Rodchenko, who made his first photomontages for Mayakovsky's poem *About This* in 1923, took charge of the periodical's layout and cover designs – in which he used photomontage – in the same year. The drive behind *LEF* was the need to link Constructivist theory with the practice of the individual artist, and to clarify the position of art within a revolutionary society. The editorial for the first issue of *LEF* addressed artists as follows: 'In dictating orders to the factory from your studios you become simply customers. Your school is the factory floor.' The battle had already been fought, in the early stages of Constructivism, with those artists like Naum Gabo or Kasimir Malevich, who believed in building up a new art which would 'match' the new society. Such 'studio dreams' were dismissed by artists like Rodchenko who felt that all forms should be shaped according to Constructivist ideals: 'The same laws of economy and material limitation should govern the production of a ship, a house, a poem, or a pair of boots.' Lissitzky, who attempted to bridge the gap between these opposing groups, described the dialectical development through which art had recently passed, reaching a positive stage in which 'art is becoming recognised for its inherent capacity to order, organise and activate the consciousness through the inner charge of its emotional energy'.[22]

Although Klutsis was right in a sense to say that non-objective art was

22 El Lissitzky, 'Ideological Superstructures' from *Neues Bauen in der Welt: Russland* (1930); reprinted in Sophie Lissitzky-Küppers, *El Lissitzky*, Thames & Hudson, London, 1968, p.371.

finished in Russia by this time, much of its magnificent energy had shifted to photomontage. In his own work, as late as the *Transport* poster of 1931, and in that of Lissitzky, the dynamic composition and the strikingly angled viewpoint characteristic of Constructivism feed ultimately on this source. Lissitzky's poster for the *Russian Exhibition* held in Zurich in 1929 uses two heads photographed from his favourite angle – below the eye-level of the subject. The soft grey tone allows the two heads to merge as though looking into the future with a single shared vision, and contrasts strikingly with the sharp black and white of the lower part, which is either drawn or drawn over a photograph. Tension is set up between the abstract pattern created by the stark black-and-white shapes and their existence as shadows and projections on the sharply receding facade of the building.

The role of art in shaping and reorganising, not reflecting, public consciousness was promoted very early in the Revolution. Visual propaganda was obviously a direct and successful way of achieving the mammoth task of educating, informing and persuading the people. The agitprop trains and propaganda boats of 1919 and 1920, which went all over the country, were covered with paintings – bold but predominantly traditional in style – and slogans. Photomontage naturally took over part of this task; as El Lissitzky said, 'no kind of representation is as completely comprehensible to all people as photography'. Confidence in the accessibility of photomontage in fact minimised the need for texts. It is interesting to compare the agitprop paintings with their direct descendants, the street posters and the great montage friezes made for exhibitions, like Lissitzky's *The Task of the Press is the Education of the Masses* from the Soviet section of the *International Press Exhibition* held in Cologne in 1928. While the posters rely on satire and opposition to make their political point, the photographic friezes celebrate and exhort, showing the great work of construction that is underway, the technological advances and the growth of Russian industry – actual and visible progress witnessed through photographs.

Once the decision had been taken by the most active group of Constructivists to repudiate 'pure art' as 'a merely emotional, individual, romantically isolated matter', its members explored different fields of industrial design and different ways of applying their skills. Rodchenko's first work in industrial typography was the designing, from 1922 to 1924, of film titles for Dziga Vertov's 'Kino-Pravda', newsreel documentaries covering the whole country. He 'approached these titles in a production spirit, treating them as part of the film itself, guided by its montage and scenario'.[23] This early experience of working with films must have influenced his photomontages, and, indeed, the dramatic development of Soviet cinema has close parallels with that of photomontage. The use in film of dynamic, rapid inter-cutting, disrupting unity of time and space and making comparisons and qualifications, the use of alternating close-up and distance shots, overlapping motifs, double exposures and split-screen projection, all have equivalents in photomontage. Hausmann described photomontage as 'static film'. Lissitzky's photographic montage for the *Press Exhibition*, in its organisation of material and its ideological structure, is similar to the documentary films of Vertov and others.

Montage in film, in the basic sense of editing, was of course an internationally established practice, and Sergei Eisenstein had been experimenting with a 'montage of attractions' in the theatre – 'attractions' in the vaudeville sense, juxtaposing unrelated acts and events. The Russian filmmaker Lev Kuleshov, however, was one of the first to develop a *theory* of montage, and his ideas are interesting in relation to photomontage techniques. He explained how he started from the simple fact that 'every art form has two technological elements: material itself and the methods of organising that material'.[24] The methods of the cinema are very complex, but basically, Kuleshov assumes, its material is reality, and the structure given to it is all-important in determining how that reality is perceived: 'The interaction of separate montage segments, their position, and likewise their rhythmic duration, become the contents of the production and world view of the artist. The very same action, the very same event, set in different places with different comparisons, "works" differently ideologically.'[25] Kuleshov himself used to synthesise details of quite disparate objects to create a sequence – once he created the presence of a woman in a film by combining different features from several different women.

23 *LEF*, no.1, March 1923.
24 Kuleshov, 'The principles of montage' (1935), in Ronald Levaco (ed), *Kuleshov on Film*, University of California Press, Berkeley, CA, 1974, p.194.
25 *Ibid.*

From about 1923 until 1931, the uses of photomontage were rapidly extended in the fields of commercial publicity and political propaganda, for posters, book covers, magazine and book illustrations and exhibition installations. It was often combined with new typographic techniques to make simple, bold and striking designs. As Lissitzky said:

> Most artists make montages, that is to say, with photographs and the inscriptions that belong to them they piece together whole pages which are then photographically reproduced for printing. In this way there develops a technique of simple effectiveness which appears to be very easy to operate and for that reason can easily develop into dull routine, but which in powerful hands turns out to be the most successful method of achieving visual poetry.[26]

Certainly, for this period, in the USSR and in Poland, under the aegis of Constructivism, photomontage had a strength and confidence which, at its best, though in a different vein, may equal Heartfield.

Though the use of photomontage continued, its distinctive character was increasingly diluted and submerged. This is made quite clear in the lecture for the opening of the exhibition of Rodchenko held in Moscow in 1957:

> Mention is often made of the asceticism of the artistic left wing... This was an asceticism of simplicity, a straight-lined asceticism which brought an end to ornamentation. Our departure from asceticism has led to the proliferation of middle-class art on a large scale. When I gaze on the posters and covers of Rodchenko, they seem to be the beginning of something which was never continued. It is sad that middle-class art, as personified by thousands of pink lampshades glowing in the windows of new flats, has managed to nip these early germs in the bud.[27]

26 Lissitzky, 'Our Book' (1926), in Lissitzky-Küppers, *op. cit.*, p.359.

27 S. Kirsanov, quoted in Szymon Bojko, *op. cit.*, p.37.

> We will sing of great crowds excited by work, by pleasure and by riot; we will sing of the multicoloured, polyphonic tides of revolution in the modern capitals; we will sing of the vibrant nightly fervour of arsenals and shipyards blazing with violent electric moons; ... and the sleek flight of planes whose propellers chatter in the wind like banners and seem to cheer like an enthusiastic crowd.[28]

Energetic and pulsating as they can be, Futurist paintings never fully matched the heroic vision of the modern world evoked by Marinetti in *The Manifesto of Futurism* (1909). The violent changes of scale and simultaneous perceptions of different things implicit in the vision of the Futurist city were, however, ideal matter for photomontage. The contrast between the surging masses in the city and its gigantic buildings, the sense of exhilaration in their very dominance, and the beginning of panic with the realisation that the city with its buildings and machines can no longer be experienced as an extension of man, but is moving swiftly out of control and into a life of its own, are all expressed in the piled images of Paul Citroen's *Metropolis* or Kazimierz Podsadecki's *Modern City: melting pot of life* (1928).

Paul Citroen made his first *City* montages in 1919, pasted together from cut-up photographs and postcards of houses, windows, staircases. He had been in contact with Berlin Dada, and from 1922 to 1925 was a student at the Weimar Bauhaus, where in 1923 he made his *Metropolis* series. There is an impression of dizzying space in these pictures, with the bird's-eye view of a street racing back into the distance in the centre, surrounded by steeply angled perspectives of buildings that stretch away as far as the eye can see. Citroen's work was perhaps an inspiration for Fritz Lang's film of the same title, a nightmare moral fable of a future society where only the rich live above ground. The skyscraper city in the film, with planes flying between the buildings, was a maquette with close similarities to Citroen's *Metropolis*. The montage of scenes from Walter Ruttmann's film *Berlin: Symphony of a Great City* (1927) suggests the clockwork rhythm of

28 F.T. Marinetti, 'The Founding and Manifesto of Futurism' (1909), in Umbro Apollonio (ed), *Futurist Manifesto*, Thames & Hudson, London, 1973, p.22.

the city. One building looms up at such a sharp and unnatural angle that it looks, ironically, more like a cathedral spire than an office block. By contrast with this work and with Podsadecki's, Citroen's, in spite of its breathless obsessional quality, is built up in ordered squares, so that there is almost a horizon line formed by an even series of joins across the centre of the picture. Within this vertical-horizontal grid, which anticipates Piet Mondrian's *Broadway Boogie-Woogie* (1942–43), each square acts like a window with its own vista; the effect is as powerful as the more obviously dynamic diagonal construction of the Podsadecki and the Ruttmann.

The use of photomontage by architects in building plans and projections is now commonplace. It has a practical use in, for example, showing the relationship between the existing environment and the projected building. In the 1920s, however, it was sometimes used in a more personal way. Citroen's *Brotenfeld* (1928) is like a mock projection, pointing up the unbridgeable gap between the country and buildings of the past, taken from an old engraving, and the city and buildings of the present and future. It is curiously hard now to judge the tone of the work – whether it was intended as a comic fantasy, or contains suggestions about appropriate building styles, or is simply a comment on the industrialisation of the countryside.

The photomontage by the Polish Constructivist architects Bohdan Lachert and Józef Szanajca, *Design and Construction of a House, Warsaw* (1928), combines plans and a view of the house – of advanced construction methods for its time – with photographs of the two architects and of the house under construction, so that in spite of its utilitarian appearance it is more like a personal record.

Many of the great architectural projects conceived in Russia in the 1920s remained unbuilt (as did in Italy the Futurist Antonio Sant'Elia's visionary cities), and perhaps the grandest of these was El Lissitzky's *Wolkenbügel* – this could be translated as 'sky hanger' or 'sky iron' – which he demonstrated in a photomontage of 1925 erected in Nikitsky Square, Moscow. Lissitzky aimed to bridge the gap between the functional group of artists and architects and those who believed in the abstract search for an ideal form, which would bring its influence to bear on functional work – as Malevich's *Architectonics*, a series of 'models' never intended to be built, were supposed to do. Lissitzky was concerned with the problems of suspending a building clear of the Earth; as he wrote in *Russland*, in 1929, 'our idea for the future is to minimise the foundations, the link to the earth'. Undoubtedly planned to be built, the concept of the *Wolkenbügel* also leans on Lissitzky's non-objective 'prouns', volumetric constructions on canvas which he described as the 'interchange station between painting and architecture', and his 'proun-room', of whose space he wrote: 'We see that Suprematism has swept away from the plane the illusions of two-dimensional planimetric space, the illusions of three-dimensional perspective space, and has created the ultimate illusion of irrational space, with infinite extensibility into the background and foreground.'[29] The *Wolkenbügel* photomontage, however, which shows the building from the point of view of a man walking in the street, is startlingly realistic, making the visionary project *actual*.

5 THE MARVELLOUS AND THE ORDINARY

Just as the greater 'reality' of the photographic image as opposed to, for example, the drawn caricature informs political photomontage, so it can the more successfully disrupt our perception of the normal world, and create marvellous images. By the juxtaposition of elements by nature strange to one another, hallucinatory landscapes are formed; commonplace objects become enigmatic when moved to a new environment. Our thought struggles to encompass them and is baffled, or a new thought is made for them. Different realities are thus revealed.

Before Dada and Surrealism began to pursue 'the systematic derangement of the senses', as Rimbaud called it, by pictorial as well as other means, the fascinating paradox of being able to distort reality with the medium that was its truest mirror had often been explored. A turn-of-the-century postcard shows a cart filled with giant Alice in Wonderland apples as big as its wheels, with the caption 'Can a photo lie?' Other postcards wistfully juxtapose an ideal and a real scene – the young sailor embracing his girl rises from the battleship on which he is serving.

29 Lissitzky, 'A. and Pangeometry', from *Europa-Almanach* (1925); reprinted in Lissitzky-Küppers, *op. cit.*, p.348.

The first works in which the disorienting power of combined photographic images was systematically explored, and where the possibilities of marvellous transformations of substance itself were pursued down to the tiniest detail, were made by Max Ernst in Cologne in 1920. In these Dada pictures, a number of which were called *Fatagagas,* Ernst opened up new areas of figuration. He knew of Berlin Dada, but had a low opinion of it, considering it a counterfeit version: 'It's really German. German intellectuals can't shit or piss without ideologies.'[30]

Ernst often combined photographic and other elements, sometimes adding imperceptible marks of crayon or gouache, and frequently intensified the poetic power of the pictures with long inscriptions or titles (some of which may have been added by Arp, who was also in Cologne at the time). When these collages were exhibited in Paris in 1921, André Breton, the future leader of the Surrealists, found in them an entirely original and exhilarating form of expression which corresponded with a quality he had been seeking in art and poetry. In his preface to the exhibition he recognised the dual role of photography, both in rendering obsolete traditional kinds of painting and in supplying the consequently lacking but indispensable element of figuration:

> The invention of photography has dealt a mortal blow to the old modes of expression, in painting as in poetry, where automatic writing, which appeared at the end of the nineteenth century, is a true photography of thought... Since a blind instrument now assured artists of achieving the aim they had set themselves up to that time, they now aspired, not without recklessness, to break with the imitation of appearances... [But] a landscape into which nothing earthly enters is not within the reach of our imagination.[31]

There is in Ernst's work that surprising confrontation present in Lautréamont's image (so much admired by the Surrealists and providing the touchstone for Surrealist poetry): 'as beautiful as the chance encounter

30 Letter from Max Ernst to Tristan Tzara, 17 February 1920, in *Max Ernst*, exhibition catalogue, Grand Palais, Paris, 1975.

31 André Breton, preface to the Max Ernst exhibition, Paris, May 1921, in Max Ernst, *Beyond Painting*, Wittenborn, Schultz, New York, NY, 1948, p.177.

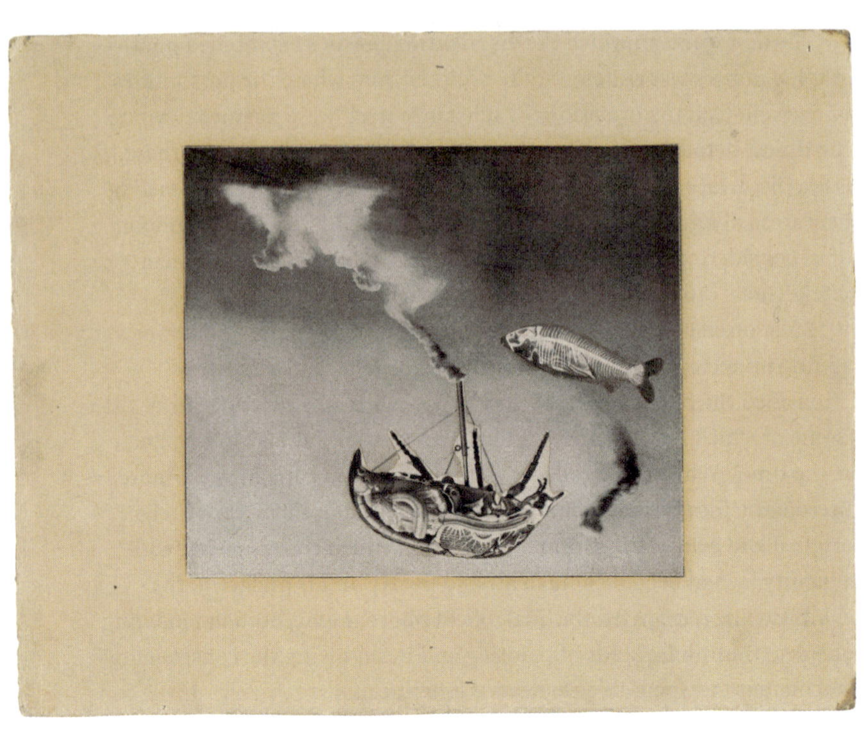

58 **Max Ernst**
Here Everything is Still Floating, 1920
Cut-and-pasted printed paper and pencil
on printed paper on cardstock
16.5 × 21 cm | 6½ × 8¼ in

on a dissecting-table of a sewing-machine and an umbrella'. As Breton put it in the preface quoted above:

> It is the marvellous faculty of attaining two widely separate realities without departing from the realm of our experience, of bringing them together and drawing a spark from their contact; of gathering within reach of our senses abstract figures endowed with the same intensity, the same relief as other figures; and of disorienting us in our own memory by depriving us of a frame of reference – it is this faculty which for the present sustains Dada. Can such a gift not make the man whom it fills something better than a poet?

In Ernst's *Here Everything is Still Floating* (1920) a ship and a skeletal fish float together in the sky, or perhaps the sea. The ship is formed of an inverted and transparent beetle, exacerbating the displacement of objects with a marvellous transformation of matter.

Max Ernst did not distinguish those of his works with predominantly photographic imagery from collages using other materials – the term 'photomontage' would at that time perhaps have smacked too strongly of Berlin Dada. But he clearly recognised the special role of the photograph in collage. As Breton said, 'He did not use materials aimed at an effect of compensation, as had been the practice hitherto (painted paper for painted canvas, snip of the scissors in place of the brush stroke, the glue itself to imitate smudges), but, on the contrary, elements endowed in their own right with a relatively independent existence – in the same sense that photography can evoke a unique image of a lamp, a bird or an arm.'[32]

Collage for Ernst was the conquest of the irrational. This is how he described its discovery, in terms that apply to both his collages from engravings and his photomontages:

> One rainy day in 1919, finding myself in a village on the Rhine, I was struck by the obsession which held under my gaze the pages of an illustrated catalogue showing objects designed for anthropologic,

32 André Breton, *Le Surréalisme et la peinture*, Paris, 1925; trans. Simon Watson-Taylor, *Surrealism and Painting*, Icon Editions, Harper and Row, New York, NY, and London, 1972, p.26.

> microscopic, psychologic, mineralogic and paleontologic demonstration. There I found brought together elements of figuration so remote that the sheer absurdity of that collection provoked a sudden intensification of the visionary faculties in me and brought forth an illusive succession of contradictory images, double, triple and multiple images, piling up on each other with the persistence and rapidity which are peculiar to love memories and visions of half sleep.[33]

Ernst's later collage novels, like *La Femme 100 têtes* (The Hundred Headless Woman, 1929), use engravings, some of which are by artists like Henri Thiriat and Auguste Tilly, who themselves worked from photographs.

The isolation of an object can be as important as its incongruous juxtapositions. As Breton said, 'If one were to displace a hand by severing it from an arm, that hand becomes more wonderful as a hand.' In a slightly different way, but one which is nonetheless related to Ernst's works, recent photomontages by Hans Hollein isolate an object or part of an object and place it in a landscape that is strange to it, but with which unexpected analogies are set up: a Rolls-Royce radiator grille rises up among the skyscrapers of Manhattan, incongruously paralleling their shapes.

While Ernst saw his collages as in some sense equivalent or parallel to automatic writing in provoking unconscious images, other Surrealist photomontages express the hallucinatory qualities of dreams. Herbert Bayer's *Lonely Metropolitan* (1932) captures the feeling of living in a waking dream, like Louis Aragon's *Paris Peasant* (1926), whose familiar city streets and shop windows are momentarily animated and transformed by extraordinary visions. Other photomontages by Bayer evoke the paintings of René Magritte.

Bayer was not in fact a member of the Surrealist group, and after the initial impulse given by Ernst's 1920 pictures, in which the special contribution of the photographic image was acknowledged, comparatively few Surrealists persisted with photomontage after initial experiments although the pages of Surrealist periodicals are filled with *photographs.* Man Ray, of course, put photography to surrealist use in a number of ways – in his 'rayograms', solarised photographs, photographs of enigmatic

33 Ernst, *op. cit.*, p.14.

objects – although he rarely used photomontage, with occasional exceptions like a marvellous four-breasted torso, and the 'self-portrait' from the journal *Minotaure*. Collages and three-dimensional objects constructed from readymade materials were very popular, but the interest of the majority of the Surrealists was in painting and in hand-operated techniques for provoking visions, like Max Ernst's rubbings from various textured materials (frottage) or Oscar Dominguez's marbling technique (decalcomania). The Belgian Surrealist Marcel Mariën, however, uses predominantly photographic material. Sometimes it is difficult in reproduction to distinguish a photomontage from a photograph of a composite object: a tap sprouts tresses of black hair, and it takes a few seconds to decide that this is in fact a photographed object. It is as though the surrealist object took over some of the functions of photomontage.

British artist Paul Nash wrote an article on the 'surrealist' monuments and happenings of Swanage ('swanage or seaside surrealism'),[34] but in his photomontage *Swanage* (c.1936) all but the lone swan buffeted at sea have been replaced by his own found objects, photographed separately but here combined to complicate and extend their individual and potent existence. As Nash said, 'The more the object is studied from the point of view of its animation, the more incalculable become its variations; the more subtle becomes the problem of assembling and associating different objects in order to create that true irrational poise which is the solution of the personal equation.'[35] Driftwood, stone and branch here loom out of Studland Bay, Dorset, on a gigantic scale.

Space can be created in an almost infinite variety of ways in photomontage. Objects of sharply differing scale can meet in an irrational space. In Ernst's photomontages and collages the alien objects never *quite* relate to the space into which they have been intruded. Superimpositions can make objects appear to exist in the same spatial plane which would otherwise bear quite different relationships with each other. Richard Hamilton goes to great lengths to ensure realistic space in his inventory of indispensable objects, *Just what is it that makes today's homes so different, so appealing?* (1956), a collage of cuttings from colour magazines which was made for the poster and catalogue of the exhibition *This is Tomorrow* at the

34 In *Architectural Review*, April 1936, pp.151–54.
35 Paul Nash, 'The life of the inanimate object', in *Country Life*, May 1937, pp.496–97.

Whitechapel Art Gallery, London, in 1956 and which, in a deadpan way, transforms readymade images so that the patterned carpet is a crowded beach scene, the ceiling an early satellite view of the Earth.

It is in this field – the creation of strange and marvellous (in the sense of magic) images, and the rendering of isolated commonplace images enigmatic – that photomontage has become most familiar today, for example in advertising, where the banal is metamorphosed with the simple aim of whetting our appetites.

6 PHOTOMONTAGE AND NON-OBJECTIVE ART

The relationship between photomontage and non-objective art is not perhaps an obvious one, but it is nonetheless reciprocal and full of productive tension. The structure of certain photomontages, for example those of the Russian and Polish Constructivists, was naturally dependent on the principles of constructive, non-objective design. Conversely, the camera and photographic processes in general were found to be capable of suggesting forms, patterns and textures independent of the visible world and rich in possibilities.

Herbert Bayer's photomontage *Metamorphosis* (1936) wittily suggests a strange relationship between non-objective and representational forms. He has taken the basic geometrical shapes that he used in his design for the cover of the first issue of the *Bauhaus* periodical in 1926 (made while he was building up the graphic design workshop at the Dessau Bauhaus), and shows them tumbling out of a dark cave towards a romantic landscape. Perhaps Bayer is also gently satirising here the Platonic assumptions of non-objective art, with its use of basic 'ideal' forms, by placing them in the mouth of a cave so that they become, as it were, Plato's ideal objects of which we, mankind, living in the dark, facing away from the light, see only the shadows on the wall.

El Lissitzky's superb and famous portrait of himself from 1924 was made by a combination of superimposed negatives and direct exposure. He has literally integrated the artist's eye and his hand holding a pair of compasses with the circle and rectangular planes on graph paper showing the alphabet of constructive forms, the abstract basis of Constructivist art.

Klutsis and Lajos Kassák, among others, based their photomontages on a dynamic, abstract framework. Klutsis's *Sport* (1922) is close to his work in other mediums such as painting and drawing, and is based on the composition in *Dynamic City*, which was inspired by Malevich's Suprematism and Lissitzky's 'prouns'. In his photomontages, figures or buildings are substituted for or added to the planes and volumes of the abstract works. It is interesting that the origins of Suprematism, which expressed the 'new environment of the artist', were demonstrated by Malevich in a montage of photographs of bird's-eye views of cities, docks, roads and dams.

Photography for Moholy-Nagy was of inestimable value in educating the eye to what he called the 'new vision'. He believed that in our efforts to come to terms with the age of technology, to become part of it and not to sink back into a retrogressive symbolism or expressionism, the camera with its capacity 'to complete or supplement our optical instrument, the eye' would help us to disengage ourselves from traditional perceptual habits. Moholy-Nagy's ideas have perhaps been more influential than his works in any of the mediums in which he experimented; but probably his most original and exciting compositions are those using photographs or photographic processes. His 'photograms', as he called them, are more distanced from the world of objects, from fantasy creations, than Man Ray's, and are closer perhaps to those of Christian Schad. The direct records of forms on light-sensitive paper were particularly fascinating for him, being almost pure experiments in light and shadow, produced with the minimum of handling, and with the bonus of surprise in the result. In a letter to American curator and writer Beaumont Newhall in 1937 he wrote: 'I would think that photogram is a better name than "shadowgraph" because at least in my experiments – I used or tried to use not alone shadows of solid transparent and translucent objects but really light effects themselves e.g. lenses, liquids, crystals and so on.'[36]

Moholy-Nagy's photomontages, or 'photoplastics' as he sometimes preferred to call them when photographs were combined with drawing, are very varied: he was fully aware of the vast range of possibilities in the field. This is how he described his photomontages in *Malerei Fotografie*

36 Quoted in Richard Kostelanetz (ed), *Moholy-Nagy*, Praeger, New York, NY, 1970, p.57.

Film (Painting Photography Film, 1925): 'They are pieced together from various photographs and are an experimental method of simultaneous representation; compressed interpenetration of visual and verbal wit; weird combinations of the most realistic, imitative means which pass into imaginary spheres. They can, however, also be forthright, tell a story; more veristic "than life itself".'[37] And he added: 'It will soon be possible to do this work, at present still in its infancy and done by hand, mechanically, with the aid of projections and new printing processes.' But it is not surprising, given his wholehearted and optimistic, though not dogmatic, commitment to non-objective art, that he should reveal new relationships between photomontage and non-objective construction. In the marvellously clear image of *Leda and the Swan* (1946), while there is an interest in the subject matter ('the myth inverted', as Moholy-Nagy said), the main interest is in the spatial possibilities of the medium. As he wrote in 'Space, Time and the Photographer': 'Linear elements, structural pattern, close-up, and isolated figures are here the elements for a space articulation. Pasted on a white surface these elements seem to be embedded in infinite space, with clear articulation of nearness and distance. The best description of their effect would be to say that each element is pasted on vertical glass planes, which are set up in an endless series each behind the other.'[38]

The idea of a photographic sequence or series, which was the basis of some of Moholy-Nagy's most striking photomontages, had a particular relation to the qualities of mechanical reproduction of the photograph: 'repetition as a space-time organisational motif, which, in such wealth and exactitude, could be achieved only by means of the technical, industrialised system of reproduction characteristic of our time'. The repetition of an image, Moholy-Nagy believed, minimised its particularity as a representation, and enabled it to become a unit, a part of an overall design: 'The series is no longer a "picture", and none of the canons of pictorial aesthetics can be applied to it. Here the separate picture loses its identity as such and becomes a detail of assembly, an essential structural element of the whole which is the thing itself. In this concatenation of its

37 László Moholy-Nagy, *Malerei Fotografie Film*, Bauhaus Books 8, Munich, 1925; English edition published by Lund Humphries, London, 1969.

38 Moholy-Nagy, 'Space, Time and the Photographer', in Kostelanetz, *op. cit.*, p.65.

separate but inseparable parts a photographic series inspired by a definite purpose can become at once the most potent weapon and the tenderest lyric.'[39] Delicately, in *The Law of Series* and with more vivid fantasy in *The Shooting Gallery*, Moholy-Nagy repeats an image, but with such variations that a counterpoint is created between its identity as a structural element and its identity as a picture. Andy Warhol, in his paintings and screen prints on canvas of Coca-Cola bottles or soup tins, repeats the same image symmetrically until it becomes a decorative overall design.

The subtle differences of exposure in each repeated image of *The Law of Series* are significant in building up an abstract pattern of light, shade, texture, not unlike the pattern set up by the repeated tractors in Vladimir and Georgii Stenberg's *To the Fallow Ground* (1928). Moholy-Nagy's emphasis on repetition as a formal device uniquely available to photomontage is really the reverse of that quality of photomontage explored by the Dadaists and Heartfield – its capacity for expressing oppositions, for dialectics. While not totally denuded of its representational qualities (the photograph is less incidental for him than it is, sometimes, in the work of graphic designers like Tschichold), the photographic image has become an essential part of, not just an addition to, the non-objective clarity of the composition.

Hausmann has been amply proved right since he wrote: 'The field of photomontage is so vast that it has as many possibilities as there are different milieux, and in its social structure and the resulting psychological superstructure the milieu changes every day. The possibilities of photomontage are limited only by the discipline of its formal means.'[40] Since Hausmann discussed photomontage, photographic processes have developed which are potential extensions and refinements of the genre. The silkscreen print, now often made photographically, can, as in R.B. Kitaj's *Addled Art* (1975), combine photographs (and, in this case, a film still from Salvador Dalí and Louis Buñuel's *L'Age d'or* of 1930). The Xerox can be used to make double prints. Curiously, so familiar are we with photomontage that a photograph can appear to be a photomontage when in fact it is not – as with Tim Head's *Equilibrium* (1975), or the photograph

39 Moholy-Nagy, 'A New Instrument of Vision', in Kostelanetz, *op. cit.*, p.50.
40 Hausmann, *op. cit.*, p.48, author's translation.

by Andrew Lanyon, *Fylingdales Early Warning System* (1966), where the reactors are giant white puffballs on the horizon.

So great is the proliferation of photomontage today, and so familiar is it in, for example, advertising that it is not possible to cover it exhaustively in a book of this length. This essay is intended to describe the historical origins of photomontage, and to outline some predominant themes.[41]

41 The advent of digital imaging, Photoshop etc., has transformed what was once the domain of photomontage. In the original publication, this essay was supplemented with an extensive documentary section.

68 Page from *Dadaco*, Munich, January 1920 with George Grosz and John Heartfield, *Der Weltdada Richard Huelsenbeck* (Worlddada Richard Huelsenbeck) or *Dadabild* (Dada Picture), c.1919

Dada–Constructivism

DADA–CONSTRUCTIVISM; The Janus Face of the Twenties, Annely Juda Fine Art, London, 1984

This is a preliminary and tentative investigation of a subject that needs closer attention than it has so far received: the relations between Dada and Constructivism. It is not difficult to see why this topic has engaged neither the attention of historians of Dada nor of Constructivism, except in special cases where there is an obvious overlap – that of Theo van Doesburg and his rogue review *Mécano*, for instance, or of Kurt Schwitters. Dada and Constructivism have at best been seen as the opposing poles of the international avant garde in the period immediately following the First World War. This view has been reinforced by the insistence on the Dada-Surrealism inheritance, with Surrealism's well-known antipathy to most forms of abstraction, an antipathy which has, with a certain justice, been mapped back onto Dada. But Dada has not always been granted the status of an 'opposing pole' to Constructivism, and has quite frequently been presented, often by Constructivists, as performing something of the role of an enema, a destructive but cleansing convulsion preceding the great task of reconstruction. In 1922 El Lissitzky and Ilya Ehrenburg wrote in an editorial in the first issue of their review *Veshch/Gegenstand/Objet*: 'The negative tactics of the "Dadaists", who are as like the first futurists of the pre-war period as two peas in a pod, appear anachronistic to us. Now is the time to build on ground that has been cleared.'[1] Naum Gabo even denied Dada a separate identity, presenting it rather as the death throes of the Cubist revolution:

1 El Lissitzky and Ilya Ehrenburg, 'The Blockade of Russia is coming to an end', *Veshch/Gegenstand/Objet*, Berlin, nos.1–2, 1922, trans. Stephen Bann, in Stephen Bann (ed), *The Tradition of Constructivism*, Thames & Hudson, London, 1974.

> There were moments in the history of Cubism when the artists were pushed to these bursting points; sufficient to recall the sermons of Picabia 1914–16 (sic), predicting the wreck of art, and the manifestos of the Dadaists who already celebrated the funeral of Art with chorus and demonstrations. Realising how near to complete annihilation the Cubist experiments had brought art, many Cubists themselves have tried to find a way out... Our generation did not follow them since it has found a new concept of the world represented by the Constructive idea.[2]

More recently critics have recognised the positive and radical nature of the Dada challenge: 'During the First World War the Dadaists had initiated an international movement that subverted the traditional categories and supposed "laws" of art. With the conclusion of the War, it seemed imperative to many artists that the dada critique be accepted and the laws of art reformulated from firm and objective bases.'[3]

It is possible to take this point further, and see the Dada critique not only as a crucial precedent to the objectives of International Constructivism but to see Dada as a continuing and active force in its own right during the early 1920s.

Richard Sheppard ends his thorough chronology of the Dada movement with two events, both of which took place towards the end of 1924: the publication of the *First Surrealist Manifesto* by André Breton, and the closure of the Bauhaus in Weimar (it was to move to Dessau in October 1925).[4] Both of these events then, standing apparently at opposite ends of the artistic spectrum, were of significance in relation to the cessation of Dada activity. By then, most Dada artists had already or were soon to enter into other allegiances. Dada's permanent state of ironic revolt was impossible to sustain, and yet most Dadaists remained nostalgically loyal to it. Jean (Hans) Arp wrote in 1927: 'dada is the basis of all art. dada is for the senseless which doesn't mean nonsense... i exhibited along with the surrealists because their rebellious attitude toward "art" and their direct attitude toward life were as wise as dada.'[5]

2 Naum Gabo, 'The Constructive Idea in Art', in J.L. Martin, Ben Nicholson, Naum Gabo (eds), *Circle: International Survey of Constructive Art*, Faber and Faber, London, 1937.

3 Bann, *op. cit.*, p.51.

4 Richard Sheppard (ed), 'Dada: A Chronology', *New Studies in Dada: Essays and Documents*, Hutton Press, Driffield, 1981.

In spite of the fact that Arp exhibited at the first Surrealist exhibition in 1925, *La Peinture Surréaliste,* his continued relations with Constructivists confirm the strength of the links Constructivism once had with Dada. In 1924 he collaborated with El Lissitzky to write the first 'dictionary' of modernism, *The Isms of Art*, and towards the end of the decade worked with Van Doesburg and Sophie Täuber on the Aubette café in Strasbourg. None of them compromised their style and the now destroyed café, its severe geometrical designs side by side with Arp's free organic forms, stood as a memorial to the creative oppositions and collaborations between the two movements. While Arp joined the Surrealists (although this barely affected his work), Hans Richter, a fellow Zurich Dadaist, took the opposite path of Constructivism. He still saw Dada as an essential element though, in the constitution of the review he founded in 1923, *G*.

> *G* as it finally appeared had the traits of Dadaism as well as of Constructivism, two seemingly unrelated movements. It offered articles by Mies van der Rohe as well as Tristan Tzara, by Gabo, Pevsner, Malevich, Lissitzky, Doesburg as well as by Arp, Schwitters, Hausmann, George Grosz, Man Ray. The fact is that the tendencies of Constructivism, or more generally speaking of structure, appeared in Dada itself; though they were not, as in Russian Constructivism, a programme or the single aim of Dada. Dada as a movement had no programme. But the tendencies for an order, a structure, appeared nonetheless as a counterpart to the law of chance which Dada had discovered. In this way the Constructivist involvement in Dada and vice versa may be understood. That is how Doesburg from *De Stijl* was at the same time a Dadaist. Eggeling made his *Generalbass* in Dada times, Richter's black and white counterpoint and even Duchamp's discs and 'roto-reliefs' (all with structural tendencies) were connected with and appeared in Dada. The aims of the new and unrestricted (Dada) and the aims of the enduring (Constructivism) go together, and condition each other. To embrace and integrate these two tendencies was the purpose of the magazine *G*.[6]

5 Jean (Hans) Arp, 'dear monsieur brzekowski' (?1927), 1st pub., *L'Art Contemporain*, n.d., *Collected French Writings*, London, 1974, p.35.

6 Hans Richter, introduction, 'Great Little Magazines no.3, *G*', *Form*, no.3, 15 December 1966.

This positive statement concerning the mutual involvement of Dada and Constructivism is confirmed in the avant-garde reviews which proliferated at this period. Not only in the relatively late *G*, but in *Ma*, for instance, the review founded and largely edited by Lajos Kassák, first in Budapest and then in Vienna, which ran from 1916–25, or the Belgrade review *Zenit* (1921–26), Dadaists and Constructivists appear side by side.[7] Although their contributions mostly remained distinct, there were particular planes where their interests and experiments coincided and collided – machine aesthetics, the practice of collage and photomontage, object-construction. Moholy-Nagy, who had become by 1923, when he began teaching at the Bauhaus, one of the most influential of the International Constructivists, was represented in the September 1921 issue of *Ma*, and some of the works, montages, for example, show strong Dada affinities. Arp is frequently present (an 'arpaden' is on the cover of the March 1922 issue) as are Raoul Hausmann and Schwitters. The presence of the Paris Dadaists is rarer, though Picabia does appear. One of the most ubiquitous presences in these reviews is the *Black Square* of Malevich. In *Zenit*, in *Ma*, in Lissitzky's *Veshch/Gegenstand/Objet*, in the issue of Schwitters's *Merz 'Nasci'*, co-edited by El Lissitzky, the *Black Square* has a prominent place. Obviously as the initial Suprematist form it has a close relationship with Constructivism, but at the same time it is probably not fortuitous that it is in those reviews which relate to Dada that the *Black Square* most commonly appears. It is as though it could stand as an icon of both destruction and construction, representing a primary urge to re-create form from scratch, a kind of Ur-form. In some respects it could be compared to the phonetic poetry of Hausmann, in which language is reduced orally to pure sound and visually to the letters of the alphabet. Both Van Doesburg and his 'Letter Sound Poems' and Schwitters, whose *Ursonate* was based on Hausmann's *FMSBW*, were closely indebted to him.

Before examining the 'structural tendencies' Richter found in Dada on the one hand, and further points of intersection between Dada and Constructivism on the other, it would be useful to attempt to define, a little belatedly, what is being understood here by 'Constructivism'. Unlike 'Dada', the terms 'constructive' and 'construction' became part of

7 It would be interesting to consider *Zenit* in relation to the Zagreb Dada reviews *Dada-Jazz*, *Dada-Tank*, *Dada-Jok* (1922, single issues).

the aesthetic terminology of post First World War progressive (or would-be progressive) artists before being adopted as the name for a movement. This is one of the causes of the confusion surrounding the term, and of the various and even conflicting theories and practices of artists associated with Constructivism. Osip Brik had to deal with the abuse of the term attendant on widespread use: 'there are artists who have rapidly adopted the fashionable jargon of constructivism. Instead of "composition" they say "construction"; instead of "to write" they say "to shape"; instead of "to create" – "to construct". But they are all doing the same old thing: little pictures, landscapes, portraits.'[8] Such traditional art had nothing to do with 'Constructivism' as it was properly understood. The term stood for an artistic practice which eschewed both the reproduction of the external world and the individualist tendencies of expressionist abstraction. (Theo van Doesburg used 'Constructivist' in direct opposition to 'Impulsivist'.) The emphasis was on the study of form and material for its own sake in both two and three dimensions, on the use of pure geometric form in mass (cubes etc.) and in line. The first group to define themselves officially under this name in Russia, and to have a specific programme, was the First Working Group of Constructivists, formed in March 1921, including Alexei Gan and Alexander Rodchenko.[9]

However, this group, although retaining the term 'constructive' from their earlier purely formal and 'laboratory' experiments, now rejected 'art' altogether. They redefined the artist as a worker, engaged in 'material–intellectual production' whose special skills would be put to use in the task of social reconstruction following the Revolution. Besides posters and books etc., for propaganda and didactic purposes, they were to shape utilitarian objects – stands, furniture, fabrics etc. It is important to distinguish between this 'Russian Constructivism' and the 'International Constructivism' of the West, which remained primarily an aesthetic movement, and maintained even at its most extreme an ambiguous relationship between the useful and the artistic. As Lissitzky wrote in the editorial in *Veshch*: 'No-one should imagine... that by objects we mean

8 Osip Brik, 'Into Production!', *Lef*, no.1, March 1923, in Bann, *op. cit.*, p.84.

9 See Margit Rowell and Angelica Rudenstine, *Art of the Avant-Garde in Russia*, exhibition catalogue, Guggenheim Museum Press, New York, NY, 1981, and Christina Lodder, *Russian Constructivism*, Yale University Press, New Haven, CT, and London, 1983.

expressly functional objects. Obviously we consider that functional objects turned out in factories – airplanes and motorcars – are also the product of genuine art. Yet we have no wish to confine artistic creation to these functional objects. Every organised work – whether it be a house, a poem or a picture – is an "object" directed toward a particular end.' This is obviously very different from the position of Rodchenko and other artists associated with the 'Productivist' wing of Constructivism.

It was with the International Constructivists that Dada was largely concerned, and the list of names given above by Richter more or less covers those involved.

Richter's point about the 'constructive' within Dada needs to be examined a little more closely. He said that a tendency to structure arose as a counterpart to the law of chance discovered by Dada. However, the relationship between structure and chance during the early manifestations of Dada, in Zurich between 1916 and 1918 especially, was more complex than that, and operated as dynamic paradox. In one of Dada's key texts, Tzara's *Dada Manifesto 1918*, published in *Dada 3/4* (December 1918) there are passages embedded within the apparently nihilistic philosophy of Tzara, which refer directly to the impersonal abstractions of Zurich Dada artists in terms which are prophetic of Constructivism but which spring from the Dada belief in a creative energy engineered by opposites:

> ...the new painter creates a world, whose elements are also its means, a sober and defined work, without argument. The new artist protests: he no longer paints/symbolic and illusionistic representation/but creates directly in stone wood iron... Order = disorder, ego = non-ego, affirmation = negation: supreme radiations of an absolute art. Absolute in the purity of ordered and cosmic chaos.

Parallels can be drawn here between the Dada artist 'creating directly in stone wood iron' and the earliest manifestations of Constructivism in Russia, in the post-Cubist non-utilitarian constructions of Tatlin, especially, constructed in wood and metal. It would be interesting to compare these with Marcel Janco's lost constructions of c.1917, which work directly in found materials, explored for their own sake. In *Construction 3* (c.1917) the freely curling, spiralling and tangling wire creates a drawing in space.

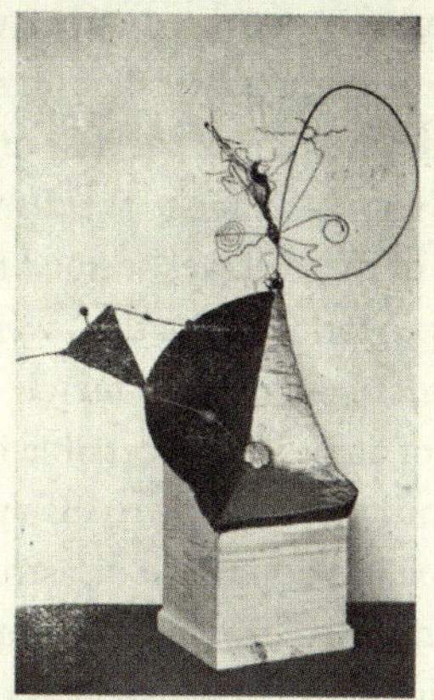

M. JANCO:
CONSTRUCTION 3

Marcel Janco
Construction 3
Page from *Dada 1*, Zurich, July 1917

But there are also in Tzara's text puzzling and seemingly nonsensical phrases like 'ordered and cosmic chaos'. This phrase can, however, be understood if it is set in the context of Arp's exploration of chance, which, far from being a random opposite to 'structure', became a 'law' on which a natural, as opposed to a mechanical or man-made order could be based. Arp introduced the concept of the 'law of chance' in relation to his geometrical collages of c.1916–18: 'since the disposition of planes, and the properties and colours of these planes seemed to depend purely on chance, I declared that these works, like nature, were ordered according to the "law of chance", chance being for me merely a limited part of an unfathomable *raison d'être*, of an order inaccessible in its totality.'[10]

If man tries to impose order, according to his own necessarily partial measure, which, Arp says, he has done with disastrous effect since the Renaissance, he will cut himself off from understanding the laws of nature ('ordered and cosmic chaos') of which he is only a part rather than ruler. Chance is one of the means by which he can regain a sense of the 'unfathomable' laws of nature, and by which he can recover equilibrium. After the impersonality of the geometrical collages, Arp actually introduced chance procedures into his work, though very differently from Duchamp, who used it among other things to test the laws of causality. In c.1917–18, Arp discovered a nature-based organic abstraction in his woodcuts and drawings, which have the appearance of a spontaneity free of individual gesture, a dynamic equilibrium based on the balance of figure/ground, black/white.

Arp and Sophie Täuber were working in isolation from the developments in Russia and especially in Holland, where the emphasis on a vertical and horizontal geometry of line and plane in the Neoplasticism of the De Stijl artists, Van Doesburg, Piet Mondrian and Bart van der Leck, has at first sight close similarities to Arp and Sophie Täuber's collages and embroideries. However, Arp's collages have attained an all-over surface in which no distinction between colour plane and line exists, whereas in Mondrian's paintings surface tensions continue between these elements and the ground, while Van Der Leck's pure colour rectangles were quickly re-adapted to represent once again specific objects, like bottles or people.

10 Arp, 'Dadaland', *XXe Siècle*, no.1, Paris, 1938, trans. *On My Way*, Documents of Modern Art, Wittenborn, Schultz, New York, NY, 1948, p.40.

Arp perceived a quite different intention between his own works and theirs, which 'though treated in an abstract manner... retain a base of naturalism.'[11] More fundamentally, he saw the work of the De Stijl artists and the Constructivists in Russia as 'in fact a homage to modern life, a profession of faith in the machine and technology'.

Dada did not share the Constructivists' faith in progress and the advance of machine technology. But they did not turn their backs on the machine – it was part of the world and could not be ignored. It could, however, be treated with humour and thereby integrated into life. Duchamp in his *Large Glass* (1915–23), Picabia in his machine paintings, created a machine aesthetic as an ironic counterpart to Futurism, in which the machine was forced to take its place within the erotic and the irrational. Duchamp went on to pursue his interest in optics with the *Rotary Glass Plates* of 1920 and the *Rotary Demisphere (Precision Optics)* of 1925, achieving, as Richter put it, 'a synthesis between scientific and artistic endeavour'.[12]

It is in the context of the playful, ironic and aesthetic use of the machine, initiated by Dada, that one of the oddest and most direct collaborations between Dada and Constructivism can be seen: the review *Mécano*, edited by the Dada persona of the *De Stijl* editor Van Doesburg, 'I.K. Bonset'. Five issues were published between 1922–23 (the last was a double issue largely devoted to describing the Dada performances in Holland put on by Schwitters and Van Doesburg early in 1923.) This review was announced in *De Stijl* as 'an international periodical for spiritual hygiene, machine aesthetics and neo- Dada.'[13] The works reproduced clearly reveal the bias of the review, for they concentrate on the abstract-machine aspects of Dada to the exclusion of, for example, Arp, or the political montages of Grosz or Heartfield. Of Ernst it reproduces a *Photo-Mechanical Composition*, of Man Ray the glass painting with machine elements *Danger/Dancer* (1917–20). Beside these are reproduced Constructivist works: Moholy-Nagy's *Nickelplastik* (1921) is reproduced in irreverent juxtaposition to Serge Charchoune's drawing *Cigarette*

11 *Ibid.*
12 Richter, *Dada: Art and Anti-Art*, Thames & Hudson, London, 1965.
13 *De Stijl*, January 1922. For a detailed account of Van Doesburg, De Stijl and Dada, see Jane Beckett, 'Dada, Van Doesburg and De Stijl', in Richard Sheppard (ed), *Dada: studies of a movement*, Alpha Academic, Chalfont St Giles, 1979.

Dadaisme et Isthme de Dada

Les grands pontes des jeux de la renommée ont revètu ces temps-ci un costume de toréador et comme Dada leur donne au ventre quelques coups de corne ils le traitent de creille vache crevée.

Dada mort ou Dada vivant? Mais Dada? Mot sans définition, à la garde robe plus luxueuse que celle de Frégoli, à la peau de cameléon, qui répond aussi bien au nom de détecteur qu'a celui de chou-de-Bruxelles ou de Balthazar; en tout cas sa vertu est d'exister, et on ne peut faire que ce mot n'existe. Et l'ennui pour ces prêtres au coeur inquient qui ont peur de mourir avant que leur âme n'ait sa paix assurée dans l'immortalité, est précisément qu'ils ont ce mot collé au derrière parce qu'ils se sont assis dessus. Ils ont beau dire: „Voyez, voyez, j'ai la peau rose." — On se penche et que voit-on? La marque de fabrique. — On ne nous la fait pas, dit le public; entendez plutôt: Pourquoi donc la voix de leur gosier chante-t-elle maintenant de si beaux cantiques, puisque celle de leur digestion gazouille encore **„Dada, dada, dada"?**

On peut bien dire en avant, en avant! L'un préconise les bateaux, les avions, l'automobile, un autre conseille l'air des grandes routes. Ah les beaux horizons romantiques! On a le coeur qui s'ouvre comme le sexe d'un orage en chaleur. On a déjà un petit spasme avant coureur de la grande lumière.

— He bien voila, c'est fini. L'acteur est indisposé et s'en tient là. Si vous n'êtes pas contents on remboursera le prix de vos places. Dada est mort mais les vers amicalement engraissés de sa décomposition sont morts aussi. Adieu.

Pour ma part, je ne sais pas du tout si Dada est mort, vivant, idiot ou miraculeux. Ce que je sais, c'est qu'il n'a pas encore donné ce qu'il contenait — et qu'il ne le donnera peut-être jamais à cause de la self-kleptomanie à laquelle aucun homme ni aucum groupement d'hommes ne peut échapper. Et la destruction ne peut passer sans qu'il subsiste au moins un nuage de fumée auquel les meteorologistes trouvent une physionomie de chameau ou de femme au profil délicieux.

Mais si la grossesse s'arrête au huitième mois, peu importe. Vous ne pensez tout de même pas qu'un joli petit ange ressemblant à son pépère ou à sa mémère allait jaillir des cuisses écartées et vous sauter au cou pour vous embrasser en chantant la Marseillaise ou le Crépuscule des Dieux? Voyez donc nos prophètes qui brandissent dans l'air embrasé leur petite nouveauté périodique dont le flux doit embaumer le siècle!

Hélas hélas. Ce n'était qu'une mèche de leurs cheveux. Pourquoi suis-je chauve? J'en ferais bien autant, et me nommerais Christ, Confucius — ou Picabia.

Je me console de la nonchalance de Dada. Ses jeux de mots, sa danse d'un pied sur l'autre, sa joie lorsqu'ayant pris ce qu'il avait dans sa poche droite pour le mettre dans sa poche gauche il le sort à nouveau, valent encore mieux que cette prédication des illusionnistes de la création. Et enfin, puisqu'on parle de la grossesse de Dada, il est doux de voir que ce sont ses assassins qui vomissent.

G. Ribemont-Dessaignes

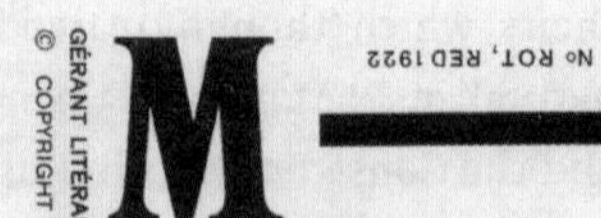

MÉCANO 3 ROUGE

No ROT, RED 1922

No ROUGE, ROOD 1922

GÉRANT LITÉRAIRE: I. K. BONSET MÉCANICIEN PLASTIQUE: THEO VAN DOESBURG

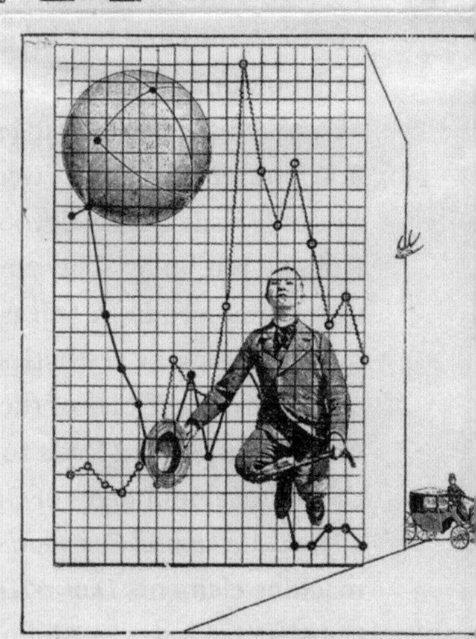

MAX ERNST PHOTO-MECHANISCHE COMP

Het contra-natuurlijke, metaphysische aspect der italian
Chirico en Carrà langs photo-mechanischen weg overtroff

 Mécano No.3 Red, Leiden, October 1922
Unfolded sheet: 32 × 50 cm | 12⅝ × 19¾ in

DADA POUR TOUS

L'Optimisme dévoilé

pour:

les thés mondains
les fabricants de boîtes d'allumettes
l'ennui d'argent
une nuit d'ordre supérieur
un cylindre d'azote couvert d'un chapeau haut de forme
un philosophe tombé dans les plaisirs des cascades vierges
un beau paysage alpin avec la lune et son ruisseau de luxe
le cow-boy qui nous entoure de son lasso de paroles
un sucre d'orge
un sucre d'orage
un missionnaire qui prêche l'insomnie
un pied de verre rempli d'eau et d'oiseaux
un clou qui sort des merveilles liquides
le scorpion qui compte les avalanches à venir
et les avalanches gardées soigneusement dans des sacs
par l'administration des postes et par une société de soldats anonymes en peau luisante tendue et quelquefois gonflée par

Notre produit spécial
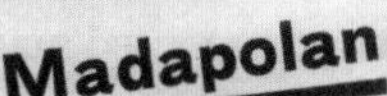
„l'INTELLIGENCE"
La moins chère et la plus résistante
En vente Partout Toujours

Tristan TZARA

Madapolan

J'ai rencontré une femme
de bois
en noir
un arbre orangé
une chambre des idôles
de chocolade
madapolan
en noir
petite fille de lait
de lait
de lait
conjuration
cirque des arabiers

i. k. bonset (hollande)

SOUSMARIN
DE LA RUE SCRIBE
S. CHARCHOUNE

L'enfant au ventre blond

C'est qu'il découvrit l'Amérique et les jupons
les pancartes et les bonnes soeurs
C'est que toutes les misères se soulèvent
autour de sa grandeur ensoleillée
Le président des achats vend le 15 pour le 15
use ses moustaches comme du verre
mange comme un chat
pisse comme un hôtel
à l'heure où le plus jeune carburateur
emploie ses derniers jonques
pour le dernier gateau
La femelle se cache dans un drapeau
autour d'un ventre
sous des lunettes.

Benjamin Péret

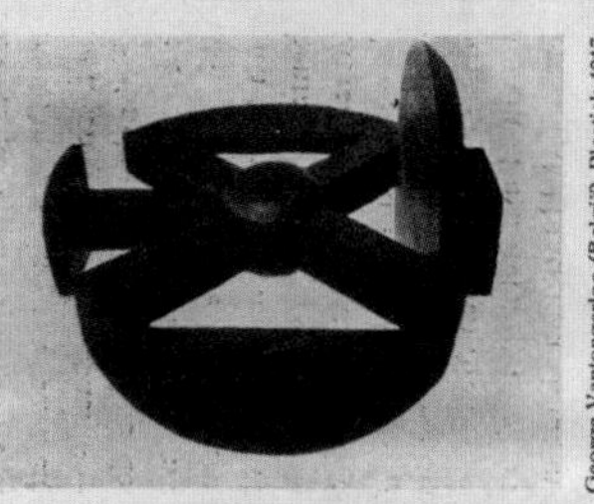
George Vantongerloo (België) Plastiek 1917

Bed-Bites

Do mosquitoes sleep
I don't know
I sleep
Mosquitoes know
I don't bite
Mosquitoes don't know
They bite
I know.

Rosie Spotts

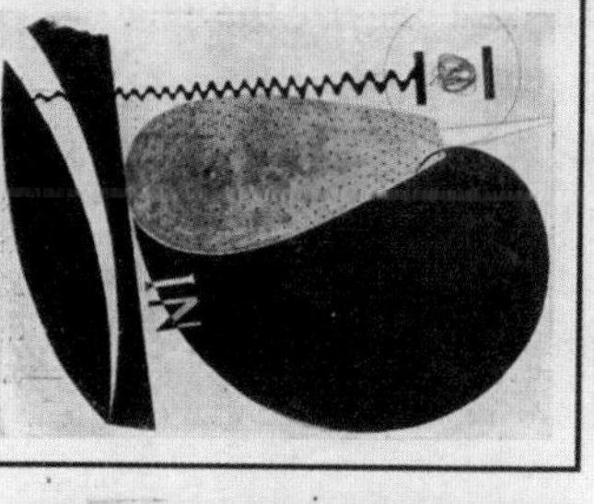
MAN Ray

Dada – partly, certainly, in a spirit of playful parody, but also, as another juxtaposition, that of Hausmann's *Mechanical Head* (1919) and a relief of Moholy-Nagy's using readymade machine elements suggests, to argue that 'their apparently opposed ideas were not irreconcilable'.[14] Certainly from this publication the Dada works stand up to the formal claims made by the Constructivist ones, and also have something to teach Constructivism in terms of the potential flexibility of human-machine relations.

Van Doesburg, with a foot in both camps, played a leading role at the Düsseldorf Congress of Progressive Artists (May 1922), where Constructivists and Dadaists came together for the first time. Here 'Hausmann (dadaist) read a protest... declaring that he was neither for the progressives nor for the artists, and that he was no more international than he was a cannibal' (*De Stijl*, no.4, 1922), while Van Doesburg, Lissitzky and Richter led a break-away group (the International Faction of Constructivists), nucleus of a further Congress of Constructivists and Dada at Weimar in September 1922, with Tzara, Arp and Schwitters in attendance. Van Doesburg's motives were complex, and partly inspired by antagonism for certain elements in the Bauhaus. The anonymous 'Chroniek' (Chronicle) of the Congress (*Mécano Red*) commented maliciously on Tzara's visit to 'The Hotel of sick artists, the "Bauhaus"'.[15]

Berlin Dada is something of an exception to the general argument concerning the relations of Dada with International Constructivism, for it deliberately took up a position of sympathy with Russian Constructivism.

At the First International Dada Fair of 1920 Grosz and Heartfield exhibited a large placard bearing the slogan 'art is dead. Long live the new machine art of Tatlin.'

Hausmann's photomontage *Tatlin at Home* (1920) depicts Tatlin (it was not in fact Tatlin, but an anonymous man cut from an illustrated paper) with a machine mounted in place of a brain. Heartfield described himself as a *monteur*, engineer, rather than artist, and a number of his and Grosz's photomontages at the time are stamped (rather than signed) 'mont',

14 Beckett, *op. cit.*, p.20.

15 Accounts of the more or less hostile reception of Dada at the Bauhaus vary. See Beckett, *op. cit.* On 25 September Tzara gave an important lecture on Dada, which made no concessions to Constructivism, and omitted the positive comments on the 'new artist' contained in his 1918 manifesto in favour of a stress on Dada's indifference, and on the fact that it was not modern.

(montiert) or 'construiert'. How much, however, of the developments in Russian Constructivism were actually known about in any detail is very hard to determine.[16]

Grosz's and Heartfield's use of the term 'construct' was clearly a means of distancing themselves from the conventions of art. Grosz's text of 1921,[17] proclaiming that art as such was a secondary consideration, and was only of value when put directly at the service of the proletariat, is perfectly in line with his communist commitment, and not necessarily ascribable to any specific influence of Russian Constructivism, though obviously the art of the new Soviet State was an object of absorbing curiosity and sympathy, even though little was known of it until 1922.

But Grosz, looking back in 1925, in *Art is in Danger*, while criticising Dada for failing to attack the system that underlay the absurdity of the capitalist world, nonetheless praised it as 'the only essential art movement in Germany for decades', while of Constructivism he said that in spite of its objectivity and clarity, its love of the circle and the line, and its dismissal of the antiquated and metaphysical, it had failed because it remained in the realm of purely artistic activity.

Photomontage is the most important area in which Berlin Dada and the Russian Constructivists meet. Priority in its invention is claimed by both Gustav Klutsis and Hausmann, and without entering this question again, it is probably the case that it was discovered independently and at about the same time in Russia and in Berlin.[18] While in the work of Klutsis and of Rodchenko photomontage was used mainly for didactic and propaganda purposes, Heartfield and Grosz turned it to political-satirical ends – a difference that obviously arises from the different conditions under which they were working. In the hands of Klutsis and Rodchenko, or of Mieczyslaw Szczuka in Poland, the montage of photographs was

16 See Martin Kane, 'George Grosz: Constructivism Parodied', in Sheppard, *New Studies in Dada*, for an interesting interpretation of Grosz's work in the early 1920s, which, however, suffers from a generalised use of the term 'Constructivism'. See also *The First Russian Show* (Annely Juda Fine Art, 1983), a commemoration of the Berlin 1922 exhibition. For contacts between Dutch Constructivism and Russia during this period, see Ger Harmsen, 'De Stijl and the Russian Revolution', in Mildred Friedman (ed), *De Stijl: 1917–31, Visions of Utopia*, Mildred Friedman (ed), Walker Art Center, Minneapolis, MN, and Abbeville Press, New York, NY, 1982.

17 'Zu meinen neuen Bildern', *Das Kunstblatt*, January 1921, quoted in Kane, *op. cit.*

18 See Ades, *Photomontage*, Thames & Hudson, London, 1986.

X

man seine Werke am besten telephonisch, vom Bett aus, bei einem Anstreicher bestellt.

SIMULTANISMUS

Die Gleichzeitigkeit der Farben, die gleichzeitigen Kontraste und alle aus der Farbe sich ergebenden ungeraden Maße, entsprechend ihrem Ausdruck in ihrer darstellenden Bewegung: dies ist die einzige Realität zum Aufbau des Bildes. DELAUNAY.

DADAISMUS

Der Dadaismus hat die schönen Künste überfallen. Er hat die Kunst für einen magischen Stuhlgang erklärt, die Venus von Milo klistiert und „Laokoon & Söhnen" nach tausendjährigem Ringkampf mit der Klapperschlange ermöglicht, endlich auszutreten. Der Dadaismus hat das Bejahen und Verneinen bis zum Nonsens geführt. Um die Indifferenz zu erreichen, war er destruktiv. ARP.

PURISMUS

Das Gemälde ist eine Maschine zur Übertragung der Gefühle. Die Wissenschaft bietet uns eine Art physiologischer Sprache, welche uns ermöglicht, beim Beschauer eindeutige physiologische Empfindungen hervorzurufen: hierauf ist der Purismus begründet. OZENFANT & JEANNERET.

NEOPLASTIZISMUS

Der Neoplastiker gewinnt durch die horizontal-verti-

mieux faire que de commander ses œuvres téléfoniquement du lit, auprès d'un peintre en décors.

SIMULTANISME

La simultanéité des couleurs, les contrastes simultanés et toutes les mesures impaires issues de la couleur, selon leur expression dans leur mouvement représentatif: voilà la seule réalité pour construire la peinture. DELAUNAY.

DADAISME

Le dadaïsme a assailli les beaux-arts. Jl a déclaré l'art d'être une purge magique a donné le clystère à la Vénus de Milo et permis à «Laocoon & fils» de s'absenter enfin après s'être tourmentés dans la lutte avec la serpent à sonnettes pendant des milliers d'années. Le dadaïsme a poussé l'affirmation et la négation jusqu'au nonsens. Afin d'arriver à l'indifférence il était déstructif. ARP.

PURISME

La peinture est une machine pour la transmission des sentiments. La science nous offre une sorte de language physiologique qui nous permet de produire chez le spectateur des sensations physiologiques précises: ce qui forme la base du purisme. OZENFANT & JEANNERET.

NÉOPLASTICISME

Par la division horizontale-verticale du rectangle le néo-

can do better than order his works by telephone from his bed, by a common painter.

SIMULTANISM

Simultaneousness of colour, simultaneous contrasts and all uneven measures issuing out of colour, conform to their expression in their representative movement: this is the only reality to construct a picture. DELAUNAY.

DADAISM

The dadaïsm has assailed fine-arts. He declared art to be a magic purge gave the clyster to Venus of Milo and allowed "Laocoon & Sons" to absent themselves at last after they had tortured themselves in the millennial fight with the rattlesnake. Dadaïsme has carried affirmation and negation up to nonsens. In order to come to the indifference dadaïsme was distructive. ARP.

PURISM

The picture is a machine for the transmission of sentiments. Science offers us a kind of physiological linguage that enables us to produce precise physiological sensations in the spectator: thereon purism is founded. OZENFANT & JEANNERET.

NEOPLASTICISM

By the horizontal-vertical division of the rectangle the neo-

Pages x–xi from Arp and El Lissitzky, *Die Kunstismen 1914–1924*, 1925

kale Aufteilung des Rechteckes die Ruhe, das Gleichgewicht der Dualität: des Universums und des Individuums. MONDRIAN.

MERZ

Alles, was ein Künstler spuckt, ist Kunst. SCHWITTERS.

PROUN

Proun ist die Umsteigestation von Malerei nach Architektur. LISSITZKY.

VERISMUS

Der Verist hält seinem Zeitgenossen den Spiegel vor die Fratze.

Ich zeichnete und malte aus Widerspruch und versuchte durch meine Arbeiten diese Welt davon zu überzeugen, daß sie häßlich, krank und verlogen ist. GROSZ.

KONSTRUKTIVISMUS

Diese Künstler sehen die Welt durch das Prisma der Technik an. Sie wollen keine Illusionen mit Farbe auf Leinwand geben und arbeiten direkt in Eisen, Holz, Glas. Die Kurzsichtigen sehen darin nur die Maschine. Der Konstruktivismus beweist, daß die Grenze zwischen Mathematik und Kunst, zwischen einem Kunstwerk und einer Erfindung der Technik, nicht feststellbar ist.

ABSTRAKTER FILM

So wie die moderne Malerei und Plastik, fängt jetzt auch der Film an, sein spezifisches Material: die Bewegung und das Licht auszubauen und zu gestalten.

plasticien obtient la tranquilité, l'équilibre de la dualité: l'univers et l'individu. MONDRIAN.

MERZ

Tout ce que l'artiste crache c'est de l'art. SCHWITTERS.

PROOUN

Prooun est la station de changement de peinture à architecture. LISSITZKY.

VÉRISME

Le vériste tend la glace devant la grimace de ses contemporains.

J'ai dessiné et peint par opposition et par mon travail j'ai essayé de convaincre ce monde qu'il est laid, malade et hypocrite. GROSZ.

CONSTRUCTIVISME

Ces artistes ne voient le monde qu'à travers le prisme de la technique. Ils ne veulent donner aucune illusion avec de la couleur sur de la toile, mais travaillent directement sur fer, bois, verre etc. Les myopes n'y voient que la machine. Le constructivisme prouve qu'entre la mathématique et l'art, entre un objet d'art et une invention technique les limites ne sont pas déterminables.

FILM ABSTRAIT

Tel que la peinture et la plastique moderne le film aussi commence à déployer et à former son matériel spécifique: le mouvement et la lumière.

plastician obtains tranquillity, the balance of the duality: universe and individual. MONDRIAN.

MERZ

All that artist spits is art. SCHWITTERS.

PROOUN

Prooun is the station for change from painture to architecture. LISSITZKY.

VERISM

The verist tends the lookingglass before the grimace of his contemporaries.

I drew and painted by opposition and by my work tried to convince this world that it is ugly, ill and hypocrite. GROSZ.

CONSTRUCTIVISM

These artists look of the world through the prisma of technic. They don't want to give an illusion by the means of colours on canvas, but work directly in iron, wood, glass, a. o. The shortsighteds see therein only the machine. Constructivism proves that the limits between mathematics and art, between a work of art and a technical invention are not to be fixed.

ABSTRACT FILM

Like modern painture and sculpture nowadays the film also begins to unfold and form its specific material: movement and light.

3

KONSTRUKTIVISMUS

73

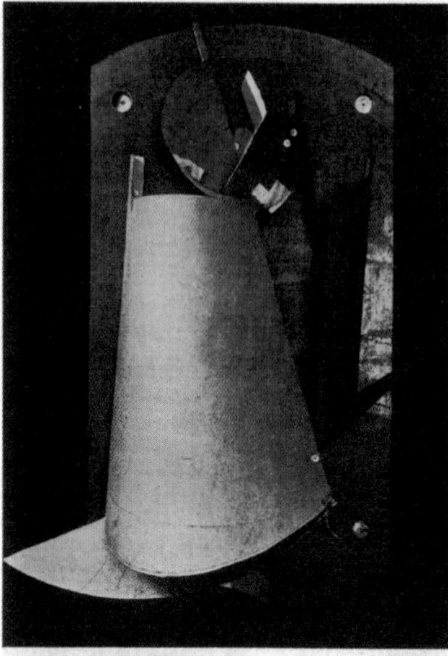

1917

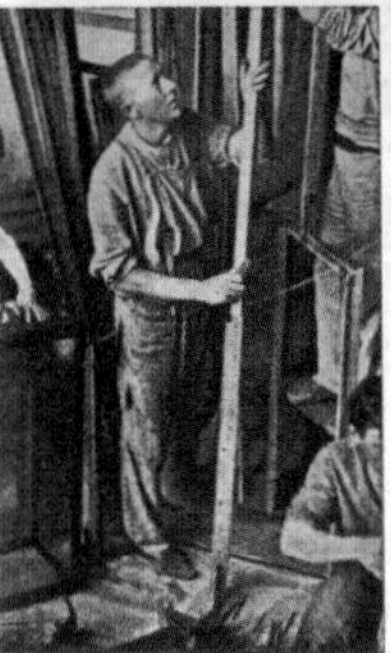

TATLIN

 Pages 3 and 17 from Arp and El Lissitzky, *Die Kunstismen 1914–1924*, 1925 with works by Vladimir Tatlin, Raoul Hausmann and Max Ernst

17

DADA

HAUSMANN
1920

29

22

ERNST
1919

still ordered according to the dynamic geometry of Constructivism, with the characteristic diagonal still dominant, legacy of the Suprematism of Malevich and of El Lissitzky. The Berlin Dadaists on the other hand used a more or less anarchic type of juxtaposition in their earliest montages, to get as close as possible to the vitality of modern life. This gave way gradually in the work of Grosz and Heartfield to a more dialectical system of contrast. The essential point, I think, is that both in Berlin and among the Russian Constructivists there was an urgent need to move away from the limitations of abstraction without slipping back into antiquated illustrational or figurative modes. The photograph obviously has a special and privileged place in relation to reality, and is also susceptible of being manipulated to re-organise or dis-organise that reality. It is for this reason that in Russia, and in Berlin, where the impetus away from a basically aesthetic movement towards social concerns was most marked, photomontage made its appearance.

One montage from the unpublished anthology *Dadaco* deserves to be mentioned, for its characteristically paradoxical and subversive spirit; it probably contains an element of parody though, as so often with Dada, it is impossible to tell for certain. A headless and footless man is set within the circles and straight lines that would seem to be a byword for Constructivism, though here they are also probably intended as an anti-expressionist device. They are the lines that construct the new world and at the same time bar the way to the 'otherworldly', to the individualistic, and metaphysical speculation. However, this model of the impersonal scientific New Man is supported on 'Dada' feet and spouts nothing from his neck but 'dadadadada'.

A common aim *was* perceived all the same, at certain points in the trajectories of Dada and Constructivism, and this led to a number of shifting alliances. The manifesto 'The Call for an Elementarist Art' of 1921 was signed by a group of highly diverse artists: Hausmann, Arp, Ivan Puni and Moholy-Nagy. It is couched in general terms that nonetheless reveal something of Dada's principle of creative opposition: 'Seized by the dynamism of our time, we proclaim the revision in our outlook brought about by the tireless inter-play of the sources of power that mould the

19 Raoul Hausmann, Jean (Hans) Arp, Ivan Puni, László Moholy-Nagy, 'A Call for an Elementarist Art', *De Stijl*, vol.4, no.10, 1922, in Bann, *op. cit.*, p.52.

spirit and the form of an epoch and that allow art to grow as something pure, liberated from usefulness and beauty.'[19]

The statement on the cover of the issue of Schwitters's *Merz* (which ran from 1923–32) entitled 'Nasci', and jointly edited by El Lissitzky and Schwitters, has something of the same dynamism, and also suggests to what extent Schwitters, in spite of his increasing adoption of a Constructivist clarity in his collages and reliefs, did not wholly abandon Dada. 'Nature, from the Latin *nasci*, signifies to become, to spring, that is to say everything which by its own force develops, forms, moves.' 'Nasci' opens with a full-page reproduction of Malevich's *Black Square*, and goes on to include reproductions of a rayograph by Man Ray, a building by Mies van der Rohe, and a series of other juxtapositions such as a painting by Mondrian and a Merz relief by Schwitters, as well as natural forms. The issue is intended to extend, perhaps, the definition of Constructivism given by Arp and Lissitzky in *The Isms of Art*, that it proves 'that the limits between mathematics and art, between a work of art and a mechanical invention are not to be fixed'. In their definition, Arp and Lissitzky went on to explain that Constructivist artists 'don't want to give an illusion by the means of colour on canvas, but work directly in iron, wood, glass.' It is an irony fitting Dada's ambiguous and paradoxical relationship with Constructivism that this is almost – but not quite – the same as Tzara's definition, quoted above, of the new artist who 'creates directly in stone wood iron.'

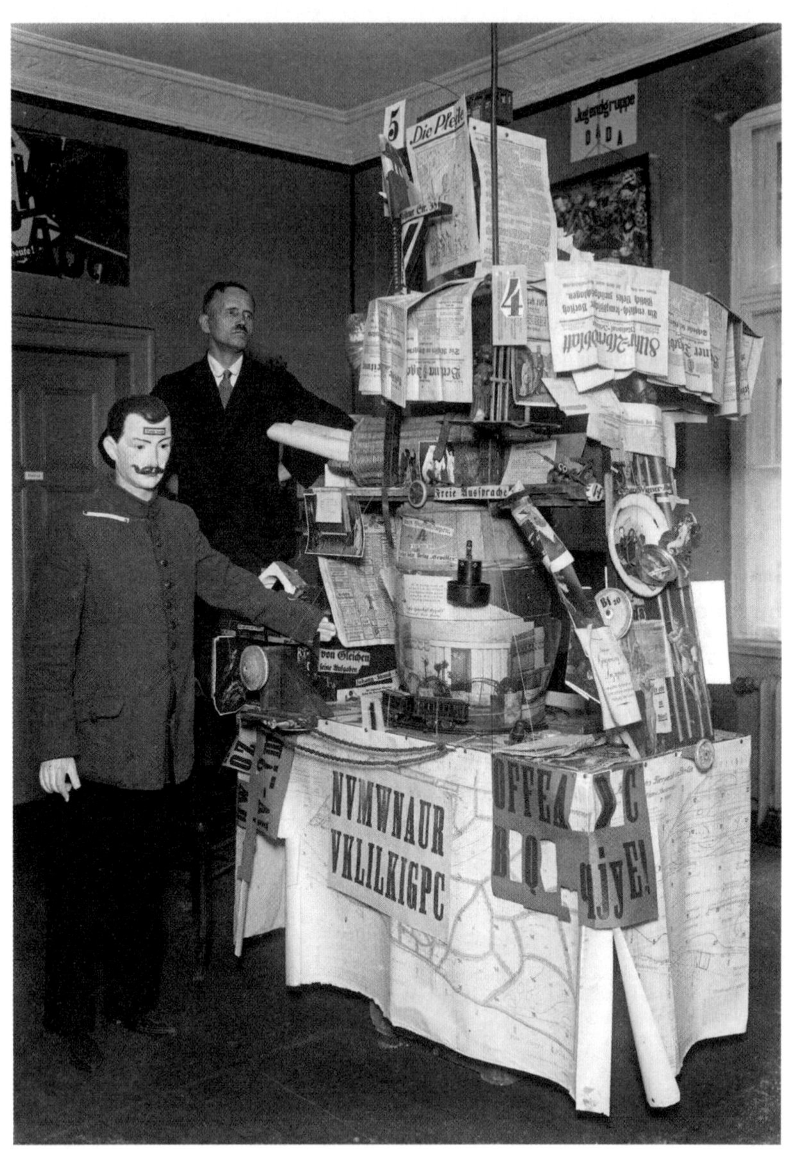

Johannes Baader
The Great Plasto-Dio-Dada-Drama, 1920
Installation view, First International Dada Fair,
Otto Burchard Gallery, Berlin, 1920

Art as Monument

Art and Power: Europe Under the Dictators 1930–1945, David Britt (ed), South Bank Centre, London

In 1940, Diego Rivera painted a mural over 22 metres long and six metres high at the Golden Gate Fair in San Francisco. It was part of the 'Art in Action' section of the exhibition, and the public paid 50 cents to watch the famous Mexican artist at work. The mural's theme, immediate context and subsequent history open up some of the problems and debates that surround monumental art in the twentieth century.

Its theme was the politically hot topic of 'Pan-American Unity', which was being actively canvassed at the time, most strongly by those anxious to keep the United States out of the Second World War. Most of the giant mural compares the creative and scientific achievements through history of 'the North and South of this continent': that is, Canada, the United States and Mexico, but one panel is dedicated to European dictators. A twisted scene of carnage, barbed wire and bodies, with the busts of the dictators – Stalin clasping the bloody ice pick that had killed Trotsky earlier that year, Hitler saluting and Mussolini clasping the fasces – emerging from a cloud of poison gas. At the centre, however, is the figure of Charlie Chaplin, whose satire *The Great Dictator* (1940) had just been released, gesticulating towards a scene from the film, with 'Hitler' holding the world balloon.

The difficulty of judging the tone of this scene, which seems compounded of both outrage and mockery, is partly explained by attitudes in the United States to the European War, which seemed to mark the end of the Old World and the collapse of its civilisation. The Golden Gate Fair itself was a frank celebration of the New World, a little regretful at the absence of some of the countries that had been swallowed up by Hitler since the Fair the previous year, but on the whole optimistic. Another factor may be Rivera's own sense of the contradictions of making monumental art in a site of ephemeral entertainment, and even perhaps of rivalry with the medium of film.[1]

This mural and its setting have been construed as the final straw for artists long suspicious of politically committed art, fearful of its descent into frank propaganda and confused by the numerous changes in the official cultural policy of the Communist Party and the Left since 1935. Meyer Schapiro's group, the Federation of Modern Painters and Sculptors, whose position was loosely based on the André Breton-Leon Trotsky 'Manifesto for an Independent Revolutionary Art' of 1938, 'rejected the politicisation of art which led to such absurdities as posters advertising the Golden Gate Park exhibition in 1940, which combined Diego Rivera with strippers from the Folies Bergère'.[2] Political art seemed to be reduced to the fairground, to pure entertainment rather than serious criticism; and, 'if this was the price of democratisation in art, then democratisation was unthinkable'.[3]

The ground was thus laid for Clement Greenberg's idea of an avant-garde art, essentially opposed to kitsch, to develop into the highly influential theory of an art whose critical function was to investigate its own medium and form.[4] The history of modern art has largely been written according to Greenberg; and monumental art, Rivera's along with that of the totalitarian regimes, has become an embarrassing footnote. It is not a question here of re-evaluating this position, but rather of attempting to shake loose the tight knot of rejection that has bound all monumental art together, whether of the fascist or communist regimes, of the Spanish Republic, of revolutionary Mexico or of the bourgeois democracies.

1 Rivera's mural was dismantled and stored; it was installed in its present location, the Theater of the City College, San Francisco, in 1961.
2 Serge Guilbaut, *How New York Stole the Idea of Modern Art*, University of Chicago Press, Chicago, IL, and London, 1983, p.41.
3 *Ibid.*
4 Clement Greenberg, 'Avant-Garde and Kitsch', *Partisan Review*, Fall 1939; Greenberg's 'Towards a Newer Laocoön', *Partisan Review*, July–August 1940, in defence of abstract art, marked a shift away from the 1939 text, which maintained that a living, avant-garde culture depended for its survival on Socialism. See Greenberg, in John O'Brian (ed), *The Collected Essays and Criticism 1939–1944*, University of Chicago Press, Chicago, IL, 1988.

A monument in the classic sense of the term commemorates a person, event or action; it can refer to a written record, a sepulchre, a boundary, or the remains or remnant of something. 'Monumental art', on the other hand, can be taken simply to mean sculpture or painting that is huge or stupendous; in other words, the term's significance as *reminder* – celebration or memorial – may be emptied out. This essay considers works of art, made in the period roughly covered by the *Art and Power* exhibition, which laid claim to be monumental in more than sheer size. An examination of these claims, how they interlocked with questions of style, function or ideology and what shifts occurred in the deployment of the word *monumental* may help to outline changes in the relations between art and its publics, public art and its patrons.

Built monuments – sculpture or combinations of architecture and sculpture – are for public spaces. Visible signs of authority, they have constituted complex and various messages to the present. They assert power in various ways: through a particular idea of history, or of nationhood, or the celebration of superior individual achievements. The shift to the frankly didactic or agitational that has occurred this century was a natural extension of the power of exhortation that was already implicit or explicit; but this has raised an important question for twentieth-century monumental art: who is being addressed and by whom? Can there be such a thing as a genuinely demotic monumental art – that is, a monumental art not addressed to, but rather of, the people?[5] Certainly, such claims were made in some quarters. Was it possible for monumental art to reinvent itself? Monumental art tried to come to terms with a newly defined 'popular', and this process had inbuilt contradictions.

Following the revolutions in both Mexico (1910–20) and Russia (1917), plans were swiftly elaborated for programmes of public art. One of Lenin's first legislative acts in April 1918 was to decree the removal of the monuments erected in honour of the Tsars ('monstrous idols'), and

5 During the Second World War in Britain, propaganda posters appeared calling on the people to 'defend your country and your homes'; all over the land the 'y' was swiftly scratched out to give 'our country and our homes'. This relatively trivial incident reveals a profound shift in popular political perceptions and attitudes to authority.

'organise a broad competition in designing monuments to commemorate the great days of the Russian Socialist Revolution'.[6] In August 1918 he drew up a list of persons to whom monuments were to be erected, which included 66 names of revolutionaries, writers, philosophers, scientists, artists and composers.[7] Sergei Eisenstein opens his filmic celebration of the October Revolution of 1917 with the dismembering of the enormous statue of Tsar Alexander III, which finally, roped and mutilated, topples ignominiously together with its chair from the high pedestal. It is notable, however, that he intercuts this scene with revolutionary groups and masses, including some 'spot lit' anonymous heroic figures, ancestors of Vera Mukhina's peacetime peasant and industrial worker, rather than with individual heroes of the revolution.

In the early years of the Soviet Union, notwithstanding Lenin's decree, the right to determine what the new monuments and monumental art should be was strongly contested, and the irrelevance of monumental figurative sculpture was argued from the Constructivist side. Nikolay Punin, writing about Tatlin's *Monument to the Third International* (1919–20) in 1920, favourably compared its dynamic creative design and use of materials with the limitations and static quality of figurative monuments: 'The agitational action of such monuments is extraordinarily weak amidst the noise, movements and dimensions of the streets.'[8] For Punin, moreover, a monument without a practical function – which Tatlin's (ideally) had – was pointless.

Punin objected to figurative monuments on the grounds that, beside their static and feeble effect, they cultivated individual heroism and conflicted with history: 'At best they express the character, feelings and thought of the hero, but who expresses the tension of the emotions and thoughts of the collective thousand?'[9] They conflict with history, because – as Eisenstein demonstrates so vividly in *October* – it is the people and not the individual hero whose acts are history.

6 Vladimir Lenin, 'Decree: On the Monuments of the Republic, 12 April 1918', in *On Literature and Art*, Lawrence & Wishart, London, 1967, p.245.

7 Lenin, *ibid.*, p.247. These included Karl Marx, Mikhail Bakunin, Henri de Saint-Simon, Robert Owen, Alexander Pushkin, Andrei Rublev, Mikhail Vrubel and Frédéric Chopin.

8 Nikolay Punin, 'The Monument to the Third International', 1920, trans. Christina Lodder, in 'Modern Art and Modernism, Supplementary Documents (Blocks VIII–IX)', Open University Press, Maidenhead, 1983, p.6.

Attacks on figurative monuments also came from very different quarters: at the end of the 1920s, Robert Desnos, the Surrealist poet, distinguishing between stone allegories and portraits, wrote: 'To erect the effigy of a being, who once lived, on a pedestal, is equivalent to raising him to the rank of a god, and in our times such an enterprise is less legitimate than ever.'[10] Statues, he suggests, should be only the accessories to life, 'with its procession of strange manifestations, miracles, deep looks, insults and warm embraces'. Desnos's proposal was to take the statue off its pedestal, and have a bronze Baudelaire strolling among the crowds or leaning on the parapet of a bridge. What both these arguments have in common is the underlying idea that the genre of the monumental figure portrait cannot hold its own in the modern age: that it is either ineffectual, illegitimate, unnatural or offensive.[11]

Although the Constructivist monument (arguably a completely new form, rather than a hybrid of sculpture and architecture) championed by Punin, Tatlin and others soon lost official support in favour of precisely the kind of figurative monument it sought to replace, the questions that Punin raised were among those that continued to be debated in relation to twentieth-century monumental art in general: the leader versus the masses, modernity versus tradition, national versus universal. In the decades that followed the revolution, the Soviet leadership went on to plan fantastic edifices topped with the giant figure of Lenin or Stalin. (The competition for the Palace of the Soviets produced perhaps the supreme examples.) In these the monument ceases to represent the ideal fusion of architecture and sculpture: the building, vast as it is, becomes the pedestal for the figure. There is a strange disjunction of scale that fails to resolve itself, except in the idea ridiculed by Desnos of a superhuman mortal. To an extent, subjects such as Stalin or Lenin as 'Leader, Teacher, Friend' can be seen as attempts to defuse and conciliate the tension between the cult of the hero and the rights of the collective.

9 *Ibid.*

10 Robert Desnos, 'Pygmalion et le Sphinx', *Documents*, vol.2, no.1, 1930, p.36.

11 Witness the furore provoked in Britain by the statue of Churchill in Parliament Square, which offended because it had swung too far towards naturalism and away from dignity, and more recently by the statue of Air Chief Marshal 'Bomber' Harris in the Strand, which was seen as a remarkably insensitive way of marking D-Day. This sculpture, interestingly, does what Desnos recommended, standing on the ground without a pedestal.

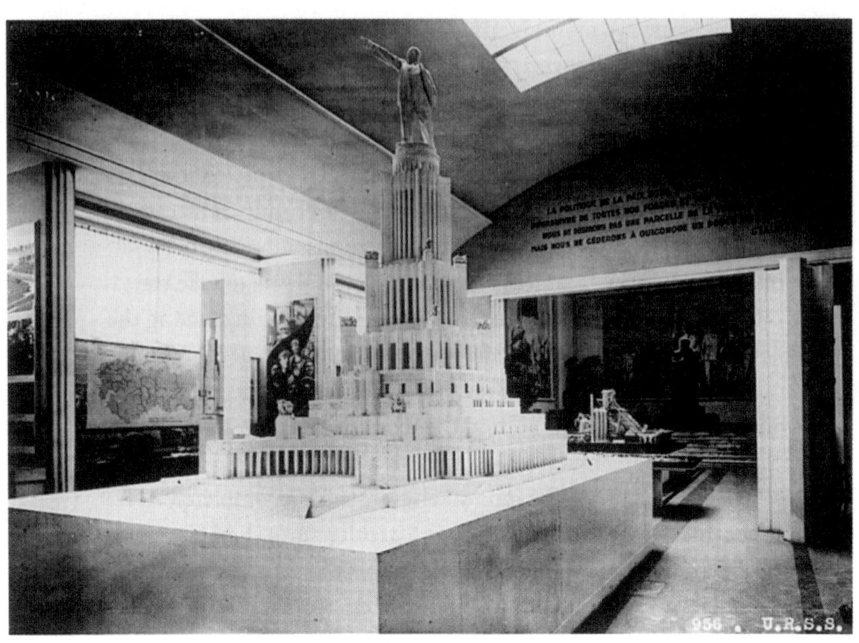

94 Model of the proposed Palace of the Soviets, Soviet Pavilion at the International Exposition, Paris, 1937

The populist rhetoric of the totalitarian regimes thus sometimes offers revealing contradictions in the context of monumental art. Perhaps surprisingly, there were no monumental figures in bronze or stone of Hitler, although his image was ubiquitous in paintings and smaller portrait busts. (Mussolini, however, did not stint in presenting himself and the King-Emperor on all scales.)

If portrait monuments were the natural expression of the cult of the leader, another major genre of monumental sculpture and painting, allegory, was intended to form the symbolic order that constructed a sense of nationhood, especially for those regimes seeking to authenticate and legitimise themselves through history and tradition.

At least since Hegel, allegory – using a human figure to represent an abstraction such as 'nation' – has been regarded as a debased device, icy, remote and inauthentic, an 'aesthetic aberration, the antithesis of art'.[12] Walter Benjamin restored interest to the term, if not to the type of official art that continued to be produced under its name. Normally banished from the modernist canon, allegory posited a relationship between modernity and history, which Benjamin as a Marxist recognised as an urgent issue. For him, though, it was not monuments but their ruins that constituted 'allegory'. This had a disjunctive, atomising character – not being whole, essential or organic – and could thus be extended to refer to collage and photomontage as well, which recycle and juxtapose materials in unexpected but significant combinations. In this light, George Grosz's montage of a bourgeois constructed of newspaper clippings, coloured lithograph and hair could be read as an allegory of capitalism.

The type of art that interested Benjamin, usually in a Dada or Surrealist context – montage, photography, film, the city street that was also the Surrealists' natural hunting ground – was as remote from Greenberg's modernism as was kitsch or propaganda. At the First

12 Craig Owens, 'The Allegorical Impulse: Towards a Theory of Postmodernism', *October*, no.12, Spring 1980, reprinted in Charles Harrison and Paul Wood (eds), *Art in Theory 1900–1990*, Blackwell, Cambridge, MA, and Oxford, 1993, p.1052.

International Dada Fair in Berlin in 1920, Johannes Baader erected a large conglomeration of material, objects, photographs, slogans, newspapers, in a heap that was described as 'Dadaist monumental architecture in five floors, three parks, a tunnel, two lifts and a cylinder end'. It has been suggested that this was an ironic comment on Oswald Spengler's *The Decline of the West* (1918);[13] certainly it revels in the appropriation of imagery that is part of the 'allegorical impulse', as later defined in postmodernist theory. From this perspective, Dada's disruptive iconoclasm is seen as a 'truer' face of the twentieth century than its faded monuments. Dada's techniques of disjunction and appropriation seem the opposite of the binding and controlling impulses of monumental art, but 'allegory' presides at the heart of each.

Both Germany and Italy laid claim to the classical tradition. Mario Sironi represented Italy as a female version of Emperor Augustus, while Giorgio Gori's equestrian statue *The Spirit of Fascism*, which fronted the Italian Pavilion at the Paris 1937 exhibition, drew upon many layers of equestrian imagery from Rome onwards. For Germany and Italy, the monument had a classical aura that reinforced its message of longevity and a continuity that was intended to legitimise the illegitimate dictatorship. By contrast with Italy, though, there was little in Germany that mediated between the classical and the modern: between the pastiche antique and the great machines and Autobahns. It is significant that the journal *Cahiers d'Art*, while attacking the aesthetic of the Third Reich, reproduced photographs of German machinery – the diesel motor and the Mannesmann tube – among its photographs of modern buildings and their interiors at the *Exposition de Paris* (Paris Exhibition). Its editor, Christian Zervos, commented on the sculpture of the Third Reich as consisting of 'beings carved out for sport, struggle, violence; depth is missing'.[14] Virtually interchangeable male nudes represent things such as Comradeship, Youth, Sport, Victory, even the *Ostmark* (Eastern Frontier). These lack depth in the sense in which Zervos understood it: that is, signs of human sensibility or specific individual being, but also signs of the elaborate culture required by allegory. The only attributes tend to be

13 See Hanne Bergius, Norbert Miller and Karl Riha (eds), *Johannes Baader*, Anabas, Lahn-Giessen, 1977, p.187; and Kate Winksell, 'Dada, Russia and Modernity 1915–1922', doctoral dissertation, Courtauld Institute of Art, London, April 1995, p.67.

helmets and cloaks, unlike the giant nudish figures in the Foro Mussolini in Rome, who are carefully identified via the signs of the modern sports they represent. Would both these cases be condemned under the one label of 'Alexandrianism', as Greenberg dubbed it, a late version of the academicism 'in which the really important issues are left untouched because they involve controversy, and in which creative activity dwindles to virtuosity in the small details of form'?[15]

These instances of monumental sculpture attempting to authenticate themselves and the idea of history they represent are in fact quite different, and both, though probably unintentionally, offend against virtuoso academicism. In the case of the Nazi sculptures, there is a clue in the *Ostmark* sculpture. This archaic term is resonant not of classical Rome but of medieval Germany, and it reminds us that the past had to incorporate Wagnerian Nordic mythology and the Teutonic Knights as much as classical antiquity. Thus these native/classical bodies had to compromise and lose specificity in order to retain both their aesthetic and their ideological character. In the Roman sculptures, by contrast, the modernised versions of allegorical attributes, which deliberately display familiarity with and capacity to ring changes on their ancient sources, become dissonant and ludicrous because what is being sought is a non-allegorical identity with the ludic nudes of the past. (Tennis is not played in the nude.)

A much more elegant response to allegory's 'conviction of the remoteness of the past, and desire to redeem it for the present'[16] is Arturo Martini's great bronze *Winged Victory* or *Victory in the Air*. This celebrated the crossing of the Atlantic by an Italian air squadron led by Marshal Italo Balbo, and dominated the *Cour d'honneur* of the Italian Pavilion at the Paris Exhibition of 1937. Fully three-dimensional, the huge female figure is suspended from the wall so that she appears to be in flight, attended by eagles flying in formation like the pilots. She honours as much the national exploit as the conquest of the Atlantic, and therefore combines the idea of the Italian nation – so often, as in Sironi's murals, represented

14 Christian Zervos, 'Réflexions sur la tentative d'Esthétique dirigée du IIIe Reich', *Cahiers d'Art*, vol.11, nos.8–10, 1936, p.212.

15 Greenberg, *op. cit.*, p.6.

16 Owens, *op. cit.*

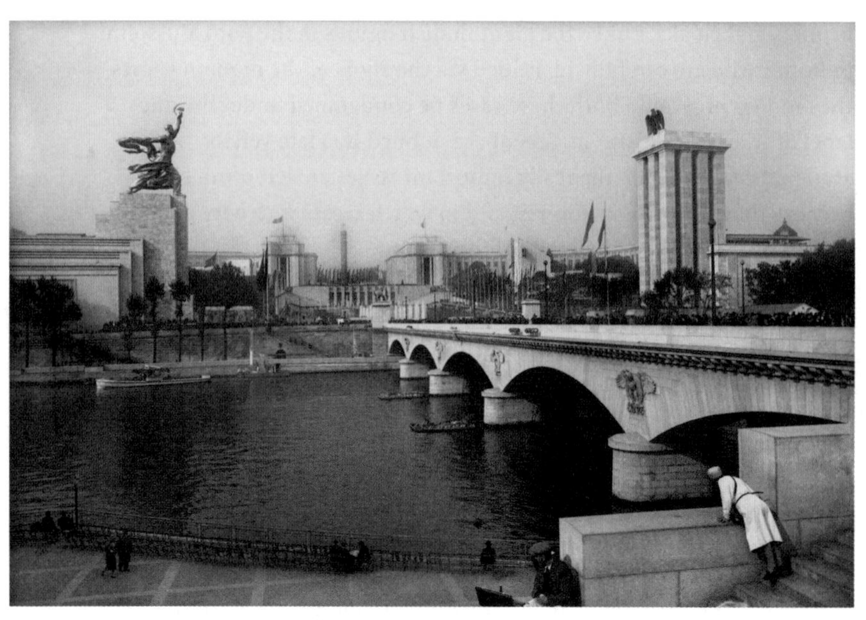

98 USSR and German pavilions at the *Exposition colonial internationale*, Paris, 1937

by a draped female figure – with a modernised version of the antique figure of Winged Victory.

Italy was not alone, of course, in rooting much of its monumental art in nationalist allegories, centred on the classicised female figure, which were then elaborated to suit the particular context (industry, transport, justice or whatever). Versions of this had long been part of the official rhetoric of many nations, including France and Britain. Marianne, the Revolutionary symbol of the French Republic, reappears at the heart of the Popular Front's 'People's Fair', the Paris 1937 exhibition. Antoine Bourdelle's bronze *La France* (c.1922), complete with spear, stood on the top terrace at the centre of the colonnades of the Palais de Tokyo, the new Musées d'Art Moderne, above bas-relief allegories elaborating on the idea of France's geographical extensions by sea and air (Imperial France).

Germany chose as its national sign the eagle, usually publicly displayed in conjunction with the swastika. Architectural decoration in the Third Reich was almost exclusively limited to these two forms. The USSR obviously needed a universal symbol of revolution; it is a matter of debate whether figures carrying the hammer and sickle could be described as allegorical. The sculptures topping the German and the Soviet Pavilions at the Paris Exhibition make an interesting comparison. The inevitable eagle faced Vera Mukhina's colossal steel-clad statue, *Industrial Worker and Collective Farm Girl*. These figures are anonymous but not abstract; they are not 'allegories' of an abstract concept or virtue, but the young heroes of a new world order. Unlike images of specific heroes, martyrs or leaders, though, they do not stand out from the crowd as individuals, for they are simultaneously of it. It is important to note that the two figures, striding and dynamic man and woman, are treated equally in terms of gender, for this is one of the many features that distinguishes Soviet imagery from that of Nazi Germany. The tendency of the latter in monumental statues, and indeed in all plastic arts, was to a ludicrous exaggeration of male and female difference, as in the towering Josef Thorak triads that flanked the entrance to the German pavilion.

What modernity should constitute in the context of monumental art was also of course inflected by the political context. For Fernand Léger, the ideal modern monument was Radio City in New York. For Punin:

> A monument must live the social and political life of the city and the city must live in it. It must be necessary and dynamic; then it will be modern. The forms of contemporary, agitational plastic arts lie beyond the depiction of man as an individual. They are found by the artist who is not crippled by the feudal and bourgeois traditions of the Renaissance, but who has laboured like a worker on the three unities of contemporary plastic consciousness: material, construction, volume.[17]

Mural painting in this century, secular offspring of religious frescoes, has taken on a more elaborate didactic function than statuary was capable of, especially in the hands of its greatest exponents, the Mexican muralists.

In Mexico, a programme of monumental art to decorate public buildings was inaugurated shortly after the revolution of 1910–20, by José Maria Vasconcelos, the new Minister of Education. However, his plan for harmoniously vague and elevating humanist allegories was rudely overtaken by the artists he had gathered together. In 1923 the newly formed Union of Mexican Workers, Technicians, Painters and Sculptors issued their Manifesto repudiating easel painting and asserting their commitment to a didactic and national mural art. Although this is not directly part of our story, it is important both as precursor and comparison in relation to the claims and practice of mural painting as a monumental art. Signed by, among others, José Clemente Orozco and Diego Rivera, but largely composed by David Alfaro Siqueiros, the Manifesto claimed that the art of the Mexican people was directly linked to their Indian traditions, was 'of the people and therefore collective… We reject so-called salon painting and all the ultra-intellectual salon art of the aristocracy and exalt the manifestations of monumental art because they are useful. We believe that any work of art which is alien or contrary

17 Punin, *op. cit.*, p.6.

to popular taste is bourgeois and should disappear because it perverts the aesthetic of our race.'[18]

What would have seemed a natural alliance, though, between the Soviet Union and the Mexican muralists came to little; plans for Rivera to paint a mural in Moscow during his visit there in 1927–28 never materialised, and official art there remained largely concentrated in the production of posters, statues and easel painting – admittedly often on a large scale – rather than murals.[19]

Appreciation of Rivera in Europe came from an unlikely quarter: the Surrealist leader André Breton, who visited Mexico in 1938, and wrote enthusiastically of Rivera's work, not only in his essay 'Souvenir du Mexique' but in letters to Surrealist friends and colleagues. André Masson wrote in response: 'I have often thought of his [Rivera's] lot (to be a great monumental painter), which has always seemed to me the best career there is for someone who wants to reveal the conception he has of the world, of life, his *raison d'être* – "by means of painting".'[20] For Masson himself, a painter who, through Surrealism, was committed to the idea of revolution but lived in a bourgeois democracy, this was impossible: 'Long live Mexico which is in harmony with Diego Rivera, and long live Diego Rivera who puts his genius at the service of an entire people.'[21]

How did Breton, whose resistance to propaganda in art, and to the very idea of a 'proletarian' art or literature, had been thoroughly honed and articulated in a series of confrontations with the French Communist Party earlier in the 1930s, justify his response to Rivera?[22] In 'Souvenir du Mexique' he talks not of the grand political vision of Rivera's murals but of their direct, story-telling character, like a popular picture-book, and their link to the pre-Columbian past.[23]

Breton refuses to relate Rivera to the issues of Socialist Realism, but

18 'Manifesto of the Union of Mexican Workers, Technicians, Painters and Sculptors', *El Machete*, Mexico City, 1923, trans. Polyglossia, in Dawn Ades, *Art in Latin America*, exhibition catalogue, Yale University Press, New Haven, CT, and London, 1989, p.324.

19 Siqueiros, who remained a member of the Communist Party, was an influential figure in Eastern Europe after the war. Among those who collaborated with him in the 1930s on mural projects such as the Electricians Union in Mexico City was Josep Renau, who was responsible for the graphic material of the Spanish Pavilion at the 1937 Paris Exhibition.

20 André Masson, letter to André Breton, 29 June 1938, in *André Breton: la beauté convulsive*, exhibition catalogue, Centre Pompidou, Paris, 1991, p.239.

21 *Ibid.*

his companion in Mexico, Leon Trotsky, does precisely that in a letter to the editors of *Partisan Review* in 1938. Trotsky contrasts Rivera's work with Stalinist Socialist Realism, whose anachronistic photographic naturalism and historical falsifications express the 'profound decline of the proletarian revolution': 'Incredible as it seemed at first sight, there was no place for the art of Diego Rivera, either in Moscow, or in Leningrad, or in any other section of the USSR where the bureaucracy born of the revolution was erecting grandiose palaces and monuments to itself. And how could the Kremlin clique tolerate in its kingdom an artist who paints neither icons representing the "leader" nor life-size portraits of Voroshilov's horse?'[24]

The 'Manifesto for an Independent Revolutionary Art', signed by Breton and Rivera, though drawn up by Breton in collaboration with Trotsky, was published in 1938. While drawing a clear distinction between Fascism and Communism, this robust assertion of the artist's need and right to complete creative independence outlines the degradation of conditions in Germany and the USSR. The Soviet Union represents 'not Communism but its most dangerous and treacherous enemy'.[25] The manifesto is an appeal to find a common ground for all the scattered and isolated revolutionary artists. Although the movement it represented, FIARI (International Federation of Independent Revolutionary Art), was short-lived and utopian, the manifesto sought to address in simple terms the conflict between the individual artist and hostile social forms, without reviving 'a so-called pure art which generally serves the extremely impure ends of reaction',[26] or losing a belief in the capacity of art to influence the fate of society.

22 See for example, André Breton. 'Position Politique du Surréalisme', *La Bibliothèque Volante*, no.2, 1971, and André Breton, Franklin Rosemont (ed), *What is Surrealism? Selected Writings of André Breton*, Pathfinder Press, London, 1978.

23 André Breton, 'Souvenir du Mexique', *Minotaure*, vol.6, nos.12/13, May 1939, pp.30–52.

24 Leon Trotsky, 'Art and Politics: a Letter to the Editors of *Partisan Review*', *Partisan Review*, 1938, p.8.

25 'Manifesto for an Independent Revolutionary Art', in André Breton, *What is Surrealism?*, *op. cit.*, p.184.

26 *Ibid.*, p.186.

The Paris Exhibition of 1937 was the last showcase in Europe before the Second World War for the display of art that was 'monumental' in a variety of different senses: that is, monuments in the classic sense of commemorative sculpture, allegorical and symbolic figures, and work in two or three dimensions that was simply on a massive scale. The works of mural painting, mosaic, stained glass and tapestry fell into both didactic and decorative categories.

The most prominent two-dimensional monumental works were those of Sironi, Picasso, Dufy, Léger and the Delaunays. Those who had publicly entered the debate – Sironi and Léger – claimed their *raison d'être* to lie in the popular, collective character of the mural. Le Corbusier, however, raised some awkward questions about the character of the spectator-public. He noted that few paused to look at Picasso's *Guernica* (1937), while Dufy's vast mural on the history of electricity, which was simply a panoramic view of individual inventors with a few illustrative anecdotes but with very little concern for structure, drew crowds who amused themselves identifying the various characters.

Both Sironi and Léger wrote about monumental mural painting, but from very different perspectives. Sironi's 'Manifesto of Mural Painting', which was also signed by Achille Funi, Massimo Campigli and Carlo Carrà, argued that art had a social function, and that mural painting was 'social painting par excellence', because it 'acts on the popular imagination more directly than any other form of painting'.[27] The manifesto is haughtily vague, however, about what exactly the social, civic, didactic function of fascist mural painting constituted. The impression that mural painting should leave on the public would not be by virtue of the subject matter – which was, Sironi argues, the error of the communists. It should rather be by the 'style'. The mural 'must give a unity of style and grandeur of contour to common life. Thus art will once again become what it was in the greatest of times and at the heart of the greatest civilisations: a perfect instrument of spiritual direction.' Through mural painting, order, control and the authority of antiquity would become the 'fascist style'.

27 Mario Sironi, 'Manifesto of Mural Painting', 1933, in Harrison and Wood, *op. cit.*, p.408.

Far from Rivera's rousing and polemical populism, Sironi dreamed of the unforced superiority of muralism, which would synthesise tradition and contemporary life. His own compositions, such as the mosaic for the Italian Pavilion of 1937, or the great stained-glass window for the Palazzo dell'Industria in Rome, avoid specific subject matter in favour of an 'ideal tension', to apply Mussolini's phrase, between grand abstractions embodied in allegorical figures and 'typical' scenes from contemporary Italian society exemplifying work and sport, home and the battlefield, etc. His images are thus intended structurally to represent Italy:

> ...the juridical and ideal structure of Italy today. This structure draws its strength from age-old tradition... and from the perpetual capacity of the Latin race for work and renewal. 'Believe, Obey, Fight': that is the inscription placed between the large silhouettes of the mosaic in which Mario Sironi represents Italy today. The manly figure of the Duce, beside that of the King-Emperor, opposite the stained glass where one sees the mystical faces of St Ambrose, St Martin and the Archangel Michael, seems to warn us that in the life of the people, what is of value is not just material riches, but above all the ideal forces of faith, discipline and sacrifice.[28]

Fernand Léger, whose huge mural *Transport of Forces* was housed in the Palace of Discovery in Paris in 1937, believed no less in the triumph of the mural as 'modern monument', but from a diametrically opposite position to that of Sironi. He regarded mural painting as a necessary response to the exigencies of modern architecture (the 'new pitiless reality' of the architect's white wall) and to public needs of a practical and psychological kind. The monument is or should be a 'popular work', which needs the collaboration of architect, painter and sculptor; but this is not a matter of 'demagogical concessions' or lowering standards to meet popular desires: 'It is a human necessity which demands that, in works or realisations that touch people, crowds, the men who direct or command them must listen to hearts beating.'[29]

28 P. Sacerdoti, in *Le Pavillon Italien, Exposition de Paris*, Paris, 1937, p.77.

29 Fernand Léger, 'Le Mur, l'architecte, le peintre', 1933, in *Fonctions de la peinture*, Éditions Gonthier, Paris, 1965, p.120.

Mural painting is artisanal and collective. The problem, as Léger saw it, was to forge a work that was monumental – in the sense that it was public, collective, and a hybrid of painting, sculpture and architecture – and would act as directly on the crowd through 'pure plastic values' as did the advertisements, shop windows and modern forms of spectacle to which people were already accustomed. Both Léger and Rivera keep to the ideal of an art that will be comprehensible to the people. But while Rivera structured his giant, multifigure canvases to present strong arguments about the evils of capitalism, the importance of its specific historical past to present-day Mexico, contrasting the oppression of the colonial period with the harmony of pre-Columbian Mexico, and revelling somewhat contradictorily in the power and magic of the machine, Léger avoided the didactic and the distracting character of figurative narrative in favour of the free use of colour on large surfaces. Wary of coercive claims, Léger saw the 'social function' of his murals in terms of a loosening of habits of thought chaining 'the ordinary man' to a subservient past. His revolution was 'not only of a plastic order, but also of a psychological order':[30] a statement which raises intriguing connections with Surrealism.

The fact that, outside the totalitarian regimes, the ephemeral International Exhibitions or World Fairs proved the most viable venue for monumental art is paradoxical. That which was conceived as embodying an idea of permanency and the constant and vital interpenetration of past and present proved even more vulnerable than portable works of art. Little of the monumental art from the 1937 Paris Exhibition found a permanent home, and much, like Léger's *Transport of Forces* and Joan Miró's *Catalan Peasant in Revolt* (*The Harvester*), disappeared. Robert and Sonia Delaunay's large paintings from the Railway and Aeronautical Pavilions were rolled up and forgotten for decades – as indeed was Rivera's huge mural for the 1940 Golden Gate Fair.

Commemorative figurative monuments in their imperishable materials of stone, bronze or steel appear to guarantee eternal fame, while reminding the spectator of mortality. 'Civic sculpture,' Carlos Monsiváis wrote, 'is the homage of the lasting to that which will never return.'

30 Léger, 'De la peinture murale', 1952, in Léger, *ibid.*, p.111.

Statues both '*are*, and *represent*'.[31] Perhaps this is one of the reasons for the violence of the reaction against them when power changes hands. As fetishes of the symbolic order that constructed them, they arouse a kind of primitive animistic awe. At least since the destruction of the idol of Baal, or the disfigurement of the stone heads of the Olmec in America over 2,000 years ago, one of the first acts of a liberated people has been the overthrow of the monuments of the previous rulership, which overnight has become illegitimate. When the Soviet Union and other Eastern Bloc regimes crumbled at the end of the 1980s, some of the most memorable images were of the dismantling of the stone effigies of the leaders and heroes; the violent destruction of the statue of the police chief – and the careful dismantling with saws, ropes and cranes of Dolezal's double statue of Lenin and Stalin;[32] photographs show Stalin almost covered with autumn leaves, and graveyards of disgraced monuments in forgotten corners of the cities.

31 Carlos Monsiváis, 'La hora cívica: de monumentos cívicos y sus espectadores', in *Los rituales del caos*, Ediciones Era, Mexico City, 1995, p.149.

32 See *Kunst und Diktatur*, exhibition catalogue, Jan Tabor (ed), Künstlerhaus, Vienna, 1994, vol.2, pp.842–45.

Abstraction

The terminology for abstract, 'non-objective', 'non-figurative' or 'objectless' – to use Kasimir Malevich's term – art has been much debated. For some artists, such as Jean (Hans) Arp, 'abstract' should be applied only to configurations 'abstracted' from things in the world, as in Cubism, which never lost its link to representation. Somewhat ironically given his preference as a sculptor for biomorphic forms, Arp argued for the term 'concrete' rather than abstract for work which had no referent outside itself.

Raising questions in relation to the discourses of abstraction in the history of twentieth-century art and design from a different approach, 'Function and Abstraction in Poster Design' looks at topics not otherwise covered in the essays here. It easily could have been placed under 'Art and Power' rather than 'Abstraction', as it addresses some of the same issues and concerns a medium particularly suited to propaganda and the harnessing of the visual to socio-political or commercial power.

One of the most original outcrops from the mass of abstract, non-objective, constructive and concrete art was Arte Madí, which emerged in Argentina in the early 1940s. I first saw examples of this in 1986 in the storage of a collection in Buenos Aires: a screen covered in strange little objects, shaped pieces of wood or canvas, painted in flat colours, some with movable parts, some in relief. Their inventive and playful geometries seemed to me to own a Dada-Constructivist genealogy.

The other two essays are about artists whose work I find constantly engaging, never settling into repetition or programmatic abstraction. Melanie Smith moved to Mexico from the UK in the late 1980s, and her work reflects the experience of another kind of modernity in dialogue with her European background. In her installations there is a tension between austerely geometrical but brightly coloured paintings and the interference from TV monitors on packing cases. The films made with her partner Rafael Ortega include street markets and a kind of homage to artist Robert Smithson, in which the megalopolis Mexico City is filmed in an endlessly receding spiral. There is no clear-cut boundary between figuration and abstraction. Abstraction can take on many guises and in the work of Richard Deacon remains as potent and open to experiment as in its earliest polemical appearances over a century ago.

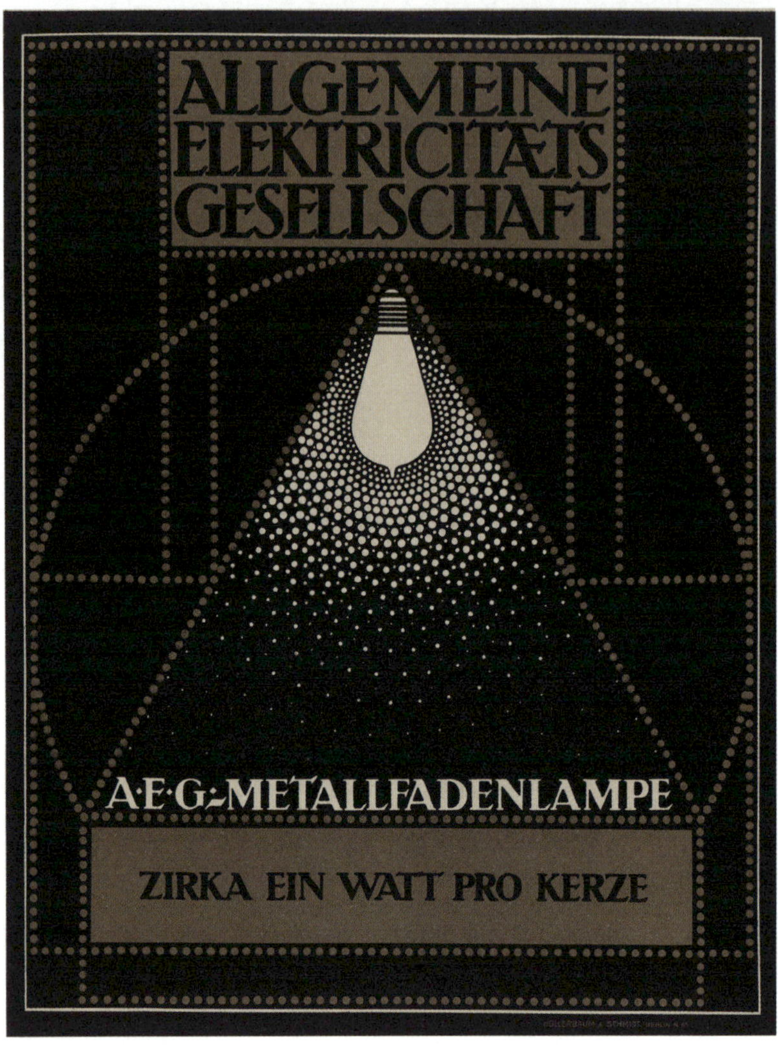

112 **Peter Behrens**
AEC – Metallfadenlampe
(AEC – Metal Filament lamps), 1907
Lithograph
69.2 × 52.7 cm | 27¼ × 20¾ in

Function and Abstraction in Poster Design

Posters: The 20th-Century Poster. Design of the Avant-Garde, Dawn Ades (ed), Abbeville Press, New York, NY, 1984

In 1936 Alfred Barr opened his book *Cubism and Abstract Art* with a comparison of two posters. Both were produced to advertise the 1928 international exhibition of printing held in Cologne. Barr's purpose was to draw attention to the contrast between the 'fairly realistic poster style common to mediocre travel posters the world over', of the one, and the 'simplicity and abstraction' of the other.[1] Here, the 'natural objects are reduced to flat, almost geometric forms arranged on a strongly diagonal axis under the influence of Russian Suprematism'. The reason that two different posters were produced was that they were intended for different markets: one for the Anglo-American, 'accustomed to an over-crowded and banally realistic style', the other for the German public, which, 'through the activity of its museums and progressive commercial artists was quite used to an abstract style'. For Barr, the superiority of the formal, abstract poster was self-evident. He ends his comment by saying: 'Today, times have changed. The style of the abstract poster, which is just beginning to interest our American advertiser, is now discouraged in Germany.' Later in the book he comments on the political cause of this discouragement, the rise of National Socialism.[2]

Certain assumptions in Barr's pictorial preface are worth spelling out. Firstly, the status of the poster: it is treated not as a secondary art but as an art form in its own right, like painting, photography, theatre, film. In his catalogue of the exhibition that the book accompanied he lists the

1 Alfred Barr, *Cubism and Abstract Art*, Museum of Modern Art, New York, NY, 1936. Barr's book accompanied the first major historical survey exhibition of modern movements in art.

category as 'typography and posters'. Secondly, there is the implication that, while the simplicity of the abstract poster was good in itself, it was particularly good in a poster where the need for simplicity had long been recognised as intrinsic. The question might arise as to whether an abstract poster is necessarily simpler than a figurative one – look at the radical simplifications of the Beggarstaffs (the pseudonym used by British artists William Nicholson and James Pryde), for example. The difference here is that the simplicity of Barr's poster is based upon abstract geometrical principles independent of the subject depicted, and the complex of ideas underlying Barr's prejudice will be examined in detail later. He implies that the more abstract design is more functionally effective than the other. Because the result of the abstraction in this case is to focus attention on the typography, it is of course especially apt, given that the poster is advertising an exhibition of modern printing. But Barr would clearly favour an abstract design, whatever was being advertised. When he uses the term 'abstraction', in this case, he does not in fact mean total non-figuration. Although it is doubtful whether an Anglo-American audience would recognise in the triangular shapes a 'reduction' or 'abstraction' of Cologne cathedral's twin towers, the fact remains that these geometrical shapes retain an element of figuration, however reduced, which has the function of keeping them distinct from the typography. But many posters in the 1920s and 1930s did use totally non-figurative designs. Does this mean that the poster image as distinct from its typography ceased to function? In other words, that in so far as it was abstract it became simply an adjunct to the typographical message?

I would like to look at the question of function and abstraction in poster design in the first three decades of the twentieth century, and to consider the ways in which the main movements within modernism influenced and absorbed the poster, and reciprocally to what extent they fed off it. To focus on these questions and narrow my argument to those

2 Barr discusses the contradictory ways in which abstract art became involved in politics, with, for example, the Nazis suppressing abstract art and international style architecture while fascist Italy welcomed them. A footnote was added, as the book was going to press, on the refusal of US customs to allow in, as art, 19 pieces of sculpture that were to be in the exhibition, because they did not represent a human or animal: 'This essay and exhibition might well be dedicated to those painters of squares and circles... who have suffered at the hands of philistines with political power.'

posters directly or indirectly connected with modernism and its roots is, obviously, to look at only a tiny fraction of the total poster production of this period. Whole areas have to be excluded, including historical and political events that spawned innumerable poster campaigns such as the two world wars. However, the inquiry will necessarily involve sociopolitical and historical issues given the interdependence of the poster and society. Why, for example, was the Anglo-American market, as Barr describes it, resistant to or ignorant of abstract design? What contributed to its success in Europe? Barr's optimism about the arrival of an abstract style in American advertising was to be short-lived. The Second World War brought to an abrupt end experimental graphic design and before the war, in Germany, the Nazis had condemned modern typography and returned to black letter gothic. On both sides, Axis and Allies alike, a conservative realism (which had of course always coexisted) swept across the entire field of poster production and more or less eliminated the abstract-constructivist style. It is, incidentally, a significant comment on the divided nature of poster studies that the literature on Second World War posters often entirely ignores this remarkable fact, leaving out the way a poster looks altogether. Although the poster has its own history and conditions, it tends to be treated in different ways according to the discipline involved: as an illustration of social or political history, as an aspect of the history of marketing and advertising, as a branch of art and design.

The poster had, during the period I want to discuss, a spectacular energy, and this energy has never really been recovered since the Second World War. Its conditions had changed for good. The poster belongs to a specific phase in the age of mechanical reproduction: for 70 or 80 years it was the most conspicuous, accessible and familiar form of pictorial production. After the First World War it was joined by the film and the illustrated weekly paper, which had, in El Lissitzky's opinion, triumphed over the easel picture. 'The invention of easel pictures produced great works of art, but their effectiveness has been lost. The cinema and the illustrated weekly magazine have triumphed.'[3] For a while the poster was the ally and support of the cinema. But it was eventually displaced by

3 'Our book' (1926), in Sophie Lissitzky-Küppers, *El Lissitzky*, Thames & Hudson, London, 1968, p.361.

television, and now, in Europe and the United States at least, its function has been taken over by print advertising.[4]

Almost from the beginning of poster history there have been the poster and the art poster. Before the 1870s, and excluding special categories like the recruiting poster, the vast majority of advertisements in public places took the form of words. A few woodcut posters included pictures, but usually with the accompaniment of a long text. Primarily it was easily printed slogans and the titles of plays, books and products that were plastered over the walls. Before the regulation of hoardings began it was virtually a war, too, to see who could get his poster on top. A comparison was drawn in an article in *The Poster* in 1900 between a hoarding of 1844 and one at the turn of the century. This was intended to show the improvement of the regulated order of the contemporary hoarding with its practice of 'blocking' or placing groups of a single poster together. Although this photograph still shows a preponderance of the typographical poster, the pictorial poster was by this time very well established. The potential of the coloured lithograph for posters had been recognised in the 1870s. Some of the earliest examples were enlarged versions of book illustrations hung up in bookshop windows to advertise new publications. It was in the late 1860s that Jules Chéret brought together his technical experience as an apprentice lithographer in England and the lesson of the Japanese colour woodblock print with its bold shapes and flat washes of brilliant colour, which had been a powerful influence on Impressionist and post-Impressionist painting in Paris, to create the conditions for the poster boom of the 1880s and 1890s. This is often described in poster histories as the 'golden age' of the poster, and with nostalgic exaggeration as the highest point reached by the poster before or since. Many of these posters were publicity for books, theatre and cabaret – much the same subjects as those on the 1844 hoardings. This was the area dominated by the artist-poster designer: Chéret, Henri de Toulouse-Lautrec, Alphonse Mucha (Sarah Bernhardt's preferred artist), Félix Vallotton. Such posters were almost immediately collectors' items, with price lists and catalogues, and they were frequently stripped

4 In the case of the firm of Guinness, which still mounts extensive poster campaigns on well-placed hoardings, the ratio of money spent on advertising is four to one in favour of film, which they find the most cost effective way of reaching their target audience.

from the walls by enthusiasts before the paste was dry. But commercial manufacturers were also quick to recognise the value of the lithographic picture poster, especially for products like food, drink or soap. By 1900 some were even using the new photographic halftone process for the image. Most such posters, though, were designed by printers, either on speculation or on commission from an advertising agency or directly from a company. The fact that artists were seldom involved was due less to the prejudice of the artist than to the prejudice of the manufacturer. The artist was not trusted to make a comprehensible and desirable image. When Henry Davray was asked by the Paris dealer Deschamps to organise an exhibition of English posters he succeeded in scraping together a few by Aubrey Beardsley, the Beggarstaffs and Maurice Grieffenhagen, but he found a constant complaint by the artists that they were hampered by the advertisers' insistence that the 'tin of cocoa or shoe polish, brand of soap or cigarettes' should be shown in its external packaging, which seldom had anything very aesthetic about it.[5] The Beggarstaffs' radical designs, that sometimes used large cutout paper shapes and drew, as did Lautrec and Chéret, on the flat colours and silhouettes of the Japanese print, were unpopular, and were even satirised as grim and gloomy. The generally conservative attitudes of the manufacturers persisted after the First World War in England and the United States, though more daring publicity came to be associated with such products as tyres and cars.

The distinction between the poster and the art poster (the *Plakat als solches* as opposed to the *kunstlerische Plakat* as the German magazine *Das Plakat* defined it in 1914) was not necessarily between the function of advertising an aesthetic as opposed to a consumer product, but was rather a reference to the status of the designer. But for such reasons as I have outlined above the term art poster was most frequently used for those concerned with cultural as opposed to commercial interests. Within this, there were posters with a specific relationship to an art movement and which therefore acted as a visual manifesto, as aesthetic propaganda, clearly displaying their status as art. Good examples of this would be the posters produced in association with the Secession in Vienna and Germany. In Glasgow, the Macdonald sisters (Margaret and Frances) and

5 *XIXth-Century French Posters,* with an introduction by James Laver and a preface by Henry Davray, Nicholson & Watson, London, 1944.

Herbert McNair designed an exhibition poster for The Glasgow Institute of the Fine Arts, which shares with the Viennese posters the highly decorative features of the pervasive Jugendstil. Within this decorative ideal the poster's specific function is realised: it is not a question of simply reproducing a representative work of art and adding some lettering. Stress is laid on the design as a whole, with close attention to the typography, which is often highly stylised, complementing the emphatic linearity of the image. Sometimes it is adapted to fit around the image, or given a separate box, and in some cases becomes the major element in the design. The stylisation of the letters sometimes leads to distortion and internal inconsistency, and even within a poster the same letter may be shaped differently (the length of the central stroke of the 'E' varies, for example, in the poster for The Glasgow Institute of the Fine Arts, c.1894, by McNair and the Macdonalds). Such lettering was to be condemned as idiosyncratic and random when the call for standardisation came in the first decade of the twentieth century.

The art poster dominated the field leading up to the turn of the century. It was a time when poster magazines and societies flourished, and hoardings were proliferating through town and country. Posters had become a pervasive pictorial presence, and as such drew strong responses from artists and critics. Ruskin, a reluctant witness to the massive growth of poster advertising, expressed the view that it would finally usurp painting: 'The fresco painting of the bill sticker is likely, so far as I see, to become the principal fine art of modern Europe: here, at all events, it is now the principal source of street effect. Giotto's time is past... but the bill poster succeeds', he wrote from Florence in 1872.[6] The poster, at certain times and for different reasons, has represented the condition to which painting itself would aspire. 'Be a poster: advertise and project a new world', was the call to a new generation of Constructivist artists in the Prague review *Disk* in 1923. This represents an extreme position which was part of a complex of ideas I shall return to.

At the beginning of the machine age the poster was 'a piece of modern

6 John Ruskin, *Fors Clavigera. Letters to the Workmen and Labourers of Great Britain*, Index, etc. (Compiled by the Rev. J.P. Founthorpe), 9 vols, G. Allen, Orpington, 1871–87.

7 *Functions of Painting*, edited and introduced by Edward F. Fry, with an article by Fernand Léger, 'Contemporary Achievements in Painting', Thames & Hudson, London, 1973.

furniture that painters immediately knew how to use'.[7] A street aesthetic had begun to replace the 'secular idealism' of the earlier nineteenth century, magnetising those who wanted art to remain in close contact with life.[8] 'We would at any price re-enter into life', the Futurist painters wrote in their 1910 *Technical Manifesto*. Apollinaire, critic and champion of the Cubists, and an admirer of the Futurists, included scraps of overheard street conversations in his poems, and located art outside its conventional lairs – the salon, museum, or review: 'You read prospectuses catalogues posters singing out loud/There's poetry for this morning...'[9]

The Fauve painters included brilliantly coloured poster hoardings in their works, and Robert Delaunay used poster signs and images as essential elements in his simultaneous visions of city life. Fernand Léger, in his writings, developed the notion that the true source of visual ideas lay in the world of industry and technology. At the Paris Fair, at the annual Aeronautical and Automobile Salons, a new kind of beauty was to be found, which put to shame the 'vast, dull, grey surfaces, stuck in pretentious frames', of the paintings in the Salon d'Automne.[10] 'I am amazed to see that all those men who arranged the splendid display boards, astonishing fountains of letters and light, powerful or precious machines... don't understand or appreciate that they are the real artists, that they have upended every modern plastic idea.'[11] It was not a matter, for Léger, of taking this modern spectacular as a subject, but of learning from it new pictorial principles. The most essential of these was contrast, and for this the poster provided the most vivid example. 'This yellow or red poster, shouting in a timid landscape, is the best of possible reasons for the new painting; it topples the whole sentimental literary concept and announces the advent of pictorial contrast.'[12] El Lissitzky described how Léger's postwar, post-Cubist painting had achieved its ideal: 'With the new canvas... the culture of painting no longer comes from the museum. It comes from the picture gallery of our modern streets

8 Albert Gleizes and Jean Metzinger, 'Cubism' (1912), in Robert L. Herbert, *Modern Artists on Art*, Prentice-Hall, Englewood Cliffs, New Jersey, NJ, 1964, p.3.

9 Guillaume Apollinaire, *Zone* (1912), in *Alcools, Poems, 1898–1913*, Paris, 1913.

10 Fernand Léger, 'The Machine Aesthetic, the Manufactured Object, the Artisan and the Artist', *Léger and Purist Paris*, Tate Gallery, London, 1971 p.92.

11 *Ibid.*, p.91

12 Léger, 'Les realizations picturales actuelles' (1914), in Léger, *Fonctions de la peinture*, Editions Gonthier, Paris, 1965, p.21.

– the riot and exaggeration of colours on the lithographic poster.'[13] The Futurist leader F.T. Marinetti celebrated the new industrial age in his 'The Founding and Manifesto of Futurism': 'We will sing of the great crowds excited by work, by pleasure and by riot; we will sing of the multicoloured polyphonic tides of revolution in the modern capitals; we will sing of the vibrant nightly fervour of arsenals and shipyards blazing with violent electric moons; greedy railway stations that devour smoke-plumed serpents.'[14]

Both Léger and Marinetti used the poster as a sign of the industrial world as opposed to the country. 'Multi-coloured billboards on the green of the fields, iron bridges that chain the hills together, surgical trains that pierce the blue belly of the mountains', Marinetti wrote in 'War, the World's Only Hygiene'.[15] The violent clash between billboard and natural landscape is also a symbolic opposition between past and present, the harmonious rural scene and the modern industrial street. The image of the brilliant hard-edged poster slicing into the 'sentimental' landscape does of course belong to a period before the spread of advertising was strictly controlled, when it was far more invasive and striking both in town and country than it is today. Ruskin grumbled about the spread of advertisements for 'prayers and wares', and was particularly distressed by the religious posters plastered all over the facade of one of the most beautiful churches in Florence, '...in and out upon the sculptured bearings of the shields of the old Florentine knights'.[16] Léger, by contrast, was outraged by attempts to control the spread of billboards, a characteristic failure, as he saw it, of the so-called 'men of good taste' to recognise the pressing if brutal demands of the new state of things. He links it to the general failure of the public to understand modern art:

> It has even given rise to a stupefying and ridiculous organization that pompously calls itself 'The Society for the Protection of the

13 El Lissitzky, 'Exhibitions in Berlin' (*Veshch* 3, Berlin, 1922), Lissitzky-Küppers, *op. cit.*, p.346.
14 Filippo Tommaso Marinetti, 'The Founding and Manifesto of Futurism' (*Le Figaro*, 20 February 1909), Umbro Apollonio (ed), *Futurist Manifestos*, Thames & Hudson, London, 1973.
15 Marinetti, 'War, the World's Only Hygiene' (1911–1915), *Marinetti: Selected Writings*, Secker & Warburg, London 1971 p.67.
16 Ruskin, *op. cit.*

> Landscape'. Can anyone imagine anything more comic than this high court of worthy men charged with solemnly decreeing that such and such a thing is appropriate in the landscape and another thing is not? By this reckoning it would be preferable to do away with telegraph poles and houses immediately and leave only trees, sweet harmonies of trees... There is nothing worse than habit, and you will find the same people who protest with conviction in front of the billboard writhing with laughter at the Salon des Indépendents in front of modern pictures, which they are incapable of swallowing...[17]

While Léger sought to emulate the effect of the poster in its environment, abstracted from its function, Wyndham Lewis, the English Vorticist writer and painter, imagined annexing it to serve directly as aesthetic propaganda. Lewis, who, like the Futurists, was fully alive to the possibilities of mobilising the new means of mass communication for his own purposes, envisaged the poster as a means of converting the public to abstract art:

> Let us give a direct example of how this revolution will work in popular ways. In poster advertisement by far the most important point is a telling design. Were the walls of London carpeted with abstractions rather than the present mass of work that falls between two stools, the design usually weakened to explain some point, the effect architects rally would be much better, and the public taste would thus be educated in a popular way to appreciate the essentials of design better than picture galleries have ever done.[18]

The poster had pushed its way into the consciousness of painters like Léger and Delaunay. It made an appearance in a much less direct way in the difficult, esoteric Cubism of Picasso and Braque. When lettering was smuggled onto late analytic Cubist canvases, hovering ghostlike on the

17 Léger, *op. cit.*, p.12. Much later, Léger recalled the dramatic intervention of posters in the landscape: 'The streets, the countryside, those impressionist landscapes, which were so melodic and pleasant, have suddenly seen "Dubonnet" signs appearing everywhere: the melody got all fucked up – there is no other word', 'La couleur dans l'architecture' (1954) in Léger, *op. cit.*, p.185.

18 Wyndham Lewis, introduction to Vorticist exhibition, Doré Gallery, London, 1911.

surface and often the only immediately 'legible' element on it, posters, like newspapers or bottle labels, could have been the occasion for it. In Braque's *Le Portugais* of 1911, the stenciled letters refer to a poster for a ball, and serve to locate the man as sitting at a café table, the poster on the glass wall of the café or glimpsed through it.

But none of these painters was interested in poster design for its own sake, and neither Cubism, nor Futurism, had a direct impact upon it. Cubism, of course, through its crucial influence on a number of artists who travelled through it on a road to abstraction (like Mondrian, or Malevich), was strongly to affect postwar art, architecture and design. Cubism itself always remained an art of realism though, and when Mondrian or Malevich developed their abstract or non-representational art it was founded upon a different set of ideas.

There is almost no evidence of a geometrising abstraction which could be ascribed to the workings of a Cubist influence in poster design until the middle of the First World War, to judge by the most important poster magazine of the time, *Das Plakat*. *Das Plakat* was published in Berlin from 1909 until 1921, its internationalism barely ruffled by the war. It covered most aspects of the poster, with theoretical articles as well as a quantity of excellent reproductions of posters from all over Europe and from the United States, including commercial, political and cultural ones. It is therefore a valuable guide to the state of the poster during this period. The Munich designer Ludwig Hohlwein was generally recognised as the dominant figure before (and indeed during) the war, and *Das Plakat* devoted its May 1913 issue to him. His work can be compared to the flattened and simplified style of the Beggarstaffs. Like them, he placed a heavy emphasis on silhouette, but while Pryde and Nicholson kept a strong linear element that bounded or complemented the large flat areas of colour, Hohlwein almost eliminated it. The formalised shapes composing the figures are defined usually by contrast with a neighbouring tone or hue; he often used a negative-positive contrast, and sometimes the effect is curiously like a painting from a halftone print. His elegant silhouetted figures were well adapted to the clothing advertisements that formed a major part of his pre-war output.

Not until June 1916 is there a hint of Cubism of any kind. In that issue of *Das Plakat* an article was published entitled 'Cubism and the Poster' by a Dr Wolf. He goes straight to the heart of Cubism with works by Picasso, both analytic paintings and collage, rather than by followers like Albert Gleizes and Jean Metzinger. The posters reproduced for comparison can only be called Cubistic. The most interesting example is by Oskar Schlemmer, in which a head is reduced to flat black-and-white geometric forms, prophetic of later developments but less like Cubist painting as it existed at the time.

Das Plakat picked up Dada, reproducing a Raoul Hausmann 'poster' in 1920, but not De Stijl. In 1920 it also published a number of Soviet posters, but these did not include examples of Suprematist or Constructivist designs.

When I mentioned the 'simplification' of Secessionist posters above, I was not referring to Cubist simplification, but rather to a quite independent influence on design in the prewar years: the German Werkbund. The Werkbund was founded by Hermann Muthesius in 1907 with the aim of improving the standards of German design and encouraging and facilitating contacts between industry and designers. It can be seen as having established certain ideas and practices that were to remain of importance after the war, in such contexts as the Bauhaus. It established architecture as the leader in the fields of design, and placed an emphasis on standardisation with simplicity, clarity and rationality as primary objectives. This led to direct conflict with Jugendstil, and such figures as Henry van de Velde, who opposed Muthesius in 'a spirited rearguard action by an outgoing type of designer'.[19] It is interesting to compare posters by Van de Velde and Hector Guimard with posters by Peter Behrens, who was the most complete example of the Werkbund designer. Van de Velde's posters for the food company Tropon use highly stylised organic shapes, reminiscent of Guimard's Paris Metro entrances, which here contrast with the linear pattern surrounding the letters and governed by them in a rather random and arbitrary way. This is an inventive and effective poster; but Jugendstil typography did not place a high premium on legibility. There are Secession posters, and those by the Glasgow 'Four',[20] whose lettering holds a fine balance between ornament and

19 Reyner Banham, *Theory and Design in the First Machine Age*, The Architectural Press, London, (1960) 1975, p.78.

20 Margaret and Frances MacDonald, Charles Rennie Mackintosh and Herbert MacNair.

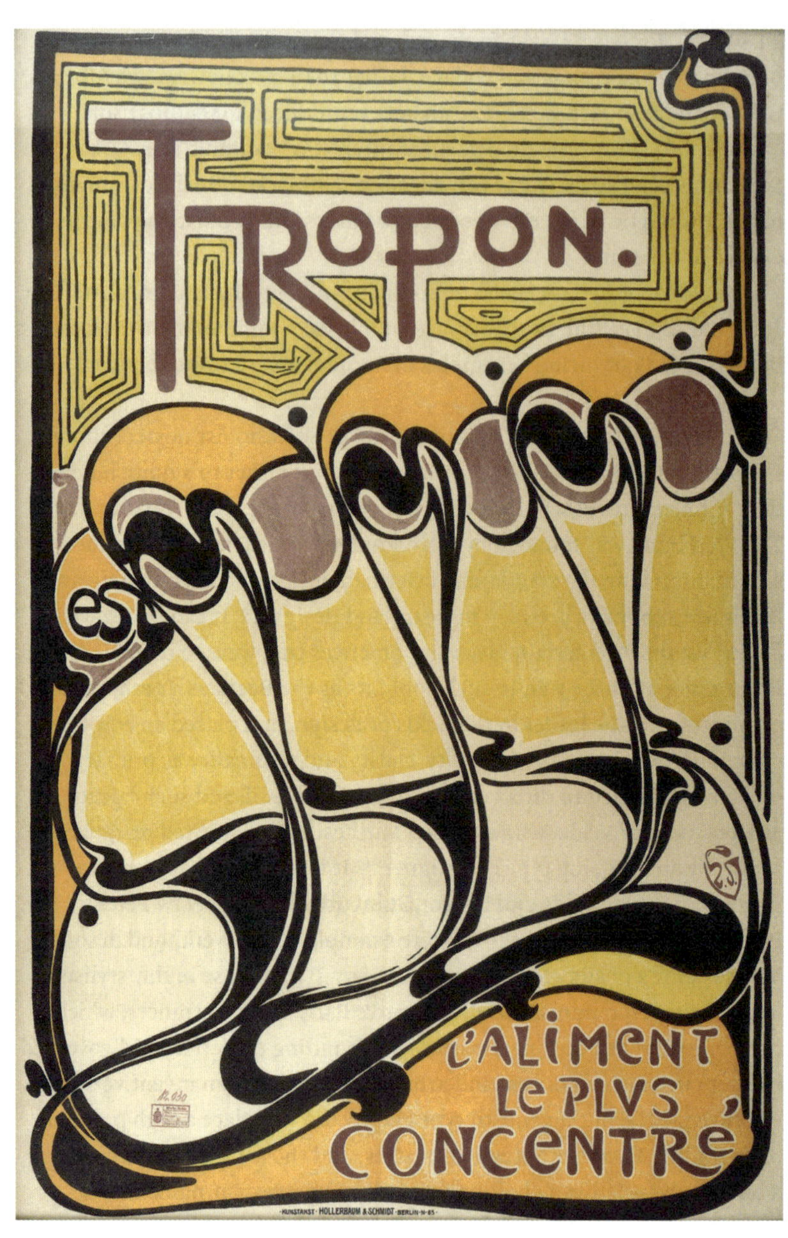

124 **Henry van de Velde**
Tropon, l'Aliment Le Plus Concentré
(Tropon, the most concentrated nourishment), 1898
Colour lithograph
112.4 × 75.5 cm | 44¼ × 29¾ in

clarity, but still could not be referred to as standardised. In Guimard's own poster it reaches an unprecedented degree of illegibility.

The Werkbund designers moved towards a simplicity governed by rational order. Behrens had joined the German electrical company AEG in 1907 as design consultant for all AEG products (buildings, manufactured objects and publicity). Initially a painter and graphic designer, he continued to produce posters after becoming an architect, as well as designing lamps, teapots and a sewing machine. His 1907 poster for AEG uses an architectural motif, but no longer as a separate image. It has become a framework for the design as a whole (p.112). The lightness of the later poster is related to a change in Behrens's own architectural practice, in that he moved from solid, heavy factory buildings to structures conceived of as envelopes over a vast industrial space. But Behrens is not here reproducing a glazed and abstracted neoclassical industrial temple, but reworking his industrial aesthetic in terms appropriate to the function of the poster. Muthesius had stressed that attention to function was to govern the search for formal solutions to problems of mechanical production. In his speech to the 1911 Werkbund Congress, whose theme was 'The Spiritualisation of German Production', he 'introduced the idea of standardisation as a virtue, and of abstract form as the basis of the aesthetics of product design'.[21] Although he did not apparently have in mind the abstract geometry of mathematical proportions, the ideas are remarkably similar to the neo-Platonic, post-Cubist Paris movement Purism, which was founded in 1918 by Amédée Ozenfant and Charles-Édouard Jeanneret (Le Corbusier), who had attended this Congress as a young architect. Purism proposed the selection of manufactured objects based upon pure geometric shapes as subjects for painting. To return to Behrens's poster, there is perhaps an incipient abstract geometry in the forms – the rectangular arch, the incomplete arc of a circle, the triangle of the lamp's rays – but they are not conceived of as primarily abstract forms independent of the object in the way that Suprematism, De Stijl and Constructivism were to do. The type of radical simplicity of Behrens's design, growing out of but rejecting the decorative abstractions of the Arts and Crafts movement, exemplifies the theory and practice of a

21 Banham, *op. cit.*, p.72.

movement concerned with industrial design in the broadest sense. It was not, in other words, the result of imposing new pictorial ideas onto the field of graphic design.

Three movements began during the First World War that were to influence, in various ways, graphic design: Suprematism in Russia, De Stijl in Holland and Dadaism in Zurich (and subsequently all over Europe). Dada inherited the Futurists' publicity methods, flooding the newspapers with stories (or fables), the public with leaflets and the art world with exhibitions and reviews, but it rejected their positive celebration of the machine aesthetic and glorification of war. Dada engaged in a wholesale rejection of society, its art and its war, that involved it immediately in a contradiction. Most of its (not very numerous) members were writers or artists, most living off the production of words and images. Dada's well-publicised nihilism, though, has often been allowed to mask its positive side. There was no identifiable Dada 'style': Dada includes the sophisticated ironies of Duchamp, the satirical anti-militaristic graphics and photomontages of John Heartfield and George Grosz, the abstractions of Jean (Hans) Arp. But certain ideas and methods were held in common. The irrational was valued in a world where sense and rationality had led to or at least been powerless to stop the 'civilised carnage' of war.[22] One method of bypassing controlling reason was chance. Feeding into experiments with chance were ideas culled from Eastern philosophies, which recognised that the flux or chaos of nature was a salutary and necessary reminder to man of his place within rather than above it. Another Dada method was to force a return to pre-cultural forms: to reduce language to its basic components of sound or letter, or to emulate children's drawing. At the other end of the scale was parody: Futurist simultaneity, Cubist collage, were subjected to various degrees of subversion. Dada also refused the conventional medium of oil paint, and its search for new materials, readymade or found or simply previously unthought of as art, was to reverberate on through the twentieth century.

Dada differed greatly in the various centres where it was active. In Zurich, where it began in 1916, Dada artists took 'abstraction as the cornerstone of their new wisdom'.[23] Marcel Janco, the Romanian artist,

22 Hugo Ball, *Flight Out of Time: A Dada Diary* (June 1916), Viking Press, New York, NY, 1974, p.67.

who at this time was making abstract reliefs in plaster and wood, made two posters for the second Dada season in Zurich in 1917. One was for the first Dada exhibition at the Galerie Corray in January, the other was for the second *Sturm* exhibition and featured a drawing by Janco of primitive sculpture. The earlier poster was, like many Dada works, composed entirely of lettering. The framework of the repeated 'Dada', characteristic of the obsessive self-publicity of the movement, is written in childishly uneven capitals, as though chalked on a blackboard. This is deliberate and significant, representing the 'primitiveness, beginning again at zero' that Dada stood for.[24] As Hugo Ball said, 'childhood as a new world; all the directness of childhood, all its symbolic and fantastic aspects, against the senilities of the adult world'.[25] 'Dada' curling round in unbroken repetition is also reminiscent of Dada sound poetry. Hugo Ball read his first sound poems in Zurich in 1916, and although these did not reach the pure phoneticism of Hausmann's or Kurt Schwitters's later work, he felt he had 'developed the plasticity of the word to a point which can hardly be surpassed'.[26]

Dada in Berlin differed radically from Dada elsewhere. Conditions were more extreme: starvation, defeat, revolution, made this one wing of Dada actively political. Much of Berlin Dada took on the aspect of street art. The montages by Grosz and Heartfield, mixing graphic elements, cut-up or complete photographs and scraps of printed text, anticipate the use of montage in posters later in the 1920s. Many of them were made for the satirical magazines put out by Wieland Herzfelde in Berlin just after the war, during the period of the abortive German revolution and the establishment of the Weimar Republic. In these the technique of photomontage was first systematically exploited for political ends. Many works looked like posters and even functioned as such. At the Berlin Dada Fair of 1920, poster placards were stuck among the works, which were themselves hung not only all over the walls but often on top of one another, so that the whole wall looked like a hoarding. The works were hung, in other words, not to facilitate individual contemplation

23 Richard Huelsenbeck, 'En Avant Dada: A History of Dadaism' (1920), in Robert Motherwell, *The Dada Painters and Poets*, Wittenborn, Schultz, New York, NY, 1951, p.37.

24 Huelsenbeck, 'Dada Lives!' (1936), in Motherwell, *op. cit.*, p.280.

25 Ball, *op. cit.*, August 1916.

26 *Ibid.*, June 1916.

and spiritual immersion, like a conventional exhibition, but to arrest, buttonhole, shock and amuse the public. Individually and collectively, in a sense, they were aiming at the condition of a poster. Hausmann printed his phonetic poems, such as *FMSBW,* on large sheets of coloured paper. Made to be declaimed, in giving them typographical form, Hausmann made them preeminently visual. One slogan at the exhibition read: 'Art is dead – long live the machine art of Tatlin', witness to the curiosity and affinity Berlin Dada felt for the as yet largely unknown art of the new Soviet Republic, and also heralding the complex relationship that was to take place between Dadaism and Constructivism after the war.

The typographical experiments, casually revolutionary, that characterise so many Dada productions, began with the third issue of Tristan Tzara's Zurich periodical, *Dada.* On the cover there is overprinting, and the lines are arranged at odd angles, disrupting our conventional reading habits from left to right, in a horizontal line. *Dada* was produced on a minute budget, Tzara paying for most of it himself with Arp and Janco subsidising four more pages. They went to an anarchist printer, Julius Heuberger, and appear to have selected the typefaces and played freely with the layout themselves.[27] Tzara's 'Salon Dada' poster, made for the exhibition during the 1921 Dada season in Paris, harks back typographically to his poem *Bulletin* in *Dada 3,* in which each line was printed in a different font. Any sequential sense the poem might have had is destroyed by the slogan-like distinctness of each line. In the 1921 poster this is taken to a logical extreme, with each separate announcement, either practical or apparently quite irrelevant, literally framed to become a sign on a signboard. In the lettering for the title of the exhibition, Tzara mixed both typefaces and upper and lowercase letters on a random basis, contradicting all accepted typographical manners.

There were, of course, precedents for Dada's typographical experiments. One that could really be seen as falling within Dada itself was an advertisement in the Berlin magazine *Neue Jugend,* for a Grosz portfolio, that scatters words and images freely across the page. There was a long

27 Dada did not discriminate in its choice of typefaces; old-fashioned and modern examples were used equally, with the occasional addition of letters from decorative alphabets. They could not afford the expense of such special printing as Marinetti's *Parole in Libertà,* nor were they sufficiently interested technically to take their involvement as far as the compositor.

tradition of adapting the printing of a poem to add a counterpointing visual dimension to the page, of which Apollinaire's *Calligrammes* (1918) was one of the most recent examples. The Futurists made spirited attacks on the rigidity of the printed word. Poems were printed to make their appearance parallel their sound, so that a crescendo in volume was indicated with an increase in the size of the letters. Futurist poems of this kind were printed in the first Dada review in Zurich, *Cabaret Voltaire,* of June 1916. Marinetti, in his manifesto 'Wireless Imagination and Words in Liberty' of 1913 challenged the whole notion of syntax, and was equally rude about the 'decorative precious aesthetic of Mallarmé', who, in *Un Coup de Dés* (1897), had his poem printed so that any natural reading order was destroyed. Marinetti wanted 'a swift, brutal and immediate lyricism', which could only be achieved in print by attacking the typographical harmony of the page. 'On the same page, therefore, we will use *three or four colours of ink,* or even twenty different typefaces if necessary. For example: italics for a series of similar or soft sensations, boldface for violent onomatopoeias.' When his 'Words in Liberty' was published in 1919 the visual effect exceeded his earlier ideas. But even the liberation of Futurist printed poetry seems systematic beside the anarchic typographical vagaries of many Dada posters and reviews. The point is that there was no Dada system, but it is not so easy as it may seem to act or construct without any system. At their most interesting, Dada works have allowed the material to be explored or simply to exist for its own sake – including typography. The notion of 'direct' creation led Dadaists to a position close to the formalist and anti-art theories of Russian Constructivism, and prepared the way for collaborations such as those between Kurt Schwitters and El Lissitzky.

Dada had, and still has, a long tailpiece. Marcel Duchamp, for one, continued to design posters, catalogues and book covers that could often be described as Dada inventions. Sometimes they comment ironically on the historicising tendency of the event they publicise or commemorate. A 1953 poster for example, whose layout was designed by Duchamp, was, when sold or sent through the post, to be, following Duchamp's instructions, crumpled into a ball. 'This could account', as Richard

28 *The Almost Complete Works of Marcel Duchamp,* exhibition catalogue, Tate Gallery, London, 1966.

Hamilton commented, 'for its comparative rarity.'[28]

De Stijl, unlike Dada, was founded on a positive set of theories. It was an international movement, which started in 1917 in Holland with the publication of the review *De Stijl,* edited by Theo van Doesburg, with, initially, the close support of the painters Piet Mondrian and Bart van der Leck. De Stijl was to become a major theoretical and practical force in graphic design, painting and architecture after the war. Its main theoretical underpinning in the first few years was provided by Mondrian, who defined his concept of Neoplasticism in the first issue as follows: 'This new plastic idea will ignore the particulars of appearance, that is to say, natural form and colour. On the contrary, it should find its expression in the abstraction of form and colour, that is to say, in the straight line and clearly defined primary colour.'

When this was written, Mondrian was still in the process of realising this ideal in practice, and was working in close contact with Bart van der Leck. In 1916 Van Der Leck had moved to Laren, near Amsterdam, where Mondrian had already settled. Van Der Leck had been working as a designer for the firm of Müller & Co. in The Hague since 1914, producing publicity, and also colour schemes for interior design. His 'Batavier Lijn' (Batavier Line) poster already shows a schematic, geometrical reduction of the objects and figures, which look ancient Egyptian, placed horizontally to the picture plane to eliminate perspective. It is interesting to compare this with his *Study for Composition 1917 no.5 (Donkey Riders).* In the final version the riders and donkeys are abstracted to a series of blue, red, yellow and black rectangles of regular width on a plain ground. The influence of Mondrian's 'plus and minus' works of 1915–16 was apparent in the two-dimensional linear patterning in earlier stages of the composition, but Van Der Leck's use of coloured rectangles seems in turn to have encouraged Mondrian to experiment with free-floating colour planes. It is significant, however, that when Mondrian began to paint following Van Der Leck's example, as in *Composition in Colour A* of 1917, he did so in terms of purely pictorial elements, with no reference to subject matter. In his plus and minus compositions a synthesis was being enacted that had, as its terms, both the earlier church facade and pier and ocean series. In other words, whereas Van Der Leck had worked progressively towards abstraction from a particular point of reference, Mondrian was striving for a universal basis for his abstraction. Both Van Der Leck and Mondrian now eliminated any residual reference to subject matter, but Mondrian was unhappy with the random appearance of the colour planes in his canvases, and commented, 'While working I discovered that the colour planes against a flat ground do not create a unity for my work. In Van Der Leck's work it seems to be possible, but he works in a totally different way.'[29] To retain unity, a concept central to his theory of Neoplasticism, Mondrian began, in 1919, to anchor his colour planes to a grid of black or grey vertical and horizontal lines, striving to retain the flatness of the actual canvas in the composition. In Van Der Leck's completely abstract canvases he, unlike Mondrian, introduced diagonals, cutting the edges of his rectangles. The effect of these compositions was, as Mondrian noted, one of balance and unity. This could be ascribed to Van Der Leck's greater decorative instinct, or what might be described as an attraction to symmetrical patterning and repetition. For Mondrian, on the contrary, unity had to be the result of a balance of *opposites.* For him, the vertical and horizontal, for example, stood for such opposing qualities as male and female, spiritual and earthly, tragic and harmonious, and the final asymmetric composition was to resolve the tension between them.

Whereas for Mondrian the introduction of the particular would destroy the abstract and therefore the universality of his painting, it was relatively easy for Van Der Leck to adapt his painting once again to the depiction of specific objects – as in the 'Plantennet Delfia' poster where the colour planes are arranged to compose the image of a bottle. Van Der Leck was always an idiosyncratic figure within De Stijl and in some ways these posters are not representative of the movement. The overwhelming De Stijl influence in graphic design was the use of strong vertical and horizontal lines and rectangles, either as typographical markers or as the arrangement of the text, or as independent abstract elements.

De Stijl was dedicated to the creation of new forms appropriate to modern man whose life, Mondrian said, 'was becoming more and more a-b-s-t-r-a-c-t'.[30] Its concerns were not primarily functional; it believed

29 Letter to Bremmer, early 1918, in Rudolf W. Oxenaar, 'Van Der Leck and De Stijl, 1916–1920', in *De Stijl: 1917–1931, Visions of Utopia*, Walker Art Center, Minneapolis, MN, and Abbeville Press, New York, NY, 1982, p.69.

30 Piet Mondrian, 'De Nieuwe Beelding in de Schilderkunst', *De Stijl*, vol.1, no.1, October 1917.

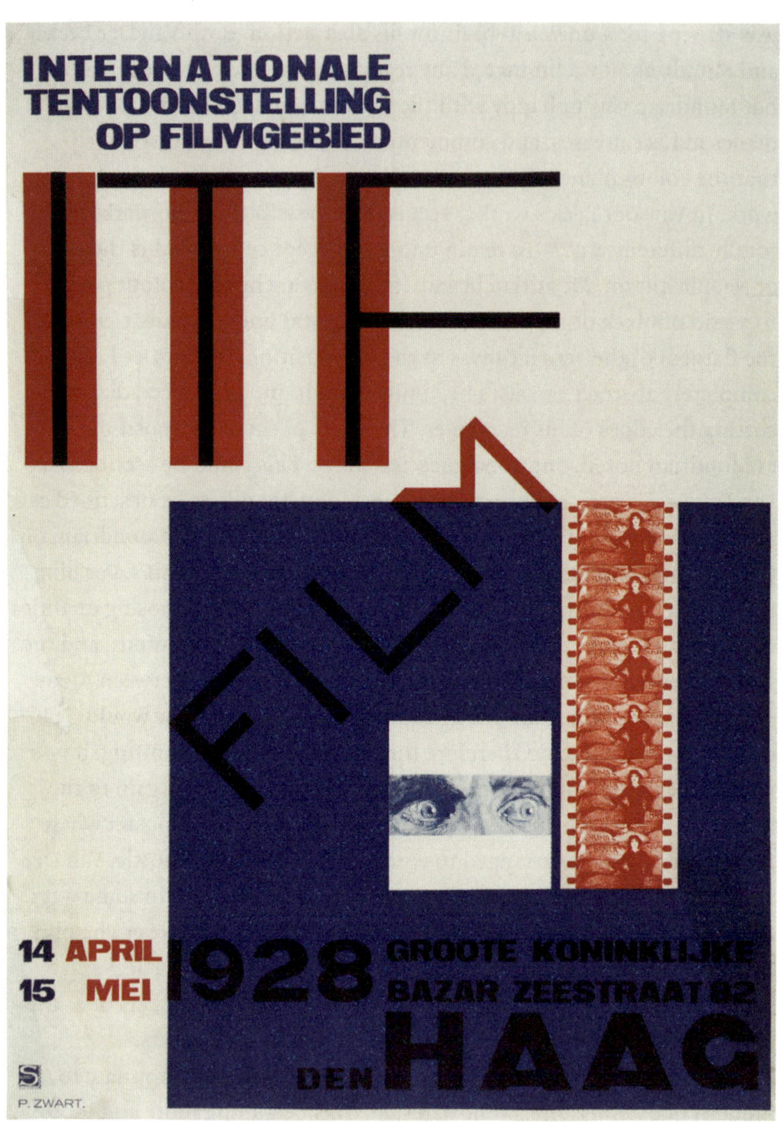

132 **Piet Zwart**
Internationale Tentoonstelling Op Filmgebied
(International Film Festival), 1928
Lithograph
107.9 × 77.7 cm | 42½ × 30⅝ in

that art should serve as a 'model for future life'.[31] Although there was dogmatism within De Stijl (Mondrian for example finally resigned from it when Van Doesburg introduced diagonals into his painting), the magazine itself, under Van Doesburg's editorship, was both polemical and highly receptive to new ideas.

Posters were a comparatively incidental aspect of De Stijl activity, but it did maintain a lively interest in typography. Van Der Leck, in his posters, fragmented his letters, stencil fashion, to parallel his fragmented planar images, but not according to any strict geometry. The lettering on Vilmos Huszár's title page for the first issue of *De Stijl* is also divided into single components, here regularly geometrical, but in the interests of matching the purely abstract woodcut design rather than creating a standardised typography. Indeed, they match the image so well that they read first as shapes and only secondarily as letters. This was quite deliberate; as Huszár said, his intention was to 'give black and white equal value, without ground', an aim hardly compatible with legible lettering.[32] Huszár continued to experiment with figure-ground egality, and in the 1929 poster for the exhibition of contemporary industrial arts it has become a positive, rather obstructive element through the introduction of a colour contrast. There were various experiments with geometrical letterforms in the 1920s which showed scant regard for legibility. Piet Zwart, for example, designed logos based on the square, rectangle and circle. There is, of course, a difference between a logo and a poster, and the distortion of the logo is much modified in the poster lettering, as can be seen in the 'Internationale Tentoonstelling op Filmgebied' (International Film Festival) poster. Van Doesburg devised a basic uppercase alphabet in 1918–19, whose proportions could be altered and exaggerated at will vertically or horizontally (for example, his 'Section d'Or' poster, 1920). Beside the basic alphabets designed at the Bauhaus in the 1920s this looks curiously mannered. Van Doesburg did not use this alphabet exclusively, but alternated happily between Dada and a more austere constructivist typography. In the 1920s new features, such as the diagonal, entered De Stijl design, which will be discussed below in the context of international Constructivism.

31 Hans L.C. Jaffé, introduction, in *De Stijl: 1917–1931, op. cit.*, p.11.
32 Cited in Kees Broos, 'From De Stijl to a New Typography', *De Stijl: 1917–1931, op. cit.*, p.147.

In both Dada and De Stijl, posters as such were relatively peripheral. They did exemplify a general typographical curiosity, or a dominant visual aesthetic, but they were produced according to local or specific demands. In Russia, from 1917, the poster was to have a crucial social and political role, and to become central to the theory and practice of a group of revolutionary artists who came to be known as Constructivists.[33] The poster held a peculiarly prominent position in Russia following the Revolution, during the Civil War and blockade, and then in the years of reconstruction. It had first of all an enormous educational and propaganda function. The need for pictures was vital in the task of reeducating the people in the aims and ideals of the new communist state. 'During the civil war and blockade, pictures outstripped and often replaced the press, the megaphone installed in a public square or the eloquence of the orator at mass meetings.'[34] Not only did they transcend the language barrier in a land with a multinational population, but they overrode the barrier of illiteracy, a gigantic problem in the construction of a new state 75 per cent of whose people were unschooled. In the early days of agitprop the task was to transform as many visible surfaces of buildings, ships and trains as possible. Huge panels hid the neoclassical facades of buildings, trains were painted with slogans and pictures of stock caricature figures designed to give a simple and immediately graspable message. Street posters, like illustrated newspapers, were there both to be looked at and, by those who could, read.

33 The term 'constructivism' is not identified with any single movement or group of artists, nor is it easily susceptible to a single definition. 'Constructive' or 'constructivist' came into general use by avant-garde critics and artists after the First World War, to explain new artistic practices in which representation was no longer a concern. In sculpture, traditional methods like carving and modelling were rejected in favour of building or constructing form out of planes, volumes and lines. There was stress on the use of new materials and on the study of material for its own sake. Many of the ideas are derived from Cubism and Futurism (in sculpture). The term can be associated with 'abstract', but the two are by no means interchangeable. In the USSR between 1920 and 1924 artists calling themselves Constructivists could hold different and even contradictory views. In Europe, *De Stijl* was a major forum for constructivist ideas in all branches of the plastic arts and in architecture. In 1922 the Congress of Constructivist Artists at Weimar included Constructivists and Dadaists such as Jean (Hans) Arp, Kurt Schwitters, Theo van Doesburg, Hans Richter, Cornelis van Eesteren and El Lissitzky. El Lissitzky's role in spreading Russian Constructivism in Europe was vital, but the more purely abstract Contructivism of Naum Gabo was more influential in England and the United States.

34 Szymon Bojko, *New Graphic Design in Revolutionary Russia*, Lund Humphries, London, 1972, p.32.

> Our younger generation of artists accumulated much latent energy during the 1917 Revolution, energy which only needed big demands on the part of the people to reveal itself. The audience was the mass of the people, the great mass of semi-literates. The Revolution has carried out colossal propagandist and educational work. The traditional book was, one might say, divided into separate pages, enlarged a hundredfold, painted in brighter colours and hung up in the street as posters. Unlike the American poster ours was not planned to be taken in at a single glance from the window of a passing car, it was meant to be read and digested at close range...[35]

Many of the posters, such as those El Lissitzky describes above, were intricate and beautifully coloured. Often woodcuts, they treat the Revolution symbolically (a peasant ploughing with a sunrise behind him and the czarist crown and jewels trampled into the ground, for instance). Many were before and after scenes of the life of the peasant and the landowner, and they sometimes took the form of an illustrated story with a series of pictures and texts. There was no tradition of the political poster in Russia, although the bloody satirical graphics and cartoons of the 1905 Revolution were a source for the agitprop posters. The major source was the printed broadside or *lubok* (a term referring either to the limewood block from which it was printed or the baskets from which it was hawked). By the mid-seventeenth century large numbers of these were being sold. They were often couched in religious symbols, and there was also a tradition of the broadside icon. There were traditional stories and legends, but also picture stories with specific local and historical significance. The *lubok* is characterised by a deliberately crude stroke, flat colour washes and a clear composition, and many of the early agitprop posters, such as those of the poet Vladimir Mayakovsky, are clearly modelled on this popular street imagery. An arsenal of stock caricatures was built up, designed to give simple and easily graspable messages: fat landowner, false priest, heroic peasant and soldier. They reflect the fact, too, that the vast majority of the population worked the land; industry was not to become a subject or object of poster campaigns immediately.

35 Lissitzky, 'Our Book' (1926), Lissitzky-Küppers, *op. cit.*, p.358.

Besides this natural extension of street culture, artists of many different tendencies mobilised to help, including the most advanced artists who had been developing radical nonobjective art under the last years of the czarist regime. They, severally, believed they had a peculiar right to determine what art appropriate to a revolutionary society should be, including its street propaganda. The Suprematists in particular flung themselves enthusiastically into the task, harnessing their abstract designs (not always successfully) to the demands of street and theatre demonstrations. A May Day parade in Vitebsk, Belarus, was transformed by Malevich and his pupils: 'The red brick of the main street is covered here with white paint. Green circles, orange squares and blue rectangles swarm over this white background.'[36] Lissitzky, who had been working with Kasimir Malevich, and Malevich himself, produced posters for the recruiting campaign on behalf of the Red Army fighting for the Bolshevik government against the White Russian threat in the Civil War. Both are examples of the pure abstract geometrical forms of Suprematism pressed into service for agitational purposes. In Malevich's poster for a ROSTA window: 'What have you done for the front?' the slogan is surrounded by Suprematist 'elements' shooting out from the curved and shaded surface of, presumably, the globe. Malevich had enthusiastically welcomed the Revolution, but saw no need to adapt his commitment to a visionary abstraction in the interests of a specific message: 'Innovators of the whole world, a new pole of the revolutionary axis is forcing our heavy sphere to turn,' he wrote, and it is this vision that his poster is intended to convey.[37] In Lissitzky's poster 'Beat the Whites with the Red Wedge' the Suprematist forms of the circle, triangle and rectangle, still based on Malevich's original source forms of 1915, are given symbolic functions, easily recognisable within the framework of the campaign: red wedge for the Red Army (whose uniform included a red star on the helmet) and white for the counter-revolutionary forces. But how recognisable would this poster have been? Would the message have been perceived as clearly as that in the famous British recruiting poster by Alfred Leete, 'Your Country

36 Sergei Eisenstein, 'Notes about V.V. Mayakovsky', in Larissa Alekseevna Zhadova, *Malevich: Suprematism and Revolution in Russian Art, 1910–1930*, Thames & Hudson, London, 1982, p.32.

37 Kasimir Malevich, 'To Innovators of the Entire Universe' (1919), in Olga Makhroff and Stanislas Zadora (eds), *Art et Poésie Russes 1900–1930, Textes Choisis*, Centre Pompidou, Paris, 1979, p.126.

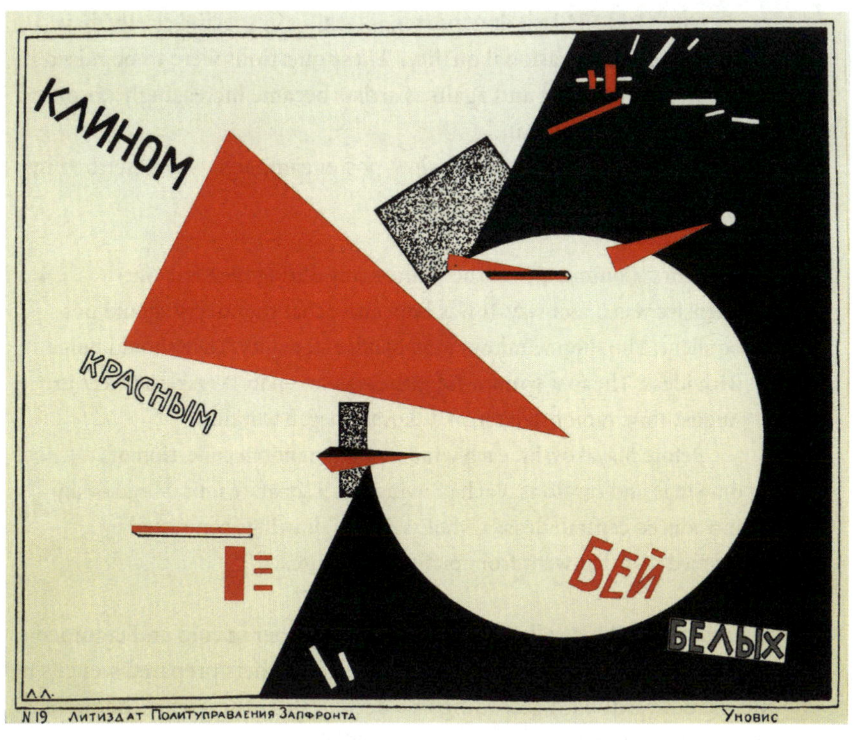

El Lissitzky
'Beat the Whites with the Red Wedge', 1920
Lithograph
49 × 69 cm | 19¼ × 27⅛ in

Needs YOU'? Did El Lissitzky's poster, if lacking in specific clarity, have a more universal inspirational quality? These questions were to be raised in theoretical terms again and again as artists became increasingly absorbed in the problem of function.

The genesis of the ROSTA window-poster campaign was described by Viktor Shklovsky:

> Denikin's (Commander of the White Army during the Civil War) offensive was under way. It was imperative that the streets should not be silent. The shop windows were blank and empty. They should bulge with ideas. The first window of satire was set up in Tverskaya Street in August 1919. A month later, Mayakovsky began working.
>
> Before Mayakovsky, each window was a random collection of drawings and captions. Each drawing was a separate unit. Mayakovsky introduced central ideas: a whole series of drawings connected by a rhymed text that went from picture to picture...[38]

Mayakovsky and his collaborators worked together in cold and cramped conditions: 'Mayakovsky made the posters, the others prepared stencils by cutting out cardboard according to a design; still others used the stencils to make copies.' ROSTA continued to publish propaganda and information posters until 1922.

Neither Lenin nor Trotsky sympathised with the claims of the advanced artists on the Left, but under Anatoly Lunacharsky, the head of the People's Commissariat of Enlightenment, in charge of both cultural and educational policy, they were encouraged with state patronage, and given posts in art schools, and within IZO (Department of Visual Arts of Narkompros).

The 'Futurists', as the avant garde in general was still termed, immediately after the Revolution, responded energetically to it, and in 1918 published 'Decree No.1 on the Democratisation of the Arts', attributed by Szymon Bojko to Mayakovsky. This is an interesting document, marking an early stage in the complex debate concerning the new role of the artist:

38 Viktor Shklovsky, *Mayakovsky and His Circle*, Pluto Press, London, 1974.

1. From today, with the abolition of the czarist regime, the existence of art is suppressed in the warehouses and hangars of the human spirit: palaces, galleries, salons, libraries, theatres.
2. In the name of the great march toward the equality of all in the face of culture, may the Free Word of the creative personality be seen at the crossroads, the walls of houses, palisades, roofs, the streets of our towns and our villages, on the backs of cars, carts, tramways and on the clothes of all citizens.
3. May pictures (colours) be hung from house to house, in the streets and on the squares, in rainbows of precious stones, rejoicing, ennobling the eye (the taste) of the passerby...[39]

It is clear that the pictures the writer had in mind are not propaganda but art, and the democratisation called for is to serve the double function of freeing the artist from his restrictive conventional audience (to allow the free play of his 'creative personality') and of bringing art within the reach of all, so that 'everyone, coming out into the street, will be enlarged and enriched by the contemplation of beauty'. Bojko quotes a passage from this to illustrate how the early agitprop activities intended to 'instil a communist awareness in broad segments of society', but this is not primarily what the writer had in mind.[40] The emphasis on collective is already there; what would have grated in particular on participants in the later stages of the debate, as it sharpened, was the emphasis on 'creation' and 'beauty'. As early as 1919, Osip Brik, the critic and fellow employee with the poet Mayakovsky of IZO, launched an attack on definitions of the artist that depended upon these concepts. Brik argues that, indissolubly welded as they are to bourgeois culture, if they are removed there are those who fear that art itself would go along with them, but that in fact there are other artists who 'know how to paint pictures and decors, they know how to paint ceilings and walls, they know how to make drawings, posters, signs, they know how to erect monuments... these artists have their place in the commune. They execute definite and socially useful tasks.'[41]

39 'Decree No.1 on the Democratisation of the Arts' (*Gaseta Foutouristov,* 15 March 1918), Makhroff and Zadora, *op. cit.*, p.107.

40 Bojko, *op. cit.*, p.32.

It was not part of Brik's purpose to discuss what form these pictures, posters, murals and monuments should take, but over the next two or three years the debate within IHKhUK (Institute of Artistic Culture) and VKhUTEMAS (Higher State Art-Technical Studios) became increasingly concerned with this question.[42] The next step was taken in November 1921, when the Production Group – 25 artists, including Alexander Rodchenko, Varvara Stepanova, Vladimir and Georgi Stenberg, Gustav Klutsis under the guidance of Brik, Boris Arvatov and Nikolai Tarabukin – withdrew from all theoretical activity. This led to a radical revision of the term Constructivism: 'Constructivism is socially utilitarian. Its application is situated either in industrial production (engineer-constructor) or in propaganda (constructor-designer of posters, logos, etc.). Constructivism is revolutionary not only in its words but in acts. It is revolutionary by the very orientation of its artistic methods.'[43]

The following phase of the Constructivists' struggle to impose their views on the visionary ideology of revolutionary society is in some ways the most extraordinary. It must be clear by now that there were groups of artists going under the name Constructivist who held very different and even opposing views, and this was equally true of postwar Constructivism in Europe. The Production Group, far from abandoning its researches into pure form and material, sought to adapt them to the production of specific objects. As Lyubov Popova said, '[We must] find the paths and methods that lead away from the dead impasse of depictive art and advance through knowledge of technological production to a method of creating objects of industrial production, products of organised, material design.' Those last three words are significant because they imply a

41 Osip Brik, 'The Artist and the Commune, The Artists' Effort', Makhroff and Zadora, *op. cit.*, p.121.

42 VKhUTEMAS (Higher State Art-Technical Studios) established in 1920, replaced the Moscow Free Schools, which had been the amalgamation in 1918 of the Moscow School and the Stroganov School. It was geared towards design and in these faculties the Constructivists were prominent. The painting faculty was more traditional, and by 1925 had adopted the realism of the AKhRR artists into its curriculum. INKhUK was a group originally founded by Wassily Kandinsky in May 1920, devoted to theory and research. Many of its members taught in VKhUTEMAS, and it became a centre of Constructivist theory.

43 Boris Arvatov, 'Two Groups' (1922), in Margit Rowell and Angelica Rudenstine (eds), *Art of the Avant-Garde in Russia: Selections from the George Costakis Collection*, exhibition catalogue, Guggenheim Museum, New York, NY, 1981, p.226 and further.

whole series of attitudes to the design of objects which we can define as 'constructive'. Nothing fortuitous, nothing uncalculated, as Alexei Gan said in his book on Constructivism. Gan himself made posters and worked on the design of his own book; he worked with the compositor on the type and layout.[44] The difference between the Productivists and Constructivists like Naum Gabo, who were influential in bringing the movement to the West, was that they eschewed the making of easel painting and sculpture altogether.

The abstract experiments of the previous years were now applied. There is a close relationship between Klutsis's Constructivist designs of 1920–22, which, like similar constructions by the Stenberg brothers, do not even have the role of a 'model', however utopian, and his designs for kiosks for the Fourth Comintern Congress (Congress of the Communist International). These obviously had a practical destination, though only two were built, but at the same time they were utilising the 'laboratory' period principles of using material according to its natural properties, eliminating all superfluous detail or ornament, emphasising the linear as opposed to the mass in space. They were to be made of wood, rope and canvas and painted red, white and black: red with its now well-established symbolic connection with the new communist state, black and white because they were symbolically constructive rather than decorative. It may be argued that they represented an ideal of utility, economy and efficiency, though they were not necessarily more economical or efficient than other forms might be.

Several of Klutsis's kiosk designs were intended as display stands

44 It was not a matter of rejecting the abstract 'laboratory' period of Constructivism except in so far as it was 'laboratory', but of utilising the research into material of that period in conjunction with industrial processes. 'A proletarian artist receives an order for a poster. What should he do to make it effective? To make it correspond to the place where it will be hung (e.g., on the surface of a wall), to the spectators to whom it will be shown, to the distance from which they will look at it, to the subject that will be depicted on it (if the poster is figurative), to the ideological influence for which it is intended, etc.? All this can be accomplished on one condition: that the artist knows how to make free use of those materials that go to make up the poster as an expressive and actively organised form; and, moreover, not to use them – as was done previously – in one definite direction (in such and such a "style"), but in any way, as a given concrete occasion dictates. Inevitably this command of material presupposed an abstract laboratory'. Boris Arvatov, 'The Proletariat and Leftist Art' (1922), in John E. Bowlt, *Russian Art of the Avant-Garde: Theory and Criticism 1902–1934*, Viking Press, New York, NY, 1976, p.228.

for posters, and the question now arises – what were the posters to be produced by the 'constructor-designers' to look like? It is significant that Klutsis in his drawings for these kiosks represents the posters in position simply with typography. Many of the Constructivists' posters at the time (for circus and theatre, for example) did rely almost entirely for their effect upon a bold use of the Cyrillic alphabet simplified to maximise its geometrical effect. Occasionally formal abstract elements are introduced subordinate to the words and acting as punctuation marks or directional signs. It is not always obvious whether these are descended from Suprematism or are ingenious uses of the printer's black line. If posters needed images, though, how were they to be reintroduced? People outside the Constructivist group were simply continuing the early agitprop style of the ROSTA posters for shop windows. But for Alexander Rodchenko, who was teaching on the 'artistic' side of the metalwork faculty while an engineer taught the technical side, there was no obvious solution to this problem. He was, at the time, producing advertisements and book and poster designs for various state institutions, in line with his Productivist beliefs, and he made a variety of different experiments in returning to the image.

One of his first designs is a horn of plenty effect, an advertisement for the GUM department store which appeared in *Izvestya* in 1923. It shows a number of isolated objects, which could have come straight out of the small ads page of an illustrated Victorian newspaper. By contrast, his poster, 'The Press is Our Weapon', slightly later the same year, clearly has in mind Klutsis's kiosk designs, and strikingly adapts formalist design to the image of papers rolling off the presses. It could be argued that the reason for the difference in design was that one was intended for small-scale consumption in the pages of a newspaper, the other for the street. However, I don't think this accounts for the radical difference between the types of images. Uncertain of his direction Rodchenko worked closely with Mayakovsky, who produced the text for the posters and advertisements, and to a certain extent Mayakovsky's own poster drawings, with their simplified, cheerful flat figures and objects influenced him. But Rodchenko's designs are always rationalised to the nearest complete geometrical form – circle, rectangle, square – as in the famous 'Baby's Dummy' (c.1923) advertisement. Another device Rodchenko borrowed from nineteenth-century advertisements was the use of the object advertised as a constructive element in the whole design. These could be fortuitous similarities, and should not be overemphasised, because one of the key positions the Constructivists held was that culture had to find new forms and methods for the new proletarian society. 'We will fight with all our power against the transfer of dead methods of work to today's new art', announced the first editorial in *LEF* (Left Front of the Arts). Their stress on the ideological soundness of the constructivist method (which sometimes involved a deliberate ambiguity in the use of the term 'materialist') was important because it was in opposition to the Bolshevist leaders' attitude to the bourgeois past: Lenin had no time for the leftists and believed, 'We must take the entire culture that capitalism left behind and build socialism with it. We must take all its science, technology, knowledge and art. Without these we shall be unable to build communist society.'[45] In 1922 a new body of artists was formed, the Association of Artists of Revolutionary Russia (AKhRR), who promoted a return to a 'realist' style, based on The Wanderers group of artists of the nineteenth century, with workers in new industries, Red Army soldiers and scenes from the recent heroic past as subject matter.

The magazine *LEF* was produced at least in part to stiffen and unify the opposition to what the Left artists considered a regressive move. This opposition, it seems to me, was posited in a particularly acute form in the medium of posters, book illustration and advertisements, because there the question of an image comes into play. How is reality to be pictured without slipping back into nineteenth-century modes? One important solution was found by Rodchenko in photography and photomontage. An unsigned article was published in *LEF* in 1924, called 'Photomontage', in which two arguments are put forward stressing the essential difference between photography and conventional pictorial representation: 'The combination of photographs replaces the composition of graphic representations... The meaning of this substitution lies in the fact that the photograph is not the sketch of a visual fact, but its precise fixing... A poster about hunger with photographs of the starving produced a much

45 Vladimir Lenin, 'The Achievements and Difficulties of the Soviet Government' (1919), quoted in Briony Fer, *Russian Art and Revolution*, *Modern Art and Modernism* series, Open University Press, Maidenhead, 1983, p.22.

stronger impression than a poster using ordinary sketches of the starving.' The second argument presents the technique of photomontage from a Constructivist point of view – it has its own proper qualities which are not simply an echo of painting: 'Photography has its own possibilities of montage which have nothing to do with the composition of paintings.' It goes on to cite Rodchenko's photomontages for Mayakovsky's poem *Pro Eto* (1923) and, in the West, the photomontages of Grosz and the other Dadaists.

The combination of photography, usually in the form of montaged photographs, with formal Constructivist design, became the basis for poster design in the hands of Rodchenko, the Stenberg brothers, Klutsis and Nikolai Prusakov. A major client was Sovkino, established to administer the newly nationalised film industry. Many of the films made under its auspices were documentary, with the function of educating the people in the aims of Soviet society and glorifying the achievements of the state in the reorganisation of agriculture and industry.

The film poster, though extraordinarily influential, was not the dominant manner of poster design in the 1920s. The ROSTA windows continued in an early agitprop style, while others reflected an AKhRR attitude with their use of a bloodless realism. One of the most interesting artists who also designed posters was Alexander Deyneka. He belonged to a younger generation, and had trained at VKhUTEMAS from 1921 to 1924 in the painting faculty, where the Constructivist influence, which dominated in the basic division and the metalworking faculty, was at a minimum. However, while advocating a return to easel painting with a proletarian subject matter, he avoided a return to the nineteenth-century Wanderer style. In posters such as 'Transforming Moscow', of 1931, he utilises formalist devices to a much greater degree than in his paintings – the flat geometrisation of certain areas is at odds with the proun-like diagonal tilt of the buildings illustrated on the right half of the poster. Deyneka's works are closely involved with Stalin's emphasis on industrialisation as the means by which Socialism would be brought about in Russia, and the consequent lessening of communist internationalism in favour of nationalism. Although Deyneka was criticised in the 1930s for his formalism, he was eventually decorated as a Hero of Socialist Labour and was made a full member of the USSR Academy of Arts.

Towards the end of the 1920s a new conflict arose between the Right and Left over photography. Rodchenko was accused of abusing the descriptive, documentary and informative value of a photograph because of the strange angles from which he chose to photograph things. The two children in his poster for Dziga Vertov's film *Kino-Eye* (1924) gazing upwards, exemplify Rodchenko's belief that:

> In photography there are old points of view, for example the angle of vision, the view of a person standing on the ground looking straight ahead, or, as I call it, belly shots with the camera held to the stomach. I am fighting against this viewpoint and shall fight it just as my comrades in the new photography are doing. Take shots from all angles except the navel until all these points of view are recognised. The interesting angles of the present are those from above down and from below up and one must work on those.[46]

Rodchenko acknowledged here the close similarities between his photography and that of Moholy-Nagy or Herbert Bayer. Boris Kushner retorted in *Soviet Photo* that 'to show a 150-metre-high radio tower looking like a bread basket made of wire is not paying attention to reality but ridiculing facts'.

Rodchenko knew that the photograph is no less a sign to be interpreted than any other image – through it reality can be presented and structured in a particular way; this structuring can be made apparent in the use of montage. But this was in direct opposition to the concept of realism advocated by the AKhRR easel painters and the *Soviet Photo* photographers, to which the great majority of posters produced conformed. Klutsis was a major exception. He continued to produce posters well into the Stalinist period, using photography and montage, and also maintaining many of the Constructivist design principles. Sometimes, as with the posters built on the symbolic motif of the hand, he took the photograph himself, using documentary photographs, which he montaged, or photographs with an angled view. Like Lissitzky's famous Russian exhibition poster, heads and whole figures may gaze upwards, but Klutsis usually succeeds in avoiding the potentially idealised, sentimental or

46 '*Novy LEF*, 1928', in Colin Osman (ed), *Creative Camera International Year Book*, Coo Press Ltd, London, 1978.

utopian nature of this gaze as it tended to be used in the realism of the 1930s, by introducing an element of confrontation (train and camel for example), or shock, which depends essentially upon montage.

> The appearance of *Veshch* (Object) is an indication of the fact that the exchange of 'objects' between young Russian and west European masters has begun. Seven years of separate existence have shown that the community of the tasks and the aims of art in different countries is not something that exists by chance. We are standing in the dawn of a great creative era.[47]

This opening statement in the first issue of El Lissitzky and llya Ehrenburg's review *Veshch/Gegenstand/Objet* outlines the common aspirations and activities of international Constructivism. The history of its early exhilarating years has often been told, but there are a few specific points I would like to make which bear on my subject. First, there was a significant interaction between Dada and Constructivism. Dada was not just an irrational nuisance, to be avoided or stamped out, situated at the opposite pole to Constructivism. There was of course the famous incident when, to the horror of the more staid participants, it was revealed at the 1922 International Congress of Constructivists in Weimar that Theo van Doesburg and the Dada poet I.K. Bonset were one and the same person. But the connections go deeper than that, and the melding of Dadaism and Constructivism created some characteristic and striking 'objects': the special number of Kurt Schwitters's periodical *Merz*, which he designed with El Lissitzky, Schwitters's *Merzbau* in Hanover, Van Doesburg's 'X-bilden' (X-picture) poems in *De Stijl*, the four issues of Bonset/Van Doesburg's *Mécano*. Nor is the Dada connection established exclusively through the double participation of Schwitters and Van Doesburg in the two movements. Dadaists in Paris like Georges Ribemont-Dessaignes, Francis Picabia and Paul Éluard contributed to *Mécano*, as did Max Ernst from Cologne, Raoul Hausmann from Berlin. Arp and Tzara contributed to both *Mécano* and to the ex-Dadaist Hans Richter's periodical *G*.

47 El Lissitzky and llya Ehrenburg, 'The Blockade of Russia is Coming to an End', *Veshch/Gegenstand/Objet*, nos.1/2, Berlin, March–April 1922; trans. in Stephen Bann, *The Tradition of Constructivism*, Thames & Hudson, London, 1974, p.54.

Richter, now working largely in film, established through the pages of *G* a striking communality of spirit between Constructivism and Dada, illustrating, for example, Duchamp's optical disc machine and including poems by Arp and Hausmann as well as articles by Lissitzky, Malevich, Mies van der Rohe and others.

Second, although as *Veshch* had announced general contacts were established between Germany and the USSR, and the 1922 exhibition of Soviet art had shown all the major Constructivists, El Lissitzky was the dominant influence, particularly on Van Doesburg and Moholy-Nagy, and particularly in the field of graphic design. Lissitzky had become a roving cultural ambassador for the new art, but at the same time he was not representative of such groups as the Productionists. As he said in *Veshch*:

> Obviously we consider that functional objects turned out in factories – aeroplanes and motor cars – are also the product of genuine art. Yet we have no wish to confine artistic creation to these functional objects. Every organised work – whether it be a home, a poem, or a picture – is an 'object' directed toward a particular end, which is calculated not to turn people away from life, but to summon them to make their contribution toward life's organisation... Primitive utilitarianism is far from being our doctrine. *Objet (Veshch)* considers poetry, plastic form, theatre, as 'objects' that cannot be dispensed with.[48]

Naum Gabo, who left Russia for good in 1922, totally rejected the 'utilitarian' bias of, say, Rodchenko or Klutsis, and it was his view of Constructivism that took root in England and the USA. There were, in other words, a number of different, rather than one monolithic Constructivism.

El Lissitzky's dynamic concept of space, which he explored through the proun, was eagerly absorbed by Western artists. 'I created the proun as an interchange station between painting and architecture. I have treated the canvas and wooden board as a building site, which placed the fewest restrictions on my constructional ideas. I have used black and white (with flashes of red) as material substance and subject matter.'[49]

48 *Ibid.*
49 Lissitzky-Küppers, *op. cit.*, p.325.

Building on Malevich's Suprematism (the *Black Square* was reproduced on the front of *Veshch* 3), Lissitzky, in the early 1920s, developed his constructive idea based on elementary bodies (cube, cone, sphere), set in 'imaginary space': 'We saw that the surface of the Proun ceases to be a picture and turns into a structure round which we must circle... The result is that the one axis of the picture which stood at right angles to the horizontal was destroyed. Circling round it, we screw ourselves into space.'[50]

Both Moholy-Nagy and Van Doesburg were fascinated by El Lissitzky's ideas, and in 1922 he published in *De Stijl*. The result was that the static, flat plane surfaces of De Stijl were spun into space ('We were approaching the state of floating in air and swinging like a pendulum'). In the essentially 'closed' fields of pages or posters, Lissitzky's concept of space led to the use of the diagonal, and floating arrangements of words, which were to have a profound influence on graphic design. A special issue of *De Stijl* (October/November 1922) was devoted to drawings and typographical designs by Lissitzky, including the whole *About 2 Squares* (1922), and his article 'Topography of Typography' was published by Schwitters in *Merz* 4, July 1923, that emphasised the idea 'optics instead of phonetics'.

Several factors contributed to the success of international Constructivism. Many of its leading theorists and artists had a pedagogical role. At the Bauhaus, with Walter Gropius and Moholy-Nagy among others, a new generation of designers was trained. For a while, too, Van Doesburg had a rogue school at Weimar where he was an important influence in turning the Bauhaus away from the expressionist individualism of Johannes Itten towards the De Stijl version of Constructivism. Second, a number of large international exhibitions were held (of printing at Cologne in 1928, and photography at Stuttgart in 1929, for example) whose catalogues, posters and so on were designed by a range of Constructivist designers. These international exhibitions had a dynamism lost from similar exercises today. Then, there were comparatively good relations with industry, which the Werkbund helped to foster. Finally, there was a steady flow of publications. In 1923, to take the peak year for reviews, there were *Merz*, *Mécano*, *Veshch*, *De Stijl* (published, as it said on the cover,

50 Lissitzky, 'Proun. Not World Visions BUT – World Reality', *De Stijl*, 1922; trans. in Lissitzky-Küppers, *op. cit.*, p.343.

simultaneously in Leiden, Hanover, Paris, Brno, Vienna and Warsaw), *G* and *MA*. From 1925 until 1931, fourteen Bauhaus books were published that were planned and edited by Gropius and Moholy-Nagy. Not only the Bauhaus staff but leading architects and artists all over Europe, including Van Doesburg, Moholy-Nagy, Malevich, Oskar Schlemmer and Kandinsky contributed theoretical essays.

At the Bauhaus, graphic design grew steadily in importance during the 1920s. Initially, while the school was in Weimar, neither typography nor commercial art was actually taught and, though the print workshop was open to students, it was comparatively weak in technical facilities and mainly concerned with the Bauhaus's own printed publicity. When Moholy-Nagy joined the Bauhaus in 1923 he took charge not only of the metal workshop, but also the printing workshop, and encouraged students like Herbert Bayer, Joost Schmidt and Josef Albers to experiment there. Posters were produced for the Bauhaus exhibitions, like Fritz Schleifer's of 1923, with its geometric head constructed from typographical lines and markers, reminiscent of the ex-Dadaist Hans Richter's constructivist drawings of heads. Oskar Schlemmer, who was in charge of the stage workshop, both at Weimar and Dessau, also worked in the print workshop making posters for his Triadic Ballet. In a 1921 poster for a performance at the Leibniz Academy, Schlemmer used his own costume studies overprinted with different capital typefaces. This has an almost anarchic, Dada look compared with the rationality of later Bauhaus designs, and Schlemmer remained comparatively untouched by the evolution of graphic design at the Bauhaus. The influence of Dada typography is still felt in the invitation for the farewell party of the Weimar Bauhaus in March 1925, before the move to Dessau – a joke for internal consumption, which looks like a sample catalogue of old and new typefaces.

The shift in importance of graphic design by the mid-1920s is reflected in, for example, the course in lettering devised and run by Joost Schmidt, which became a compulsory part of the general education programme at Dessau. Success in this area was both technical and commercial. Many firms began to commission Bauhaus designers to produce posters and printed publicity, and also, an important aspect of this field, to design displays and stands for exhibitions.

Bayer, originally a student in the wall-painting workshop, ran the print workshop at Dessau until 1928, when Joost Schmidt took it over, renaming it the Commercial Art Department. Schmidt worked in particular on exhibition design, carrying out displays at large exhibitions such as the Dresden hygiene exhibition of 1928, and a gas and water exhibition for the Junkers Works in 1929. Schmidt favoured a restrained, informative and scientific method of presentation. The relationship between displays of this kind, like the poster relying on the mutual supplementation of image and text, and the poster itself, would be interesting to explore further. Schmidt also designed commercial publicity for, for example, cigarette and chocolate manufacturers. Xanti Schawinsky, a student in the mid-1920s, who was active on the Bauhaus stage as a designer and an actor, produced posters for clothing and hat manufacturers, and in the 1930s for Olivetti.

Professional recognition accompanied commercial success, with, for example, the Association of German Advertising Specialists holding part of an instruction course on advertising art in association with the Bauhaus at Dessau in 1927. These factors, together with support from the German Werkbund, contributed to the dominance of modern abstract design on the Continent praised by Alfred Barr in 1936.

The stimulus of Moholy-Nagy was crucial. On joining the Bauhaus he immediately directed some of his energy to both the theory and practice of graphic design, in which he emphasised the importance of communication and the immense changes technological advances would bring in this field. His first ideas on typography in the Bauhaus context were published in an article on 'The New Typography', in which he stressed clarity and legibility: 'Communication must never be impaired by an *a priori* aesthetics. Letters may never be forced into a preconceived framework, for instance, a square.'[51] This sounds like an attack on the dogmatic aesthetic of De Stijl, and is a valuable signal to the emphasis placed by the Bauhaus on pragmatic considerations. The rationalisation of design and typography was not to be subject to a particular aesthetic programme, nor was it to drive out experiment and variation. In the same article of 1923 Moholy-Nagy wrote: 'We use all typefaces, type

51 László Moholy-Nagy, 'The New Typography' (1923), originally published in *Staatliches Bauhaus in Weimar, 1919–1923*; trans. in Richard Kostelanetz (ed), *Moholy-Nagy*, Praeger, New York, NY, 1970, p.75.

sizes, geometric forms, colours, etc. We want to create a new language of typography whose elasticity, variability and freshness of typographical composition is exclusively dictated by the inner law of expression and the optical effect.'

Herbert Bayer paid special attention to the creation of a new typography. The Bauhaus had always used the Roman as opposed to the Gothic alphabet, and had often favoured sans-serif lettering, but now research was specifically directed towards unified lettering systems, with no distinction between upper and lowercase. A single alphabet would be easier, cheaper and quicker; it would simplify the compositor's job and be more economical in the design of typewriters and typesetting machines. In his 1925 article 'Bauhaus and Typography', Moholy-Nagy appealed to precedents, such as the architect Adolf Loos, who had written, 'One cannot speak a capital letter. Everyone speaks without thinking of capital letters. But when a German takes a pen to write something, he is no longer able to write as he thinks or speaks.'[52] The Bauhaus revolution was particularly striking in Germany, where the old, complicated Gothic alphabet was still widely used in printing, with all nouns dignified by the use of capitals, and was greeted with a storm of protest in the press, although, as we noted, commercial firms recognised the enormous advantages for advertising. One of the most significant alphabets was Herbert Bayer's Universal type, based on geometrical shapes, which was widely used on Bauhaus publicity.

The production of radical new typefaces was facilitated at the Bauhaus because every stage of the printing process was under the control of the designers. Particular attention was paid to the demands of large-scale lettering for posters and exhibition displays. Bayer designed a contourless shadow script specifically for use on posters, and Albers designed a stencil script easily legible from a distance and intended for lettering on billboards. It was constructed from three basic geometric shapes: the square, the triangle as half of the square, and the quarter circle radius. The elements of the letters were placed beside one another without connection, and the unequal sizes of the spaces between the letters were deliberate, 'to liven up its appearance as the capital letters in the middle

52 *Ibid.*, p. 76.

of a word did in the Baroque period'.[53] Like Lissitzky, Moholy-Nagy and Bayer tended to use bold lines rather than typographical symbols (which belonged to the 'craftlike' mentality of the hand-set type) to aid the clarity and expressive function of the layout in both book and poster design. Bayer sometimes used an additional colour, or printed over a tinted base.

Jan Tschichold, an independent typographer who also saw the design of new typefaces as an essential element of graphic design, published the influential book *The New Typography* in 1928. He later criticised Lissitzky for paying insufficient attention to the actual typography of his posters and book designs and, rather, 'accepting the conventional shapes of the letters'. Much of his work, 'original and powerful though it might be, betrays the struggle of the amateur typographer with the ancient, intractable mysteries of printing'.[54]

Although attention was paid to typography as an active and fundamental element it would be misleading to suggest that it was at the expense of other elements. Emphasis was on the overall design (with, where relevant, integration of image and text) which Moholy-Nagy characterised as aiming at 'dynamic-eccentric equilibrium' as opposed to the 'centuries old static-concentric equilibrium'. The dynamic overall arrangement (for example, turning the text, or part of it, at 90°) should neither destroy the mutual relationships between the individual elements nor override their legibility.

Attention to the visual impact of typography, which of course at the Bauhaus extended to all printed matter and not just to posters, had in a sense been provoked by the poster. As Moholy-Nagy said:

> A new stage of development began with the first posters... One began to count on the fact that form, size, colour and arrangement of typographical material (letters and signs) contain a strong visual impact. The organisation of these possible visual effects gives a visual validity to the content of the message as well; this means that by means of printing, the content is also being defined pictorially.[55]

53 Josef Albers, in Hans M. Wingler, *The Bauhaus*, MIT Press, Cambridge, MA, and London, 1969, p.448.
54 Jan Tschichold, 'El Lissitzky (1890–1941)' (1965), Lissitzky-Küppers, *op. cit.*, p.355.
55 *Ibid.*

The text, in other words, took on the function of the image, and at no other time in the history of the poster, with the exception of Dada, had the plasticity of the word been developed so far.

One of the greatest changes in poster production was affected by processes and techniques involving photography. In 1926 Lissitzky looked forward to collotype, the transfer of 'composed type matter on to a film, and a printing machine which copies the negative on to sensitive paper'. For the first time the same production process would be available for word and illustration. 'Letterpress belongs to the past. The future belongs to photogravure printing and to all photomechanical processes. In this way the former fresco painting is cut off from the new typography. E.g. advertisement pillars and poster walls.'[56] Technical journals everywhere, like *Penrose's Annual*, debated the relative merits of the new printing techniques, but the implications in design were only fully realised on the continent, particularly in Holland and Germany. Moholy-Nagy saw photography as an integral part of poster design:

> An equally decisive change in the typographical image will occur in the making of posters, as soon as photography has replaced poster painting. The effective poster must act with immediate impact on all psychological techniques, such as retouching, blocking, superimposition, distorting, enlargement, etc., in combination with the liberated typographical line, the effectiveness of posters can be immensely enlarged.
>
> The new poster relies on photography, which is the new storytelling device of civilisation, combined with the shock effect of new typefaces and brilliant colour effects, depending on the desired intensity of the message.[57]

While many Constructivist posters still used exclusively typography and abstract geometrical 'markers' (Walter Dexel's 'Sport' poster of 1929, for example), by the end of the decade pictorial elements were increasingly made up of photographs or photomontages. This was particularly appropriate in film posters, and can be seen in the work of, for example,

56 Lissitzky, 'Typographical Facts' (1925), Lissitzky-Küppers, *op. cit.*, p.355.
57 Moholy-Nagy in Kostelanetz, *op. cit.*

Tschichold and Piet Zwart. Moholy-Nagy's distinctive photomontages, sparser and more structured than the photomontages of Berlin Dada, were well suited for poster design and were an important influence on the combining of typography and photographs (see the 'Tanz Festspiele' poster). The dramatic change is underlined in the 1929 Stuttgart *Film und Foto* exhibition poster. Its sharply angled viewpoint derived from the work of Bauhaus photographers like Bayer or Florence Henri, again under the influence of Moholy-Nagy. Bayer included photographs in his posters, which he sometimes printed in non-naturalistic 'alienated' colours. During the Bauhaus's brief and threatened life in Berlin from 1932–33, Walter Peterhans was in charge of both the commercial art department (now called the 'professional field of advertising') and the photography workshop. This was, by then, a natural alliance, and opportunities increased for designers to work with photography.

Photography and, in particular, photomontage, became a staple for commercial and political poster designers. For both it could serve as a 'fact' in a different way from the representational or expressive character of drawing or painting. The potential of photomontage in building upon or destroying the 'factual' nature of reality has been exploited in both commercial and political poster campaigns. The use of the photograph, acceptable to many Constructivist designers in a way that figurative painting was not, certainly contributed to the re-emergence of a strong pictorial element in posters of the 1930s.

The Constructivist attitude to posters was functional in the sense that the medium was expected to fulfil its function efficiently. It demanded clarity, legibility and forcefulness of design, but this was part of a general overhaul of all visual production in accordance with the new technologies. For the Constructivists in Russia, in a context where political and social campaigns (to reach production targets, to combat drunkenness) were largely conducted through posters, they had an important ideological function. Within international Constructivism no particular weight was given to the nature of their function.

In England and America, as Barr noted, there was a general failure to adopt modernist design, but, parallel to the vision of a new society pushed by the Constructivists with a crusading zeal, there was a feeling that a new age was dawning in which the poster had an important role.

Nowhere is this clearer than in US President Calvin Coolidge's address in 1926 to the American Association of Advertising Agencies. He accorded commercial advertising a potentially utopian function: it 'makes new thoughts, new desires, new actions', and 'by changing the attitude of mind it changes the material condition of people', but it is idealistic according to the ideals of capitalism, for the educational or informational role of advertising is dependent upon its commercial function: 'advertising ministers to the spiritual side of trade.'[58]

As E. McKnight Kauffer wrote in *The Art of the Poster,* the commercial dominates completely. His statement in the first issue of the *Bulletin* of the newly formed Arts League of Service, in 1919, is obviously trying to shift the function of the poster away from pure commercialism, but is vague about what might go in its place: 'Few people realise the importance of the hoardings. It is from them that the masses gather ideas for a great many things that directly influence them. Now that England, after a pause of a dozen years, is again interested in the poster, let this feeling be so genuine and broadcast as to make the hoardings amusingly interesting and vitally important.'[59]

Only a handful of people were concerned to make the hoardings 'amusingly interesting'. Of these, in England, the most dynamic and influential was Frank Pick, who was in charge of publicity for the Underground Railway Company from 1908. Not only did he carefully organise the advertising space inside and at the entrances to his stations, but he began a policy of commissioning designers to produce posters on specific themes: rural England within reach of the city dweller, museums and galleries, winter sales, all available through this means of cheap and efficient transport. He selected the best designers, and even commissioned a new alphabet in 1913 from the calligrapher Edward Johnston, and, when it appeared in 1916, the Johnston sans serif was revolutionary.

McKnight Kauffer, the best of his designers, had no illusions about the philanthropic nature of his intentions, however, and in 1926 Roger Fry had some acid comments to make about such campaigns:

58 Calvin Coolidge address delivered at the annual convention of the American Association of Advertising Agencies at Washington, DC, 27 October 1926. Quoted in Frank Presbrey, *The History and Development of Advertising*, Doubleday, Devan & Co., New York, NY, 1929.

59 Quoted in Mark Haworth-Booth, *E. McKnight Kauffer: A Designer and His Public*, Gordon Fraser, London, 1979, p.29.

> The big companies pose as the friends and advisers of the public, they appear filled with concern about their welfare, they would even educate them, and show them the way to higher and better things. The Underground tells the slum dweller of the beauties of nature in the country, it reveals the wonders of animal life at the zoo, it inspires the historical sense by pictures of old London...
>
> No doubt this has got to do with another interesting recent discovery of commerce. The early industrialist believed in increasing output and decreasing price. For some reason the modern industrialist finds his advantage in restricting output and increasing price. Advertisement is used not so much to induce us to buy as to make us willing to pay more for things than they cost to produce. Thus the railway companies give us progressively worse and worse accommodation but, by advertisement, they produce in the public a non-critical state of romantic enthusiasm for the line...[60]

Having thus attacked the invidious and illusionary nature of 'the spiritual side of advertising', Fry goes on to suggest that a possible way out for the advertisers is to turn their 'philanthropy' not to the public but to artists. Having driven them out of the field of designing textiles, pottery, etc. through mass production, business could re-create a role for the designer of posters, because the poster is a relatively inexpensive object to produce, and the industrialist would not be taking the same risks as he would in setting up the design of objects for large-scale and expensive production. The poster could, he suggests, become a medium in its own right within the field of 'opifacts': 'There is as yet no Royal Academy of Poster Designers, there is no fixed and traditional notion of the kind of thing a poster ought to be. There is as yet no pedantry, no culture, no lecturing, until tonight to hamper and harass the man who happens to have a gift in this medium.'

Fry was in fact not quite right, for there had been a Poster Academy, founded in 1901, when poster magazines and societies had flourished, but when these faded away the poster had remained in an undeveloped state. Fry was apparently unaware of the new theories of graphic design

60 Roger Fry, *Art and Commerce*, Hogarth Press, London, 1926, originally given as a lecture on the occasion of an Arts League of Service poster exhibition at Oxford, 1925.

associated with Constructivism, but was conscious of a revitalisation in this 'new opifact industry' involving 'experiments in the possibilities of printing, and in the effect of colour arrangements'.

McKnight Kauffer had the reputation in England of having helped to convert the public to modern art. He was often indeed taken by conservative opponents like the advertising manager of Pears Soap as an example of extreme and incomprehensible modernism. But McKnight Kauffer himself was quite aware of the mildness of his 'modernism':

> The terms 'Cubistic', 'Futuristic' and the like are too often applied to the present day poster in error. Practically in every case these terms are confused by the user, and to many advertising people the use of them produces a shudder of fear. They somehow suggest that such ideas and the users are slightly, if not entirely insane. The antipathy to newer developments in design and colour has its reason, no doubt, but I am bound to say, with but two or three exceptions, no such design has made its appearance, in England at any rate. For my part, the brief research I have made in these movements as a painter, has been very beneficial to me in the designing of posters. It has made it possible to make newer translations of old forms, and it has assisted me to emphasise the qualities and importance of the use of colour, and helped to simplify my arrangements of ideas.[61]

McKnight Kauffer was closely associated with Wyndham Lewis (whose use of bold uppercase typography in *Blast* was praised as a forerunner by Lissitzky) in his early career as a painter. One of his best designs, a poster for the *Daily Herald*, based on a woodcut called *Flight*, is close to Vorticism in its flat but dynamic abstraction of birds. After he devoted himself to poster design, the links between his work and modern painting become, as he suggested, pragmatic. It is possible to pick out certain specific influences in certain posters, such as Delaunay's colour discs, but on the whole the influence is very general, prompting him towards flattening form and simplifying colour. The book jacket for H.G. Wells's *The Open Conspiracy* (1928), with the diagonal slant to the typography, and the use

61 E. McKnight Kauffer, 'The Poster and Symbolism', *Penrose's Annual*, Lund Humphries, London, 1924.

of abstract typographical markers like the circle and rectangle, show that he was familiar with some Constructivist design, and he used diagonally set typography several times – for Imperial Airways, or the Post Office telephone series; in other words where he felt it would be effective and significant, but by no means as an invariable aesthetic principle.

He believed that the symbol was the essential element in poster design, which would be simple and swiftly recognised. In this he was not unlike A.M. Cassandre, and both owe a certain debt to the Purists Ozenfant and Le Corbusier, in their adoption of a vocabulary of simple forms. Both McKnight Kauffer and Cassandre recognised that there was an essential difference between the function of a poster and the function of a painting, and that the conception must therefore be different too. The dangers of ignoring this simple fact are evident in some of the Shell posters of the 1930s. In 1933 Shell approached a number of artists in their studios to produce posters on the theme 'Everywhere you go you can be sure of Shell'. *Commercial Art and Industry* magazine published the results under the title 'A Great Adventure in Posters'. Those that do not work are those that are simply a transposition – not even a translation – of a picture into a poster.

Poster design in Paris had on the whole remained decorative, often using flat colourful patterned abstractions with exotic overtones. Cassandre, like McKnight Kauffer in England, was the most imaginative and successful in adapting contemporary development in painting to posters. Unlike Auguste Herbin, who favoured a flat decorative abstract style, Cassandre always based his design on people or objects, however dramatically reduced or simplified they might be. Cassandre's affinities lie above all with Léger and the Purists. The 'Wagon-Bar' poster of 1932 plays on the purist concept of basing a pictorial language on the forms of certain manufactured objects, which, because they are geometrical, are perceived as closer to pure or ideal form. This poster could be compared with Léger's painting of a soda siphon. Like that, it is a slightly tongue-in-cheek homage to Purism, and demonstrates again how various abstract and Constructivist ideas, in theory and practice, acted upon poster design, and how, reciprocally, the special, practical demands of the poster tested and provided the impetus for these ideas.

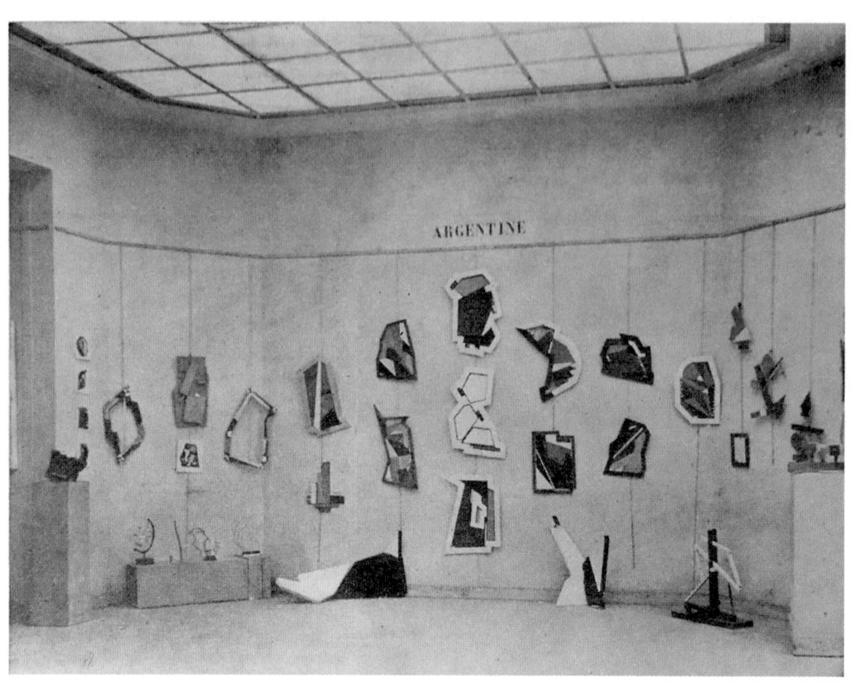

160 Installation view, *Salon des Réalités Nouvelles*, Musée d'Art Moderne, Paris, 1948

Arte Madí/Arte Concreto-Invención

Art in Latin America: The Modern Era 1820–1980, Dawn Ades (ed), Yale University Press, New Haven, CT, and London, 1989

One of the most active and inventive periods in the history of non-figurative or 'concrete' art in Latin America began with the publication of the review *Arturo* in Buenos Aires in the summer of 1944. Although it only ran to one issue, it brought together the artists and poets who were shortly to form the movement MADÍ (or Madí) and the Arte Concreto-Invención Asociación. *Arturo* described itself as a 'review of abstract arts', and was edited by Carmelo Arden Quin, Rhod Rothfuss, Gyula Kosice and the Argentinian poet Edgar Bayley.[1] It included reproductions of works by Tomás Maldonado, Rhod Rothfuss, Maria Helena Vieira da Silva, Augusto Torres, Lidy Prati, Joaquin Torres García, Wassily Kandinsky and Piet Mondrian. *Arturo*'s editorial announcement, 'Afirmaciones', announced its commitment to abstract art, 'pure imagery, free from determinism or justification', and attacked, in rather eccentric terms, Surrealism.

Torres García, then living in Montevideo, contributed a text to *Arturo*, 'concerning a future literary creation', and a poem. He was an important source of encouragement and inspiration for the younger artists, both in Uruguay and Buenos Aires: he welcomed them to his studio, showed them reproductions of the work of the European avant garde, and urged them to develop their personal voice; his weekly lectures on the radio were widely listened to. In the same year, the Taller Torres García (Studio Torres

1 See Gyula Kosice, *Arte Madí*, Ediciones de Arte Gaglianone, Buenos Aires, 1982; Nelly Perazzo, *El Arte concreto en la Argentina eu la década del 40*, Ediciones de Arte Gaglianone, Buenos Aires, 1983; Jorge B. Rivera, *Madí y la Vanguardia Argentina*, Paidós, Buenos Aires, 1976. An interesting open letter from César Paternosto, 'Pioneros ignorados', *Arte en Colombia*, no.33, May 1987, criticised the *Contrasts of Form* exhibition at the Museum of Modern Art, New York, for ignoring the South American constructivist/concrete artists.

García) made an important series of murals for the Hospital of Saint Bois, later tragically destroyed by fire. His text in *Arturo*, as relevant to visual as to literary creation, proposed in general terms a move to structure which could easily be interpreted as a move to abstraction:

> Now we are less interested in the thing than in the structure where it is situated. The house, the sun, the tree we can see now live there in another way: like stones in a wall. We are more interested in the wall we have built, in the construction, than in the things and events we were pursuing. And so we realise that what belongs to us and originality both are on that construction's side. It is no longer the things but the rhythm where they are now that is the essentiality of poetic creation.[2]

Although different currents are present in the visual material in *Arturo*, with two extremes represented by Maldonado on the one hand and Rothfuss on the other, all share a basic commitment to non-figuration. Maldonado's cover has the appearance of an aggressive automatic drawing, a violent swirl of lines with just visible Torres García-like signs. The vignette on the title page was also by Maldonado, but this time strongly recalls the biomorphic abstraction of Jean (Hans) Arp's woodcuts and reliefs. Rothfuss's highly original text 'The Frame: A Problem of Contemporary Art', on the other hand, locates itself more within a Cubist/ Constructivist tradition. Rothfuss, who taught drawing in Montevideo, and had become aware of Cubism and Picasso through Emilio Pettoruti, had, it seems, held an exhibition in 1942 of Cubist paintings with irregular edges, which Arden Quin baptised '*cubisme decoupé*'.[3]

In 'The Frame', Rothfuss presented, in rather elliptical terms, an argument for the abolition of the conventional rectangular frame, which he associated with a naturalist tradition of the picture as window. Rothfuss outlines a progression from Cézanne through Cubism, to

2 Quoted in Perazzo, *op. cit.*, p.58. Precursors in Argentina in the field of abstraction included Juan del Prete, and Pettoruti; although the latter was rarely purely abstract. In his Futurist-inspired paintings and drawings, his intention was rather to express speed and dynamism.

3 Conversation with the author, Paris, October 1988.

Constructivism, in which the move to abstraction is identified with the search for greater reality:

> Cubism was succinctly defined by Guillaume Apollinaire in 'Le Temps' of 14 October 1914, when he referred to the 'geometric aspect of those paintings where the artist wanted to restore, with a great purity, the essence of reality'. And it was that desire to [express] the reality of things which made painting more and more abstract, passing through Futurism and culminating most recently in Cubism, Non-Objectivism, Neo-Plasticism, and also in its most abstract form, Constructivism. And now, just when the artist seems to be furthest from nature, Vicente Huidobro has said: 'Man has never been closer to nature than the present, when he no longer tries to imitate it superficially but, like nature itself, imitates it in the depths of its constructivist laws, in the realisation of a whole.'

Although Rothfuss might not have known Albert Gleizes and Jean Metzinger's treatise on Cubism, *Du Cubisme*, (1912), which stated that a painting 'carries within itself its *raison d'être*',[4] he reached a similar conclusion, but with more radical results, by arguing that geometrical forms like circles, ellipses or polygons, put in an oblong frame, 'dominate the composition' and by implication, by remaining discrete elements, are in conflict with the base shape of the picture, preventing it from becoming a whole: 'A painting with a regular frame suggests a continuity of theme, which disappears only when the frame is rigorously structured according to the painting's composition. That means the edge of the canvas plays an active role in the work of art. A role it must always have. A painting should begin and end with itself. Without continuity.'

Rothfuss's ideas were shared by the artists who formed the Arte-Concreto Invención movement the following year, 1945, and in the photographs of the two exhibitions held that year in private houses – they found it impossible to get exhibition space in the galleries, and, it is said, resorted to hanging their work in the street – the walls are covered with irregularly shaped canvases, whose edges are determined by the lines of

4 Albert Gleizes and Jean Metzinger, 'Cubism' (1912), in Robert Herbert (ed), *Modern Artists on Art*, Prentice-Hall, New York, NY, 1964, p.5.

the composition. A torrent of invention had been let loose: in some works the frame itself became the composition, while the idea of movement was introduced in a variety of ways. Wall pieces in wood and metal had movable parts, and freestanding constructions could be taken to pieces and reassembled, or shifted into different configurations, as in Kosice's *Royi* (1944).

The first exhibition took place at Dr Enrique Pichon Rivière's house on 8 October, and the invitation stated: 'Concrete-elementary Theory, resolutions, music, painting, sculpture and poems. Ramón Melgar, Juan C. Paz, Rhod Rothfuss, Estéban Eitler, Gyula Kosice, Valdo Wellington and Arden Quin.'

The second exhibition, again with the title 'Arte Concreto-Invención', was in the photographer Grete Stern's house on 2 December, and included music and 'elementarist dances'. Although they appear in the photographs of the event, Raúl Lozza and Alfredo Hlito did not exhibit. Following disagreements among the artists, Maldonado, who had not participated in this exhibition, formed the Arte Concreto-Invención Asociación, which Alfredo Hlito, Manuel Espinosa, Enio Iommi, Claudio Girola, Raúl and Rembrandt van Dyck Lozza, Oscar Nuñez and Jorge Souza also joined.[5] This group held its first exhibition at the Peuser exhibition room in March 1946, and the same year brought out two issues of a bulletin.

The original group, including Kosice, Rothfuss, Quin, Martin Blaszko, Diyi Laañ and Eitler, now took the name Madí, to distinguish itself clearly from Maldonado's Arte Concreto-Invención. The origins of this term are as much in dispute as those of Dada. The *Madí Manifesto* says that the term 'concrete' was dropped because it still retained the static elements of the old art; this might suggest that the name evolved from Movimiento de Arte de Invención. Others have held that the letters MA/DI stand for MArxisme or MAtérialisme DIalectique, or that the name is basically a nonsense vocable, like Dada.[6] Three exhibitions were held during 1946; the first, which launched the movement, took place at the French Institute in August. The third exhibition, in November 1946 at the Bohemian Club

5 Whether Maldonado and his group split before or after the private exhibition at Grete Stern's house in the autumn of 1945 is a matter of disagreement.

6 Arden Quin, one of the original and most influential members, older than the others, has been interested in Marxism since the 1930s. He has spoken of his commitment to dialectical materialism, which informs his text in *Arturo*.

in Buenos Aires, was advertised in the following terms: 'Madí has invented the trimmed and irregular frame, breaking for ever with the taboo of the pictorial "Frame"; it invented painting and sculpture with movement, articulated universal and linear; *it created Plural and Ludic Plastic art*.'

Obviously, the two groups initially had a great deal in common; to begin with, both had taken the term Arte Concreto, which clearly signalled their adherence to the broad alliance of non-figurative artists within the European avant garde who rejected the term 'abstract', because it implied abstracting from a given reality in the way Cubism, say, did, and adopted instead the term 'concrete'. The first full public use of the term had been in the title of the *Manifesto of Concrete Art* founded by Theo van Doesburg in 1930.[7] The manifesto on its front page declared:

1. Art is universal.
2. The work of art must be entirely conceived and formed by the mind before its execution. It must receive nothing from nature's given forms, or from sensuality, or sentimentality. We wish to exclude lyricism, dramaticism, symbolism, etc.
3. The picture must be constructed from purely plastic elements, that is, planes and colours. A pictorial element has no other meaning than 'itself' and thus the picture has no other meaning than 'itself'...[8]

Although this group was short-lived, Max Bill and Arp later picked up the term. In 1936 Bill wrote, 'We call concrete art the works of art created according to a technique and laws entirely their own... without intervention of any process of abstraction. Concrete art... is an expression of the human spirit'.[9] And in March 1944 Max Bill organised the exhibition

7 The Constructivist Max Burchartz had first used the term 'concrete' in an artistic context. Antonio Berni apparently had a copy of the *Manifesto of Concrete Art*, which he showed to Maldonado.

8 Translated in Stephen Bann, *The Tradition of Constructivism*, Thames & Hudson, London, 1974, p.193. The manifesto was signed by Carlsmund, Van Doesburg, Hélion, Tutundjian and Wantz.

9 Max Bill, quoted in Perazzo, *op. cit.*, pp.24–25.

Konkrete Kunst at the Kunsthalle in Basel; the catalogue contained a version of Arp's vivid account of the practice of the concrete artist, who aims for a 'direct' as opposed to 'illusionistic' art: 'We don't want to copy nature. We don't want to reproduce, we want to produce. We want to produce like a plant that produces a fruit, and not to reproduce. We want to produce directly and not by way of any intermediary. Since this art doesn't have the slightest trace of abstraction, we name it: concrete art.'[10] Arp goes on to mention not only Kandinsky and Delaunay, but also Marcel Duchamp, Man Ray and Joan Miró (among others), and the resistance to orthodox divisions among the modernist tendencies (Abstraction versus Surrealism) demonstrated by Arp was echoed in the Madí group's free manipulation of sources.

Arturo had proclaimed: 'INVENT; to find or discover through ingenious thinking or mediation or mere chance something new or unknown./ To find out, imagine, create his work the poet or the artist/... INVENTION AGAINST AUTOMATISM'. Both Madí and the Arte Concreto-Invención Asociación laid stress on invention: Kosice published a pamphlet entitled *Invención*, in 1945, and Raul Lozza gave a lecture in 1946 at the third exhibition of the Arte Concreto-Invención group on 'The inventive as concrete reality in art', while the *Inventionist Manifesto* was published in the first issue of the Association's bulletin (August 1946).

The two groups also shared the aim of incorporating music and poetry, but Madí went further in this direction, and, as the *Madí Manifesto* signed by Kosice indicates, extended its ideas also to theatre, dance and architecture.

The Madí group also began to emphasise the movement and articulation of its constructions, dropping, as we saw, the term 'concrete', and explored numerous ways of undermining or subverting the conventional, static easel painting or sculpture. Its combination of aggression and playfulness recalls Dada, and especially the little magazines of the early 1920s in which Dadaist and Constructivist artists mingled side by side: Arp, László Moholy-Nagy, Kurt Schwitters, El Lissitzky, Francis Picabia,

10 Jean (Hans) Arp, 'Concrete Art', preface to *Konkrete Kunst*, exhibition catalogue, Kunsthalle Basel, March–April 1944. This was an extract from an article first published in English as 'Abstract Art, Concrete Art', in Peggy Guggenheim, *Art of This Century*, exhibition catalogue, New York, NY, 1942, but probably written earlier.

Hans Richter and so on. In this respect, it is worth noting that the relations between Dada and Constructivism were not simply those of polarised opposites. For instance, Arp, one of the leading Zurich Dadaists, and Van Doesburg, theoretician of Neoplasticism, collaborated in the late 1920s, and Van Doesburg, first propagator of 'concrete art', literally incarnated the apparently opposed spirits of Dada and Constructivism: not only did he edit the international Constructivist review *De Stijl*, but also, under his Dada persona 'I.K. Bonset', the neo-Dada review, *Mécano* (1922–23), and wrote Dada poetry. While there were, of course, profound differences between many of these artists in terms of their attitudes to nature, technology, man and the machine, their work often looked, in reproduction in the magazines, quite similar. They shared a radical rejection of past art, the refusal of representation and the abandonment of the figure, the search for new forms and experiments with new materials, the blurring of traditional distinctions between painting and sculpture.

With complete freedom, the Madí artists used a broad spectrum of avant-garde European art – Dada, Russian Constructivism, Mondrian, and so on – as a springboard for invention. Variations on the shaped and irregular canvas, and on the frame as structure in its own right, continued. Arden Quin made a series of canvases which he called *Cosmopolis*, not only with shaped edges, but sometimes also a curved surface, as well as articulated wall constructions.

The introduction of movement led to a proliferation of formal inventions. Kosice, in whose work the impulse to dematerialise the static or solid – introducing space, light, water, movement – has been most pronounced, made sculptures out of neon lights, probably the first artist to do so.[11] Biedma, Laañ, Kosice and Arden Quin, among others, made sculpture with movable parts, which variously call to mind the transformable toys of Torres García, Russian Constructivism, Futurism and Arp's Dada objects – the early wood reliefs like *The Egg Board* (1922), or *Clock* (1914), in which the idea of movement is humorously but not literally present.[12] But it would be a mistake to imply any great dependency or

11 Lucio Fontana, who was in Buenos Aires at this time, maintained a genial interest in the young Madí and concrete artists, and had his students publish his *White Manifesto* in 1946. On his return to Europe, he too began to work in neon.

derivation, for the Madí works remain unique and quite original. The articulation of the idea of play with structural inventiveness is one of the most striking characteristics of these artists' work.

Sandú Darié, a Romanian artist settled in Cuba, made increasingly complicated versions of his 'Pintura transformable Madí', strips of painted wood nailed together which could be formed into an almost infinite variety of configurations. Darié had exhibited in New York and at the Venice Biennale, and was invited by Kosice to send work to the Madí group in Buenos Aires, though he never went there himself. The American critic Clement Greenberg recognised the spirit of invention in Darié's work, but sought to draw it into a more orthodox modernist project: writing to Darié in 1950, he said, '...the reproductions in the catalogue struck me by the originality they evidenced. Not as realisations, but as promises, the beginning of something in the form of bas-relief constructions that will be a real expansion of the medium.'[13]

In Cuba, Darié has continued to invent: chairs that fold up and can become pictures on the wall; moving and kinetic sculptures, using the simplest forms of light and energy, a 'primitive technology', he says, as a form of challenge to the industrialised consumer world.[14]

A sense of play was central to the Madí group's inventiveness. The presence of the ludic, and the capacity for movement led to a kind of continuing irresolution, a permanent sense of possibilities. The Arte Concreto-Invención artists pursued a more rigorously formal direction, initially with a strong affinity to Mondrian, and later moving close to Max Bill and Georges Vantongerloo.

Maldonado met Max Bill in 1948 on a visit to Europe, and subsequently was invited by Bill to teach with him at Ulm.[15] Maldonado had explained

12 The role of the Futurist manifestos should be mentioned here: Arden Quin has spoken of his admiration for them as a continual source of new ideas, especially Umberto Boccioni's *Manifesto of Futurist Sculpture*, (Conversation with Arden Quin, Paris, October 1988.)

13 Clement Greenberg, letter to Sandú Darié (collection of the artist, Havana).

14 Conversation with Sandú Darié, Havana, May 1988. Darié died in 1991.

15 Bill intended to resume the Bauhaus tradition at Ulm School of Design. Maldonado remained a professor there until 1967.

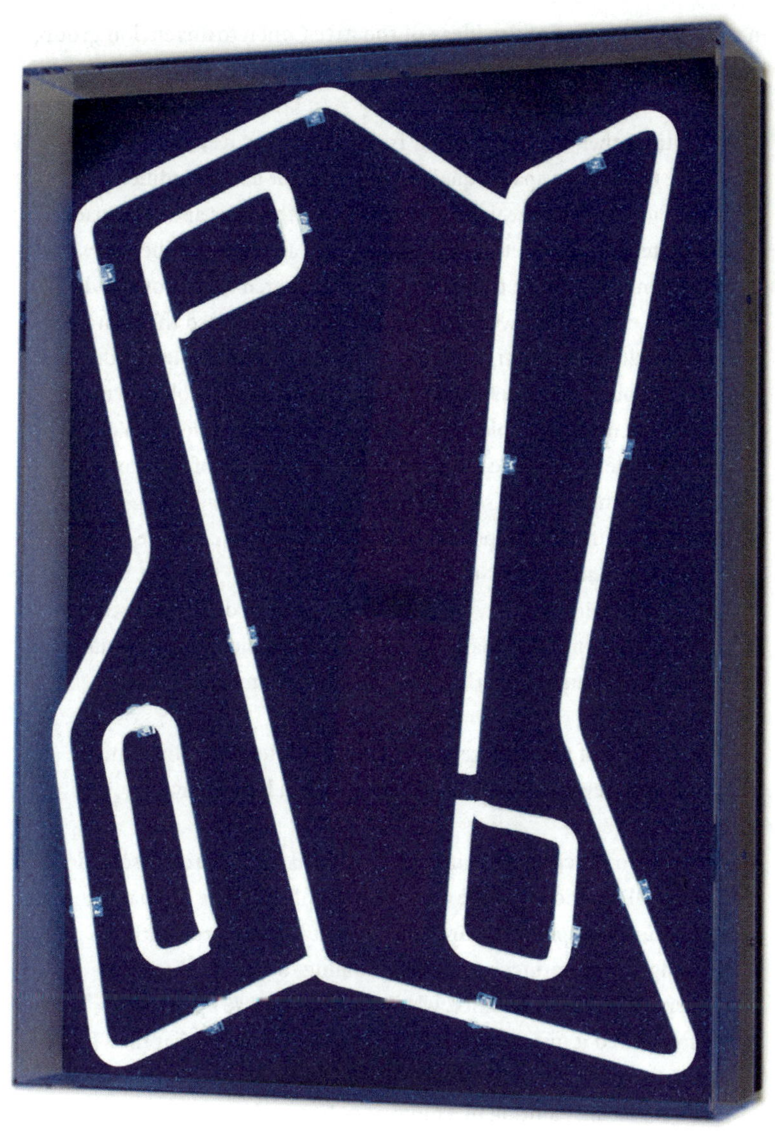

Gyula Kosice
Madí Light Structure, 1946
Neon gas, Plexiglas, wood
64 × 47 × 17 cm | 25¼ × 18½ × 6¾ in

in 1946 the evolution of the ideas of the Arte Concreto-Invención group, from the point of adopting the cutout frame, and the shaped canvas:

> We noticed then that the 'cut-out frame or picture', as we had called it, gave the frame a spatial quality; we could not remain indifferent to the fact that we were, in this way, opening the gates and that space penetrated into the picture and participated as a more aesthetically belligerent element. At the same time, we repeated Nicholson's and Domela's experiences: we materialised figures, we turned them into forms (Maldonado, Prati, Raúl Lozza, Antonio Caraduje). But at this point we found ourselves looking for a tri-dimensional solution to the bi-dimensional problem: we were repeating the same mistake... and we made a stop... We resumed in depth the study of the problem concerning the 'cut-out frame or picture'. We started by giving more importance to the penetrating space than to the picture itself (Molenberg, Raúl Lozza, Nuñez).
>
> And following this way we came to the greatest discovery made by our movement: the separation in space of the picture's constituent elements without leaving their co-planar arrangement...'[16]

The destruction of the picture plane as a still potentially illusionistic space, led to a new problem. As Hlito wrote in a later essay:

> The walls to which those paintings were fixed immediately assumed the optical function that the canvas had fulfilled before, so that the background reappeared again. These objects participated both in painting and sculpture, but without coming to have a coherence of their own. This experience, which some of us gave up because we considered it unsatisfactory, at least served to prove that the requirement for a plane could not be taken beyond certain limits without placing painting in a blind alley.[17]

16 Tomás Maldonado, in *Revista Arte Concreto-Invención*, Buenos Aires, no.1, 1946; trans. in Perazzo, *op. cit.*, p.88.

17 Alfredo Hlito, 'El tema del Espacio en la pintura Actual', *Nueva Visión*, Buenos Aires, no.8, 1955; trans. in Perazzo, *ibid.*, p.89.

In 1947 Raúl Lozza had separated from the Arte Concreto-Invención Asociación and formed a new movement, 'Perceptism'; he sought a solution to the problem of the dispersed planes and the wall by placing his dynamically shaped coloured planes on a background large enough to form a 'field', but in a sense he now returned the problem back to the fixed picture surface.

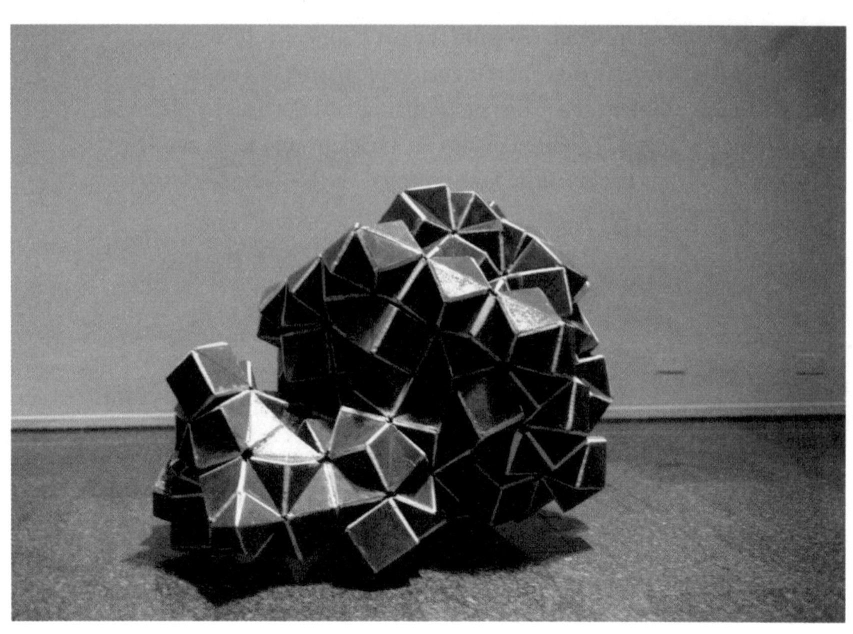

172 **Richard Deacon**
Beauty and the Beast D, 1995
Epoxy resin and cardboard
90 × 112 × 98 cm | 35⅜ × 44⅛ × 38⅝ in

Beauty and the Beast: The Sculpture of Richard Deacon

Richard Deacon: Esculturas 1984–95, The British Council, London, 1996, n.p.

Deacon's use of the term sculpture, in the titles of exhibition catalogues as in conversation, is deliberate, polemical and not without irony. His current definition of sculpture is a single object made of a single material, with the emphasis on made. Intention and meanings are important but inhere in the material and its structure rather than precede it. Deacon calls himself a 'fabricator': 'Material and its manipulation are core areas in what I do. Matter, stuff are the words I tend to use'.[1]

Although Deacon may not always have held to his definition of sculpture – for instance to the single material – there is a consistency to his work that goes back to the period of open experiment at St Martins. *Stuff Box Object* (1970–71) records an 'exchange' of location and materials with a fellow student and the series of operations with the 'stuff' he inherited (a large wooden box, an amount of raw flax joined by strips of fibreglass, straw, chicken shit and scraps of wood). These included various types of transformation, concealment, construction and destruction together with elements of performance, starting with Deacon climbing into the box and adopting a foetal position, and culminating in a lengthy apprenticeship in plastering the surfaces of the box. The ritually repetitious and satisfying nature of these activities asserts itself even through the deadpan documentary writing:

> At 4.30 I fetch a bucket of water, pour a little into the bowl and mix up a small amount of dental plaster. I flick this plaster with my hands

1 Jon Thompson, Pier Luigi Tazzi, Peter Schjeldahl (eds), *Richard Deacon*, Phaidon, London, 1995, p.15.

against one of the slatted sides of the object. I continue working alternately from end to end until the bucket is empty. I wash my hands and the bowl and leave the Studio to fetch a carton of tea. I sit and look at the plastering whilst I drink the tea.[2]

A suite of drawings, *It's Orpheus When There's Singing* (1978–79), bridged the gap between *Stuff Box Object* and two exhibitions in 1985 of Deacon's large laminated wood sculptures; *For Those Who Have Ears* and related works at the Tate Gallery, and *Blind Deaf And Dumb* at the Serpentine. The sculptures hark back in form and title to the drawing suite and to Rilke's *Sonnets to Orpheus* (1922). They have a strong sexual charge, rooted in the very openness of readings, paradoxically both direct and allusive, rather than in specific sexual symbolism.

Deacon called the drawings 'anticipatory'; they are not drawings for sculpture, although they are very large, grand works, positing a sculptile sense of gesture in space. Given that nothing was given, they are a series of visibly experimental marks, concerned with the generation of meanings in form. Deacon's description of his procedure denotes a kind of rationalised automatism:

> There was no object being drawn, so in order to get to a point where I could draw what I wanted, it seemed necessary to have rules. These were a means of avoiding some decisions about the appearance of the drawing as it developed. The drawings were constructed using a string, a pin and a pencil – this was the rule. All the curves were then built up from arcs or segments of circles of varying radii. This construction created a very fine mesh of marks, from which a final form slowly emerged, almost as if it had been captured.[3]

The search is for ways of investing potentially sculptural ideas of a general kind: enclosure, aperture, with metaphorical – or perhaps better,

2 Richard Deacon, *Stuff Box Object 1971–72*, Chapter Arts Centre, Cardiff. Published to coincide with the exhibition of Deacon's sculpture at the Lisson Gallery, London, July 1984.

3 Deacon, *Silence Exile Cunning*, exhibition catalogue, Carnegie Museum of Art, Pittsburgh, PA, 1988. Extract republished in Deacon, *op. cit.*, p.117.

analogical – significance. The forms finally captured in these drawings, Deacon says, can be thought of as the head of Orpheus but also any number of other objects. The aperture could relate to the body, or 'other very domestic objects particularly pots and pans, shoes, hats – there are lots of objects which have a volumetric shape with an opening.'[4]

Deacon commented that 'the drawings seemed to show that what was enclosed had a relationship to the contour. This functioned like a skin over the interior, and the interior remained a hollow resonant space'.[5] This idea, taken in conjunction with such works as the open slatted bell-like *Untitled* (1980) with its extra vulva-like opening, brought the eighteenth-century artist William Hogarth and his treatise *The Analysis of Beauty* (1753) to mind. The comparison was with Hogarth's imaginary model for draughtsmen. All too often, Hogarth argued, the artist considers only that part of the surface of an opaque object that is presented to the eye. To understand the whole object, we need an idea of its inside too; thus we should imagine the inward contents of an object scooped out to leave only a thin shell, made up of very fine threads so that the two surfaces actually coincide. Hogarth pursued this notion of the identity of the interior and exterior surfaces by suggesting that the imagination would 'enter the vacant space within this shell and... view the whole form within'.[6]

Hogarth based his idea of beauty in an abstract form, rather than in an idealised human shape: the serpentine line. This opens up precisely those possibilities of play between contour and volume that generate metaphor or analogy in Deacon's work, while grounding these and always returning to the material. It is not that Deacon pursues an aesthetic based on the serpentine line, but bringing it into play does help to float his work free of comparisons with biomorphism, with its fixed nexus of organic plant/human body/earth meanings. It also points to a different type of spatial modality from that of Naum Gabo, who constructed volume not through mass but through plane. With Deacon, once the contour is established as a spatial boundary it is freed of the notion of a defined space without thereby simply becoming drawing in space. The notions of an identity of

4 Deacon, 'Talking about *For Those Who Have Ears No 2* and other works', interview by Richard Francis in *Richard Deacon*, exhibition broadsheet, Tate Gallery, London, 1985, p.7.

5 *Ibid.*, p.119.

6 William Hogarth, *The Analysis of Beauty*, 1753, reprinted by Scolar Press, London, 1971, p.8.

interior and exterior, of the relation of skin to contour, of contours that are boundaries, volumes that are hollows, continue to provide a fertile ground for the paradoxical ways in which Deacon plays with the relations of space to structure.

In *Feast for the Eye* (1987) the three enclosing elements are discrete boundaries – only with difficulty linked to each other. We find ourselves at a point where structure as surface – that is the notion of a contour related to the volume implied by the three elements – can only be conceived as a kind of formlessness which dramatically contradicts the powerful steel 'ducting', a 'packing case for space'.

Between The Two Of Us (1984) is unlike the lithe, open shapes of laminated wood pieces such as *For Those Who Have Ears No 2* (1983) or *Turning A Blind Eye* (1984) in its compacted wholeness; yet this appearance of wholeness is deceptive because, like the other works, it is founded in symmetry, in other words in a doubling. It reads in several ways: as a butterfly, or perhaps as the concentrated dynamism of a dancer. It is not just the title that connotes sexuality, but this certainly helps to keep the various visible analogies vibrating against one another. The edges of the upper and lower wing/limbs are crucially different; while both are meticulously riveted, the steel edges of the upper set are bent upwards, while those of the lower wings are folded down along the curve. They thus seem to push against each other, forcing or emphasising upward and downward motion. The canvas or sacking (the lettering 'London' just visible, suggesting a mercantile origin) hangs like a cape, or a bag or the empty skin of a chrysalis between the wings.

Troubled Water of 1987 is an unexpected work. It is unusual for Deacon to take a readymade element as he has taken the A-shaped beams here; it is also unusual for him so openly to parody the modernist sculptural discourse of part and whole. The hint of calipers, the wooden segment, the odd relation between geometrical forms and the nose-like pod or protrusion on which the whole barely balances recall the moment of the coming into being of the geometry-generated spontaneous drawings.

It is simultaneously comic and grand, the nearest, in some ways, to the idea of a machine aesthetic, not of the modern technological world but that of the huge pistons, pumps and hammers of the early industrial age now preserved at the Science Museum.

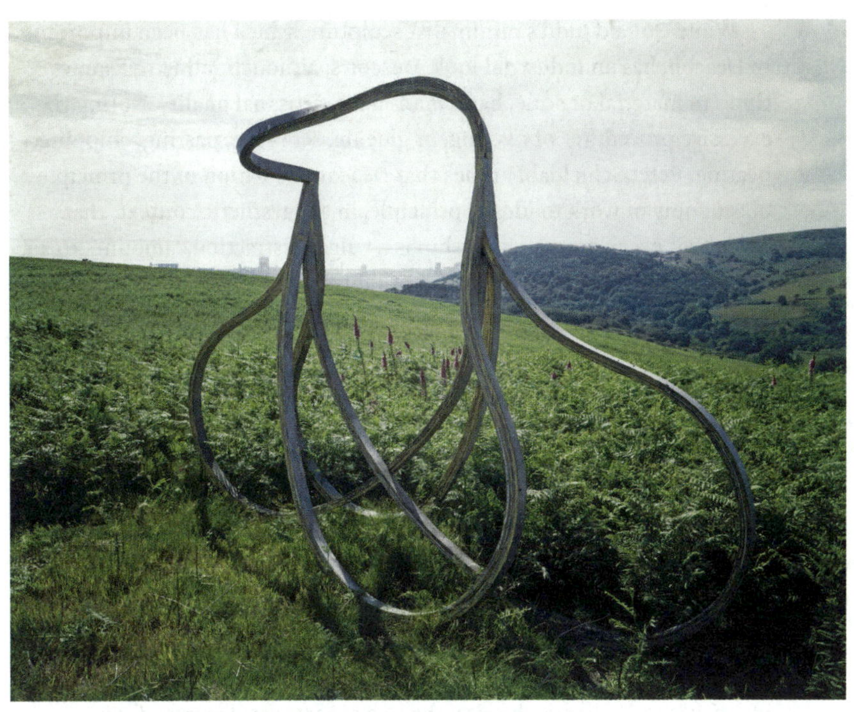

Richard Deacon
For Those Who Have Ears No 2, 1983
Laminated wood
274 × 366 × 153 cm | 107⅞ × 144⅛ × 60¼ in

While Donald Judd's minimalist sculpture, which has been important to Deacon, has an industrial look, Deacon's, although industrial sometimes in material or scale, has a man-made, artisanal quality. Noting the excessive procedures of riveting, or glueing, screwing, pasting, chipping, beating, Peter Schjeldahl argues that Deacon's violation of the principle of economy of work to idea, a principle, in the aesthetic context, that holds that excessive craftsmanship is a vulgar distraction, 'amounts to an original sculptural dictum that is both formally impressive and comical'. Schjeldahl calls this the 'tone of labour'[7] and connects it with work of an old-fashioned small-industrial-workshop kind.

The autonomy of the sculptural object can be conceived more readily than it can be either experienced or demonstrated. Deacon confronts the question of site-specific sculpture for reasons of practical necessity, not as chosen procedure. He contests Henry Moore's dictum that the proper place for sculpture is out of doors, but is equally disturbed by the proposition that 'the proper home of the autonomous modernist sculpture is the museum'.[8] This is not only prescriptive, but based on a highly reductive sense of 'autonomous'. Neither exterior nor interior sites are a priori conditions for sculpture. One way to posit its autonomous identity is to challenge the site: the two separate sculptures of *Blind Deaf And Dumb* at the Serpentine Gallery, one inside, the other outside, appeared to contain the architecture, rather than vice versa. The identity of interior and exterior, always a concern for Deacon, was thus brought into question. A further problem in this context is the dependence of the object in purely physical terms on its setting. While Minimalists like Robert Morris, Donald Judd or Carl Andre took 'the ground plane... [as] the necessary support for the maximum awareness of the object',[9] Deacon minimises the physical contact with the ground. There are no pedestals, and works are curved to keep the point of contact with the ground tenuous.

Solid or volumetrically enclosed works like *Beauty And The Beast C*

7 Peter Schjeldahl, *Richard Deacon*, exhibition catalogue, Marian Goodman Gallery, New York, NY, February 1988.

8 Deacon, 'What Car? Correspondence with Lynne Cooke 1992', in *Richard Deacon*, 1995, *op. cit.*, pp.129–30.

9 Robert Morris, 'Notes on Sculpture', *Artforum*, February 1966, reprinted in Gregory Battcock (ed), *Minimal Art, A Critical Anthology*, E.P. Dutton, New York, NY, p.224.

(1995) and *In The Flesh* (1992) are also concerned with the relation between contour and surface. The beauty of the clear plastic material of the former, polycarbonate, is lost or corrupted by manipulation. It is impossible to realise the potential of this manipulable substance, its animation into contour and transparent volume, because in the very practice of heating and bending it the pristine transparency is lost.

In the 'Back Of My Hand' series (1991) the steel surfaces are often pitted so that light animates them; here, and to a greater degree in *Beauty And The Beast*, hollows and protuberances are on a perceptually shifting scale that at times gives one the sense of the small and intimate (like the back of one's hand), at others expands into a landscape of hills and valleys.

This strange capacity to shrink and expand, like Alice alternating between potion and cake, is a persistent quality in Deacon's work and can strike whatever the actual dimensions may be. It is partly a measure of the success of establishing the object's autonomy, for scale is something we experience as determined by distance and perspective, which normally fix an object.

The idea of an invented map, which is visibly part of the 'Back Of My Hand' series, is at one end of a continuum of ideas about surface and boundary which is marked at the other by *In The Flesh*, a formless form, a seductive wooden substance without identity. In so far as a map has boundaries, *In The Flesh* might be seen as its contradiction, for the formless is a transgression of boundaries. The need for differentiation, order and purity which the very idea of the formless affronts is 'the enemy of change, of ambiguity and compromise'.[10] The paradoxical value of formlessness is that it is 'an apt symbol of beginning and growth as it is of decay'.[11]

Beauty And The Beast D (1995; p.172), a tumble of convex/concave planes, hinged like children's fortune-telling folded papers, places the very notion of manipulation at its metaphorical centre. And with the irony never far from Deacon's practice, *Beauty And The Beast D* succeeds in making of inherently structured, neat and geometrical shapes a virtually form-less mass.

10 Mary Douglas, *Purity and Danger*, published by Routledge and Kegan Paul, 1966, extract reprinted in Richard Deacon, 1995, *op. cit.*, p.105.

11 *Ibid.*, p.101.

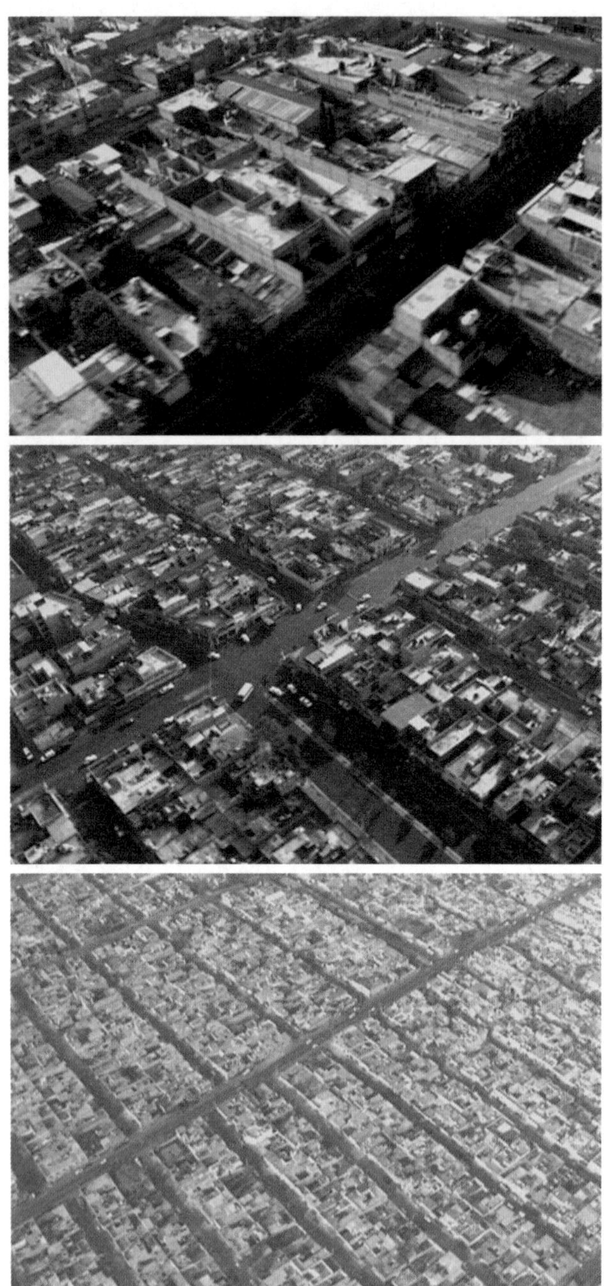

Melanie Smith
(in collaboration with Rafael Ortega)
Spiral City, 2002
Single channel video, projection
5 min 50 sec

Messing Up Abstraction

Melanie Smith: Spiral City and Other Vicarious Pleasures, Turner/A&R Press and Colección Jumex, Mexico City, 2007

Since the late 1980s Mexico City has been the base for an active and independent artistic community, a mixture of Mexican and foreign artists, critics and curators. It is not a group, though there are groups among it, nor can it be identified with any one particular viewpoint or practice. Several of the artists have well-established reputations on the international circuit. Paradoxically, while the city itself, its vast and varied urbanism, is predominantly the source and theme of these artists' work, they have fully shaken off the cultural nationalism and the weight of tradition that dominated art in post-revolutionary Mexico. Their immediate reaction was against the neo-Mexican revival of the 1970s and 1980s, which, even if often ironic in tone, still seemed to reinforce the old stereotypes and was easily institutionalised. If, for the foreign artists, the encounter with Mexico produced a powerful response, it was not to the ancient or picturesque but to an urban situation outside their European experience. The conditions of life in Mexico City were a constant challenge but also a kind of explosive liberation. For Melanie Smith, this has been a fundamental motor to her work: mixing up abstraction, as she put it, in response to new surroundings where 'aesthetic ornamentation seems irrelevant when compared to the question of daily survival'.[1]

In 1989 Smith went to Mexico for six months and is still there. Recently out of art school in England, she had no particular reason for choosing Mexico – the intention was just to work outside Europe for a while. Shortly after she arrived, she was included in the first exhibition

1 *Six Steps To Reality* (2002), in *Melanie Smith: Spiral City and Other Vicarious Pleasures*, p.153.

in Mexico to feature installations, *A propósito*, curated by Guillermo Santamarina with Gabriel Orozco and Flavia González, at the Museum of the Ex Convento de los Leones, a former Carmelite monastery in a forest on the outskirts of Mexico City. The exhibition, a kind of homage to Joseph Beuys, was an open-ended group of projects, which interacted with the architectural and natural environment. Smith at the time was making small wooden boxes by hand, using found materials, and her installation consisted of wood and wax objects. 'The piece was in a room that had no roof, and so the wax parts were exposed to the sun and melted into a pool of wax that hardened at night', very Beuys, as she says.

Informality and experiment, questing and critical practices aware of minimal and conceptual art but not dependent on them, and a great diversity of materials and mediums characterise the work of this loose community of artists. Smith's work has engaged directly with the city and especially those aspects of the life of the giant but oddly intimate megalopolis that differentiate it from European cities. Her responses to the street, the markets and the day-to-day working environment are in dialogue with that of other members of the artistic community but have a distinctive character. One unusual feature of her working practice in this context is that she paints, and painting is a constant reference in unexpected and original ways. Another is the focus on labour and the intensive effort of producing any work which she often makes apparent, as in the final video installation in *Six Steps To Reality*. Her videos/films, made in collaboration with her partner Rafael Ortega, who shot them, realise completely and effectively the possibilities of the medium, in that they are not records of an action or performance but are in themselves that action.

The links between an early group of works, 'Orange Lush', and the video *Tianguis II* (2003) are very interesting and pertinent to her relationship to abstract and minimal art. They concern not just the take on colour as a form of structuring a confusingly abundant and multifarious environment – one might mention as precedents, though not as influences, works like Boris Mikhailov's 'The Red Series' (1968–75), snapshots of urban scenes in which red objects predominate, or Richard Hamilton's beach photographs

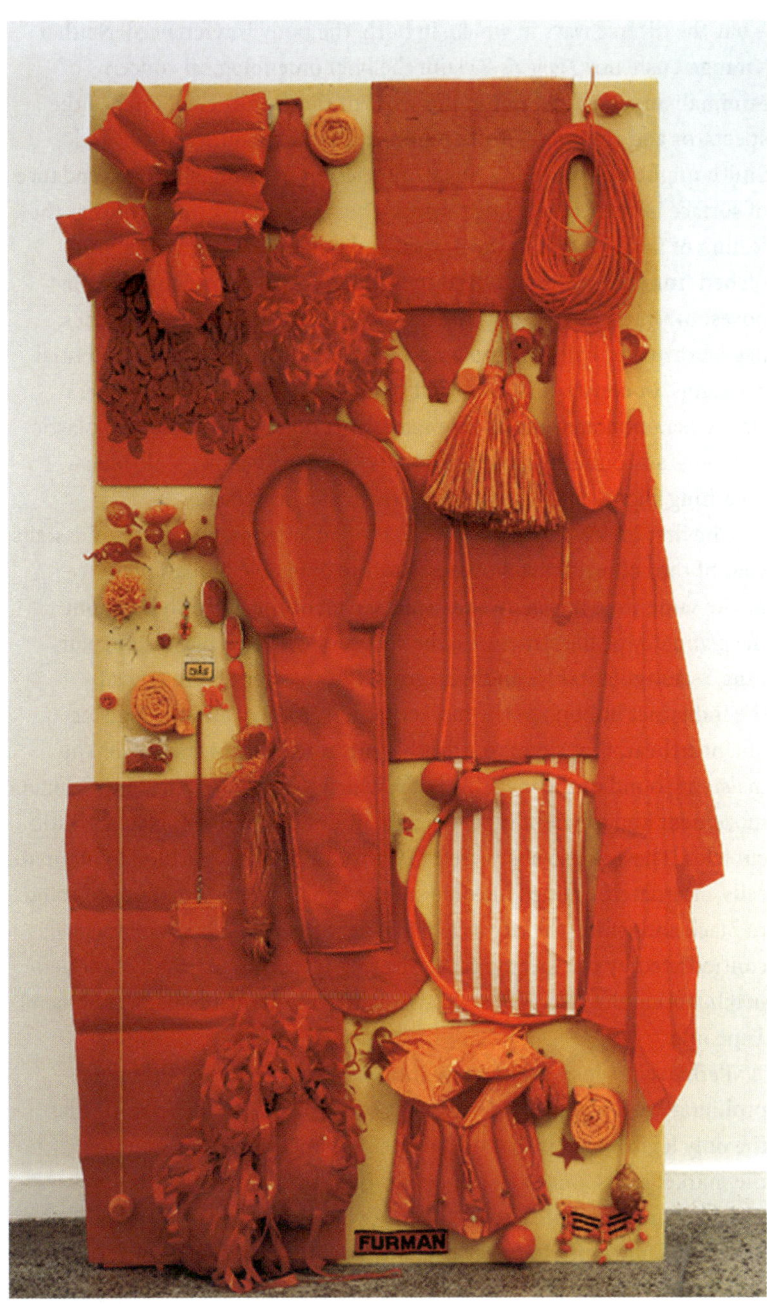

Melanie Smith
Orange Lush I, 1995
Plastic objects, wood
244 × 124 × 25.5 cm | 96⅛ × 48⅞ × 10⅛ in

– but the diverse ways in which, in both, the body is referenced. Neither 'Orange Lush' nor *Tianguis II* claim the phenomenological concerns of Minimalism, or at least not in the sense of the 'bodily encounter of the spectator and the work'. Bruce Nauman dubbed paintings 'lush' and Smith might be countering this denunciation of drunken over-abundance of surface in the 'Orange Lush' series. The name wonderfully conveys the feeling of fleshy excess in the draped and puffy orange plastic objects filched from the street and fixed to wooden boards or accumulated in boxes. In *Orange Lush I* (1995) the plastic tubes, fabrics, wires, pouches, bags, brush and balls have an ambivalent relation to the body: potential coverings, or constraints, or sexual symbols. In *Tianguis II* the camera slowly perambulates one of the many street markets, its coloured plastic sheetings surrounding the empty stalls – orange, yellow, pink, blue – breathing slightly against the soundtrack of a heartbeat.

The first impression in *Tianguis II* is of an entropic emptiness, the stalls void of the colourful mass of merchandise or visible human presence. At the same time this allows the split screen of the video to bring out the geometry of the structures, the sheets of coloured plastic, circular cans, rectangular tables and wire grids. But the sounds are crucial – the indistinct hubbub of the market traders, a siren, and the register of a heartbeat, that slows to a deathly pip at the end of the video. The insistent sound of the invisible body, which seems both part of the camera movement and inherent in its object, invades the slightly pulsing plastic cubicles. These are so abstracted that they begin to evoke blood-coloured cells, alternately drained of colour as the split screen switches from colour to black and white, the city as a living creature, which is simultaneously contradicted by the vacant scene. The fragile, temporary market shelters perch among the streets of solid two-storey modernist houses, ephemeral as people.

Perhaps it is just one of those instances of objective chance that proliferate in a place like Mexico City, but it seems wholly in spirit that the only legible sign is that on a white building in the street behind the market stalls: *Clínica médica-quirúrgica*, which becomes a fleeting but uncanny accomplice to the heartbeat, a reminder of actual bodies monitored and suffering. (Perhaps the orange of 'Orange Lush' recalls the orange marigolds that adorn graves on the Day of the Dead.) In terms of messing up or mixing up abstraction, this is a kind of post-phenomenological, 'corrupted Minimalism'.

Abstract art, the readymade, the moving image and installation are combined in *Six Steps to Abstraction* (2002) whose collage-like incongruity is buried under the bland term 'multimedia assemblage'. A series of paintings are stacked against (rather than neatly hung on) the wall, much as I had seen them in her studio in Mexico, partially obscuring one another; the vertical stripes of beautifully modulated colour across their surfaces having no particular beginning or ending or scale. Television monitors are casually floored or parked on their own cardboard containers. Suspended from the ceiling is a tangled mass of pink plastic threads, which visually resembles a pot of pink paint flung at the ceiling and, physically, a muddled skein. The ends trailing loosely above the paintings seemed an affront to their clean bands of colour, in upright stripes. The (lack of) correspondence went both ways: the pink threads might be originary to the canvases, like a jumbled skein drawn into order, or alternatively contaminating the paintings so that what at first appeared carefully regimented surfaces began to disintegrate like a television screen suffering interference. One of the television monitors showed men apparently setting up just such a three-dimensional arrangement of coloured threads in a room-space; another monitor showed a typical workshop of the kind characteristic of Mexico City, crowded with tools, open to the street: a small-scale industrial immediacy long-lost to London. Smith described the project as installed at the South London Gallery as a 'melting pot of other works that had been trying to reinterpret and mix up abstraction'.[2]

The formless pink plastic tangle recalled a short text by Georges Bataille, one of the 'Critical Dictionary' entries from his magazine *Documents*, on the word *informe*, or formlessness. This term, Bataille suggests, affronts philosophers who need to be able to categorise, to

2 *Six Steps Towards Abstraction* was shown in the exhibition *Twenty Million Mexicans Can't be Wrong* at the South London Gallery (2002), curated by Cuauhtémoc Medina. (Footnote added 2014.)

name and thus give form to things in the world. It is a term that serves to declassify, and what it designates has no rights and 'gets crushed like a spider or a worm'. 'Informe' is part of Bataille's attack on the philosophical certainties and linguistic hierarchies that assert order, but it was also written at a moment when abstraction, or non-objective art, was no longer being seen in absolute opposition to figuration, but was opening up to a world of ambiguities, of potencies, fantasies and metamorphoses. This latter aspect of 'informe' touches Smith's work in that the formlessness of the pink thread is like a collapse of the geometrical and other orders that once governed abstraction.

In 2003 Smith and Rafael Ortega made the video *Spiral City*, a highly personal response to a city they were about to leave and, at the same time, to Robert Smithson's earthwork and related film, *Spiral Jetty* (1970). Whereas the film *Spiral Jetty* follows the movement of the artist along the in-turning spiral, Smith's film plays off the counterpoint of the city grid against the upward movement of the helicopter flying in widening spirals. It was shot all in one take, and the camera produces movement as it turns, a cartwheel effect on the urban grid, with perpendicular streets becoming diagonal on the screen, but the initial perspectival effect evaporates as the camera draws away from the endless and undifferentiated grid formations. If the grid as a form is potentially open, always exceeding its own boundaries, the spiral curve has basically two formations: the equable spiral and the equiangular or logarithmic spiral. In both cases the curve starts from a point of origin and its curvature diminishes as it recedes from that point into infinity. However, it is possible to imagine moving in the opposite direction: into rather than outwards from the spiral. This is the entropic movement in *Spiral Jetty* in which the artist is filmed running inwards to the starting point of the spiral, as the camera rises away from him (and parodied in Damián Ortega's *Hágalo usted mismo: Spiral Jetty* (1993), a miniature version of the earthwork with a toy car at the end of the jetty). Smith's 'Spiral City' resembles the spiral target/shield Alfred Jarry drew on the belly of his monstrous anti-hero Ubu, and on the entropic spiral Smithson quotes Samuel Beckett: 'I must have got embroiled in a kind of inverted spiral, I mean one the coils of which, instead of widening more and more, grew narrower and narrower and finally, given the kind of space in which I was supposed to evolve, would come to an end for lack of room.' In Melanie Smith's film the movement is in the opposite direction, with the camera in flight upwards in a widening spiral movement. Although the film ends in a dazzle of light like *Spiral Jetty*, this has none of the grandiose cosmic references of Smithson's film. There is rather a continuous contradiction between the metaphysical invitation of the ever-widening logarithmic spiral and the paradoxical, insistent enclosure of the grid.

Even from a great height and even as its configurations dissolve in the light, there is no end to this city; this is saturated urbanism, drained of colour, no monuments, no green spaces, no river. The starting point was Ixtapalapa, a very poor, satellite city of endless identical streets of low-rise houses. Smith called it 'apocalyptic city', but it does not at all resemble those 'cities on the move' of the Far East, whose gigantic skyscrapers with rift valleys of streets virtually realise what used to be called the 'futuristic' 1960s fantasies of Archigram. It is the megalopolis in the abstract, and the video functions like the dramatic close-ups so dear to photographers of the 1920s, in bringing to the surface of the image patterns and abstractions normally invisible to the naked eye.

Spiral City is not based on construction-heavy interventions in the landscape or the studio, nor does it feature the artist herself – her personal/impersonal trace is the spiral flight recorded in the film, and the material, the urban landscape of a totally non-European city. It is as unlike the European capitals from the air as it is on the ground. Mexico City is an awe-inspiring gigantic urban sprawl, filling its volcano-fringed valley on a scale far surpassing any European city. It is for the European visitor a mass of vivid but half-legible signs, compounded by a deep history (for example, the vast Zócalo, not this size from modernist aspirations but left over from the mightier central plaza of the Aztecs) and serial rushes of modernisation, an ongoing confrontation between capitalist expansion and socio-cultural conditions of huge complexity.

There is nothing sentimental about Smith's pursuit of the modern spectacle in Mexico, the massed aerobics classes, the curiously staged photographs of sado-masochistic scenes in *Farce and Artifice* (2006), dances, the crowded workshops on the streets. No reference to history and the weight of the past. This is modernity of a shattered, intimate kind, already old, past its expiry date, but always still to happen. While it would not

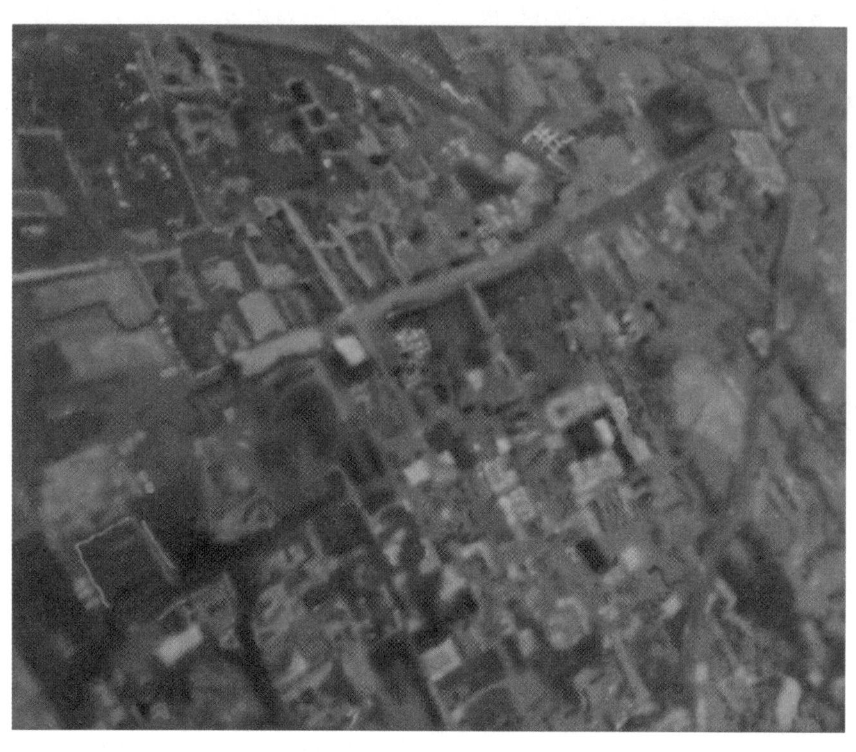

188 **Melanie Smith**
Pintura para Ciudad espiral
(Painting for Spiral City), c.2004
Oil on board
50 × 40 cm | 19¾ × 15¾ in

be true to say that the UK has entirely lost its local traditions, handcraft production – inventive popular forms of culture outside the mass media –are rare and need the eye of a Jeremy Deller to bring them into focus. In Mexico, the markets and small workshops teeming in the streets immediately behind the gigantic highways produce a quite different relationship between the globalised economy and the make-do-and-mend world, practical or fantastic, of the ordinary citizen.

In thinking of Smith's responses to modern Mexico largely in terms of the disruptions to aesthetic purities of one kind or another, I found that among the numerous initiatives in abstract art that could be brought in, it was the Russian Constructivist and Productivist artists with their utopian projects who insistently came to mind. Not simply as polar opposites to a dystopian modernity but because their attempt to re-fashion life in terms of an ideal abstract language, which conflated the object and pure forms, is seen, as it were, through strange mirrors, which reverse the movement. This is not to suggest that Smith is in search of pure forms, but that there is a dialectic between form and the stuff of the street that is subtly embedded in the diversity of her mediums.

This somewhat far-fetched comparison with the rigorously impersonal Constructivists does not, however, allow for the question of the person of the artist herself. In the movement between intimacy and objectivity in much of her work, there is rarely a reference to her identity. *Parres II* (2004) came as a complete surprise because it is, apparently, a self-portrait. Like *Parres I* (2004) it is shot in the semi-urban *terrain vague* of Parres, a sub-industrial settlement visible from the highway between Mexico City and Cuernavaca, at the top of the high volcanic ridge that separates the polluted city from the flowering and temperate valley to the south. The road divides, one route leading to Cuernavaca, the other to Tepoztlán, a community with strong indigenous roots. Tepoztlán is now home to many artists, including Smith and Rafael Ortega, and was successful in a famous battle to retain its autonomy and prevent, among other things, its water being diverted to nourish a Cuernavaca golf course. In these dramas, Parres is forgotten, a non-place of no interest to the thousands who make the mountain crossing every day.

In the film/video, Smith stands alone in a rough yard, facing the camera, which gradually draws back from a close-up of her face, away from her immobile figure while dogs and passers-by run to shelter from the tropical downpour, eventually so intense that it almost obliterates her, the intensity of the water operating like the spray-paint in *Parres I*, which finally whites out the camera lens. Whether her face is wet with tears or just the rain is impossible to say. The film lasts 3'42", just the length of the song on the soundtrack, which startlingly evokes quite a different world. It is a rural complaint, performed, it seems, by a female English country singer though the protagonist is a young Irish servant clapped in jail for daring to aspire to the hand of his employer's daughter. 'When I was young and in my prime…': the poignancy of this displaced song, with a displaced protagonist of the wrong gender in a distant setting, is virtually indistinguishable from the irony of its context. What I took at first for a self-portrait (literally as the subject of the film, then culturally referenced with an Anglo-Irish song) became a moving, ambiguous and even hilarious play with cultural and political identities.

Surrealism

Neither Dada nor Surrealism could be reduced to a single set of propositions or principles; in the case of Dada, over a very short time span this word expanded to cover anti-art, and iconoclastic and revolutionary impulses across Europe and in New York, which often manifested themselves in very different ways. Surrealism, on the other hand, had a kind of central spine in Paris, where it was formally launched by André Breton with the *First Surrealist Manifesto* in 1924, but remained in a constant state of becoming over decades. A recurring point is that, unlike other modern movements, there is no such thing as a surrealist style in the visual arts, each artist finding his or her own route in relation to chance, automatism or to dreams, experimenting in many mediums from paint to objects.

I wrote '*Documents*' for the catalogue of the exhibition *Dada and Surrealism Reviewed* (Hayward Gallery, 1978) which presented the work of Dada and Surrealist artists in the context of the reviews, or magazines, that were the life-blood of the movements. The magazine *Documents* was edited by Georges Bataille, and has been a major source for his writings and ideas. In recent decades these have been pitted against Breton and the so-called orthodox Surrealists, widely appealed to in support of a new aesthetic in contemporary art and have influenced ethnographic and anthropological approaches to culture. How far Bataille's ideas have overridden those of Breton, and to what extent they were seriously divided is open to question. Although quite raw in terms of more recent scholarship and critical writing, the essay seemed worth reprinting as an early attempt to grapple with the fundamental philosophical, aesthetic and ethnographical issues raised by *Documents*.

The exhibition *Lost Magic Kingdoms* was created by Eduardo Paolozzi from the collections of the British Museum for its Museum of Mankind in London in 1986. He mixed an extraordinary range of objects and tools with interventions of his own, inspired by the recycling and crossing-over of materials. He drew, as he said, on the legacy of Surrealism, and was especially keen to exorcise the idea of authenticity in so-called 'Primitive art', an attitude he shared with *Documents*.

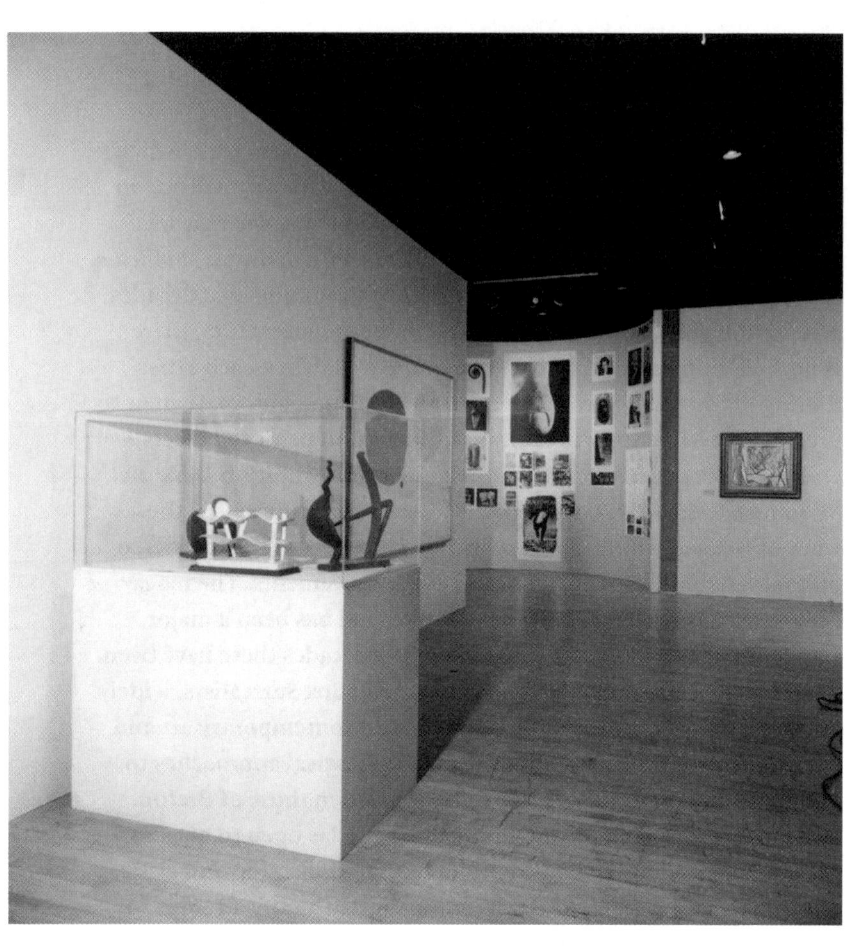

 Installation view of *Documents* display, *Dada and Surrealism Reviewed*, Hayward Gallery, London, 1978

Documents

Dada and Surrealism Reviewed, Dawn Ades (ed), Hayward Gallery, Arts Council of Great Britain, London, 1978

Documents was not a Surrealist magazine, nor was it para-Surrealist in the manner of the journal *Le Grand Jeu*. But, under the guidance of Georges Bataille, who later described himself as Surrealism's 'old enemy from within', and with the collaboration of dissident Surrealists like Michel Leiris and André Masson, a major part of the review presented an internal opposition to Surrealism.

Georges Wildenstein, the picture dealer and director of the *Gazette des Beaux-Arts*, founded *Documents*, probably with the idea of creating a rival to Christian Zervos's *Cahiers d'Art*. An editorial committee was set up, including prominent members of the Institut, museum officials, and representatives from the fields of archaeology, ethnography, music and art history. Bataille was the *secrétaire générale*, and the chief animators, apart from him, were Georges-Henri Rivière, Assistant Director of the Museum of Ethnography at the Trocadero (where Leiris also worked) and Carl Einstein, the outstanding writer of the time, both on modern European painting and on African art. Leiris was for a time during the second year *gérant* (manager) of the review.

Leiris and Bataille met in 1924, the year in which Leiris was introduced to André Breton, and joined the Surrealists.[1] Through Leiris, Bataille made the acquaintance of a circle of friends who gathered at the rue Blomet in Paris, where Joan Miró and Masson had adjoining studios. Apart from the painters, the group included Robert Desnos, Georges Limbour and Antonin Artaud, and all had in the course of 1924 given their allegiance

1 Michel Leiris, 'De Bataille L'Impossible à l'impossible Documents', *Brisées*, Gallimard, Paris, 1966.

to Surrealism except for Bataille. He met the Surrealist group for the first time in 1925 at the Café Cyrano, felt profoundly ill at ease with them, and thenceforth held aloof, although remaining a close friend of Leiris. Bataille was already remarkable for the depth and diversity of his culture and for his highly non-conformist mind, marked by a distinctive black humour. In some ways, he shows a close affinity with Dada, although, always extreme, he felt Dada had not gone far enough. 'Dada? Not idiotic enough', he once said to Masson. He suggested to Leiris that they should start a movement 'Oui', which would oppose to Dada's puerile 'Non' a perpetual acquiescence to everything. Bataille and Leiris had also nourished an abortive project for a review to be run from a brothel, and they began to record the dreams of its occupants for eventual publication. But Bataille did not intend to form a counter movement to Surrealism – indeed, Leiris has said that he was not suited to such an undertaking. He was unable either to gather and orchestrate a group of people, as Breton did, or to submit to another's domination.

Perhaps Bataille's long and uneven relationship with the Surrealists is best expressed by his own opinion of his work, which he situated 'at the side of Surrealism' maintaining that it contained the best of Surrealism, and by his desire to be more Surrealist than the Surrealists.

There is no question of the accord he felt with the revolutionary sweep of Surrealist activity, with its ability 'to go beyond the limits', and particularly the limits imposed by reason. He is most strikingly different from Breton, however, in his massive pessimism. In this he comes closer to the Surrealism of Desnos and Artaud in 1925. The despair and violence of *La Révolution surréaliste* at that time had made Breton uneasy; he wanted Surrealism to offer more hope than despair, and by the late 1920s he felt he had succeeded in establishing a more positive base. It is paradoxically true that in spite of the irrationality of the movement, Breton himself had a measured and harmonious spirit. He saw Bataille as an *obsédé* (an obsessive), not unlike Artaud. Bataille's only contribution, which had a strong Dada element, to *La Révolution surréaliste*, was a series of nonsense poems or *Fatrasies* of the thirteenth century which he selected and accompanied with an anonymous note [*La Révolution surréaliste* no.6, 1 March 1926]. By 1929, his suspicion of Surrealism had hardened. At the beginning of the year, his reply to Breton's invitation to help determine some common ground of positive action for intellectuals on the Left was: 'too many fucking idealists.'

Only a few weeks after the meeting at the Bar du Château in Montparnasse, which followed Breton's appeal and from which Bataille had so definitively disassociated himself, the first issue of *Documents* appeared, with contributions from the dissident Surrealists Leiris and Limbour. Others were soon to gather round Bataille, and even more in the wake of Breton's *Second Surrealist Manifesto* (1929). *Documents* is an extraordinary complement to the official Surrealist reviews, although it falls at a time when Bataille was personally least close to Surrealism, whose current political activism and artistic optimism jarred on him. Where *Documents* differed from *La Révolution surréaliste* was that the latter offered openly highly personal and individual experiences, its field of action being 'the operations of the mind', while in *Documents* Bataille is exploring the 'obscure intelligence of things'. Bataille, as we have seen, was not at all convinced by the Surrealists' conversion, with the *Second Surrealist Manifesto*, and *Le Surréalisme au service de la révolution (SASDLR)*, to the principle of historical materialism.

Had Bataille wished to establish a Surrealist review in opposition, it would have been necessary to engage in arguments relating explicitly to the theory and ideology of Surrealism, as the Belgian group did, but this did not interest him. There are polemics between *Documents* and firstly *La Révolution surréaliste* and then *SASDLR*, but they are very one-sided.

In the publicity handout for the review, Bataille's presence is clear in certain passages:

> The most provocative works of art, which are not yet classified, and certain eccentric productions, neglected until now, will be the subject of studies as rigorous and scientific as those of archaeologists... envisaged here in general are the most disquieting facts, whose consequences are not yet defined. In these various investigations, the occasionally absurd character of the results or the methods, far from being disguised, as it normally would be in conformance with the rules of propriety, will be deliberately underlined, as much from a hatred of platitude as from humour.

Clearly, *Documents* was to be no more of a conventional art review than *La Révolution surréaliste*, although certain articles would not be out of place in the *Gazette des Beaux-Arts*.

On the yellow cover of the first issue with its emphatic typography is the explanatory subheading: 'Doctrines, Archéologie, Beaux-Arts, Ethnographie', and a summary of the contents. Leiris has said that he and Bataille were determined to 'put all their ingenuity into utilising the review as a war-machine against received ideas', although this ambition was clearly not shared by the editorial committee. For the first three numbers, Bataille prudently held his hand, but with the fourth, the subheading was altered to read 'Archéologie, Beaux-Arts, Ethnographie, Variétés', and with the new category of 'variétés', Bataille introduced articles on the African-American troupe performing at the Moulin Rouge, 'Lew Leslie's Blackbirds', a 'chronique du Jazz', and photographs of film and music-hall stars, an area *Documents* continued to explore with gusto. Dada reviews had occasionally included pin-ups – *Die Schammade* had printed photographs of 'beauty American cyclists', but not on Bataille's scale, while the Surrealist reviews had not so far shown this kind of interest in popular culture. With the sixth issue, the editorial committee disappears from the title page, and Bataille's name appears alone. His articles should be examined first for the context of aggressive anti-idealism they create within *Documents* against the sober background of archaeology, ethnography and fine arts.

Bataille's articles in the first two issues, 'The academic horse' and the 'Apocalypse of Saint-Sever', are unexceptionable from the point of view of subject matter, and are perfectly in line with the other archaeological and historical contributions. The first, a study of Celtic versions of the classical horse on Greek and Roman coins, is at first sight not unlike the studies he, as a numismatist working in the Cabinet de Médailles at the Bibliothèque Nationale, had contributed to *Aréthuse*.[2] However, Bataille's subversive intentions, his *double jeu* (double game), as Leiris called it, are revealed in his trenchant and personal interpretations: 'The dislocation of the classic horse, finally reaching a frenzy of forms, transgresses the rule and realises

2 Between 1926 and 1929, Bataille contributed various articles including 'Les monnaies des grands Moguls au Cabinet de Médailles', *Aréthuse*, nos.13 and 14, October 1926 and January 1927.

the exact expression of the monstrous mentality of these people living at the mercy of suggestions', these people whose barbaric choice of other ignoble subjects 'represents the definitive answer of the human night, burlesque and frightful, to the platitudes and arrogance of the idealists.' The second article describes the senile beatitude of the figures on the medieval manuscripts of Saint-Sever before the most savage and brutal scenes.

Bataille now, after the second issue, abandoned the archaeological alibi. He turned to a series of phenomena eccentric and provocative only through the disquieting attention he paid them. 'The language of flowers' and 'The human face', which would seem to be reassuring, even idyllic, subjects, are used by Bataille to challenge the very idea of placing nature within the rational order. The photographs accompanying the articles now assume an almost monstrous importance: they include details of vegetal forms magnified into incongruous and disturbing shapes, and turn-of-the-century photographs of a petit-bourgeois wedding and of theatrical and music-hall figures in obsolete and ridiculous guise. The latter, for Bataille, destroy the idea that there are certain permanent human qualities, transcending changes in fashion, which are necessary for a belief in human nature. For Bataille, on the contrary, these dim figures, who might be our fathers and grandfathers, are monstrous apparitions who are in our terms barely human. As for the general use of flowers to represent the human ideal, Bataille destroys not the concept but the assumption that it is ideal beauty that the flower contains: on the contrary, the flower 'abruptly returns to its primitive ordure: the most ideal is rapidly reduced to a tatter of aerial manure'.

Bataille pursues his brilliant tragicomic attack on idealism in 'Le gros orteil' (The big toe), where he develops his idea of *bassesse* (baseness). The big toe is the most human part of the body in the sense that it is the least like the corresponding element in the anthropoid ape; it is also the most firmly fixed in the mud. The article, accompanied by brutal enlargements of photographs of toes, by Jacques-André Boiffard, examines the ecstatic 'low seduction' they offer, inherent in the old taboos about women's feet. Becoming more and more insistent through the black humour is the idea that while we feel malaise and horror when certain spectacles confront us, we are also seduced by them ('Les écarts de la nature', The Deviations of

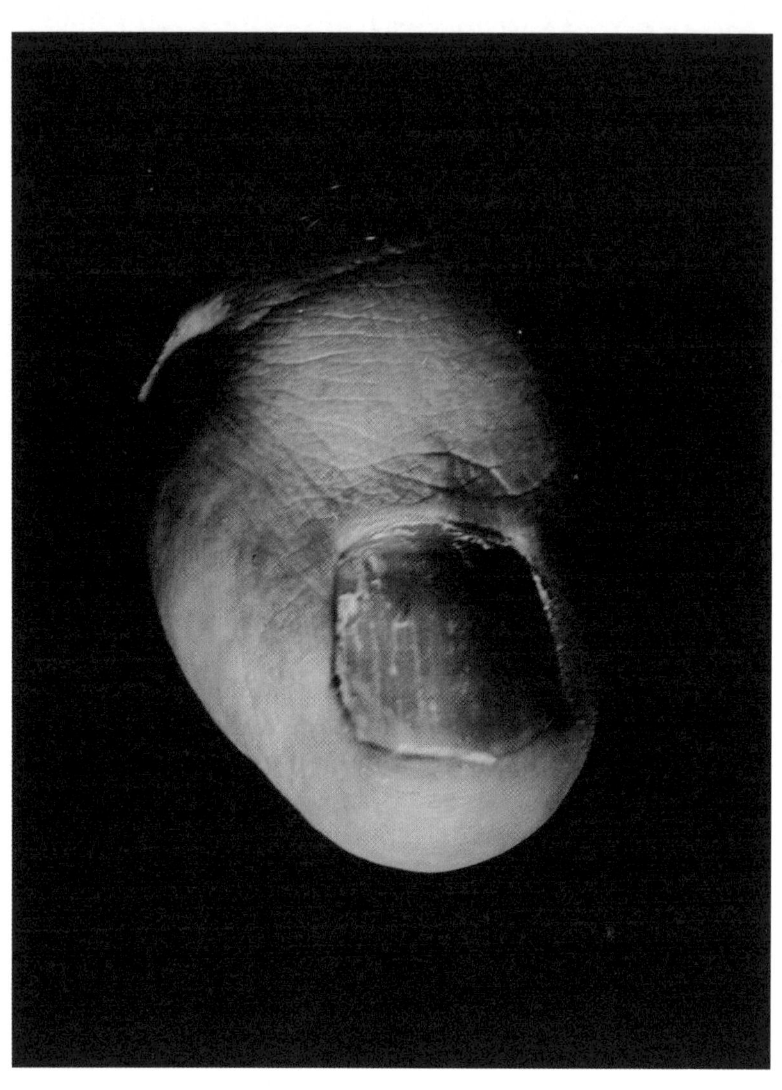

202 **Jacques-André Boiffard**
The Big Toe
Documents, no.6, Paris, 1929

Nature). Without this emphasis on the fascination of the repugnant, 'Le bas matérialisme et le gnose', (Base Materialism and Gnosticism) in which Bataille develops most fully his idea of anti-idealist materialism, would sound rather like the fulminations of the Early Church Fathers against that sect which believed in matter as an active principle with an autonomous existence. 'It is difficult to believe that Gnosticism does not witness above all a sinister love of darkness, a monstrous taste for obscene and lawless headless figures, for the head of the solar ass (whose cosmic and desperate braying is the signal of a shameless revolt against the idealism in power).'[3]

Beginning in the second issue is the 'Dictionnaire critique' (Critical Dictionary), a series of entries on selected words by Bataille and some of his closest associates on the review, Michel Leiris, Carl Einstein, Marcel Griaule, Jacques Baron. They are cast, not in the form of ironic epigrams like Flaubert's *Le Dictionnaire des idées reçues* (Dictionary of Received Ideas, 1911–13), but as short essays. Three of the most significant by Bataille are on 'Abattoir', 'Informe' and 'Materialisme'.[4]

'Abattoir' is illustrated with three extraordinary photographs by Eli Lotar of Paris slaughterhouses. These are for Bataille the descendants of temples in the sense that originally the buildings served as places of religious offerings and as slaughterhouses. That they are regarded now as cursed is because people cannot bear the sight of their own ugliness, but, with an unhealthy need for cleanliness, they have banished themselves into an 'amorphous world where there is nothing horrible any longer'. Ideas of slaughter and sacrifice obsessed Bataille for a long time. In the 'Apocalypse of Saint-Sever' he noted the 'physical optimism' that characterised butchers, and he later explored self-mutilation in the case of Van Gogh as an example of the surfacing of an ancient and suppressed need for sacrifice and self-sacrifice.

Bataille's essays on 'Informe' and 'Materialisme' both turn on the apparent inability of man to exist without systems; without them, the world opens into a terrifying abyss of formlessness, 'something like a spider or a blob of spittle'. Most materialists, even, still erect a system of hierarchies in which they have simply placed the 'ideal form of matter'

3 Georges Bataille, 'Le bas matérialisme et la gnose' (Base materialism and Gnosticism), *Documents*, no.1, 2nd year, 1930, p.6.

4 *Documents*, no.6, November 1929, no.7, December 1929, and no.3, June 1929.

at the top. The word materialism should be used to designate 'to the exclusion of all idealism, brute phenomena'. In these essays, Bataille is performing an 'operation on language' not unlike that of the Surrealists except that he pushes it further.

Breton examined *Documents*, and in particular Bataille's essays, with the attention demanded by a review which had gathered so many of his former friends and associates, and found them offensive. He wrote in the *Second Surrealist Manifesto* of December 1929:

> M. Bataille professes to consider in the world only what is vilest, most discouraging and corrupted, and he invites man to avoid making himself useful for anything specific 'to run absurdly with him – eyes suddenly dim and filled with unavowable tears – towards haunted provincial houses seamier than flies, more depraved and ranker than barbers' shops.' If I relate such remarks, it is because they seem to me to implicate not only M. Bataille but also those ex-surrealists who wanted to be fully free to involve themselves anywhere and everywhere... Already lined up at the starting gate for the race which M. Bataille is organising are: Messrs Desnos, Leiris, Limbour, Masson and Vitrac: it's difficult to explain why M. Ribemont-Dessaignes isn't there yet. I maintain that it is extremely significant to see reunited all those whom a defect of one sort or another has removed from a given initial activity because there is a good possibility that all they have in common is their dissatisfaction.

Breton attacks Bataille's 'offensive return to the old antidialectical Materialism' emphasising his pessimism and drawing attention to his 'delirious abuse of adjectives: soiled, senile, rank, sordid, lewd, decrepit... (which) far from serving as descriptions for him of insupportable things, are those by which his pleasure is most lyrically expressed'. He also notes rather tartly Bataille's free use of Freud. Those denounced and excommunicated in the *Second Surrealist Manifesto*, most of whom had already left the movement at least by the spring of 1929, were followed by others, like Jacques Prévert and Raymond Queneau, who had subsequently contributed, even briefly, to *Documents*. Bataille masterminded the pamphlet 'Un cadavre' (ironically modelled on the Surrealists' 1924 pamphlet of the same name attacking Anatole France), which is a bitter denunciation of Breton, pictured in the front as a martyred Christ, and is signed by the dissident Surrealists – Limbour, Max Morise, Baron, Leiris, Queneau, Boiffard, Desnos, Prévert and Bataille himself. Outraged as many were by their treatment in the *Second Surrealist Manifesto*, others recognised the necessity of getting out from Breton's shadow, breaking his almost paternal dominance. As Leiris wrote in *Documents*: 'Strange vermin we are, still fastening ourselves under the armpit of genius.'

For the dissident Surrealists, Bataille offered a new means of going beyond the limits imposed by reason and conventional morality, which was as far removed from 'aesthetic and moral preoccupations' as was Surrealism. Leiris's article on 'Man and his interior', is interesting, in showing how although certain figures like Marquis de Sade were honoured in common, *Documents* took a much more extreme view: 'Masochism, sadism, almost all vices in fact are only ways of feeling more human' because they are in a deeper and more abrupt relationship with the body. 'Humanity, besides, has nothing to do with happiness, any more than with goodness, we are very far here from any idea of charity, the most atrocious visions and the cruellest pleasures are entirely legitimate if they contribute to such a humanity.'[5]

Within *Documents* as a whole, Bataille introduced a kind of free taste, which was not limited to what could properly be called 'variétés' but spread through all parts of the review. Leiris's own articles on the 'Musée des Sorciers' in issue no.2 (1929) and on eighteenth-century anatomical plates in no.5 (1930) derive from preoccupations shared by both men. Leiris contributed articles which belong to but consort very oddly with the ethnographical side of *Documents*. In no.6 (1930) 'L'oeil de l'ethnographe' (The ethnographer's eye) is a record of his ideas about ethnography (and he quotes the full text of Helen Bannerman's *Story of Little Black Sambo*, 1899) when on the verge of leaving Europe with the Mission Dakar-Djibouti, and in the last issue there is an essay on William Seabrook (ethnographer, traveller and practitioner of black magic) whose book on voodoo in Haiti Leiris had reviewed in issue no.6 (1929). It was Leiris who drew Desnos's attention to the mystery of Abraham Juif (no.4, 1929).

5 Leiris, 'L'homme et son intérieur', *Documents*, no.5, 2nd year, 1930, p.266.

Robert Desnos also wrote about the statuary of Paris in 'Pygmalion and the Sphinx', in an odd, sociological tone which echoes Bataille's. This is illustrated with photographs by Boiffard, and it is interesting to compare them with Boiffard's photographs in Breton's *Nadja* (1928). While an atmosphere of mystery and the 'marvellous' – a word which barely appears in *Documents* – spills into the photographs in *Nadja* of the secret places of Paris where Breton experiences strange encounters and coincidences, the Paris statues of 'Pygmalion and the Sphinx' have an emphatically material and human presence. ('Bronze breathes and marble has veins.') Desnos imagines a Paris full of statues without pedestals – a bronze Baudelaire leaning on the parapet of the Île Saint-Louis, famous modern fetishes, advertisements like the Cadum baby and the child on the Chocolat Meunier cover, realised in alabaster and stone – an alter ego of visionary Surrealism, denuded of symbolism.

Popular and curious subjects especially intrigued Bataille and the ex-Surrealists. Raymond Queneau in issue no.5 (1930) contributed an article on the eccentric English publication by E.V. Lucas and George Morrow, *What a life!* (of 1911 but just then reprinted) whose comic illustrations are entirely composed from the department store Whiteley's general catalogue. Limbour wrote an article on carnival masks, with disturbing illustrations by Boiffard, comparing them with Aeschylus's comic and tragic masks, and suggests that the only authentic modern one is the gas mask. Bataille introduced American comic strip cartoons (*Les Pieds nickelés*) and Desnos wrote about the *Fantômas* books, of which he himself had a collection. In the fifth issue (1929), Bataille inaugurated what was intended to be a series on places of pilgrimage. The first two chosen were Hollywood and Notre-Dame de Liesse; those promised for the future included Chicago, Salt Lake City and Lourdes. The kind of iconographic and sociological attention paid to religion in *Documents* is not unlike that in Alfred Jarry's *L'Ymagier*, a periodical he founded with Remy de Gourmont which ran from 1894–95, and was largely devoted to particular themes in religious prints and woodcuts. There are a number of articles on Hollywood films, with a profusion of stills and photographs of stars, in the choice of which Georges-Henri Rivière was also involved. At Desnos's instigation, the Cuban writer Alejo Carpentier contributed an article on indigenous Cuban music, and jazz is paid a good deal of attention, with a notable review of Duke Ellington. This was a taste which *Documents* had in common with Dada, but it was entirely foreign to Surrealism.

Leiris has recently pointed out which articles in the review, within the catalogue of fine art and archaeology, were in line with the particular interests of Bataille and his friends.[6] Leiris's own article on the then unknown sixteenth-century French painter, Antoine Caron, in no.7 (1929) was prompted by Bataille, and the painting chosen was a grim Roman massacre. Carl Einstein wrote, in his peculiarly ardent tone, about the virtually forgotten Hercule Seghers in no.4, Jean Bourdeillette wrote about Franz Messerschmidt, the sculptor of old age, in no.8 (1930), and Sacheverell Sitwell wrote on the Mexican baroque in no.5 (1930). Clive Bell discussed Constable and French painting in no.7 (1930), and also in this category fall articles on Piero di Cosimo, Piranesi, and the doors of San Zeno in Verona. There are also important articles on Courbet and Manet, both by Marie Elbe, in no.2 and no.4 for 1930, which use contemporary documents to examine the scandals each provoked in their time. An article on Cycladic figures, however, unexpectedly does not fall into the category of those of special interest to Bataille.

Documents did fulfil its role as an art magazine, but not without thoroughly disturbing its natural public by the proximity of film stars, comics, jazz and the grotesque and often terrible photographs, not to speak of Bataille's own articles, a mixture unheard of in serious magazines of the time. The unexpected as a method was not new, indeed it was a staple of Dada and Surrealist magazines, but this 'côté farfelu' (wacky side), as Leiris called it, had never been used so effectively in such a context.

The real strength of *Documents* as an art magazine lay in its articles on modern painting and sculpture, largely, though not exclusively, the work of Carl Einstein. Young artists like Alberto Giacometti and Salvador Dalí were introduced here before they appeared in Surrealist reviews; Gaston-Louis Roux, a friend of Vitrac, was one of the younger painters attached to Kahnweiler's gallery. Leiris had known Giacometti since 1928, but his article on him in no.4 (1929) had given him his first opportunity to visit Giacometti's studio. It was precisely at this time that Giacometti was moving away from Cubist sculpture, influenced by Henri Laurens and

6 Ades in conversation with David Sylvester, 1976 and 1977.

Jacques Lipchitz, towards the figures drawn from his imagination which led him towards Surrealism. Contact between the ex-Surrealists and the newcomers was close. In the summer of 1929, Masson and Giacometti were working on a double commission from Pierre David-Weill to decorate his apartment; Masson was working on panels at his studio in the Midi, and Giacometti on two andirons and a pierced bas-relief in Paris.

Major articles appeared on Miró, with very extensive illustrations (including one of the Dutch interiors and the extraordinary abstract *Peinture* of 1930), and on Masson and Jean (Hans) Arp. Picasso dominated the review, and had one special issue devoted to him (no.3 in the second year), to which the great sociologist Marcel Mauss, one of the strongest influences on Bataille, contributed. Both Picasso's linear pictures with bone-like figures, and the monumental biomorphic bathers and heads of the late 1920s are shown. Thus, for a time, the new work of three of the strongest artists associated with Surrealism, together with the work of Picasso, who was still of supreme importance to Breton, appeared outside the official Surrealist context.

One interesting result of the peculiar contagion that spreads through *Documents* is the way that the reliefs of Arp and the sculptures of Giacometti, Laurens and Lipchitz, gain from Bataille's texts and photographs emphasising objects and things, so that their presence as material bodies is stressed rather than their artifice. To a certain extent, though in a different way, the same is true of the paintings – this is very far away from Breton's statement that painting (and presumably sculpture too) was a 'lamentable expedient'. One might remember Louis Aragon's criticism of Arp and Miró's 'imbecile harmonies' – *Documents* is almost like a refuge for those artists who still enjoyed the doing and making. What, tentatively, seems to link those modern artists present in *Documents*, Paul Klee, Juan Gris and Fernand Léger as well as Picasso, Giacometti, Arp, Miró and Masson, is not so much the obvious balance between abstraction and representation, but, given the extended morphology offered by Cubist and biomorphic abstraction, the metamorphoses of the human form, explored in different ways in the violence of Giacometti and Picasso whose figures are absorbed in a threatening sexuality, and in the gentler, witty visual puns of Arp. Bataille wrote that the dislocation of Picasso's forms led to the dislocation of thought.

Bataille felt at this time a close affinity with Dalí, and this led him to interpret Dalí's fantastic imagery in a way radically different from that of Breton. One of the rare direct clashes between *Documents* and Surrealism arose over Dalí, who on returning from Paris after the summer of 1929 opted definitively for Surrealism, much to Bataille's disappointment, and promptly refused Bataille permission to reproduce *Le Jeu lugubre* (The Dismal Game, 1929), forcing him to rely on a schematic drawing instead. Bataille first refers to Dalí in no.4 in his entry under 'Oeil' in the 'Dictionnaire critique', headed 'Cannibal delicacy', and reproduces three paintings including *Blood is sweeter than honey*, a title that could not fail to appeal to him. In a note to the entry on 'Oeil', he refers to the famous scene of the slit eye in *Un Chien andalou* (An Andalusian Dog, 1929), and gives a clear explanation of what he means by horror: 'How is it possible not to see at what point horror becomes fascinating and also that horror alone is brutal enough to break what is stifling.'

What kind of approbation Bataille meant by describing Picasso's paintings as hideous and those of Dalí as of a frightening ugliness is forcefully explained at the opening of his essay on *Le Jeu lugubre* (no.7, 1929): 'Against half measures, evasions, deliriums betraying the greatest poetic impotence, only a black anger and even an undeniable bestiality can be opposed.' Against these 'evasions' (by the Surrealists, quite clearly) Dalí's 'horrible shadows' express shame and disgust. In his preface to Dalí's exhibition at the Galerie Goemans, Breton had said that here for the first time the windows of the mind had opened wide; Bataille, aghast, asks where on earth they can be: 'Those who see here for the first time the mental windows open wide, placing an emasculated poetic complaisance where there is only the crying necessity for a recourse to ignominy.'

In the third issue of 1930 (the 'Hommage à Picasso'), a rare editorial note announced a new and sensibly larger format for the future, with colour plates and more articles on earlier artists, placing them in the critical context of their time. Such optimism was misplaced; Wildenstein had had enough of the review which was by turn 'carp and rabbit' as Leiris put it, and closed it down after the eighth issue of 1930. Two further issues did appear: no.1 of a third series in 1933, and no.1 of a fourth series in 1934, but with the elimination of Bataille and the old contributors, the review appears as a pale imitation of the *Gazette des Beaux-Arts*, and is virtually without interest. At the period of *Contre-Attaque* in the mid-1930s, Bataille and Breton briefly drew together, and Bataille contributed once to the periodical *Minotaure*. But Bataille remained essentially a lone figure, whose most important works, with the exception of the great erotic masterpiece, the novella *Histoire de l'oeil* (Story of the Eye, 1928), were still to come at the time of *Documents*. From a refusal that is Dada in nature, Bataille's works move in a way that is parallel to and then goes beyond Surrealism; as Leiris wrote:

> having been the impossible man fascinated by the discovery of what was most unacceptable and who made *Documents* in undoing it, he enlarged his vision (according to the old idea of going beyond the *no!* of the child stamping his foot) and, knowing that man is only wholly a man if he seeks his measure in that excess, made himself the man of the Impossible, avid to attain the point where – in dionysian vertigo – high and low are mingled and distance is abolished between the all and the nothing.[7]

7 Leiris, 'De Bataille L'Impossible à l'impossible', *op. cit.*

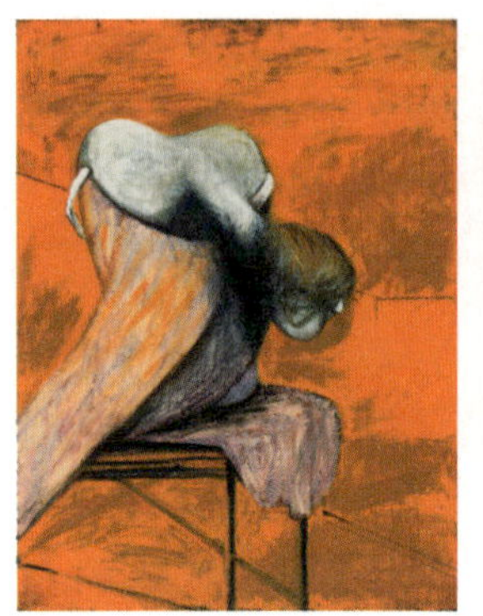
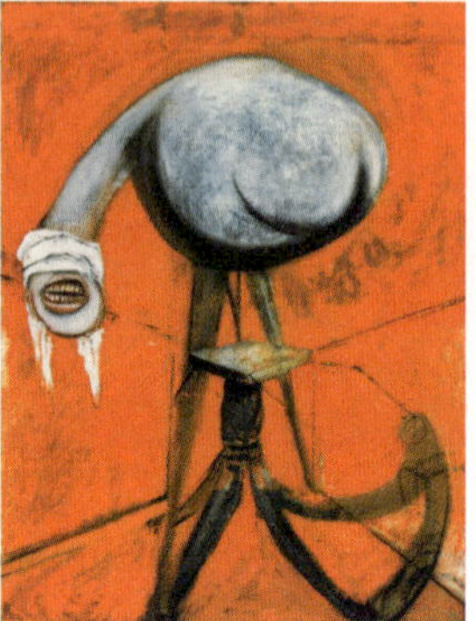
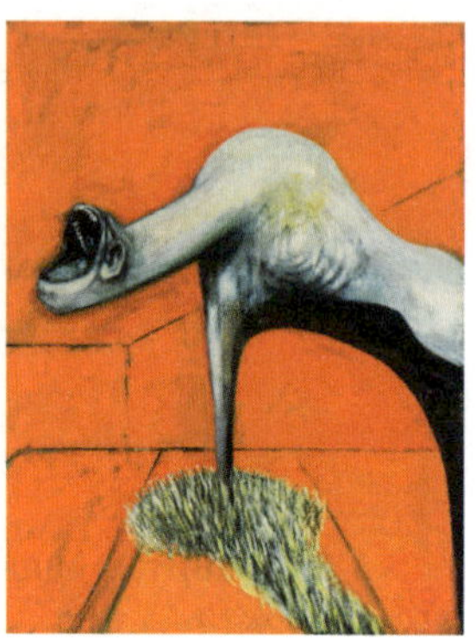

212 **Francis Bacon**
Three Studies for Figures at the Base of a Crucifixion, c.1944
Oil on board, three panels
Each: 94 × 73.7 cm | 37⅛ × 29⅛ in

Web of Images

Francis Bacon, Thames & Hudson, in association with the Tate Gallery, London, 1985

Too much has been made of the 'horror' in Francis Bacon's paintings both by critics and by the public. Bacon has always found this an irrelevant problem, denying that he ever intended to be 'horrific'. Yet he has, on the other hand, admitted that violence was central to his art, although the violence he is talking of only incidentally has anything to do with the 'horrific' in his work. When the disturbing and disquieting elements in his painting are discussed, it is usually in terms of subject matter, and a moral stance may be adopted towards his apparently grim imagery. 'I find the vision of man he uses his undeniable painterly talents to express quite odious', one critic recently wrote.[1] Others, still with the effect of making the paintings 'reflect' horror or violence in the world, describe it as mirroring the alienation and misery of mid-twentieth-century man. While, obviously, it is undeniable that Bacon has lived through and witnessed, in the common currency of our knowledge – films, news reports, photographs – the horrors of war, of concentration camps, and has experienced more directly the effects of violence in Ireland where he grew up, this does not mean that his painting is the mirror of this. Were it so, then John Berger's condemnation of his lack of indignation, such as Picasso expressed in *Guernica* (1937), would indeed give grounds for disquiet.[2] Bacon makes the distinction between this 'mirrored' violence, and the mode in which he feels that violence enters his paintings, quite clear when answering David Sylvester's question about the 'distinct presence or threat of violence' conveyed in his work:

1 Peter Fuller, 'Ludic Hope', *Vanguard*, April 1984.

'This violence of my life, the violence which I've lived amongst, I think it's different to the violence in painting. When talking about the violence of paint, it's nothing to do with the violence of war. It's to do with an attempt to remake the violence of reality itself. And the violence of reality is not only the simple violence meant when you say that a rose or something is violent, but it's the violence also of the suggestions within the image itself which can only be conveyed through paint.'[3]

The main points here are, first, that violence in painting has nothing to do with illustrating violence; second, that the violence he is talking about can only be realised in a painted image; third, that it is not to do with the violent application of paint, with 'expressionist' violence, but comes out of 'suggestions within the image itself'.

Bacon has always been strongly opposed to painting as illustration, to painting which tells a story or becomes narrative. 'Illustrational form tells you through the intelligence immediately what the form is about, whereas a non-illustrational form works first upon sensation and then slowly leaks back into the fact.'[4] The opposition between intelligence and sensation is crucial for Bacon. Sensation may include intelligence but the intellect can bypass sensation. Bacon wants his painting to operate primarily through sensation, otherwise it becomes a mere vehicle: 'I want very, very much to do the thing that Valéry said – to give the sensation without the boredom of its conveyance. And the moment the story enters, the boredom comes upon you.'[5]

Bacon is very conscious of the peculiar conditions of painting today, which he describes as both very complicated and primitive, and which are partly a result of the advent of photography. 'As the thing's in such a terribly complicated stage now, the story that is already being told

2 Berger's comments were made during a discussion at the ICA, a report of which by Lawrence Alloway, 'Points of View: Bacon and Balthus', was published in *Art News and Review*, 26 January 1952, p.7. The panel, chaired by David Sylvester, included Berger, Robert Melville, Michael Ayrton, Colin McInnes, Angus Wilson and Herbert Read. Berger was reported as introducing 'tangled moral considerations: we look at Bacon instead of going to Belsen, and this is not a "constructive attitude". He complained of a lack of indignation in Bacon's art which does not stir the conscience.'

3 David Sylvester, *Interviews with Francis Bacon 1962–1979*, Thames & Hudson, London, 1980, p.81.

4 *Ibid.*, p.56.

5 *Ibid.*, p.65.

between one figure and another begins to cancel out the possibilities of what can be done with the paint on its own.' One problem is that the language in which we can talk of 'figurative' painting now has been impoverished, partly because of the simple opposition we are used to setting up between non-objective or abstract painting and figurative or representational painting. Bacon has seemed an isolated figure, his paintings set in a direction counter to most postwar art. Bacon considers abstract painting to be a wholly aesthetic thing, and any 'visceral' response we may claim to have to it is, he robustly asserts, just 'fashion'.[6] But this was not the only reason why he seemed to painter and critic Andrew Forge to be, in the 1950s, violating 'every taboo that existed in English painting'. As Forge wrote, his paintings 'were concrete, worldly and grand and there was no precedent for them where everything from Ben Nicholson's abstract reliefs to Graham Sutherland's landscapes was in some sense or another romantic, ideal and intimately lyrical'.[7] There is no real precedent for the kind of tightrope walk he enacts between abstraction and figuration. The point is that he is trying to keep the 'recording' character of painting without slipping into illustration or storytelling.

The elements of his painting can be isolated as follows: there is the material ground (the surface structure of the painting), there is the figure itself, and there is the setting or siting of the figure, more or less allusively established, and sometimes performing no more than a function of holding or isolating the figure. Sometimes the surface is painted with a single hue, sometimes areas of canvas (which he always uses reversed) are left naked. The variations of surfaces both within a single canvas and between different canvases is very striking. Two recent triptychs provide a good example: one, *Triptych* (1983), is painted in vivid liquid pastel, a hue of orange-red unobtainable in oil paint, giving a rich, smooth surface. The other, *Studies for a Portrait of John Edwards* (1984), has a surface so light it is almost conjured out of air. The ground is divided, the upper part a very pale green-grey, the lower brown. The surface is dry, and as delicate as the

6 *Ibid.*, p.60.
7 Andrew Forge, 'The Paint of Screams', *Art News*, October 1963, pp.38–41, 55–56.

portrait itself is tender, and in places it is powdered or lightly rubbed with paint. In earlier paintings in particular he would add sand to paint to manufacture a thick-textured surface, and occasionally the sand is heaped or clustered in certain areas to give a surface uneven in texture. At this point a further element should be mentioned: the glass behind which Bacon insists the painting should be placed as soon as it is finished. In a note to his gallery he explained that this was 'to give a unified texture to the painting without having to alter the abruptness of the technique in the painting… also to preserve the surface'.[8] The glass, then, is an essential element in the material surface of the paintings.

There is no illusion of real space for the figure to exist in; the body is isolated in its own localised space, which may be a chair or a bed, or may be just a frame of lines, sometimes visibly derived from the tubular 1930s furniture he himself used to make.

Since we so readily read a story into images, it is understandable that Bacon often deliberately destroys potential narrative or story content in his work, wilfully disrupts relationships between figures or between the figure and its setting. This is one reason for the predominance of the single figure in his canvases: once there are two or more figures the danger of the story 'talking louder than the paint' becomes that much greater.[9] It is possible to have several figures in a canvas without setting up a narrative, but under special conditions of figuration. Figures may, for example, be isolated from one another in the canvas, separated in their own, discontinuous spatial location. Another presence may be introduced through the device of a portrait within the painting, or by a reflection in a mirror – as in *Study of a Nude with Figure in a Mirror* (1969) – and this reflection may not necessarily be that of the figure(s) in the canvas. Two figures may be so closely locked in physical embrace that their flesh is melded and dissolved, and their struggle becomes a single sensation – as in *Three Studies of Figures on Beds* (1972). Finally, there is the triptych itself, which both separates and links the figures within each panel.

The figure – and here I am not thinking so much of the portraits, though some of what I want to say of distortion and its origins also relates to the portraits – is first and foremost a body with a head. Often it has no

8 *Francis Bacon: Recent Paintings*, Marlborough-Gerson Gallery, New York, NY, 1968.

9 Sylvester, *op. cit.*, p.22.

face, and may be lacking part of its body or even its head. It is as though it is still in the process of realising itself as a figure – it is not fully figurative. The French philosopher Gilles Deleuze suggests the term 'figural' to describe a process which both avoids abstraction and the illusionism of complete figuration.[10]

In the portraits and self-portraits, where the face is necessarily important and cannot be ignored or destroyed in favour of the head alone (which is an appendage of the body rather than, like the face, a structure in its own right), Bacon uses rather different means of avoiding illustration.

There are several ways by which he 'destroys' appearance in order to remake a likeness. One is the use of non-rational marks, marks which have no obvious representational relationship with those areas of the face they are intended to depict. Bacon is obviously not the first painter to do this, and himself invokes the Rembrandt self-portrait in Aix-en-Provence, in which 'there are hardly any sockets to the eyes... it is almost completely anti-illustrational.'[11] The irrational marks may be a matter of chance: what was not accidental was Rembrandt's 'profound sensibility, which was able to hold onto one irrational mark rather than onto another'.

Bacon describes the involuntary marks that may begin the painting as a graph, and within this graph there are an enormous number of possibilities for 'planting facts' like the mouth or the eyes. 'Appearances are ambiguous' and endless in their possibilities: 'in a way you would love to be able in a portrait to make a Sahara of the appearance – to make it so like, yet having the distances of the Sahara.'[12] (This is reminiscent of the anxiety that gripped Giacometti when he contemplated the enormous distance that he felt when trying in a sculpture to cross from one side of the nose to the other.[13]) While in a painting of a 'figure' rather than a portrait the head may be so blurred as to have no features, in portraits the marks are often more specific. Sometimes, as I said, these may be irrational in terms of representation but nonetheless convey the fact of a nose or a mouth or a cheekbone. Sometimes Bacon may destroy one set of more or less precise marks with another – not blurring or smudging but painting

10 Gilles Deleuze, *Francis Bacon: Logique de la sensation*, Seuil, Paris, 1981.

11 Sylvester, *op. cit.*, p.58. (The authenticity of this Rembrandt is in doubt.)

12 *Ibid.*, p.56.

13 See Giacometti's letter to Pierre Matisse, 1947; trans. in *Alberto Giacometti*, Museum of Modern Art, New York, NY, 1965.

against, as though to destroy a likeness perhaps of a photographic kind. In the 1964 *Study for Portrait (Isabel Rawsthorne)*, an almost photographic likeness is overlaid with streaky white or grey strokes, which seem to delineate not just an alternative face but a different, nearly feline, head.

Distortion, fragmentation, isolation, then, are on one level the result of a pictorial battle against illustrative figuration, against a type of representation aimed solely at the intelligence. In his frequent uses of photographs – photography of almost any kind – the implications of these distortions can be seen as an attack on the too simple, too restricted, 'too ordered, too coherent' picture that photography 'gives of the interaction between man and his environment or one man and another',[14] or, indeed, of a single person.

Bacon's comments on the particular meaning of violence in his paintings quoted above continue directly into a consideration of problems posed by the portrait. 'When I look at you across the table', he says to his interviewer David Sylvester, 'I don't only see you but I see a whole emanation which has to do with personality and everything else. And to put that over in a painting, as I would like to be able to do in a portrait, means that it would appear violent in paint. We nearly always live through screens – a screened existence. And I sometimes think, when people say my work looks violent, that I have from time to time been able to clear away one or two of the veils or screens.'

The clearing away of these screens or veils relates, as I hope to show, not only to the portraits. The point is that distortion is the result of an effort to convey a presence beyond likeness, to be able to bring into play a whole nexus of associations relating to that image, to convey the fact of a sensation as directly as possible: 'I'm just trying to make images as accurately off my nervous system as I can.'[15] As a materialist, Bacon deliberately says 'nervous system' rather than any more elevated or vague term like soul, or personality.

14 Mark Roskill, 'Francis Bacon as a Mannerist', *Art International*, 15 September 1963, pp.44–48.
15 Sylvester, *op. cit.*, p.82.

The distortions in his painting have sometimes been seen, rather lazily, as 'Expressionist'. But it is far from true to read them as a result of inflicting personal agitation or anguish onto people or objects so that they become deformed through frenzied or uncontrolled paint marks. Both chance and control are operating in Bacon in deliberate ways very different indeed from those of the Expressionists.

Bacon's figures, and not just those which are clearly engaged in action (usually sexual), but also those which are just standing or sitting, seem to be in the grip of a muscular force, a spasm of energy, which intensifies rather than diminishes their living presence. They are painted not as self-controlled, social creatures, but as beings driven by those urges or instincts Bacon describes as the irresistible counterpoint to the despair of contemplating death.

Bacon's seemingly violent and sometimes disquieting imagery has also been read as a direct result of a nihilistic attitude to life. The American writer Donald Kuspit, for instance, after describing the isolation of Bacon's figures 'sick with death – not necessarily literal death, but rather the feeling of being nothing', accounts for it as the result of a 'compulsive attention to the inevitability of death'.[16] Their loneliness, he suggests, communicates a 'general sense of oblivion' resulting from a deliberate cultivation of nihilism. 'Bacon, who has been called an existentialist... is simultaneously a decadent, in the sense of cultivating a nihilistic perception of and attitude to life.'

A different though still partial account of the isolation and distortion of Bacon's figures has been proposed above, which so far has not confronted the question of Bacon's 'nihilism', though it has suggested a strong response to physical presence. Bacon has made a number of comments about the futility or meaninglessness of life which have fed the view of him as nihilistic, but if they are considered more closely they are almost always carefully qualified: 'I think of life as meaningless; but we give it meaning during our own existence' [...] 'we are born and we die, but in between we give this purposeless existence a meaning by our drives.'[17]

The sense of futility is always countered by a profound exhilaration, springing not from any perverse obsession with 'death in life' or joy in

16 Donald Kuspit, 'Francis Bacon: The Authority of Flesh', *Artforum*, summer 1975.
17 Sylvester, *op. cit.*, pp.133–34.

death, but from life itself: 'I'm greedy for life; and I'm greedy as an artist. I'm greedy for what I hope chance can give me far beyond anything that I can calculate logically. And it's partly my greed that has made me what's called live by chance – greed for food, for drink, for being with the people one likes, for the excitement of things happening...'

The meaninglessness that Bacon takes for granted is that of life lived without belief in an afterlife, or in any moral absolutes. Many other systems of belief or codes of action, obviously, have been proposed to take the place of once dominant religious ideas, and the absence of these does not necessarily imply pessimism. Bacon is not particularly interested in subscribing to any other given set of beliefs, although he is profoundly interested in the philosophical problems involved. Like so many European artists of the earlier part of this century, he has been greatly attracted by Nietzsche, in particular by *The Birth of Tragedy* (1872) and *On the Genealogy of Morals* (1887). Nietzsche's passionate rejection of Christianity, in for example the later critical preface to *The Birth of Tragedy*, is expressed in terms of an affirmation of life with which Bacon would have much in common:

> From the very first, Christianity spelt life loathing itself, and that loathing was simply disguised, tricked out, with notions of an 'other' and 'better' life. A hatred of the 'world', a curse on the affective urges, a fear of beauty and sensuality, a transcendence rigged up to slander mortal existence, a yearning for extinction, cessation of all effort until the great 'sabbath of sabbaths' – this whole cluster of distortions, together with the intransigent Christian assertion that nothing counts except moral values, has always struck me as being the most dangerous, most sinister form the will to destruction can take.[18]

Bacon may share something of Nietzsche's hypothesis of a 'strong pessimism',[19] but he phrases it for himself as a kind of internal dialectic: 'Ah well, you can be optimistic and totally without hope. One's basic nature is totally without hope, and yet one's nervous system is made out of optimistic stuff.' Deleuze formulated this as 'cerebrally pessimist,

18 Friedrich Nietzsche, *The Birth of Tragedy and The Genealogy of Morals*, trans. Francis Golffing, Anchor Books, New York, NY, 1956, p.10.

nervously optimist' (the original French *nerveusement* meaning 'of the nerves, sinews, sensations', rather than 'timidly').[20]

Since it has often been suggested that Bacon is in some sense an existentialist, this should perhaps be looked at a little more closely. (Parallels have often been drawn between the claustrophobic windowless interior of Sartre's play *Huis Clos* (No Exit, 1944) and the trapped space in Bacon's painting.) However, there is a real difference between his attitude to life and the stoic philosophy of Sartre, his 'stern optimism'.[21] In *L'Existentialisme est un humanisme* (Existentialism and Humanism, 1946), Sartre defended Existentialism against the various charges made against it: that it led to the 'quietism of despair', that it emphasised human ignominy and the futility of the human enterprise, that it denied human solidarity by insisting on man's isolation. Sartre's answer to the Marxist and Catholic critiques – that by defining man in relation to his acts alone, rather than by any system of abstract values, he is affirming man's complete liberty, his moral freedom – stresses the optimism of Existentialism, and affirms it as a humanism. This is couched, in a sense, too much in terms of man's moral dilemma as a social being to appeal to Bacon. For Bacon any answer lies not in a harsh or dogged optimism, but in the tension between 'cerebral pessimism' and 'nervous optimism'.

In considering Bacon in relation to Existentialism, connections are necessarily of a tenuous kind, given that it was primarily a theoretical and literary movement. With Surrealism, however, with which, again, Bacon has been associated, more specifically visual connections have

19 *Ibid.* Nietzsche argued that pessimism was not of necessity a sign of decadence: 'Is there such a thing as a *strong* pessimism? A penchant of the mind for what is hard, terrible, evil, dubious in existence, arising from a plethora of health, a plenitude of being? Could it be, perhaps, that the very feeling of superabundance created its own kind of suffering: a temerity of penetration, hankering for the enemy (the worthwhile enemy) so as to prove its strength, to experience at last what it means to fear something? What meaning did the tragic myths have for the Greeks during the period of their greatest power and courage?'

20 Deleuze, *op. cit.*, p.31.

21 Jean-Paul Sartre, 'Dureté optimiste', in *L'Existentialisme est un humanisme*, Nagel, Paris, 1946; trans. *Existentialism and Humanism*, Methuen, London, 1948.

been drawn. Bacon himself is more interested in surrealist ideas and in surrealist poetry than in surrealist painting, and it is perhaps only in the apparent incongruity of the imagery of *Painting* (1946) that something like surrealist juxtaposition has been allowed to stand. The transformation involved in the genesis of this painting has also been seen as bearing witness to an early disposition towards Surrealism: 'I was attempting to make a bird alighting on a field. And it may have been bound up in some way with the three forms that had gone before, but suddenly the lines that I'd drawn suggested something totally different, and out of this suggestion arose this picture.'[22] It is clear, then, that if this painting is to be associated at all with Surrealism, it is in the process of transformation through accident and suggestion.

Bacon's use of accident and chance, his natural acceptance of the transforming and motivating powers of the unconscious, can in a sense be related to Surrealism, but they do not come out as a commitment to the Surrealists' ideas and beliefs in any systematic way. His use of chance marks, and of accident, has a different genesis and is subject to different procedures from Surrealist automatism or from Duchamp's controlled philosophical experiments with chance. While the Surrealists aimed to 'trap' images from the unconscious through automatic drawing, or in the unwilled figurations thrown up by techniques like frottage, images which could have the character of revelation and of the marvellous about them, Bacon is not interested in quarrying the unconscious in this sense. He may at any point in a painting make random paint marks – throwing, scrubbing or sponging the paint (or all three), sometimes to break a spell when the painting is not going well, or to destroy the conventional, the pictorial cliché ('half my painting activity is disrupting what I can do with ease').[23] In some ways this is only to intensify the already unpredictable behaviour of the fluid medium of paint. He may at the last minute add a streak or dash of randomly splashed paint – then either leave it or not. It is not a matter of accepting unquestioningly what chance or the unconscious throws up and valuing it then for its own sake. If the random marks work, it is because they have a 'kind of inevitability' about them, and the result in the end is a balance between immediacy and control.

22 Sylvester, *op. cit.*, p.11.
23 Sylvester, *op. cit.*, p.91.

Bacon is not interested either, by contrast with the Surrealists, in the potential of symbolism, in the kinds of visual paraphrase of dream processes after Freud that were created by Ernst or Dalí. He is interested rather in things themselves, enriched as they may be by associations, or in facts that he is attempting to trap: 'Now I feel that I want to do very, very specific objects, though made out of something which is completely irrational from the point of view of being an illustration.'[24]

Bacon's position *vis à vis* Surrealism is clarified if it is approached from what may seem to be a tangential comparison: with Georges Bataille, who once described himself as Surrealism's 'old enemy from within'. Bacon shares a number of Bataille's preoccupations, during above all a specific period when Bataille was engaged in a polemic with Surrealism; while, that is, he was editing and writing in the magazine *Documents* between 1929 and 1930. *Documents* was the refuge for several disaffected Surrealist writers and painters, including Michel Leiris, a long-standing friend of Bacon's, who has also written on him and whose portrait Bacon has painted, as well as Joan Miró and Alberto Giacometti's.[25] A number of Bataille's texts in *Documents* can be read as implicit attacks on Surrealism, particularly on what Bataille felt was an evasive and poetic idealism in Surrealism which conflicted with its stated commitment to dialectical materialism. Breton counter-attacked in his *Second Surrealist Manifesto* (1929), and the terms in which he castigates Bataille are not dissimilar to those used by some critics against Bacon: 'M. Bataille professes that he only wants to consider the vilest, most discouraging and corrupted things in this world...'[26]

Bacon possessed copies of *Documents*, and has talked specifically about the effect some of the illustrations reproduced in them had upon him, notably those of slaughterhouses, which will be discussed below. It was not just the illustrations, however, but the whole context of ideas in which these illustrations were situated, that must have touched Bacon. To clarify the implications of this, I want to take a specific image which obsessed Bacon almost from the start of his painting career: the mouth.

24 Sylvester, *op. cit.*, p.11.

25 See, for example, Michel Leiris, *Francis Bacon: Full Face and in Profile*, Phaidon Press, Oxford and New York, NY, 1983.

26 André Breton, 'Second manifeste du surréalisme', *La Révolution surréaliste*, Paris, no.12, 15 December 1929, p.16.

Stretched in a grimace or a cry, or even perhaps in a smile, the mouth was often the most prominent or even the only feature in some of the earliest of Bacon's heads and figures. Some of Bacon's direct sources for the human cry have been identified by a number of critics – the wounded, screaming nursemaid from the Odessa steps sequence of Eisenstein's *Battleship Potemkin* (1925), the desperate mother in Poussin's *Massacre of the Innocents* (c.1629), perhaps too Caravaggio's *Medusa* (c.1597). He has also spoken of his fascination with a 'second-hand book which had beautiful hand-coloured plates of diseases of the mouth, beautiful plates of the mouth open and of the examination of the inside of the mouth, and they fascinated me, and I was obsessed with them.'[27] Later, he thought his screams were too abstract, that they might have been more successful had they 'been more conscious of the horror that produced the scream.'[28] But Bacon's avoidance of the direct products of horror has already been explained in the context of his determined avoidance of a kind of figurative painting which could slide into illustration. The photographs and texts in *Documents* could have been a source in that one of their main characteristics was that of presenting a material sensation as directly as possible, and in the process stripping away some of the veils or screens, some of the hypocrisies, with which we try to conceal and make palatable bald existence.

One of the photographs by another ex-Surrealist, Jacques-André Boiffard, reproduced in *Documents*, was of an open, screaming mouth, and it accompanied a short text by Bataille, one of his 'Critical Dictionary' entries, 'Bouche' (Mouth).[29] This focuses on the fact that it is through the mouth that our most concentrated experiences of agony or ecstasy are physiologically expressed, and also that in this expression the human draws particularly close to the animal. Bataille wrote: 'On great occasions human life is concentrated bestially in the mouth, anger makes one clench one's teeth, terror and atrocious suffering make the mouth the

27 See, for example, Sylvester, *op. cit.;* Roskill, *op. cit.*; John Russell, *Francis Bacon*, Thames & Hudson, London, 1979; Robert Melville, 'Francis Bacon', *Horizon*, London, December 1949/January 1950. Melville also instances Buñuel and Dalí's silent Surrealist film, *Un Chien andalou* (1929), a film which deeply impressed both Bacon and Bataille).

28 Sylvester, *op. cit.*, p.35.

29 Georges Bataille, 'La Bouche', *Documents*, Paris, no.5, 1930, pp.299–309.

organ of tearing cries. It's easy to observe on this subject that the stricken individual, in stretching out his neck, frantically lifts up his head, so that the mouth comes to be placed, so far as is possible, in the extension of the vertebral column, that is to say in the position it normally occupies in the animal constitution.'

It is possible to trace in Bacon's early images concentrating on or significantly including the mouth, several characteristics which run parallel with Bataille's text; first, the presence of the mouth alone among the features of a figure; second, the peculiar animal-extension of the neck instanced by Bataille; and third, a more general and deliberate dwelling upon the shared characteristics of man and animal.

The cry shares the character of the laugh in that it is, as Julia Kristeva says when writing about Bataille, both 'evaporation of meaning and the only possibility of communication'.[30] Speech may be the sign of human intelligence, eyes the window to the soul, but the cry, visibly speechless, is an instinctive spasm of the body. The figures of the Eumenides, in Bacon's 1944 triptych, *Three Studies for Figures at the Base of a Crucifixion*, have no eyes, but only mouths. The creature in the centre panel, which resembles a huge flightless bird rather than a human, has its eyes bandaged. In that on the right, the upper part of the face is lacking, an absence accompanied by or produced by another severe distortion: the neck is abnormally prolonged, ending in a savage jaw/mouth. This is suspended horizontally like an animal snout, though the rest of the body is vestigially, in spite of its posture, closer to that of a human. The bird-animal aspect of the Eumenides, the Furies who pursued the matricide Orestes in the final part of the *Oresteia* of Aeschylus, is implicit in the broken and ambiguous description of them:

> an amazing company –
> women, sleeping, nestling against the benches...
> not women, no,
> Gorgons I'd call them; but then with Gorgons
> you'd see the grim, inhuman...

30 Julia Kristeva, 'Bataille, l'expérience et la pratique', *Bataille*, (Direction Philippe Sollers: Communications Roland Barthes, et al.), Paris, 1973.

I saw a picture
years ago, the creatures tearing the feast
away from Phineus –
These have no wings,
I looked.[31]

In a series of heads of the late 1940s, the cry effects the same anatomical distortion, though now the subject is clearly human. In *Head I* of 1948 the mouth is tilted sideways as though to emphasise the spinal extension Bataille describes, the neck and cheek bulging massively as though attempting to contain and suppress the bestial spasm. It is possible to read into the neck at the right a configuration which is not just bulging flesh but a second neck culminating in the mouth, which itself thereby becomes, as in the right-hand panel of the earlier triptych, the substitute for the complete head. When painting this head, Bacon was looking at a photograph of a chimpanzee, and it is clear that the extended canine teeth are animal, not human. This is true also of *Head II* (1949). In *Head IV* (1949) the chimpanzee or monkey appears on the man's shoulder.[32] When Bacon painted the chimpanzee itself in 1955, it had the same mouth, with the head also tilted sideways and up, for the chimpanzee shares most of its anatomy with man, and therefore would, ironically, share the same distorting extension to achieve expression of the cry.

Bacon's man/animal imagery could now be brought back to Bataille's treatment of this theme. In the first sentence of 'Mouth' Bataille brought into direct rapport 'great human occasions' and 'bestially', and as the passage goes on is clearly challenging the value normally placed on the terms 'human' and 'animal'. This might be clarified if we look at another characteristic set of themes: noble/ignoble/base. Bataille distends or subverts the usual value accorded the term 'base', in the paradigm noble/base, and may use it either in a positive and laudatory way, as for example in the title of one of the *Documents* texts, 'Le bas matérialisme et la gnose' (Base Materialism and Gnosticism), or negatively, but in a context in which this negation itself is shocking: 'l'orientation *bassement* idéaliste

31 Aeschylus, 'The Eumenides', *The Oresteia*, trans. Robert Fagles, Viking, New York, NY, 1975, l.50.
32 This series began in 1948 and was numbered successively into 1949; normally numbering is successive within a year.

du Surréalisme' ('the basely idealistic direction of Surrealism'). The violent pulling together of man/beast in such a way that the traditional distinction between them is brought into question was part of Bataille's continual attack on the 'idealist deception' that man practises upon himself. In this case it involves the revelation of the animal or near-animal in man in those situations above all when he believes himself to be at his most human or noble. A comparable idea could be at work in Bacon. Deleuze suggests that the animal traits of certain figures and heads in Bacon involves a double significance: man becomes animal, but not without the animal taking on something of the *esprit* of man. There is, in other words, a zone of non-discrimination between man and animal. But this is not to be seen as a 'lowering' of man to the level of beast.

Bacon has said that the *Head* of 1948 was in fact a woman – was it perhaps then thematically related to the Eumenides? The upper part of the head is engulfed in black, so that all attention is focused on the mouth. It is not a question of the dehumanising of the human figure, but of giving the human characteristics of an animal in a moment of extreme experience. *Head III*, in the 1949 series, is a striking reversal of the two earlier heads: the mouth is gripped tight shut, and everything is concentrated in the piercing gaze, vivid black pupils framed in the pince-nez, which echoes that of the stricken nursemaid in *Battleship Potemkin*. The difference between this and the earlier heads, the physical contrast, is again illuminated by Bataille in 'Mouth':

> This... puts into relief the importance of the mouth in physiology or even in animal psychology, and the general importance of the upper or lower extremity of the body, orifice of profound physical impulses: one sees at the same time that a man can liberate these impulses in at least two different ways, in the brain, or in the mouth, but the moment the impulses become violent he is obliged to turn to the bestial manner to liberate them. Whence comes the narrowly constipated character of a strictly human attitude, the magisterial aspect of the face with its mouth closed, beautiful as a strong-box.

This in a sense completes the argument, for it is not that man in his scream sinks to the level of animal, but that this animal element is necessary and a part of him, and without it he is restricted or 'constipated'.

When Bacon painted his versions of Velázquez's *Portrait of Pope Innocent X* (c.1650), immediately after the 'Heads' discussed above, several works similarly have mouths stretched wide in a cry: *Study after Velázquez* (1950) for example, or *Pope I* and *Pope II* (1951). Perhaps his idea was to test one of the greatest portraits ever painted, of a man set highest above his fellow men (the archetypal father, verging on the divine) in the grip of a feeling so intense that the only expression of it brought him close to the beasts.

It must be emphasised that it is not the intention here to suggest that Bacon was in any sense illustrating Bataille, but rather that their concerns, preoccupations and attitudes run parallel. Bacon's obsession with the image of the mouth moves also in other directions. To a certain extent it is concerned with a purely visual response to the mouth irrespective of its human construction in either cry or laugh. He has spoken of liking the 'glitter and colour that comes from the mouth, and I've always hoped in a sense to be able to paint the mouth like Monet painted a sunset.'[33] Being thoroughly aware of Freudian ideas, he is also probably aware of an explicit sexual symbolism connected with the mouth: 'I've always been very moved by the movement of the mouth and the teeth. People say that these have all sorts of sexual implications, and I was always very obsessed by the actual appearance of the mouth and teeth, and perhaps I have lost that obsession now, but it was a very strong thing at one time.'[34]

It is a commonplace of Freudian theory that sexual repression as it is manifested, for example, in dreams, frequently 'makes use of transpositions from a lower to an upper part of the body'.[35] Bacon is certainly not making any deliberate call on psychoanalysis, in which he does not have much interest; there are no direct transpositions of one part of the body to another in any self-conscious or systematic way, and indeed he expresses a definite scepticism about the whole problem of interpretation

33 Sylvester, *op. cit.*, p.50.
34 Sylvester, *op. cit.*, p.48.
35 Sigmund Freud, *The Interpretation of Dreams*, trans. James Strachey, Allen & Unwin, London, 1954, p.387.

of this kind. Talking of the problem of explaining what chance is and how it operates, he said, 'I don't think one can explain it. It would be like trying to explain the unconscious. It's also always hopeless talking about painting...'

Nonetheless, there are certain pictorial means by which a particular image is invested with a sexual potency of a special kind, and one which quite often involves the mouth/teeth/head. There is, for example, a curious kind of inversion in certain paintings of nude figures on a bed, in which the nude is turned so that the head is towards the lower edge of the picture frame, the legs and genitals to the upper edge: *Studies from the Human Body* (1975), for example, or *Lying Figure* (1969), or *Lying Figure with Hypodermic Syringe* (1963). In the latter two, the facial features and the genital areas are so indistinct as to blur any notion of gender or specific personality, but in the *Studies from the Human Body* teeth and sex are distinct. Although the mouth/teeth/head are in the correct position, there is nonetheless a concentration of sexual energy and aggression in them that seems partly to spring from their inverted positions. In another figure, the lowest in *Three Figures and a Portrait* (1975), the body itself is so vague, its physical components so fluidly defined, that the mouth/teeth are the only clear feature, but their relation to the other parts of the body – whether, in other words, they are located in the head or the genitals – is impossible to determine.

One further comparison in connection with the motif of the mouth could be made between specific figures in two paintings: the figure in the central panel of the *Oresteia* triptych of 1981 and the left-hand figure in *Three Figures and a Portrait*. The relationship between the head and the body is similar, defined by the strongly marked vertebrae, which, in the *Oresteia* figure, also form a neck. The humped shoulders, incidentally, from which the vertebrae sweep down, trace back to a 1944–45 painting, *Study for a Figure*, one of those that immediately followed the Eumenides triptych, and reappear recently (anatomically vague, sexually suggestive and figurally potent) in the nude figures with cricket pads. The figure in *Three Figures and a Portrait* has an unusually complete head (such heads are more common in recent paintings), and is a posthumous portrait of Bacon's close friend George Dyer. This is singled out from the rest of the body by the use of the radiographer's 'target' circle.[36] This circle, drawn round the part of the body to be photographed in medical guides to aid the correct positioning of bodies for radiography, is used here to demarcate a change of focus in the painting, although this change is not consistent. The beige ground of the room-space darkens and changes in texture, as though suddenly magnified through a strong lens; the head, though, does not change in scale in relation to the rest of the body, nor is it made transparent as though in an X-ray. It is, however, clearly defined in feature both in relation to its own body and to the other figures in the room, including the portrait. In keeping with this, the figure starts off neatly dressed – in the area defined by the circle – with a white collar, but outside the circle the figure is naked, the backbone clearly visible, as though the X-ray is operating perversely in the area outside the circle. When, as we tend to do by analogy with the top right-hand figure whose circled area is clearly magnified, we try to read Dyer's head as *closer* to us, we are immediately confronted by a sharp white splash of paint, manifestly on the surface of the painting, unresolvable as anything but a splash of paint and yet also a disrespectful substitute for the tie that should have been there, which pierces the circle and pins the head back into submission to the body. In the central figure of the *Oresteia* triptych, the head is also swept downwards on an extended neck and placed in what is now clearly a genital position, teeth glowing in hollowed flesh set in a dark circle, a dab of cloudy white paint dribbling from between them. So the 'displacement' of mouth or teeth to the genital area, and a condensation there of sexual energy, is accomplished without gratuitous or wholly irrational distortion.

There is one final 'charge' or association possessed by the mouth for Bacon, which rises from the fact that this orifice is the most prominent visible opening in the head and the body. Bacon said, 'one could make a mouth in a way – I mean it comes about sometimes, one doesn't know how – I mean you could draw the mouth right across the face as though it was almost like the opening of the whole head, and yet it could be like the mouth...'[37] In the *Seated Figure* of 1979 the mouth stretches across the whole width of the jaw, almost like the teeth/jaws of a skull, revealed by

36 Bacon has talked of his interest in K.C. Clark's *Positioning in Radiography*, W. Heinemann, London, 1939.

37 Sylvester, *op. cit.*, p.107.

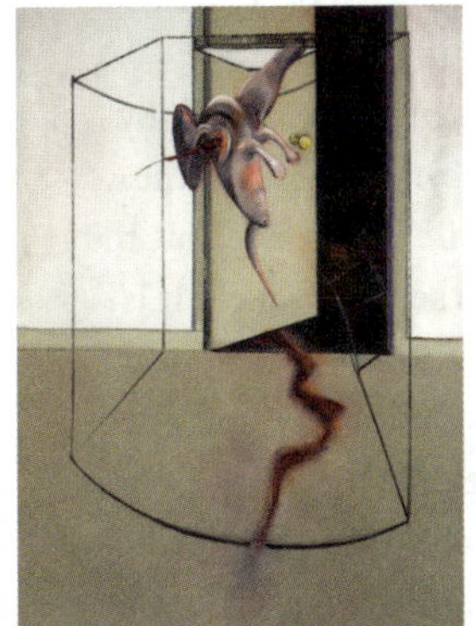
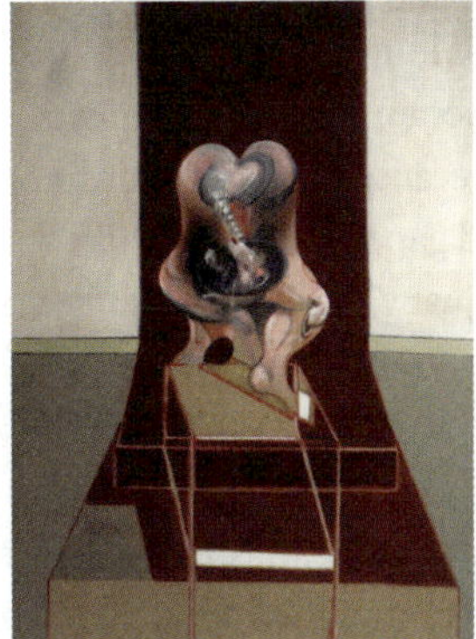
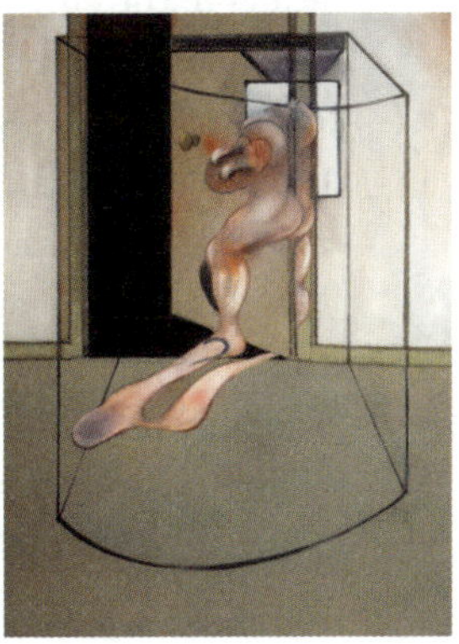

Francis Bacon
Triptych Inspired by the Oresteia of Aeschylus, 1981
Oil on canvas, three panels
Each: 198 × 147.5 cm | 78 × 58⅛ in

X-ray if we imagine the head seen frontally, but if read as a profile head in line with the black shadow profile it is as though the mouth stretches right across the head. This emphasises the mouth in relation to the head as bodily organ, not the mouth as one of a set of features defining an individual personality. But the sense of 'opening' goes further than this, for the mouth itself can also be metaphor for a wound. A line from the *Oresteia* which has haunted Bacon for some time is that spoken by the leader of the Furies, or the Eumenides, as they track Orestes to Athena's sanctuary: 'the reek of human blood smiles out at me'.[38]

This line shocks because of the clashing of disgust ('reek') and joy ('smiles'), but more because of the extraordinary synaesthesia of the metaphor: the wound gapes in the flesh like a smile in the face, but the blood is present not just visually but through the sense of smell. It is this kind of image, its knotted complex of associations which appeal to a totality of bodily sensation, that obsesses Bacon in poetry, and above all in Aeschylus. A very early painting by Bacon exhibited in 1934, and which he regretted destroying, was *Wound for a Crucifixion* – a painting of a specimen wound mounted on a sculptor's armature, against the wall of a hospital corridor or ward. A more recent painting of a wound occurs in the left-hand panel of *Triptych – Studies of the Human Body* (1979), a red streak in a painting otherwise remarkably hygienic and athletic. Bacon does not make any direct metaphoric or symbolic use of the wound/ mouth images, but in many images appeals in some way, however distant, to a nexus of associations they may share as openings in the body.

Among the photographs in *Documents* are two from a series taken by Eli Lotar when he accompanied the painter André Masson to the slaughterhouses at La Villette. Masson was about to do a series of works based on the theme of massacres. In 1937 he illustrated Bataille's text *Sacrifices* with five etchings representing Mithra, Orpheus, the Sacrificed,

38 Aeschylus, *op. cit.*, l.252. This line is rendered as 'the reek of human blood – it's laughter to my heart!', which is a rationalisation of Aeschylus's shocking image. The line as Bacon quotes it is translated in W.B. Stanford, *Aeschylus in His Style: A Study in Language and Personality*, Dublin University Press, Dublin, 1942.

the Minotaur and Osiris. Other ink drawings he made for Bataille's review *Acéphale* represent the headless man, the Minotaur and scenes of cosmic and Dionysian sacrifice.

The photographs by Lotar were reproduced to accompany another of Bataille's 'Critical Dictionary' entries, 'Abattoir' (Slaughterhouse). Slaughter and sacrifice were, Bataille argued, once linked; they were aspects of the same act and happening in one place: 'The slaughterhouse rises out of religion in the sense that the temple of distant epochs served a double function, being used at the same time for supplication and for killings. From this resulted a disturbing coincidence between mythological mysteries and the lugubrious grandeur of places where blood flows.'[39] The real thrust of the text, however, is not really towards a dubious nostalgia, but towards an exposure of the insipid, blinkered, hypocritical and hygienic life of modern man. The 'quarantine' that hides abattoirs from our sight is a sign of our inability, in Bataille's view, to tolerate our own ugliness.

There are enough points of comparison on this subject between Bataille and Bacon to warrant closer examination. A recurrent subject of Bacon's from the 1930s has, of course, been the Crucifixion. One Crucifixion, showing the strong influence of Picasso, who also probably guided him in the choice of subject, was the first work by Bacon to be reproduced (in Herbert Read's *Art Now*, of 1933). Although painted over ten years before the point at which Bacon considers his serious painting career to have begun, with *Three Studies for Figures at the Base of a Crucifixion* of 1944, this Crucifixion already shares some of the preoccupations of later paintings. The figure (its reduced stick-like forms harking back to Picasso) is isolated against a dark ground, and there appear to be lines or markers of space round it, besides the dark form of the cross itself, which anchor it to the edges of the canvas without providing any kind of 'illusionistic' space. Most striking, though, is the light-coloured form sweeping out around the body of the figure, almost like a second figure or the aura of another figure. At the lower end of the figure to the right, there are three broad strokes, parallel and oriented at an angle which must suggest a rib cage, though whether that of emaciated human or carcass

39 Bataille, 'Abattoir', *Documents*, Paris, no.6, November 1929, p.329.

would be impossible to say. In *Painting* (1946) such a conjunction is again suggested. The huge carcass framing the grinning demagogue is hung in such a way that it clearly evokes a crucifixion. Bacon was not the first artist to bring into play, however distantly, this connection. The strange dignity of Rembrandt's carcass of beef and the intensity of Goya's, both suggest distant associations with each artist's treatment of the crucifixion. Bacon, in his 1933 *Crucifixion*, like Picasso, empties the theme of any religious significance, but does not appear to put the same emphasis on the pain, anguish and horror of the event. In *Three Studies for a Crucifixion* (1962), and in the central panel of the crucifixion triptych of 1965, the man/flesh/carcass theme is quite ambiguous. The figural form as a whole was prompted by Cimabue's Santa Croce *Crucifixion*, which Bacon says he always thought of 'as an image – as a worm crawling down the cross'. In the right-hand panel of *Three Studies of a Crucifixion*, the flesh and the rib cage make the carcass explicit. The undulating slabs of flesh in the central panel of the 1965 triptych are less obviously animal carcass, but Bacon has added here two rigid limbs, encased in plaster splints, but ending in the kind of formless knobs of a flayed carcass. Bacon in his paintings makes an explicit connection between the crucifixion and the abattoir, which has certain things in common with Bataille.

When Bacon was asked why he chose the theme of the crucifixion for the 1962 triptych, he replied as follows:

> I've always been very moved by pictures about slaughterhouses and meat, and to me they belong very much to the whole thing of the Crucifixion. There've been extraordinary photographs which have been done of animals just being taken up before they were slaughtered; and the smell of death. We don't know, of course, but it appears by these photographs that they're so aware of what is going to happen to them, they do everything to attempt to escape. I think these pictures were very much based on that kind of thing, which to me is very, very near this whole thing of the Crucifixion, I know, for religious people, for Christians, the Crucifixion has a totally different significance. But as a non-believer, it was just an act of man's behaviour, a way of behaviour to another.[40]

There is, running through this, the idea already discussed that there is a 'zone of non-discrimination' between man and animal – and even the thought, in the passage above, that the animal's awareness depends on senses that we may have lost. It is possible that the figures in the 1944 triptych are also animals lifting their heads as they sense death and their own fate. Bacon also shares with Bataille to a certain extent the idea that the grand sites of religious sacrifice cannot be separated from the slaughterhouses, though this is not intended to suggest that he shares Bataille's ritual/sacramental idea that man needs sacrifice. He does, however, share Bataille's revulsion against the hypocrisy of averting one's eyes from the slaughterhouses: 'When you go into a butcher's shop and see how beautiful meat can be and then you think about it, you can think of the whole horror of life – of one thing living off another. It's like all those stupid things that are said about bull-fighting. Because people will eat meat and then complain about bull-fighting covered with furs and with birds in their hair.'[41]

Many artists and writers have over the last hundred years gone back to the image of the crucifixion but for reasons that are extra-religious and in a non-Christian context. It has been used to express spiritual or transcendental attitudes, or, as in the case of Picasso, pain or anguish. Bacon talks of it as an 'armature' on which to hang 'feelings about behaviour and the way life is'. These feelings are very private, and involve a whole nexus of associations and sensations, and Bacon even suggests that painting the crucifixion is akin to painting a self-portrait.

The Greek myths are more distant from us even than the crucifixion, but are brought closer to us again through the writings of those like Nietzsche and Freud, who used them to validate their own ideas about man in his aesthetic and psychic relation to life. Freud hung a theory central to psychoanalysis on the myth of Oedipus, whose actions in killing his father and marrying his mother were, in Freud's opinion, expressive of a universal impulse, one of the 'primeval wishes of our childhood'. In Jung's view, one

40 Sylvester, *op. cit.*, p.33.
41 Sylvester, *op. cit.*, p.48.

of Freud's great services to mankind was the rescuing of Greek mythology from the dusty recesses of literary history. Nietzsche, in *The Birth of Tragedy*, 'claimed that art, rather than ethics, constituted the essential metaphysical activity of man',[42] and analysed the development of Greek tragedy in terms of the opposing Dionysian and Apollonian forces in art.

Bacon has referred to Greek tragedy at least since the 1944 triptych, where he brought it into direct relation to the crucifixion by describing the figures at the base of the cross as Eumenides. He is referring already to the tragic myth of Orestes, who killed his mother Clytemnestra in revenge for her murder of his father Agamemnon, and as a result was pursued by the Eumenides whose function was the punishment of 'incestuous' murder. It is significant that he, like Bataille, preferred this to the Oedipus tragedy. This is attributable not just to his response to the myth itself but to his preference for Aeschylus over Sophocles or Euripides. A book that he has valued for a long time is a study of the literary rediscovery of Aeschylus, by W.B. Stanford, *Aeschylus in his Style: A Study in Language and Personality*, which was published in Dublin in 1942. Stanford argues that, although Aeschylus was much respected in theory as the founder of Greek tragedy, his 'rough, bold poetics' were relegated in favour of the polished perfection of Sophocles from the time of Sophocles himself until the nineteenth century. Aeschylus's imagery offended against the classical ideal of lucidity, coherence and rationality, and the rediscovery of his work only began with Romanticism. Stanford's account of Aeschylus provides considerable insight into both Bacon's imagery and his concept of conveying the 'facts' of sensations. Aeschylus's obscurity, Stanford points out, is the result of the expression of 'half-formed thoughts', which are in fact skilful ways of conveying the inarticulacy or incoherence caused by extreme emotion. His imagery is violent to express the inner effects of emotion: fear makes the heart turn black and vibrate, 'these inner sensations of tossing, tearing, darkening, raving, burning, freezing, prophesying, oozing, came from his own passionate heart'. Aeschylus was the Dionysian in Nietzsche's sense, and Stanford also proposes a parallel with the obscurity of twentieth-century poets, who have themselves, like T.S. Eliot, rediscovered Aeschylus. Stanford describes Aeschylus as

42 Nietzsche, *op. cit.*, 'A Critical Backward Glance', preface of 1886 to *The Birth of Tragedy*.

trying to express the participation of all the senses, as in the line 'the reek of blood smiles out at me'. He tended to prefer metaphor to simile: 'metaphor is a concentrating intensive figure, congenial to a mind that seizes broad analogies without pausing to reflect on accompanying dissimilarities of detail', and relies far less than Sophocles or Euripides on synecdoche or metonymy, types of imagery which, in Stanford's opinion, show a desire for variety rather than imagination. He favours synesthetic imagery, and sustained and mixed metaphor. He was capable of shocking travesties of conventional simile, as in his treatment of the spring/birth simile in the following passage. Clytemnestra, rejoicing over the dead body of Agamemnon, whom she has just drawn to his death over the blood-red tapestries, says:

> And squirting out a sharp death-gush of blood,
> He strikes me with dark drizzle of murderous dew,
> And I rejoiced as the sown corn-fields rejoice
> At the god-sent glistering when the buds are born.

This, Stanford observes, is 'as dark a piece of literary blasphemy as has ever been uttered'. Bacon painted his 1981 triptych while reading the *Oresteia*, and it has been given the title *Triptych Inspired by the Oresteia of Aeschylus*. The three images cannot, nor should we expect them to, be located in any specific scene from the *Oresteia*. Nor can each separate painting be linked serially in a dramatic progression following the three-part structure of the trilogy, although the trilogy form of classical Greek tragedy may have confirmed Bacon in his preference for the triptych.

Painting, obviously, obeys different laws from those of drama, and it is natural that what would be a climax in drama, occurring at or near the end of an act should in a triptych be placed in a central panel, just as the crucifixion is placed centrally in an altar piece; Bacon by no means always invests a central panel of a triptych with any greater or climactic value than the other panels, but in the 1981 triptych the central panel is dominant. The whole image conveys the 'lugubrious grandeur of places where blood flows', and, although the central figure cannot be specifically identified, the whole image seems to refer to the first part of the *Oresteia*, *Agamemnon*. It condenses the scenes where Agamemnon, victorious in the Trojan War, is welcomed home by Clytemnestra, who leads him into the palace and murders him in revenge for the sacrifice of their daughter Iphigenia at the start of the war. Clytemnestra and her women have spread dark red tapestries before Agamemnon, which Aeschylus describes in a characteristic metaphor of blood:

> Let the red stream flow and bear him home
> To the house he never hoped to see – Justice
> lead him in...

The carpet flows and is the colour of blood, home is both the palace, and the death which awaits him within. The great slab of dark crimson paint, both carpet and royal dais, surrounding and raising the figure, is the same colour as the blood that trickles under the door in the left-hand panel. Both Agamemnon, and at the end of the second part of the trilogy, *The Libation Bearers*, Clytemnestra, are murdered offstage, though the bodies of each are revealed at the end. The presence of the curious bird creature in the left-hand panel suggests one of the Furies, who appear only after Orestes has killed Clytemnestra.

Each image in the triptych condenses sensations which can thematically relate to several scenes in the play, but which, like Aeschylus's own imagery, are to do with obscure and generalised emotions: fear, prophesy, defiance, desire.

But, of course, it would be ludicrous to try to establish any full equivalence between Greek tragedy and Bacon's painting. Without lessening the grandeur of the central image, Bacon brings us up sharply against the distance that separates the modern world from the ancient myth, in the left-hand panel, by including a very modern and unusually distinct tubular chair, propping open the door. This immediately brings to mind T.S. Eliot, who, too, looked back to the *Oresteia*, and based on it his play *The Family Reunion* (1939). The following lines from Eliot's poem *Sweeney Among the Nightingales* (1920), in a very general sense, could be cited in connection with Bacon:

> The host with someone indistinct
> Converses at the door apart

The nightingales are singing near
The Convent of the Sacred Heart

And sang within the bloody wound
When Agamemnon cried aloud
And let their liquid siftings fall
To stain the stiff dishonoured shroud.

Bacon has always considered that he was influenced by Eliot, or certainly that reading Eliot's poetry was a fruitful source, not directly of specific images that he would translate into paint, but of images which awoke a series of associations in Bacon himself and fed in that way into his painting.[43] He was particularly responsive, perhaps, to the combination in Eliot of nostalgia for classical mythology, the abruptness of modern manners, the threat of the unseen and the eruption of casual violence; Sweeney, in the poem *Sweeney Erect*,

Tests the razor on his leg
Waiting until the shriek subsides...[44]

Although not specified in the titles, other images in Bacon's painting refer to the *Oresteia*: in the central panel of the 1976 triptych black birds tear the flesh of a clearly human, even living 'carcass'. Its leg is raised in just the gesture of the Agamemnon figure from the 1981 triptych, and might evoke the lines of the shocked chorus confronted by the murderous Clytemnestra:

You empower the sisters, Fury's twins,
Whose power tears the heart!
Perched on the corpse your carrion raven
Glories in her hymn...

43 A detailed study of Bacon's imagery in relation to T.S. Eliot has recently been republished by Rolf Læssøe, 'which pays particular attention to the *Triptych Inspired by T.S. Eliot's Poem 'Sweeney Agonistes'* (1967), and to parallels between Bacon's themes and Eliot's play *The Family Reunion*. Rolf Læssøe, 'Francis Bacon and T.S. Eliot', Hafnia: *Papers in the History of Art*, Copenhagen, no.9, 1983.

44 T.S. Eliot, *The Complete Poems and Plays*, Faber and Faber, London, 1969.

The brimming bowl certainly suggests libation, and the Eumenides or Furies seem to be present. It is also possible that this image of the bird tearing flesh could be to do with the Prometheus myth. In revenge for Prometheus's act of stealing fire from the gods to give to men, he was condemned to be chained for ever to a rock with a vulture gnawing his flesh. Prometheus is the epitome of the tragic hero, both winner and loser in a hopeless battle against fate and the gods.

Bacon insists that all he wants to do is make images; people can then read into them what they will.[45] To take the first part of this apparently innocuous statement only, it is perhaps not as straightforward as it seems. From what are these images constructed? What kind of relationship with the natural world is implied? What sort of sources does he choose, and how does he treat them? What measure of factuality enters the images, and what is 'fact' measured against?

The catholicity of Bacon's sources has already been mentioned, and his acknowledged or implicit use of poetry, drama, other paintings and photography of various kinds. Bacon himself has pointed to his use of Velázquez, Van Gogh and Ingres, which is quite explicit. Art historian Mark Roskill has instanced the borrowing of the figure of the sergeant in Manet's *Execution of the Emperor Maximilian* (1867–69) in Bacon's *Study of Van Gogh I* (1956), and has suggested, surely correctly, that there may be many other such borrowings.

The issues raised by Bacon's use of photographs, with which I should like to conclude this essay, are of particular interest in his works; photographs are a different kind of visual source from the images other painters have created, and this is because of their status as record, as fact, or history. Bacon was intrigued by the 'candid camera' snaps of famous people in unguarded moments that became a source of popular amusement in the 1930s, and has also 'used' news photographs, photographs from wildlife studies, from medical books, polyphotos of himself, photographs of friends, and perhaps most significantly of all photo-

45 Conversation with the author, September 1984.

graphic studies of movement by Eadweard Muybridge. Most of this has, as John Russell said, 'been composted beyond the point of no recovery.'[46] But it is not so much the fact that he uses them, but what he does to them in using them that is interesting.

It is both because the Muybridge sources are still traceable, but also because of the special nature of these studies in relation to the real world, that Bacon's paintings based on them need special attention. Muybridge's first experiments were intended to document the actual movement of the horse, the movement of the legs while galloping. In the 1870s and 1880s, with a more sophisticated camera (he had first used a series of cameras with threads attached to their shutters which were broken and released by the horse), he turned his attention to the study of normal and abnormal locomotion using a variety of subjects. The enormous contemporary interest in his work reflects the nineteenth-century passion for and belief in scientific objectivity, and in a new kind of verisimilitude. But there was also the passion for curiosities, an element of the circus, which ran almost unconsciously beside the scientific; the wonders of nature could, after all, so easily brush the fantastic. So, among the stranger of Muybridge's studies of 'actions incidental to everyday life' were 'Chicken Scared by a Torpedo', 'Man Heaving a 75 lb. Rock' and 'Man Walking, after Traumatism of the Head'. One, at least, of Muybridge's studies of abnormal movement was used by Bacon, in his study of the paralytic child walking on all fours.

But the first point to make is that Bacon is not so much using the photograph as attacking it, challenging its status as record or fact through his transformations. The photograph may claim to capture or present reality, but is in fact only reflective of a – restricted – visual fact. It cannot record sensations, emotions, experience or associations, above all not the intense life of the body. It is understandable that Muybridge should have so fascinated Bacon, for he was above all concerned with the body. Paintings after Muybridge include the following: *Triptych – Studies from the Human Body* (1970), *Two Figures* (1953), the dog in *Man with Dog* (1953). Bacon used Muybridge's studies of naked wrestlers several times, transforming

46 Russell, *op. cit.*, p.65. Russell gives an excellent account of Muybridge and of Bacon's use of his photographs. [After Bacon's death, contact sheets of photographs of figures in movement in the style of Muybridge, commissioned by Bacon, were found in his studio. Footnote added 2014.]

them into a couple locked in a sexual rather than athletic embrace. The distance after all is not that great and the aggression is more emphatic in the sexual encounter. Through the studies of the wrestlers Bacon found he could reach the fact of embrace more accurately or, as he put it, return fact on to the nervous system more violently. It is not just a matter of refusing the movements that Muybridge so laboriously separated to reveal the greater 'reality' of movement, because the distortions of the upper body in *Two Figures* are not a matter of thickening or repeating forms to suggest physical bodily movement, as the Futurists did, but of trying to give the muscular sensation of spasm or contraction; it is sight, touch, tension, orgasm, together. It is a way of rendering visible invisible forces. Secondly, the photograph proved for Bacon an invaluable ally in the fight against cliché. Deleuze saw in Bacon a parallel with Cézanne who, unable 'to accept the readymade clichés that came from his mental consciousness, stocked with memories and which appeared mocking at him on his canvas, spent most of his time smashing his own forms to bits'.[47] Ready-made and not subject to aesthetic convention, the photograph lies outside cliché. Bacon makes use of both the restricted and the non-aesthetic fact of the photograph, and the free marks made by accident or chance, to create the 'graph' of his painting.

Finally, the photograph, in spite of its pretensions to record, often paradoxically contains a curious slippage from reality, or from what we expect to see. Looking at photographs is often a process of discovery rather than simple recognition, and this odd slippage is often what provides Bacon with a peg or key. 'I think it's the slight remove from fact, which returns me on to the fact more violently. Through the photographic image I find myself beginning to wander into the image and unlock what I think of as its reality more than I can by looking at it. And photographs are not only points of reference, they're often triggers of ideas.'[48]

47 D.H. Lawrence, 'Introduction to These Paintings' (1929), *Selected Essays*, Penguin, London, 1950, p.337.
48 Sylvester, *op. cit.*, p.30.

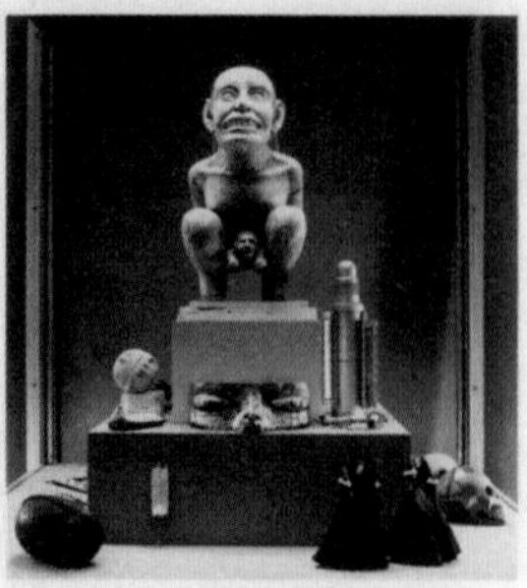

◇11◇

Here again there's a mixture of nice objects, things that are quite small, though significant. And just to punch it up a bit I made that figure, a goddess of childbirth. Some of the other objects are Eskimo, or North American Indian including the sun goggles and toggles. The two *papier maché* figures are from a Mexican Day of the Dead Festival.

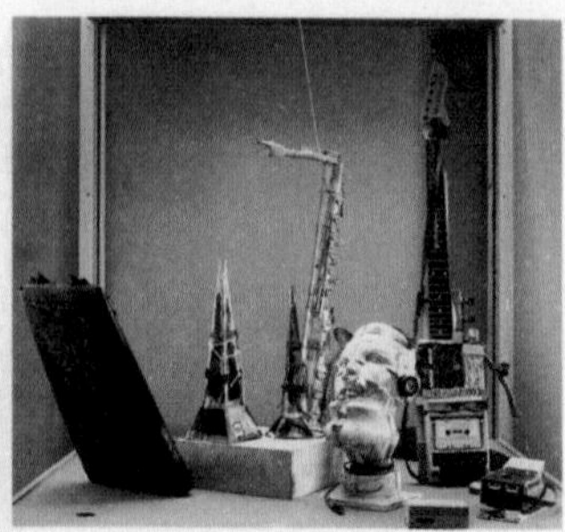

◇12◇

This is what I call the music case. There's an Indian rattle and a rather good finger piano and clay pipes. And then there's my imaginary idea about the East where the transistor is taking over from the harp or the guitar: as a kind of crossing of them I made a guitar with a tape recorder built in. Once you press the button it plays through a loud-speaker and you can pretend to play it, so that everybody – and this is another form of magic – becomes a musician.

Pages from the exhibition booklet for Eduardo Paolozzi, *Lost Magic Kingdoms and Six Paper Moons*, Museum of Mankind, London, 1985

Paolozzi, Surrealism, Ethnography

Lost Magic Kingdoms and Six Paper Moons from Nahuatl: An Exhibition at The Museum of Mankind, Eduardo Paolozzi, British Museum Publications, London, 1985

> The ancient magician and the modern artist are in a sense situated face to face in relation to the world they scrutinise. The image presented by the former corresponds to that contemplated by the latter, but the one is inverted in relation to the other. An inexhaustible desire animates them. Real is hardly more distinguishable from imaginary than morning from evening. One can only consider them as two states of the same phenomenon. The sorcerer seeks to transform it by direct action, the second by ricochet.[1]

This was part of the reply of the poet Benjamin Péret to a questionnaire by the Surrealist leader André Breton on the nature of 'magic art', and was published, together with the replies of a number of other writers, artists and ethnographers in his *L'Art Magique* in 1957. Several took a harsher line with Breton; Georges Bataille challenged his apparent idealism, and Lévi-Strauss argued for a rigorous and rationalist distinction between the terms 'art' and 'magic'.[2] To use the term 'magic' was, as Breton was aware, to raise a Tower of Babel in response. This book brought together works from many cultural traditions, non-Western and Western, including the European occult. Behind it, and the diverse response it provoked and included, lies a long history of Surrealist involvement with other cultures,

1 Benjamin Péret, in André Breton, *L'Art Magique*, Club Français du Livre, Paris, 1957.

2 Bataille argued that the idea of 'material efficacy' was normally linked to magic, and not to art; Lévi-Strauss shared the idea that magic has an 'inoperational' character. He was strongly critical of the generalised context of Breton's questionnaire: 'art' and 'magic' could, he said, mean quite different things and relate in quite different ways in different societies; they could only be defined within their specific context.

and also a history of complex interactions between ethnography and the artistic and literary avant garde in France, in which questions of cultural order and identity were at issue. It is in relation to that history that the present exhibition, *Lost Magic Kingdoms*, selected by Eduardo Paolozzi from the collections of the Museum of Mankind, can be situated, and differences between this exhibition and that recently mounted at the Museum of Modern Art (MOMA) in New York, *Primitivism in 20th Century Art; Affinity of the Tribal and the Modern*, may be understood.

The primary purpose of the MOMA exhibition was 'the further illumination of modern art'[3] – it was concerned both with the direct and 'invisible' influences of tribal art and with a vaguer concept of affinities. This concept of affinities is very different from the image Péret presented of the magician and the artist, and was governed by a further purpose of the exhibition: to demonstrate the formidable artistic strength of 'primitive' art.[4] Works were, wherever possible, chosen for their 'high aesthetic quality', with the assumption that there exists a common aesthetic sensibility in mankind.

In *Lost Magic Kingdoms*, Paolozzi has not primarily been concerned with objects which fall into any conventional idea of what is beautiful in 'primitive' art but he has, he says, even gone for the ugly – for what resists incorporation in given canons. He has shown a particular interest in objects with a function – in tools of day-to-day as well as of ritual use. When the collections of the Museum of Mankind were being established in the eighteenth and nineteenth centuries, distinctions between art and artefact were irrelevant for the collectors in the context of the 'tribal' curiosity, and moreover because the artefacts belonged to a 'lower', in an evolutionary sense, technology, they were an index of the backward

3 William Rubin, 'Modernist Primitivism: An introduction', *Primitivism in 20th Century Art*, Museum of Modern Art, New York, NY, 1984, vol.1, p.2.

4 Rubin, wary of the pejorative sense that, in spite of Lévi-Strauss and others, still attaches to the term 'primitive', uses by preference 'tribal', and specifically rejects the 'court' art of South and Meso-America from his consideration, although for modern artists 'primitive' included these as well as the art of Japan, Cambodia, Egypt, etc, well into the 1920s. It was for aesthetic rather than anthropological or socio-historical reasons that Picasso, for example, avoided Pre-Columbian art, 'finding it too monumental, hieratic, and seemingly repetitious' (Rubin, *ibid.*, p.3). No distinction between 'tribal' and 'court' art governed the Surrealists' interests in American Indian art, nor has one operated for Paolozzi within the present context.

or 'primitive' nature of the culture responsible. It is with a very different perspective that Paolozzi has approached these objects, tools of various kinds; his admiration is active, and, after years of working with the 'high' technology of engineering he finds the suggestions of a different way of working – less wasteful, less expensive of material and energy – enormously important. Here too Surrealism offers an unexpected precedent: André Breton said, in a lecture given in Haiti towards the end of 1945, 'mechanical progress tends to isolate man in an abstract world... He will have to learn everything all over again from the peasant.'[5] Paolozzi's interests in this context, though, are quite independent of hidden formal ethnographic distinctions between civilised and primitive – one of his most fruitful finds was the paper squeezes made by the archaeologist A.P. Maudslay, by means of which precise moulds were taken of many of the Maya monuments, their figurative sculpture and glyphs, which he then brought back to England with the idea of eventually making casts from them. This provoked in Paolozzi a chain of thoughts about paper as material for sculpture (examples are included in the exhibition) and the possibilities of recycling. (Although of immense value for students of the Maya, these paper squeezes, because they were unfortunately not genuine ethnographic objects, languished for years in dusty obscurity, as, themselves, a kind of bulky archaeological curiosity. They were shown at *The British and the Maya* exhibition in 1973, which is where Paolozzi first came across them).

A sheet of drawings of 1945 of African sculpture from the Pitt Rivers Museum in Oxford testifies to Paolozzi's early interest in 'primitive' art. These careful studies were succeeded by fully worked drawings, like *Three Men in a Boat*, and *Fisherman and Wife*, in which the masks are integrated into the subject of the picture as a whole. *Horse's Head*, a sculpture of 1946, is a remarkable invention in which the gouged lines in the neck are a transposition of the striated planes derived from Pablo Picasso. In 1947 Paolozzi went to Paris and came into contact with the Surrealists and ex-Surrealists. He began to read the classic texts by or valued by them. On Tzara's recommendation, for instance, he read Raymond Roussel's *Impressions of Africa*, an imaginary account of a group of travellers trapped

5 Quoted in J. Michael Dash, *Literature and Ideology in Haiti 1915–61*, Macmillan, London, 1981, p.157.

in an African kingdom; their conditions of freedom depend upon the construction of various incredible objects and sculptures, the technical ingenuity of which is no less remarkable than their imaginative genesis – which turned out in the end to be based on a series of linguistic games.[6] But what interested Paolozzi above all was a sensibility, crucially determined by the Dada and Surrealist aesthetic, which was based on the association and juxtaposition of the disparate. The Surrealist poetic image, central to the preoccupation of Breton's *First Surrealist Manifesto* of 1924, was to be born of the encounter of two or more different 'realities' on a plane foreign to all. The touchstone for Breton was the image by the nineteenth-century poet Lautréamont, rendered famous through Surrealism: 'as beautiful as the chance encounter of a sewing machine and an umbrella on a dissecting table'. The process of disorientation, 'depriving us of a frame of reference' as Breton described it in connection with Max Ernst's collages in 1921, rendered unfamiliar the familiar.[7] Its principle is that of disconnection rather than connection.

This holds as true in the context of the Surrealists' involvement in ethnography as in their other activities, and is explicit in the mode of presenting material in their reviews and exhibitions. Their preference for Oceania and for Pre-Columbian and Native America over Africa was motivated partly by the existing formal assimilation of the latter into modern art. Anyway, it was no longer a question of perpetrating again an 'audacity of taste', as Apollinaire had described the process by which African 'idols' came to be accepted among Europeans as 'genuine works of art'.[8]

The Surrealists' love of Oceanic and American objects brought them naturally into association with ethnography. Paul Rivet and Georges-Henri Rivière, who at the time of the Dakar-Djibouti Mission were director and assistant director of the Ethnographic Museum in Paris – the Trocadéro – were contributors to *Documents,* the review edited by Georges Bataille, which provided a forum for many dissident Surrealists, and the whole of

6 See Raymond Roussel, *Comment J'ai Ecrit Certains de mes Livres*, Librairie Alphonse Lemerre, Paris, 1935.

7 André Breton, 'Max Ernst', in *Max Ernst: Beyond Painting*, Wittenborn, Schultz, New York, NY, 1948, p.177.

8 Guillaume Apollinaire, 'A propos de l'art des noirs', *Sculptures Nègres*, Paul Guillaume, Paris, 1917.

the second issue of *Minotaure* (1933) was devoted to the Dakar-Djibouti Mission.[9] *Documents* had on its title page the rubric 'Doctrines – Archéologie – Beaux-Arts – Ethnographie'; *Minotaure* the slightly smoother and more Catholic 'Arts Plastiques – Poésie – Musique – Architecture – Ethnographie et Mythologie – Spectacles – Études et Observations Psychanalytiques'. To share the attitude of the ethnographer, too, was to locate themselves firmly outside the conventional art movement. 'Ethnography', as Marcel Griaule, leader of the Dakar-Djibouti Mission wrote a little earlier in *Documents*, 'is interested in the *beautiful* and the *ugly*, in the European sense of these words... Ethnography is suspicious, too, of itself – for it is a white science, ie strained with prejudices – and it will not refuse aesthetic value in an object because it is up to date or mass produced.'[10]

So the Surrealist magazines extended the ethnographers' method to the collection and study of 'documents' from their own culture. As they presented these in reviews and exhibitions, juxtaposing things and ideas from the most disparate fields, the method itself becomes that of collage.

One of the first instances of this approach in relation to a specifically ethnographic subject, was in the first of the Surrealist reviews *(La Révolution surréaliste*, 1924–29), and was a photograph identified as a ritual scene from New Britain reproduced without any further explanation and without any thematic context. It is there, not to illustrate a text, but as a 'text' in its own right (as were the other visual works in this issue – among them paintings by Yves Tanguy, Jean (Hans) Arp and André Masson, a collage by Picasso and photographs by Man Ray). Nor is there any attempt

9 *Documents 1929–30; Minotaure* 1933–39. The Dakar-Djibouti expedition, whose team included the ex-Surrealist Michel Leiris, not only 'produced one of the most complete descriptions of a tribal group (the Dogon and their neighbours) on record anywhere' (Clifford, *op. cit.*, below) but brought back, among other things, to enrich the nation's collections, 3,500 'ethnographic objects' and the mural paintings of an entire Abyssinian church (Rivet et Rivière, 'Mission ethnographique et linguistique Dakar-Djibouti', *Minotaure*, no.2, 1933). Rivet's vision of a new 'museum of humanity' was realised with the opening in 1938 of the Musée de l'Homme, which brought together the ethnographic collections of the old Trocadéro, scientific laboratories from the Musée d'Histoire Naturelle, and the Institut d'Ethnologie; selected exhibitions of the world's races and cultures were displayed in succession. A comparative history of the Museums of Art, Ethnography and Natural History in London and Paris would be interesting; (the Museum of Mankind in London was not separated from the British Museum until 1970).

10 Marcel Griaule, 'Un coup de fusil', *Documents*, no.1, 2nd year, 1930; trans. in James Clifford, 'On Ethnographic Surrealism', *Comparative Studies in Society and History*, October 1981, vol.23, no.4, p.550.

to mediate the strangeness of the ritual scene. The most aggressive of the reviews was *Documents*, which not only maintained the closest links with ethnography as a science, but in which, paradoxically, Bataille put forward his profoundly anti-idealist view of mankind in which the primitive and the ancient-sacred were ironic allies. *Documents* no.1, 1930, for instance, contains photographs of an 'ignoble initiation rite' of the Nandi people (for Bataille 'ignoble' was not necessarily a pejorative term in terms of his attack on his own culture's value systems), covers of the popular magazine series *Fantomas* and photographs of decadent Parisian monumental sculpture. Other subjects covered in *Documents* included articles on ethnographic methods, detailed studies of non-Western music and musical instruments, Hollywood films and reviews, Japanese Neolithic art, and recent paintings by Joan Miró. *Minotaure* too covered a wide and disparate field, but was more humanist in tone, in common with Breton's Surrealism, and contained a strong bias towards psychoanalysis. It is significant that the rubric of *Minotaure* included 'mythology' with 'ethnography', for this was a crucial dimension. The ideas, the poetry and the literature; the cosmogonies and cosmologies of 'other' peoples were of no less importance than their material culture.[11] In the last issue, before the Second World War broke up the surrealist world, Kurt Seligmann published *Conversation with a Tsimshian* (a North-West Coast shaman).[12] After the war, Breton clung to the idea that it was possible to have access through the art and thought of the American Indian (by far the most exploited of all) 'to a new system of knowledge and relations'.[13]

A similar point may be made about Surrealist exhibitions. In 1927 an exhibition was held at the Galerie Surréaliste of paintings by the Surrealist artist Yves Tanguy and of American objects from the Surrealists' own collections: from British Columbia, New Mexico, Mexico, Colombia and Peru. Reproduced in the catalogue was a small version of the great statue

11 Péret, for instance, translated a prophetic-historical Maya text, *Livre de Chilam Balam de Chumayet*, Editions Denoël, Paris, 1955.

12 *Minotaure*, nos.12–13, 3rd series, 1939, p.66.

13 Breton, *Entretiens 1913–52*, Gallimard, Paris, 1952, p.245. 'The only chance', Breton says, 'that the European artist in the 20th century has of warding off the desiccation of the sources of inspiration brought about by rationalism and utilitarianism is by renewing relations with the so-called primitive vision, synthesis of sensorial perception and mental representation... Monnerot, in *La Poésie Moderne et le Sacré*, has proved... the affinities of surrealist thought and of Indian thought...'

of Coatlicue, wearing her necklace of hands and hearts and a serpent skirt. The Surrealist exhibition of objects of 1936 included objects of all kinds: made or found by the Surrealists themselves and also Oceanic and American objects including Eskimo masks, Hopi dolls and Peruvian pots. At the time of the first postwar international exhibition of Surrealism, *Le Surréalisme en 1947*, Breton emphasised that the true perspective of both the current exhibition and that of the last major exhibition in Paris of 1938 was not that of art, but should be understood within their aim of 'rendering generally accessible the terrain of agitation which lies at the confines of the poetic and the real'.[14]

Surrealism had always been in direct conflict with the traditions of European thought that valued rationality above all else. The attention paid to other cultures was a measure of the increasing depth of disillusionment with the culture of which they were a part. This had its political dimension; in 1931, for example, the Surrealists mounted an anti-colonial exhibition, *The Truth About the Colonies*, in opposition to the huge official colonial exhibition. Installations were devised in such a way as to subvert conventional assumptions about cultural norms, to emphasise the relativism of ethnographic study, and to attack the missionary ethos. A display including a statue of the Virgin and Child is labelled *European Fetishism*.

The Surrealist 'ethnographic' method, in reviews, exhibitions and elsewhere, challenged any fixed notion of cultural value and cultural identity, and also a belief in a 'common humanity'.[15] It subverted conventional symbols and categories by placing them in unusual contexts. It was a kind of raw ethnography, paradoxically kinned with the 'extensive Ethnography' practised by Marcel Griaule and his team on the Dakar-Djibouti Mission, whose limitations he is willing to admit: 'to extract from the imbroglio of social facts a documentation relating solely to one of them, is like wanting to extract one element from the game of pic-a-sticks without disturbing the whole.'[16] The Surrealists did not hesitate to extract elements, because the very idea of the whole was under suspicion. The point of juxtapositions from an extensive field, too, like the point of the

14 Breton, 'Devant le Rideau', *Le Surréalisme en 1947*, Maeght, Paris, 1947, p.13.
15 See Clifford, *op. cit.*
16 Marcel Griaule, 'Introduction Methodologie', *Minotaure*, no.2, 1937, p.7.

Surrealist image (verbal or visual collage) was not to seek affinities but to disorientate and shock through difference.

> To write ethnographies on the model of collage would be to avoid the portrayal of cultures as organic wholes, or as unified, realistic worlds subject to a continuous explanatory discourse... The ethnography as collage would leave manifest the constructivist procedures of ethnographic knowledge; it would be an assemblage containing voices other than the ethnographer's, as well as examples of 'found' evidence, data not fully integrated within the work's governing interpretation. Finally it would not explain away those elements in the foreign culture which render the investigator's own culture newly incomprehensible.[17]

When Paolozzi reached Paris in 1947 the attitudes of 'ethnographic Surrealism', either in a historical sense (*Minotaure* was still available) or in its active postwar continuations, were sufficiently strong, and sufficiently different from the English environment to have a lasting impact. It provided a different perspective from which to understand his own early interest in primitive art, and was to affect him as a method that extended beyond the artistic medium of collage. In 1952 he gave a lecture at the ICA which was 'the first time... that pictures had been shown blam, blam, blam – without recognisable order or logical connection'.[18] There was no linking commentary: Paolozzi did not speak. Such a slide-show lecture was certainly new in England, and new in its technology, but a parallel can be found in the 'ethnographic Surrealism' described above. It treated our culture as a collection of documents, but Paolozzi refused to intervene or interpret. Later the material from this lecture was assembled, partly constructed as collages, in the portfolio *Bunk*. An actual ethnographic presence in his collages was infrequent, though by no means absent: there is a *Collage over African sculpture* of 1960 (in which the collaged machinery both invites and then resists attempts to read it as the statue's head). Images from *The History of Nothing* juxtapose the modern (West) and the

17 Clifford, *op. cit.*, p.563.
18 Quoted in Wieland Schmied, 'Bunk, Bash, Pop – the graphics of Eduardo Paolozzi', *Eduardo Paolozzi*, Arts Council of Great Britain, London, 1976, p.21.
19 Eduardo Paolozzi, 'The Iconography of the Present', *ibid.*, p.27.

exotic/primitive. What Paolozzi described as the 'problems of selection and presentation which face the artist in today's ever-changing society',[19] can to a large extent be understood in the context of 'ethnographic Surrealism'. There are obviously other perspectives in which his work can be seen, but none in which his own work and the collections of the Museum of Mankind which he has quarried can be brought so dramatically into conjunction.

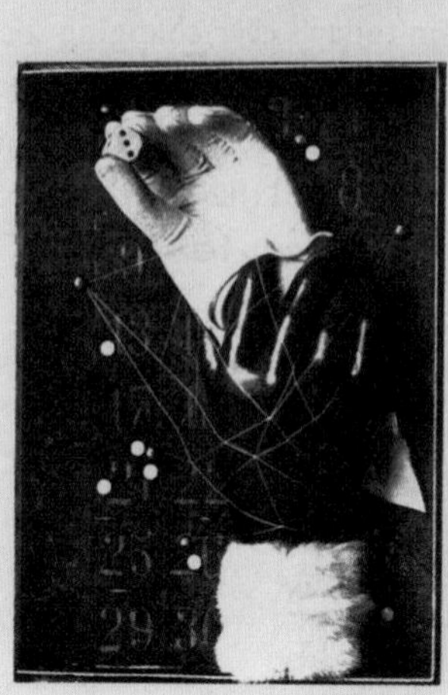

VALENTINE HUGO.

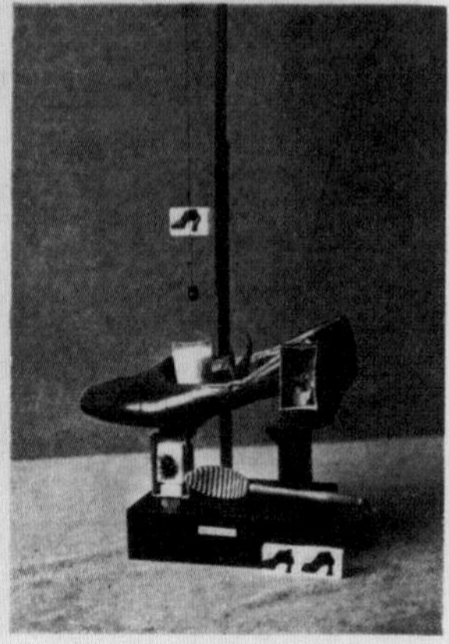

SALVADOR DALI.

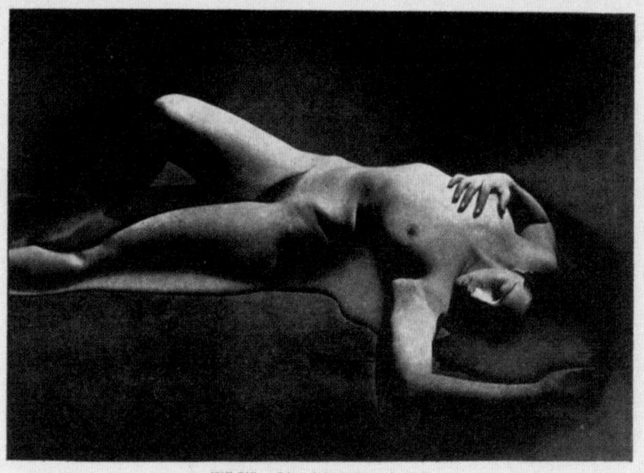

MAN RAY. — Primat de la matière sur la pensée.

Spread from *Le Surréalisme au Service de la Révolution*, no.3, December 1931 with Man Ray, *Primat de la matière sur la Pensée*, 1929 and two Surrealist objects by Valentine Hugo and Salvador Dalí

Surrealism: Fetishism's Job

Fetishism: Visualising Power and Desire, Anthony Shelton (ed), South Bank Centre, London and The Royal Pavilion, Art Gallery and Museums, Brighton, in association with Lund Humphries, London, 1995

Georges Bataille once proposed that the proper scope of a dictionary should not be the passive act of defining the meaning of a word, but that of addressing the job of work it had to do: 'A dictionary's job would begin from the moment that it stopped giving the meaning, but rather the tasks, of words.'[1]

The word 'fetishism', of obscure origins and disputed etymology, has worked its way through the rationalising discourses of the European Enlightenment; connoting over-valuation and displacement, its job was to signal error, excess, difference and deviation. Perhaps one of the key phantoms of the Enlightenment's 'dream of reason', it helped to structure and enforce distinctions between the rational and irrational, civilised and primitive, normal and abnormal, natural and artificial. Thus the adoption of the term successively by Karl Marx, and nineteenth-century psychologists, to refer to forms of irrational valuation within their own society, had a satirical edge. In Surrealism, however, there is a change in its fortunes. Having served to affirm the powerlessness of mind and body to act rationally, fetishism was to intervene in the Surrealist subversion of utilitarian and positivist values, or, as writer and critic Carl Einstein put it, 'to change the hierarchies of the values of the real'.[2]

The peculiar capacity of the word both to adapt to and resist change may be a function of the very obscurity of its origins, which has prompted an obsessive interest in its etymology. A contrast might be drawn with

1 'Un dictionnaire commencerait à partir du moment où il ne donnerait plus le sens mais les besognes des mots', Georges Bataille, 'Informe', *Documents*, no.7, 1929, p.382.

the word 'taboo', which could be seen as belonging to the same type of mysteries relating to power, desire and superstition as those to which 'fetishism' was initially attached. The difference lies in the fact that taboo, however its meanings may have developed, was a word that belonged to the same cultural space as those concepts to which it referred. Taboo is a Polynesian word. As Freud said in *Totem and Taboo* (1913): 'It is difficult for us to find a translation for it, since the concept connoted by it is one we no longer possess. It was still current among the ancient Romans, whose "sacer" was the same as the Polynesian "taboo"...'[3] Unlike 'fetish', taboo was a term internal to the culture whose beliefs it connoted. The term fetish evolved in the course of encounters between Africans and Europeans on the coast of West Africa from the sixteenth century on, but, as anthropologist and post-colonial historian William Pietz has argued, 'These cross-cultural spaces were not societies or cultures in any conventional sense. From this standpoint, the fetish must be viewed as proper to no historical field other than that of the history of the word itself, and to no discrete society or culture, but to a cross-cultural situation formed by the ongoing encounter of the value codes of radically different social orders.'[4]

Our idea in this exhibition [*Fetishism: Visualising Power and Desire*] was to assemble objects to which the term 'fetish' has been applied, in some of its disparate arenas, tracing the history of the word's activities and investigating continuities and discontinuities. We divided the exhibition into three parts: first, those things described as 'fetishes' by European traders and explorers in West Africa; second, a room devoted to Surrealism; and finally a section including street culture and fashion that has been dubbed fetish, and works by contemporary artists which could be related to any of the usages of the term. These are divisions that could correspond roughly to the concerns of ethnography, psychoanalysis and sexual politics. They were, though, intended to be porous, not watertight.

An obvious reason for the centrality of Surrealism in this exhibition is its involvement in both ethnography and psychoanalysis, in which notions of fetishism have played such a crucial role. Surrealism was constituted

2 Carl Einstein, 'André Masson: Étude Ethnologique', *Documents*, no.2, 1929, p.95.
3 Sigmund Freud, *Totem and Taboo*, Routledge, London, 1965, p.18.
4 William Pietz, 'The Problem of the Fetish', *Res*, no.9, spring 1985, pp.10–11.

in an awareness of what Foucault later called the 'confrontation, in a fundamental correlation' of ethnology and psychoanalysis. As Foucault commented in *The Order of Things: An Archaeology of the Human Sciences* (1966), 'Since *Totem and Taboo*, the establishment of a common field for these two, the possibility of a discourse that could move from one to the other without discontinuity, the double articulation of the history of individuals upon the unconscious of culture, and of the historicity of those cultures upon the unconscious of individuals, has opened up, without doubt, the most general problems that can be posed with regard to man.'[5]

The Surrealists' embrace of other cultures was defined by their rejection of the values of their own; André Breton, for example, wrote in 1925 that 'Latin civilisation has passed its zenith, and for my part I demand that we forgo, unanimously, any attempt to save it. It seems just now to be the last rampart of bad faith, senility and cowardice.'[6] Their attitudes, though not wholly escaping the primitivising stance of the colonial world, are more complex than is sometimes admitted. Recent critiques of the Surrealists' attitudes to non-Western cultures are a useful corrective to a romanticisation of their position, but do not necessarily take into account the full complexity of this position historically.[7]

The pejorative character of the term was put to subversive effect in the counter exhibition organised by the Surrealists and the French Communist Party at the time of the huge International Colonial Exhibition (*L'Exposition coloniale internationale*) in Paris in 1931, which celebrated the extent of French territorial colonisation. African and Oceanic art were exhibited, and mural paintings by French artists allegorised the supposedly harmonious and patriotic relations between France and its colonies.[8] The Surrealists joined the anti-colonial campaign to expose these as myths and protest against exploitation and repression

5 Michel Foucault, *The Order of Things: An Archaeology of the Human Sciences*, Tavistock Publications, London, 1985, p.379.

6 André Breton, 'Introduction to the discourse on the paucity of reality' (1925), in Franklin Rosemont (ed), *What is Surrealism?*, Pluto Press, London, 1978, p.27.

7 See for example Marianna Torgovnick, *Gone Primitive: Savage Intellects, Modern Lives*, University of Chicago Press, Chicago, IL, 1990, or Nicholas Thomas's 'Colonial Surrealism: Luis Buñuel's *Land Without Bread*', *Third Text*, spring 1994, p.25.

8 See Charles-Robert Ageron, 'L'Exposition coloniale de 1931: mythe républicain ou mythe impériale?', *Les Lieux du mémoire*, vol.1., 1984.

in the colonies, preparing and distributing a tract, 'Ne visitez pas l'exposition coloniale!' (Don't visit the colonial exhibition), and helping devise an exhibition entitled *La Vérité sur les colonies* (The Truth About the Colonies). A photograph reproduced in the journal *Le Surréalisme au service de la révolution* shows a vitrine of exhibits labelled 'European Fetishes' containing three statues including a Catholic image of the Virgin and Child, and a charity collecting box in the form of a black child.

The use of the term 'fetish' is doubly provocative. To describe these European objects as fetishes exposes the Western ideological assumptions behind the term, and by redirecting its object backwards, as it were, to Western things, serves to defamiliarise and denude them. Moreover, to juxtapose the Virgin with the black child begging-bowl was to make comparisons between religious and economic 'fetishism', a complex relationship which precisely inheres within the term itself. Whether or not the organisers of the Anti-Colonial Exhibition (*L'Exposition anticoloniale*) were aware of it, the term did initially contain the Protestant viewpoint that Catholic idols compared in a number of ways with African *fetissos*.

The Surrealists were inveterate collectors of things from all over the world, from Paris flea market detritus to grand sculptures from Oceania or pre-Columbian America. Photographs of Breton in his studio show him surrounded by objects of all kinds, massed like charms to protect him from things modern and utilitarian. However, only a few of these are actually described as 'fetishes'.[9]

The 'correlation through confrontation' of ethnology and psychoanalysis is especially vivid in the review *Documents*, which was published between 1929–30; edited by Georges Bataille together with Carl Einstein, this gathered many dissident Surrealists, such as Michel Leiris, Robert Desnos and André Masson, in its pages. Although the juxtaposition of

9 A major sale of Breton's and Éluard's collections, 'Sculptures d'Afrique, d'Amérique, d'Océanie' at the Hôtel Drouot in 1931, coincided with the International Colonial Exhibition. The catalogue listed two masks described as 'Fétiches M'Gallé' from the Ogoué region of Gabon. Éluard's list of ethnographic objects sold to Roland Penrose in 1937 describes only three of the African sculptures, the Gabon 'reliquaries', as fetishes, thus suggesting an attempt (if misplaced) to be precise in the use of the term.

cultures characterises all Surrealist reviews, in *Documents* – and partly because, unlike the official Surrealist reviews, it was never the organ of a movement with its own project – contrasts, contradictions and comparisons force a radical revision of the hierarchies and values created by man and his artefacts, from whatever culture.

Documents represents a reaction against treating ethnographic objects as art; this serves, not to enforce a distinction between them and 'Western art', with only the latter properly entitled to such 'elevated' concepts as 'beauty', but to propose a similar process of addressing art as part of a specific cultural continuum among other artefacts. But there is also, in *Documents*, a strong sense of loss in much of the writing about modern art; as Bataille says in a key text in the last issue of *Documents*, 'L'esprit moderne et le jeu des transpositions' (The modern spirit and the play of transpositions), even the best of modern art belongs more to the history of art, emasculated and academic, than to human urgencies. It lacks the capacity to express either admissible or inadmissible experiences or needs. 'I defy', he writes, 'any lover of modern art to adore a painting as a fetishist adores a shoe.'[10] By 'play of transpositions' Bataille means, as Denis Hollier points out, the symbolism of psychoanalysis, especially dream symbolism, targeting thereby the Surrealists.[11] The opposition Bataille sets up between symbolic transpositions and the fetish is clear, and this points to a crucial issue in relation to the Surrealist object. Bataille's polemic also throws into relief two important earlier pieces of critical writing in *Documents*: Carl Einstein's 'André Masson: Étude ethnologique',

10 Bataille, 'L'esprit moderne et le jeu des transpositions', *Documents*, no.8, 1930, p.489. Taking a cue from Mauss, the term 'fetish' is occasionally queried in *Documents*. A photograph of three rare Benin forged iron sculptures is reproduced (opposite, significantly, an anamorphic painting and two of Dalí's androgynous/body fragment paintings of 1928, *Bathers* and *Female Nude*); the commentary asks: 'Fetish trees? but perhaps also genealogical trees, or even trees flowering with freshly cut heads: it is difficult for the ethnographers to decide the nature of these most mysterious of trees.'(*Documents*, no.4, 1929, p.230). See James Clifford, 'On Ethnographic Surrealism', in *The Predicament of Culture*, Harvard University Press, Cambridge, MA, 1988, for a further discussion of *Documents* and ethnography, and Jean Jamin, 'L'etnographie mode d'inemploi: de quelques rapports de l'ethnologie avec le malaise dans la civilisation', in Jacques Hainard and Roland Kaehr (eds), *Le mal et la douleur*, Musée d'Ethnographie, Neuchâtel, 1986.

11 Denis Hollier, *Against Architecture* (1974), MIT Press, Cambridge, MA, and London, 1989, p.112.

12 Einstein, *op. cit.*, p.93; Michel Leiris, 'Alberto Giacometti', *Documents*, no.4, 1929, p.209.

and Michel Leiris's 'Alberto Giacometti'.[12] Under pressure from similar preoccupations each chooses a term from outside traditional aesthetic rhetoric, both of which in different ways are implicated in the drawing together of psychoanalysis and ethnology: Einstein takes the term totem, while Leiris places fetishism at the heart of his short piece on Giacometti. Each centres on issues of identity, the relation between self and the external world and the problem of creativity, which the words totem and fetish focus in quite different ways.

There is a somewhat contradictory character to the section of this exhibition that focuses on Surrealism.[13] While ideas and themes that can be seen to correspond to various usages of the word fetish abound in Surrealist writing and visual manifestations – above all, as we shall see, in the Surrealist object – there is a certain reserve in the use of the term itself. The reasons for this are probably rooted in a new awareness, itself a consequence of the opening of ethnology into psychoanalysis, of the prejudicial character and the nature of the power relations that fetishism had signified.

The prevalence of 'fetishism' as an explanatory tool in the study of 'primitive religion' came under attack from French sociologist Marcel Mauss by the end of the nineteenth century. He pointed out that the term should only ever be addressed to the thing itself and not to a spirit distinct from it; in his 1898 review of Mary Kingsley's *Travels in West Africa* he argued that 'fetish' should designate at most certain amulets, and subsequently rejected it altogether, on the grounds that it prejudiced the understanding of the specific conceptions of magic within a given society.[14]

Effectively, he was banning the word; 'so-called fetish-objects', he

13 There were three sections in the exhibition *Fetishism: Visualising Power and Desire*: 1. African Works; 2. Surrealism; 3. Contemporary Artists.

14 Marcel Mauss, *Oeuvres Complètes*, vol.1, Editions de Minuit, Paris, 1968, p.560. To Mauss's disgust, Mary Kingsley persistently used the term 'joujou' ('French, used by the natives'). Curiously, this was the subject of one of Marcel Griaule's 'Critical Dictionary' entries, which he discusses in terms close to those one might expect for 'fetish'. 'The first Portuguese... who landed on the African coast, facing the immense problems of the beliefs, mysteries, powers, gods, black spirits, resolved them all immediately into a single word: DjouDjou... A ridiculous word from an ethnographic point of view but a very elegant one if put in its place, that is if one considers it as nothing but a term of African *lingua franca* [*sabir*] and the *lingua franca* [*sabir*] of exhibitions.' *Documents*, no.6, 1930, pp.367–68.

argued, 'are never any old things chosen at random; this could only be true for the superficial eye of an outsider. On closer inspection it should be obvious that such objects are "always defined by the code of magic or religion" in question.'[15] Mauss's ideas were a powerful influence on the Surrealists and on that overlapping group that included Georges Bataille, centred on the review *Documents*. It was the apparently arbitrary character attached to the notion of the fetish that persuaded Mauss to drop the term as a dangerous caricature: a caricature with its roots in such notorious travellers' accounts as that of the Dutch merchant William Bosman in 1703. Bosman's African informant (significantly, an educated man, aware of the gulf between different social, religious and economic structures) told him that:

> ...the number of their Gods was endless and innumerable. For (said he) any of us being resolved to undertake anything of importance, we first of all search out a God to prosper our designed Undertaking; and going out of doors with this Design, take the first creature that presents itself to our Eyes, whether Dog, Cat, or the most contemptible Animal in the World, for our God; or perhaps instead of that any inanimate that falls in our way whether a Stone, a piece of Wood, or anything else of the same Nature.[16]

William Pietz comments on the puzzlement of early travellers and traders at exchange practices which operated so massively in the Europeans' favour: 'Gold is much prized among them, in my opinion more than by us, for they regard it as very precious: nevertheless they traded it very cheaply, taking in exchange articles of little value in our eyes.'[17]

It was precisely this radical disjunction, this gap between estimations of the value of a material object signalled by fetishism as a key term in the study of primitive religions that had led to its 'figurative' adoption by Marx and then by nineteenth-century psychologists. In the fourth section of the first chapter of *Capital* (1867), 'The mystery of the fetishistic character of commodities', Marx's use of the term is, as Pietz has argued,

15 Adrian Pettinger, 'Why Fetish?', *Perversity: New Formulations*, no.19, spring 1993, p.92.
16 William Pietz, 'The problem of the fetish 1', *Res*, no.9, spring 1985, p.8.
17 Pietz, *op. cit.*, p.41.

both 'theoretically serious and polemically satirical':[18]

> The mercantilists (the champions of the monetary system) regarded gold and silver, not simply as substances which, when functioning as money, represented a social relation of production, but as substances which were endowed by nature with peculiar social properties. Later economists, who look back on the mercantilists with contempt, are manifestly subject to the very same fetishistic illusion as soon as they come to contemplate capital. It is not so very long since the dispelling of the physiocratic illusion that land-rents are a growth of the soil, instead of being a product of social activity![19]

The fetishisation of capital, not less than the fetishisation of commodities, which Marx argues was a simpler form of bourgeois economic production, is an illusion, whose mysterious origins are analogous to 'the nebulous world of religion. In that world, the products of the human mind become independent shapes, endowed with lives of their own, and able to enter into relations with men and women. The products of the human hand do the same thing in the world of commodities, I speak of this as the fetishistic character which attaches to the products of labour, so soon as they are produced in the form of commodities.'[20]

What is striking about these passages in which the notion of fetish is used as a satirical weapon to attack the value systems of bourgeois society is the way in which distinctions between what is natural and what is produced by human labour seem almost fortuitously to reverberate with the etymological complexity of the term itself. Whether or not Marx bore this in mind, the proposed derivation of fetish via the pidgin *fetisso*, from the Portuguese *feitico*, meaning witchcraft or charm, which derived from the Latin *factitius*, meaning 'made' or 'manufactured', gives the adoption of this term an interest exceeding that of the surface or foreground satirical analogy with the superstitious overestimations of primitive religious forms of belief. Although apparently buried deep beneath the sense of

18 Pietz, 'Fetishism and Materialism', in Emily Apter and William Pietz (eds), *Fetishism as Cultural Discourse*, Cornell University Press, Ithaca, NY, 1993, p.130.
19 Karl Marx, *Capital*, Lawrence & Wishart, London, 1942, p.57.
20 *Ibid.*, p.46.

witchcraft, the Latin and then early Christian meaning of *factitius* as 'man-made', as opposed to the God-made natural world, often therefore with the sense of something fabricated, artificial or deceptive as opposed to genuine, further thickens the value-constructions loading the word.

Like Marx, the nineteenth-century psychologists of sexuality adopted the term fetishism from the study of religions. They show a fascination characteristic of the nineteenth century with its etymology. Psychologist Alfred Binet, for instance, who first proposed it in his 'Le Fétichisme dans l'amour' (Fetishism in Love), published in *Revue Philosophique* in 1887, as an appropriate term for a particular sexual deviation within psycho-sexual research, gave alternative derivations. To his own etymology of the word, 'from Portuguese *fetisso*, enchanted, magic thing ('*chose fée*'); *fetisso* from *fatum*, fate', he adds a footnote to the effect that Max Müller attached the word *fetisso* to the Latin *factitius*, '*chose factice, sans importance*' (something artificial, without importance), rather than *fatum*.[21]

Binet is confident that it has a real object within the scientific study of religions. Fetishism, he argues, which was disdainfully called by Max Müller the '*culte des brimborions*', (the worship of knick-knacks) played a capital role in the development of religions, and even if they did not start with it, all were involved with it in some way and some ended there. The great battle of images, that has raged since the early Christian era, 'sufficiently proves the universality and the power of our tendency to confound the divinity with the material, palpable sign which represents it. Fetishism holds no less a place in love.'[22]

There is an interesting stress here on the importance of the material sign, the embodied character of the amorous illusion. Binet's analysis of fetishism quickly spread in the growing literature on the psychology of sex, and it is in this context rather than in the sense that Freud was to give the term, that we should begin to examine Surrealism's use of it.

21 Alfred Binet, 'Le Fétichisme dans l'amour', *Revue Philosophique*, part 1, August 1887, part 2, September 1887, p.144. Mutations in the etymology of fetishism continue: the catalogue to the 1994 V&A Museum, London, exhibition *Revolt into Style* gives the meaning 'charming', a novel derivation from 'charm' in the magical sense.

22 *Ibid.*, p.145.

Binet emphasised that what was described was not a 'psychological monstrosity'; 'everybody is more or less fetishist in love'. He defined a *grand* and a *petit* fetishism, of which only the former could be described as a form of 'genital madness'. The fetish object could be an inanimate object or any fraction of the body. Some parts of the body, though, were more likely to become fetishes than others: hand, foot, hair and eye. Binet's examples, many of which are taken from physicians Jean-Martin Charcot and Valentin Magnan's clinical studies, do include cases of women fetishists. Richard von Krafft-Ebing, however, who extensively revised his *Psychopathia Sexualis* (1886) to incorporate fetishism, notes that cases where fetishism assumes pathological importance have so far only been observed in men.[23] He does not rule out the possibility of female instances, although such, he says, have not yet been the object of study. Krafft-Ebing's purpose in classifying pathological forms of sexuality was, unlike Binet, in large measure forensic: he was concerned with its potentially criminal extensions, ranging from theft (of handkerchiefs, hair etc.) to violence on the body. But he agrees with Binet on the crucial point that fetishism is proof of the intimate connection between mind and body. Fetishism, Krafft-Ebing argued, can only be acquired; it cannot be congenital: 'Every case requires an event which affords the ground for the perversion.'[24] It can only be individual, and he quotes Binet: 'In the life of every fetishist there may be assumed to have been some event which determined the association of lustful feeling with the single impression.'[25] Almost certainly this was an event in early youth, connected with the first awakenings of the *vita sexualis*, whose circumstances were usually forgotten, although the result of the association was retained.

Here we are obviously on the threshold of Freud's discovery, or claim, as to what that event invariably was (for the male child): shock at the discovery of the lacking maternal penis. However, the conditions for that discovery – that is the existence of the castration complex – were still absent. There was agreement that the associations were subjective, probably not wholly accidental, that the imagination was a key ingredient,

23 Dr Richard von Krafft-Ebing, *Psychopathia Sexualis* (1886), translation by Francis J. Rebman of the revised and expanded 12th German edition, Heinemann, London, n.d. [c.1922], p.218.

24 *Ibid.*

25 *Ibid.*

and above all that the fetish object took on an independent value – that it was, in terms of normal sexuality, irrationally overvalued.

The fetish-object may be articles of female attire, as in the case of the nursemaid's costume, frequently boots and shoes (Octave Mirbeau's *Diary of a Chambermaid* (1900), on which Buñuel's film *Le Journal d'une femme de chambre* (1964) was based, could well have been drawn from one of these case studies), gloves or underclothing.[26] Attachment to such inanimate objects should not be confused with the normal love of man for a handkerchief, shoe or glove etc. which 'represented the mnemonic symbol of the beloved person – absent or dead – whose whole personality is reproduced by them. The pathological fetishist has no such relations. The fetish constitutes the entire content of his idea.'[27] Only the presence of the fetish could allow for erotic experience with a person, and often the presence of another was unnecessary for erotic stimulation. Merely the sight of such an object could be enough, though other senses were often involved – smell, touch and hearing.

Parts of the body particularly likely to become the object of fetish worship were hair, foot, hand and eyes. Binet gives the case of a young man whose sexual interest was displaced onto the eye, and he imagined the nostrils as the seat of the female sexual organs – a case which seems to involve a double displacement. Another example in Krafft-Ebing was the young man who loved the foot of a lame woman. His ambition was to marry a chaste, lame girl who would free him of his crime by 'transferring his love for the sole of her foot to the foot of her soul'.[28] This attraction to the base, which is often a part of the fetish's attraction, formed an important part of Bataille's analysis of seduction, whose relation to the fetish we shall examine below.

The power of the word is rooted in a certain set of constants, which William Pietz argues provide continuity despite the variability of the arenas in which it operates.[29] He defines these as follows: first, its

26 As Krafft-Ebing pointed out (in *Psychopathia Sexualis*, *op. cit.*), his examples were all of female clothing because most of the cases he and other psychologists had studied were men, but he did not rule out the possibility of female fetishists, and indeed among Binet's examples, drawn from Charcot's and Magnon's cases, was one of a woman who developed a fetishistic attachment for a man's voice.

27 *Ibid.*, p.218.

28 *Ibid.*, case 95, p.230.

29 Pietz, 'The problem of the fetish 1', *op. cit.*, p.7.

irreducible materiality; the fetish is not identical with an idol, which is an acknowledged stand-in. Second, it is characterised by what Pietz calls 'singularity and repetition'; 'The fetish has an ordering power derived from its status as the fixation or inscription of a unique originating event that has brought together previously heterogeneous elements into a novel identity.'[30] This apparently is characteristic of African culture of the fetish, where Pietz quotes anthropologist Wyatt MacGaffey's statement that 'a "fetish" is always a composite fabrication'.[31] We need to distinguish two aspects to this 'ordering power of the fetish' in the context of Surrealism: there is both the unique and singular event, which invested a material object or body part with special power, which in psychoanalytic terms was compulsively repeated, and also the notion of heterogeneity, which was endowed with an illusion of unity or meaning (social, religious, psychological) through the operation of desire. The third constant is the notion of value: the displacement, reversal or overestimation of value, which is attached to the term 'fetish' and is perhaps its clearest and most consistent feature. Finally, the relation between fetish and the human body, whose functions and health the former may control and order.

As what Michel Foucault called the 'model perversion', fetishism had become, in the move to classify and control the deployment of sexuality, 'the guiding thread for analysing all the other deviations'.[32] The Surrealists, whose emphasis on pleasure and the body deliberately flouted the 'socialisation of procreative behaviour', were nonetheless ambivalent about sexual fetishism. The fact that fetishism had been so obsessively studied as a type of pathological sexual aberration in the context of a France paranoid about falling birth rates, and insistent on reproduction as a moral and patriotic duty and the only proper aim of sexual activity, invested it for the Surrealists with a positive value.[33] Their insistence on

30 *Ibid.*

31 *Ibid.*

32 Michel Foucault, *The History of Sexuality*, Penguin Books, London, 1984, p.154. Surrealism itself profoundly influenced later radical critiques such as Foucault's *History of Sexuality*, and was responsible for publishing some of the first writings of two of the most influential figures in Structuralist thought in the fields of psychoanalysis and ethnography: Jacques Lacan and Claude Lévi-Strauss.

33 See Robert Nye, 'The medical origins of sexual fetishism', in *Fetishism as Cultural Discourse*, *op. cit.* The poet Apollinaire, who coined the term 'surréaliste', wrote a play entitled *Les Mamelles de Tirésias* (1903), a piece of mildly satirical propaganda for childbearing, presented as a 'drame surréaliste'.

erotic pleasure as an aim in itself quite unmarked by any sense of patriotic or familial duty takes on in this light a clearly oppositional quality to the pathologisation of deviance. However, the Surrealists – above all, Breton himself – were bound to the idea of the reciprocity of heterosexual love; although there is some debate in the 'Recherches sur la sexualité' (Research on Sexuality, 1928–32), limits to the free discussion of the body exist although they are different from those imposed by the notion of normality.[34] Fetishism is in effect pressed into service in different ways by Surrealism, the very ambivalence of the term, occupying a kind of *terrain vague* between public and private spaces, dream and waking, the interior and the exterior, Europe and its others, matching Surrealism's own situation.

Surrealism's relationship with the fetish depends crucially on the latter's materiality, and was closely bound up with the emergence of the Surrealist object. As Dalí put it: 'What matters is the way in which the [Surrealist] experiments revealed the *desire for the object*, the tangible object. The desire was to get the object at all costs out of the dark and into the light, to bear it all winking and flickering into the full daylight. That is how the *dream objects* Breton first called for in his 'Introduction to the discourse on the paucity of reality' were first met with.'[35] This introduction contains one of Breton's rare usages of the term 'fetish', and also, not by chance, the first formulation of the idea of the Surrealist object:

> Do not forget if for no other reason the belief in a certain practical necessity prevents us from ascribing to poetic testimony an equal value to that given, for instance, to the testimony of an explorer. Human fetishism, which must try on the white helmet, or caress the fur bonnet, listens with an entirely different ear to the recital of our expeditions. It must believe thoroughly that it *really has happened*. To satisfy this desire for perpetual verification, I recently proposed to fabricate,

34 *Recherches sur la sexualité*, Archives du Surréalisme, Paris, 1990, translated as *Investigating Sex*, José Pierre (ed), Verso, London, 1992. The first two 'conversations' were published in *La Révolution surréaliste*, nos.10/11, 1928.

35 Salvador Dalí, 'The object as revealed in Surrealist experiment', *This Quarter*, 1932, p.199. I have slightly altered the translation, which rendered Breton's 'Introduction au discours sur le peu de réalité' as 'Introduction to the discourse on the poverty of reality'.

> in so far as possible, certain objects which are approached only in dreams and which seem no more useful than enjoyable. Thus recently while I was asleep, I came across a rather curious book in an open-air market in Saint-Malo. The back of the book was formed by a wooden gnome whose white beard, clipped in the Assyrian manner, reached to his feet. The statue was of ordinary thickness, but did not prevent me from turning the pages, which were of heavy black cloth. I was anxious to buy it and, upon waking, was sorry not to find it near me. It is comparatively easy to recall it. I would like to put into circulation certain objects of this kind, which appear eminently problematical and intriguing. I would accompany each of my books with a copy in order to make a present to certain persons. Perhaps in that way I should help to demolish these concrete trophies which are so odious, to throw further discredit on those creatures and things of 'reason'.[36]

Breton is interested in the fetishist not, in the first instance, because of his sexual obsessions per se, but as someone who is convinced by his imagination. This can best be illustrated with reference to the almost contemporary and much better known *Manifesto of Surrealism* (1924), where Breton outlines the two types of being who do not suffer from sclerosis of the imagination: children and the insane. For them, the world is not restricted to the purely utilitarian and functional. Things outside the immediate reach of the waking senses can be experienced as real. In his example of the fetishist who is compelled to touch the white helmet or the fur, it is the conjunction of the actual material substance, the 'irreducible materiality' of the fetish object, and the imaginative leap at a moment of intense experience that has given it such power, whatever its psychological roots. That which had been bracketed as outside rational behaviour and activity became almost by definition the arena of Surrealist exploration. The fetishist offered a supreme example of the reconciliation of imagination and reality. The fetish object – fur, bonnet, apron; the examples from the case studies are numerous and specific – was an undeniable material substance, but at the same time could not register in the world of utilitarian reality. It had individual psychological value

36 Breton, 'Introduction to the discourse on the paucity of reality', in Rosemont, *op. cit.*, p.26.

but no social value. As Breton put it: 'Must poetic creations assume that tangible character of extending, strangely the limits of so-called reality?'[37] In this sense, then, the fetishist, as Breton said in the passage quoted above, could understand the Surrealist poet, exploring the tangible inventions of language, loosened from its utilitarian function. 'What is to prevent me from throwing disorder into this order of words, to attack murderously this obvious aspect of things? Language can and should be torn from this servitude. No more descriptions from nature, no more sociological studies.'[38] Since conviction of the reality of social conventions is riveted in us through its clichés, for 'it is from them we have acquired this taste for money, these constraining fears, this feeling for the native land, this horror of our destiny', to destabilise language is to shake these convictions, and also to question the assumed border between real and imaginary.

Breton's attack on the despised objects of utility sets the Surrealist object in direct confrontation with Le Corbusier's 'type-objects', hygienic and prosthetic.[39] Dalí's proposal for the construction of Surrealist objects, as a new form of communal activity for the movement, was directly prompted by Breton's dream object. Dalí, however, reforges the direct link with psycho-sexual concerns, which was marginal to Breton's invocation of the fetish, through his notion of the 'Surrealist object functioning symbolically'.[40] These composite, elaborate constructions touch at several points upon the themes noted above for the fetish, although they should not be simply collapsed into it. The very fact that Dalí describes them as 'symbolically' functioning objects opens up some distance between them and the classical fetish, pulling them into relation with dreamwork. Dalí divorces these objects from any formal considerations, and they have nothing in common with the early constructivist experiments in kineticism.

37 *Ibid.*, p.25.
38 *Ibid.*
39 Le Corbusier, *L'art decoratif d'aujourd'hui*, Editions Crés, Paris, 1925. See also Briony Fer, 'The hat, the hoax, the body', in Kathleen Adler and Marcia Pointon (eds), *The Body Imaged: The Human Form and Visual Culture Since the Renaissance*, Cambridge University Press, Cambridge, 1993.
40 Dalí, 'Objets surréalistes', *Le Surréalisme au service de la révolution*, no.3, 1931, p.16.

OBJECTS OF SYMBOLIC FUNCTION

> *These objects, which have a minimal mechanical function; are based on phantasms and representations susceptible of being provoked by the realisation of unconscious acts...*
>
> The incarnation of these desires, their manner of objectivising themselves by substitution and metaphor, their symbolic realisation constitute the typical process of sexual perversion, which resembles in every respect the process of poetic fact.[41]

In his 1931 text 'Objets surréalistes', Dalí simultaneously sets up a psychoanalytical context through the classificatory terminology of 'normal' and 'perverted' sexuality, and then subverts it, by equating the object with Surrealism's poetic aims, thereby bringing into question the scientific aims of the psychologists: 'the object itself and the phantasms that its functioning can unleash always constitute a new and absolutely unknown series of perversions, and consequently of poetic facts'. The idea of an almost endless inventiveness at the service of a perverse erotic imagination, the categorising psychologist's nightmare, serves to underline the gap between the Surrealists' interests in the research and experimentation in sexuality and that of the 'scientists'. It was part of the project of the Surrealist object in the early 1930s that it should be 'practised by all'. Coming closer to fetishism than to dream symbolism, Dalí proposes that everyone should produce their own object, given the irreducible individuality of the erotic imagination. The objects depend only on the amorous imagination of each person and are 'extraplastic' – that is, outside formal and aesthetic considerations. Of the four objects reproduced, two are by men, two by women (André Breton, Valentine Hugo, Dalí and his companion Gala). As far as Dalí was concerned, there was no gender bar to the realisation of these desires.

Dalí's 'Objets surréalistes' concluded with accounts of these four objects, which are basically descriptive rather than analytical, and were necessitated by the very complexity of the objects, the details of whose materials, construction and mobility were quite hard to determine from the photographs. He described his own 'article' as follows:

> Inside a woman's shoe is placed a glass of warm milk in the centre of a soft paste, coloured to look like excrement.
>
> A lump of sugar on which there is a drawing of the shoe has to be dipped in the milk, so that the dissolving of the sugar, and consequently of the image of the shoe, may be watched. Several extras (pubic hairs glued to a lump of sugar, an erotic little photograph, etc.) make up the article, which has to be accompanied by a box of spare sugar and a special spoon used for stirring leaden pellets inside the shoe.[42]

Dalí's comments in 'The Object as Revealed in Surrealist Experiment' on an object by the poet Paul Éluard are intriguing in the very direct link he sets up with the ethnographic objects. Éluard had included a wax taper in his object, and Dalí says 'wax was almost the only material which was employed in the making of sorcery effigies which were pricked with pins, this allowing us to suppose that they are the true precursors of articles operating symbolically.'[43] Art critic and author Herbert Read's comment in the foreword to the 1937 exhibition *Surrealist Objects and Poems* at the London Gallery makes a more general link between the Surrealist object – whether found, made or chosen – and ethnographic objects. He does so in terms that unintentionally highlight the contradiction that lies at the heart of Surrealism's embrace of the other – the 'savage': 'Imagine, therefore, that you have for a moment shed the neuroses and psychoses of civilisation: enter and contemplate with wonder the objects which civilisation has rejected, but which the savage and the Surrealist still worship.'[44]

The Surrealist object has a rich ancestry; apart from Breton's dreamed object, the bearded book dwarf mentioned above, there were other both verbal and visual sources: the classic Surrealist image based upon the conjunction of two or more dissimilar realities on a plane foreign to

41 *Ibid.*
42 *Ibid.*
43 Dalí, 'The Object as Revealed in Surrealist Experiment', *op. cit.*, p.206.
44 Herbert Read, 'Foreword', in *Surrealist Objects and Poems*, London Gallery Ltd, London, 1937.

them ('beautiful as the chance encounter of the sewing machine and umbrella on a dissecting table'); collages governed by a similar principle of displacement and disorientation; the game of the *cadavre exquis*; a variety of Dada objects and constructions, and Duchamp's 'assisted readymades'. Its immediate origin, though, was Giacometti's *Suspended Ball* (1930), a source Dalí acknowledges but distinguishes from his own proposal of the symbolically functioning object on the grounds that it was still a sculpture, while the Surrealist object was exclusively made from found or readymade materials, and had nothing to do with aesthetics.

A drawing of *Suspended Ball* is included among the 'dumb, mobile objects' by Giacometti reproduced in *Le Surréalisme au service de la révolution*. *Suspended Ball*, which exists in both the original plaster form and in a wooden version, shockingly links violence to desire; the cleft pendant ball seems to hover over a curved wedge, which is waiting to slice further into the ball, but is also perhaps a magnified segment of it. Analogies between the ball and both eye and genitals point to a long obsession of the Surrealists, and most immediately to Buñuel and Dalí's 1929 film *Un Chien andalou* (An Andalusian Dog), whose opening scene of the slitting of the young woman's eye was celebrated in *Documents* by Georges Bataille: 'The eye could be brought closer to the cutting edge, whose appearance provokes at the same time acute and contradictory reactions: precisely what the makers of *Un Chien andalou* must horribly and obscurely have experienced when in the first images of the film they determined the bloody loves of the two protagonists.'[45] *Suspended Ball*, as has often been noted, confuses gender in its analogies with the human body and the motions of sex.[46]

A comic-horror sequence in *Un Chien andalou* also plays on fetishistic displacements and substitutions across gender. A young man and young woman confront each other; the man suddenly clasps his hand to his mouth as though his teeth were about to fall out, and then removes it to reveal the lower part of his face as though wiped clean, as if he has no mouth. The girl reacts by furiously applying lipstick to her own mouth;

45 Bataille, 'L'oeil', *Documents*, no.4, 1929, p.216.

46 See Yves Bonnefoy, *Giacometti*, Flammarion, Paris, 1991, p.196; and Hal Foster, *Compulsive Beauty*, MIT Press, Cambridge, MA, and London, 1993, p.92; also Rosalind Krauss, 'Alberto Giacometti', in William Rubin (ed), *Primitivism in 20th Century Art*, Museum of Modern Art, New York, NY, 1984, for a discussion of Giacometti and 'hard primitivism'.

however, hairs now grow on the man's face. The young woman claps her hand to her mouth in dismay and quickly examines her armpit, which is now completely hairless. The man continues to look at her with hair growing on his mouth; she puts her tongue out at the man, and leaves the room, returning to put her tongue out once again at the hairy-mouthed man. This hilarious sequence compresses an extraordinary range of sexual signifiers into a dance between genders, starting with the horror-provoking castration symbol of the empty face (the original film direction was that the man should pucker his mouth until it appeared like a slit), through the masquerade as the woman frantically applies lipstick, to the final display by the woman of a comically waving phallic tongue.

Breton's 'L'Objet fantôme' (The Phantom Object), published in the same issue of *Le Surréalisme au service de la révolution* as Dalí's 'Objets surréalistes' and later incorporated into *Les Vases communicants* (The Communicating Vessels, 1932), included a critique of these elaborate constructions.[47] Breton begins by drawing a sharp distinction between fantasy prompted by religious fear and modern monsters of the imagination like Picasso's *Clarinet Player* (1911), Duchamp's *Bride* (1912) or Dalí's *The Great Masturbator* (1929). He opens with a quotation from Engels: 'The beings outside time and space created by the clergy and nourished by the imagination of ignorant and oppressed crowds are only the creation of a morbid fantasy, the subterfuges of philosophical idealism, the bad products of a bad social regime.' Breton wants to refute charges brought against the Surrealists by the dissident group centred on *Documents*, which had been leading a campaign to discredit the Surrealists by implicating them as idealists.

The deviation of works such as those by Duchamp or Dalí, modern monsters, which at first sight appear 'repellent and indecipherable', should not be confused with the metaphysical imaginary of Hieronymus Bosch or William Blake. 'The variable theory which presides over the birth of this work shouldn't let us forget that preoccupations rigorously personal to the artist, but essentially linked to all people, here find a means of expression through a form of deviation.' Breton argues that such works can be analysed for their latent content, and then proceeds to do so for his drawing of an envelope with eyelashes and a handle – the phantom

47 Breton, 'L'Objet fantôme', *op. cit.* p.20 (author's translation).

object. Favourable though he is to the idea of the Surrealist object, whose adoption, he says, he recently insisted upon, he nonetheless finds it loses in power through being too systematically determined.

> They offer to interpretation a less vast scope... than objects less systematically determined. The voluntary incorporation of latent content – filleted in advance – into the manifest content serves here to weaken the tendency to dramatisation and magnification used in the opposite case by censorship. Without doubt such objects, too particular and too personal in conception, will always lack the astonishing power of suggestion enjoyed by chance by certain quite ordinary objects, for example the gold-leaf electroscope...[48]

Out of Breton's objection to the symbolically functioning objects – his own as well as Dalí's – emerged the simpler type of Surrealist object, such as Méret Oppenheim's *Le Déjeuner en fourrure* (Fur Breakfast, 1936). Here there is an elision between fetish and dream object, in which the condensation and displacements typical of dreamwork take on material form.

Michel Leiris's 'Alberto Giacometti', published in *Documents* in 1929, continues the challenge to Surrealism posed by that review, which took the form of contesting value and meaning across a similar field of objects. Facing the problem of the 'private and particular' – the relation between individual expression and communicability – Leiris eschews the idea of the universalising function of the symbolic dreamwork. Fetishism alone occupies the central place in his argument.

Fetishism, for Leiris, now as in ancient times, 'remains at the basis of our human existence'.[49] He distinguishes, however, between a true fetishism, and a counterfeit version to which too much of our lives is devoted, in the form of the worship of 'our moral, logical and social imperatives'. True fetishism is a different order of relation between the self, and the outer world altogether. It is desire in its true form – love which demands another pole, external to itself and is projected from the interior, 'clad in a solid carapace which imprisons it within the limits of a precise thing... into the vast strange chamber called space'.[50] Few works

48 Breton, 'L'objet fantôme', *SASDLR*, no.3, 1931, p.22.
49 Michel Leiris, 'Alberto Giacometti', *Documents*, no.4, 1929, p.209 (author's translation).

made by the human hand respond to the exigencies of this true fetishism; most art is deeply boring. The reason that certain moments, objects or events stand out with inexplicable force and clarity in our memory is that they witnessed this sudden confirmation of desire from the outside, in what could be truly called a crisis. 'It is a matter of moments when the outside seems brusquely to respond to the summation that we launch towards it from the inside, when the external world opens up for our heart to enter into it and establish with it a sudden communication.'[51] Leiris delicately builds up a framework for perceiving Giacometti's *Man and Woman* (1929), *Reclining Woman* (1928) or *Personnages* (1929) as material traces of such moments of intense experience.[52] They are essentially autonomous, and unjustifiable from any logical or rational perspective which may demand of art a comfortable copy or ideal model of the external world. Leiris's description of the figure and its fetish alone in space closely corresponds to the open cage-like tracery of Giacometti's sculptures and the mysterious interpenetration of their forms.

The memory traces left by these moments of crisis are often embodied in events that appear in themselves 'futile, denuded of symbolic value and in some way gratuitous', like the fetish object. Leiris instances some of his own memories of this order: 'In a luminous street in Montmartre, a negress from the Black Birds troupe holding a bunch of roses in her two hands, a steamer I was aboard moving slowly away from the quay... meeting in a Greek ruin a strange animal which must have been a kind of giant lizard.' Leiris finds Giacometti's sculptures, like *Man and Woman* or *Reclining Woman*, the precise equivalents of this type of memory – records of a psychical crisis, a confirmation of one's existence in a space not bounded by the imperatives of false fetishism but outlined rather by the operation of our own desire, which can be nothing other than 'l'amour réellement amoureux – de nous-mêmes...' (Love – real love – for ourselves).

And yet – what price should we give the capricious character of Leiris's own memories? They seem in effect to be almost too perfectly structured,

50 *Ibid.*

51 *Ibid.*

52 *Femme couchée*, now known as *Femme couchée qui rêve* (Reclining Woman Who Dreams), is dated 1928 in Leiris's essay; the photograph titled 'Personnages' includes several sculptures: *Man and Woman, Reclining Woman Who Dreams, Man* and *Three Figures Outdoors.* The works were arranged by Giacometti and photographed by Marc Vaux.

corresponding to three of his – and Bataille's – preoccupations at the time: with the implications of 'negrophilia' in Paris (such as the Black Birds troupe), with the overturning of old notions of 'the primitive mind' (travel from here to there), and finally with the collapse of Latin civilisation (dinosaur in the ruins of Greece). Perhaps it should be enough to note that they operate in this text as a hint of another layer behind the psychoanalytical discourse of the fetish. Leiris was reading Freud's *Totem and Taboo* at the time, and comments in his diary a couple of months before finishing the Giacometti article:

> The theories of contemporary psychologists and sociologists (Freud, Durkheim, Lévy-Bruhl) on primitive mentality are necessarily subject to caution, these scholars having made no direct observations but worked from materials provided by the ethnographers. As far as totemism is concerned, for example, the different observers bring out very different forms, depending upon the country... Moreover, these observations cannot have been made in an absolutely objective frame of mind; they are tendentious, and falsified in origin by the interpretation whose germ they already contain.
>
> It seems that to explain the life of primitives most of these people have invented '*robinsonnades*' which represent in their field the equivalent of those that Marx mocked in the classical economists.[53]

Leiris was evidently aware of the tainted nature of the term fetishism within ethnographic discourse, whose shadow he nonetheless invokes. Dalí once referred to the philosopher Ludwig Feuerbach's 'conception of the object as being primitively only the concept of the second self... Accordingly it must be the "you" which acts as "medium of communication", and it may be asked if what at the present moment haunts Surrealism is not the possible body which can be incarnated in this communication.'[54]

Hans Bellmer's object-sculptures are haunted by this idea of the 'possible body'. They have their origins both in the 'little fetishism' that Binet described as inseparable from all human love, but also undeniably

53 Leiris, *Journal 1922–1989*, Gallimard, Paris, 1992, p.157.

in the sadism that Krafft-Ebing argued could be closely related to fetishism. In 'L'Anatomie de l'amour' (The Anatomy of Love), Bellmer claims that desire has its point of departure not in the whole, but in the detail. The body fragment isolated and compulsively repeated also points to male anxiety about lack in the Freudian sense of the fetish. In Bellmer, this overlaps with the earlier type of sexual fetishism – desire takes the fragment 'fatally' for the whole: its efficacy relies above all on the fact that it has an independent identity. Only thus, Bellmer writes, can it be doubled, multiplied, displaced in the realisation of the image of desire:

> From the moment that the woman reaches the level of her experimental vocation, accessible to permutations, algebraic promises, susceptible of yielding to transubstantial caprices, from the moment that she is extendible, retractable... – we shall be better instructed as to the anatomy of desire, than the practice of love itself could do.[55]

Bellmer imagines removing the barrier between woman and her image. He gives a fearful example of this; a photographic document of a female victim who had been wrapped in wire: 'Tightly criss-crossed, it produced swollen cushions of flesh, irregular, spherical triangles, incising her body with long creases and impure lips, creating hitherto unseen multiplications of breasts in indescribable places',[56] which Bellmer compares with the multi-breasted Diana of Ephesus. This document prompted Bellmer's own experiments of photographing the body wrapped in string, one example of which was used for the cover of *Le Surréalisme, même* in spring 1958. Comparisons have been made between Bellmer's 'monstrous dictionary of analogies/antagonisms' of body parts and the decadent dream-fantasy of one of the male lovers in Remy de Gourmont's book *Le Songe d'une femme* (1899). However, there is a crucial difference. Paul Pelasge dreams of plants and bodies that metamorphose into one another in a cinematic slow

54 Dalí, 'The object as revealed in Surrealist experiment', *op. cit.* p.202

55 Hans Bellmer, 'L'Anatomie de l'amour', *Le Surréalisme en 1947*, Pierre à Feu/Maeght, Paris, 1947, p.108 (author's translation).

56 *Ibid.*, p.109. 'Provoquant des saillants bour-soufflés de chair, des triangles sphériques irreguliers, allongeant des plis, des lèvres malpropres, multipliant des seins jamais vus d'emplacement inavouable.' Hans Bellmer, *The Doll*, trans. Malcolm Green, Atlas Press, London, 2005, p.129.

motion of inflated fragments: 'now her two small sharp breasts become irritated and tremble; they become balloons; they stifle the naked woman who was offering herself, they settle down on their short stem; they are two large white mushrooms topped with a pink shell'.[57] Bellmer's body parts multiply and are displaced, but never metamorphose into something else. The leg, for example, 'perceived in isolation and in isolation appropriated by memory, should go forth to live its own life in triumph, free to double itself, to attach itself to a head, to sit down, cephalopod, on its open breasts while straightening the backbone that is its thighs';[58] but it remains, essentially and irreducibly, like the fetish, itself.

Parallels have often been drawn between the Surrealist object and photographs – parallels that are clearly laid out in *Le Surréalisme au service de la révolution* when the objects were reproduced facing Man Ray's photograph *The Primacy of Matter over Thought* (1929). But if we draw in the idea of fetishism, some intriguing differences emerge. The body is the site for much of Surrealist photography, usually the female body. Brassaï's nudes, acephalous and phallicised, themselves seem to symbolise the fetish as Freud defined it. The Surrealist object – especially in its first incarnation as Dalí's notion of the symbolically functioning object – posits rather the absence of the body: shoe, gloves, a mirror, a bicycle seat. They are like symbolic narratives of erotic sensations, each highly personal in character.

Jacques-André Boiffard's photographs of three big toes, which accompanied Bataille's 'Le gros orteil', are photographic paradigms of a fetishised body fraction. The heavy chiaroscuro isolates the toe from its body; as reproduced in *Documents* in 1929, the toe is cropped from the original photograph of the foot and enlarged, dramatised and magnified in a wholly fetishistic process. The toe itself, though, is erect, its aggressive verticality confounding the base horizontality of its normal position. In the text, Bataille turns the 'classic fetishism of the foot' to account in terms of his

57 Remy de Gourmont, *Le Songe d'une femme*, Meurcure, Paris, 1916, p.145 ('Voilà que ses deux seins menus et aigus s'exasperent et tremblent; ils deviennent des ballons; ils étouffent la femme nue qui s'offrait; ils se couchant sur leur tige courte; ils sont deux grands champignons blancs surmontés d'une coque rose...')

58 Bellmer, *op. cit.*, p.109.

arguments about 'base seduction' contrasting with the seduction of ideal beauty. The 'sacrilegious charm' of the foot of the Spanish Queen, which obsessed the Count of Villamediana and led to his death at the hands of the King, rested, Bataille argues, in the fact that it did not significantly differ from the hideous and deformed foot of a tramp.[59]

Five photographs of Paris monuments by Boiffard, illustrating Robert Desnos's essay 'Pygmalion et le sphinx' (Pygmalion and the Sphinx, 1930),[60] rather blank belly-shots of elaborate lumps of stone, raise the notion of the fetish in the context of the 'ethnological journeys' the Surrealists made in the heart of their own city. Like the statue of Étienne Dolet, in La place Maubert, which, Breton recounts in *Nadja* (1928), always simultaneously attracted him and filled him with an insupportable malaise, there is a disproportion between their apparent role and their effect.[61] Desnos is interested in the contradiction between the materiality, the heavy weight of these statues and the elevated aspirations they are meant to symbolise, underlined grotesquely in monuments to speed, flight or telecommunications. They may, even more appropriately, be taken as fetishes to a nation's idea of progress, military might and glory, and thus classic examples of the mechanism of disavowal – that, at any rate, is the way the Surrealists saw them. Monuments, it was once suggested, are to history as the fetish is to the maternal phallus. In order to deny the absence of something that doesn't exist, you fill the gap, blanking out the absence and endowing this material object with the lineaments of your desire.

Louis Aragon, in *Paris Peasant* (1926), imagines the stone statues of capital cities becoming idols of a new religion, before which the people would come to worship and sacrifice. 'We have the phallophoria of Trafalgar Square, where one-armed Nelson is the witness of a nation's hysteria. And Frémiet's Joan of Arc... not to mention the magnificent apotheosis of Chappe at the foot of a telegraphic scaffold.[62] Boiffard's photographs of these monuments are reminders that the fetish could work for the Surrealists in playful and satirical, as well as perverse and sexual, ways.

59 Georges Bataille, 'Le gros orteil', *Documents*, no.6, 1929, p.297.
60 Robert Desnos, 'Pygmalion et le sphinx', *Documents*, no.1, 1930, p.33.
61 Breton, *Nadja* (1928), Livre de Poche, Paris, 1964, p.25.
62 Louis Aragon, *Paris Peasant* (1926), Jonathan Cape, London, 1971, p.167.

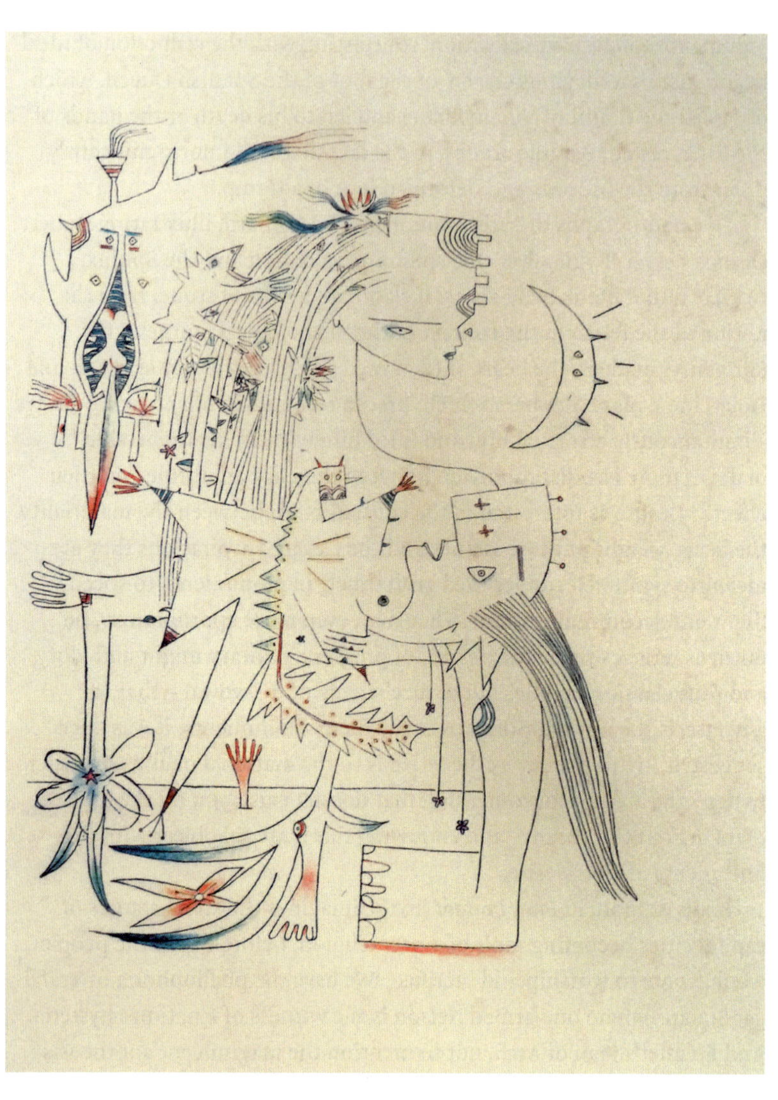

280 **Wifredo Lam**
Untitled
Ink and pencil on paper
27.9 × 18.7 cm | 11 × 7⅜ in
Illustration for André Breton, *Fata Morgana*, 1942

Wifredo Lam and Surrealism

Wifredo Lam in North America, The Patrick and Beatrice Haggerty Museum of Art, Marquette University, Milwaukee, WI, 2008

Accommodez-vous de moi. Je ne m'accommode pas de vous.
AIMÉ CÉSAIRE, *Cahier d'un retour au pays natal*, 1939

Wifredo Lam's connections with Surrealism have in recent years been minimised in favour of an Afro-Cuban context for his work. Placing him within a Surrealist framework has been seen as an imposition by Eurocentric art history. The argument has been made for a change of viewpoint, which would provide a critical and art historical account of Lam's work viewed 'less as a product of Surrealism or in terms of the presence of "primitive" African or Afro-American elements in modern art, than as a result of Cuban and Caribbean culture and as a pioneering contribution to the role of the Third World in the contemporary world.'[1] Although this is a salutary exercise, these viewpoints are not necessarily incompatible. The problem lies partly in the negative associations of 'primitive' in the Western ethnographic discourse combined with Surrealism's experimental interest in the irrational, in the unconscious, and in ideas banished by Western rationalism as superstition. Surrealism becomes a scapegoat for the primitivising gaze of the West: 'The permanence of a certain exoticism typical of the astonished Western vision, particularly among the Surrealists, which extends to everything "primitive", aestheticised as "mystery", "magic", "night", "darkness", "fantastic" etc.'[2] The assumption that Surrealism was an 'aestheticising', even anaesthetising, influence in the complex story of modern art outside

1 Gerardo Mosquera, 'Modernism from Afro-America: Wifredo Lam', in Gerardo Mosquera (ed), *Beyond the Fantastic*, Iniva, London, 1995, p.121.

the Western centres ignores the political commitments of this movement, whose anti-colonial stance differentiates it from an earlier avant garde that fed simply on the formal inventiveness of African art. Moreover, when some acknowledgement of Surrealist links, in the case of a painter like Lam, becomes unavoidable, it is reduced to the issue of 'style', a concept which is extremely problematic in the context of Surrealism.

That there was a change in Lam's work c.1941, which heralded its magnificent flowering in the paintings he made in Cuba between 1942 and 1952, is undeniable. It would be a mistake, however, to equate escaping Europe with abandoning Surrealism, and I would argue that, on the contrary, Lam discovered in Surrealism unexpected resources precisely as a result of its displacement and the loss of its former centre, Paris. Lam's greater intimacy with the Surrealists and with Surrealist ideas while in Marseilles over the winter of 1940–41 and during the voyage to the Caribbean was to have a lasting effect on his work. In Marseilles he was in daily contact with Breton and with Surrealist artists like Victor Brauner, participating in collective games and projects; he then travelled with Breton to Martinique, where the painter André Masson joined them. Of special significance for Lam was the revival of automatism in Surrealist discourse at this time, which Lam was to interpret in a distinctive way and of which he was one of the last great practitioners.

In Martinique the Surrealists unexpectedly encountered a parallel movement that matched their own opposition to European colonialism. The poet Aimé Césaire had started a review, *Tropiques*, which had close affinities with Surrealism. Césaire gave the Surrealists copies of his long and passionate poem, *Cahiers d'un retour au pays natal* (Notebook of a Return to the Native Land), published just before he returned to Martinique from Paris in 1939. Surrealism is all too often cast as a mystificatory influence which failed to resolve the contradictions of its own situation within a colonial Western culture. The encounter in the Caribbean presents Surrealism in a different light. It allows us to escape from thinking in terms of the influence of Surrealism, of Surrealism as a movement that selectively appropriated from other cultures and imposed its name, and to regard it as a point of view that opened up communication between different

2 *Ibid.*, p.130. Alejo Carpentier countered Surrealism with the proposition of 'magical realism' as a 'natural' Latin American experience.

cultures and sensibilities, between Europe and the Americas, the Old and New Worlds. The encounters changed Surrealism and the Surrealists. One should not forget how completely isolated Surrealism was politically, as well as displaced geographically, in 1941. Its watchword, 'Neither your war nor your peace', expressed its position clearly. Finding allies in the world was supremely important. For Lam, Surrealism in a new guise was bound to his return to his native land.

In March 1941, Wifredo Lam, together with the Surrealist poet André Breton and his family, Claude Lévi-Strauss, and other refugees from the fall of France, embarked from Marseilles for America. The last sight of Europe was a grim reminder of its fate: 'I did not begin to understand the situation until the day we went on board between two rows of steel-helmeted guards, with machine guns at the ready, who cordoned off the quayside and cut the passengers off from any contact with the relatives and friends who had come to say goodbye.'[3] Three hundred and fifty passengers, mostly artists and intellectuals under threat from the Vichy regime, crammed onto a small steamer with only two cabins and seven berths; 'it was more like the deportation of convicts'.[4] But it was not so much the appalling conditions of the voyage, the uncertainty of Europe's future under the shadow of the war and the totalitarian dictatorships, nor concerns about their own precarious existence that colour Breton's and others' accounts of this long and tortuous journey, but rather the unexpected discoveries, enthralling encounters with like-minded poets and intellectuals, and the experience of the flora and fauna of a different, tropical clime. At the end of April the overcrowded ship reached the island of Martinique, a French colony under Vichy control, and many of the passengers, including Breton and Lam, were promptly locked up in what was effectively a prisoner-of-war camp, in a former leper hospital.

On 16 May 1941, Lam, Helena Holzer, and Breton, Jacqueline Lamba and their daughter Aube left Martinique, stopping in Guadeloupe, St Thomas, and Santo Domingo. From there Breton and his family sailed

3 Claude Lévi-Strauss, *Tristes Tropiques*, Penguin, London, 1976, p.25.
4 *Ibid.*

to New York, while Lam and Holzer eventually left for Cuba, arriving in late July or early August. During their stay in Martinique, however, there had been a momentous meeting with profound repercussions for the Surrealists, not least Lam himself. Breton managed to get permission to leave the camp to explore the streets of Fort-de-France; chancing to enter a haberdasher's shop, he picked up a local publication on display there. To his astonishment he found himself reading texts that shared the political and aesthetic views of the Surrealists. The voice in this modest journal 'said exactly what needed to be said, not just in the best way but with the greatest force! All those mocking shadows were torn aside and dispersed; all the lies and derision fell in tatters. It was proof that, far from being broken or stifled, here the human voice rose up like the very shaft of light. Aimé Césaire was the name of the one speaking.'[5] The journal was *Tropiques*, its chief animators Césaire and René Ménil, whose sister happened to own the little shop and quickly put Breton in contact with them.

It is not hard to recognise what so moved Breton in Césaire's opening text for the first number of *Tropiques*. It was not so much the totally unexpected references throughout the review to his own poetic universe (Césaire prefaces a poem with Rimbaud's *Je dis qu'il faut être voyant, se faire voyant* (I say one must be a seer, make oneself a seer)), though this counted a lot, but the discovery of a political voice that believed in poetry, an opposition from within on a moral and social as well as aesthetic level to the Vichy regime, which was also a black voice, one that spoke from within the colonised. Even more, it was a voice of vigorous protest, unlike the feeble and masochistic publications Breton had encountered in France in the months preceding his departure. Césaire's text is a passionate protest against a colonial power subservient to Fascism and what he felt was a cultural void: 'A silent and sterile land. I am speaking about ours. And my hearing measures by the Caribbean Sea the terrifying silence of man. Europe. Africa. Asia. I hear screaming steel, drumbeats in the bush, temples praying amidst banyan trees. And I know it is man speaking. But here is the monstrous atrophy of the voice, the age-old exhaustion, the incredible mutism. No city. No art. No poetry.'[6] But, he goes on, 'we are

5 André Breton, 'Martinique charmeuse de serpents: Un grand poète noir', *Tropiques*, no.11, May 1944, p.119.

the kind who refuse the shadow'.[7]

Tropiques is an extraordinary journal, censored by the Vichy regime and thus disguising its political critiques in various ways, publishing incendiary poetry, scientific studies of local flora and fauna, Leo Frobenius on African civilisations, Afro-Cuban folk tales gathered by Lydia Cabrera, poems and texts by Césaire, Breton, Pierre Mabille and Benjamin Péret. There was no sudden adoption of Surrealism, because it was unnecessary for the journal to change its direction in any sense, and with *Tropiques* the Surrealists encountered a movement of a new kind whose championing of the black population and cultures and challenge to colonial, classical French values seemed so unexpectedly to endorse and justify their own intransigent position *vis à vis* European nationalist and colonialist positions. If *Tropiques* was for the Surrealists a guarantee of their position, Césaire was clear about the reciprocal value for him of their support. 'Breton brought us boldness; he cut short our uncertainties. I would say that the meeting with Breton was a confirmation of the truth of what I had discovered by my own reflections.'[8] He also gives the most moving description of Breton not just as poet but as one who sought out poetry: 'He literally fascinated me... he had an *astonishing* sense of poetry. He sensed poetry, he sniffed it, like pollen in the air... A poet... and a philosopher... the meeting with Breton was a VERY IMPORTANT thing for me.'[9]

As Suzanne Césaire wrote in her text in *Tropiques* nos.8 and 9, '1943: Le Surréalisme et nous' (Surrealism and Us), Surrealism was an activity whose dynamism could assist human emancipation: an activity that could 'liberate man by revealing his unconscious assisting the liberation of peoples by clarifying the blind myths that have governed them hitherto'. For *Tropiques,* Martinique was not only a cultural void but a society haunted by memories of slavery and run by a pro-fascist government. 'The arrow of history indicates our human task: a society tainted in its origins by crime, supported at the present time by injustice and hypocrisy,

6 Aimé Césaire, 'Presentation', *Tropiques*, no.1, April 1941, p.5, trans. Michael Richardson and Krzysztof Fijalkowski, in Michael Richardson (ed), *Refusal of the Shadow: Surrealism and the Caribbean*, Verso, London, 1996, p.88.

7 *Ibid.* This phrase inspired the title for the anthology *Refusal of the Shadow*.

8 'Entretien avec Aimé Césaire par Jacqueline Leiner', introduction to the facsimile edition of *Tropiques*, Jean-Michel Place, Paris, 1978, p.V1.

9 *Ibid.*

rendered fearful of its future by bad conscience, must morally, historically, necessarily disappear… And among the powerful war machines that the modern world has placed at our disposal… our audacity has chosen surrealism which offers the best chance of success.'[10]

I have dwelt on *Tropiques* because the ideas of its contributors, the way in which it fostered an evolution, an expansion of Surrealism in new territories, together with the Césaires' and Ménil's ambition to regain black consciousness and pride in African culture, undoubtedly affected Lam's own return to Cuba. Lam's *The Jungle* (1943) and the related paintings from the 1940s could, indeed, be seen as the visual partners to Aimé Césaire's *Retour au pays natal,* which was translated into Spanish by Lydia Cabrera and published in Cuba in 1942 with illustrations by Lam and a preface by the Surrealist poet Benjamin Péret. 'I have the honour to salute a poet, the only great poet of the French language to appear for 20 years. For the first time a tropical voice resounds in our language, not to produce an exotic poetry, ornament of bad taste but an authentic poetry.'[11]

> *Qui et quels nous sommes? Admirable question.*
> *Haïsseurs. Bâtisseurs. Traîtres. Hougans. Hougans surtout.*
> *Car nous voulons tous les démons*
> *ceux d'hier ceux d'aujourd'hui*
> *ceux de carcan ceux de la houe*
> *ceux de l'interdiction du marronnage*
> *et nous n'avons garde d'oublier ceux de négrier*[12]

The recognition and admiration was mutual. Lam is first mentioned in the second issue of *Tropiques,* July 1941; following the welcome to Breton and Masson, Lam is named: 'the astonishing black Cuban painter in whom we meet, at the same time as the best of Picasso's tutelage, Asiatic and African traditions curiously and intelligently mingled'.[13] In February 1943, *Tropiques* nos.6 and 7, there is a more substantial commentary on Lam

10 Suzanne Césaire, '1943: Le Surréalisme et nous', *Tropiques*, nos.8/9, October 1943, p.17, trans. in Richardson, *op. cit.,* p.123.

11 Benjamin Péret, preface to Césaire, *Cahiers d'un retour au pays natal*, Havana, 1943, quoted in *Tropiques*, nos.6/7, February 1943, p.60.

12 Césaire, *Cahiers d'un retour au pays natal*, Paris, 1939, in J.L. Bédouin, *La poésie surréaliste*, Seghers, Paris, 1964, p.107.

by Pierre Loeb, concerning his first solo show in New York at the Pierre Matisse Gallery in November 1942. Loeb locates Lam's work in the context of the long affair of the modern artists with non-Western art, mentioning a dazzling range of works with which he had surrounded himself in Paris: Ivory Coast masks, New Hebrides tree fern carvings, Easter Island fetishes, sculptures from Papua New Guinea. Loeb had met Lam through Picasso, who insisted that he visit the young painter's studio, and tells the following anecdote against himself: needing to make some judgement about the work, he remarked to Picasso: '"he is influenced by negro art." Picasso, furious, replies brusquely: "He has the right, him, He is Black!"'[14]

Lam eventually arrived in Cuba, seven months after leaving Marseilles, in late July 1941. He had brought virtually nothing with him and had to start again from scratch. His first impression on his return to Havana was 'one of terrible sadness... The whole colonial drama of my youth seemed to be reborn in me.'[15] While there were parallels with Martinique, the situation was different in many respects. Cuba was an independent country, not a colony, but had become a playground for the rich, where most Cubans of African descent lived in poverty. Lam was appalled by the conditions, and by the cultural as well as economic forms of exploitation: 'Havana at that time was a land of pleasure, of sugary music, rumbas, mambos and so forth. The negroes were considered *picturesque*.' The absence of respect, the 'trafficking in the dignity of a people is hell'.[16] The bold position of *Tropiques* must have supported him in his chosen direction, which he described in a famous passage from his conversations with Max-Pol Fouchet:

> Poetry in Cuba then was either political and committed, like that of Nicolás Guillén and a few others, or else written for the tourists. The latter I rejected, for it had nothing to do with an exploited people, with a society that crushed and humiliated its slaves. No, I decided that my painting would never be the equivalent of that pseudo-Cuban music

13 'À la Martinique', *Tropiques*, no.2, July 1941, p.77. Lam was at this point on his voyage home to Cuba; *Tropiques* anticipates his return in a vague celebration of Picasso, Asia and Africa. Asiatic is evidently a reference to his Chinese father and has no serious purchase on his work.

14 Pierre [sic], 'Wifredo Lam', *Tropiques*, nos.6/7, February 1943, pp.61–62.

15 Max-Pol Fouchet, *Wifredo Lam*, Poligrafa, Barcelona, 1989, p.187.

16 *Ibid.*

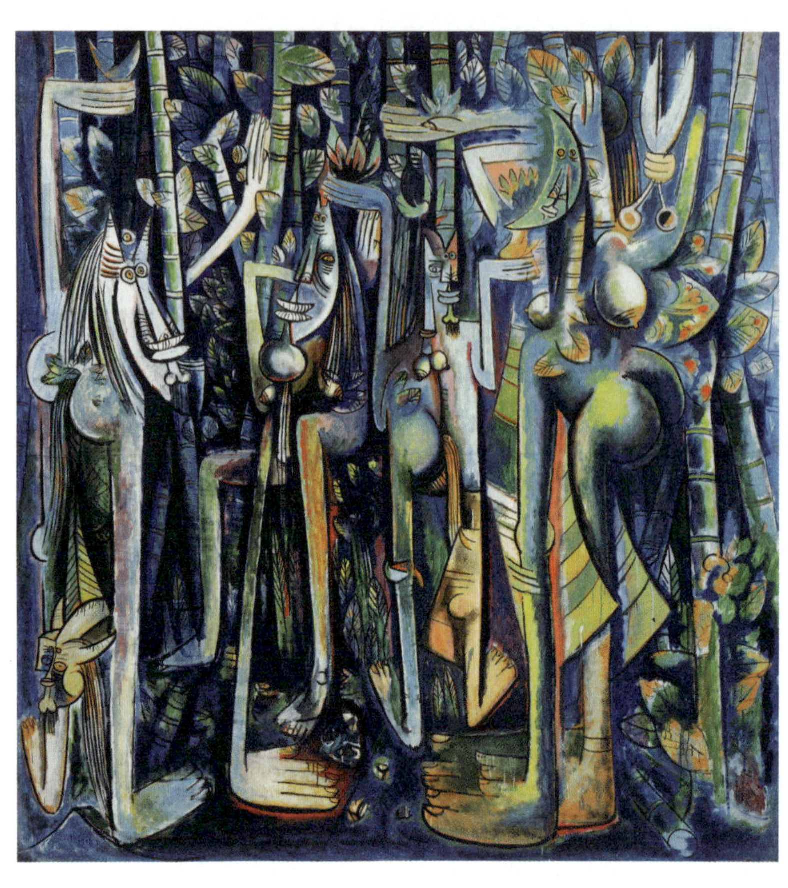

288 **Wifredo Lam**
The Jungle, 1943
Gouache on paper, mounted on canvas
239.4 × 229.9 cm | 94¼ × 90½ in

for nightclubs. I refused to paint cha-cha-cha. I wanted with all my heart to paint the drama of my country, but by thoroughly expressing the negro spirit, the beauty of the plastic art of the blacks. In this way I could act as a Trojan horse that would spew forth hallucinating figures with the power to surprise, to disturb the dreams of the exploiters.[17]

Tropiques is often seen as precursor of *Négritude*, but in fact its chief animators were to take very different stances on this issue. While Césaire became one of its foremost exponents, Ménil was 'one of its more trenchant critics'.[18] For Ménil it became a dangerously reductive political ideology based on an essentialist notion of identity that merely inverted black/white values. Lam's position, while still sympathetic to the poetic uses to which Césaire put *Négritude*, basically agreed with Ménil. Responding to the accusation of 'black racism', Lam replied, 'It's a false accusation. They say that because I don't paint like a European, because I try to paint with the idiosyncrasy of my people. The personages in my paintings are neither white nor black, they lack race. I am not in agreement with the doctrine of négritude either. It is not a matter of race, but of the class struggle.'[19]

Standing out against a vibrant, pulsating canvas of yellows, blues and greens, a blanched, moonlit arm with long fingers gestures towards a group of strange, sometimes menacing, figures, half-hidden among the sugar canes. The raised arm belongs to a character on the left of the painting who is, Lam remarked, 'as if it will experience a revelation at the sight of the other personages in the painting, astonished by the discovery of this whole universe'.[20] The picture in question is, of course, *The Jungle*, celebrated as Lam's masterpiece. He painted it on his return to Cuba, between December 1942 and the beginning of the following year. The

17 *Ibid*, p.192.
18 Michael Richardson, introduction to *Refusal of the Shadow*, p.8, *op. cit.*
19 Mosquera, 'Mi pintura es un acto de descolonización', interview with Wifredo Lam, in *Exploraciones en la plástica cubana*, Havana, 1983, p.189.
20 *Ibid.*, p.182: 'como si encontrara una revelación al ver a estos otros personajes del resto del cuadro, se asombra ante el descubrimiento de todo ese universo.'

'tipo' Lam describes is encountering a revelation, which, he goes on to explain, is that of Caribbean culture: 'It is a symbol of the revelation of our cultural world. Some say this is the first canvas that was painted as a demonstration of the Third World.'[21]

The language Lam uses here echoes that of Césaire, for example at the end of 'Introduction à la poésie nègre américaine' (Introduction to Black American Poetry), where the latter evokes the difference between the felt totality of a people's experience and its representation as spectacle for consumption: 'To create a world – is that a minor thing?... There, where the exotic inhumanity of a junk shop spread out its wares, to make a world appear!'[22] Césaire, like Lam, rejected the picturesque treatment of their common predicament and honours the poet who is not content with presenting the human spectacle 'picturesquely from the outside', but is, rather, 'not above, but among'.

The Jungle frankly quotes Picasso's *Les Demoiselles d'Avignon* (1907), but its reference to Picasso is different from the broadly formal resemblance between Lam's paintings of the late 1930s and Picasso's, with their flattened figures, strong, simplified black outlines, and often mask-like features. *The Jungle* deliberately sets up a dialogue with the *Demoiselles* in which the ambiguity of the latter's subject with its rough overlay of alien heads on the pink bodies of the prostitutes, is transposed into a new tropical setting. The five figures are similarly ranged in shallow relief across the picture surface; the gesture of the one on the left, in the *Demoiselles* (its dark head derived from a primitivist Gauguin) as in *The Jungle,* acknowledges the scene and presents it to the spectators. Lam's figures are also life-size and confront us with a mixture of lewd sexuality and impenetrable ritual masks. A comparison with a celebrated painting by Mario Carreño, *Afro-Cuban Dance* (1943), highlights the differences with Lam's approach. Carreño depicts two figures, a bare-breasted nightclub dancer and a *diablito,* the latter a popular subject in nineteenth-century *costumbrista* paintings. It is the stereotype of an exotic tropical scene to entertain the viewer with a *frisson* of lust and danger. Lam, by contrast,

21 *Ibid.*, p.182: 'Es un símbolo de la revelación de nuestra mundo cultural. Hay quien dice que este es el primer cuadro que está pintado como una demostración del Tercer Mundo.'

22 'Créer un monde est-ce peu de chose?... La où s'étageait l'inhumanité exotique de magasin de bric à brac, faire surgir un monde.' Aimé Césaire, 'Introduction à la poésie nègre américaine', *Tropiques*, no.2, p.42.

confronts the viewer just as Picasso does, with an ambiguous challenge to their expectations.

The transformation of Lam's imagery and style on his return to Cuba involved not so much a rejection of his Paris period as an extraordinary breakthrough in which Surrealist ideas found a wholly original expression. If we compare *Composition (The Three Oranges)*, which he completed in Paris in 1940, with paintings like *The Jungle* and its related studies *The Fascinated Nest* (1944) or *Personnages*, we see a dramatic change in the way in which the paint is applied and the hybrid creatures emerge out of or meld into their settings. In *Composition*, although colour is not naturalistic, it is contained within the severely outlined figures and their internal divisions. (The three oranges, Matisse-like, are pure yellow circles.) In the later paintings, colour is applied in loose streaks, dabs, and washes, or in luminous shifting clouds of bright pigment dusted over the surface. This is not to imply an abstraction or separation of colour from the subject of the paintings, but rather to point to a freeing of the hand, a spontaneity of gesture that seems to be integral to his representation of the world of *orishas* and other personages of the imagination. Lam credited automatism with releasing memories from his Cuban childhood: 'in an automatic manner, as the surrealists say, this world leaked out from me. That is to say, I carried all this in my subconscious, and, letting myself get carried away by automatic painting... this strange world sprang out.'[23]

This loosening of the paint and freedom in the colour rhythms of the surfaces is probably due to the renewed interest in automatism among the Surrealists in the early 1940s. Even in the appalling conditions aboard the *Capitaine Paul-Lemerle,* Breton was absorbed in questions of art and expression. Lévi-Strauss recalled their exchanges of letters 'in which we discussed the relationships between aesthetic beauty and originality'.[24] In Martinique the Surrealists were joined by André Masson, who arrived a few days after the first Marseilles contingent and was, like Breton, bowled over by its tropical beauties; their lyrical 'Creole Dialogue' was published in *Martinique, charmeuse de serpents* ('The liana flower is too slender, too white, to be a star: it could only slip from a sylph's letter. When you manage to make out their forms in their entirety, these lianas – I'm

23 Mosquera, 'Mi pintura', *op. cit*, p.186.
24 Lévi-Strauss, *Tristes Tropiques, op. cit*, p.26.

talking about those that are so upright, so tall – are truly the harp of the earth.'[25]) Masson's paintings and drawings inspired by Martinique were a fervent rediscovery of free and spontaneous gestures, though interestingly his line, as in his earlier automatic drawings, is unlike Lam's: it is nervous and sketchy with abrupt changes in rhythm, while Lam's is usually even and enclosing. On his arrival in New York, Breton immediately published 'Artistic Genesis and Perspective of Surrealism', which reaffirmed the old founding principle of Surrealism, 'pure psychic automatism', but with a new tolerance for an automatism that was not strictly 'pure' (as it had rarely been anyway for the artists):

> Automatism, inherited from the mediums, has remained one of Surrealism's two great directions. Since it is automatism that has aroused, and still arouses, the most violent controversy, it cannot be too late to seek to analyse its function rather more deeply and so try to sway the argument decisively in its favour. Contemporary psychological research has suggested that a comparison can be drawn between the construction of a nest by a bird and the beginning of a melody that is in the process of establishing a definite theme... Without prejudice to the deep individual tensions that graphic and verbal automatism brings to the surface and is to some extent able to resolve, I maintain that it is the only mode of expression which gives full satisfaction to both eye and ear by achieving *rhythmic unity* (just as recognisable in an automatic drawing or text as in a melody or a bird's nest), the only structure that corresponds to the by now widely acknowledged non-differentiation between sympathetic and formal qualities, to the by now widely acknowledged non-differentiation between sensory and intellectual functions... I will concede that it is possible for automatism to enter into the composition of a painting or a poem with a certain degree of premeditation. But the converse holds true that any form of expression in which automatism does not at least advance under cover runs a grave risk of moving out of the Surrealist orbit.[26]

25 Breton and André Masson, 'Creole Dialogue', trans. in Richardson, *op. cit*, p.187.
26 Breton, 'Artistic Genesis and Perspective of Surrealism' (1941), in *Surrealism and Painting*, trans. Simon Watson-Taylor, Icon Editions, London, 1972, p.69.

Over and above the evidence of the paintings and the fact that Breton frequently wrote about Lam, a brief statement by Lam himself, although rather compressed, is an unambiguous expression of his continued commitment to this idea: 'I am not painting for the colours as such but I want my work to give the impression of three dimensions. One of my works represents primitive things of my land in pre-Columbian times. Another is a drawing of rhythm of automatic work in process.'[27]

Awkwardly though Lam's words have been recorded, this phrase that links rhythm to automatism is clearly an echo of Breton's text, while the admission Breton made that automatism could run 'under cover' and coexist with a degree of conscious planning encompasses Lam's own position. When Lam suggests that *The Jungle* was intended to 'communicate a psychic state',[28] his words can be understood in relation to the notion of 'psychic automatism', that is a form of expression, in this case visual, of thoughts outside conscious control.

The ambiguity of what is understood as Surrealist art colours the following important comment by Lam. By the time this interview took place the notion of a 'Surrealist manner' was probably that of Salvador Dalí. 'Surrealism helped me to find an opening but I didn't paint in a surrealist manner although I gave a solution to surrealism. Miró and I renewed surrealism. Here in Cuba there were things that were pure surrealism. For example, Afro-Cuban beliefs; in these you can see poetry preserved in its magical, primitive state.'[29] In claiming to have brought a solution to Surrealism, Lam is stating the truth, and in aligning himself with Miró, it is clearly in the context of automatism, of which in painting Miró was the greatest explorer in the 1920s. Here the problem of 'style' in Surrealism arises. Surrealism was not and never became a visual formula. To the early experiments of the 1920s with automatism, which produced results as brilliant and varied as Miró's blue paintings, Max Ernst's *frottages*,

27 *The Chicago Sun-Times*, 28 September 1958. In 1958, Lam was awarded a fellowship by the Graham Foundation for Advanced Studies in the Fine Arts, one of nine artists, architects and sculptors thus honoured, including the architect and exhibition designer Frederick Kiesler and the Spanish sculptor Eduardo Chillida. The newspaper reported the awards and printed short statements from each artist, 'evaluating the moods or messages they were trying to portray through their creations'.

28 Fouchet, *Wifredo Lam*, *op. cit*, p.202.

29 Mosquera, 'Mi pintura', *op. cit*, p.189.

and Masson's sand paintings, were added the hyperrealist dreams of Dalí and new procedures such as the construction of Surrealist objects with readymade and found materials. Now Lam was to look for his own visual deployment of the Surrealist notion of 'psychic spontaneity' in the context of the poetry of Afro-Cuban religions.

More than any other painter associated with the Surrealist movement, Lam merged through painting hitherto unrelated ideas, images and belief systems. When Breton said that 'in the case of Lam, we are concerned as never before with *painting*,'[30] he may have had in mind the fact that the visible expressions of Afro-Cuban culture and Santería beliefs had previously involved very little in the way of two-dimensional, pictorial imagery. Painting as such was an original mode in this context. Although Catholic pictures of, say, Santa Barbara or Saint James may have been absorbed into the syncretic Afro-Cuban religion, it was three-dimensional figures, attributes, and paraphernalia that largely dominated its palpable manifestations. In other words, there was no indigenous pictorial tradition for Lam to discover and adopt on his return to Cuba. The situation was similar in relation to voodoo in Haiti; here, the priest/artist Hector Hyppolite was 'the first ever to record actual voodoo scenes and divinities'.[31] Breton met Hyppolite at the Centre d'Art in Port-au-Prince, and asked him what he thought of Lam's paintings, then in the process of being hung for an exhibition. Hyppolite 'affirmed a vigorous and deferential interest in them while still retaining a slight air of reserve because in his view it was "Chinese magic" rather than the "African magic" which was, he implied, his own province of knowledge.'[32] It was not the difference, I would argue, between voodoo and Santería that caused Hyppolite's reservation, but the specific character of Lam's painting. Hyppolite, in his paintings, clearly seeks to convey information about the orishas, their powers, associated rituals, and symbols in the unprecedented form of two-dimensional representations. His paintings, which have initiated an extensive pictorial tradition in Haiti, are primarily concerned with representing the deities or spirits and possibly in the

30 Breton, 'Wifredo Lam: The long nostalgia of poets...' (1941), in *Surrealism and Painting*, *op. cit*, p.171.

31 Breton, 'Hector Hyppolite' (1947), in *Surrealism and Painting*, *op. cit*, p.311.

32 *Ibid.*

process making of them icons. Lam draws on a similar body of belief and its material expression, but in quite different interests, and, moreover, his sources are not exclusively from the Afro-Caribbean world, but include Africa itself, Mesoamerica, Melanesia, not to speak of European art with which he was familiar. Lam's paintings constitute a multiple, complex imagery that has the power to convey contradictory meanings, to encompass satire and humour as well as politics. It is far both from the religious interests of Hyppolite and from simply revelling in the mysteries and marvels of a 'primitive' world.

What struck Hyppolite as strange, foreign, about Lam (he probably said 'Chinese magic' because he knew Lam's father was Chinese) was the extreme remoteness, even exoticism, of his representations of Afro-Caribbean deities or 'spirit-powers'. They were present but in quite another context from that with which he was familiar, and this context is a visual language in which poetry and the unconscious, the core of Surrealism, are the key concerns. Hyppolite was a *houngan*, Lam was not. Familiar as he was with the ceremonies and objects associated with his country's most widespread (if occasionally censored and suppressed) religious practices, he was not a practitioner. Like the Surrealists, he took a relaxed attitude to the contradictions in their position, of trying to combine dialectical materialism with a defence of superstition and magic. Lam explored the poetic as well as the political in his paintings. Speaking of the presence of the symbol of Shango, God of Thunder, in *The Eternal Presence* (1944), Lam said, 'This is exceptional in my painting, for I do not usually employ a specific symbology. I have never created my pictures in terms of a symbolic tradition, but always on the basis of a poetic excitation. I believe in poetry. For me it is the great conquest of mankind. Revolution, for instance, is a poetic creation. I say everything through the pictorial image.'[33]

Lam's hybrid figures and creatures first appear consistently in the drawings he made for Breton's long poem *Fata Morgana* in Marseilles in 1940–41. The longhaired woman with stars in her hair, shield-headed birds, hammer-headed humans, a bat woman, which echo the imagery of the poem, are all drawn in a clear clean line. This striking ability to

33 Fouchet, *Wifredo Lam*, *op. cit.*, p.208.

outline imaginary, dream-like beings so confidently is related to several of the Marseilles experiences: the heraldic style of the alternative playing cards produced by the group, *Le jeu de Marseille*; the drawing game of *cadavre exquis;* and also probably the composite creations of Victor Brauner, human-animal or androgynous, influenced by alchemy and hermetic traditions. Some features that appear regularly in the Cuba paintings figure here for the first time, such as the curious bony appendage suspended from the lips of the mask-heads, from the end of which hair sprouts. To the unusual juxtapositions of these drawings Lam added from the rich sources of material transformations he encountered in Cuba: the shell lips and eyes, for instance, typical of the heads of Eleggua.[34] In *Personnages*, what appear to be the heads of Eleggua are linked and reversible, recalling both the sacred twins of Haitian voodoo and the reversible half-length figures of the court pictures in playing cards. Frequently elements in Lam's paintings are, like Freudian dream objects, 'over-determined' – that is, they are inscribed with many meanings and associations. The scissors, for example, in *The Jungle*: pairs of scissors are sometimes lashed, open, to magic bottles. Sharp and dangerous, they are also anthropomorphic, with four 'limbs', and form part of a system of symmetries and oppositions characteristic of Santería and voodoo.[35] But in Lam's painting they also clearly have an aggressive, castrative implication familiar to the psychoanalytically informed Surrealist. Lam also continued to draw on a wide range of 'first nation' sculptures, not least the grand New Guinea carvings so dear to the Surrealists and of which he possessed a fine collection. The reference to the indigenous, pre-Columbian cultures of the Caribbean is also intriguing and reflects the serious scholarly interest of Surrealists like his friend Péret.

The freedom to transpose and fragment, to construct scenarios which can combine humour and magic, springs from Lam's re-invention of

34 See Julia P. Herzberg, 'The Development of a Style and a World View, The Havana Years 1941–1952', in *Wifredo Lam and his Contemporaries 1938–1952*, exhibition catalogue, The Studio Museum in Harlem, New York, NY, 1992, for a more detailed discussion of his Santería references and relationship with Lydia Cabrera; also Dennis Moreno, *Cuando los Orichas se vistieron*, Havana, 2002.

35 See Donald J. Cosentino, *The Sacred Arts of Haitian Vodou*, UCLA Fowler Museum of Cultural History, Los Angeles, CA, 1995, p.307, and Alex Farquharson and Leah Gordon, *Kafou: Haitian Art and Vodou*, Nottingham Contemporary, Nottingham, 2012.

Surrealism. If he was able, unlike the Surrealists themselves or Picasso, to speak from within the culture of the African Caribbean, he was not restricted to it. Like Césaire, he could be both defender and challenger of the Third World, speaking from within and without.

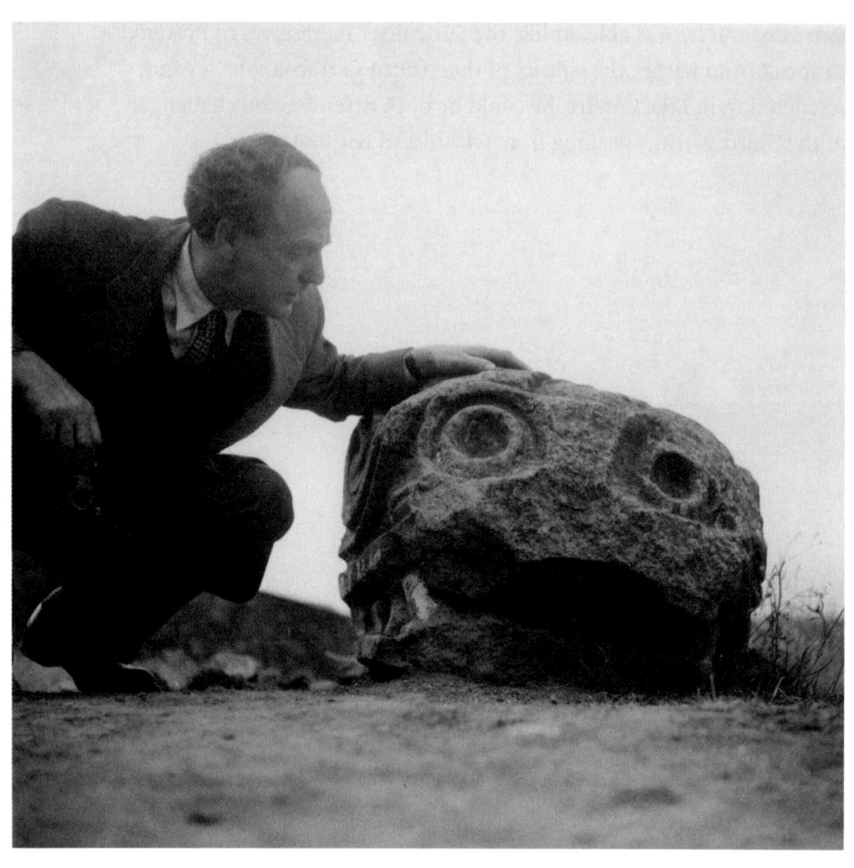

 Henry Moore in Teotihuacán, Mexico, c.1953

'A new friendship between art and anthropology': Henry Moore, Surrealism and Mexico

Henry Moore and the Classic Canon of Modern Sculpture, Kremlin Museums, Moscow, 2012, first published in Russian

Henry Moore's involvement in the Surrealist movement during the 1930s is well known, as is his admiration for the sculpture of pre-conquest America, especially Mexican.[1] This essay explores the ways in which these two aspects of his work are linked, which involves a discontinuous history but a long-lasting thematic continuity. My starting point is Moore's presence in the journal *DYN*, published in Mexico between 1942 and 1944 by the Austrian artist Wolfgang Paalen. This marked the end of Moore's formal association with Surrealism. Paalen, who had been active in Paris before the war and was a close friend of the Surrealist leader André Breton, had just publicly seceded from the movement. But *DYN* is also one of the high points in the long history of the Surrealists' engagement with pre-Columbian and First Nations art, with its anthropological and aesthetic perspectives.[2] The magazine brought together contemporary and what it called 'Amerindian' art, and was the mouthpiece for a significant grouping of post-Surrealist poets and artists in exile in the war years.[3] There were some interesting connections with Moore beyond the journal itself: Paalen's close friend and collaborator the English artist Gordon

1 See Christa Lichtenstern, 'Henry Moore and Surrealism', *Burlington Magazine*, vol.123, no.944, November 1981, and Barbara Braun, 'Henry Moore and pre-Columbian art', *Res*, nos.17/18, 1989.

2 Paalen and his wife, the artist Alice Rahon, left Europe, anticipating the war to come and settled in Mexico in 1939, having travelled to British Columbia to research and collect First Nations art. Rahon was a close friend of Valentine Penrose, Roland Penrose's first wife, then living in London. Her poems were published in *DYN*.

3 These included Gordon Onslow Ford and the Peruvian poet César Moro. Other Surrealists in exile in Mexico – Péret, Remedios Varo, Leonora Carrington, Kati Horna – remained on good terms despite Paalen's 'theoretical' break with Surrealism.

Onslow Ford, also then in Mexico, had bought Moore's elmwood *Reclining Figure* (1939) for £300, which enabled Moore to buy the house in Perry Green, Hertfordshire, where he lived for the rest of his life. As he wrote to Paalen, who was concerned about his safety, with England under bombardment at the height of the war: 'I am pleased to say that I am able to go on working all right. It has been difficult in the last year or so to have the proper facilities and conditions for making sculpture so I have been obliged to do more drawing and painting, but here at our new country address I am now converting an outhouse into a studio and am looking forward to making sculpture again soon, I hope.'[4] Paalen urged Moore to escape war-torn Europe and come to Mexico,[5] but it was only long after, in 1953, that Moore finally made his one and only trip to the country whose history and art so fascinated him.

The conjunction of anthropology, archaeology and modern art has a rich and contentious history in the twentieth century. As Moore said later, the 'new friendship... between art and anthropology has been of fundamental importance to twentieth-century art.'[6] The Surrealists by no means had exclusive rights to this 'new friendship', but it is fair to say that in their magazines and exhibitions and those of artists and writers linked to Surrealism or moving in its orbit, many of the fundamental issues concerning the relationship between the West and its others were explored, and the revaluation of so-called primitive art, which had a fundamental impact on the aesthetic and cultural assumptions of the West, was debated and championed. The problems of using this term 'Primitive art' have long haunted critics, historians and artists. Moore himself said in his essay of that title, 'The term "Primitive Art" is generally used to include the products of a great variety of races and periods in history, many different social and religious systems. In its widest sense it seems to cover most of those cultures which are outside European and the great Oriental civilizations. This is the sense in which I shall use it here, though I do not much like the application of the word "primitive" to art...'[7] Without denying the unavoidable and virtually unconscious

4 *DYN*, no.2, 1942, back page.
5 Paalen to Moore, letter 19 July 1942, Henry Moore Foundation, Perry Green.
6 Philip James, *Henry Moore on Sculpture: A Collection of the Sculptor's Writings and Spoken Words*, Macdonald, London, 1966 p.201.

colonialist and even racist attitudes of the time, there is, as artist Susan Hiller has said, a positive and optimistic register to the 'discoveries' made by artists like Picasso, Moore, Jacob Epstein, Constantin Brancusi, Alberto Giacometti and so on, for they also mark the dissolution of cultural boundaries and acceleration of cultural influences, and 'prefigure and enable the increasing hybridisation of Western culture.'[8]

Moore's engagement with Surrealism had various different aspects, which, while not exactly contradictory, deserve clarification. The most striking is the fact that, while there is no question of his active membership of the movement between 1936 and c.1942, there is no dramatic change in the appearance of his sculptures. The rhythm of his creative development remained quite consistent, with its own internal pulses and counterpoints – the relationship between the 'abstract' and the 'figurative', for example. Not only does this mean that with one or two exceptions his affiliation made little visible change to his sculpture in the 1930s (although there was a change in his drawings), but the corollary is also true – that whatever the aspect of his art was that linked it to Surrealism, was not contained within this period but began earlier and continued throughout his life. Moore himself affirmed that Surrealism had been a liberating force with a lasting influence.[9] But it was on Moore's terms.

One point needs clarification: Surrealism never tried to impose and can never be identified with any particular style in the visual arts. It is therefore a mistake to pick out 'Surrealist' elements in Moore's work in terms of stylistic quirks or mannerisms adopted from Surrealism. In this sense Surrealism is different from the other 'isms' of modern Art, from Cubism, Futurism and Purism, for example, which can be recognised and categorised according to a particular range of visual characteristics. Surrealism for many reasons cannot be adequately accounted for in a similar way, both because it extended more broadly into other areas of activity (could, as is often said, be described as a way of life rather than an art) and also because the emphasis was on the process (of writing,

7 Henry Moore, 'Primitive Art', *The Listener*, 24 April 1941, pp.598–99 in Alan Wilkinson, *Henry Moore Writings and Conversations*, Lund Humphries, London, 2002, p.102.

8 Susan Hiller, '"Truth" and "Truth to material": Reflecting on the sculptural legacy of Henry Moore', in Jane Beckett and Fiona Russell (eds), *Henry Moore: Critical Essays*, Ashgate, Burlington, VT, 2003.

9 Lichtenstern, *op.cit.*, p.645.

drawing, speaking, painting) rather than the final expression. Surrealism was an invitation to explore, to find ways of tapping into the unconscious, of trapping dreams; it appealed to chance in order to escape clichés and conventions; it celebrated surprise, the direct, the spontaneous, and the works of children, the mad and the primitive, which surpassed the polite cultural fashions of the West. There was no given means of doing any of these things. Artists aspiring to be part of the Surrealist adventure when it began in 1924 were launching into the unknown: André Masson's automatic drawings, Max Ernst's collages with their startling juxtapositions, Joan Miró's free washes of paint, Man Ray's 'cameraless' photographs with direct imprints of objects – all are part of Surrealism. In a sense artists are self-defined as Surrealist – or suddenly find themselves so defined, like Eileen Agar or Frida Kahlo.[10] Moore articulated his comment on the unconscious origin of some drawings in terms, broadly, of the Surrealist concept of automatism, but although it was made at the height of his Surrealist involvement, in 1937, it could just as easily apply to his work before and after:

> The violent quarrel between the abstractionists and the surrealists seems to me quite unnecessary. All good art has contained both abstract and surrealist elements, just as it has contained both classical and romantic elements – order and surprise, intellect and imagination, conscious and unconscious. Both sides of the artist's personality must play their part. And I think the first inception of a painting or a sculpture may begin from either end. As far as my own experience is concerned, I sometimes begin a drawing with no preconceived problem to solve, with only the desire to use pencil on paper, and make lines, tones and shapes with no conscious aim; but as my mind takes in what is so produced, a point arrives where some idea becomes conscious and crystallises, and the control and ordering begin to take place.[11]

10 Eileen Agar was invited by Read and Penrose to exhibit at the *International Exhibition of Surrealism* in London in 1936, thereby becoming 'overnight a Surrealist', in her words. Frida Kahlo was admired and written about by André Breton when he saw her work on his visit to Mexico in 1938.

11 Moore, 'The Sculptor Speaks, *The Listener*, 18 August 1937, in James, *op.cit.*, p.67.

For Moore, it was natural to align himself with the artistic and intellectual group in England whose politics and tastes he shared. The public side of Moore's affiliation with Surrealism is relatively straightforward. He was a member of the 'English Committee' of the *International Surrealist Exhibition* in London in 1936, together with Hugh Sykes Davies, David Gascoyne, Humphrey Jennings, Rupert Lee, Paul Nash, Roland Penrose (who was Honorary Treasurer) and Herbert Read. He was already an old friend of fellow Yorkshireman Herbert Read, the intellectual leader of the group, who had written the introduction to the catalogue for the *Unit One* exhibition in 1934. Both Moore and the artist Paul Nash had been part of Unit One, a grouping significant for understanding Surrealism in England. As Nash wrote in a letter to *The Times* quoted by Read, the 11 artists concerned were various and individual, but had in common a commitment to 'a truly contemporary spirit' in painting, sculpture and architecture.[12] Not all were abstract artists, but all championed modernism against a generally regressive conservatism in the visual arts in the UK, where fidelity to nature was still the yardstick.

Moore exhibited four sculptures and three drawings at the International Surrealist Exhibition and two sculptures at the *Surrealism* exhibition organised by the Cambridge University Arts Society in 1937. Benjamin Péret, in the preface to the Cambridge exhibition, evoked Moore in the following words: '...the horizon bristling with Henry Moore's figures, who menace the heavens with sexual fists...[13] In the same year Moore contributed his *Object to Hold* to the London Gallery exhibition *Surrealist Objects and Poems* – to which I will return. Moore, like his Surrealist colleagues, was prominent in anti-fascist manifestoes, demonstrations and protests. He had taken part in the Artists International Association (AIA) exhibition, *Artists Against Fascism and War*, in 1935, which followed the shift of the AIA away from being an organ of the Communist Party to a broader Popular Front organisation. He signed the Surrealist Declaration on Spain in 1936, protesting against the Franco rebellion, and continued to campaign in support of the Republican cause in the

12 Herbert Read (ed), 'Introduction', *Unit 1 The Modern Movement in English Architecture, Painting and Sculpture*, Cassell, London, 1934, p.10.

13 Benjamin Péret, 'Preface', *Exhibition of Surrealism*, exhibition catalogue, Cambridge University Arts Society, Gordon Fraser's Gallery, Cambridge, 1937.

Civil War. A manifesto of 1937, *We Ask Your Attention*, which attacked the non-intervention policy of the Western nations, had a drawing by Moore overprinted on the front. This manifesto was published at the time of the First British Artists' Congress and accompanying exhibition organised by the AIA. The huge exhibition of almost one thousand works was a 'mass demonstration by and gathering of everyone engaged in the political struggle against the suppression of culture'.[14] Three juries were appointed to select the works, for Surrealism, abstraction, and a Working Men's Group. Moore, with Roland Penrose and Paul Nash, was one of the group selecting works for the Surrealist section, including a special category of sculpture.

Works by Moore, like *Composition* of 1934, with their 'decomposed' elements, draw fruitfully on two distinct sculptural practices in Surrealism: on the one hand the biomorphic carvings of Jean (Hans) Arp, which included 'Human Concretions', organic forms often photographed lying in the grass, and also works with movable or separated parts, like *Head with Annoying Objects* (1930); on the other hand Giacometti's plasters, like *Reclining Woman Who Dreams* (1929), *Suspended Ball* (c.1930) or *Project for a Passage* (1932). Moore melds them into his own distinctive formal language, which although pre-dating his affiliation with the Surrealists naturally aligned him with them. A photograph of the 1936 *International Surrealist Exhibition* in London shows Moore's *Figure* of 1934 in front of one of Hans Bellmer's photographs of his dismembered, polymorphous doll, so shot as to confuse the two in a thoroughly disturbing way.

Despite collecting and studying things from the natural world – pebbles, bones, shells, branches – Moore never made objects in the Surrealist sense, preferring to stick to what Salvador Dalí described, in his text launching the 'Surrealist object' in 1931, as 'the means proper to sculpture'.[15] This was how Dalí referred to Giacometti's *Suspended Ball*, which otherwise corresponded to his definition of the 'surrealist object functioning symbolically'. Such objects, in Dalí's view, had to be constructed of found and readymade things rather than created using stone, plaster, wood. The 'dumb, mobile objects' Giacometti presented in the same issue of *Le Surréalisme au service de la révolution* (Surrealism in

14 Michel Rémy, *Surrealism in Britain*, Ashgate, Aldershot, 1999, p.109.

15 Salvador Dalí, 'Objets surréalistes', *Le Surréalisme au service de la révolution*, no.3, 1931, p.16.

support of the revolution), are, like *Suspended Ball*, aggressive, suggestive and heavily inflected by the primitive. Henry Moore knew Giacometti in Paris, though by the time he joined the Surrealist movement Giacometti had left it. But Moore's friend Roland Penrose owned one of Giacometti's dumb mobile objects, the wooden *Disagreeable Object (To be Disposed Of)* (1931), which used to lie around on a low table inviting one to pick it up. Its function was symbolic rather than utilitarian, and it occupies a kind of disturbing *terrain vague* between sculpture and the everyday. Moore's *Object to Hold* belongs in this category, and is the nearest Moore came to the 'Surrealist object'; it was included in the section of 'Constructed Objects' in the London Gallery exhibition *Surrealist Objects and Poems* of 1937, Moore's only contribution. (Irina Moore exhibited a 'Natural Object'). There are many possible ways of reading the sculpture *Three Points* (1939–40), but one would be as the counterpart of the *Object to Hold* with connections to Giacometti's *Point to the Eye* (1932). Its violence is understandable in relation to the declaration of war against Germany in September 1939.

After the war, a reconstituted Surrealist group in England attacked Moore and Herbert Read in a 'Declaration' published in the catalogue of the exhibition *Le Surréalisme en 1947*, which was held at Galerie Maeght in Paris: Read's eclecticism had reached monstrous proportions, while Moore had forfeited any right to call himself a Surrealist because of his 'fabrication d'ornements sacerdotaux' (fabrication of priestly ornaments).[16] The Surrealists' horror of the Church was deep rooted and Moore's acceptance of the commission to carve a Madonna and Child for the Church of St Matthew in Northampton put him beyond the pale.

But by then for many of those who had joined Surrealism in the 1920s and 1930s it had lost its immediacy and relevance, and there was a sense that it was necessary to move on, to find a new reason for making art. DYN, in which Moore featured prominently, is an interesting mouthpiece and showcase for this moment. In the first issue, Paalen published a 'Farewell au surréalisme', in which he paid homage to Surrealism's essential contribution, its heroic ambition to create a synthesis between

16 'Declaration du groupe surréaliste en Angleterre', *Le Surréalisme en 1947*, Galerie Maeght, Paris, 1947. The only signatories left from the founding group from 1936 were Penrose and E.L.T. Mesens.

art and poetry, and poetry and life, but argued that its theoretical base in dialectical materialism was untenable and that it was time to move on. 'I am convinced that the great surrealist poets and painters will continue to create essential works but I no longer believe that it is Surrealism that will be able to determine the position of the artist in the world today nor to formulate objectively art's *raison d'être*'[17] Paalen's own painting was an attempt to visualise the dynamic physical forces in the universe revealed by science. In DYN, Moore is in the company of an international array of artists who, Paalen clearly felt, belonged to the future, but who also had undeniable links to the Surrealist past. They included Alexander Calder, Robert Motherwell, Jackson Pollock, David Smith, William Baziotes, Carlos Mérida, Alice Paalen (Rahon) and Gordon Onslow Ford. Moore, whose *Drawing for Metal Sculpture: Two Heads* (1939) was reproduced in DYN, no.2, in 1942, is entirely at home in this company of artists whose work at this period occupies a loose borderland of abstraction, of considerable expressive power and not afraid of some degree of figuration. As well as *Two Heads*, the lead and wire sculpture *The Bride* (1939–40) and a pastel *Reclining Figure* were reproduced in DYN no.2; *String Figure no.4 (Mother and Child)* (1938),[18] a *Reclining Figure* and two recent drawings including the important 1939 *Two Figures (drawing for metal and wood sculpture)* in no.3 in 1942; and in the final issue, no.6 in 1944, *Two Figures (drawing for wood sculpture)* (1940). His influence, interestingly, is felt strongly by the final issue of DYN: in the drawings by Alexander Calder and in Onslow Ford's painting *The Marriage* of 1944, which depicts biomorphic and mechanical forms linked by rows of strings or wires.

Paalen and Moore shared more than a belief in the essential value of art in the modern world. Paalen also had a passionate interest in both First Nations art from British Colombia and in pre-Columbian art and architecture, and DYN contains some of the most important research at the time in both fields.[19] There are magnificent photographs of Haida

17 Wolfgang Paalen, 'Farewell au surréalisme', DYN, no.1, 1942, p.26.

18 Then in the possession of Mrs Edward Wadsworth. The version in lead and string now at the Henry Moore Foundation is titled *Stringed Mother and Child* (1938).

19 Paalen published 'Paysage totemique' (Totemic landscape), 'Totem Art' and 'Rencontre totemique' (Totemic encounter), inspired by the work of the anthropologist Franz Boas and based on his own field trip to British Columbia in 1938, in DYN, nos.1–6. No.4/5 was a special Amerindian issue.

wood carvings, huge totem poles from the North-West Coast of America, Olmec giant heads and jade figurines; they form extraordinary visual counterparts to the works by contemporary artists – Moore's drawings 'for sculpture' in particular taking on a scale and grandeur by the juxtaposition. But there is no suggestion of direct influence. The material on the North-West Coast First Nations art and on Mesoamerican and Andean art and architecture is there primarily for its own sake, not as sources for contemporary artists to plunder. Comparisons can be made but are not insisted upon.

At the same time that Paalen was publishing *DYN*, the Surrealist poet Benjamin Péret, also a refugee in Mexico City, was gathering material for his anthology of myths and legends from all over the Americas. It was a work of painstaking scholarship but his fundamental purpose was to show their poetic quality. The Surrealists' interest in the art, the architecture and the literatures of Ancient America had both anthropological and poetic strands, but it was fuelled always by a sense of the poverty of Western culture and the 'failure of Western beauty'.[20]

Modern artists, Roger Fry wrote, had started to look to Aztec and Maya sculpture for inspiration, one result 'of the general aesthetic awakening which has followed on the revolt against the tyranny of the Greco-Roman tradition.'[21] For Moore, recognition that the ideal of Greece was not only outdated but peripheral, gave him the sense of rejoining a wider sculptural world: 'the realistic idea of physical beauty in art which sprang from fifth-century Greece was only a digression from the main world tradition of sculpture, whilst, for instance, our own equally European Romanesque and Early Gothic are in the main line.'[22] On a drawing of 1926 he scribbled: 'Development of sculpture from now/not back to Maillol & archaic Greek/& modelling.'[23]

Moore's independent discovery of the sculpture in the Ethnographic Room at the British Museum in London, his research in books on Mexican art and his thoughtful interrogation of what he perceived as its special

20 Paalen, 'Paysage totemique', *DYN*, no.1, 1942, p.48.

21 Roger Fry, 'Ancient American Art, *Burlington Magazine*, 1918, in Roger Fry, *Vision and Design*, Chatto and Windus, London, 1920, p.92.

22 Henry Moore.

23 Ann Garrould (ed), *Henry Moore, Complete Drawings 1916–29*, vol.1, Henry Moore Foundation, Perry Green, and Lund Humphries, London, 1996, p.139.

qualities and their relevance for himself carried him on to a parallel track with the Surrealists. In the British Museum, the Ethnographical Room 'contained an inexhaustible wealth and variety of sculptural achievements (Negro, Oceanic Islands, and North and South America), but overcrowded and jumbled together like junk in a marine stores, so that after hundreds of visits I would still find carvings not discovered there before... Of works from the Americas, Mexican art was exceptionally well represented.'[24] This was a consequence of the English explorers and archaeologists who had brought back their treasures in the nineteenth and early twentieth centuries from the major Mesoamerican sites. Like many of his Surrealist comrades, Moore collected pre-Columbian art but not on the scale of Breton, Paul Éluard and Paalen. His fascination with pre-conquest American sculpture dates from the early 1920s, before his awareness of Surrealism:

> Mexican sculpture, as soon as I found it, seemed to me true and right, perhaps because I at once hit on similarities in it with some eleventh-century carvings I had seen as a boy on Yorkshire churches. Its 'stoniness', by which I mean its truth to material, its tremendous power without loss of sensitiveness, its astonishing variety and fertility of form-invention and its approach to a full three-dimensional conception of form, make it unsurpassed in my opinion by any other period of stone sculpture.[25]

Both drawings and carvings testify to his close attention to Mexican sculpture, whether seen reproduced in books or in the collections of the Musée du Trocadéro in Paris or the Ethnographic Room at the British Museum. The blocky forms of the 1922 *Mother and Child*, draws on the British Museum's seated man as well as Tlazolteotl giving birth; the sinuous and compact curves of Moore's *Snake* (1924) has Aztec 'Coiled Serpent' ancestors; masks are related to those of the Aztecs and earlier civilisations such as Teotihuacán and Tula; simplified animal forms look both to Mexico and to the sculpture of Henri Gaudier-Brzeska.[26]

24 Moore, 'Primitive Art', *op. cit.*, p.104.
25 *Ibid.*
26 See Braun, *op. cit.* for a fuller survey of Moore's borrowing from Mexican art.

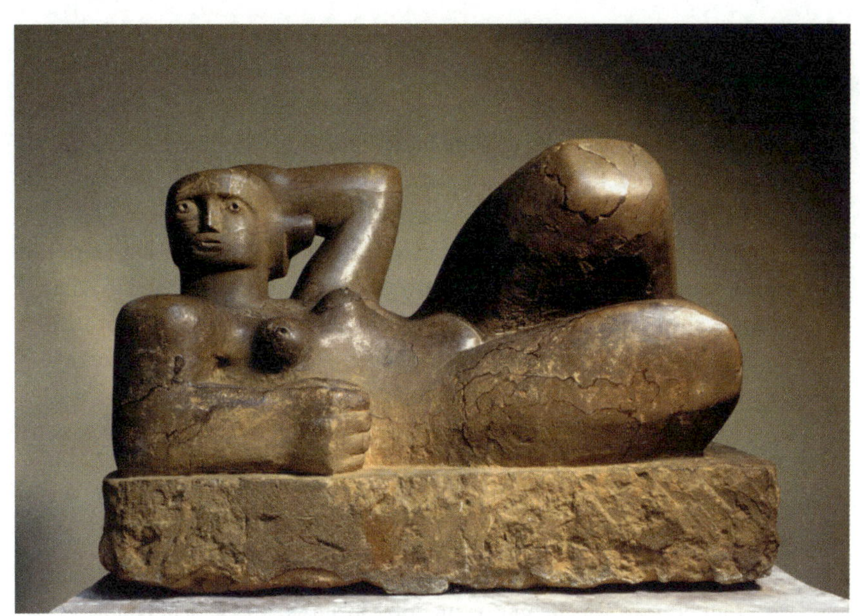

Henry Moore
Reclining Figure, 1929
Brown Hornton stone
Length: 83.8 cm | 33 in

The extraordinarily alert, possibly alarmed figure of *Girl with Clasped Hands* (1930) has a resemblance to the Toltec and Aztec 'standard-bearer', but also, unusually for Moore, has been given coloured eyes, the whites created by chipping at the alabaster, and most surprisingly inset red stones for pupils. This practice of adding paint or some other material like shell or pearl to the features of a face was widespread in Oceanic as well as Mexican sculpture. However, it is extremely rare for Moore; whether or not he was aware that most of the now-bare stone was once covered in paint, jewels, shell, coral and so on, when he writes about Mexican sculpture it is its stoniness and austerity he emphasises, which obviously spoke to the modern artist's pursuit of 'truth to materials'.

Mexican sculpture played a truly vital role in Moore's early career, as he commented in 1947:

> For six months after my return [from Italy, 1924] I was never more miserable in my life. Six months exposure to the master works of European art which I saw on my trip had stirred up a violent conflict with my previous ideals. ...I found myself helpless and unable to work. Then gradually I began to find my way out of my quandary in the direction of my earlier interests. I came back to ancient Mexican art at the British Museum. I came across an illustration of the Chacmool discovered at Chichen Itza in a german [sic] publication – and its curious reclining posture attracted me – not lying on its side, but on its back with its head twisted around.[27]

The chacmool was fundamental to one of Moore's recurrent themes, the reclining figure, and makes its imposing presence clear in the 1929 *Reclining Figure*. The exact date of his 'discovery' is unclear, because as early as 1922 he made two tiny sketches of a reclining figure on a rectangular base which undoubtedly suggest a chacmool. But perhaps it had not hitherto made the impact on him that was produced by the stark contrast with the recently seen 'masterpieces of European art'.

The chacmool is a generic stone-carved figure on a rectangular base that typically was positioned at the entrance to a temple. Common at the

27 James, *op. cit.*, p.42.

time of the Aztec, it seems to have originated in the Valley of Mexico with the Toltecs of Tula though one of its most famous examples is from the Maya city of Chichen Itza in the Yucatan, which at one period became a 'Tula in the East'. The statue was intimately concerned with sacrifice; the figure half-lying on its back holds a bowl on its stomach which was to hold the blood of the victim, human or animal. It is not itself a deity, but a warrior, and the examples from Tula and Chichen Itza have carved on the chest the butterfly symbol that indicated the dead hero. The squared headdress and earpieces typical of most examples of the chacmool enhance the abrupt twist of the head and its frontal stare at those who would see it from the base of the pyramid steps.

Unlike Roger Fry, but like the Surrealists, Moore far preferred Aztec sculpture to that of the Maya. The British Museum had extensive collections from Mesoamerica covering civilisations over two thousand years, but the long and complex history of the pre-Spanish world tended to get condensed into an opposition between the Maya, who, because they had a script, and their sculpture was relatively naturalistic, were regarded as 'civilised', and the Mexica or 'Aztecs', who were not, primarily because they were identified with the practice of heart sacrifice. Moore admired Aztec sculpture for its 'truth to materials', which encompassed its often grim subject matter.

> Toltec sculpture is the connecting link between Mayan (which is mostly in relief and highly decorative) & Aztec sculpture. Toltec is rather florid & conventionalised. Aztec sculpture became more & more a style of its own and very distinct from Mayan. It reflects the character of the Aztecs in its rigorous simplicity, power, almost fierceness. I prefer Mexican to Mayan sculpture. Mexican stone sculptures have largeness of scale, and a grim, sublime austerity, a real stoniness. They were true sculptors in sympathy with their material & their sculptures have some of the character of mountains, of boulders, rocks and sea-worn pebbles."[28]

28 Moore, 'Mexican Sculpture', this passage from the otherwise unpublished notes is in Wilkinson, *op. cit.*, 2002, p.97.

Although Moore writes largely about the formal qualities of the sculpture he admires from other times and other periods – the wonderful phrases 'form-invention' and 'form-knowledge' recur – he was also curious about the civilisations that made them. No one whose attention was caught by Aztec art in the 1920s could have been unaware of its fearsome and bloody reputation for human sacrifice. Reaction to this among artists and intellectuals was varied and, taken in conjunction with the challenge to Western aesthetics posed by objects like the chacmools, throws an interesting light on the new 'friendship between art and anthropology'. Sculptor Leon Underwood, who gave life-drawing classes at the Brook Green School attended by Moore, remained in contact with the young sculptor, publishing prints by him in the journal *The Island* in 1931. Underwood was passionately interested in and collected primitive art, African and Mexican, and in 1928 went to Mexico. His satirical drawing of a chacmool with sacrificial victim reminds us that the subject matter of much Mexican sculpture was not wholly over-ridden by its formal qualities. When Moore drafted an essay about Mexican sculpture, probably intended for a student or colleague at some time in the early-mid 1920s, he took a cool view of human sacrifice and very interestingly deflected the practice on to sculpture itself.

> The Religion of Ancient Mexico from our point was perhaps cruel. Human sacrifice played a large part in their ritual. They had numerous gods and goddesses. When for any reason a new likeness of a god or goddess was wanted, the Mexican sculptors were separated alone away from the rest of the people, given food enough to last them till the work was done, and at the end of the set period they were brought out & the priests chose the one they thought the best and the rest were destroyed.[29]

Taking on the known fact that sculptors were professionals in the Aztec world, as the early Spanish commentators like Fray Durán and Bernardino de Sahagún had recorded, and unlike what was known of African sculpture, where it was assumed that its makers were anonymous and

29 Moore, 'Mexican Sculpture' manuscript, Henry Moore Foundation, Perry Green.

undifferentiated, Moore identifies with this unusual form of commission, and the idea of destroying the unsuccessful images seems unconsciously to link to the destruction of human life. Moore's precise source for this story is unclear, but, matter of fact as his telling of it is, his sense of the social and religious urgency, the close ties between ritual, religion, icon and artist is striking.

In 1927, before Moore made contact with them, the Surrealists put on an exhibition at the Galérie surréaliste in Paris combining one of their new artist-recruits and objects from the Americas: *Yves Tanguy et objets d'Amérique*, in which works from British Columbia, New Mexico, Mexico, Colombia and Peru were shown, including a version of the great Aztec deity Coatlicue. Paul Éluard contributed a short essay fantasising about human sacrifice:

> So the Aztecs believed that on the eve of the end of the world, pregnant women would be changed into jaguars and would eat men. Locked into reality and tragically persuaded that they could never get out of it, they peopled tombs with images of cruelty and pain, they decorated idols with torn out hearts still beating, blood intoxicated them and on the red river of life, they paid homage to all the pure powers of the soul. Nothing could be done without the outpouring of blood.[30]

Moore visited Paris at least once a year from 1922 on though there is no evidence he saw this exhibition, nor the huge show of pre-Columbian art the following year at the Musée des arts décoratifs that included over 1,200 objects, of which half were lent by the Trocadéro and the rest from private collections and museums all over the world including Mexico. However, the fact that he bought, in 1928, *L'Art précolombien* by Adolphe Basler and Ernest Brummer, which was published to coincide with the exhibition, suggests that he at least knew of it. *L'art précolombien* was abundantly illustrated and aimed at 'scholars, artists, antiquarians and the general public', giving them the opportunity to 'make contact with civilisations that only yesterday were still unknown, and whose threshold modern investigations are only beginning to clear.' The romance of the lost worlds

30 Paul Éluard, 'D'un véritable continent, *Yves Tanguy et objets d'Amérique*, Galerie Surréaliste, Paris, 27 May–15 June 1927.

of American civilisations was a powerful lure and the fact these were 'high civilisations' (city dwelling, literate and so on) was much commented on by the various audiences in the west. Moore himself noted:

> At the time of the Spanish Conquest there was in America a people at a high state of civilization and evidences [sic] proving that there had been even higher civilizations there. Historians are still searching for clues which will enable us to read their language – until some such discovery as the Rosetti [sic] stone (which gave us the key to the Egyptian hieroglyphics) our knowledge of them is bound to be very limited, & it will be impossible to date with certainty their architecture & sculpture chronologically with ours.[31]

Another scholarly publication that appeared at the same time as *L'Art précolombien* contained an essay by Georges Bataille, 'L'Amérique disparu' (Extinct America), which was the first salvo of a radical approach to anthropology. Bataille had a close but contentious relationship with Surrealism, (of which he declared himself its 'old enemy from within'). In 'L'Amérique disparu' Bataille contrasts the art of the Maya, 'certainly more human than any other in America', with that of the Mexicans (Aztecs), who 'were probably as religious as the Spanish, but who mingled with religion a sentiment of horror, of terror, linked to a kind of black humour even more terrible than horror'.[32] Already in his approach the overturning of conventional values that characterised his journal *Documents*, which was published between 1929–30, is felt: Mayan art is stillborn despite the 'perfection and richness of the work'. The horrific Aztec gods, by contrast, who have an undeniable kinship with the devils and demons of medieval

31 Moore, 'Mexican Sculpture', *op. cit.* Since Moore wrote these unpublished notes in the mid 1920s the state of knowledge of the Aztec and Toltec, but most particularly of the Maya and Olmec, has changed dramatically. Over the last three decades or so Maya hieroglyphic writing has been, thanks to the Russian epigrapher Yuri Knorosov and others, largely deciphered, allowing us to date cities, battles, kings, queens, monuments and art. The great antiquity of the Olmec, who had writing and a complex calendar, at the beginning of the first millennium BC, was finally agreed in 1942 and the latest research published in *DYN* nos.4/5 and 6.

32 'L'Amérique disparu', in Jean Babelon, Georges Bataille, Alfred Métraux, *L'Art précolombien: L'Amérique avant Christophe Colomb*, Cahiers de la république des lettres, des sciences et des arts XI, Les Beaux-Arts, Paris, 1928, p.10.

Christianity, are born of a different attitude to the 'human', in which the reality of human frailty, its helplessness before the god-phantoms it has created to express the terror of the implacable void of heaven, is vividly expressed. Mexico-Tenochtitlán was not only a slaughterhouse running with blood but a remarkably beautiful city with decorated temples, flowers and canals. This welcoming, even celebration of the inevitability of death in life had, Bataille infers, more human reality in it than the elegant realism of the Maya. Although here Bataille doesn't draw direct connections with modern Europe, shortly afterwards in *Documents* he was to return many times to the theme, for example in his 'Critical Dictionary' entry on 'Abattoir'. Starting from the archaeological point that once temple and slaughterhouse were the same place (the Aztec model perhaps uppermost in his mind), he points out that in contemporary European cities slaughterhouses are tucked away in remote corners, as though quarantined, because modern man is unable to face the ugliness of the bloodshed that he nonetheless depends on for his daily meat.[33] Bataille's position may have been extreme in the turning of the anthropological gaze from the distant strangeness of alien societies to those at 'home' in Europe, but he certainly contributed to a different reading of the 'primitive', in which it is the stark visceral horror (and humour) that is valued, rather than the poetic and imaginative qualities celebrated by Surrealists like Péret and Breton.

Although there is no suggestion of a direct link between Moore and Bataille, there is, notwithstanding Moore's more measured and rational means of expression, some common ground, especially in the drawings of the late 1930s when Moore was forced to contemplate the approach of another war.

Art historian Andrew Causey has persuasively argued that Moore's drawings in the second half of the 1930s, during his affiliation with Surrealism, have a different relationship with his sculpture from usual, and that this is constituted by the 'Uncanny'. Freud's notion of the Uncanny has frequently been applied to Surrealist work but in Moore's case it is very convincing. The Uncanny, Causey says, is a property of Moore's drawings but not of his sculpture. Drawing may be able to

33 Georges Bataille, 'Abattoir', *Documents,* no.6, November 1929, p.329.

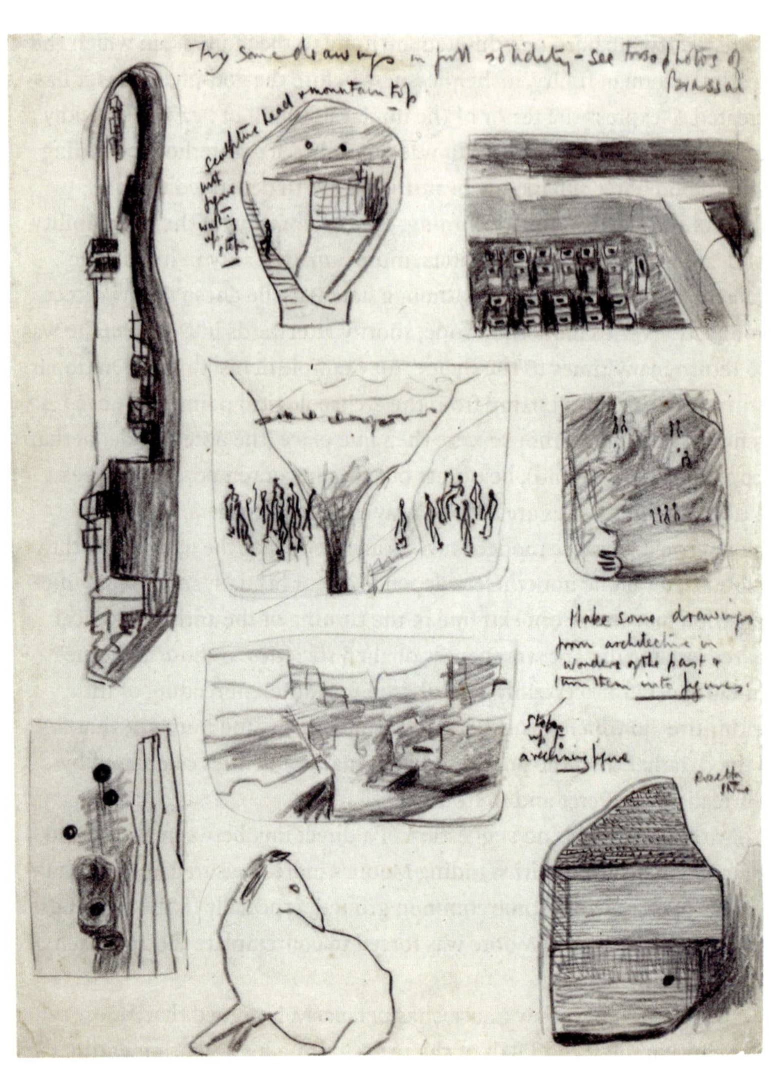

316 **Henry Moore**
Ideas for Drawing Subjects, 1937
Pencil, crayon, wash on cream lightweight wove paper
26 × 19.9 cm | 10¼ × 7⅞ in

summon the Uncanny in a way sculpture, which by its nature 'shares the space of everyday life', cannot.[34] Drawings of this period, such as the series of *Drawings for Metal Sculpture* (1938), *Four Forms* (1938) and *Ideas for Sculpture in a Setting* (1938), create fictive spaces for the objects that are thereby rendered strange, uncertainly real, like figures in a dream. Some are in vaguely landscape settings, others in interiors, or in dark and sinister spaces like some underground version of Tanguy's ambiguous terrains, as with *Drawing for Metal Sculpture: Two Heads.* As a result one of the key properties of the Uncanny as Freud described it is enacted: their identity is ambiguous, no longer familiar; once clearly inanimate, as sculpture, these personages might be alive. Robert Melville, the surrealist writer and critic, recognised the unusual importance of these drawings which reveal 'the sinister, melancholy, serene and tragic life of sculptural communities in worlds of dream and reality that are equally strange'.[35] Moore is closer to Surrealism here, rather than in the self-conscious oddness of his occasional suggestions for a 'surrealist object', notably the table pierced by an outsize safety pin and flower-personage, with the scribbled note 'safety pin/magic/table/in/odd/setting'. Such bizarre conjunctions of objects, based on the collage-principle, were popular among his colleagues but never 'took' for Moore. Nonetheless, the new direction of his drawings indicates that he was sensitive to the ambivalent position of sculpture within Surrealism, as a medium not naturally disposed to the expression either of the rapid gestures of automatic drawing or the recording of dreams.

On one sketchbook page from 1937 the potential of the drawn image to follow the imagination into realms difficult for sculpture to follow takes several fascinating directions, and shows Moore experimenting with double images. One of these also has a bearing on the chacmool/reclining figure conjunction. A note at the top says 'Try some drawings in full solidity – see torso photos of Brassaï'. The Brassaï Moore probably has in mind is *Ciel postiche* (False Sky, 1932–34) that was reproduced in *Minotaure* no.6. It makes a fascinating comparison with Moore's desire to combine

34 Andrew Causey, 'Henry Moore and the Uncanny', in Jane Beckett and Fiona Russell (eds), *op. cit.*, p.85.

35 Robert Melville, 'Communities of Statuary', in *Henry Moore: Figures in Space, Drawings*, Institute of Contemporary Arts, London, 1953, quoted in Causey, *op. cit.*, p.86.

figure and landscape; Brassaï has juxtaposed front and back views of a nude torso photographed against indeterminate backgrounds thereby turning them into landscape – mountain and sea. This brilliant visual play clearly fascinated Moore, and two of the sketches on this page pursue the idea of the double image, which derived from Salvador Dalí. At top left an elongated landscape with building is turned 90 degrees with the potential to become a vertical abstract figure like those Moore endlessly sketched. At the centre top is a small, contained sketch which doubles as head and architecture; 'sculpture head and mountain top/with/figure/walking/up/steps'. The head, with two dot-eyes and a grill-form (Parthenon, prison, teeth) could be seen as an ancestor for the metal sculpture heads, and for Moore's 'forms within forms'. But it is a small drawing towards the bottom of the sheet in the centre that brings quietly to the surface an underlying resonance of the reclining figure theme. A quite crowded architectural scene is annotated 'steps up to a reclining figure'. The structure with the steps to the right of the sketch is unmistakably that of a Mexican temple platform, from what were known in Moore's time as ceremonial centres – Teotihuacán, Tula or one of the Aztec sites. The chacmool/reclining figure, a tiny dark note on the page, is half enclosed by walls, and there is a rough indication beyond it of a rising temple. This evocation of a Mexican ritual building with all its implications of sacrifice and bloodshed is a rare, perhaps unique instance of the reclining figure shown in its original context. Moore had not forgotten this, even if the reclining figure has already by repetition become accepted in more humanist, not to say female, terms. It brings us back to the original chacmool and its fascination for Moore – 'about as good a piece of sculpture as I know.'[36] Did Moore have a sense of the Uncanny in this sculpture, in which symbol, gesture and posture build up to the death in life, or life in death ambiguity? The shock of the abruptly turned head, above a neck that is clearly severed; the hard rectangular ear pieces, the combination of incision, low relief and carving in the round, the whole figure of a piece with its pedestal out of which it rises, formal qualities which marry so perfectly with its terrible alertness.

36 Wilkinson, *op. cit.*, p.97.

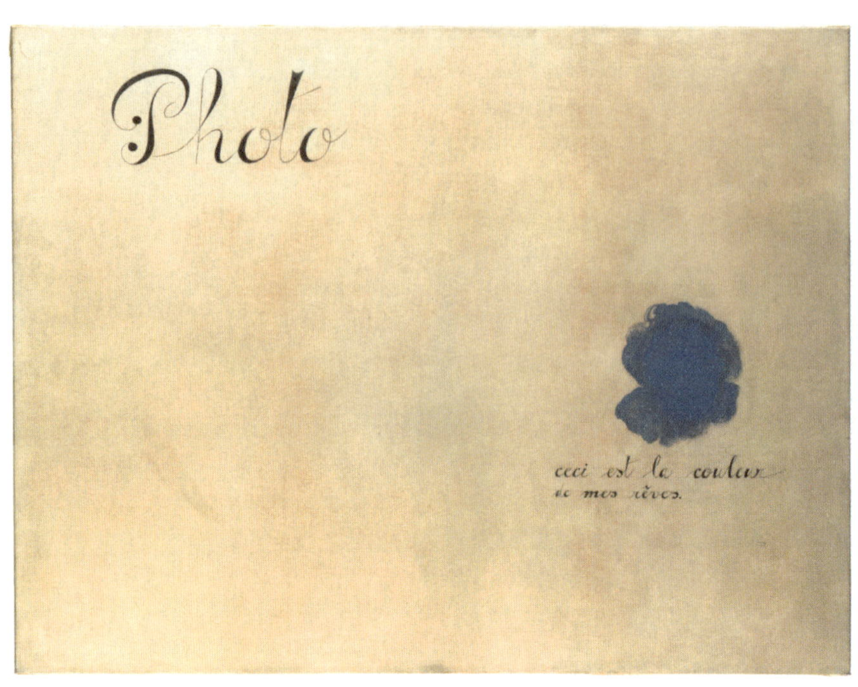

320 **Joan Miró**
Photo: Ceci est la couleur de mes rêves
(Photo: This Is the Colour of My Dreams), 1925
Oil on canvas
96.5 × 129.5 cm | 38 × 51 in

Dreams in Surrealist Discourse and the Unusual Case of Miró's *Photo: Ceci est la couleur de mes rêves*

Surrealism and the Dream, José Jiménez (ed), Museo Thyssen-Bornemisza, Madrid, 2014, here published in a revised form

Joan Miró's *Photo: Ceci est la couleur de mes rêves* (Photo: This is the Colour of my Dreams, 1925) is a strange work, barely even a painting. The conjunction of the apparently innocent, offhand but carefully lettered assertion 'Photo: this is the colour of my dreams', and the formless smudge of blue pigment on an otherwise bare canvas is enigmatic to the point of obscurity. Words dominate the canvas, and although Miró frequently added inscriptions to his canvases of this period, which he called poem-paintings, they rarely take over so completely. It is nothing if not a challenge to the concept of representation. Photography, painting, dreams and automatism all seem to be brought into question. *Photo: Ceci est la couleur de mes rêves* lacks the luscious washes of blue pigment that flood other paintings of the period. And yet it is still a remarkably satisfying picture rather than a conceptual work of art. It is also an original and humorous response to contemporary Surrealist debates, during the ferment of the first months of the movement, about dreams and their role in what the Surrealists had begun to see as the problem of painting, especially of painting dreams.

Dreams have puzzled and fascinated every human culture in every age and each one has found some measure of an explanation according to their reliance on physical, metaphysical or psychological factors. For the modern era there is no doubt that Sigmund Freud's *The Interpretation of Dreams* (1899) has been the fundamental text. Freud himself, as the founder of psychoanalysis, regarded dream interpretation as his capital discovery. 'Freud very rightly', André Breton wrote in the *First Surrealist Manifesto* (1924), 'brought his critical faculties to bear upon the dream.'

What attracted the Surrealists above all was the revelation that dream is a major portion of our psychic activity – our mental life including the unconscious. Freud showed that the 'dream-work' was responsible for transforming latent thoughts into the manifest content of the dream – that is, what we are conscious of when we wake up, what appears in the manifest dream (what we remember). The transformations occur through the processes of condensation and displacement, together with other irrational effects of the dream-work. Freud's arguments about the nature of the dream and the relationship between its manifest and latent contents were crucial for the Surrealists, but they followed their implications in a totally different direction from psychoanalysis, with whose aims they were not in sympathy.

Dreams were at the heart of Surrealism's foundation in 1924; they were collected and recorded as 'récits de rêve', dream narratives, and like the notion of 'pure psychic automatism' were presented by Breton in his *First Surrealist Manifesto* under the authority of Freud. In the manifesto Breton gives dreams equal weight if not equal billing with the notion of automatism, to which they are related. The 'dictionary' definition of Surrealism introduces the question of thought, *pensée*, whose relationship to the dream is a key issue for the Surrealists: 'Pure psychic automatism, by which it is intended to express, either verbally, or in writing, or in any other way, the true functioning of thought. The dictation of thought, in the absence of any control exerted by reason, and outside all aesthetic or moral considerations.'[1] It is only in the following 'encyclopaedia' definition that dream is introduced: 'Surrealism is based on the belief in the superior reality of certain forms of association hitherto neglected, in the omnipotence of the dream, in the disinterested play of thought...'

Breton invokes Freud both in the context of automatic writing and of the dream, but at the same time firmly distinguishes his and Surrealism's interest in the mental world that was opened up by Freud's discoveries from that of the doctors and analysts: no method, he insists, has been designated a priori for the investigation of 'les profondeurs de notre esprit' (the depths of our mind), and the conduct of this investigation 'peut passer pour être aussi bien du ressort des poètes que des savants...'

1 André Breton, *Manifeste du surréalisme*, Editions du Sagittaire, Paris, 1924, p.42, author's translation.

(can be as much the province of poets as of scientists). The poets have just as much right to follow Freud's discoveries, to experiment and explore, as the specialists, the psychologists and psychoanalysts.

It has often been averred that Breton misunderstood Freud, but it would be fairer to say with philosopher and psychoanalyst Jean-Bertrand Pontalis that he 'took from psychoanalysis only what he wanted'. As far as the dream is concerned, Breton dismissed most of the voluminous literature that had from the mid-nineteenth century addressed dreams from biological, philosophical and literary points of view in favour of Freud's discoveries. Nonetheless, he had no scruples in giving space to the manifest dreams in their own right, which Freud found pointless.

There were some among the Surrealist group, notably Louis Aragon, who resisted Freud and psychoanalysis altogether. Aragon's great account of this period is a prose-poem essay called 'Une Vague de rêves' (A Wave of Dreams, 1924) in defiance of the author of *The Interpretation of Dreams*. In 'Une Vague de rêves' Aragon captures the fluidity in the experience of states of mind beyond the simple everyday consciousness, whether to do with daydreams, hallucinations, narcotics or dreams, that carried over from the 'époque des sommeils' (period of hypnotic trances) to the early years of the Surrealist movement. Aragon said that Breton's interest in dreams was to solve a particular poetic problem and nothing to do with psychoanalysis. He argues for a concept of reality that is neither idealist nor commonplace, and understands 'dreams' in the widest sense. 'Dreams, dreams, dreams, with each step the domain of dreams expands. Dreams, dreams, dreams, at last the blue sun of dreams forces the steel-eyed beasts back to their lairs...'[2]

In a striking section in the *First Surrealist Manifesto,* Breton challenged the greater value normally placed on our waking life than on dreaming, which is reduced to a mere parenthesis. Dreams, he says, 'give every evidence of being continuous and show signs of organization.' Memory seems able only to excerpt from dreams and depicts for us 'a series of dreams rather than the *dream itself*'. In a very interesting passage Breton changes Freud's notion of 'manifest' and 'latent' content to that of depth. 'Account must be taken of the *depth* of the dream. For the most

2 Louis Aragon, 'Une Vague de rêves' (1924), trans. Susan de Muth, *Papers of Surrealism*, no.1, winter 2003, p.7.

part I retain only what I can glean from its most superficial layers. What I most enjoy contemplating about a dream is everything that sinks back below the surface in a waking state, everything I have forgotten about my activities in the course of the preceding day, dark foliage, stupid branches. 'In "reality", likewise, I prefer to fall'.[3] It may be, he proposes, that it is the waking state that is the phenomenon of interference in our lives, not the dream.

The reception of psychoanalysis in France, as Élisabeth Roudinesco has argued, came as much through literary as medical channels. 'Starting in 1914, an interest in psychoanalysis could be found in a large sector of French thought.'[4] The Surrealists were the most prominent of those in the literary world in France who were interested in Freud and it was above all the Surrealists who distanced themselves from the physicians – somewhat ironically as Breton, Aragon and Théodore Fraenkel had met while doing medical studies, and had encountered Freud in that context. Although there were hardly any translations of Freud's writings into French until 1921, his ideas had filtered through earlier. Marguerite Bonnet, in *André Breton, Naissance de l'aventure surréaliste* (André Breton, Birth of the Surrealist Adventure, 1988), unpicks the complicated process of Breton's discovery of psychoanalysis during the First World War and its influence on his theories of automatism, which she argues is indebted less to Pierre Janet's *L'Automatisme psychologique* (Psychological Automatism, 1889) than to Dr Emmanuel Régis's *Précis de psychiatrie* (1914) and to Régis and Angelo Hesnard's *La Psychanalyse des nevroses et des psychoses* (Psychoanalysis of Neuroses and Psychoses, 1914). Their summary of Freud's ideas and Breton's own experiences as a young medic specialising in nervous diseases were crucial for the latter's first experiments in automatic writing, *Les Champs magnétiques* (The Magnetic Fields, 1919).[5] Régis discussed the 'translation of the unconscious into the conscious' and emphasised mental associations

3 Breton, *op. cit.*, p.20 and following. *Manifestos of Surrealism*, trans. Richard Seaver and Helen R. Lane, The University of Michigan Press, Ann Arbor, MI, 1969, p.11.

4 Élisabeth Roudinesco, *Jacques Lacan & Co.: A History of Psychoanalysis in France, 1925–1985*, University of Chicago Press, Chicago, IL, 1990, p.3.

and the flow of thought, *la pensée parlee*, rather than dreams, in the treatment of the subject under analysis.

Breton began to turn his attention to dreams a few years later, in 1922. *Die Traumdeutung* (The Interpretation of Dreams, 1899) was only translated into French in 1925, as *Le Rêve et son interpretation*) but Freud's ideas about dreams were sufficiently well known to spark a fashion in Paris for dream interpretation in the early 1920s. Yves Delage's *Le Rêve, Etude Psychologique, Philosophique et Litteraire* (The Dream, a Psychological, Philosophical and Literary Study) of 1919, a compendium of ideas and examples of dreams which includes a fairly detailed critique of Freud's theories about the dream, is a good example of the porous boundaries between science, philosophy and literature at the time. Delage discusses in some detail Freud's notion of the manifest and latent dream, the 'modifications' of ideas in dreams (Condensation, Displacement, Symbolisation and Dramatisation) and his theory, as Delage put it, that dreams are a realisation of an infantile wish. He does not agree with Freud, claiming that the latter fails to present any proof of his ideas: 'The problem consists in discovering the latent content hidden beneath the manifest content of each dream. Freud shows with numerous examples that this latent content can be an infantile desire, but nowhere does he prove that this is really what it is.'[6] There had been no lack of studies of dreams since the mid-nineteenth century, which replaced the 'interminable litanies' of the 'clefs des songes' of antiquity, as Roger Caillois put it in the preface to his anthology *Puissances du rêve* (Powers of Dreams, 1962), and which took an apparently more scientific and systematic approach. Two of the most remarkable were those by Alfred Maury and by the great sinologist the Marquis d'Hervey de Saint-Denys, whose *Les Rêves et les moyens de les diriger* (Dreams and Ways to Steer Them, 1867) was the starting point for Breton's *Les Vases communicants* (The Communicating Vessels, 1932). The independence of Breton's approach to Freud's ideas about dreams was clear already from the first manifesto. In *Les Vases communicants* he surveys the principal theoreticians of the dream, according to their

5 Marguerite Bonnet, *André Breton, Naissance de l'aventure surréaliste*, Corti, Paris, 1988, pp.102–07.

6 Yves Delage, *Le Rêve: Etude psychologique, philosophique et littéraire*, Presses universitaires de France, Paris, 1919.

various schools: the adepts of primary materialism, the positivists and the idealists. The positivists regard dreaming as a degradation of the waking state, the idealists as liberation from it. Breton dismisses Delage as a 'partisan of the theory according to which dream is only, strictly speaking, partial waking, its value purely organic.[7]

On more than one occasion Freud expressed his bewilderment at the Surrealists' adoption of and interpretation of his ideas about dreams. In *Les Vases communicants*, in which Breton 'provocatively', as Roudinesco says, analysed his own dreams, letters from Freud are included. 'Although I have received many testimonies of the interest you and your friends show for my research, I am not able to clarify for myself what surrealism is and what it wants. Perhaps I am not destined to understand it, I who am so distant from art.'[8]

The Surrealists persisted in their independent study of dreams, publishing 'récits de rêve' and on occasion 'analysing' them. In *Les Vases communicants* Breton recounts several of his own dreams and provides analyses of what Freud would call their 'manifest' content, that is, what is remembered on awakening. In 1938 *Trajectoires du rêve, documents recueillis par André Breton* (Trajectories of dreams, documents gathered by André Breton) was published. This anthology opened with Albert Béguin's essay on dream and poetry ('Le rêve et la poésie') and included historical as well as contemporary examples: dreams by Paracelsus, Dürer and Lichtenberg as well as Paul Éluard, Breton himself and Benjamin Péret. (Béguin was the author of *L'Ame romantique et le rêve* (The Romantic Soul and the Dream), a study of German Romanticism and French poetry, published by Cahiers du Sud in 1937). But at the end of the anthology Breton reproduces a devastating letter from Freud, whom he had invited to write an introduction, in the original German:

7 André Breton, *Les Vases communicants* (1932), *Communicating Vessels*, trans. Mary Ann Caws and Geoffrey T. Harris, University of Nebraska Press, Lincoln, NE, 1990, p.11.
8 *Ibid.*, p.152.

I have nothing more to say about dreams. I ask you to note that the interpretation of dream which I call the manifest dream has no interest for me. I was occupied with it to discover the latent dream, which can be won by analytical probing from the manifest dream. A collection of dreams without comments, attached associations, without knowledge of the circumstances under which it was dreamed means nothing to me. I can hardly imagine what it could mean to anyone.

It is graspable that the manifest dream according to the unsurpassed insights of Aristotle is nothing else than the continuation of our thoughts in the state of sleep...[9]

The gulf between scientific and poetic attitudes to the dream remains today. Hélène Cixous, for example, is in the surrealist tradition when, in *Rêve je le dis* (2003), she introduces her 'book of dreams without interpretation'. Her words recall those of Breton in the first manifesto, thinking dreaming as of at least equal importance to the waking state. 'I live in, I used to live in two countries, the diurnal one and the continuous discontinuous very tempestuous nocturnal one... I couldn't have said which was the main, the primordial one.' Dreams, for her, are necessary, magic, a land of grace; 'without dreams death would be mortal'. By contrast, *The Dream Discourse Today*[10] is concerned exclusively with the function of dreams in psychoanalysis and with clinical examples. Whether or not the dream has declined in clinical importance is discussed, and there are some interesting reflections on the manifest dream and the dream as object. Only Pontalis comments plaintively that 'In a way, psychoanalysis is strangling the eloquence of oneiric life.'[11]

It was precisely the 'eloquence of oneiric life' that the Surrealist artists embraced. There is nonetheless an interesting parallel, between the role of the dream in psychoanalysis and the situation of the visual arts in Surrealism. In each case there is a bias towards the verbal. 'La psychanalyse', as Marguerite Bonnet writes, 'met l'accent sur la parole'

9 See André Breton, *Trajectoires du rêve, documents recueillis par André Breton*, GLM, Paris, 1938.

10 Jean-Bertrand Pontalis, 'Dream as an Object' (*The International Review of Psycho-Analysis*, 1974) in Sara Flanders (ed), *The Dream Discourse Today*, The New Library of Psychoanalysis, Routledge, London, 1993, p.17.

11 *Ibid.*, p.116.

12 Flanders (ed), *op. cit.*, p. 67.

(psychoanalysis stresses the word). At the same time, dreams are 'essentially a visual experience'.[12] For Freud the translation of the visual experience of the dream into words as it is remembered by the patient was a crucial source for the analyst. Surrealism was founded by poets and writers and there was inevitably a bias towards the word. As André Breton wrote in *Le Message automatique* (The Automatic Message, 1933):

> I consider verbal inspirations infinitely richer in visual meaning, infinitely more resistant to the eye, than visual images properly speaking. *In poetry, verbo-auditory automatism has always seemed to me to create the most thrilling visual images for the reader. Verbo-visual automatism has never seemed to me to create visual images that are in any way comparable.* Suffice it to say that today, as ten years ago, I am entirely devoted to, and continue to believe blindly in (blindly... with a blindness that simultaneously covers all visual things), the triumph of the auditory over the unverifiable visual. Now that I've made my point, it goes without saying that the floor should be turned over to the painters...[13]

The poetic images Breton had in mind sprang from and spoke to the imagination, independent of the external world. There is an important distinction to draw between the visual images rather denigrated here by Breton, and what historian and writer Martin Jay called 'the high modernist ethic of pure opticality.'[14] Dreams would seem to be a natural berth for Surrealist artists, being fundamentally a visual experience but not an optical one.

However, the process of translating Surrealism's basic tenets, always intended to be of the widest possible application to every aspect of life and from the start speculative and experimental, from verbal to visual, was far from straightforward. A theoretical problem arose concerning dreams in the Surrealist context which came to a head in the Surrealist journal *La Révolution surréaliste*, and which was to have a considerable, if temporary, influence on the Surrealist possibilities of painting.

13 André Breton, 'Le Message automatique', *Minotaure*, nos.3–4, December 1933, 'The Automatic Message', in André Breton, *Break of Day*, trans. Mark Polizzotti and Mary Ann Caws, University of Nebraska Press, Lincoln, NE, 1999, p.141.

14 Martin Jay, *Downcast Eyes*, University of California Press, Oakland, CA, 1994, p.246.

Photo: Ceci est la couleur de mes rêves in no way resembles what is now thought of as a 'dream image'. (Dalí's hand-painted 'trompe l'oeil' dreams were still to come). Miró's work of the mid-1920s was influentially described as 'dream painting' because of his close association with the Surrealists and because of what French poet and critic Jacques Dupin describes as their 'purely oneiric atmosphere'.[15] But how the 'dream image' was understood in the context of Surrealism is no simple matter. It might be assumed that, whether rudimentary or meticulous, it would be by its nature figurative. However, this was not necessarily the case as *Photo: Ceci est la couleur de mes rêves* proves.

Whatever the Surrealists expected initially from their experiments in the wake of Freud's discoveries about the dream, it was not to begin with in the interests of literature – or art. It was ironic that Freud could only see what they were doing under the banner of art and literature, as is evident from his letters, while the Surrealists sought to divest themselves of this label. While not aligning themselves with psychoanalysis and the medical, they felt that making their debt to Freud clear would be one of the guarantees of their extra-literary project.

In October 1924, shortly after the publication of the first manifesto, the Surrealists acquired their own space and opened the Bureau de recherches surréalistes, in the ground floor of a building at 15, rue de Grenelle, rented from the father of Pierre Naville, one of the group. This was the centre of their collective activities, and was known also as the Centrale; it was open to the public from 4.30 to 6.30 pm every day, staffed by a changing rota of two of the Surrealists, who would welcome visitors, encourage them to tell their dreams, and answer their questions. It was a 'porte ouverte vers l'inconnu', a door open onto the unknown. A ledger (cahier de la permanence) recorded the events, visits and comments by the changing pairs of Surrealists in charge, and is an invaluable source for the first months of the movement and the production of the first review, *La Révolution surréaliste*. Breton noted in the 'cahier de la permanence' that they should exchange their review, *La Révolution surréaliste*, with the

15 Jacques Dupin, *Joan Miró Life and Work*, Harry N. Abrams, New York, NY, 1962, p.157.

principal scientific publications, the philosophical reviews, and so on.[16] *La Révolution surréaliste* did not resemble a literary or art magazine nor the visual anarchy of its Dada forebears, and its cover was modelled on that of the popular science journal *La Nature*.[17] For a time, in the first months of the Surrealist movement, as the records of the 'cahier de la permanence' make clear, the experimental activities that the first manifesto had boosted but not prescribed are directed away from art and literature. The Declaration of 27 January 1925, a manifesto published as a leaflet, signed by the whole group but written entirely by Antonin Artaud, stated:

> We have nothing to do with literature.
> But we are perfectly capable of making use of it
> like everyone else, if necessary.

Everything, in the months following the publication of the first manifesto, was open to experiment and investigation. The only sure project was the review, *La Révolution surréaliste*. Breton commented critically to his colleagues on the current plans for the contents of the review in the *cahier* on 30 October 1924. Too many Surrealist texts, he says, and not enough dreams: '...no news in brief, no anonymous communications, no small ads, no publicity, no trouvailles, nothing that bears witness to a real, non-literary life. The whole thing, as we feared, will be artistic. Not enough dreams, either.' What he hoped for was some real life, the hidden underworld of the unconscious that might manifest itself in the actual underworld of the street, news reports, *faits divers*, chance encounters – and more dreams. Plans for the third issue of *La Révolution surréaliste* were already being discussed in December 1924: it was to be devoted to the dream, and members were asked to carefully edit their dream narratives. Artaud asked everyone to 'isolate and note down everything in their dreams that seems to belong to a system, the whole unconscious systematic of the dream.[18]

16 Paule Thévenin (ed), *Archives du surréalisme, vol.1, Bureau de recherches surréalistes: cahier de la permanence, Octobre 1924–Avril 1925*, Gallimard, Paris, 1988, p.75.

17 See Dawn Ades (ed), *Dada and Surrealism Reviewed*, Hayward Gallery, Arts Council of Great Britain, London, 1978.

18 Thévenin, *op. cit.*, p.97.

The first issue of *La Révolution surréaliste*, which appeared mid-December 1924, placed dreams at the forefront of the unprecedented mixture of experiment and document that launched the first full collective expression of the movement. The first sentence of the preface written by Jacques-André Boiffard, Paul Éluard and Roger Vitrac claimed 'le rêve seul laisse a l'homme tous ses droits a la liberté, (Dreams alone leave man with all his rights to freedom) but goes on, 'We are all at the mercy of the dream and must suffer its power when awake. It's a terrible tyrant clothed in mirrors and lightning. What are paper and ink, what is it to write. What is poetry in the face of this giant that has muscles of clouds in its muscles?'. An advertisement for the 'Bureau de recherches surréalistes' invited anyone to join in, announcing that 'We are at the dawn of a REVOLUTION'. The nature of this 'revolution' and of the dream experience are two of the major preoccupations of the contributors to the *cahier* during these early months.

La Révolution surréaliste divided its contents into sections with clearly marked headings: 'Rêves', 'Textes surréalistes', 'Chroniques', 'Revues' and 'Suicides'. Following the preface, it opens with a dream sent in by Giorgio de Chirico, who was close to the group at the time, one of two he had submitted, and three dreams from Breton. In the last of these Breton is at home, Picasso seated on a sofa drawing furiously in a notebook, and the shadow of Apollinaire stands upright by the door – an image echoing De Chirico's *Portrait of Apollinaire* of 1914, in which a shadow profile of the poet appears behind the classical bust. Several of De Chirico's early paintings, 'which enjoyed unequalled prestige in the eyes of the Surrealists',[19] hung on the walls of the 'Bureau des recherches surréalistes', and Breton himself owned De Chirico's *The Child's Brain* (1914), the painting that haunted the work of both Max Ernst and Salvador Dalí. De Chirico was at this moment the artist Breton most admired, after Picasso. However, in the 'Chroniques' section of the review, under the 'Beaux-arts' rubric, an article by Max Morise, 'Les Yeux enchantés' (Enchanted Eyes), raised fundamental questions about the relationship between Surrealism and the visual arts, in particular with reference to the dream. This article marks, and must have influenced, a turn away from the exploration of visual equivalents

19 André, Breton *Entretiens 1913–1952*, NRF, Paris, p.108.

to the 'recits de rêve' towards the more spontaneous and visceral automatism.

Morise lays out the problem and its implications for visual procedures very clearly. Breton's *Les Champs magnétiques* is, Morise says, so far the only precise example of Surrealism; it is a form of 'exteriorisation de la pensée' (exteriorisation of thought) which is what Surrealism, as Breton explained it in the first manifesto, seeks. Morise argued that 'What surrealist writing is to literature, visual surrealism must be to painting, to photography, to everything made to be seen': thought cannot be static, and 'la succession des images, la fuite des idées' (the succession of images, the flight of ideas) are basic to any manifestation of Surrealism.[20] Whereas we approach a written text in time, he argues, it is in space that we perceive a painting or sculpture. The point he is trying to make is less to do, in fact, with the perception of a painting or sculpture, than with the process of its making. Although the making is 'in time', it does not, in his opinion, have the immediacy of 'writing thought'; '...To paint a canvas you have to start at one end, and continue elsewhere, a process that favours the arbitrary, taste, and tends to lead the "dictation of thought" astray.' The clear division between automatism and the dream in the visual arts had not yet been made. Morise goes on to take the dream as posing the problem of 'representation' in Surrealism most acutely:

> Surrealism's confrontation with the dream has not brought us much guidance. Painting like writing is suited to telling a dream. A simple effort of memory is enough (brings it through)... strange landscapes appeared to De Chirico; he had only to reproduce them, to trust the interpretation provided by his memory. But this effort of secondary intention which inevitably deforms images as it floats them to the surface of consciousness shows us that we must renounce this as the key to surrealist painting. Indeed, though no more than a dream narrative, a painting by De Chirico cannot be accepted as typical of Surrealism: the images are surrealist, their expression is not...

20 Max Morise, 'Les Beaux arts: les yeux enchantés', *La Revolution surréaliste*, no.1, Paris, 1924, p.26.

Morise's strictures apply as much to the 'dream stories', the 'récits de rêves' that were so prominent in *La Révolution surréaliste*, as to paintings; the problem, in his view, was where to find the equivalent of the Surrealist text, of automatic writing. In the 'waking dream' that characterised the 'Surrealist state', thought was revealed as much in words as in visual images. But, he argues, while words can be quickly written, the traces of the brush only translate, in a form of mediation, the mental image. But – and here he begins to make a case for the visual, 'We have every reason in the world to believe that the simple, direct element constituted by the touch of the brush on the canvas intrinsically has meaning, that the mark of the pencil is the equivalent of a word.' The unexpected example he gives is Cubist pictures – which is where, interestingly, Breton was also to start his great defence of painting the following year: *Le Surréalisme et la peinture* (Surrealism and Painting). In Cubist pictures, Morise writes, there was no preconceived idea, no question of representation to bother about: 'The lines get organised as and when they appear and so to speak *by chance*... At every moment the painter may take a cinematic snapshot of his/her thought...' He then suggests two possible routes: either the most rudimentary representation of a thing or person, or – and here 'we touch a truly surrealist activity – forms and colours dispense with an object, get organised according to a law that is completely unpremeditated, that develops and is undone even as it appears...' As illustration, there is one of Masson's automatic drawings in the review (unfortunately it was reproduced upside down), which is not only one of Masson's most abstract but also most Cubist-like in appearance.

Morise effectively demolished for a time the assumption that De Chirico's paintings offered a possible model for the expression of 'dreams'. The distinction he drew between automatism and the dream must have seemed quite rigid and restrictive for many of the Surrealists and especially the artists. Max Ernst had painted some of the most haunting pictures related to the experiences of the 'époque des sommeils' such as *Pietà or Revolution by Night* (1923), which for Breton was a 'revelation'. Much has been written about *Pietà*, its relationship to the 'époque des sommeils' and to the ideas of Freud.[21] In paintings like *Pietà* and *Resurrection of the Flesh* (1919) Ernst follows De Chirico's example, but in a more explicitly Freudian way. Whether the strange images – a son held in the arms of his father, a kind of homage to De Chirico's *The Child's Brain*, or the male nude rushing through an abattoir, both explicitly iconoclastic – were attributable to the hypnotic trances or to a dream is impossible to say. But either way they would be subject to the objection Morise raised, that the image would be dependent on efforts of memory and skill in representation. Apart from the work of children and the mad, whose rudimentary image-making Morise accepts as closer to the 'Surrealist method', the main exception to his caveat were the paintings by Robert Desnos, which in a very rudimentary way captured episodes of the exchanges made while he was in a hypnotic trance.

I have talked about Morise's text at some length because it sharply exposes debates within Surrealism about dreams and the visual arts and the bias against painting. It also offers some insights into Miró's *Photo: Ceci est la couleur de mes rêves*. Although Morise is seeking a solution for the artists – how the traits of the pencil and traces of the brush might constitute Surrealism – running through the article are hints that it is photography and film that might be the true Surrealist medium, and this is his metaphor for Cubism: 'un cliché cinématographique de la pensée' (a cinematographic snapshot of thought). 'A photo', Miró writes, 'of the colour of my dreams.' Morise's conclusion that the spontaneous marks of a brush and the forms and colours that arise were closer to the movement of thought also must have struck a chord; the splash of blue pigment could hardly be further from the premeditated, preexisting image criticised by Morise. (This does not preclude the poetic associations of the colour blue and its wider significance in Miró's paintings, as shown by Rosalind Krauss and Margit Rowell in *Joan Miró: Magnetic Fields* of 1972).

Miró had already begun to strip his canvases down to the minimum before making *Photo: Ceci est la couleur de mes rêves*; he wrote to his friend Michel Leiris in August 1924:

> More or less total destruction of everything I left behind last summer… Still too real! I am moving away from all pictorial conventions (that poison). In spreading out my canvases I noticed that the ones that have

21 See Ades, 'Between Dada and Surrealism: Painting in the Mouvement flou', Terry Ann R. Neff (ed), *In the Mind's Eye: Dada and Surrealism*, Museum of Contemporary Art, Chicago, IL, 1984.

> been painted touch the spirit less directly than the ones that are simply drawn (or that use a minimum of colour…). There is no doubt that my canvases that are simply drawn, with a few dots of colour, a rainbow, are more profoundly moving.[22]

Miró had been in the habit of jotting down words, names of colours, on the drawings in his notebooks, sometimes simply the word 'yes' if he decided he would carry out the idea. Adding words to the canvases themselves began in the summer of 1924, more or less at the time he wrote to Leiris. This was, Miró said, the only period at which the words came to him first. These 'poem-paintings', as he called them, which began with *Bouquet de fleurs ('Sourire de ma blonde')* (Bouquet of Flowers ('My Blonde's Smile'), 1924), may indeed have been inspired by his close association with the Surrealist writers. Miró's passionate rejection of realism coincides with the Surrealists' challenge to what is understood by 'the real', a challenge that importantly included the question of dreams. As Louis Aragon wrote, most people fail to understand the true nature of reality, that it is just an experience like any other, that the essence of things is not at all linked to their reality, that there are other experiences that the mind can embrace which are equally fundamental such as chance, illusion, the fantastic, dreams. These different types of experience are brought together and reconciled in one genre, Surreality.[23]

In the build up to the publication of this first issue of the review, the 'cahier de la permanence' records the visits of several artists to the Bureau – Masson, Man Ray, Max Ernst, and the mysterious character Dédé Sunbeam, who arrived with the painter Pierre Roy. On 22 October 1924 Max Ernst brought in a drawing 'made following the surrealist method on a narrow and very long roll of paper which unrolls'. Two long drawings by Ernst have survived: one, untitled, is more spontaneous and looser in appearance and could be the one 'made according to the surrealist method', in other words, automatic. The other, to which he gave the title *L'aimant est proche sans doute* (The magnet is near, no doubt), is more figurative, and it could be that the two drawings demonstrate

22 Joan Miró, *Selected Writings and Interviews*, Margit Rowell (ed), GK Hall, Boston, MA, 1986, p.86.

23 Aragon, *op. cit.*, p.3.

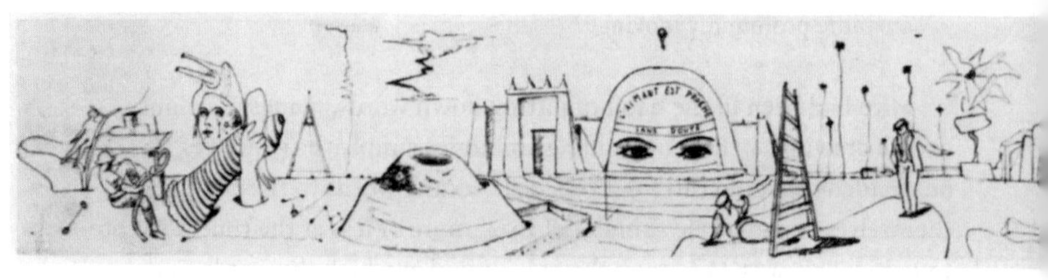

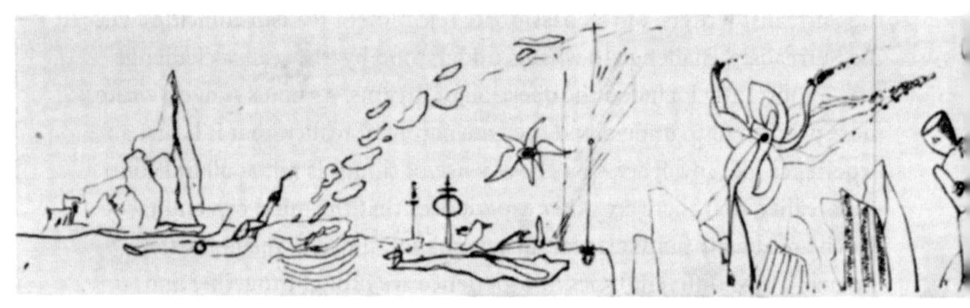

top:
Max Ernst
Lesson in Automatic Drawing (The Magnet is Close No Doubt), c.1923
Pen and ink on paper
17.3 × 169 cm | 6¾ × 66½ in

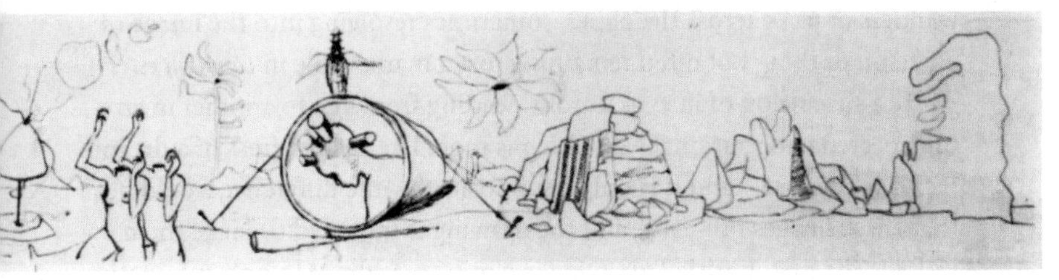

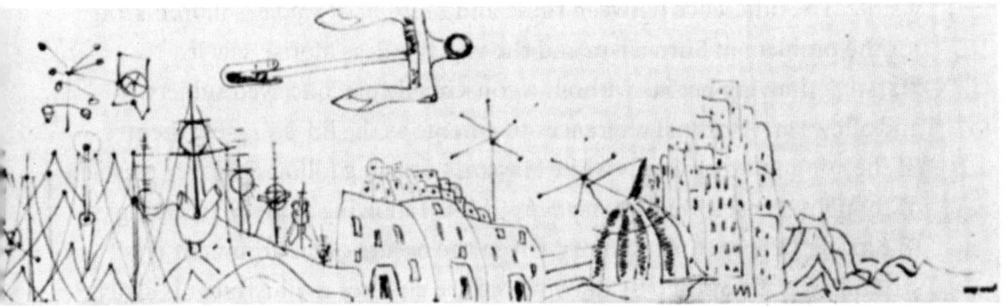

bottom:
Max Ernst
Lesson in Automatic Drawing, c.1923
Pen and ink on paper
17.3 × 169 cm | 6¾ × 66½ in

different methods, equivalent on the one hand to automatic writing – 'the Surrealist method', on the other to the 'récit de rêve', the dream narrative. In the untitled drawing, there is a freedom in the line, which wanders or jerks across the paper, sometimes resolving into the image of a person or thing but often remaining just a mark, while in *L'aimant est proche* a succession of images unrolls, leading from one to another in an unexpected and irrational way which is more like the progress of a dream. If this is the case – and it is only a supposition – the difference would be that these images pre-exist, and the drawing is intended to make them visible. The first, untitled, drawing is closer to André Masson's automatic drawings, one of which was reproduced in the first issue of *La Révolution surréaliste*. Both Masson and Ernst allude to time through the process of drawing, making the progression of line and its metamorphosis very visible. The difference between these and *L'aimant est proche* is illuminating for the problem of Surrealism and the visual arts as Morise saw it. Masson's drawing begins without a consciously preconceived subject, and allows any external references to emerge as the lines suggest them (if they do). In other words while Masson's drawing follows the free play of thought, Ernst's *L'aimant est proche* (if it is following a dream) is trying to capture images from memory. Given the nature of his argument it is striking that the automatic drawing Morise chooses to illustrate his article is one of the most abstract Masson ever made.

Breton took control of *La Révolution surréaliste* in July 1925 and started to publish his essays on Surrealism and painting, which were a response to Morise and to the even more negative position of Pierre Naville who denied there could be any such thing as '*surrealist painting*'.[24] Breton mentions and then glides over the controversy about the incompatibility of painting dreams, in which the image pre-exists, and the 'Surrealist method' of automatism, simply fastening on the ancient need to 'fix' images. 'The need to fix visual images, whether or not these images pre-exist, has manifested itself throughout time and has led to the formation of a real language which seems to me no more artificial than the other one...'[25] Painting was thus re-established as an *echt* (real) Surrealist activity, though no rules were laid down.

24 Pierre Naville, 'Beaux-Arts', *La révolution surréaliste*, no.3, April 1925, p.27; 'Everyone knows now that there is no such thing as *surrealist painting*.'

The debates culminating in Breton's 'Surrealism and Painting' were the background to *Photo*. Though there is no doubt that Miró took his own route, he was aware of the rich Surrealist discourse around the problem of translating into visual terms dreams, daydreams, and unconscious thought. Morise had begun to question the problem of the 'dream image', which was essentially still considered in terms of rather than opposed to automatism. Much later, in 'Artistic Genesis and Perspective of Surrealism' (1941), Breton contrasted the (still essential) automatism with the 'other road available to surrealism... the stabilizing of dream images in the kind of still-life deception known as *trompe l'oeil* (and the very word "deception" betrays the weakness of the process), has been proved by experience to be far less reliable and even presents very real risks of the traveller losing his way altogether.'[26] The 'dream painting', in 1925, was not yet the popular metaphor for visual Surrealism.

In 1925 Miró began the series of paintings on a blue ground, so blue as 'the colour of my dreams' is also the colour of his paintings. He did not otherwise add words to his 'blue' paintings. Blue seems to have a natural affinity with dreams: the 'blue sun of dreams' as Aragon said.

The writing on the canvas in *Photo: ceci est la couleur de mes rêves* is more carefully lettered than in any of the other 'poem-pictures', which has the paradoxical effect of on the one hand underlining their graphic nature and on the other the divorce between line/word and colour. It is as though Miró is meditating on the Surrealist tendency to give the word primacy over the image. In 'Une Vague de rêves' Aragon describes the 'nature of the troubled mental states brought on by Surrealism, by mental fatigue, by narcotics, and the way these resembled dreams and mystical visions together with the semiology of mental illness' which 'led us to evolve this proposition which, alone, can explain and link all these factors: the existence of a mental substance.' Eventually, he says, 'it gradually dawned on us that the mental substance described above was, in fact, vocabulary itself. *There is no thought outside words:* the whole surrealist experience evidences this proposition...'[27]

25 Breton, 'Le surréalisme et la peinture', *La révolution surréaliste*, no.4, Paris, 16 July 1925, p.26; Breton's articles on Surrealism and painting were published as a book *Le Surréalisme et la peinture*, NRF, Paris, 1928.

26 Breton, *Le Surréalisme et la peinture*, Gallimard, Paris, 1965, p.70.

27 Aragon, *op. cit.*, p.7.

This question of the primacy of words or of images in thought, in dreams and in the phenomenon of phrases or pictures surging suddenly into consciousness at the moment of falling asleep was obviously of interest to artists as well as the theoreticians and poets of the movement. In the *First Surrealist Manifesto* Breton talks of an insistent phrase that suddenly was present in his mind – his words for this were that it 'cognait à la vitre', knocked on the window pane. He couldn't quite remember the phrase but it was something like, 'Il y a un homme coupé en deux par la fenêtre (There is a man cut in two by the window). He then adds an important footnote: 'Were I a painter, this visual depiction would doubtless have become more important for me than the other. It was most certainly my previous predispositions which decided the matter.'[28] Subsequently he focused on similar apparitions, visual, as clear to him as the auditory ones – a tree, a wave, a musical instrument, whose contours he was easily able to follow, because it was not a matter of drawing, but of *calquer*, fixing. This is a term that was to reappear in the context of Salvador Dalí's notion of the hand-painted dream picture. In a later text, Breton returns to this question, and admits the vast unknown hinterland of 'thought' before it becomes conscious. He is talking about the relationship between Surrealist automatic writing and that of the mediums, and between their respective auditory or visual perceptions.

> Not only do I think that there is almost always complexity in imaginary sounds – the unity and speed of the dictation remain active concerns – but it also seems certain that visual or tactile images (primitive, not preceded or accompanied by words, like the representation of whiteness or elasticity without any prior, concomitant, or subsequent intervention of words that express them or derive from them) freely operate in the immeasurable region that stretches between consciousness and unconsciousness.[29]

In the context of the long debates about perception and representation within Surrealism, in which the visual tends to be regarded as inferior, this comment resonates with Miró's painting. *Photo: Ceci est la couleur de mes rêves*

28 Breton, *Manifestos*, *op. cit.*, p.21.
29 Breton, *Break of Day*, *op. cit.*, p.140.

sets up a threefold dance between painting, photography and writing, three forms of expression each of which claims to 'represent' the world. None does so in a conventional way in this work. The 'blue', 'the colour of his dreams' is the wordless appearance in that 'immeasurable region' that remained the Surrealists' hunting ground, between consciousness and unconsciousness.[30]

30 See Anne Umland, 'Painting as Object', in Ades, *The Colour of My Dreams: The Surrealist Revolution in Art*, Vancouver Art Gallery, Vancouver, 2011, for a discussion of this painting in connection with the Surrealist object.

Gender and Identity

The questioning of identity runs as a live wire through the works of Dada and Surrealist artists and writers. Changing sex was a familiar Dada game: Duchamp, Man Ray and Francis Picabia all on occasion adopted female personae, with photography as the performative medium that endorsed Duchamp's alter ego Rrose Sélavy. Hannah Höch in her photomontages, on the other hand, challenged a binary male/female switch; gender, profession, race, nationality and sexuality were thrown into confusion and presented visually with as much ambiguity as possible.

Surrealism became something of a lightning rod for gender critiques. The Surrealists have been condemned for placing women at the heart of their project but denying them a voice, for lauding love exclusively in terms of heterosexuality, for the violence done to the female body in their work, for homophobia and even for being a boys' club. I am not the only person to try to disentangle this knot of displeasure and defend them against these charges. In the essay 'Surrealism, Male-Female' I attempt to argue that Surrealism's position was more complex and that its transparency in questions of desire, its privileging of the erotic and curiosity about sexual preference could release both male and female artists from gender stereotypes. The Surrealists probed sexuality in parallel to the investigations by psychologists and psychoanalysts but still placed love at the centre of their ideas.

In recent years the active presence of women in the movement has been recognised, and exhibitions like art historian and curator Whitney Chadwick's *Mirror Images: Women, Surrealism and Self-Representation* (MIT List Center, Cambridge, MA, 1998) have helped to flush them out from long historical neglect. Claude Cahun, for example, almost completely forgotten until the 1980s, was one of the most brilliant and extreme artists to challenge the notion of a unitary self. That her photographs were collaborations with her partner Marcel Moore has now become clear. Not only did women indeed have a voice – many voices – within Surrealism, but they also produced some of its most original expressions.

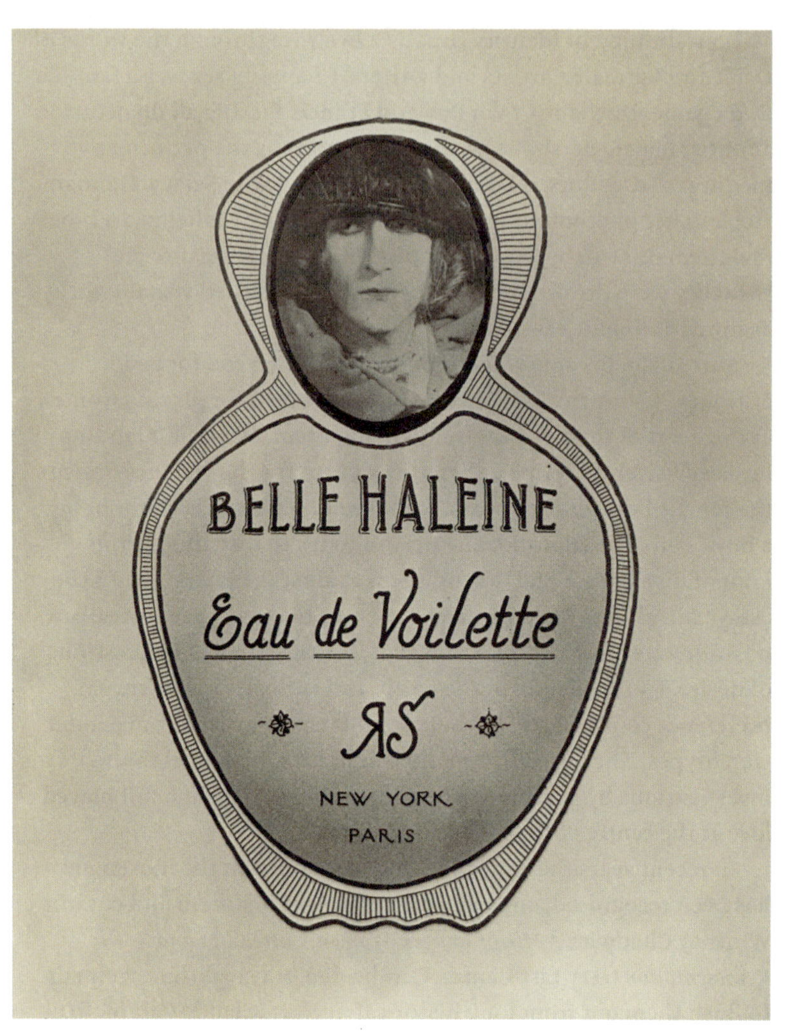

346 **Marcel Duchamp and Man Ray**
Belle Haleine, Eau de Voilette
(Beautiful Breath, Veil Water), 1921
Gelatin silver print
22.4 × 17.8 cm | 8⅞ × 7 in

Duchamp's Masquerades

The Portrait in Photography, Graham Clarke (ed), Reaktion Books, London, 1992

The numerous photographs of Duchamp by friends and admirers inhabit a curious and ambiguous space in relation to his work. Although not technically his, the photos have begun to command a regular place in books and catalogues about him. In many, there is a high degree of connivance between Duchamp and the photographer. Duchamp was clearly instrumental in the conception of the photographs and stage-managed their effects. Some, like Man Ray's shots of Duchamp *en femme* dressed as Rrose Sélavy, have with obvious justification been discussed more frequently in the context of Duchamp's art than in the context of Man Ray's. A few photographs were incorporated into a specific work: Man Ray's image of Duchamp with shaving soap in his hair, for instance, which was used in Duchamp's *Monte Carlo Bond* (1924), or the shot of Duchamp dressed as a woman, which was incorporated into the assisted readymade *Belle Haleine, Eau de Voilette* (Beautiful Breath, Veil Water, 1921) and reproduced on the cover of *New York Dada*. But the level of engagement and, in some sense, of manipulation, remains high even in casual snapshots.

Duchamp posed willingly all his life for photographs, but there is a particular concentration of energy in his involvement with the camera in the period during and just after the First World War; significantly, two of the most interesting series – the shaving-soap portraits and the second set of Rrose Sélavy pictures mentioned above, date from 1923–24, the year following his final abandonment of work on the *Large Glass* (1915–23), and his decision to give up art for chess. It was a period in which he was able fully to indulge his interest in the camera – in both photography and film – as a consequence of his close collaborative friendship with Man Ray.

His practical involvement, however, seems to have gone no further than taking a few lessons from Man Ray, and once contemplating becoming an assistant cameraman. In fact his interest in photography has some parallels with the readymades, in that he partly saw it as a new way of realising ideas outside the exercise of traditional skills. Although in this sense relishing photography's 'automatism', it is also clear from his notes that he was fascinated by the technical side of the craft.

Evidently, the photographs we are talking about are portraits, in the elastic sense of the term (that is, not confining the term to studio poses). However, the conventional sense in which a portrait must bear a likeness to the sitter quickly comes under uncomfortable scrutiny. A comparison between the photo-portraits in question and other contemporary instances of the practice of portraiture highlights the ambiguity of Duchamp's self-presentations in photographs.

During the period we have been discussing, c.1917–24, Duchamp was the subject of portraits in a variety of mediums apart from photography, some conventional, others not. Several were by women friends. Florine Stettheimer painted him; Elsa von Freytag-Loringhoven constructed her *Portrait of Marcel Duchamp* (1919) out of feathers and other found materials which sprout from a goblet.[1] This object seems to emerge from a marriage between the readymade and that odd family of Dada portraits whose most famous examples include Picabia's object-portraits of his friends (Alfred Stieglitz as a camera, his wife Gabrielle as a windscreen, and so on). But the fact that it is constructed of objects fragmented and recombined rather than being a single object bearing a symbolic relationship to the person represented, in the manner of Picabia's portraits, results in a suggestiveness that has more in common with the Surrealist object.

Equally remarkable, though in a more conventional avant-garde mode, is Katherine Dreier's abstract painted portrait of Duchamp. Dreier, a close friend and patron, reproduced this portrait in her study of Western art, published in 1922, to provide a contrast with an 'old style' portrait of Duchamp in silverpoint by Joseph Stella. In the new style, she argues, the painter tries to express the character of the sitter through 'abstract form and colour': 'Thus through the balance of curves, angles and

1 *The Little Review*, winter, 1922.

squares, through broken or straight lines, or harmoniously flowing ones, through colour harmony or discord, through vibrant or subdued tones, cold or warm, there arises a representation of the character which suggests clearly the person in question, and brings more pleasure to those who understand, than would an ordinary portrait representing only the figure and face.'[2] Dreier's rather over-anxious assertion of faith in the psychological potential of the painted portrait, provided the modern portrait painter possessed the deeper knowledge of psychology necessary in order to 'make a more profound study of his subject', attempts to recoup for painting the area that photography above all had usurped: the likeness, but now expressed in terms of abstractions inimitable by photography. This claim that abstract painting can be more psychologically true than photography might have helped provoke Duchamp's ironic response, in using photography as a disguise or mask to construct alternative identities. Dreier's text, though, certainly indicates that the question of psychological likeness in portraiture was still being debated, in this case in terms of the expressive potential of abstraction.

The photographs of Duchamp that we are discussing challenge, in different ways and with different consequences, precisely those assumptions made by Dreier about the potential of a portrait to summon up a sitter, and reveal the 'truth' about him or her, whether physical or psychological. Indeed they seem to declare the whole debate about 'likeness', as touched on above by Dreier, to be no longer relevant – or perhaps, more correctly, to be exploitable in ways that shift the centre of interest away from the sitter/subject and towards the mode of representation. Rather than revealing a unitary nugget of identity, these photographs disguise, dissolve, multiply and contradict.

Photography was the ideal alibi for changes of identity. In apparently introducing a measure of authenticity, it was also prone to the kind of paradox Duchamp enjoyed – as in the altered *Wanted* poster (1923), to which Duchamp added two mugshots, full-face and profile, smudgy and almost illegible in the heavy tonal contrast, as though to demonstrate how drained of identity even identity photos can be.[3]

2 Katherine Dreier, *Western Art and the New Era*, Bretano's, New York, NY, 1923, pp.112–13.

3 See also Richard Brilliant, *Portraiture*, Reaktion Books, London, 1991, for a discussion of this as 'anti-portrait'.

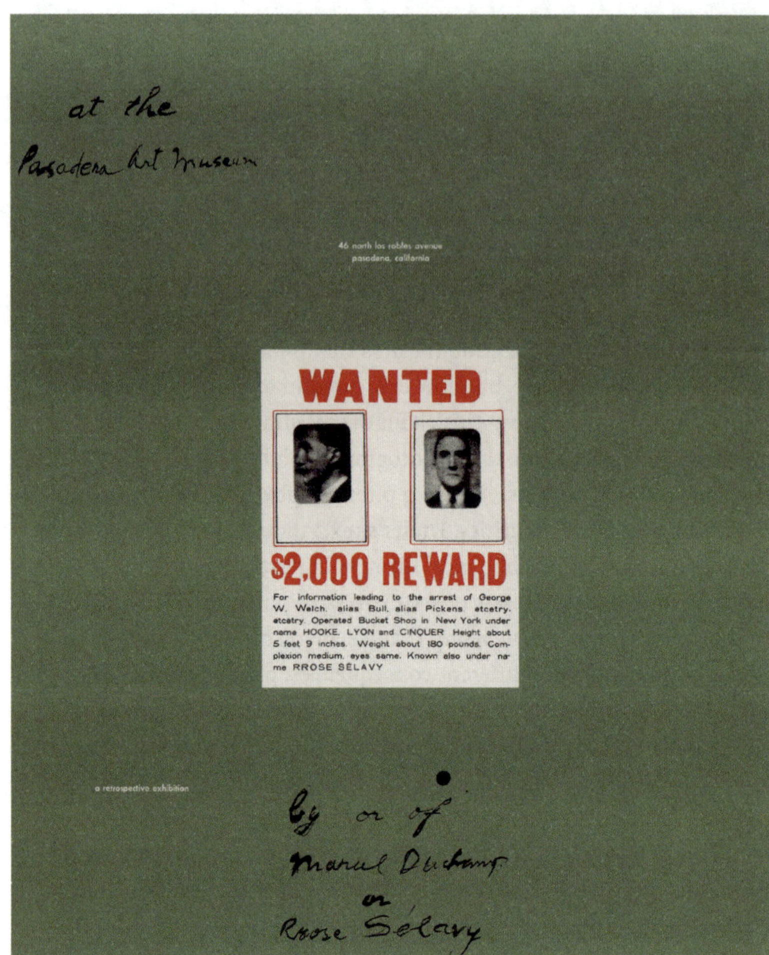

350 **Marcel Duchamp**
Wanted $2,000 Reward, A Retrospective Exhibition by or of Marcel Duchamp or Rrose Selavy, 1963
Offset lithograph
87.6 × 68.5 cm | 34½ × 27 in

Both Duchamp and Man Ray dressed up before the camera to change identity. Duchamp masqueraded as his female alter ego; Man Ray, in photographic self-portraits, posed both as a woman, and also as a priest. (In the Surrealist circles in which Man Ray moved his priest pose was a deliberate act of sacrilege, a challenge to the social order to be understood as parallel to the reversal of gender.)

Sometimes Duchamp used pose or props to suggest mythological or legendary associations, classical or modern. Robert Lebel mentions St Sebastian, 'ce patron des artistes dont il a pris ironiquement la pose dans une photographie de 1942' (the artists' patron saint whose posture he has taken on in a photo of 1942);[4] Duchamp acephalic on his 81st birthday and 'se couvrant à son niveau pubien d'un "birthday cake" planté de bougies érectiles' (covering her pubic area with a "birthday cake" planted with erect candles);[5] and the series of photographs taken in London in 1937 with Mary Reynolds, in which Duchamp is mysteriously swathed in a towel, only his head visible, like a shaved Medusa, with a tape measure round his neck or protruding from his mouth.

These photo-portraits – almost self-portraits – are not a fixed group, merging as they do at one end with the bona fide works and at the other with family snapshots, but they constitute an arena in which Duchamp's interest in gender and in representation intersect.

I

Photo: Wall (morning):
My portrait in the bathroom mirror[6]

There is no satisfactory solution to the problem of how to photograph oneself looking at oneself in the mirror – that is, if the photographic apparatus is to remain concealed or an awkwardly angled shot is to be avoided. Such a photograph would, however, be the best way to represent Duchamp's observation that:

4 Robert Lebel, *Marcel Duchamp*, Belfond, Paris, 1985, p.133.
5 *Ibid.*, p.131.

On peut regarder voir,
On ne peut pas entendre entendre
(see)
one can look at seeing
one can't hear hearing[7]

Duchamp hints, by giving alternative words to the action (*voir, regarder*), that although doubled it may not be identical. To photograph oneself and retain the look, to separate that look from the camera's eye, is evidently impossible. To be photographed looking into and in a mirror is possible.

Duchamp and his friend Henri-Pierre Roché discovered one version of a photographic mirror-trick in the popular photo-booths in Manhattan in 1917. With the aid of mirrors, and with the photographer and his apparatus concealed in the darkness behind the subject, 'as if the latter were the "mask" projected on the print', multiple simultaneous views were produced on a single negative.[8] However, it is rather the absence of the mirror plane than its presence that is remarkable here. Duchamp appears to be looking at himself, but not at himself looking at himself. Duchamp's interest in the problem of the mirror self-portrait was shared by a number of photographers in the 1920s. But instead of experimenting with the kinds of technical and formal artifice or the games with reflection and reality practised by someone like Florence Henri, Duchamp sometimes chose to have himself photographed by his friend Man Ray in poses and guises that imply the presence of a mirror. There is no mirror visible, but the presence of one is a necessary component of the staging. The implied, but not actual, presence of the mirror also allows, as we shall see, a metaphorical dimension to the image to emerge.

In one such series of photographs, Duchamp posed for Man Ray with shaving soap rising messily up from its accustomed place to cover his hair

6 Marcel Duchamp, *Notes and Projects for the Large Glass*, Arturo Schwarz (ed), Thames & Hudson, London, 1969, p.98. A spoof text entitled 'Man Before the Mirror', written by a German friend of Man Ray's and signed by Rrose Sélavy, was published in Man Ray, *Photographies 1920–1934*, Cahiers d'Art, Paris, 1934. It described men standing before the mirror absorbed in their secret vice of vanity.

7 Duchamp, 'La Boîte de 1914', in Michel Sanouillet and Elmer Peterson (eds), *The Essential Writings of Marcel Duchamp*, Thames & Hudson, London, 1975, p.23.

8 Jean Clair, *Méduse*, Gallimard, Paris, 1989, p.166.

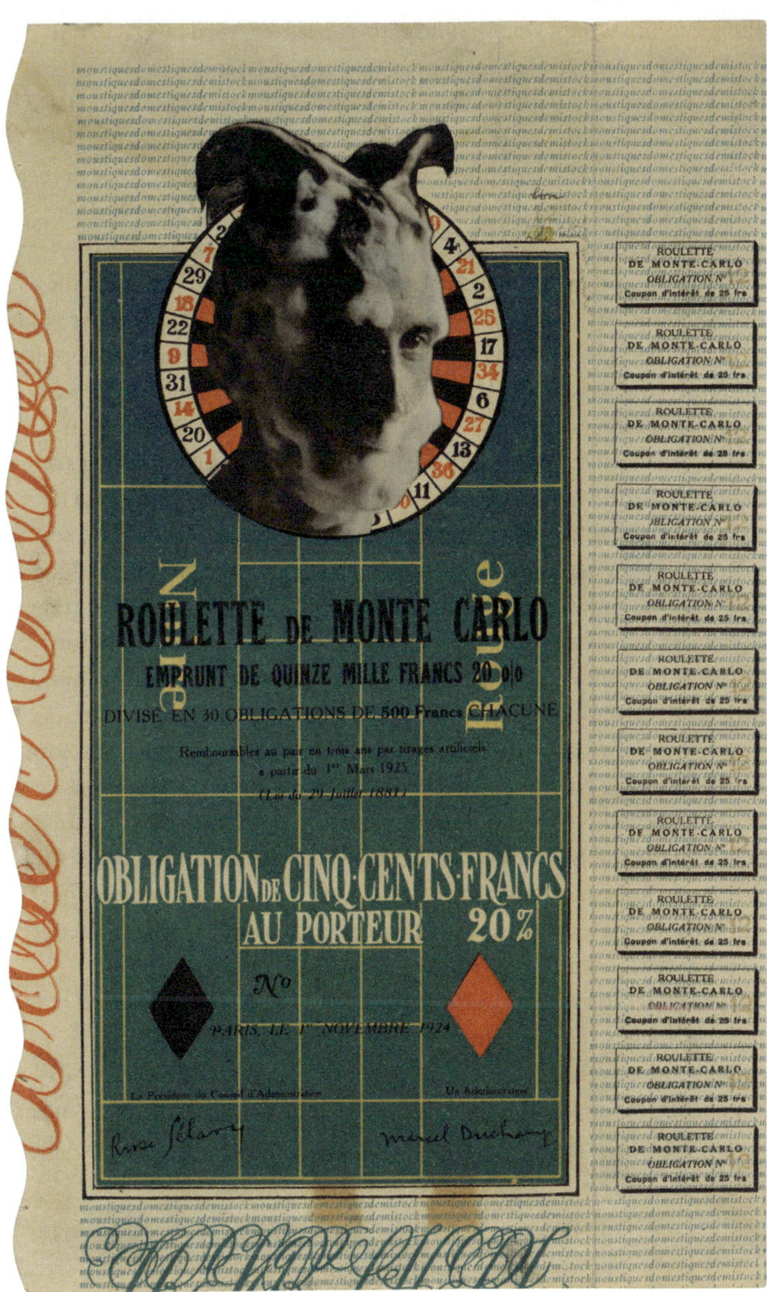

Marcel Duchamp
Obligations pour la Roulette de Monte Carlo (Monte Carlo Bond) No.12, 1924
Cut-and-pasted gelatin silver prints on lithograph with letterpress
31.2 × 19.3 cm | 12¼ × 7½ in

and lift it into wings. One shot from this series was used by Duchamp for his *Monte Carlo Bond* in 1924. Another has him staring fiercely straight ahead, not unlike a battered Wagnerian hero, in a pose which is in creepy contrast to the fluffy white soap.[9]

The image must have sprung from the idea of the 'self-portrait in the bathroom mirror' that Duchamp proposed, in his notes, as a possible subject for a photo – the place is specific and the action, the shaver's intimate scrutiny of his reflection, private. The bathroom mirror is the male counterpart to the dressing table looking glass, and in another group of photographs by Man Ray, which also, I would argue, imply (perhaps less obviously) the presence of a mirror, Duchamp presents himself dressed as his female alter ego, Rrose Sélavy. Although not the first time Man Ray recorded Duchamp on film dressed as a woman, this particular set of images are the most emphatically self-admiring. They were taken in 1924, the same year as the male shaving-soap images, to which they act in quite direct ways as pendants. In the Rrose Sélavy photos, everything that signifies conventional femininity is emphasised, and the gaze at the camera lens operates as a replay of the mirror's confirmation of beauty.

There is a hidden linguistic pun that supplements the visual connection between these two photo-portraits. There was, Duchamp once noted, a *'femmes-savantes'* (intellectual woman, blue-stocking) side to Rrose Sélavy: her male counterpart, then, would be an *'homme-savant/savon'*, or soap-man. This pair – the *'homme savon'* and the *'femme savante'* – are counterparts to one another. But are they just generated from linguistic games à la Roussel? Or do they represent one possible pair of poles out of which the male/female elements of the personality are constructed? Could they reveal hidden aspects of the subject?

The rendering strange in a mirror, though not quite obliterating likeness, invites speculation about recognition and identity. 'For the *imagos* – whose veiled faces it is our privilege to see in outline in our daily experience and in the penumbra of symbolic efficacity – the mirror image would seem to be the threshold of the visible world.'[10] The mirror enables

9 There is a print of this version in Mme Duchamp's collection.

10 Jacques Lacan, 'The Mirror Stage as Formative of the Function of the I as Revealed in Psychoanalytic Experience', *Ecrits; A Selection*, trans. Alan Sheridan, W.W. Norton, London, 1977.

the double to appear, 'in which psychical realities, however heterogeneous, are manifested',[11] and Duchamp forces the mirror to realise those other identities, or psychical realities, fragmentary, ghostly, bizarre as they may be, which would usually only be accessible through those dreams or hallucinations which present us with what Lacan called the 'imago of one's own body'.

Duchamp's lathered head, about to be shaved (another portrait shows him with closely shaven head, and yet another with a star/comet shaved into his hair), penitentially inverts his own whiskering of the Mona Lisa in *LHOOQ* (1919), though it simultaneously demonstrates that the inversion or reversal cannot work – to shave a male does not reverse the bearding of a female.[12] But it de-sexualises/re-sexualises if understood as a symbolic equivalent to the castrative blinding of Oedipus.

These pendant photo-portraits, of the *'homme savon'* and Rrose Sélavy, hint at the Classical myths connected with mirrors and reflections – the myths of Medusa and Narcissus.[13] Each of these stories is laden with sexual ambiguity and threat. The myth of Medusa explores the threat of death by looking, concealing by one horror the other primal fear; in the other legend the hero brings about his own death by falling in love with his reflection in a pool. In the *'homme savon'*, the soapy hair rising into wings at the side of the head resembles certain images of Medusa or the Gorgon's head, which have, above their snake curls, wings.

Duchamp, although aware certainly of Freud's spectacular and then still scandalous modernisation of ancient myths as bearers of his theories about primordial sexual complexes, was equally aware of the rupture between the modern world and the Classical tradition, a gap he signals by the comic and derisory translation of snakes into soap.

'We have an imperfect idea', Breton wrote in *Littérature* in 1920, 'of the

11 *Ibid.*, p.3.

12 During the brief New York Dada period in 1911, Man Ray made a short film for Duchamp, which was ruined while being developed, in which a barber shaved the pubic hairs of the Baroness Elsa von Freytag-Loringhoven. Man Ray sent a salvaged shot in a letter to Tristan Tzara. (See Robert Reiss, '"My Baroness": Elsa von Freytag-Loringhoven', in Rudolf Kuenzli (ed), *New York Dada*, Willis Locker & Owens, New York, NY, 1986.

13 See Clair, *op. cit.*, for a discussion of the Medusa legend, and the way it exemplifies the face/genitals substitution. He also brings forward evidence that the Medusa face was originally male.

Seven Wonders of the ancient world. In our times, a few wise men: Lautréamont, Apollinaire, have offered the umbrella, the sewing machine, the top hat, to universal wonder... With the belief that nothing is incomprehensible, and that anything, if necessary, can serve as symbol, we expend treasures of the imagination... I reckon that a true modern mythology is in the course of being formed.'[14]

More sceptical perhaps than Breton, Duchamp's photographs seem to relate to a modern mythology whose text is lacking or partial. They hint at fragments of a modern version of myths of sexuality and gender, man and machine, chance and order, identity and loss of identity, memory and forgetting ('make an allegory of forgetting', Duchamp once noted).

II

Il y a celui qui fait le photographe et celle qui
a de l'haleine en dessous[15]

In the version of the pun, 'Il y a celui qui fait le photographe et celle qui a de l'haleine en dessous', published by Breton in his *Anthologie d'humour noir* (Anthology of Black Humour, 1940), Duchamp harks back to the title of his first appearance 'en femme', *Belle Haleine, Eau de Voilette*, with its overtones of concealment and death. The pun genders the relationship between photographer and sitter. 'There is he who acts as photographer, and she who has breath/wool beneath.'

The issue of gender identity was at the origin of the scandal created by Duchamp's *Nu descendant un escalier* (Nude Descending a Staircase, 1912). An interview in New York in 1916 under the headline 'Cubist Depicts Love in Brass and Glass: More Art in Rubbers than in Pretty Girl!' reported the following exchange between Duchamp and the woman interviewer: '"Is it a woman?" this young but very world-weary Frenchman repeated after me... "No. Is it a man? No... T*he Nude Descending a Staircase* is an abstraction of movement."'[16]

14 André Breton, 'Giorgio de Chirico', *Littérature*, no.11, January, 1920, p.28.
15 Quoted in Breton, *Anthologie de l'Humour Noir*, Éditions du Sagittaire, Paris, 1940, p.223.
16 *The Evening World*, 4 April 1916.

Duchamp later gave a less teasing explanation of the significance of the Nude's motion: 'The origin (of the painting) is the nude itself. To make a nude different from the classical nude, lying down, standing up, and set it in motion.' In motion, the nude loses the passive quality necessary for it to be an object of erotic contemplation.

It was precisely at this point of his interest in studies of movement, that photography first became important to him, in the form of the chronophotography of Étienne-Jules Marey. After 1912, when, as he said, 'my hand became my enemy', photography became a resort, like the mechanical drawing he adopted at the same time, 'against the easy splashing way' of oil painting. The rigour, precision and impersonality of mechanical drawing was a corrective against the sentimental expenditure of pigment; on several occasions Duchamp implicated painting as a male activity whose 'splashing' way metaphorised so readily. He wrote to Stieglitz: 'You know exactly how I feel about photography. I would like to see it make people despise painting until something else will make photography unbearable.'[17]

In the major work on which Duchamp was still sporadically engaged until 1923, *La Mariée mise à nu par ses célibataires, même* (The Bride Stripped Bare by her Bachelors, Even), commonly known as the *Large Glass*, photography is implicated, utilised or posited at many levels.[18] This cynical commentary, as Breton called it, on love, an elaborate metaphor of eroticism and passion, plays with ideas of sacrilege, art and the machine, through, among other things, active and passive modes. This tension between active and passive is one of the arenas in which photography is brought into play. In *The Green Box* notes (1934) Duchamp described the whole thus: 'in the dark, we shall determine (the condition for) the extra rapid exposition (allegorical appearance) of several collisions seemingly strictly to succeed each other according to certain laws.'[19] In the end, the contrast between the painstaking and labour-intensive methods used to transfer the planned images onto the glass surface, and the theoretical possibilities of the (extra rapid) photographic imprint,

17 Duchamp, *Essential Writings*, *op. cit.*, p.16.

18 Clair has discussed the relationship between photography and perspective in the *Large Glass* in 'Opticeries', *October*, no.5, summer, 1978.

19 Duchamp, *Essential Writings*, *op. cit.*, p.28.

perhaps contributed to its final abandonment. The notes also indicate an oscillation between the notion of photographic plate and mirror, this analogy leaking into the very texture of the glass (part of the glass was silvered, and Duchamp referred to tarnish, or rust, appearing through the ground glass). 'Photograph', he suggests, 'mirror effects...'

Many of the more specific references to photography in the notes to the *Large Glass* relate to the upper half, the domain of the Bride; Duchamp planned, in fact, to transfer the image of the Bride from his painting of 1912 photographically onto the glass.[20] This proving impractical, he painted it on in black and white. Photography is, in a sense, to the upper half of the *Large Glass* what mirrors and moulds are to the lower half. Photography, mirrors and moulds are all methods of reproduction:

> Given the object, considered in its physical appearance (Colour, mass, form).
> Define (graphically i.e. by means of pictorial conventions) the mould of the object.
> By mould is meant: from the point of view of form and colour, the negative (photographic); from the point of view of mass a plane.[21]

Thus, the very format and material of the *Large Glass* is a photographic analogue – two huge glass plates mounted above one another which recall the plate cameras using glass negatives that were still the normal mode at the time for portrait photography. In fact, the suspicion that the two halves of the glass are in some way self-portraits seems more and more relevant in the context of the photographs under discussion. The fact that Duchamp presented himself as both male and female in photographs might allow us to identify the Bride with Rrose Sélavy, the Bachelors with the male artist. This is in no way intended as an exclusive reading, but suggests a further dimension to the closed circuit of the work.

20 See Duchamp, *Essential Writings*, *op. cit.*, p.38.
21 See Duchamp, *Notes and Projects for the Large Glass*, *op. cit.*, p.212.

III

PC: When you were only 25 years old people already called you the 'bachelor'. You had a well-established anti-feminist attitude.
MD: No, anti-marriage but not anti-feminist. On the contrary I was normal to the highest degree! I had, rather, antisocial ideas...[22]

Duchamp explained to Pierre Cabanne the genesis of Rrose Sélavy as follows:

> I wanted in effect to change identity and the first idea that came to me was to take a Jewish name. I was Catholic and it would be quite a change to pass from one religion to another! I didn't find a Jewish name I liked or found tempting, and suddenly I had an idea: why not change sex? It's much simpler! So, that was the origin of the name of Rrose Sélavy. Nowadays it may be alright, christian names change over time, but Rose was a really stupid name in 1920. The double R came from Francis Picabia's picture, you know, *L'Oeil cacodylate* which Francis asked all his friends to sign... I think I put Pi Qu'habilla Rrose – arrose needs two Rs, and I liked the second R that I added – Pi Qu'habilla Rrose Sélavy. It was all word games.[23]

In the 1960s, asked whether Rrose Sélavy made her last appearance with the *Jeux de mots* published by GLM in 1939, Duchamp replied: 'She's still alive; manifests herself little or not at all'.[24] Rrose Sélavy occasionally signed works, but her most prominent manifestations were through the photographs; as the female mannequin dressed in Duchamp's jacket and hat in the street leading to the International Surrealist Exhibition in Paris in 1938; and as the author of the puns whose double meanings are paralleled in Duchamp's own double identity.[25]

22 Pierre Cabanne, *Entretiens avec Marcel Duchamp*, Pierre Belfond, Paris, 1967, p.54 (author's translation).

23 *Ibid.*, p.118. Picabia's painting, *L'Oeil cacodylate*, was exhibited at the Autumn Salon of 1921; Picabia had invited friends and visitors to his studio to sign it. Duchamp probably signed it upon returning to France in June 1921, after the brief episode of New York Dada. The first manifestation of Rose Sélavy accompanied the work *Fresh Widow*, signed 'Copyright Rose Sélavy 1920'. The double R, to transform the common christian name into 'arroser', first appeared on Picabia's painting.

24 Serge Stauffer, *Marcel Duchamp: Die Schriften*, Regenbogen-Verlag, Zurich, 1981.

These female masquerades have been discussed in terms of Duchamp's interest in the creative androgyne.[26] Arturo Schwarz, for example, quotes Lebel's comment that 'Man Ray made several photographic studies for this image which might suggest, in particular, the artist's inherent androgyny in the manner of Leonardo da Vinci, to whom Duchamp had paid homage in his own way by providing the Mona Lisa with masculine attributes',[27] and goes on to draw on Henry Lowenfeld, Freud and Jung to support his contention that Duchamp's apparent bisexuality is (as with other great artists) the symbol of a creative union of opposites. Schwarz quotes from Jung's *Archetypes and the Collective Unconscious* (1959) as follows:

> As civilisation develops, the bisexual primordial being turns into a symbol of the unity of personality, a symbol of the self, where the war of opposites finds peace. In this way the primordial being becomes the distant goal of man's self-development, having been from the very beginning a projection of his unconscious wholeness. Wholeness consists in the union of the conscious and the unconscious personality. Just as every individual derives from masculine and feminine genes, and the sex is determined by the predominance of the corresponding genes, so in the psyche it is only the conscious mind, in a man, that has the masculine sign, while the unconscious is by nature feminine.[28]

There is no denying the force of the Leonardo comparison, and there is plenty of evidence to support Duchamp's recurring interest in the alchemical androgyne. However, before accepting this rather final blanketing of Duchamp's interest in gender under the heading of androgyny, I would like to consider some supplementary possibilities in connection

25 In the 1942 *First Papers of Surrealism* exhibition catalogue in New York, Duchamp reproduced a photograph of an emaciated woman, a sign of the American Depression, to identify himself. He had played a similar game with false identities, although with a reverse effect, in 1924, when Picabia reproduced on the cover of the final issue of his magazine *391* a drawing of the boxer Georges Charbonnier; everyone thought it was a portrait of Duchamp, because the two resembled one another 'like two drops of water' (Duchamp, *Entretiens*).

26 See, for instance, the *Marcel Duchamp* exhibition catalogue, edited by Gloria Moure, Fundació Miró, Barcelona, 1984.

27 Arturo Schwarz, *The Complete Works of Marcel Duchamp*, Thames & Hudson, London, 1969, p.484.

28 Quoted in *ibid.*

with these particular photographs, which link them to a more extensive and pointed interest in contemporary debates about identity and gender difference. The androgyne is defined as uniting the physical characteristics of both sexes, or hermaphroditic. But, unlike Tiresias with his/her withered dugs, or the suspicious bulge Lyotard claims to see in the groin of the splayed nude of Duchamp's *Étant donnés: 1. Le gaz d'éclairage, 2. La chute d'eau*,[29] there is no evident dual sexuality in the photographs of Rrose Sélavy. Rather, pains seem to have been taken to disguise his gender, though with what success may be a different issue. If she is intended to 'reveal' the female side of the man, how far does this conform to the Jungian notion of the equation of the female and the unconscious? Are these the appropriate terms with which to approach these images? Or were there contemporary socio-anthropological debates in which Duchamp's transvestism could be seen as engaging with sexual difference in ways that challenge those stereotypes?

The first photographs Man Ray took of Duchamp dressed as a woman were part of the brief Dada campaign in New York in 1921.[30] The oval photograph in Duchamp's collection that was used for *Belle Haleine, Eau de Voilette*, is described on the back 'Marcel Duchamp en femme pour New York Dada (photo Man Ray) Spring 1921'.

From the start, then, this image was intended as a public manifestation in the context of Dada. The chosen photograph was added to an altered perfume label and pasted onto a glass bottle, which was then photographed for the cover of *New York Dada*.[31] The title of the single issue of this review was then printed repeatedly upside down, giving an effect not unlike elegant wallpaper. This *monde renversé* (world upside down) trope is continued in the mock 'statement, authorisation' by Tristan Tzara,

29 J.F. Lyotard, *Les transformateurs Duchamp*, Éditions Gaililée, Paris, 1977.

30 Modernism in New York, where Duchamp had spent most of the First World War, was largely produced by women, and the avant garde was marked by a 'jocular feminism' quite different from Dada in Zurich and Paris. The public interpreters of Duchamp's *Fountain*, during the Independents scandal of 1917, were his female friends Louise Norton and Beatrice Wood. See Ades, 'Introduction', *3 New York Dadas and The Blind Man*, A. Brotchie (ed), Atlas Press, London, 2013; Jay Bochner, *The Marriage of Rogue and The Soil, Little Magazines and Modernism*, Ashgate, London, 2008. (Footnote added 2015.)

31 It was this object and not the photo-collage, as Schwarz states, that was used for the cover. The glass-stoppered bottles used for perfume, incidentally, are almost identical to those used for certain scientific experiments, especially those adapted into a triangular shape for the experiments in stereometry that so interested Duchamp.

standing in for an editorial, whose addressee is consistently female. 'Therefore, Madam, be on your guard and realise that a really dada product is a different thing from a glossy label.' Dada's irritant iconoclasm and subversion is hilariously presented in this 'authorisation' as an article of intimate hygiene in a running metaphor drawn from fashion magazines: 'you need look no further than to the use of articles prepared without Dada to account for the fact that the skin of your heart is chapped; that the so precious enamel of your intelligence is cracking; also for the presence of those tiny wrinkles still imperceptible but nevertheless disquieting.'

The photograph of Duchamp as a fashionable woman recalls the frequent use of fashion as metaphor among Dada artists ('change your ideas as you would a pair of trousers', as Picabia said), which both signals the ephemerality of taste and parodies the importance of fashion in the construction of the 'new woman' and the 'new man'.[32]

Duchamp was not the only Dadaist to play with gender changes in self-portraits. Both Johannes Baargeld, member of the Cologne Dada group, and Erwin Blumenfeld constructed photomontages in which their own head is placed on a female torso – in Baargeld's case, atop a Classical stone Venus, in Blumenfeld's, his own naked but veiled torso terminates in the lower half of a female nude. Neither attempts a full disguise, emphasising rather the comic of the impossible conjunction. By including references to the Classic female nude, however, they evidently allude to an artistic tradition whose dignity and superiority Dada specifically sought to undermine ('Dada has given the Venus de Milo an enema', as Jean (Hans) Arp said).[33] In the Dada context, a similar intention could be posited for Duchamp. In his case it can be traced back through a long and combative engagement with the nude of high art, whose classic double role as bearer of the ideal and of the erotic he progressively undermines. Photography was to play a part in this engagement at a number of levels.

The 1921 versions of 'Duchamp en femme' are not obviously transvestite images in the pantomime dame sense; anything monstrous in

32 The heavy, feathered velvet hat Duchamp wears could well have figured among Herman Tappé's creations of the previous winter. *New York Dada* also reproduced Stieglitz's 'double exposure' of a bare leg wearing a high-heeled shoe, and the face of Dorothy True, the feminist and suffragette.

33 Jean (Hans) Arp, 'I become more and more removed from aesthetics', *On My Way*, Wittenborn, Schultz, New York, NY, 1948, p.48.

them derives rather from what Bataille called the anti-humanism of outdated masquerades.[34]

In the photographic portraits taken a little later of Rrose Sélavy,[35] again by Man Ray, the image is more finely crafted, the pose no longer the awkward head-on view, but seductively modulated, hands framing the face or stroking the fur. The hands were, in fact, those of Germaine Everling, Picabia's companion. Francis Naumann has mentioned Charlie Chaplin's film *A Woman* (1915), in which Chaplin 'impersonates a woman in order to gain entrance to the boarding house where his girlfriend lives',[36] as a likely inspiration for this photograph. This is quite convincing, but the pose and manner also bear a striking resemblance to the portrait studies of actresses and international beauties that alternated in the pages of *Vanity Fair* with articles by Gertrude Stein, Robert Benchley, Dorothy Parker and so on. Man Ray, who had taken up portrait photography in 1922, was now well established in the social and intellectual world epitomised at the time by *Vanity Fair*.[37]

Naumann comments on Rrose's 'affected manner and poorly disguised Identity', but in fact her manner/pose relates closely to fashion/theatre portraits in *Vanity Fair*, which emphasise a certain type of femininity, and which contrast markedly with other images of women in the journal. For example, those who made the Hall of Fame pages for outstanding achievements, such as Edith Wharton or Willa Cather, exhibit a direct gaze and business-like stance; they do not present themselves as objects for others' gaze in the same way as the actresses do. The photographers revelled in the actresses, manipulating their flesh and the light to create often quite fantastic, almost abstract, studies of a neck or a cheek (see, for instance, Arnold Genthe's portraits of Garbo). In such portrait studies the lens/mirror ambiguity is emphasised, as the narcissistic absorption in the

34 Georges Bataille, 'La Figure Humaine', *Documents*, no.4, September, 1929.

35 The second set of photographs is often dated, like the first, to 1921, but a later date, between 1922 and 1924, seems more likely. They were made in Paris rather than New York, but as will be argued below, were affected by the New York milieu.

36 Francis Naumann, 'Marcel Duchamp: a reconciliation of opposites', in Rudolf Kuenzli and Francis Naumann (eds), *Marcel Duchamp: Artist of the Century*, MIT Press, Cambridge, MA, and London, 1989, p.11.

37 The editor of *Vanity Fair*, Frank Crowninshield, was a friend of Beatrice Wood's family, and advised her when the New York review *The Blind Man*, jointly edited by herself, Duchamp and Henri-Pierre Roché, looked set to create a scandal.

specular image is exploited by the photographer/viewer's enjoyment of erotic promise.

However, while the pose Duchamp/Rrose Sélavy adopts may resemble that of the more feminine portraits, the eyes, it could well be argued, give the game away. They seem to assert control and consciousness, and it is there that the efficacy of the disguise falters. Perhaps therefore this does clearly indicate the male presence, but rather than uniting in a Jungian wholeness, it is an interruption which emphasises difference.

Recent studies have brilliantly revealed the ways in which Duchamp's 'Cubist' works – especially the *Large Glass* – make explicit the aggressive misogyny, perhaps unintentional, of Cubist renderings of the female body, and also how far the scientific and religious framework in which the *Large Glass* is held, in the context of early twentieth-century France, exposes the socially constructed nature of gender.[38]

The photographs of Rrose Sélavy in fact coincide with Duchamp's temporary abandonment of art, the 'other' of the male painter. Rrose Sélavy, appearance carefully gauged to reveal the socially constructed nature of attitudes to sexuality, radically opposes the timeless beauty of the classical female nude.

Duchamp's interest in making this explicit may have received a stimulus from the different context of New York. It is possible that a different climate of gender relations had its effect on Duchamp's thinking about the subject. Duchamp remarked on his arrival in New York:

> The thing which has struck me most in this country, which has undoubtedly the most beautiful women... is the lack of really strong emotions in your men. An American, for instance, if he has to choose between a business appointment and an engagement with the woman he loves, rings her up on the telephone. 'Hello, dear', he says, 'I can't see you today; I must go to the bank instead.' To a Frenchman that seems very stupid.[39]

38 See David Hopkins, 'Hermeticism, Catholicism and Gender as Structure: A Comparative Study of Themes in the Work of Marcel Duchamp and Max Ernst', unpublished PhD thesis, University of Essex, 1989.

39 See interview by Nicola Greeley-Smith, 'Cubist depicts Love in Brass and Glass: More Art in Rubbers than in Pretty Girl!', *The Evening World*, 4 April 1916.

This casual comment on cultural difference might be seen to mask some ambivalence on Duchamp's part towards the different relationship between the sexes as expressed socially.

Debates about female emancipation and equality between the sexes were more intense in the United States and in England at the beginning of this century than in France. (It is significant that in both countries some women had received the vote by 1920, whereas in France there was no female emancipation until after the Second World War.) Concomitant with this was a sharper debate about the nature of 'womanliness', which frequently took the form of an attempted reconciliation between the notion of enduring feminine qualities and the 'new woman'. In the English magazine *Vanity Fair,* the 'new woman' was advised on the true nature of 'womanliness': 'the truly womanly woman is she who is resolved that her life shall be the full and free expression of the best that is in her.'[40] James Joyce expresses some of the male anxiety at the collapse of the clear equation between biological and social difference, and at the recognised presence in varying degrees of male and female characteristics in everyone. Leopold Bloom, in his nightmare, is medically affirmed as a 'finished example of the new womanly man'.[41]

Havelock Ellis first published *Man and Woman: a study of secondary and tertiary sexual characteristics* in 1894, and it has rarely been out of print since. Havelock Ellis was moved to undertake his massive research project for social reasons, in order, as he put it, to clear away superstition and prejudice and knock on the head once and for all the absurdity of speaking of the superiority of one sex over another.[42] His careful and sceptical scrutiny also has the effect of destabilising stereotypes. There is obviously much of interest here, but two arguments in particular might have struck Duchamp. Firstly, Havelock Ellis's socio-anthropological

40 Laurence Housman, 'What is Womanly?', *Vanity Fair*, London, 1917. (Not to be confused with Crowninshield's publication, New York, 1914–36.)

41 James Joyce, *Ulysses*, The Bodley Head, London, 1960, p.613.

42 The detachment of masculine and feminine qualities from the biological characters of man and women was summed up by Freud in the 1915 footnote to *Three Essays on Sexuality*; that the biological characteristics of masculinity – aggression, greater muscular development and greater intensity of libido – were not necessarily assigned to the male in the animal species, and so on. Duchamp's close friends and patrons in New York, Walter and Louise Arensberg, possessed a full set of Freud's works, and it is reasonable to assume that they also possessed a copy of Havelock Ellis's book.

account of one of the causes of the subjection of women: 'While women have been largely absorbed in that sphere of sexuality which is Nature's, men have roamed the earth, sharpening their aptitudes and energies in perpetual conflict with Nature. It has thus come about that the subjugation of Nature had often practically involved the subjugation, physical and mental, of women by men.' While holding to the inevitability of some equation of nature/female, Havelock Ellis situates it in terms of a historical process which leaves man in possession of anachronistic characteristics and an unjustifiable assumption of superiority.

The second point would demand more space to discuss fully in relation to Duchamp, but can be seen to throw a somewhat unexpected light on his play with mechanisation and his machine/gender metaphors: 'Savagery and barbarism have more usually than not been predominantly militant, that is to say, masculine, in character, while modern civilisation is becoming industrial, that is to say feminine in character, for the industries belonged primitively to women, and they tend to make men like women.'[43] After an exhaustive psychological and anthropological investigation of the sexual differences between man and woman, Havelock Ellis concludes that it was not possible to determine the 'radical and essential characters of men and women uninfluenced by external modifying conditions'.[44]

The new conditions in which sexual and social equality were freely debated were accompanied by a greater degree of female independence. Katherine Dreier, in her account of a journey to Argentina, where Duchamp was also spending some time, described her shock at the treatment of women there, and their lack of freedom by contrast with their position in the United States.[45] But these conditions also created new tensions. 'The woman movement', as the feminist Ellen Key wrote in 1912, 'has now raised a partition between the sexes such as is found in the aquarium, where it becomes necessary to teach the pike to allow the carp, also, to live.'[46]

43 Havelock Ellis, *Man and Woman; a study of secondary and tertiary sexual characteristics*, Scott, London, 1904, p.448.

44 *Ibid.*, p.440.

45 Dreier, *Five Months in the Argentine; From a Woman's Point of View*, Sherman, New York, NY, 1920.

46 Ellen Key, *The Woman Movement*, G.P. Putnam's Sons, New York, NY, 1912, p.138.

Where can Duchamp's female persona, then, be positioned in relation to this state of affairs? How far might he be sharing the sociopolitical concerns of Havelock Ellis, Dreier or Ellen Key? As a deliberate display of socially constructed, artificial, sexual difference, how far can Rrose Sélavy be seen as critical of socially determined attitudes to femininity and womanliness? The photographs of Rrose Sélavy could be seen to focus on difference in a logical extension of Duchamp's enquiries into identity and the challenges to the symbolic order. As Julia Kristeva says, 'the apparent coherence which the term "woman" assumes in contemporary ideology... essentially has the negative effect of effacing the differences between the diverse functions or structures which operate beneath this word.'[47]

The exaggerated femininity of the Rrose Sélavy photographs, curly hair touched in with a pen, and so on, calls to mind Joan Riviere's text from the end of the 1920s: 'Womanliness as Masquerade': 'In daily life types of men and woman are constantly met with who, while mainly heterosexual in their development, plainly display strong features of the other sex. This has been judged to be an expression of the bisexuality inherent in us all... I shall attempt to show that women who wish for masculinity may put on a mask of womanliness to avert anxiety and the retribution feared from men.' The subject of this case study was an intellectual woman (a *femme savante).* As Riviere notes: 'Not long ago intellectual pursuits for women were associated almost exclusively with an overtly masculine type of woman... This has now changed. Of all the women engaged in professional work today, it would be hard to say whether the greater number are more feminine than masculine in their mode of life and character.' Riviere's patient was given to excessive displays of coquetry after successful professional engagements, which are analysed as an unconscious attempt to ward off reprisals from the father figures whose masculinity she had stolen. She dreamt of people putting on masks to avert disaster:

> Womanliness therefore could be assumed and worn as a mask, both to hide the possession of masculinity and to avert the reprisals expected if she was found to possess it... The reader may ask how I define

47 Julia Kristeva, 'Women's Time', in Toril Moi (ed), *The Kristeva Reader*, Columbia University Press, New York, NY, 1986, p.193.

womanliness or where I draw the line between genuine womanliness and the 'masquerade'. My suggestion is not, however, that there is any such difference; whether radical or superficial, they are the same things.[48]

Duchamp's Rrose Sélavy might, then, be positioned in relation to such contemporary sociopolitical and psychological debates about gender and identity, which contributed to the destabilisation of assumptions about masculinity and femininity. Both Duchamp's first idea of switching religious identities, and then his idea about changing sex, were deliberately disruptive and also denote an imagined shift away from a position of dominance, but to test out the freedom to change identity is to introduce in a characteristically ironic form the limits reached immediately by such an appeal to freedom. So perhaps, after all, Duchamp's apparent attempt at disruption is simply the assertion yet again of his control. As the anarchist Max Stirner, whom Duchamp admired, wrote: 'The craving for a particular freedom always includes the purpose of a new dominion.'[49]

48 Joan Riviere, 'Womanliness as a Masquerade', *International Journal of Psychoanalysis*, no.10, 1929, pp.303–13.
49 Max Stirner, *The Ego and His Own*, A.C. Fifield, London, 1912, p.209.

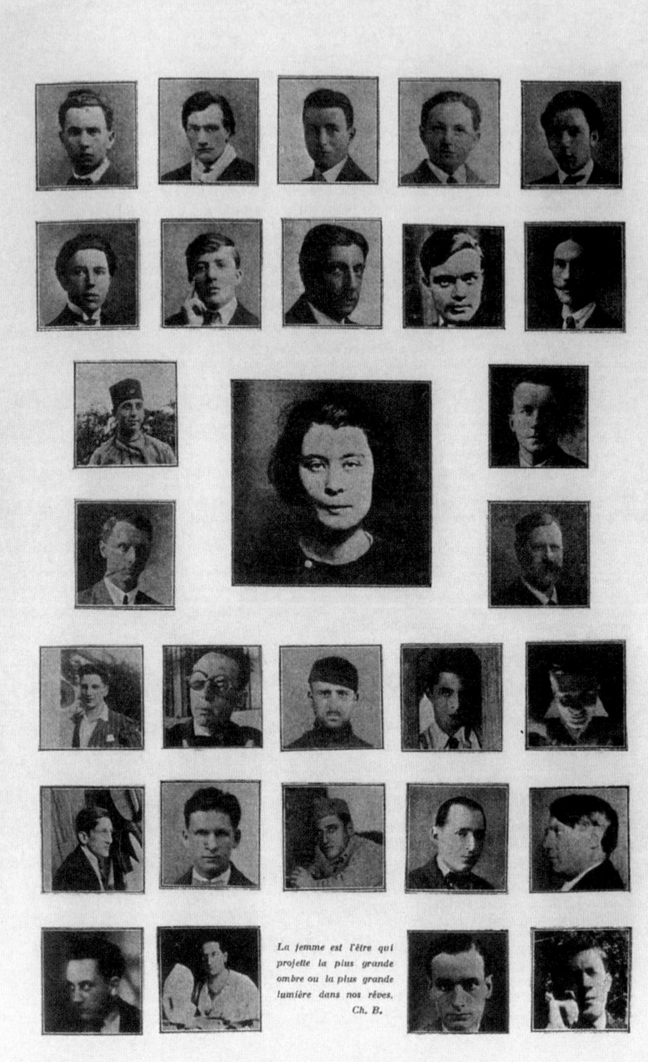

La femme est l'être qui projette la plus grande ombre ou la plus grande lumière dans nos rêves.

Ch. B.

Page from *La Révolution surréaliste*, no.1, December 1924

Surrealism: Male-Female

Surrealism: Desire Unbound, Jennifer Mundy (ed), Tate Publishing, London, 2001

The case against Surrealism and its attitude to women has had powerful advocates in the last few decades. Surrealism has been criticised for idealising woman while marginalising real women, for its indifference to female artists and writers, for the celebration of heterosexual love at the expense of other sexualities, and for a pervasive misogyny, especially in the apparent violence done to the female body in representation.[1]

In the process there has been a tendency to reduce Surrealism to a single voice and forget its complex and extra-artistic character as what the Czech artist Toyen (Marie Čerminovà) called a 'community of ethical views'.[2] Argued from different positions, however, this case has had the positive consequence of bringing back to light the works of many women artists and writers closely associated with the movement but sidelined by it or forgotten by its historians.[3] It is less often acknowledged, however, that questions of female creativity and the representation of woman in Surrealism are inseparable from its wider concerns about gender, and that male anxieties as well as same-sex desire are integral to them.

1 Xavière Gauthier, *Surréalisme et sexualité*, Gallimard, Paris, 1971, was the first full-scale attack on the movement's sexism. See also Mary Ann Caws, Rudolf Kuenzli and Gwen Raaberg (eds), *Surrealism and Women*, MIT Press, Cambridge, MA, and London, 1991.

2 Toyen, response to questionnaire about the situation of painting, in *Médium*, no.4, 1955, quoted in Penelope Rosemont (ed), *Surrealist Women*, University of Texas Press, Austin, TX, 1998, p.81.

3 The seminal study was Whitney Chadwick, *Women Artists and the Surrealist Movement*, Thames & Hudson, London 1985. See also Whitney Chadwick (ed), *Mirror Images: Women, Surrealism and Self-Representation*, MIT Press, Cambridge, MA, and London, 1998. The disappearance of Surrealist women (except as muses and lovers) from the movement's history has much to do with the selective nature of that history as it was written in the movement's latter years. Penelope Rosemont (see note 2), using journals, catalogues

The very transparency Surrealism attempted to establish in this area of sexual desire and identity produced contradictions in its own discourse about love and the idealisation of woman, and raised questions about masculinity and femininity, sexual preference, deviance and normality that simultaneously began to dismantle Surrealism's own myths. Through debates on sexuality, through the privileging of the erotic and the condition of madness, through ambiguities raised by the question of 'woman as nature' seen in Surrealist terms, through an insistent troubling of gender identity, through the attempts to make representations of the body speak as revolutionary signs, and through the apparent clash between the celebration of the lover in Surrealist poetry and the violence done (largely to 'her') in its visual arts, the possibility of a different view of human relations and the potential of radically new forms of expression were opened up.

As the dust clears from the debates it is becoming evident that some women artists and writers have spoken with great force from positions

---

etc., totted up 300 women who had taken part at some point in the Surrealist movement. Ninety-seven were included in her anthology.

Many exhibitions about Surrealism have overlooked women Surrealists in spite of the fact that they were, from the 1930s and increasingly in the postwar years, highly visible in Surrealism's own exhibitions, reviews and as signatories of manifestoes. For example, in *Dada and Surrealism and Their Heritage*, curated by William Rubin at the Museum of Modern Art in New York in 1968, only three women, Hannah Höch, Méret Oppenheim and Sophie Taueber-Arp, were included (apart from Niki de Saint Phalle in 'Heritage') while EROS (*Exposition Internationale du Surréalisme*) of 1959–60, had included 16. Rubin's frank intention was to forge a modernist identity for Surrealism, emphasising his conviction that Surrealist painting was of fundamental importance for Abstract Expressionism by ending his exhibition with the work of the lyrical painter Arshile Gorky. Forcing a narrow trajectory through the multitudinous products of Surrealism and those areas of activity in which women had played a prominent part, such as photography and the Surrealist object, the exhibition passed the baton to postwar painting.

The greater prominence of women in Surrealism's later phase has also been attributed to the eagerness of the older males 'to welcome young women like Joyce Mansour, Nelly Kaplan, or Annie Le Brun' – they brought new blood at a time when the young male turks of the avant garde were founding their own alternatives to Surrealism such as Situationism and *Tel Quel* magazine (see Susan Rubin Suleiman, *Subversive Intent: Gender, Politics and the Avant-Garde*, Harvard University Press, Cambridge, MA, 1990, p.2). As attractive disciples of a second or even third wave of Surrealism, they were, according to this argument, only tolerated by a movement in decline, but had been allowed no voice in its founding and heroic phase in the 1920s. Susan Rubin Suleiman drew the conclusion that if women want to be part of an avant-garde movement they should found it themselves.

within Surrealism that opened up new ways of writing, experimented with verbal and visual language and invested problematic modes like parody with new significance. The interrogations of culture and sexual identity by Claude Cahun in her book of essays and writings illustrated with her own collages *Aveux non avenus* (1930), the experiences of madness written by Leonora Carrington (*Down Below*, 1944) and Unica Zürn (*L'Homme-jasmin*, 1971), for instance, rank with the better-known texts by André Breton such as *Nadja* (1928) or *L'Amour fou* (1937) and Louis Aragon's *Le Paysan de Paris* (1926). Many women Surrealists resisted the invitation to abandon their special place as female icons: in 1957 Nora Mitrani argued against the tenets of Simone de Beauvoir's *La Deuxième Sexe* (The Second Sex, 1949) in an article in the Surrealist periodical *Le Surréalisme, même*.[4] Others, however, refused to allow gender to force a wedge between male and female creators, disavowing difference. Méret Oppenheim criticised the ghettoising of women artists, and Dorothea Tanning mocked what she perceived as irrelevant biological determinism: 'medical examination should be a condition for inclusion – above all today when imposture is so rife that a woman exhibitor could be only a man.'[5] Like the poet Joyce Mansour, Carrington questioned the sexual polarities that seemed to order the universe of passion: 'In *l'amour-passion*, it is the loved one, the other who gives the key. Now the question is: Who can the loved one be? It can be a man or a horse or another woman.'[6] A recent commentator, Marie-Claire Barnet, has proposed a wider exploration of the 'theories of love called surrealist', insisting on the diversity of their expression. 'It is necessary to insist on their changing character, despite critical analyses which have tended to fix the surrealist movement, or, in the wake of [the feminist writer] Xavière Gauthier, reduce them to a limited list of positions on sexuality. How can one define love through sexuality?'[7]

4 Nora Mitrani, 'Des esclaves des suffragettes du fouet', *Le Surréalisme, même*, no.3, autumn 1957, p.60. Annie le Brun likewise defended Surrealism against feminist critics such as Xavière Gauthier.

5 Dorothea Tanning, *Birthday*, The Lapis Press, San Francisco, CA, 1986, p.177.

6 Leonora Carrington, in Chadwick, *op. cit.*, p.105.

7 Marie-Claire Barnet, *La Femme cent sexes ou les genres communicants*, Peter Lang, Bern, Berlin, New York, Paris, 1998, p.231.

The 'problem of woman' increasingly became the focus of Surrealist energies, from political as well as ethical and sexual perspectives. Woman is placed in a position of spectacular prominence: 'The problem of woman is all that is marvellous and troubling in the world. And that is to the degree that it is restored to us by the faith that an uncorrupted man must be capable of placing not just in the Revolution but in love', Breton wrote in 1929.[8] But even if the Surrealists agreed with Marxism that female emancipation was a bourgeois issue, and that the exploitation of woman had primarily economic causes, the importance they accorded to love and to sexuality remained irreconcilable with the aims of the Communist Party in the interwar years. For the Communist Party, not only was the emancipation and full equality of women necessarily dependent upon the social equality of all, but sexual problems were regarded as a distraction and deviation, and love a luxury. Lenin said: 'The Revolution demands the concentration, the tension of forces... It does not tolerate orgiastic states.'[9]

It is possible that the 'Recherches sur la sexualité' (Investigating Sex, 1928–32), conversations of startling frankness on sexual practices and preferences, recorded verbatim, were undertaken not just in a sociological spirit but also as a materialist investigation, in keeping with the spirit in which several of the group (Aragon, Breton, Paul Éluard, Benjamin Péret, Pierre Unik) had joined the Party in 1927. The 'Recherches' would thus constitute an attempt to adapt to the Party's demands that the Surrealists recognise the revolution as 'of the world of facts' and not just linked to 'the purgation of the inner life', without giving up their identity as Surrealists.[10] Two of the conversations were published in *La Révolution surréaliste* in 1928. In the following year the final issue of the review published, rather than the promised sequel to the 'Recherches', a questionnaire on love and the *Second Surrealist Manifesto,* which made the Surrealists' difficulties with the Party public.

8 André Breton, *Second Surrealist Manifesto* (1929), trans. in Richard Seaver and Helen R. Lane (eds), *André Breton, Manifestoes of Surrealism*, University of Michigan Press, Ann Arbor, MI, 1969, p.180.

9 Vladimir Lenin, *De l'emancipation de la femme*, quoted in Gauthier, *op. cit.*, p.41.

10 Breton, 'Legitimate Defence', trans. Richard Howard in Maurice Nadeau, *History of Surrealism*, Jonathan Cape, London, 1968, p.251. *Recherches sur la sexualité*, trans. Malcolm Imrie in José Pierre (ed), *Investigating Sex: Surrealist Discussion 1928–1932*, Verso, London, 1992.

Nonetheless, Breton still struggled to reconcile his faith in love with dialectical materialism: reciprocal love, the only sort he believed in, could only be realised, he said, through radical social change 'whose effect would be to suppress, along with capitalist production, the conditions governing ownership which belong to it'.[11] The revolution might produce the conditions necessary for reciprocal love, but the Surrealists had no intention of 'meanwhile' abandoning their interest in love, sexuality and the myth of woman as the ideal mediator and muse.[12]

The gap is striking between the Surrealist rhetoric about woman and the discourse on gender equality and sexual difference within the French socialist tradition established by the philosopher Charles Fourier. This tradition, embracing the Saint-Simonians, writer and artist Flora Tristan and the anarchists of the Paris Commune, placed a high priority on the issue of sexual difference in the construction of the new society.[13] The Surrealists' disillusionment with the Communist Party was followed by a surge of interest in Fourier, but Breton's poem *Ode á Charles Fourier* (1947) celebrates above all the utopian socialist thinker's extraordinary capacity to imagine in complete and vivid detail a new society rather than his insistence on female equality. Simone Debout, in the catalogue of the *EROS* (Exposition International du Surréalisme) exhibition of 1959–60, suggested that for Fourier women played the role that the proletariat did for Marx. She explores the consequences of this idea at some length: 'If women are to be the lever for total effective liberation, they would not

11 Breton, *Les Vases communicants*, Cahiers Libre, Paris, 1932, p.83. Luis Buñuel's last film, *That Obscure Object of Desire* (1977), explores these ideas.

12 Breton's use of the term 'Meanwhile', *En attendant*, in *Légitime defense* (1926), encapsulated the gulf between the Surrealists and the CPF; they all, he wrote, sought to shift power from the bourgeoisie to the proletariat, but 'Meanwhile, it is nonetheless necessary that the experiments of the inner life continue, and do so, of course, without external or even Marxist control.' 'Legitimate Defence' in Rosemont (ed), *What is Surrealism? André Breton Selected Writings*, Pluto Press, London, 1978 p.39. (Footnote added 2015.)

13 Among the manifold propositions of the Saint-Simonians about equality and female sexuality, some of the most radical were those of Claire Demar who believed in total sexual freedom. She went far beyond the 'New Women' of *La Tribune des femmes* (Women's Tribune) (1832–34), who struggled for social equality and practical, material improvements. Demar, and those who accepted the idea of free love, wore a red ribbon as symbol of their ardent passions, and 'condemned the hypocrisy of men, who sought to "restrain women within the bounds of Christian morality" formulated by men, while having neither the desire nor the strength to exercise that morality themselves'. See Susan K. Grogan, *French Socialism and Sexual Difference*, Macmillan, London, 1992, p.196, p.121.

be able, like the proletariat, to assure its triumph by violence: internal maturity alone can give it birth: conditioned by economic transformations, it relies on the progressive dismantling of prejudices. Fourier leads us to an unheard of place where no human being is treated as a means, but only ever as an end.'[14] Women would be in charge of their own destiny and the unnatural monogamy of marriage would be replaced by free amorous relations. However, Fourier, in his objective interest in manias and perversions, in the variety of sexual proclivities and in the notion that masculine and feminine qualities were independent of gender, could be seen as the precursor of Freud rather than of Marx.

The feminist author Simone de Beauvoir placed Breton's elevation of the feminine within the Fourier tradition, and highlighted the problem of the woman who is always spoken for but has no voice herself. In *La Deuxième Sexe* (The Second Sex, 1949) De Beauvoir examined the myth of woman in the work of five authors, one of whom was Breton. It is not just as the incarnation of nature that Breton sees woman, but as the channel capable of releasing its magic. For him she is the 'indispensable mediatress', according to De Beauvoir, who can recreate and recolour the world through love and poetry: 'Woman has no vocation other than love; this does not make her inferior, since man's vocation is also love. But one would like to know if for her also love is key to the world and revelation of beauty... She is poetry in essence, directly – that is to say, for man; we are not told whether she is poetry for herself also. Breton does not speak of woman as subject.'[15] Although reciprocity in love is always the ideal, the absence of the female voice means that she can neither confirm nor deny her position.

The Fourierist evaluation of a feminine world view served to reinforce a romantic Surrealist myth of the child-woman/fairy Mélusine. In his book *Arcane 17* (1945) Breton wrote:

14 Simone Debout, 'La Plus Belle des Passions, in *L'Exposition Internationale du surréalisme (EROS)*, exhibition catalogue, Galerie Daniel Cordier, Paris, 1959–60, p.23.
15 Simone de Beauvoir, *The Second Sex* (1949), Jonathan Cape, London, 1953, p.267.

> I can see only one solution: it is high time for woman's ideas to prevail over man's, whose bankruptcy is clear enough in the tumult of today. It is up to the artist, in particular, to privilege as much as possible the feminine system in opposition to the masculine system, to draw exclusively on woman's faculties, better, to exalt, to appropriate so far as to make them jealously his own, everything that distinguishes her from man in terms of modes of appreciation and will.[16]

Breton's appeal could be said to demasculinise as much as to feminise social values. It is neither produced by nor responsive to woman's role in society and her right to full political and economic equality. Significantly, though, Breton is not speaking of woman as irrepressible natural creature: it is in terms of culture, not nature, that he seeks to privilege the 'feminine system', whose intellectual properties, 'modes of appreciation and will', would oppose the masculine values of 'père, patron, patrie'; family, work and state.

However, the idea of the child-woman, fey object of desire, tends to dominate, and renders his argument ambiguous. In the aftermath of the Second World War a group of revolutionary Surrealists sought to expose the surrealist myth of woman as complicit with patriarchal control. Philosopher and artist René Passeron's 'Introduction à une érotique révolutionnaire', which appeared in the one and only issue of *Le Surréalisme révolutionnaire* in 1948, was also a critique of *Arcane 17*.[17] Both Eve and the Virgin Mary, he wrote, are myths

> from which we must free our mentality. The child-woman, in her reign here below on earth – what is she? A sentimental sublimation which, substituting a pedestal for an altar, maintains woman in her Marian position. Without doubt, woman's sensibility 'once her infinite servitude is finally broken', will confound the old masculine

16 Breton, *Arcane 17*, Brentano, New York, NY, 1945, pp.62–63.

17 The Peruvian Surrealist poet César Moro criticised *Arcane 17* for its single-minded promotion of heterosexual love; see Ades, '"We who have neither church nor country": César Moro and Surrealism', in Ades, Rita Eder and Graciela Speranza (eds), *Surrealism in Latin America: Vivísimo muerto*, Getty Research Institute, Los Angeles, CA, 2012. (Footnote added 2015.)

> fatuity. But it is not in sublimating a being that one liberates them. Sublimation has always had its inverse, oppression... It is not by celebrating Mélusine that we shall advance a step towards the reign of desire, but by subjecting to materialist method the myths by which woman is lulled the better to be exploited.[18]

If woman is a mediator for the experiences and experiments of the Surrealists with language both verbal and visual, is she able ever to become herself a speaking subject? And if she does, on what terms?

Rather than addressing this as a separate issue, I propose to frame it in a discussion of the complex and diverse ways in which sexual difference is mobilised, challenged or ignored in Surrealist works, and to consider the extent to which a crisis in masculine identity is interlinked with the problematic of feminist identity and the female artist. Acceptance, assertion and denials of difference and of a 'normative' sexuality will be set within a context of Surrealist opposition to bourgeois values.

Two images which appear to reinforce gender stereotypes and 'the myth of woman' in fact problematise them in different ways, raising questions about displays of sexual difference in terms of male-female divisions. Both works introduce ambiguities about the nature of these divisions. Visually utterly dissimilar, Marcel Duchamp's *The Bride Stripped Bare by her Bachelors, Even (The Large Glass)* (1915–23) and René Magritte's *Je ne vois pas la [femme] cachée dans la forêt* (I Do Not See the [Woman] Hidden in the Forest, 1929) apparently present similar scenes incarnating a myth of woman: a lone female *vis à vis* a group of males. *Vis à vis* is a convenient term to cover the different and ambivalent relations between these emphatically gendered parties, for they are embedded in the respective

18 René Passeron, 'Introduction à une érotique revolutionnaire' in *Le Surréalisme révolutionnaire*, no.1, 1948, p.39. Passeron quotes from Rimbaud's letter to Paul Demeny (1871); 'When the unending servitude of woman is broken, when she lives by and for herself, when man – hitherto abominable – has given her her freedom, she too will be a poet! Woman will discover part of the unknown! Will her world of ideas be different from ours?' Arthur Rimbaud, *Arthur Rimbaud Collected Poems*, trans. Oliver Bernard, Penguin Books, London, 1962, p.13.

visual schema without a clear relationship necessarily being conveyed. In the *Large Glass* the Bride is skied above her bachelors, harking back to a sacred iconography of visions of the Assumption of the Virgin Mary, depicted in a heavenward ascent above clouds and male worshippers. The masculine domain in the *Large Glass* also contains a group of 'oculist witnesses', symbolised by Duchamp in the form of ellipses scratched in silvered glass, as a species of 'peeping toms' observing but not participating in the elaborate erotic encounter between the Bride and her Bachelors. Magritte's collage of photographs of the male Surrealists arranged in a tight rectangle around his painting *I Do Not See the [Woman] Hidden in the Forest*, by contrast, encloses and contains the female as a popular pin-up, a secular icon. The nude seen here, erect rather than reclining, parodies the tradition of the nude in painting with its sublimated values of beauty, from Titian to Renoir, its masculine audience made visible, an embarrassingly public self-reflexive daydream.

Both images appear to present isolation and non-communication between the sexes, but also homosocial solidarity. In the case of the Magritte, it has been argued that Surrealism is here revealed as a 'men's club': 'The surrealists lived in their own masculine world, with their eyes closed, the better to construct their male phantasms of the feminine... These masculine dreams play an active part in patriarchy's misogynist positioning of women.'[19] But the confrontation between the single female and a group of consenting males is quite ambiguous. To begin with, making the (male) viewers of the female nude visible is unusual – apart from scenes based on the biblical story of Susannah and the Elders, there is little iconographical precedent. To represent both object and subject of desire introduces an unaccustomed mode of reflection on the dynamic of the male gaze, here veiled and turned inwards. The woman enfolds herself narcissistically, while the group of males is far from representing a confident and exclusively masculine club. There is no celebration here of virility: if not quite 'malic moulds', as Duchamp described his Bachelors, the insistence on the ties worn by Magritte's male Surrealists, which recalls the 'male mannequin' in the Paris Dada exhibition of 1921, suspended from a balcony along with a fringe of

19 Rudolf Kuenzli, 'Surrealism and Misogyny', in Caws, Kuenzli and Raaberg (eds), *op. cit.*, p.18.

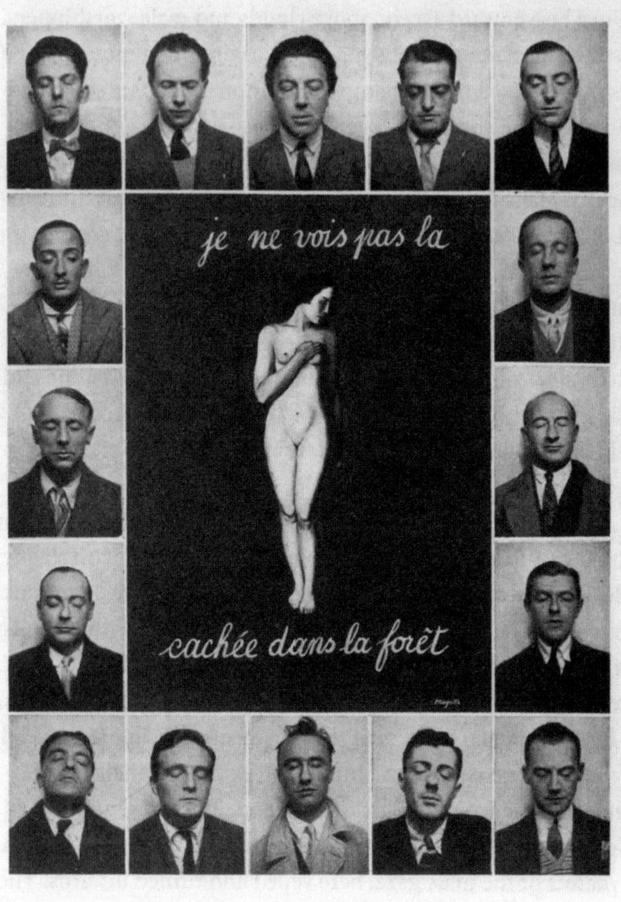

Page from *La Révolution surréaliste*, no.12, December 1929
with René Magritte, *Je ne vois pas la [femme] cachée dans la forêt* (I Do Not See the [Woman] Hidden in the Forest), 1929

carefully knotted ties, hints at a kind of male masquerade, a symbolic show. There may be an element of intense male friendship presented here, in which it is tempting to see a satirical cast, given Magritte's position as something of an outsider in the group. But consciously or unconsciously Magritte's image addresses a crisis in masculinity rather than the misogynist comfort of a male club.

Magritte's most immediate points of reference are internal to Surrealism. *I Do Not See...* is a part of his response to the questionnaire on love published in the final issue of *La Révolution surréaliste* in 1929. He makes it a pendant to the photo-collage in the journal's first issue, in 1924, in which the Surrealists and a group of chosen 'fellow travellers', including Picasso and Freud, are loosely arranged around a mugshot of the anarchist Germaine Berton, with an epigraph taken by Éluard from the nineteenth-century poet Charles Baudelaire: 'woman is the being who casts the greatest shadow or the greatest light into our dreams'. Magritte's image may also refer to Breton's equivocal desire 'to meet, at night and in a wood, a beautiful naked woman or rather, since such a wish once expressed means nothing, I regret, beyond belief, not having met her'.[20]

Magritte's montage can be seen in terms of a negative encounter, like the paradox of the title. If the woman is passive and self-absorbed, so are the males. Perhaps, by contrast with Magritte's response to the questionnaire, in which he answers to the question 'What kind of hope do you place in love?' that it is only a woman who can give love reality, *I Do Not See...* reflects upon the gap between desire and reality. Breton did not share Magritte's certainty. In *Les Vases communicants* (Communicating Vessels, 1932) he recognises, in the misery of a failed love, that 'I did not know how to make, of the immediacy of a being whom I thought I knew by heart, a real being.'[21] For Breton this posed in the acutest form the 'problem of problems', that of objective chance, which was the philosophical problem of the relationship between need and freedom, between natural necessity and human necessity.[22] In its concrete form it governed the encounter, the magical spark of a chance attraction, the

20 Breton, *Nadja* (1928), trans. Richard Howard, Penguin Books, London, 1999, p.39.

21 Breton, *Les Vases communicants*, *op. cit.*, p.89.

22 Breton, *Entretiens 1913–1952*, Gallimard, Paris, 1952, p.136.

unpredictable resolution of an unconscious need. But the difficulty was reconciling the real woman with the ideal type – in Breton's case above all, the Delilah of the late nineteenth-century symbolist painter Gustave Moreau:

> My discovery, at the age of sixteen, of the Musée Gustave Moreau influenced for ever my idea of love. Beauty and love were first revealed to me there through the medium of a few faces, the poses of a few women. The particular 'type' of these women plunged me into a state of complete enchantment and probably prevented me from recognising any other type. A great part must have been played, too, by the myths which in these pictures were endowed with miraculous new power.[23]

This is what lies behind Breton's question in *Nadja*, 'whom do I haunt?' Who is it that will recognise him as their inner necessity? And if it is not reciprocal?

A similar story to that told from Breton's perspective in *Nadja*, the meeting with a woman whom in the end he did not love, and whose mysterious attraction had its dark roots in a mental instability that in the end overtakes her, is told from the woman's perspective in Unica Zürn's *L'Homme-jasmin*. This is an example of the creative voice of a woman not echoing but speaking out, and speaking to the complex discourse in Surrealism on love and madness, on, in fact, *l'amour fou*. By contrast with the simulations of madness in Breton and Éluard's book *L'Immaculée conception* (1930), Zürn gives a detailed account, in the third person, of the progress of her breakdown, with its delusions, hallucinations and lacunae. The encounter with the Man of Jasmine was Zürn's first secret, a childhood vision of love: 'The Man of Jasmine! Boundless consolation! Sighing with relief, she sits down opposite him and studies him. He is paralysed! What good fortune. He will never leave his seat in the garden where the

23 Breton, *Surrealism and Painting*, trans. Simon Watson Taylor, Harper and Row, New York, NY, 1972, p.363.

24 Unica Zürn, *The Man of Jasmine* (1977), trans. Malcolm Green, Atlas Press, London, 1994, p.25.

jasmine even blossoms in winter... this man becomes her image of love.'[24] Much later, as a grown woman:

> ...in a room in Paris she finds herself standing before the Man of Jasmine. The shock of this encounter is so great that she is unable to get over it. From this day on she begins, very very slowly, to lose her reason. The image of her childhood vision is identical with this man's appearance. With the sole difference that he is not paralysed and that here there is no garden with jasmine blossoms surrounding him.[25]

The encounter between the compulsion of the inner vision and its object has no purchase in the real world; the person whom she haunts fails to reciprocate, as does Breton with Nadja, whose phrases of love as fleetingly reported by Breton curiously resemble those of Zürn.

The closer one looks, indeed, at the ways in which the idea and the experiences of love, *l'amour fou* and sexuality work through Surrealist texts, the greater is the divide between the stereotypes built up by later criticism and their real complexity. Duchamp's *Large Glass* destabilises the gender stereotypes that it purports to set up, through a process of invention based on a system of oppositions in which gender difference plays its part. It is worth recalling the degree to which every aspect of life, activity and occupation was gendered still in the early decades of the century: at school, for instance, boys learned a different method of drawing from that taught to girls.[26] Thus resistance and challenges to the stultifying and rigid educational and social as well as artistic codes reverberated across each other. Dry (male) mechanical drawing was introduced by Duchamp as a corrective to personal expression and the over-valuation of the purely 'retinal'. This in turn was to generate an iconography with the machine as metaphor for human sexual relations, which produced comic, sadistic and satirical scenarios. In Francis Picabia's hands, these often reinforce a 'laddish' masculinity.

25 *Ibid.*, p.27. Zürn also recognised Bellmer as the 'Man of Jasmine', and cut off her hair to make her face resemble his, but it was Henri Michaux, whose initials matched those of Zürn's beloved Herman Melville, who was her conclusive incarnation of the 'Man of Jasmine'.

26 See Molly Nesbitt, 'Readymade Originals: The Duchamp Model', *October*, no.37, summer 1986, and Dawn Ades, Neil Cox and David Hopkins, *Marcel Duchamp*, Thames & Hudson, London, 1999, chapter 4.

A fantasy of male procreation, the bearing as well as engendering of children, was one of the odder consequences of the social pressures of the calls for female emancipation and greater sexual equality as well as more broadly an expression of a crisis in industrial society. A text by photographer and writer Paul Haviland in the American proto-Dada review *291* in 1915, prominently adorned with symbolic machine portraits by Picabia, was crammed with references to male procreativity:

> We are living in the age of the machine. Man made the machine in his own image... The machine is his 'daughter born without a mother'. That is why he loves her. He has made the machine superior to himself. Photography is one of the fine fruits of this union. The photographic print is one element of this new trinity: Man the creator, with thought and will: the mother machine-action: and their product, the work accomplished.[27]

As a response to a sense of impotence, of the passing of power and control to the machine, this idea of a 'girl born without a mother' can be seen as a kind of return of repressed virility. The shadow of misogyny here would be a response to and defence against emasculation as well as a reaction against feminism.

This fantasy had antecedents in the utopian visions of the Saint-Simonians of a new social order both begotten and borne in labour by its male progenitors, in a metaphor specifically aimed at restoring a central role to men. On the other hand, women in the group had attacked the Napoleonic Code that treated women as minors and gave men the right to appropriate children at birth, claiming that children should bear the mother's name. Woman's 'natural' function as wife and mother was increasingly challenged at the same time that a 'natural' right to sexual freedom was proclaimed. Eleanor Marx and Edward Aveling argued in their 1886 essay 'The Woman Question' that, 'There is no more a

27 Paul Haviland, '291', *291*, no.1, March 1915.
28 Eleanor Marx and Edward Aveling, *The Woman Question*, Swan Sonnenschein & Co., London, 1886, p.7.

"natural calling" of woman than there is a "natural" law of capitalistic production.'[28]

Conservative anxiety about the threat to the family posed by such ideas and by the emergence of a 'new woman' who emphasised her freedom by adopting masculine attitudes, was satirised by Guillaume Apollinaire in his 'drame surréaliste', *Les Mamelles de Tirésias* (The Breasts of Tiresias, 1917). The plot is succinctly summarised by art historian David Hopkins:

> Thérèse, the main character, announces her conversion to feminism, declaring, 'I want to make war... not children'. As a result she changes into Tirésias, during which her bosom (two balloons) falls off and she grows a moustache and beard. She moves house, taking with her a chamber pot, a basin, and a urinal, leaving her husband tied up, wearing her skirt. With women off-stage shouting 'No more children, no more children', the husband decides he will personally have to set about repopulating Zanzibar (the setting for the play). He consequently produces 40,049 offspring. Tirésias eventually returns and is welcomed back by her husband with a gift of balloons and rubber balls with which to rebuild her figure.[29]

Apollinaire said the idea went back to the early years of the century, and it is possible that he had in mind, as well as national alarm about the falling birth rate, the feminist demonstrations in 1904, following the failure of a suffrage bill, when balloons were released during the anniversary celebrations of the Napoleonic Code.[30]

Apollinaire shared with Duchamp and Picabia a fascination with gender reversals, male procreation and both male and female separatism. In Duchamp's case the ancient metaphor of the male artist 'bearing' the fruits of his genius takes an original twist as he devised new methods of invention, which included linguistic puns and an oppositional logic the results of which were as bizarre as its operations were mechanical.

29 David Hopkins, *Marcel Duchamp and Max Ernst: The Bride Shared*, Oxford University Press, Oxford, 1998, p.83.

30 See Eugen Weber, *France: Fin de Siècle*, Harvard University Press, Cambridge, MA, 1986, p.93.

The Bachelors, for example, in the *Large Glass*, were the result of designing 'a direct opposition to the theme of the Bride'.[31] Duchamp's system produces not a husband, which would simply make a binary pair, but a plurality of unmarried males – the bachelors. Bride and Bachelors are then theoretically (or poetically) inscribed in a complex narrative of sexual interaction, powered by every imaginable form of energy, but remaining forever separate in their irreconcilable spheres (air and earth, ideal and material, natural and mechanical), visibly gendered by different means of representation – the Bachelors and their machines drawn according to strict laws of perspective, the Bride anamorphic and abstract.

The bride, subject of Duchamp's 1912 painting *Bride*, whose central form was transferred to the upper half of the *Large Glass*, had her roots in Symbolist types of femininity: carnal bride, spiritual bride and femme fatale. But Duchamp represents her as a pulsing mass of internal organs with hints of mechanical parts, an image which harks back to Leonardo da Vinci's drawings of copulation and the female womb, in a partly humorous reflection on male fascination with female mystery masking a desire to appropriate its procreativity. Curiosity disguises envy rather than lasciviousness. In the *Large Glass* this takes on another dimension, as the Bride's identity merges with that of the Virgin Mary, who gave birth to Christ parthenogenetically: the son born without a father. His miraculous conception could thus offer, in a spirit of humorous blasphemy, a potentially reversible prototype for the masculine fantasy. Moreover, Duchamp remarked that 'Christ' was also linked to the idea of 'stripping', for he, too, was stripped, thus conflating iconoclastically male and female eroticism.[32] Paradoxically, then, the logic of oppositions can produce a destabilisation of gender, as meanings and identities multiply and oscillate. But more radical interrogations and even denials of sexual difference were to follow: the reversible masquerades of Rrose Sélavy; the ambiguities in Man Ray's photographic portraits; the complexities of same-sex desire in the poetry of Valentine Penrose or the work of Claude Cahun; confusion of conventional attributes and values as in Joyce Mansour's 'virile woman or veiled man'. To loosen the principle of identity 'like a bad tooth' was their aim.[33]

31 Jean Schuster, 'Marcel Duchamp vite', *Le Surréalisme, même*, no.2, spring 1957, p.143.
32 Marcel Duchamp, BBC interview, 1966.

Both Man Ray and Duchamp experimented with cross-dressing before the camera, but Duchamp did so in the context of a carefully worked out female persona, Rrose Sélavy (the pseudonym is a pun on the French phrase 'Arroser la vie', 'Water life/To make a toast to life' or 'Eros, c'est la vie', 'Eros, that's life'). The first group of photographs by Man Ray of Rrose Sélavy of 1921 are somewhat grotesque, but Duchamp nonetheless used one for his 'assisted readymade' *Belle Haleine, Eau de Voilette* (Beautiful Breath, Veil Water, 1921), so that it becomes a hallmark of female luxury. The second series of photographs of c.1924 are far more successful in conveying an aura of femininity: hat, fur, make-up and hands (belonging to Picabia's companion Germaine Everling) combine to produce a seductive portrait resembling those of film stars and actresses, mementoes for an admirer.[34] With Rrose Sélavy Duchamp activates a dialogue with the ever-renewed 'New Woman' of the time. In Victor Margueritte's best-selling novel *La Garçonne* (The Bachelor Girl, 1922) the main character, Monique, flees her bourgeois home and looming marriage; she cuts her hair and opens a successful interior design shop, becoming part of an avant garde of actors, artists and dancers. Although not a *homme-femme*, she does temporarily defeminise herself in order to move freely. She crosses the gender boundaries that structure her background, and meets Fourierist academics such as Dr Vignabos, who argues that, 'If the natural desires of women had not been suppressed for centuries, there would be more sexual balance in the world.'[35] The imbalance exacerbated the effects of sexual difference: 'In our time it is this discordance between feminine idealism and male brutality which has engendered the sexual anarchy

33 'In the world's structure dream loosens individuality like a bad tooth': Walter Benjamin, 'Surrealism, The Latest Snapshot of the European Intelligentsia' (1929), in Walter Benjamin, *Reflections: Essays, Aphorisms, Autobiographical Writings*, Schocken, New York, NY, 1986, p.179.

34 On Rrose Sélavy see also Hopkins, *op. cit.*; Dawn Ades, 'Duchamp's Masquerades', in Graham Clarke (ed), *The Portrait in Photography*, Reaktion Books, London, 1992; Amelia Jones, *Postmodernism and the Engendering of Marcel Duchamp*, Cambridge University Press, Cambridge, 1994. Rrose Sélavy also bears more than a passing resemblance to Charlie Chaplin in the film *A Woman* (1915), where the comedian dresses as a woman to gain access to the girl he loves: see Francis Naumann, 'Marcel Duchamp: a reconciliation of opposites', in Rudolf Kuenzli and Francis Naumann (eds), *Marcel Duchamp: Artist of the Century*, MIT Press, Cambridge, MA, and London, 1989.

35 Victor Margueritte, *The Bachelor Girl* (1922), trans. Hugh Burnaby, Alfred A. Knopf, New York, NY, 1923.

which prevails.'[36] Rrose Sélavy takes the female masquerade to its furthest point; while the New Woman or Bachelor Girl would take their sexual life into their own hands in a form of empowerment, Rrose Sélavy seems in this set of photographs to invite the male gaze, and see what it is like to be an object of desire – coolly observing from the observed position.[37]

In *Photographs by Man Ray 1920–1934 Paris* Man Ray further inverts and plays with gender categories. Dividing two of the carefully organised sequences of photographs is a strange text 'Men Before the Mirror', accredited to, and possibly appropriated by, Rrose Sélavy.[38] Preceding it are close-ups of carefully accoutred women, some sexually ambivalent, culminating with that doyenne of the *femme-homme*, the writer Gertrude Stein. Facing her to start the second section is Man Ray himself with his camera, and the subsequent series of male portraits ends with the American female impersonator Barbette. 'Men Before the Mirror' exposes male vanity and insecurity as 'they stare at the landscape which is themselves, the mountains of their noses', as 'the mirror looks at them'. 'What is most poignant in the text', writes David Hopkins, 'is the way that the conventionalised image of the strong, outward-looking male is deconstructed in favour of an evocation of male self-reflexiveness and insufficiency. This in turn is predicated on an unusual view of men as peculiarly prone to self-objectification; to a paralysing internalised rift between self-image and body image.'[39] As in Magritte's montage *I Do Not See...*, the active, purposive male is substituted by a passive, uncertain dreamer.

---

36 For a study of gender and culture at the *fin-de-siècle* see Elaine Showalter, *Sexual Anarchy: Gender and Culture at the Fin-de-Siècle*, Bloomsbury, London, 1991.

37 It was notable that in 1917 Duchamp orchestrated the *Fountain* scandal using women's voices in the little magazine *The Blind Man*. Dada in New York, and its predecessors such as *Rogue*, had a strongly female character, unlike Berlin Dada. See Ades 'Introduction', *Three New York Dadas and The Blind Man*, Atlas Press, London, 2013. (Footnote added 2015.)

38 For the full text and analysis see David Hopkins, 'Men Before the Mirror: Marcel Duchamp, Man Ray and Masculinity', *Art History*, vol.21, no.3, 1998.

39 *Ibid.*

Photography was one of the most fruitful allies in Surrealism's exploration of desire and gender identity. The human body and human face, massively enlarged through close-ups, dislocated from one another and left separate or recombined across a single surface, become the intimate coinage of Surrealist photography's examination of intersubjective spaces and sexual ambiguities. The camera lens in the service of Surrealism is a mobile agent which alters and displaces its objects, blurs clear-cut identities and contracts and expands space. Its natural affiliation with the mirror opened up new forms of dialogue with self-images.

Claude Cahun challenged 'the verities of sexual difference' in her photographs and photomontages, in her book *Aveux non avenus*, and in her objects.[40] Her relationship with Surrealism, however, has come under scrutiny in the context of her lesbianism and the perceived insistence by Surrealism on heterosexuality. This reopens the wider issue of Surrealism's attitude to homosexuality, and the assumption that Surrealism spoke and was perceived as speaking with one voice about it. Breton's notorious dismissal of the subject in the 'Recherches' of 1928 is always cited, but the full transcript shows a strong case put by Aragon for the discussion of 'all sexual inclinations', and attitudes ranging from enthusiasm through indifference to violent objection.[41] The range of Surrealism's investigations of sexual identity and the operations of desire, in poetry and photography especially, must raise doubts about the assertion that 'the surrealists opposed heterosexual freedom to bourgeois repression' and that their 'antibourgeois sentiments – at least in the realm of gender and sexuality – sustained the dichotomies between heterosexuality and homosexuality, pure and impure, and fantasy and reality they sought in theory to challenge'.[42] Breton may indeed have subscribed to the view, traceable back to Fourier, that bourgeois moral values produced vice (adultery, prostitution, betrayal and double standards), but like Fourier Surrealism did not oppose this to a 'pure' heterosexual love, but rather opened up

40 Steven Harris discusses Cahun's object *La Marseillaise est un chant révolutionnaire* in 'Coup d'oeil', *Oxford Art Journal*, vol.24, no.1, Oxford, 2001, pp.89–112. He translates *Aveux non avenus* as 'Abrogated Vows' or, less accurately but more pithily, 'Disavowals'.

41 Objections to the discussion of homosexuality were voiced by Breton, Péret and Unik, who had all recently joined the Communist Party. Breton's dislike of the 'homosexual milieu' was also probably influenced by his antipathy to Jean Cocteau.

42 Carolyn J. Dean, 'Claude Cahun's Double', *Yale French Studies*, no.90, 1996, p.89.

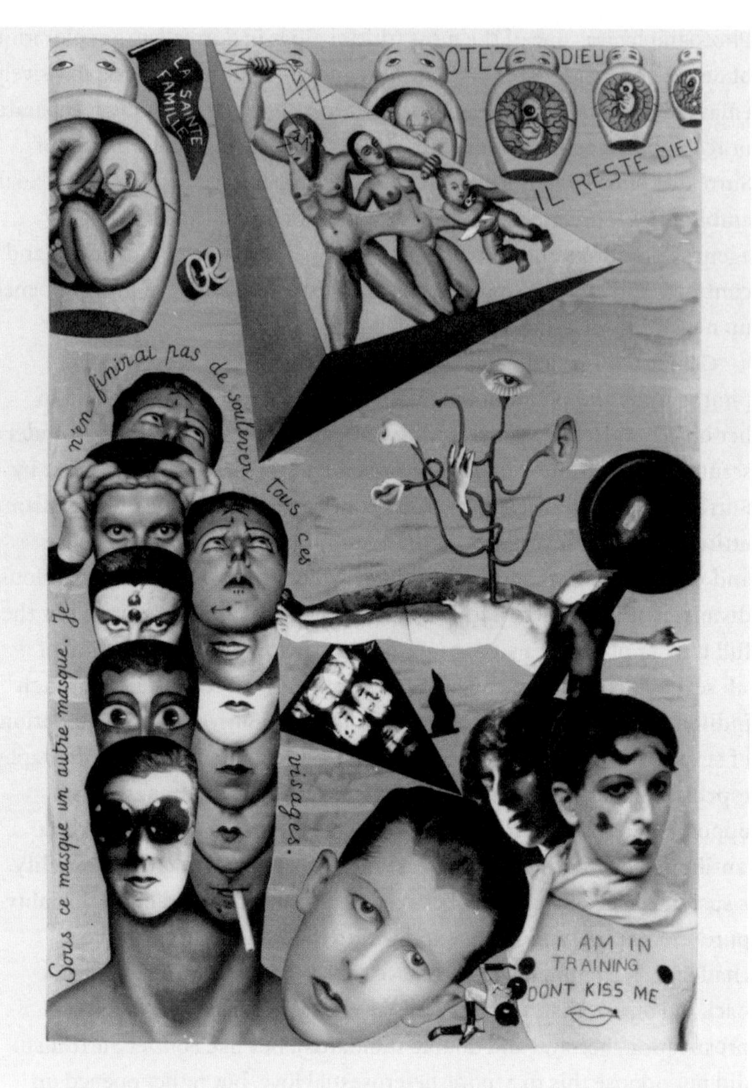

390 **Claude Cahun**
I.O.U. (Self Pride), 1929–30
Gelatin silver print
15.2 × 10.3 cm | 6 × 4⅛ in

radical questions about the 'normal' and fixed poles of sexual identity. To distance on these grounds Cahun's work from Surrealism when it so evidently inscribes itself within it at many levels is to resort to an essentialising view of Surrealism which its experimental practice denies.

In the photomontage heading the second section of *Aveux non avenus*: 'Myself. The Siren Succumbs to her own Voice', there is a mirror reflecting a half-veiled face; the mirror/window becomes the trope through which she explores and criticises the myth of Narcissus:

> Sash window
> Glass sheet. Where shall I put the silvering? On this side or the other; in front of or behind the pane? In front. I imprison myself. I blind myself. What does it matter to me, Passer-by, to offer you a mirror in which you recognise yourself, even if it's a deforming mirror and signed by me... Behind. I am equally shut in. I shall know nothing of the outside. At least I shall know my own face and perhaps it will be tolerable enough to please me.
> Leave the glass clear, and according to chance and the hours see, confused and partially, sometimes fugitives and sometimes my own look. Then, break the glass panes... with the fragments, compose a stained glass. Byzantine work!
> Transparency, opacity. What a vow of artifice![43]

There is a difference between Narcissus and her own self-love: 'The death of Narcissus always seemed to me the most incomprehensible. There is only one explanation: Narcissus did not love himself. He allowed himself to be deceived by an image.'[44] He fails to recognise himself beyond the mirage in the water/mirror, which could just as well have been a nymph. The image of the 'other' forecloses the convulsive and simultaneous recognition and loss of identity: on the one hand, 'Self-love. A hand clenched on the mirror – a mouth, palpitating nostrils – between swooning eyelids, the mad gaze of enlarged irises';[45] and on the other, a dispersal of the self in all of nature. The photomontage seethes with

43 Claude Cahun, *Aveux non avenus*, Editions du Carrefour, Paris, 1930, p.29.
44 *Ibid.*, p.36.
45 *Ibid.*, p.37.

sexualised visual metaphors: eye, parted legs, and an arm doubled up and squeezed together are all inscribed with the form of the female sex.

Cahun's photomontages are frequently elaborations on her own photographic self-portraits. In one photomontage from *Aveux non avenus*, Cahun includes among the self-portraits a column of overlapping heads showing only eyes or mouths, with the inscription; 'Under this mask another mask. I shall never finish stripping away all these faces.' Unlike Rrose Sélavy's reversible masquerade, Cahun dissolves herself into a never-ending series of masks that have no 'real' underneath. These are not so much disguises as adoptions of the socially imposed shells of feminine or masculine identities (like the doll-woman) which need first to be displayed in order then to be stripped.

Cahun's attacks on the 'myth of the family', motherhood and the church, for example, as in the photomontage introducing the ninth and final section of *Aveux non avenus* entitled 'I.O.U. One Has the God one Deserves, Too Bad', are obviously identical with Surrealist concerns. The question as to whether it is a specifically lesbian desire that is articulated by Cahun has been raised.[46] If the dialogue with Narcissus – who following Freud's analysis, was widely accepted as the signifier of homosexual identity – would indicate the wish to differentiate between male and female same-sex desire, Cahun also stages Oedipal conflict in her work (Oedipus was another of the myths she taunts and tests in *Aveux non avenus*). Whereas reversibility, as in Man Ray's photographs, maintains difference in play, Cahun 'disturbs the normal terms of sexual difference, both recalling and refusing castration'.[47] Here the idea of any stable identity is resisted, and the uncanny doubles that figure in several of her manipulated photographs, as in the photomontages from *Aveux non avenus*, have been described as a way of producing herself as a fetish. She does this in a conscious spirit of parody. 'Through the trope of the body double, Cahun uses substitution not simply to trouble or transgress binary distinctions between genders, but to deprive those distinctions (and hence the relationship between gender and sexuality) of a referent even as she (again parodically) leaves them intact... The parody permits

46 Harris challenges the suggestion that Cahun articulates a specifically lesbian desire (Harris, *op. cit.*).

47 *Ibid.* p.94.

her to remain happily and benignly castrated, to "be" the phallus in order to escape the economy of meaning organised round the phallus.'[48] Parody is an important mode within Surrealism; as an always debased aesthetic, it serves to bring down the myths of, and the myths created by, a transcendental notion of art and culture. Because it occludes a 'true' authorial voice without substituting even a fictional alternative, it is peculiarly apt for the refusal of fixed meanings, and the production of uncertain laughter. 'It seems likely that the surrealism of creative women, if it thinks itself subversive, passes via a revision of the new clichés of subversion, by a subversion of the "masculine" surrealist subversion',[49] Marie-Claire Barnet has written. Cahun subverts the notion of castration anxiety, revealing it as a cultural myth. The poet Joyce Mansour parodies the celebration by the male Surrealists of the hysteric's 'passion', itself subversive of the supposed clinical detachment of doctor and patient.[50]

Parody is a form of subversion, but only one of the modes through which men and women artists responded to the sexual anarchy produced in part by the rift between socially acceptable forms of sexuality and the dramatic revelations of psychoanalysis regarding such issues as child sexuality. If psychoanalysis itself led to renewed exclusions of women from the symbolic order of patriarchy, Surrealism and its artistic legacies have helped to keep the routes open to the expression, if not the solution, of the riddle of gender, sexuality and love.

48 Dean, *op. cit.*, p.89.
49 Barnet, *op. cit.* p.106.
50 Mansour, *Le Grand Jamais* (1981), in *Prose et poésie*, Actes Sud, Arles, 1991, p.570.

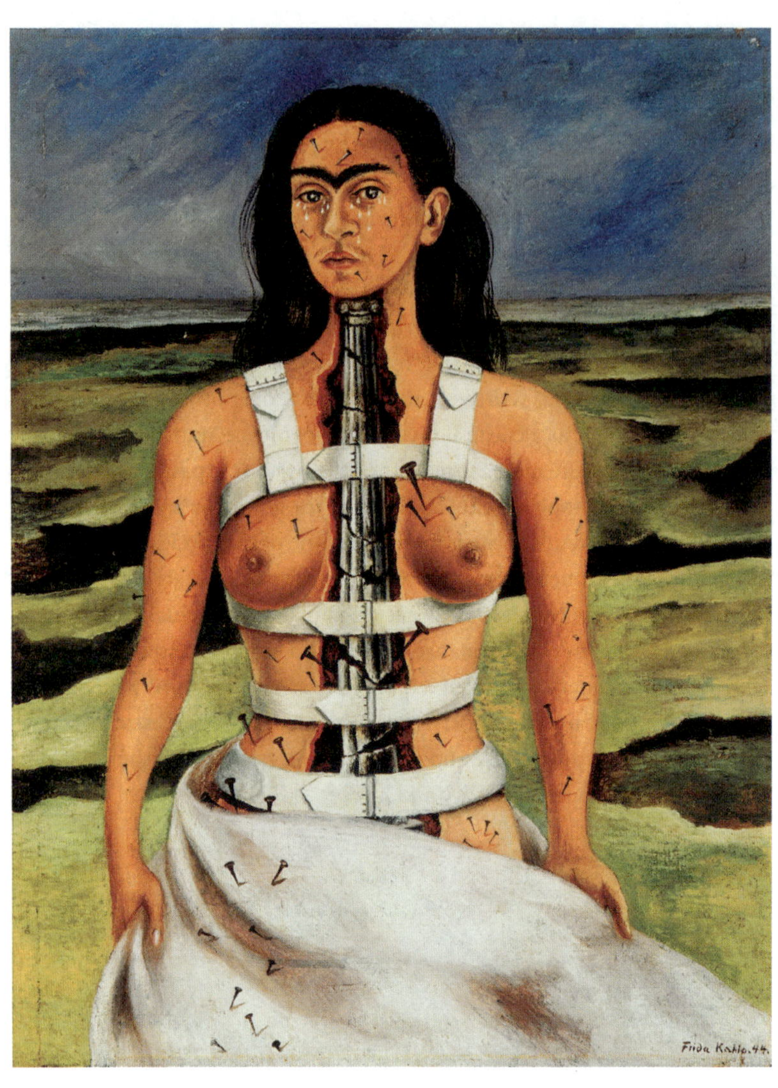

394 **Frida Kahlo**
La Columna Rota (The Broken Column), 1944
Oil on hardboard
40 × 30.5 cm | 15¾ × 12⅛ in

Orbits of the Savage Moon: Surrealism and the Representation of the Female Subject in Mexico and Postwar Paris

Mirror Images: Women, Surrealism, and Self-Representation, Whitney Chadwick (ed), MIT Press, Cambridge, MA, and London, 1998

Je voleria je volerai
L'orbite de la lune sauvage...
JOYCE MANSOUR[1]

The male Surrealists' probings of identity implicated women in ways that seem to militate against any independent explorations of their own. The very importance of woman in the Surrealist lexicon and of the female body in Surrealist iconography – the body erotic and fetishised, the sublime celebrations of *l'amour fou* – threatens to squeeze out any possibility for women in the Surrealist orbit to see themselves as other than the object or complement of male desire.

The group of self-portraits selected for this essay brings together images produced in very different circumstances both in relation to Surrealism and to localised attitudes and responses to female and sexual identity. Two of the artists are Mexican – Frida Kahlo and María Izquierdo – and their connection with the Surrealist movement is of a different character both from the other artists chosen and from each other. The purpose here is to explore intersections and coincidences as well as contrasts with the work of women artists operating in closer proximity to the movement in Europe and to inquire into the postwar period in which women's voices achieve greater prominence within Surrealism. While there are undoubtedly points of similarity in the construction of the

1 'I shall fly I shall fly/The orbit of the savage moon...' Joyce Mansour, 'Du doux repos', *Carré blanc* (1965), in *Joyce Mansour: Prose et poésiei, oeuvre complete*, Actes Sud, Paris, 1991, p.460.

subject as self-image, different factors govern how identity is experienced and addressed, and indeed how it is deemed to be constituted.

For whereas it could be argued that Paris-centred Surrealism reveals a movement towards the dissolution rather than affirmation of identity, in Mexico there was a strong need to establish identity, which was as marked in cultural as in political debates and affected artists and writers associated with Surrealism. Octavio Paz, for instance, wrote his influential study of the problematic of Mexican identity, *The Labyrinth of Solitude: Life and Thought in Mexico,* at the same time as he was associating as a poet with Surrealist circles in Paris.[2] In the different context of Europe any expression of national cultural identity was on the whole repudiated by the Surrealists. There were historical as well as cultural dimensions to these debates in Mexico, which sought to predicate national unity through a revaluation of the past and in which modern Mexico acknowledged the violently ruptured periods of the pre-conquest, colonial, and independence eras and of the present, in which the cultural synthesis of 'Indian' and European was argued against the recognition of cultural difference. Paz, for instance, argued that the figure of La Malinche haunts the Mexican sense of identity, while Mexican feminists invoked the Aztec goddess Malinalxochitl as a model of female independence and strength.[3]

The formation and experience of Frida Kahlo and María Izquierdo as women artists was enacted not in the context of a movement that, however problematically, gave special value to sexuality and eventually to a feminine revolution but in the context of an artistic renaissance powered by a cultural nationalism that was as pressing in unofficial modernist circles as in the official world of mural painting. For Kahlo and Izquierdo the experience of marginalisation both as women and as artists was played out against this dominant artistic culture, muralism,

2 Octavio Paz, *The Labyrinth of Solitude: Life and Thought in Mexico*, Grove Press, New York, NY, 1961; expanded from version originally published in the journal *Cuadernos Americanos*, Mexico, 1950. Some of Paz's statements about woman recall the worst kind of self-indulgent mystification about the eternal feminine: 'Woman is another being who lives apart and is therefore an enigmatic figure. It would be better to say that she is the Enigma. She attracts and repels like men of an alien race or nationality', p.66.

3 See Francesca Miller, *Latin American Women and the Search for Social Justice*, University Press of New England, Hanover, NH, 1991, p.117.

in which the needs of the Mexican revolution were always privileged over the individual.

Precisely their position on the borderline brought Kahlo, and to an extent Izquierdo, within range of the Surrealist gaze but also endowed them with another dimension in terms of identity. Even Kahlo's marginal position, and the assertion of herself as subject against the utopian allegorical visions of her husband Diego Rivera, found a voice within the discourse of 'Mexicanness'. Kahlo's Tehuana costume in *My Dress Hangs There* (1933) or *The Two Fridas* (1939) can be understood not just as an identification with the native American cultures whose existence and whose plight had been spot-lit by the Mexican Revolution of 1910–20 but also as a deliberate selection of a regional costume coming from an area of Mexico renowned for its matriarchal society.[4] *My Grandparents, My Parents and I* (1936) engages in a question of roots quite alien to Paris Surrealism. This is not to say that certainties are proposed, for Kahlo often challenged and ironised popular modes of representation to make them function at both personal and political levels. She drew from many sources, including popular Catholic imagery like the *retablo* or ex-voto, as well as from the metaphorical iconography of European emblem books, to construct a self or selves in which private will and pain, sexuality, as well as the Mexican land and its history confront us.

Her self-portraits challenge the privileges of so-called reality. This was what enchanted André Breton on his visit to Mexico in 1938 and made her rather than Diego Rivera the capital discovery. Her 'pure surreality' had been achieved, as Breton said, without the slightest knowledge on her part of the work of himself and his friends. Although Kahlo later rejected an affiliation with Surrealism, as did the Cuban writer Alejo Carpentier,[5] this does not lessen the value of her work for Surrealism, reminding us not only of Surrealism's non-prescriptive nature, but also of its alertness

4 See Sergei Eisenstein's unfinished film *Que Viva Mexico* (1930–32) and Oriana Baddeley, '"Her Dress Hangs Here": De-frocking the Kahlo Cult', *Oxford Art Journal*, vol.14, no.1, 1991, p.10.

5 See Michael Richardson, 'Introduction', in Richardson (ed), *The Dedalus Book of Surrealism: The Identity of Things*, Dedalus, Sawtry, UK, 1993, p.11; Hayden Herrera, *Frida: A Biography of Frida Kahlo*, Harper & Row, New York, 1983; Ida Rodriguez Prampolini, 'El Surrealismo y la Fantasía Mexicana', *Los Surrealistas en México*, INBA, México, 1986; Alejo Carpentier, *El reino de este mundo*, México, 1949; María Clara Bernal, *Mas allá de lo real maravilloso: El surrealismo y el Caribe*, Universidada de los Andes, Bogotá, 2006.

to the possibilities of finding 'Surrealism' in other places. It may be that a part of Kahlo's seduction lay in the directness and freedom with which she conjured her identities, always coloured with the textures of her sources: sacred, hermetic, pagan, revolutionary. Interesting comparisons and contrasts can be drawn with the postwar poetry of the Surrealist Joyce Mansour, which also occupies a paradoxical relation to the male Surrealist subject. In Mansour's work identity slides between male and female, past and present, the dead and the living, mother and daughter, but often along paths that intersect with Kahlo.

The traditional modes of self-interrogation or self-dramatisation on the part of the male artist disappear or come under intense scrutiny in Surrealism in response to new kinds of inquiry about who or what the self might be. The challenges and promises attendant upon the uncharted unconscious to which the Surrealists eagerly responded brought uncertainties that shook stable notions about gender and sexual and cultural identity and intersected with new forms of female consciousness.

One of the questions raised by this topic is whether women's self-representations evince the same degree of anxiety as those of male Surrealists. Although not numerous, self-images by male Surrealists are haunted by the dissolution of identity: Dalí's self-image in paintings like *The Great Masturbator* or *First Days of Spring* (both 1929) appears as a literally melting head among a plethora of other Dalís, some androgynous. Breton, in the opening passage of *Nadja* (1928), famously rephrased the question 'Who am I?' as 'Whom do I haunt?'; he went on, 'I can understand that what I take to be the objective manifestations of my existence are only what passes, in the limits of that life, as an activity whose true field is wholly unknown to me.'[6] How to set about discovering this 'field' without taking for granted a self already fully formed in one's thought? How to distinguish between unwitting repetitions and true memory, to distinguish between what is given and what may be an aptitude peculiar to him; 'Beyond all the tastes I know in myself, affinities I feel, events that happen or not to me, emotions I alone experience, I force myself to know in what consists, if not to what belongs, my differentiation.' But how can this other self ever be known?

6 André Breton, *Nadja*, Gallimard, Paris, 1928, p.11.

This hidden unconscious core can never be the subject of reflection and thoughtful consideration; it appears in chance moments, through devastating coincidences, unforeseen recognitions, and sudden affirmations to which the conscious self can only be a 'témoin hagard' (haggard witness). How then can the self-portrait, which would be predicated on a unitary reflected self-representation, be even a possibility within Surrealism? Women's self-representations, moreover, within the orbit of Surrealism face not only the self but the numerous images of women produced by the male Surrealists.

The Surrealist repossession of the woman is a complex affair that often involves an ambivalence about male and female sexuality, ranging from a furious assertion of heterosexuality to a hysterical uncertainty about gender. The dissolution of identity that is one of the strangest and most paradoxical aspects of Surrealism may sometimes be enacted as the annexing of female qualities (women erased or masculinised). While women for the Surrealists were on the whole the erotic object (or fetishised part-object), they were also as for Rimbaud, precursor to so much in Surrealism, another kind of 'other', in which a new and non-patriarchal order might be found: 'When the unending servitude of women is broken, when she lives by and for herself, when man – hitherto abominable – has given her freedom, she too will be a poet! Woman will discover part of the unknown! Will her world of ideas be different from ours? She will discover things strange and unfathomable, repulsive and delicious. We shall take them unto ourselves, we shall understand them.'[7]

Participant in collective activities, in questionnaires and games, with some exceptions they were celebrated, valued, and feared as muse, *femme-enfant*, femme fatale – as Gradiva, Galatea, and occasionally Medusa. As accomplices or recipients of some form of masculine grace they were thus almost always implicated in terms of erotic partnerships. Breton's insistence on reciprocity and equality is interesting in terms of some aspects of female identity within Surrealism, though it is firmly rooted in his strictly binary approach to sexuality. In the questionnaire on love published in the final issue of *La Révolution surréaliste*, there is a classic instance of the double-edged operations inherent in his ideal union.

7 Arthur Rimbaud, letter to Paul Demeny, 15 May 1871, in Oliver Bernard (ed), *Rimbaud*, Penguin, London, 1962, p.13.

Under Breton's name in the responses to the questionnaire are answers to the four questions, starting with: 'What sort of hope do you place in love?', to which he responds: 'The hope of never recognising any other reason for living outside it.' 'His' answers are, however, framed in inverted commas, and it turns out that they are those of his companion, Suzanne Muzard; Breton concludes, after her signature, with: 'No response different from this could be held as mine.'[8] A momentary sense of the desired inseparability of their respective responses and wonder that the poet accepted another's words as his own is erased by the recognition of a stolen identity (her response is [as] mine).

Surrealism lived a paradox of its own making in the years after the Second World War when women's voices were heard fully for the first time in the organs of the movement. From the start it had sung the supreme value of *l'amour fou*, of fetishism, exhibitionism and free love, with the woman watched always as the object. Now precisely this arena of frank sexuality attracted a new group of women, among them Joyce Mansour and the writer Nora Mitrani, whose work appeared in postwar Surrealist journals like *Médium* and *Le Surréalisme, même.* Their presence is sometimes accounted for in terms of the ageing male Surrealists' need for new blood on any terms, and it must be said that on their part attitudes barely changed. To judge from the writing of women like Mansour and Mitrani, however, they chose actively to side with the Surrealists, rather than simply passively accept Surrealism as a convenient platform.

Mansour and Mitrani addressed the female subject in more direct terms than had previously been the practice in Surrealism and often but not always struggled against oppressive modes of sexual recognition to assert desire on their own terms. Their attitudes to postwar French feminism, for instance, and the ideas of Simone de Beauvoir, whose study of female subjection *The Second Sex* was published in 1949, are ambivalent.

A measure of the different tone of the postwar reviews is signalled by the ubiquitous questionnaires, such as that on striptease; the excuse was the recent essay by Roland Barthes that had argued that striptease desexualised women. The questionnaire devised two sets of questions, one for women, one for men. None of them raised Barthes' point that

8 *La Révolution surréaliste,* no.12, 1929, p.71.

striptease is a way of inoculating society, effectively negating the flesh; they focus on the question of erotic effectiveness in terms of both male and female sexuality. The painter Monique Watteau observed that the proposition 'man likes looking at woman' is not reversible. Nora Mitrani, evidently quite familiar with the genre, notes an ambivalence in her own response, tending more to masculine appreciation than identification. Mansour, who considered the public spectacle too abstract, was the only one to comment on the gap between the image of the stripper as a stereotypical male construction and a woman's sense of herself: 'I think woman should hide herself in the imaginary, indecisive folds of her own reflection.'[9] The emphasis on the reflection in the mirror here, which is both imaginary and her own, recalls those self-portraits by Kahlo that frankly posit the mirror as the mode of representation – paintings with multicoloured decorative borders like the painted tin surrounds of Mexican mirrors.

Nora Mitrani, by contrast, called for an escape from the mirror. In 'Diptyque de l'amour et du sang-froid' (Diptych of love and self-control) she wrote: 'Never has the necessity been as urgent as today for man to break the mirror, to move away from himself.'[10] For those, she goes on, who 'wish to lose themselves in order better to learn to live, there are other experiences [than the exotic marvellous] which threaten in a more direct manner the integrity of being' of which the erotic is the most powerful. This answer is complicit with the long thread of eroticism in Surrealism, but there are interesting modulations in postwar Surrealism, when the condition, for women, became the individual exploration of sexuality. In 'Des esclaves des suffragettes du fouet' (The slavery of the suffragettes to the whip) Mitrani, again, analyses the 'infinite unhappiness of being a woman' still (despite suffrage, which unbelievably women had only achieved in France after the Second World War).[11]

Mitrani's solution to the impasse she describes is both shocking and mocking: for woman, if not taking to the whip herself, to enjoy it. Some aspects of the painter Leonor Fini's work fit Mitrani's notion of a point

9 'Une enquête sur le strip-tease', *Le Surréalisme, même,* no.4, spring 1958, p.56. 'Je trouve que la femme devrait se cacher dans les replis imaginaires, indécis, de son propre reflet.'

10 Nora Mitrani, 'Dyptique de l'amour et du sang-froid', *Médium,* no.3, May 1954, p.38.

11 Mitrani, 'Des esclaves des suffragettes du fouet', *Le Surréalisme, même,* no.3, autumn 1957, p.60.

within eroticism between domination and consent freely given: 'She throws in men's faces her scandalous manner of living. Woman become object, consenting up to that point, because such is her pleasure… but that represents a manner of aggression toward men: they no longer recognise themselves.' However, there is a certain narcissism in Fini's self-images in which the erotic attraction to the specular image, as Lacan defined that stage in the development of the ego, is projected in reflections, as in *At the Ends of the Earth* (1949), or the multiplication of self-images.

A fluidity between male and female identity as well as between specific female identities is one of the most remarkable features of Mansour's poetry. The publication of *Cris* immediately brought her to the attention of the Surrealists. *Cris* was welcomed by Jean-Louis Bedouin in *Médium* in 1954: 'Stripped of all artifice, the poems… recall the savage grandeur of those rare surviving hymns to Selene.' The shifts of identity flow from subtle verbal associations and lines that often bear double meanings. So the first verse, which may be a lament for a dead mother, ends:

Tout ceci me venge enfin
Des hommes qui n'ont pas voulu de moi,

a phrase that in one context concerns sexual rejection but whose echoes of a dying divinity then lead to an identification not just with Actaeon-Christ but also with Procne-Medea:

Le clou planté dans ma joue céleste
Les cornes qui poussent derrière mes oreilles
Mes plaies saignantes qui ne guérissent jamais
Mon sang qui devient eau qui se dissout qui embaume
Mes enfants que j'étrangle en exauçant leurs voeux
Tout ceci fait de moi votre Seigneur et votre Dieu.[12]

12 Mansour, *Cris*, from 'Faire signe au machiniste' (1977), in *Prose et poésie*, Actes Sud, Paris, 1991, p.309. 'So at last I take vengeance / On the men who rejected me / The nail planted in my celestial cheek / The horns growing behind my ears / My bleeding wounds that will never heal / My blood become water which dissolves and embalms / My children whom I strangle in fulfilment of their prayers / All this makes of me your Lord and God.'

Mansour's invocation of myth, both Christian and Classical – above all Ovid, whose metamorphoses often involved not just translations of humans into trees and constellations but also of gender – allows her dazzling shifts of identity.

'Celle qui paraît être, suis.'[13] This line from Mansour's poem *Lettre morte* could serve as an inscription for some of the ways in which the genre of the self-portrait was transformed in the hands of the women artists within or associated with Surrealism. It is the final line of a fairly atypical short poem composed of a spare sequence of puns playing on the verbs *être* and *paraître* ('to be' and 'to appear'):

Etre ou paraître
Etre ou ne pas être
Etre ou peu(t) être.

'Celle qui paraît être, suis' is a feminised version of Rimbaud's *Je est un autre* (I is another); in Rimbaud's phrase, the ungendered neutral personal pronoun is mirror-sliced into the Other. Mansour rejigs the phrase to produce a gendered subject without personal pronoun: a very ambiguous 'I'. The subject is female but distanced, without becoming Other. Here appearance – which can be changed, masked, adopted at will – is what is, and the eschewal of the first-person pronoun may be a subtle rejection of male Surrealists' pursuit of the Other, often in the form of the woman. It recalls Carolee Schneemann's problem with theorists such as Jacques Derrida, whose 'language is exclusively male: he has only one pronoun!'[14]

'Celle qui paraît être, suis' can be taken in various ways, depending on how we understand the phrase *paraît être* (appears to be). Either *celle* (she) exists through how she appears to others, her identity given by the way others see her, in other words she is given her identity from others, or she could be understood to be assuming an identity that will be what she chooses and gives to others to accept as 'her'. Either way, and

13 'She [that female] who appears to be, am [I].' Mansour, *op. cit.*, p.554.

14 'I find him female-phobic also, with a very elaborate "re-construction" which involves repossession... a way to dominate and reincorporate the female principle. Baudrillard is equally creepy! Lacan, Freud, Jung, Engels – they all have to be subjected to a more thorough analysis.' Carolee Schneemann, interview, in Andrea Juno and V. Vale (eds), *Angry Women*, Re/Search Publications, San Francisco, CA, 1991, p.74.

notwithstanding the poem's ironic tone, what is effected at the end is a merging of *paraître* and *être*. Being, in other words, is only appearance, a proposition that immediately recalls Joan Riviere's famous 1929 essay 'Womanliness as Masquerade': 'Womanliness therefore could be assumed and worn as a mask... The reader may now ask how I define womanliness and the "masquerade". My suggestion is not, however, that there is any such difference; whether radical or superficial, they are the same thing.'[15]

Riviere argues that adoption of extreme forms of femininity in dress and behaviour may hide the woman's possession of power in a traditional male realm, in psychoanalytical terms to avert reprisals from the father for her assumption of the phallus. Obsessional forms of feminisation, however, are only one of the types of masquerade purveyed through the many modes of self-representation. Whether these relate to sexual identity or to appearances that reinforce or collapse difference, and whose complexity and multivalence cannot be foreclosed by psychoanalytic readings, attention needs at least initially to be placed on the medium of enactment itself: photograph, painting, object, mask.

The idea of masquerade, of appearance as artifice, strikes at the very heart of the idea of identity inhabited as a natural skin. This is as intrinsic to photography as is its claim to document, to have a privileged relation to the real. An interesting comparison lies in the construction of female alter egos by Duchamp and Man Ray (who was in both cases the photographer) and the self-portraits by Claude Cahun. While Duchamp's Rrose Sélavy exists as a phantom female alternative, a switched identity, Cahun constructs a series of masks of either exaggerated or indistinct gender, which bewilderingly proffer feminine or masculine faces or personae, from rouged doll to boxer. 'No', she wrote in *Aveux non avenus* (1930), 'I shall trace only sketches. When the mechanics are finally dismantled, the mystery remains intact.'[16] The extraordinary *Self-Portrait* (1930) from *Bifur* – shaved head and sharp profile like the 'little bird of prey' Marcel Jean remembered – erases such markers of gender identity as hair, but the singleted body seen from the back seems soft with a

15 Joan Riviere, 'Womanliness as Masquerade', *IJPA*, vol.10, 1929, p.306.

16 Claude Cahun, *Aveux non avenus,* Editions du Carrefour, Paris, 1930, as quoted in Laurie J. Monahan, 'Radical Transformations: Claude Cahun and the Masquerade of Womanliness', in M. Catherine de Zegher (ed), *Inside the Visible*, MIT Press, Cambridge, MA, and London, 1996, p.128.

breast-like crease. Both body and face trouble any normative sense of gender while being at the same time intensely sexual. This image hovers between the idea that the lesbian is a 'third sex', neither male nor female but combining attributes of both, and the annihilation of the bodily subject altogether: 'I shave my hair, tear out my teeth, breasts – anything that disturbs or irritates my gaze – stomach, ovaries, the conscious and encysted brain. Then when I have no more than a card in the hand, a heartbeat to note… I shall have won.'[17]

Cahun's photographs exposing the self image as a construction present obvious parallels with Cindy Sherman's early 'Untitled Film Stills', although there are also interesting sociological differences in the types of womanliness. The 'Film Stills' were produced to look as authentic as possible. Sherman did not construct entire narratives around them, but rather limited scenarios rooted in one or other of the womanly tropes peddled by Hollywood and television during the 1950s and early 1960s, which focused on the postwar return of woman to the domestic setting. Her favoured territory was the B-movie – an excellent place to observe the endemic Hollywood conflict between the rival demands of glamour and domesticity. The genre she chose to appropriate above all was the horror film, where just these conflicts are exposed as the heroine-victim is displaced or disoriented, as in the horror movie's ancestor the Gothic novel (so admired by the Surrealists). Sherman's pleasure in the scenario she constructs – the very meticulousness and completeness of its details – exposes the masochistic viewpoint of the female spectator.

Dorothea Tanning put the problem differently: 'I think everything we do is autobiographical. So one of my reasons for painting was really to *escape* my biography.'[18] One of the imaginary dimensions she used to enforce distance from the mirror image is the Gothic. She read the Gothic novels illicitly as a girl in her local library, thus revealing an unconscious affinity with Surrealism. The Gothic novel is the inverse of the chivalric epic; though the texture is medieval (castles, tapestries, helmets) as well as romantic (ruins, wild mountains, inaccessible forests), there is usually a female protagonist, who is either demonic (Matilda in Matthew Lewis's

17 *Ibid.*, 127.

18 Dorothea Tanning, interview with Alain Jouffroy, *Dorothea Tanning*, Malmö Konsthall, Malmö, 1993, p.49.

The Monk, 1796) or victim (Emily in Mrs Radcliffe's *Mysteries of Udolpho*, 1794). In the latter, which long fascinated Tanning (a painting of 1988 is titled *Mrs Radcliffe Called Again, Left No Message)*, the whole terror is in the unknown threat; nothing ghostly or monstrous ever materialises. It establishes an almost perfect metaphor for the unconscious, setting up an intense concentration on what is behind the curtain, which can never be wholly revealed.

In some ways the doors in Tanning's paintings represent her obsession with the enigma, the hidden. Although in her majestic self-portrait *Birthday* (1942) the doors are open ('I had been struck, one day, by a fascinating array of doors... crowded together, soliciting my attention with their antic planes, light, shadows, imminent openings and shuttings'),[19] they conceal and promise (or threaten) as much as they reveal. Her antique dress and the woody roots creeping round her skirt belong to the same Gothic dream; it is not Daphne, the transformed wood nymph of classical mythology, but herself. The bat-bird, too, is positioned as though to transport her, like a black parody of Parsifal's swan. It could also be read as a signifying attribute, like Juno's peacock.

There is a degree of irony in Marianne van Hirtum's drawing from the postwar Surrealist review *Bief*. Van Hirtum, who is better known for her delightful and fantastic short stories and dreamlike texts, here ironically replays the traditional poles of female identity in the forms of nature and fashion. Rooted at one end like a tree in the earth, at the other she is poised in magnificent artifice; a fringed tortoise-hat sprouting a smart feather-hand while her body dissolves into the wavering lines of the tree culminating in a wound mass of lines like a giant and formless bloom. The emphasis on the head and the multiplication of the eyes contrast with the familiar headless and fetishised female body in Surrealist imagery. The mouth-pansy, which neatly concludes with a thin profile, quotes Masson's mannequin from the 1938 International Surrealist Exhibition in Paris, which had a *pensée* (the French means both 'pansy' and 'thought') in its mouth.

However, this is hardly an escape from the male consumption of the female body; drawings by the Swedish artist Max Walter Svanberg, to whom the third issue of *Médium* (May 1954) was devoted, depict fantastic

19 Tanning, *Birthday*, Lapis Press, San Francisco, CA, 1986, p.14.

women-animals bristling with eyes. Breton describes the seductive marvellous in his monsters; his 'Hommage à Svanberg' evokes Isabelle of Egypt, heroine of Achim von Arnim's remarkable story, who 'wanted to plant a dozen eyes in her little friend Cornelius' though only succeeding in placing a pair in the back of his neck.[20] But an essay by Man Ray in the catalogue of the 1959–60 *EROS* (Exposition Internationale du Surréalisme) exhibition lays out a much franker account of the seduction of the eye: poets 'have bravely seen in a woman's eye the reflection of her sex. They realised that the head contains more orifices than the rest of the body, so many supplementary invitations to poetic, that is to say sensual, exploration.'[21] Van Hirtum's eyes fringed by her hair and then multiplying among her roots situate themselves within the Surrealist erotic but divert the depersonalising gaze that consumes woman by framing them with very personal individual details. Thus the ironic references to woman as nature are contradicted by her fashionable masquerade.

Revolutionary Mexico had nourished a strong national artistic culture dominated by the mural movement, from which both María Izquierdo and Frida Kahlo were excluded. It was to their work, however, which is concerned with issues of identity at a number of levels – personal, social, sexual and artistic as well as national – that first the former Surrealist Antonin Artaud and then André Breton, on his visit in 1938 to this revolutionary country par excellence, were drawn, and both Izquierdo and Kahlo in turn responded to Surrealist ideas that complemented their inherent tendency toward a 'Surrealist' imagination.

María Izquierdo, who was the first woman in twentieth-century Mexico to sustain a successful professional career as a painter, reflects upon female identity in *The Wise Cat* (1943). This is apparently a still life, whose fruits opened, gaping, and half-eaten parody the metaphor of female flesh. Juxtaposed with the fruit are other objects that play on the presence or absence of a female subject. The red drum-like shape half-obscured by the bunch of bananas is in fact a hat that appears also in the strange painting *The Bridal Veil* (1943), which contains the bridal clothes, jewels and bouquet but not the woman herself. *The Bridal Veil* also features a ghostly head like

20 Breton, 'Hommage à Max Walter Svanberg', *Médium*, no.3, May, 1954, p.2.

21 Man Ray, 'Inventaire d'une tête de femme', *EROS* (Exposition Internationale du Surréalisme), Galerie Daniel Cordier, Paris, 1959–60, p.14.

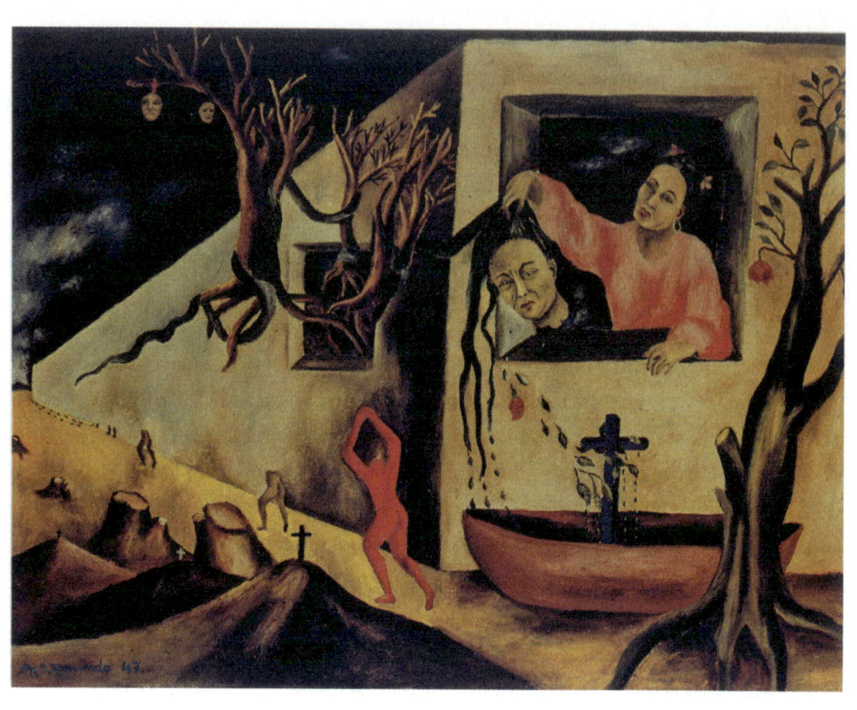

408 **María Izquierdo**
Sueño y presentimiento (Dream and Foreboding), 1947
Oil on canvas
45 × 60 cm | 15¾ × 23⅝ in

a hat maker's dummy, shown in profile, resting on a table beside jewels, hat and perfume. In *The Wise Cat* a similar head takes on an uncanny resemblance to a living head, or perhaps the living head is truncated to look like a dummy. Dark-skinned and staring, it resembles Izquierdo herself; however, the Tehuana dress that hangs over the back of a chair is recognisably that made famous by Frida Kahlo in *The Two Fridas* of which a slightly different version appears in *My Dress Hangs There* (1933). A curious set of juxtapositions, then, which may be a quite deliberate invocation of Surrealist practice.

The white cat reading a catechism may be intended as a sardonic contrast to Kahlo's adoption of the *retablo* format; it may equally refer to Surrealism as dogma. In the foreground beside the unmistakable pipe of Magritte's *La Trahison des images (Ceci n'est pas une pipe)* (The Treachery of Images (This is not a pipe), 1928–29) lie some marguerites, a pun on Magritte's name. Izquierdo's connection with Surrealism has certain parallels to that of Kahlo; she became close to Antonin Artaud on his visit to Mexico in 1936; Artaud believed that in her he had found an 'authentic' indigenous painter, wrote about her work, and took some paintings to Paris for an exhibition.[22] This endeavour lacked the type of backing Breton brought to Kahlo, and Izquierdo was not included in the Surrealist exhibition in Mexico City in 1940. The odd juxtapositions could therefore have a knowing and slightly malicious air; this painting may accumulate satirical attributes that take the place of a masquerade. The self is ironically subsumed in a mix of still life and self-portrait.

Relatively rare among women's self-portraits in any context is the tautological mode of the artist as artist. Even an apparent exception like Kahlo's *Self-Portrait with Dr Farill* (1951) revalues in ironic form the notion of self-expression by turning the palette into her heart, complete with arteries. Such an image is made possible within the non-naturalistic framework that Kahlo drew from both the *retablo* tradition in the Catholic world and from the seventeenth-century emblem books so popular in Spain and its dominions and in the Low Countries. A number of her images can be

22 Antonin Artaud, 'La pintura de María Izquierdo' (*Revista de Revistas,* 1936); 'Mexico y el espiritu primitivo: María Izquierdo', *L'Amour de l'Art,* no.7, Paris, October 1937, in *María Izquierdo, Monografia*, Gobierno de Jalisco, Departamento de Bellas Artes, Guadalajara, 1985; see also Antonin Artaud, *Oeuvres complètes*, Gallimard, Paris, 1956.

traced to the emblem and more general hermetic traditions, in which a picture is accompanied by a poem and sometimes a longer interpretive text.

In the painting *The Little Deer* (1946), for instance, Kahlo shows herself as a hunted deer stuck with arrows. The deer hunted and wounded frequently appears in emblem books with various meanings. The arrows in the heart/hart can stand for Cupid's love shafts, but a fascinating and more characteristic example reproduced in the publication *The Hermetic Garden of Daniel Stolcius* (1623) shows a huntsman chasing a stag-man, with human head and stag body, like Kahlo.[23] The huntsman, the text argues, hunts his own essence; he must kill the stag of male forces within himself, and this inner act will give him the freedom to experience the more feminine facets of being found in Diana's grove and spring. There may be a reference to a conflict of male and female forces in Kahlo's painting, as well as to an idea of suffering, given that she endows herself with stag horns.

María Izquierdo's *Sueño y presentimiento* (Dream and Foreboding, 1947) is one of those rare pictures that could convincingly be of a dream – enigmatic, irrational and complete – rather than one that posits its dream credentials through a mass of symbols. It is often taken as a narrowly autobiographical prognostication, foreshadowing the stroke that was to cripple her the following year. However, a more attentive examination suggests that this bleak scene with doubled self-portrait concerns Izquierdo's sense of struggle for an identity within the specific and problematic situation in Mexico.

A rare preliminary drawing, a bare but meticulous outline of the whole scene, may confirm a dream origin, the need to fix a complex evanescent image. But this is not to suggest that the painting's value for Izquierdo resided in the fact that it was a dream image, with some privileged route to the unconscious, as it would have been within a Surrealist context. Its dream status does, however, explain its unusual character in relation to the rest of her work, to which it is nonetheless related in intricate and peculiar ways. This complex self-representation includes at one level a tragic perception of her artistic identity.

The painting contains transformations and reversals of both the

23 Daniel Stolcius, *Hermetic Garden of Daniel Stolcius*, Magnum Opus Hermetic Sourceworks, Edinburgh, no.5, 1980.

Catholic imagery that Izquierdo had firmly adopted as her own and of the iconography of the Revolution (and possibly also of the Cristero rebellion) as established by the muralists. Leaning through a windowless embrasure Izquierdo holds up her own head by the unbound hair as though presenting it to a crowd; the tresses wind away snakelike, suggesting the Medusa whose gaze turned men to stone. But unlike most representations of the Medusa, whose open mouth and glaring eyes must have contributed to Freud's understanding of the terror inspired by Medusa as castration anxiety, this mouth is closed and mute. She is, moreover, weeping like the Mater Dolorosa whom Izquierdo had often depicted in startling, portrait-like close-up framed by the offerings on her own altar. The other famous weeping woman in Mexican mythology is La Llorona, whom Octavio Paz identified as one of the Aztec earth goddesses Cihuacoatl, 'the long-suffering Mexican mother' who 'wanders the streets late at night weeping and crying out'.[24]

Not only are the eyes weeping, but also the hair. Hair is the most uncanny of the body's parts in that it continues to grow after death and also is the most faithful recorder of the body's consumption. Here the hair has grown monstrously after death and weeps as though the body is made of tears. The tears metamorphose into leaves, and at the centre is a leaf painted red as a heart. In Catholic imagery the heart burns or bleeds but does not weep; but the heart pulses at the centre of the Aztec as of the Christian religion and in each is the paramount symbol of sacrifice. Izquierdo thus represents herself presenting her own image, using eclectic and even contradictory iconography as sacrificial victim or martyr.

As a suffering woman there is a clear contrast with Frida Kahlo (although Kahlo's *Self-Portrait with Unbound Hair* (1947) could conceivably also be a referent here). In Kahlo's *Arbol de la esperanza mantente firma* (Tree of Hope Stand Firm, 1946) the barren fissured land is an empathetic extension of her own bodily suffering. In Izquierdo's case, the personal significance is more obscure, and there is a sense in which it might be concerned with women's situation in Mexico in the decades following the Revolution. Elena Poniatowska gives a bleak picture of Mexican women outside the home as anathematised,[25] though as Ana Macías comments,

24 Paz, *op. cit.*, p.75.

there were, against all odds in the patriarchate that revolutionary Mexico still was, important struggles by and on behalf of women for suffrage and the right to education and a career.[26]

Izquierdo was involved in the feminist movement, which in Mexico had a distinctly nationalist tone. 'Though contemporary historians generally agree that the revolutionary phase of the Mexican Revolution ended with the administration of Cardenas in 1940, and label the Revolution as "moribund" by 1946, Mexican women were still struggling to be full participants in national politics. And they identified with the inclusive rhetoric of the revolution, with the concept of *la raza cósmica,* the idea of Mexicanness.'[27] This analysis bears upon Izquierdo's painting, but in a negative way. Her engagement at a national level with cultural politics had recently come to a bitter conclusion. In 1945 a longed-for mural commission was suddenly rescinded. In 1947, the year of *Dream and Foreboding,* she published a breathtakingly bold attack on the three great figures of muralism who had forbidden her the right to paint a mural: Diego Rivera, José Clemente Orozco and David Siqueiros. The same year, Siqueiros delivered his notorious lecture in which he affirmed the mural movement as the 'root and trunk of the whole of modern Mexican painting', condemning as a serious deviation painters who accentuated art of a 'Christian, archaeological, folk-art, essentially picturesque nature'.[28] Izquierdo's sense of exclusion from the mural movement – she looks but cannot speak, her hair locked into the dead 'roots and trunks' floating away from the bare unpainted walls – seeks expression in a deliberate echo of the only anti-utopian and unsentimental imagery of the Revolution, that of Orozco. The devastated land, ruined house and stormy black sky look directly back to Orozco's *The White House* (1925–28), a painting depicting the suffering and fear of the Revolution rather than its promise of national prosperity.

Izquierdo's personal narrative thus parallels and intersects the violent history of the country: the headless trunks, bodies and trees, other heads

25 Amy Conger and Elena Poniatowska, *Compañeras de Mexico: Women Photograph Women*, University of California at Riverside, Riverside, CA, 1990, p.45.

26 See Anna Macías, *Against All Odds: The Feminist Movement in Mexico to 1940*, Greenwood Press, Westport, CT, 1982.

27 Miller, *op. cit.*, p.117.

28 David Alfaro Siqueiros, 'The Historical Process of Modern Mexican Painting' (1947), in *Art and Revolution*, Lawrence & Wishart, London, 1975, p.12.

hanging on branches as in the Cristero rebellion, the humped cross-marked graves. The martyrdom is of herself as woman and painter: she was the first professional woman painter in revolutionary Mexico but was unable to exercise her profession in the highest recognised mode. *Dream and Foreboding* is a bitter counterpart to her passionate defence of the right to paint: 'Mexican painting remains alive, always virginal, always born of itself, suspended from its living branches, renewing itself in political and historical accidents – unavoidable law of art – but not arising out of them.'[29]

Although embracing the idea of 'Mexican' painting, Izquierdo argued the freedom of the individual painter to construct her or his own version of it. In self-images both Izquierdo and Kahlo in diverse ways challenged the political-historical narrative of Mexicanidad as constructed through the orthodoxy of muralism. There is something both detached and intimate about these unique images, which are shadowed by both personal and national histories. In asserting the rights of the imagination as the means of expressing their own reality, and thus moving in very general terms into the Surrealist orbit, Kahlo and Izquierdo challenged the official cultural ideology in Mexico. In a sense they had first to assert their right to a share in the concept of Mexicanidad, which all too often excluded women; but then precisely because they were less burdened by ideas of a self bounded by race, history and politics, they could freely explore.

Mexicanidad provided the frame for an examination of gender, of status and of aesthetic responsibility which then prompted forms of resistance and opposition; within Surrealism, a new female subject began to emerge, but this time from a challenge to a Surrealist ideology in which the female was no longer the token of male identity. The work of Mansour, Mitrani, Louise Bourgeois, Dorothea Tanning, Claude Cahun and others used the modes of Surrealism, such as the Gothic and the dream, and its mediums – collage, photography, the object – to assert identities above and beyond that invested in the passive body.

29 María Izquierdo, 'María Izquierdo vz. Los Tres Grandes', *El Nacional*, Mexico City, 2 October 1947.

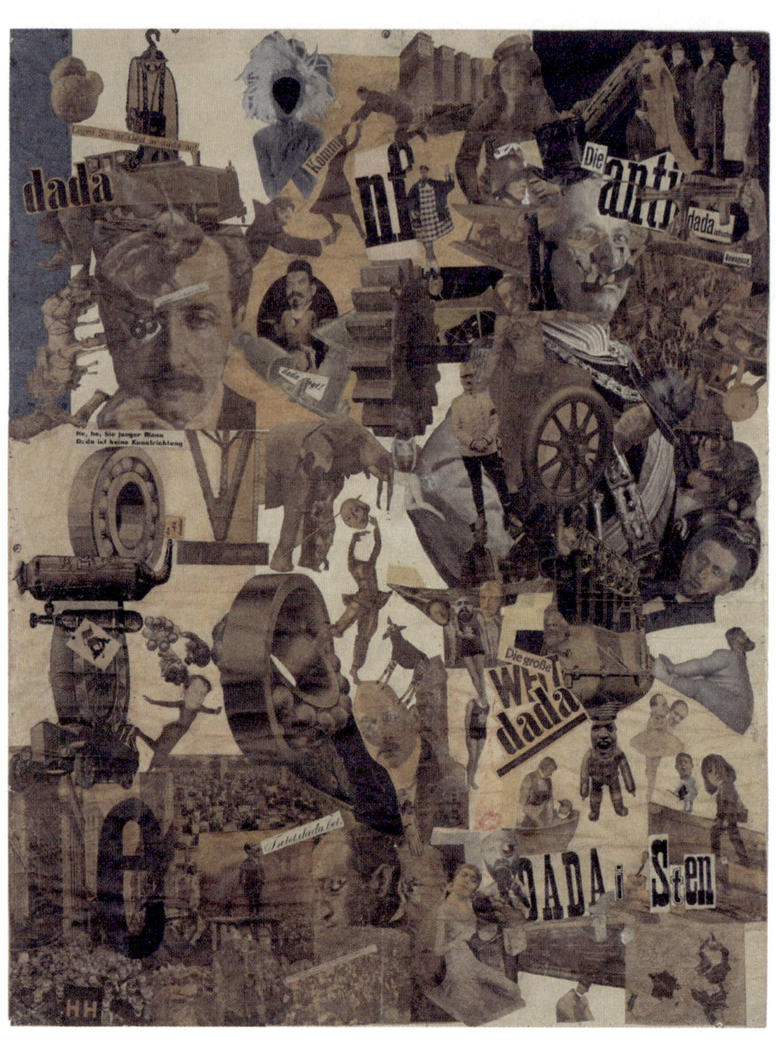

414 **Hannah Höch**
Schnitt mit dem Küchenmesser Dada durch die letzte Weimarer Bierbauch-kulturepoche Deutschlands (Cut with the Dada Kitchen Knife through the Last Weimar Beer-Belly Cultural Epoch in Germany), 1919
Collage
114 × 90 cm | 44⅞ × 35⅜ in

Hannah Höch and the 'New Woman'

'Hannah Höch and the "New Woman"', *Hannah Höch*, Dawn Ades, Emily Butler, Daniel F. Herrmann (eds), Whitechapel Gallery and Prestel, London, 2014

In the short grotesque tale *Der Maler* (The Painter), written around 1920, Hannah Höch pinpointed the way the critical debate about gender equality plays out in the domestic sphere, where it comes down to the question: do you take turns with the washing-up? Her story of the painter-genius, thwarted by his wife because he was asked to wash the kitchen dishes on four occasions in four years, apart from remaining relevant today (although of course so much else has happily changed), is fascinating for its merciless exposure of the limits (in the home) of the much trumpeted freedom of the *Neue Frau* or New Woman, the gap between public rhetoric and private reality, and the instinctive male backlash. On the first occasion, in her story, the painter's wife had asked for help with the washing-up because she was giving birth to their first son. The other three occasions had not seemed absolutely necessary to the painter, who was called Heaven.[1]

> During the nights after the days in question he became obsessed with certain ideas. He kept seeing Michelangelo washing up cups. He had looked into psycho-analysis in enough detail to feel that he could directly confront his wife with the fact that, whatever reasons there might be for what she had done, demands of this kind only ever arose from a lust for power and, even if he, as a modern man, would in

1 The model for the painter seems to have been Raoul Hausmann, an expressionist painter when Höch met him at the start of their relationship in 1915. His friend Johannes Baader described himself as, 'the Superdada, President of the Globe and Heavenly Sphere...', Richard Huelsenbeck (ed), *Dada Almanach*, Atlas Press, London, 1993, p.100.

theory stand up for the equality of the sexes, well, nevertheless – in the cool light of day – and in any case – in his own four walls – and – any similar demands on her part would surely be tantamount to the enslavement of his spirit...[2]

The breaking down of the sentences in the final part of this extract, as the argument within the painter's mind proceeds, brilliantly and hilariously captures the irrational swing from confident modern (public) person to private (threatened) genius. Setting aside for the moment the wider gender issues raised by the image of the New Woman, Höch's *Der Maler* posits the problem of equality in the home. The painter's wife might be the other, private face of the New Woman or her opposite, an unreformed *Hausfrau* – Höch doesn't specify. The central irony of the story concerns an oil painting in which the artist represents the essential likeness between chives and the female soul, thus expressing his resentment at ever being asked to help in the kitchen. The painting, in which he eventually abandons the attempt to paint the female soul, ends up an unremitting green, but is a surprise hit. The President, 'ferrying his presidential belly' round the exhibition, declares it a masterpiece. Its creator then omitted any mention of chives and 'proudly declared "The Soul of Woman".'

The title of her justly famous collage *Schnitt mit dem Küchenmesser Dada durch die letzte Weimarer Bierbauchkulturepoche Deutschlands* (Cut with the Dada Kitchen Knife through the last Weimar Beer Belly Cultural Epoch of Germany, 1919), takes on another dimension in the light of this satirical story. The kitchen is still the domain of the woman/wife, but she is now wielding the Dada kitchen knife (or the kitchen knife called Dada), slicing the beer belly of male culture. The title hints at the intimate domestic arena in an image otherwise full of women (and men) prominent in the public sphere. Perhaps times are changing, not least because this slice of life is to be seen from a female perspective. Höch's generation saw women newly taking their places in the public realm – in theatre, dance, politics, sport, art and literature. In *Schnitt mit dem Küchenmesser Dada...*, Höch is

2 *Der Maler* was unpublished during her lifetime. See *Hannah Höch: Eine Lebenscollage*, vol.1, 1889–1920, Berlinische Galerie/Argon, Berlin, 1989, pp.747–49; See also translation by Fiona Elliott in Dawn Ades, Emily Butler and Daniel F. Herrmann (eds), *Hannah Höch*, Whitechapel Gallery and Prestel, London, 2014, pp.74–75.

able to draw on an impressive number of female stars from the worlds of art and theatre for her collage, celebrating thereby their position in the new order. Women are literally at the centre of her collage: the headless body of the dancer Niddy Impekoven, juggling the head of the artist Käthe Kollwitz. But they look very fragile, as giant wheels, cogs and even an elephant circle round and crowd in on them.

It is very interesting to compare the pictorial structure of *Schnitt mit dem Küchenmesser Dada...* with Raoul Hausmann's photomontages of the time, such as *Tatlin at Home* or *Dada Conquers*, both from 1920. In these, following on from his caricature heads of burghers constructed with snippets of newspaper texts, sliced-up woodcuts and fragments of photos, he returns to an illusionistic pictorial space based on De Chirico's paintings. By contrast, *Schnitt mit dem Küchenmesser Dada...* is highly original, replacing illusionistic space with the blank of a page as its basis, onto which Höch pastes her photo fragments in a centrifugal fashion, mobilising them so that the whole image appears like a wheel turning on the Impekoven/Kollwitz pair. Höch's satirical spirit is largely at the expense of the males massed in the upper right of the collage, running from the Kaiser, whose moustaches have metamorphosed into the rear ends of two boxers, to her then-partner Raoul Hausmann, who is being extruded like a sausage, with a tiny robot-puppet body, from a giant mechanical cylinder. The collage is thus perhaps a modified celebration of the modern woman, who is at the heart of things but whose triumphs are frail and possibly transitory.

Where the 'Dada' in this snapshot of Weimar culture comes in is another question, because despite its radical politics, Berlin Dada was not notably geared to the female voice. The sheer scope, density and boldness of *Schnitt mit dem Küchenmesser Dada...* is all the more impressive when not only Höch's isolation as the only woman in Berlin Dada is taken into account, but its dominantly masculine if not macho nature is also considered. The public face of Berlin Dada, unlike that of Dada in New York or Paris, was almost unremittingly male. There is a range in the way the Berlin Dadaists represent man (usually themselves), from the dandy to the revolutionary, but in the Dada magazines there are very few representations of women (let alone representations by women), with the exception of George Grosz's wedding celebration montage *'Daum' marries her pedantic automaton 'George' in May 1920, John Heartfield is very glad of it (Meta-Mech. Constr. after Prof. R. Hausmann)* (1920), and his erotic and often violent street, café and brothel scenes. Photographs of Hausmann proclaiming his phonetic poems, sometimes with raised fists, contrast with those of him dressed as a dandy or even in a half-naked dance. A particularly striking photograph for *Dadaco* (unpublished, 1919; p.68), shows a headless 'new man' nattily dressed in a three-piece suit, with the words 'dadadada' issuing from his neck and feet.

A photograph of the installation of the *First International Dada Fair* of 1920 shows Höch together with Raoul Hausmann in front of their respective works. It is startling to see the size of Höch's *Schnitt mit dem Küchenmesser Dada...* in comparison with the other collages. It is unusually large – more or less the size of a poster, such as those filling the walls of the gallery, indicating a confidence and an independent vision that do not square with her otherwise relative invisibility in Berlin Dada and its subsequent histories. Two of the members of the Dada group, George Grosz and John Heartfield, had, it seems, opposed her participation in the exhibition, but were overruled. In later histories of Dada by former participants, she is virtually absent. Astonishingly, she is not mentioned at all by Richard Huelsenbeck in his account of Berlin Dada, *Memoirs of a Dada Drummer* (1969), nor in the English edition of *The Dada Almanac* (1993) and was slightingly referred to by Hans Richter in *Dada: Art and Anti-Art* (1964). She was not included in the key publication that revived interest in Dada: Robert Motherwell's *The Dada Painters and Poets* (1951), despite or perhaps because of the fact that those whom Motherwell described as the old warhorses of Dada had taken a close interest in the book.[3] Nonetheless, despite the fact that she was still active as an artist at the time of her rediscovery, the interviews that followed almost all concentrated on her Dada times and her memories of her more famous fellow Dadaists. Poet and writer Edouard Roditi's interview with Höch published in *Arts* 34, no.3 of 1959 was one of the first to kindle interest in her work, and was probably responsible for her presence in William Rubin's massive Museum of Modern Art, New York exhibition, *Dada,*

3 Höch is mentioned in passing as having exhibited *The Dictatorship of the Dadaists* [sic] and other collages, with Hausmann, at the *First International Dada Fair*, Berlin, 1920. She does not figure in the index in Robert Motherwell's *The Dada Painters and Poets*, G.K. Hall, New York, NY, 1951, p.148.

Surrealism and Their Heritage in 1968, where she was one of only three female artists to be included.[4] A paradigm shift starting in the 1970s, away from the study of art through its 'isms', together with a surge in cultural studies of Weimar Germany, has tended to align Höch with the 'New Woman', and her work has opened up to feminist analysis.

The New Woman as she appeared in the first decades of the twentieth century embodied hard-won freedoms: the right to a professional life, to vote, to enter politics, to enjoy sexual liberty, to play sports. She existed in other democratic countries beside Germany. Suffrage, though obviously important, was not the sole issue. Women were given the vote in Germany in 1918 but not until after the Second World War in France, where the *garçonne* was much debated in the 1920s and 1930s. But in Germany several factors have brought the New Woman during the period of the Weimar Republic into particular prominence, heightened by her almost complete elimination after 1933 by Nazism, which was anti-Semitic, anti-feminist and homophobic.[5] 'Our movement', National Socialism declared, 'places woman in her natural sphere of the family and stresses her duties as wife and mother.'[6] The movement prided itself on emancipating women from the women's emancipation movement, as they put it. The contrast with the Weimar years was all the more striking: 'In the atmosphere of the 1920s freedom and tolerance were in the very air you breathed. Defeat in the war and subsequently the arrival of hyperinflation left people frantically eager to enjoy life to the full... Culture flourished as never before, while the country tumbled down into the abyss. It was a time of exuberant erotic pleasure, of intellectual fun and games...'[7] Germany had been in the forefront of scientific and scholarly studies of sex, and the work in particular of Magnus Hirschfeld contributed to the demystification of sexual preferences and promoted the idea that gender variability was natural. (Hirschfeld's *Sexuelle Zwischenstufen* (Sexual Borderline Cases) was mentioned by one of the witnesses in the lawsuit charging the Dadaists

4 Höch, Méret Oppenheim and Sophie Taeuber-Arp, see p.372, note 3 in present volume.

5 The unprecedented access for women to the professions: law, medicine, the church, during the Weimar Republic was not wholly eradicated after the Nazi take-over. I am grateful to Professor Cornelie Usborne for her generous help on these topics.

6 Erwin Haeberle, *The Journal of Sex Research*, vol.17, no.3, August 1981.

7 Charlotte Wolff, quoted in Shearer West and Marsha Meskimmon (eds), *Visions of the 'Neue Frau': Woman and the Visual Arts in Weimar Germany*, Scolar Press, Ann Arbor, MI, 1995 pp.81–82.

with distributing indecent publications, as part of a 'disquisition on the relationship between satire and sexual pathology'.)[8]

The New Woman in Germany was often seen as deviating from the 'normal'; she was identified with '*männliche Frauen*', mannish women, and also often represented as androgynous and linked to transvestites. But at the same time, the 'normal' was seriously open to question. Class was too, and the New Woman was 'overlaid with the expressive proletarian woman'.[9] The new freedoms and attendant anxieties that the accelerated modernity brought in Weimar Germany were not only fully explored but also partially created by the combination of serious scholarly research into sex and gender and the proliferating illustrated press. The New Woman was part of this process and was a very visual phenomenon. The illustrated press in Germany – especially the *BIZ* (*Berliner Illustrierte Zeitung*) and the *MIP* (*Münchner Illustrierte Presse*) – were fascinated by 'the partly mythical notion of a sexually emancipated working woman'.[10] There were also a number of lesbian-oriented magazines, such as *Frauenliebe und Leben* and *Die Freundin*, which encouraged the exploration of lesbian identity as well as being outlets for the problematic questions of female pleasure and female desire.

How far this liberation reached from the public into the private realm of intimate gender relations is one of the questions raised by Höch's collages and photomontages, as well as by her story. *Der Maler* shows the other side of the postwar liberation of women, or rather the inequity of this liberation. The New Woman may have been identified as such because she seemed to have joined the male political and cultural world; she may even have begun to try to feminise it, at the same time as the mannish woman and the androgyne make an appearance – all possibilities are amply attested to in the many illustrated magazines of the 1920s and 1930s in Germany. But privately, as many women other than Höch must have experienced, 'liberation' did not translate into equality. Rather than subscribing to a singular view of the modern woman in the modern demo-

8 Walter Mehring, quoted in Hans Richter, *Dada, Art and Anti-Art*, Thames & Hudson, London, 1965, p.112.

9 Patrice Petro, *Joyless Streets: Women and Melodramatic Representation in Weimar Germany*, Princeton University Press, Princeton, NJ, 1989, p.154.

10 Richard McCormick, *Gender and Sexuality in Weimar Modernity,* Palgrave Macmillan, New York, NY, 2001, p.2.

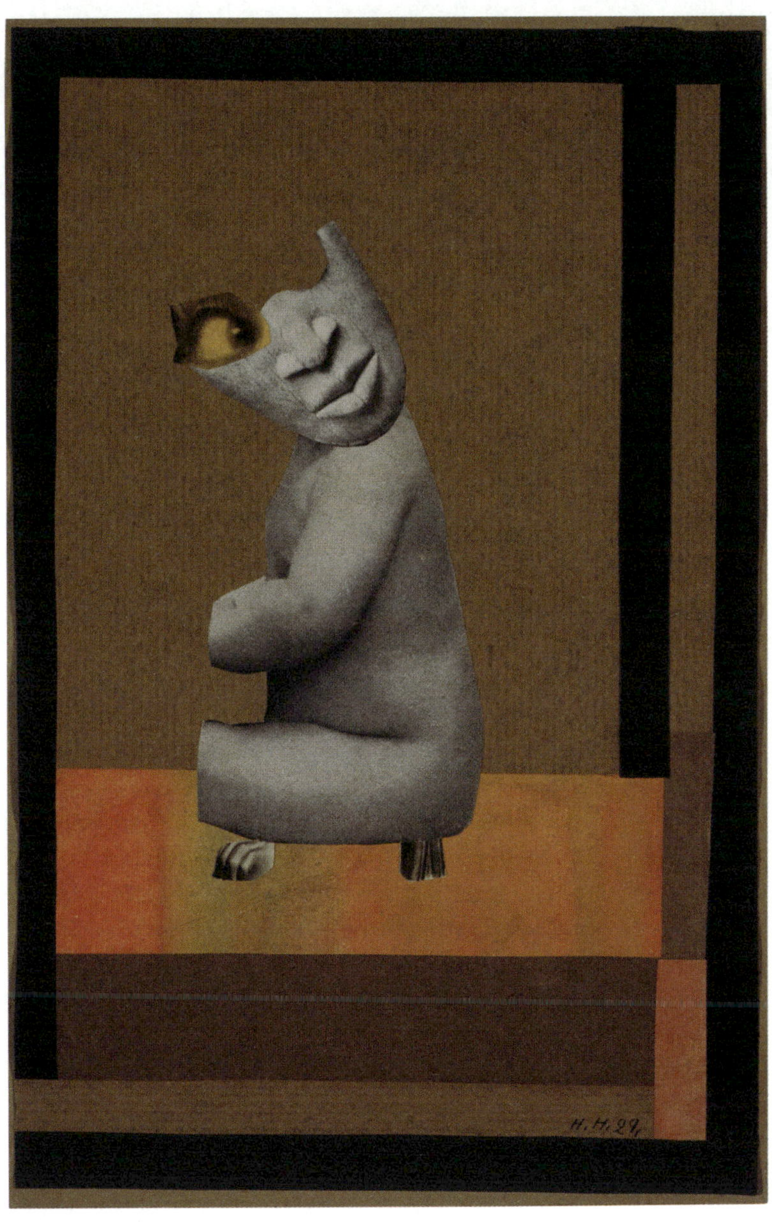

Hannah Höch
Aus der Sammlung: Aus einem ethnographischen Museum
(From the Collection: From an Ethnographic Museum), 1929
Collage and gouache on paper
26 × 17.5 cm | 10¼ × 6⅞ in

cratic republic, Höch observes and lives her ambiguous position, especially the contradictions between the public and private dimensions of the equality debate. She is acutely aware of the ways the illustrated magazines constructed and manipulated the image of woman inside and outside the home, and she is merciless in her treatment of the ironies involved.

In *Da-Dandy* (1919), Höch has chosen photographs of expensively clad and shod women, with the fixed half-smiles and come-hither eyes of a model, wearing pearls and elegant hats, which she has cut up and recombined. As the originals were of different scales, the arms, heads, legs and eyes cannot match and don't add up to a complete body, even of the mismatched kind that appears in many photomontages, such as *Der Vater* (The Father, c.1919), *Fröhliche Dame* (Happy Lady, 1923), *Auf dem Weg zum siebenden(!) Himmel* (On the Way to Seventh(!) Heaven, 1934), or *Deutsches Mädchen* (German Girl, 1930). What she shapes them into is not another body but the head of a man, whose outline is created by a thin red line around the women's heads. Is she drawing attention to and lampooning the way fashion magazines dictate how women should look, a glamour promoted for the delectation of men? The man's head is stuffed with the stereotypical female image, far, one might add, from the way Höch herself dressed, 'in avant-garde clothes, plain and drop-waisted, possibly of her own design'.[11]

In the *Portrait of Gerhart Hauptmann* (1919), the face of the German playwright and Nobel Prize-winner, hugely respected in the Weimar period, is cut in two, making him appear two-faced and undermining the otherwise dignified pose; between the two halves of his head is the face of a woman, while several male and female faces swarm in the formal shape of the stock at his neck, perhaps a reference to the social realism of his early plays. The identity of the woman is unknown, but Höch is surely alluding to the contrast between his public persona as the literary figurehead of the new order in Weimar and the mess of his private life and the lives of the women in it.

Unlike the *Portrait of Gerhart Hauptmann*, the central male figure in

11 Maud Lavin, *Cut with the Kitchen Knife: The Weimar Photomontages of Hannah Höch*, Yale University Press, New Haven, CT, and London, 1993, p.37.

Der Vater, also a Dada period photomontage, appears to be anonymous. The structure of the image here is very interesting; unlike *Schnitt mit dem Küchenmesser Dada...*, with its strongly centrifugal composition circling round the head of Kollwitz, the abstract and figurative fragments are subtly arranged to create the figure of a rocking horse, or perhaps a merry-go-round horse, its neck created by the curved tyre on the left, with arched 'legs' pointing to the lower left and right corners, with the central mismatched figure seated upon it clasping a baby. It's possible that Höch is here playing with the French meaning of the word *dada*, 'gee-gee', or child's hobby horse. The head of the 'father' is male but the rest of the body is made of disjointed female parts, with notably glamorous legs and high heels; none of the elements constructing this monstrous figure is classically maternal or associable with baby care. To the left of the head is a letter cut from one of Hausmann's printed phonetic poem-posters, 'U', though unlike his own self-portraits proclaiming his poems, this male's mouth is firmly closed. There are many possible readings of this witty montage and it is difficult to reconstruct how its contemporary viewers might have seen it, let alone its more private implications. However, the contrast in the illustrated papers between the New Woman engaged in all kinds of sports, represented here with the photos of female swimmers, dancers and gymnasts together with the muscular 'new man' boxer (aiming a blow at the baby's head) and celebrations of the family might have given Höch the idea for this ironic photomontage.

Although quite prominent in the *First International Dada Fair*, Höch was almost invisible in the Dada magazines. In the exhibition she showed (at least) four works: the catalogue listed no.15 *Zwei Dada Puppe* (Two Dada Dolls, 1916–18), no.23 *Schnitt mit dem Küchenmesser...*, no.24 *Da-Dandy* and no.25 *Dada-Rundschau* (Dada Review, 1919). Höch's Dada puppets received considerable press attention, but it was the male artists' Dada puppets that figured in the Dada magazines: the bourgeois and militarist caricatures by Grosz and Heartfield. In fact, she is included only once in any of the Dada magazines in Berlin – in *Der Dada* no.2 (December 1919) an abstract woodcut by 'M. Höch' [sic] appears in the advertisement for *Dadaco*, 'Dadaistischer Handatlas'.[12] However, this was not entirely the fault of the male Dada editors: a letter from Johannes Baader invited 'graphic or literary contributions' to *Der Dada* (10 June 1919) and on 13 June

1919, he asked her to contribute another woodcut, which she either failed or refused to do. The explanation is at least partly personal. The charming photograph of Höch and Hausmann at the *First International Dada Fair*, in which she inclines gracefully to read something he holds, emphasising their closeness, tells us nothing of their turbulent, difficult love affair over the previous five years, which ended in 1922. A few days after his note asking Höch for another woodcut, Baader wrote a long letter to her trying to resolve yet another crisis between them, pleading with her to be less intransigent with Hausmann.

Höch's collages reveal her sophisticated attitude to debates about the sensual and the intellectual components of female experience. At the centre of *Schnitt mit dem Küchenmesser Dada...* is the figure of the dancer and former child star Niddy Impekoven, cut from a photo in the *BIZ* (9 November 1919), pirouetting in the costume of a 'Pritzel puppet'. She is headless, but is gently juggling the head of the artist Käthe Kollwitz between her raised hands. Art historian Hanne Bergius and others have pointed to the mind/body division in Höch's fragmented women: 'In separating the head from the body and in often drastically displacing the eyes, the artist poses the question of the possibilities of the intellectual and sensual identity of the woman...'[13] The detached head and body in *Schnitt mit dem Küchenmesser Dada...* are a particularly striking example of this, and Höch is undoubtedly giving her own take here on a widespread debate in Germany, which was fed by the discoveries of psychoanalysis, by the psychological and sexual studies of gender and the whole phenomenon of the New Woman, which she was experiencing very directly herself. The letters from Hausmann and from his friend Baader to Höch are constantly analysing their intense and troubled relationship in terms of the body and the intellect:

12 Höch contributed twice to her close friend Kurt Schwitters's magazine *Merz* (1923–1932): *Merz*, 1 January 1923, p.10, *Zeichnung* by Höch; *Merz*, 7 January 1924 [*Merz ist form*], *Astronomie* by Höch. *Merz* became a remarkable platform for the international Dada-Constructivist axis in the post-Dada period.

13 Hanne Bergius, *Hannah Höch: Collages, Peintures, Aquarelles, Gouaches, Dessins/Collagen, Gemälde, Aquarellen, Gouachen, Zeichnungen*, Musée d'Art Moderne de la Ville de Paris and Nationalgalerie Berlin, Staatliche Museen Preußischer Kulturbesitz, Paris and Berlin, 1976, p.35.

> You two love each other. What does that mean: love each other? Sexuality, the magnetism of mutual attraction, binds you to each other. Where the very adversity that your intellectual selves automatically create drives you apart, it just as much draws you together again once it has polaristically overcome that same intellect.[14]

Unlike the other (male) Dadaists, Höch did not sign manifestoes. However, she does admit in her interview with Suzanne Pagé that she wrote 'grotesques' which on occasion she performed with Hausmann and Mynona (Salomo Friedländer).[15] During her long and happy relationship with the Dutch writer Til (Mathilda) Brugman, from 1926–36, Höch illustrated Brugman's writings, and there is a close link thematically between the latter's grotesques and Höch's collage practice.[16] The 'grotesques' are a literary genre of a fantastical satirical character: they could be compared to Jonathan Swift's *Modest Proposal* (1729), itself chosen by André Breton as an example of dark humour in *Anthologie de l'humour noir* (Anthology of Black Humour, 1940). Höch collaborated with Brugman on her *Scheingehacktes* (1935), a comic tale of a man compelled to buy everything he sees, totally under the sway of the advertising regime of the commodity culture in which he lives. Brugman's *Himilia* (1927) is even more directly linked to Höch's photomontages, many of which anticipate the theme of this grotesque about a bride who is surgically reconfigured to be made perfectly beautiful, and is operated to death. In Brugman's *Tempora lehren mores* (Time teaches manners), from the 1920s, a wife, in her attempt to remain attractive to her husband, purchases a miraculous beauty product; she applies the whole jar to her body and the rejuvenating powers are such that she turns into a foetus.

In Höch's interview with Suzanne Pagé, the latter asks for Höch's opinion of feminist interpretations of her work. 'One can nowadays make a feminist reading of some of your works: biting irony against marriage and the family... exaltation of the modern woman...'[17] Höch's response

14 Johannes Baader to Höch, 22 June 1919, in *Hannah Höch: Eine Lebenscollage, op. cit.*, p.589.
15 Interview with Suzanne Pagé in *Hannah Höch, op. cit.*, 1976, p.25.
16 See Julie Nero, *Hannah Höch, Til Brugman, Lesbianism and Weimar Sexual Subculture*, 2013. PhD dissertation, Case Western Reserve University (online).
17 Interview with Suzanne Pagé, *op. cit.*, p.27.

is unexpectedly measured. Irony: yes, she agrees that this is certainly an important part of her work. But marriage and the family she does not regard as 'useless institutions'. They can be 'good brakes' against uncivilised behaviour, and it could be that here is an echo of her refusal to bear Hausmann's children when he was still married to someone else, despite his urging and his theoretical pronouncements about women's freedom.[18] She approves totally of the Rights of Woman, but denies that she sought to glorify modern woman in her work. She was, she says, more concerned in her collages with the suffering of women. When, on the other hand, she wished to give a face to the epoch, she would then include what she called the contribution of women. She frequently insisted on this point that she was working with the images of things that were around her.[19] The materials she used included not just photos from newspapers and the illustrated magazines, but new developments in photography, like aerial views, microscopy, radiography, and also those more specifically associated with women (though not the *Neue Frau*), such as lace designs and dress patterns. These often form the background to her collages, the interrupted lines in the patterns, like those on a star chart, paralleling the broken and cut fragments of the photomontages. They may have originally been documents, but she turns them all to the service of her independent vision.

Höch's collages throughout her life show an acute and independently minded attitude to the position of women in modern society, to gender, to social and sexual identities, to beauty and difference, to the technological manipulation of the body, and to the contradictions between public and private 'equalities', all of which remain relevant today.

18 Höch had two abortions, in May 1916 and January 1918, against Hausmann's wishes.
19 A point she insisted on in an interview with the author, Berlin, 1976.

Dalí

The two artists whose work I have written about most extensively, Marcel Duchamp and Salvador Dalí, would seem to be at opposite ends of the spectrum from moral as well as artistic points of view. Dalí was excluded from the Surrealist movement in 1938 for cynically exploiting his public and for his increasingly right-wing remarks, and cold-shouldered by critics and historians after the Second World War for aligning himself with Franco, painting in a regressive manner and cultivating a celebrity persona. Duchamp on the other hand remained admired and courted by the Surrealists to the end of his life. He ceased to paint on canvas in 1918 and while his interventions – such as the readymades – were relatively few and far between, his influence as the instigator of Conceptual art has been massive. But they were in fact close friends and had a surprising amount in common. Each responded in their own way to a sense that art was in crisis in an age of new visual technologies. They shared interests in science, optics and eroticism, experimented with film and photography and tested identity in terms of gender as well as the persona of the 'artist'. Each artist could have had his own section in this collection. However, Duchamp's work threads through several sections and he is less often the sole subject of an essay.

I met Dalí in the late 1960s and found myself in the position of defending him and writing seriously about his work. Homing in initially on his Surrealist period I gradually came to appreciate the later paintings, which Duchamp virtually, and uniquely within the avant-garde, supported. The first essay here is concerned with the intricate relationship between Dalí's painting and writing during the 1920s, a turbulent time in which he was expelled from art school, had phenomenal early success as a painter, gave up art, made the film-masterpiece with Luis Buñuel *Un Chien Andalou*, joined the Surrealist movement and returned to painting. The range of Dalí's activities is extraordinary: painting, sculpture, objects, prints, films and film scripts, poems, psychoanalytical essays, theoretical texts, a novel, an autobiography, advertisements, fashion, videos and other uncategorisable projects. *Salvador Dalí: the Centenary Exhibition* at the Palazzo Grassi in 2004 gave the fullest account so far of these multifarious activities. The other two essays here concern film and film scripts; Dalí is also at the heart of 'Little Things: Close-up in Photo and Film', in the final section on The Photographic Image.

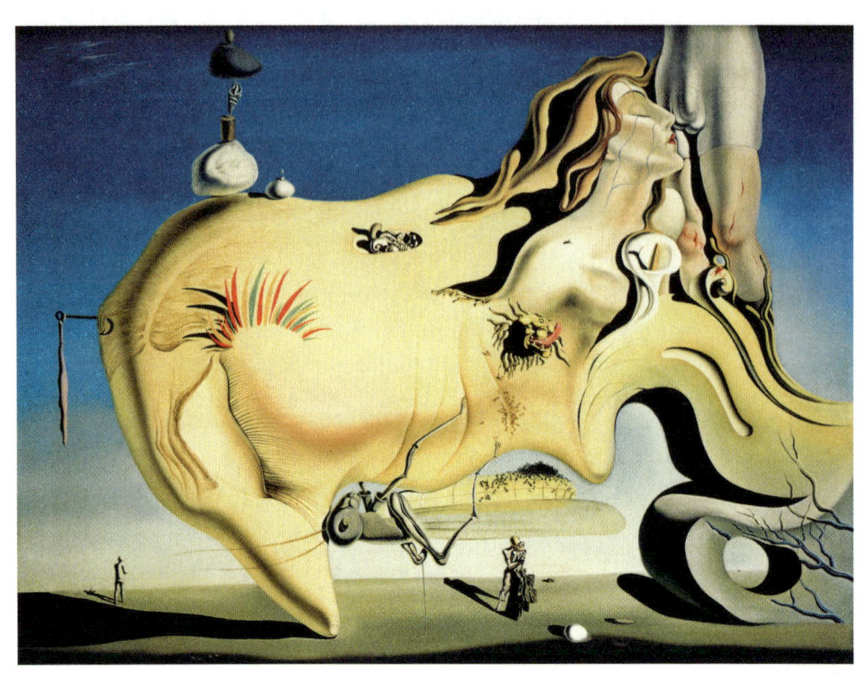

432 **Salvador Dalí**
The Great Masturbator, 1929
Oil on canvas
110 × 150 cm | 43¼ × 59⅛ in

Morphologies of Desire

Salvador Dali: The Early Years, Michael Raeburn (ed), South Bank Centre, London, 1994

The cluster of paintings that marked Dalí's entry into the Surrealist movement in 1929 are usually seen as the starting point – and, in some ways, apogee – of his career. Startling conjunctions of ideas and images drawn from Surrealism, psychoanalysis and natural history, they immediately placed him at the centre of the Paris movement. However, both in their aspect – that hyperreal fixing of the imaginary – and in their themes, their roots lie in Dalí's work of the preceding decade. But their relationship to his previous work is quite complex – there are continuities, but also transformations and even reversals of the earlier material. The transformations and reversals owe much to Dalí's growing familiarity with Freud and with the works of French psychiatrists, and to some extensive self-analysis. The paintings seem, overwhelmingly, to be concerned with sex: not just sexual desire, but fears, phobias and obsessions, and problems of sexual identity. Readings of these pictures have been dominated by their evident rootedness in psychoanalysis – whether they are taken as deliberate constructs by Dalí, utilising his familiarity with that science, or as 'pathological documents' bearing witness to his actual neuroses or obsessions. But the tendency to scan the pictures for symbols and to read these off like a chart of symptoms obscures other kinds of ideas and associations, which stand out in relief when linked to his earlier work.

One set of ideas was to lead to his lifelong fascination with morphology: 'Glory be to Goethe for having invented this word of incalculable moment, a word that would have appealed to Leonardo!'[1]

1 Salvador Dalí, *The Secret Life of Salvador Dalí*, Dial Press, New York, NY, 1942, p.3.

Morphology is the term used to describe the structures, homologies and metamorphoses of form in animals and plants, or in language. Although as the study of shapes it is of obvious interest to artists, for Dalí morphology was possessed of a range of significant ideas. Categories of form, such as hard and soft structures, came to magnetise crucial qualities, even of a moral and psychological character. And, as the study of hidden forces that govern the structures and transformations of bodies, Dalí made morphology into a materialist analogue to the notion of the hidden forces of the unconscious mind. His vigorous description of the dynamic operation of matter awakens echoes of the powers of repression in the individual psyche: 'Form is always the product of an inquisitorial process of matter – the specific reaction of matter when subjected to the terrible coercion of space choking it on all sides, pressing and squeezing it out, producing the swellings that burst from its life to the exact limits of the rigorous contours of its own originality of reaction.'[2]

Through the 1920s he developed his ideas about hard and soft, form and formlessness, the conscious and the unconscious, and eventually about paranoia. To consider the 1929 paintings in the context of his deliberate stylistic contradictions, his equivocal relations with Surrealism and modernism, with machinism and *L'Esprit Nouveau*, and of his initial deployment of Surrealist ideas *vis à vis* photography and film, is to get a sense of the nature of the convulsions that produced them.

'MINERAL CADAQUÉS'

If Federico García Lorca can be seen as the modern poet of Granada (a Granada, though, as Dalí said, without trams or railways), it looked for a time as if Dalí was to become the modern artist of Catalunya. Cadaqués, and especially the strange geology of the landscape round Port Lligat were to remain important to him, though not in the direction his early work had pointed.

As early as 1923, the critic Eugenio Montes, in the Madrid newspaper *La Tribuna*, regretted that a recent poster display celebrating the lands of

2 *Ibid.*, p.2.

Castile and Portugal had not also included a poster by Dalí to give a taste of the 'Mediterranean spirit'. This suggests that Dalí was regarded as the latest young recruit to Catalan Noucentisme. Although his work does have elements of this Mediterranean classicist movement, the early paintings most strongly marked by a 'Catalanist' sensibility are the bright, poster-like watercolours and gouaches of popular and picturesque subjects. The paintings of gypsies, market scenes and fairs show the influence of paintings of similar subjects by Ramon Pichot, but also his own direct involvement with local life and popular culture that Dalí's sister Ana María notes in her memoirs.[3] In 1921 he made posters for the Fires i Festes de la Santa Creu, which aroused some controversy because of their bold, flat modern colours; he also, with his friend Joan Subias, decorated a float for the Procession of the Three Kings in Figueres so magnificent that it attracted the attention of the local press.

In January 1922 he showed in Barcelona for the first time, in a mixed exhibition of work by the Catalan Students' Association with paintings that included *Smiling Venus* (1921), *Fiesta at the Hermitage* (c.1921) and *Olive Trees* (c.1922). One critic noted his 'formidable artistic personality'[4] but not the remarkable fact that this manifested itself already in such diverse styles. For, as was to be almost invariably the case over the coming years, Dalí exhibited, simultaneously, paintings in markedly different manners. On the one hand, there was the direct but slightly caricatural picturesque style, often with simple black outlines and clean, flat colours; on the other, evidence of an awareness of Impressionism and post-Impressionism, also gained largely through the work of Ramon Pichot, who moved regularly between Paris and Cadaqués.

Smiling Venus is a curious amalgamation of the two: a seaside idyll with a raven-haired Venus reclining before a divisionist view of the bay at Cadaqués. How far this painting suggests a sardonic attitude to the revival of the Mediterranean Venus in *noucentista* classicism is an open question. But an inclination towards satire is notable in several works of this period, especially those dealing with popular or Catalanist subject matter. In this, Dalí was still very much within a Catalan tradition.

3 Ana María Dalí, *Salvador Dalí visto por su hermana*, Ediciones del Cortal, Barcelona, 1983, pp.73f.

4 *L'Empordà Federal*, Figueres newspaper, 21 January 1922.

This could best be explained with reference to the Catalan graphic artist Xavier Nogués, to whose work Dalí's frontispiece for a special number of *El Día Gráfico* of 1921, devoted to 'the divine restorer of the *sardana*', Pep Ventura, was compared. Nogués's album of drawings *La Catalunya Pintoresca* (1919) 'contains grotesque figures... who make up satirical scenes, which, without imitating them, were done in the spirit of traditional popular Catalan prints'.[5] A work that fits this model is Dalí's watercolour of the popular Catalonian dance, *Sardana of the Witches* (1921), which is closely related to his title-page illustration for Carles Fages de Climent's *Les Bruixes de Llers* (1924). The poem that gives the book its title celebrates, in the same satirical-picturesque spirit, the legend that on a Friday night, if the *tramuntana* wind has blown all week, wizards and witches come out to dance the *sardana*:

> Wizards and witches crazily ranged
> dance the sardana in open spaces.
> Their ill-omened manes of hair fly in the wind
> sweeping across the clouds.

The revival of the *sardana*, a 'miracle of Nationalism' endebted to Pep Ventura, was part of the cultural renaissance sponsored by the Catalan government and enthusiastically supported by Dalí's father, a Catalan federalist of the Left.

The satirical spirit Dalí absorbed from within this tradition was later to be turned against it. By 1928 rejection of the Catalan or indeed of any picturesque was a prominent element in his 'anti-artistic' campaign. A much-quoted lecture by Dalí of that year called for the abolition of the *sardana*, and the demolition of the Gothic Quarter of Barcelona. When he and Ana María took lessons in and had themselves photographed doing the charleston, it was a quite deliberate rejection of the national Catalan dance in the name of the modern age.

Fiesta at the Hermitage, picturesque as it is, also shows another side of Dalí's political interests as a young man, as recorded in his diary for 1920. A subtle sense of social division is revealed in the separation of the gypsy

5 Francesc Fontbona, 'The Art of Noucentisme', *Homage to Barcelona*, exhibition catalogue, Hayward Gallery, London, 1985–86, p.177.

with headscarf in the centre from the group of townspeople to the right, which includes Dalí himself talking to two young girls seen from the rear, a motif that appears frequently through the early 1920s. As in several drawings of the period, such as *My Family* (1920), Dalí portrays himself as a bohemian young artist; the similarity between the caricatural, triangular face with almond eyes and the later *Self-Portrait with L'Humanité* (1923) is striking. It is noteworthy that, although one of Dalí's preferred subjects is, undoubtedly, himself, he rarely exhibited self-portraits unless, as we shall see, they were in a more or less disguised form.

The third work in the 1922 exhibition was a landscape of olive trees, regarded by at least one critic (*Alt Empordà*), as the best in the show. Views of Cadaqués, its harbour, olive groves, stone-bordered lanes, bays and wild rocky headlands, as well as of the Empordà plain with its cypresses and wide vistas, were to remain favoured subjects through many radical stylistic transformations. Dalí was increasingly identified with Cadaqués, where his family had a holiday house and where he always painted in the summer. One admirer predicted that he would be 'the poet-painter of our sea'. But Cadaqués also had its connections with international modernism: Picasso at the height of his Cubist period, and André Derain in his later 'classical' Cubist mode had both worked at Cadaqués, an association noted by critics who commented on the shifts in Dalí's landscapes between the stippled post-Impressionist manner, a silvery naturalism and a sombre, harder, green-brown Cubist style clearly indebted to Derain.

Cadaqués, Cap Creus and the rocky coastal landscape continue to figure in many paintings in the 1920s, from the detailed realism of *Cliffs* (1926), where the human body is overwhelmed by the mass of rock, to 'academic Cubist' pictures like *Composition with Three Figures (Neo-Cubist Academy)* (1926), where the Cubistic bodies and the sharp rocks are equally hard-edged.

Cadaqués became for Dalí the geographical epitome of a morphological category: the hard and crystalline in form. He wrote to Lorca in January 1928, after a visit there, that the village was 'more mineral than ever, the olives grow straight from the smooth shale, like machines, objectivity closed its teeth with force'[6] Mineral hardness is linked to

6 Dalí, *Letters to Lorca*, letter 34, 15 January 1928, p.82.

the notion of objectivity, which Dalí connected with rigour, order and measure in an increasingly elaborate but finally equivocal schema.

PURISM, MEASURE AND MATHEMATICAL LYRICISM

Dalí consistently and provocatively exhibited paintings in two apparently contradictory styles; in his very early work, the switch was between a flat, 'popular picturesque' manner and Impressionism/post-Impressionism. From the mid-1920s, it was between Cubism and realism. Un-remarked earlier by critics, from the mid-1920s it was this cool switching of manners, rather than the extreme vanguardism of his Cubism, which contributed to his controversial reputation.

Although there were inevitably critics who disliked Cubism and Futurism, and whose nostalgia for a comfortable academic naturalism, or in Catalonia for the classicism of Noucentisme, guaranteed an unfavourable reception for the various brands of modern art, Dalí was by no means the only artist working in this manner. Barcelona's familiarity with the latest French art, from Cubism to Picabia's Dada and neo-Dada abstractions, is well known, and Madrid was more familiar with Cubism than Dalí suggests in his autobiography (though perhaps not in the Special School where he was studying, whose professors, he noted in his text 'New limits of painting', were still locked into teaching the primacy of the retinal whether with respect to academic or to Impressionist painting). Rafael Barradas's 'Vibrationism', for example, a highly individual form of dynamic Cubism, was familiar from the pages of the art reviews. In 1922, one of the lecturers in the programme put on in the Residencia in Madrid, to which eminent scholars from a variety of fields contributed, was on 'Some problems of modern painting', by Marjan Paszkiewicz. The key section on 'The Cubism of Pablo Picasso' was extracted for publication in *Horizonte*,[7] a short-lived avant-garde review to which Dalí's Residencia friend Luis Buñuel also contributed.

Some critics regarded Cubism as already passé, although Dalí, who visited Picasso in Paris in the spring of 1926, must have realised that his

7 'El cubismo de Pablo Picasso', *Horizonte*, no.5, 1923.

famous compatriot treated it as an alternative visual language, not just a style. There is a very tenacious as well as adventurous quality to Dalí's various experiments in Cubism, and in Cubism's successor Purism, which still inform the condensed and collage-like space of certain works of 1928 like *Thumb, Beach, Moon and Rotting Bird*.

However, it was not his Cubism or Purism that provoked the critics, but the systematic contrast in the modes of the works he exhibited: the Cubist or Cubist-related manner and the careful realism dubbed by a critic 'miniaturist'. In May 1925, for example, he sent paintings which included *Purist Still Life, Bather* and his *Portrait of Luis Buñuel* (all 1924) to the salon of the Sociedad de Artistas Ibéricos in Madrid. The exhibition as a whole provoked a certain amount of reactionary comment. *Buen Humor* ran a double spread of illustrations of works by various artists with satirical captions. Dalí's *Purist Still Life* was described as 'one of the clearest pictures in the exhibition: it represents a meal after the meal' (an involuntary recognition of Dalí's interest at the time in the pictorial possibilities of hollows rather than masses). *Bather*, though, is in a trim, hard-edged neoclassical manner with prominent signs of modernity: the male figure is clad in a bathing dress and seen from a dramatically foreshortened viewpoint in front of a large touring car. Several critics noted with approval the shift such works appeared to represent from Cubism to a more classical naturalism; Moreno Villa saw Dalí abandoning Picasso in favour of Derain, who himself by now had abandoned Cubism, and others noted the influence of the artist Josep de Togores. Eugeni d'Ors, author of *La Ben Plantada* (1911) and chief inspiration of Noucentisme, welcomed his return to nature, adding that if Dalí had, 'in the time of Cubism', constructed like a watchmaker, now he had returned to nature and was 'creating like a mother'.

But they spoke too soon. Dalí was still far from abandoning Cubism and vanguard experiment. At his first solo show at the Galeries Dalmau in Barcelona, in November 1925, the paintings again fell broadly into these two groups, with extremely clear and precise portraits of his sister and father on the one hand, and Cubism of varying degrees of abstraction on the other. *Pierrot and Guitar* and *Venus and Sailor (Homage to Salvat-Papasseit)* (both 1925) represent the extremes of the latter. Although the catalogue of this exhibition did not identify *Venus and Sailor* as a 'Cubist painting', as it did the *Pierrot*, at an exhibition in January 1926 it was described as 'academic Cubist'. *Venus and Sailor* is a lyrical merger of the clean planes of classical postwar Cubism with Mediterranean classicism. The combination of ancient and modern is not out of keeping with the spirit of Noucentisme (see, for example, Enric-Cristofol Ricart's woodcuts in the magazine *L'Amic de les Arts*), but for his friends in the Residencia, familiar with his more scabrous drawings of sailors in brothels and remarks about modern Venuses, *Venus and Sailor* perhaps possessed a satirical edge. This exhibition was an unexpected success, selling well and attracting widespread critical attention, being especially admired by the intellectuals of the Barcelona Ateneu and the literary world.

Dalí's dual manners may have represented the different spaces he inhabited as an artist: realism at home with his familiar subjects, Cubism as part of the professional challenge of a vanguard career in Madrid. But the contrast was deliberately maintained and systematically presented to his public. At the exhibition organised by the newspaper *Heraldo de Madrid* at the salon of the Círculo de Bellas Artes in January 1926, Dalí put in *Venus and Sailor* and one of his most celebrated realist paintings, *Figure at a Window* (1925), which made the front cover of *D'Ací i d'Allà* (January 1926). At his second one-man show at the Galeries Dalmau the following winter, the duality of his production was emphasised by placing the 'Cubist and neo-Cubist' works and the 'miniaturist' ones in separate spaces. The latter included a portrait of his sister *Girl Sewing* and *Girl from Figueres* (both 1926) – a painting of a young lace-maker that more than any other at this time honours Vermeer: 'the greatest painter who has ever been.'[8]

Such subjects as *Girl Sewing* were in fact quite commonplace in Spain at the time. Intimate portraits, domestic interiors, careful still lifes of simple, isolated homely objects like Dalí's *The Basket of Bread* (1926) abound in the illustrated reviews of the time, but none have Dalí's tight precision, the quality of 'miniature' – not necessarily referring to the actual size. The difference could be described as that between a naturalism in which nature is filtered through the artist's temperament, with some degree of expressive gesture and the emphasis on individual perception of the external world, and a realism which involves a notion of objective

8 Dalí, *Letters to Lorca*, *op. cit.*, letter 12 March 1926, p.34.

exactitude according to a pre-existing conception. Dalí's desire for precision is so strong that the frozen effect leads to a degree of un-naturalism. It comes as no surprise that his next favourite painter beside Vermeer was the Douanier Rousseau, whose idea of realism was to paint every individual leaf on a tree. Like Dalí's description of spending all day painting 'seven waves as hard and cold as those of the sea itself',[9] this is the very reverse of naturalism.

Opposed as these styles of Dalí's may appear to be in the light of modernist aesthetics, in that realism approximates 'window' and Cubism 'surface', they are in fact entirely homologous with respect to his ideas about morphological categories, to which he gives psychological and even moral overtones. Purism, Cubism and 'realism' all belonged for Dalí to the category of the 'hard': the objective, ordered, lucid and controlled. They belong to the world of the senses, not of the emotions, which for Dalí were a realm of terrifying unpredictability and confusion: '...while I have always known exactly and with premeditation what I wished to obtain of my senses, the same is not true of my sentiments, which are light and fragile as soap bubbles.'[10] Whether or not one accepts Dalí's confident assertion here that he knew what he wanted to get from his senses, the distinction he makes was a crucial one. But it was not simply physical, but what he called a 'spiritual sensuality', opposed to nature. By 1926 art had crystallised for Dalí into the opposite of nature. Writing to Lorca in the early summer of 1926, he noted that two thinkers he much admired, Goethe and Le Corbusier, both 'said that art and nature are two distinct things'.[11] Rejecting the academic idea that nature has its superior laws for the artist to discover as dangerously fringing the realm of faith and religion, he wrote of his relief at being free of 'this nightmare of being submerged in nature, that is, in mystery, in confusion, in unintelligibility; settling down finally within the limits of a few clearly organised truths, preferences which satisfy my spiritual sensuality.'[12]

Although Dalí's readings of Jean Cocteau, Raymond Radiguet and Élie Faure were important, it was above all the language of Purism that

9 *Ibid.*, letter 18 September 1926, p.44.

10 Dalí, *The Secret Life of Salvador Dalí*, *op. cit.*, p.10.

11 Dalí, *Letters to Lorca*, *op. cit.*, letter 16, summer 1926, p.42.

12 *Ibid.*

helped him to formulate his ideas. References to measurement and to mathematics in both writings and paintings have their origin in Le Corbusier and Amédée Ozenfant's 'Le Purisme'. Talking of the hierarchy of aesthetic sensations, they write: 'The highest level of this hierarchy seems to us to be that special state of a mathematical sort to which we are raised, for example, by the clear perception of a great general law (the state of mathematical lyricism, one might say).'[13] This notion of mathematical lyricism undergoes a dramatic sea-change in Dalí's hands in the proto-Surrealist text, 'Saint Sebastian', which was published by *L'Amic de les Arts* in 1927, and in the paintings related to it.

He explained the relationship between Cubism and these ideas in 'New limits of painting' (published in three parts in *L'Amic de les Arts* in the spring of 1928 and effectively announcing his adherence to Surrealism).[14] Charting his journey through the visual languages of the time, he wrote of Cubism that 'the intelligence served not to render the mind visible, but rather to sensualise it and reduce it to the significance of a number, or a sign, which, by the power of mathematical abstraction, could move us aesthetically, by a measure and a rhythm in harmony with architecture but never in harmony with the most violent needs for the absence of cohesion'.

The final sentence here signals the potential disruption of the calm assurance of the Purists' 'higher aesthetic order' of mathematical lyricism; there are other, violent and unconscious needs pulling in the opposite direction, away from order and towards disorder, dispersion and abjection. The disorder and repellent formlessness of the 'absence of cohesion', initially expressed in terms of the '*putrefact*', which will be discussed below, was to be recognised by Dalí as a compelling need, while the notion of mathematical order came by 1929 to be treated with an ambivalent, almost derisory literalness. In *Dismal Sport* (1929), for example, the plinth of the statue of the troubled, hermaphroditic, young man has as an inscription three terms for measuring weight: 'gramme, centigramme, milligramme'.

13 Le Corbusier and Amédée Ozenfant, 'Le Purisme', *L'Esprit Nouveau*, no.4, 1920.

14 Dalí, 'Nous límits de la pintura', *L'Amic de les Arts*, nos.22, 24, 25, 29 February 1928, pp.167–69; 30 April 1928, pp.185–86; 31 May 1928, pp.195–96. In these articles Dalí moves much closer to Surrealism, and there are many echoes of Breton's *Le Surréalisme et la peinture*, the series of articles that were published from 1925 in *La Révolution surréaliste* and as a book in 1928.

At the opposite pole to the clarity, mathematical order and what he called 'astronomy', to which Dalí attached both the Cubist and the 'miniaturist' works of the mid-1920s, he and his friends elaborated the notion of the *putrefact.* In a letter of December 1925 to Pepín Bello he proposed that the key to their particular 'atmosphere' was 'astronomy'. Hence, 'we oppose astronomy to Putrefaction – PUTREFACTION – ASTRONOMY – are two symbols, 2 categories'.[15]

Astronomy, as the science of the measurement of the heavens, was an anti-transcendental and rigorous category of thought applied to the unknowable and therefore not without its 'mathematical lyrical' side. Putrefaction was the category of decay and formlessness, identified with sentiment rather than the senses.

The satirical-picturesque strand in Dalí's adolescent works, like *Sardana of the Witches*, helped prepare the ground for the visual expression of the idea of the *putrefact*, which emerged from the milieu at the Residencia in Madrid. Initially a private joke among the group that included Pepín Bello and Lorca, it was pursued with particular vehemence by Dalí. Negatively defining their anti-art position, the idea of the *putrefact* has clear echoes of Dada, though Dalí took care to distinguish it from the Berlin Dada version. George Grosz, Dalí wrote to Lorca in the summer of 1925, had claimed to depict putrefaction, but his '*señor tonto*' (Mr Idiot) was painted 'with hate, anger, rage in a (*social*) sense.[16] They, on the other hand, had elevated the *señor tonto* and 'made of idiocy a lyrical category. We have arrived at the lyricism of human stupidity.' Unlike the targets of Grosz's political satire: horrific militarists and fat capitalists, Dalí's were largely, though not exclusively, from the artistic and literary world. He invented a double-edged, satirical celebration of the exaggerated, sentimental, picturesque and emotional, in drawings with an outrageously soft, wobbling line. In 'Saint Sebastian', his first published text, he clinically details 'the whole world of the putrid figures: the blubbering, transcendental artists, far removed from all clarity, cultivators of all germs, unaware of the precision of the double, measured decimetre; the families

15 Rafael Santos Torroella, *Dalí Residente*, CSIC, Madrid, 1992, p.122.
16 Dalí, *Letters to Lorca*, *op. cit.*, letter 6, summer 1925, p.16.

who buy *objets d'art* to go on top of the piano; the public works clerk; the associate committee member; the professor of psychology...'[17]

Dalí and Lorca planned to publish a 'Book of Putrefaction'; Dalí apparently finished his contributions, but Lorca failed to produce the promised preface, and the book never appeared. As well as drawings, Dalí contemplated including some of the collages which he sent in letters to Lorca, such as the *Book of Varicose Veins* (1926) or *Homage to Fra Angelico: Birth of the Child Jesus* (1927), with their spare and frankly Dada humour. Writing to urge Lorca to produce his preface, he asks about putting in the 'Buster Keaton collage'.

José Moreno Villa, another friend from the Residencia and co-member of Buñuel's 'Ordén de Toledo',[18] wrote a newspaper article on the non-publication of Dalí's 'Book of Putrefaction', and located its origins in a Madrid literary group of the type they nicknamed '*putrefacto*'. This type was a bit 'pompier' in character: 'a mind that is punctilious and peevish, hollow, full of commonplaces, of routine and idiotic prudence. But at the other times it wasn't a question so much of his character as his appearance. The painter Dalí designed a whole book, and I saw drawings in which the "putrefact" was really disgusting. Apparently his most characteristic feature was his moustache.'[19]

But Dalí did not relinquish his idea. Letters to friends bristle with references to *putrefacts*, who wallowed in the transcendental and sublime, and adopted the tics of the artistic establishment. One whom Dalí pursued relentlessly was the poet Juan Ramón Jiménez, 'great hairy *putrefact*'. In its strategy there are similarities between Dalí's attack on this respected modern poet, and Dada's characteristic opposition to the prevailing avant garde. Dada, wherever it manifested itself during and just after the First World War, regularly took on what might have seemed to be their own nearest allies against the bourgeois or salon art world: Berlin Dada against the Expressionists, Paris Dada against the postwar Cubists.

17 Dalí, 'Sant Sebastià', *L'Amic de les Arts*, no.16, 31 July 1927, pp.52–54.

18 The Ordén de Toledo was a mock heroic 'order' founded by Buñuel while he was at the Residencia, of which Pepín Bello, Lorca, Maruja Mallo and Dalí were all members. They professed devotion to the ancient capital, centred their excursions there on eating and drinking at a famous inn and took the opportunity to dress up, often impersonating religious characters. It is possible that Lorca's and Dalí's self-dramatisations as Saint Sebastian had their origins here.

19 *Ley / (entregas de capricho) / Ley a algo, a la poesía, por ej. / España / 1 / Un día / 1927.*

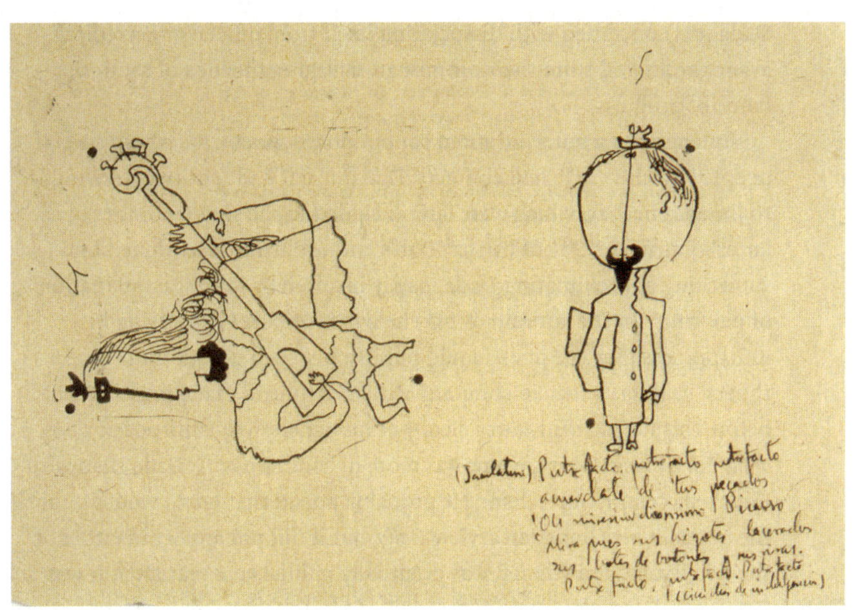

Salvador Dalí
Los Putrefactos (The Rotten), c.1925
Ink on paper
11.5 × 16.6 cm | 4½ × 6½ in

Dada was concerned with dissociating itself from official or accredited avant gardes and from their promise of salvaging the idea of art in the name of progress.

Jiménez was a much-admired contemporary poet with whom several people in Dalí's circle had contacts. Dalí himself had sent two drawings to Jiménez in 1925, which were later included in the single number of the latter's journal *Ley*,[20] but by 1927 Dalí's anti-art attitude hardened into something approximating Dada, partly inspired by Miró's 'assassination of painting'. In the autumn of 1927 he wrote to Lorca expressing his unhappiness that the poet should publish his 'such unique and sincere things' in *Verso y Prosa*, in company with that 'putrid marasmus'. Shortly before this he had sent Lorca a copy of his aggressively anti-poetic *Poem of the Little Things* (1927), which has more in common with Dada than with Dada's successor, Surrealism. He probably hoped that Lorca would publish the poem in his Granadan review *Gallo*, but it did not appear in either of the two issues, and when it was eventually published a year later, it was in Catalan in *L'Amic de les Arts*, with a dedication to Dalí's co-signatory to the Dadaist *Yellow Manifesto* (1928), Sebastià Gasch:

> ...Little things, little things, little things, little things, little things, little things, little things, little things, little things, little things, little things... THERE ARE LITTLE THINGS, AS STILL AS A LOAF OF BREAD.[21]

Dalí explicitly contrasted his *Poem of the Little Things* with Jiménez, who 'has never ever seen anything, only receives mangy emotions from things'.[22] Dalí had just re-read Jiménez's famous story *Platero y Yo* (1917), 'which gave him a good idea; it's a farce all this ecstasy worked up in front of things that he can't see, that he can't see at all'. *Platero y Yo* is the tale of the poet and his beloved companion Platero, a donkey, with whom he wanders through the country and villages, meditating on life and describing pastoral and picturesque scenes and characters in a series of vignettes. The donkey dies from eating a poisoned root and is buried

20 *Ibid.*
21 Dalí, 'Poema de les cosetes', *L'Amic de les Arts*, no.27, 31 August 1928, p.211.
22 *Letters to Lorca*, *op. cit*, letter 30, October/November 1927, p.71.

in a flowering orchard, but is still addressed by the poet, who imagines his soul in paradise. Dalí's violent dislike of this gentle, sentimental story must have contributed to the appearance of the obsessional theme of the rotting donkey in paintings like *Honey is Sweeter than Blood* (1927) and *Apparatus and Hand* (1927). The rotting donkey is an ambivalent concept, for Dalí signs himself in a letter to Lorca of early December 1927 'your ROTTING DONKEY' and adds, 'may Juan Ramón's donkey (Platero) die'. In this inversion of the *putrefact*, Dalí as himself 'rotting donkey' represents the abolition/destruction of the sentimentalised and idealised death of Platero. So the *putrefact* here comes to represent its opposite, the clean objectivity of the non-sentimental, anti-putrefaction of Dalí's own ideas. Platero was the 'decorative stylisation of donkeys, anti-realism of donkeys, which, as you'll know, are usually made of cork swarming with ants like crystal'.

In 'New limits of painting' the following year Dalí elaborated the inversions of this theme – and the character of his symbolism – in a passage that is a remarkable premonition of Georges Bataille's attack on romantic idealism in the text 'The Language of Flowers', first published in *Documents* in 1929. Answering critic Rafael Benet's objections that his painting is illogical and absurd, Dalí points out that, 'The life of creatures who people the surface of canvases and the world obeys laws of existence that are very different to those who people the surface of the earth.'[23] Only a point of view drawn from the narrowest realism would fail to see the different laws (which may or may not be precisely symbolic in character) that govern art and poetry. He reminds Benet that, 'a decapitated figure in the world of art or poetry is not a figure without a head... we could add that a figure without a head is more suitable to be interlaced with rotting donkeys, and that flowers are intensely poetic precisely because they resemble rotting donkeys'. Flowers are anti-romantic because they are, as Bataille put it later, 'tatters of aerial manure'.[24]

The rotting donkey that appears in the canvases of 1927 takes centre stage in *L'Âne pourri* (The Rotting Donkey, 1928) and figures also in the film *Un Chien andalou* (An Andalusian Dog, 1929), and the painting *William Tell*

23 Dalí, 'Nous límits de la pintura', *op. cit.*, p.167.

24 Georges Bataille, 'Le langage des fleurs', *Documents*, no.3, June 1929; trans. in Allan Stoekl (ed), *Visions of Excess*, University of Minnesota Press, Minneapolis, MN, 1989.

(1930). In later accounts of the rotting donkey Dalí omits any mention of Jiménez and stresses the bizarre coincidence that Pepín Bello and Buñuel wrote to him separately and independently, as he recounts in the essay 'The Liberation of the Fingers' (1929) and in his autobiography *The Secret Life of Salvador Dalí* (1942), describing an almost identical image. However, given their shared interest in the *putrefact*, a similar complex of associations was probably operative. The rotting donkey, as epitome of decay, is also a form of the 'simulacra' Dalí was to describe in his book *La Femme Visible* (The Visible Woman, 1930).

SAINT SEBASTIAN

The iconography in *Honey is Sweeter than Blood*, *Apparatus and Hand* and *Little Ashes* (1927–28), all of which contain the 'rotting donkey', is closely related to ideas Dalí associated with Saint Sebastian (the patron saint of Cadaqués), and also, though now in a more perverse form, to the concept of mathematical lyricism.

Simultaneously with these canvases and with the new manner he adopted to paint them, Dalí published his first text, 'Saint Sebastian', dedicated to Lorca. Since 1926 Saint Sebastian had been an emblematic figure for both Dalí and Lorca, part of a shared language which offered a channel for self-dramatisation, though the connotations of the martyr were different for each. For Dalí, Saint Sebastian was a symbol of objectivity: 'another time I'll tell you about St Objectivity, whose name is now that of St Sebastian.'[25] He links this with his idiosyncratic concept of irony, which he claims to derive from writer and artist Alberto Savinio and traces back to Heraclitus. As sado-masochistic object, Saint Sebastian becomes the sign of a private language of sexuality: 'As you can see, I "invite" you to my new type of St Sebastian, consisting of the pure transmutation of the Arrow by the Sole. The principle of elegance is what made St Sebastian agonise so deliciously.'[26]

In 'Saint Sebastian', Dalí describes a rapport between passion, inaction and patience, which seems to be a modern version – or a travesty or

25 Dalí, *Letters to Lorca*, *op. cit.*, letter 16, early summer 1926, p.42.
26 *Ibid.*, letter 19, 18–20 January 1927, p.46.

transgression – of the neoclassical aesthetic. Dalí suggests that Saint Sebastian presents an image of suffering not as anguish but as endurance: 'I am referring to the patience in the exquisite agony of St Sebastian.' This recalls Johann Winckelmann's celebrated description of the statue of the Laocoön, which he chose as the unlikely epitome of his classical ideal, focused on the male body – suffering endured with the minimum of fuss, and represented with 'noble simplicity and calm grandeur'. Excluding the qualities of simplicity and grandeur, the parallel lies in the desire to control emotion.

Dalí's description of Saint Sebastian is framed as though it is a dream: 'I realised that I was in Italy, because of the black and white marble paving of the staircase...'. There he sees the figure of Saint Sebastian, which is at once a surrealist object and a Cubist construction. Half of his head is 'formed of a substance similar to that of a jellyfish', the other half reminds Dalí of 'someone very familiar'. He is tied to an old cherry tree trunk, his feet resting on the broken capital of a column (perhaps, as has been suggested, a memory of Mantegna's versions of *St Sebastian* (1456–90)). Around him on a shell-strewn beach are instruments of an unknown science, intended for measurement. These instruments, as Dalí paints them in *Honey is Sweeter than Blood* and *Apparatus and Hand* resemble Tanguy's enigmatic geometrical forms as well as Giorgio de Chirico's metaphysical constructions, and are predominantly variations on a set square.

In a drawing which appeared in the previous issue of *L'Amic de les Arts*, in June 1927, it is Lorca himself who is shown on a beach in the position of the dreamed Saint Sebastian, with broken classical heads hideously veined to one side, and measuring instruments to the other. The beach is identified by Dalí in the inscription as Empúries, the huge antique site, once a Greek harbour town, to the south of Figueres on the coast of the Empordà plain. The broken veins of the truncated limbs were inspired by the illustration from an advertisement for a cure for varicose veins, which Dalí had used in his *Book of Varicose Veins*. The poet is thus sited between emblems of a corrupted physicality on one side and of mathematical order on the other – the latter perhaps signs of that 'spiritual sensuality' that he preferred to an idealised spirituality.

In August 1927 *L'Amic de les Arts* announced that Dalí had been working during the summer on two pictures: *The Wood of Gadgets* and *The Birth of*

Venus.[27] These were probably the two pictures he sent to the Barcelona Saló de Tardor, the Autumn Salon, in October 1927, renamed *Honey is Sweeter than Blood* and *Apparatus and Hand*, although it is possible that *The Birth of Venus* became the painting known as *Cenicitas* (*Little Ashes*), a word Lorca used in a letter to Dalí.[28] The three paintings are closely related, though there are some new and significant elements in *Little Ashes.* This must have been one of the paintings he was working on when he wrote to Lorca in December of 'some pictures which make me die of happiness; I'm inventing in a way which is purely natural, without a trace of artistic consideration… now I'm painting a beautiful woman, smiling, convulsed with multi-coloured feathers, supported on a small base of marble in flames; the marble base is supported in turn by some tiny smoke, a little flattened and silent; and there are donkeys in the sky with heads of tiny parrots, grass and the sand of the beach…'[29]

The paintings at the Autumn Salon provoked a scandal, which centred on the question of his relationship with Surrealism. Critics like Joan Gols had dubbed the two canvases 'surrealist', but Sebastià Gasch, the young Barcelona critic who was close to Dalí at this time, asserted that they were on the contrary 'the very type of anti-surrealist painting'.[30] This supported Dalí himself, who wrote a defence, 'My Pictures at the Autumn Salon', published as an insert in *L'Amic de les Arts* in October 1927. Here Dalí somewhat ambiguously proclaimed his distance from Surrealism – ambiguously, because he admits that the subconscious may have played a role in his work: he had indeed been experimenting with automatism, and admired the work of Miró and Tanguy. Dalí lays out his grounds for distancing himself from Surrealism in arguments that reappear several times in his own writings of the time and in those of other Catalan critics

27 Although performing his military service in Figueres between February 1927 and February 1928, Dalí lived at home and seems to have been able to paint, certainly over the summer. However, the fact that he turned to writing in the summer of 1927 may have been both to do with an interest in exploring verbally the surrealist process of automatism, and to do with the time restrictions military life posed on painting.

28 Torroella, *op. cit.*, p.177. The painting, which appears to have had other titles previously, has also been titled *Senecitas* (Old Age) – probably in error. It is now known as *Els esforços esteriles (Cendretes)*, Futile Efforts (Little Ashes).

29 Dalí, *Letters to Lorca*, *op. cit.*, letter 33, December 1927, p.80.

30 Sebastià Gasch, 'Butlletí: l'exposició collectiva de la Sala Parés', *L'Amic de les Arts*, no.19, 31 October 1927, p.95.

in *L'Amic de les Arts.* To a certain extent they represent a prejudice against Surrealism that was to evaporate over the coming months, but there are also vital distinctions which Dalí maintained and which underpin the originality of his eventual contribution to the movement.

Dalí argues that his painting is perfectly well understood by the uninstructed public: children and the Cadaqués fishermen. This is because his painting is 'anti-artistic' and possesses qualities that are in opposition to the complex, lyrical and intellectual qualities of 'artistic' painting. The latter depends upon preparation and convention, while his painting is direct: the consequence of looking at the normal and the everyday as objectively as possible, without the intervention of stereotypical modes of looking. He refers the reader to his 'Photography, Pure Creation of the Mind' (1927), in which he had argued that 'to look is to invent'.[31] It was not just the simple fact of objectively observed reality that he was advocating, but the idea that objects thus seen ('a living eye, the most anodyne and insignificant vegetable, a fly'), bore in themselves the marvellous, the unexpected and the mysterious. He is, in other words, seeking, like the Surrealists, the marvellous, but not according to the same means. The 'poetic transposition of the purest subconscious' was best sought, in Dalí's opinion, not through the automatism advocated by Surrealism, but through more objective means, such as photography and film. He prefaced 'Photography, Pure Creation of the Mind' with René Crevel's words, 'Painting is not photography, the painters say. But photography is not painting either.'

Dalí's appreciation of the special qualities of photography was prompted, not by Surrealism, but by such publications as Moholy-Nagy's Bauhaus book *Painting Photography Film* (1925). He swiftly grasped the implications of the distortions or enlargements of reality achieved through close-ups, slow motion, X-ray and so on. He lifted photos from *Painting Photography Film* to illustrate his own and other texts: in the final issue of *L'Amic de les Arts* in March 1929, of which he was co-editor, the eye

31 Dalí, 'La Fotografia pura creació de l'esperit', *L'Amic de les Arts*, no.18, 30 September 1927, pp.90–91.

32 The two photographs were originally published by László Moholy-Nagy in his *Painting Photography Film*, Bauhaus Press, Weimar, 1925 (reprinted by Lund Humphries, London, 1969). 'La dada fotogràfica' was published in *Gaseta de les Arts*, February 1929.

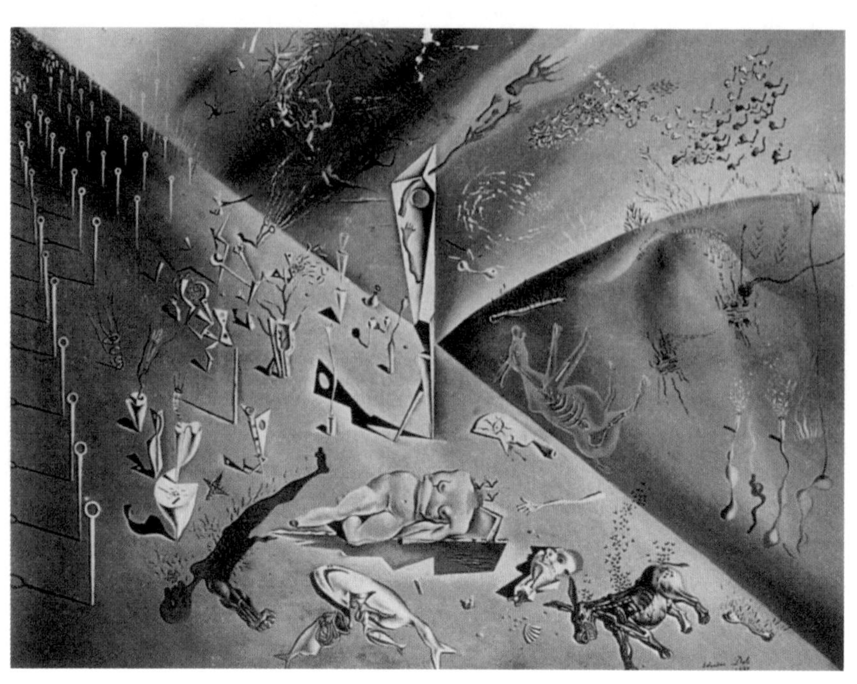

452 **Salvador Dalí**
Honey is Sweeter than Blood, 1927
Oil on unknown support
Unknown dimensions

of a marabou, which Moholy-Nagy had captioned, 'There is extraordinary concentration in a singled out detail', accompanied Lluis Montanyà's text 'Punt i apart (Full-stop and paragraph)', and a racing cyclist from the same source illustrated 'The Photographic Donnée' (p.481).[32]

There was clearly a connection between Dalí's interest in film and photography and the new manner of the 1927 paintings. *Honey is Sweeter than Blood* was reproduced in the magazine *La Gaceta Literaria* (15 December 1927) with the subtitle 'cinematismo de Dalí'. In the same issue his 'Art Films and Anti-Artistic Films' was published, and there were regular contributions on the film pages of this review from both Dalí and Buñuel. Paintings like *Honey is Sweeter than Blood,* and especially *Little Ashes* do seem to be trying to achieve in paint effects more natural to the manipulative possibilities of the camera and photographic techniques: superimpositions, montage, fades and dissolves, as well as the objective mystery of close-up or X-ray. In *Little Ashes,* for instance, the lumpen pink torso seems to be dissolving, metamorphosing, from one form to another; it is also bristling with little brightly coloured spines or needles, a direct reference to Dalí's 'surrealist' 'Two Prose Pieces', in which he 'misreads' an object in a chain of bizarre interpretations. The very difficulty of achieving these effects in paint on canvas led to a crisis of expression for Dalí in 1928; there was a further division in his painting styles, with dramatic fluctuations between an aggressively reductive 'anti-painting' like *Four Fishermen's Wives of Cadaqués* (1928), heavily sexualised semi-figurative paintings like *Female Nude* (1928) or *Two Figures on a Beach (Unsatisfied Desires)* (1928), and a confident post-Cubist style in *The Rotting Donkey* or *Thumb, Beach, Moon and Rotting Bird.* As we have seen, Dalí courted stylistic variation, but the crisis at this point is exacerbated by the new possibilities of photography and the challenge this posed to painting. As we shall see, and in spite of his proclaimed distance from Surrealism, Dalí was becoming more and more enmeshed in Surrealist ideas, but needed to find his own visual mode of expression. Experiments with automatic drawing, which seem to have begun as early as 1926, had not transferred very successfully to painting – *Nude Woman in an Armchair* (1927), for instance. It must have looked for a time as if Dalí would find a solution in film rather than painting, and in a use of film and indeed of photography that Surrealism itself had not yet realised.

Little Ashes, which Dalí completed early in 1928, is an important stage between *Honey is Sweeter than Blood* and the surrealist paintings of 1929. It combines the influence of Miró and the Purism of Le Corbusier in a context foreign to each. As in Miró's blue-ground paintings of 1924–25, the canvas is loosely streaked with blue, though this is restricted to the upper, sky area. The lighter handling of the ground is repeated in some of the painted marks, specks and doodles which, in their appearance of spontaneity, resemble the drawings in Dalí's letters and the rare 'automatic' drawings of the period rather than anything that had previously appeared on canvas. Such drawings, probably dating to the summer of 1927, suggest that he was interested in the classic Surrealist process of automatism. The tense co-existence in *Little Ashes* of these automatist marks and the meticulous miniaturism of other forms is the continuation in exaggerated form of the stylistic duality we have noted; but the fact that they occur on the same canvas supports the contention that there was a crisis of expression at the time.

Little Ashes is a very curious construction. It is a painting within a painting, but in an inverted sense, for the painting 'within', just above the horizon to the left, is in fact that which engenders the rest of the forms swarming over the surface. This tiny picture, signed and dated 1928, depicts the simplified forms of five guitars in a vaguely purist, machinist style, together with a mysterious pair of floating breasts which recall Man Ray's photograph from *La Révolution surréaliste*. The torso-like form of the yellow guitar 'produces' the towering torso of pink flesh, which swings forward with its other limb touching and casting a shadow upon the horizon line. In this movement, the torso recalls not so much the figure of Venus rising from a seashell as the flying figure of the winged messenger of the gods, Mercury.

Almost every element in the painting is doubled or further multiplied. To an extent this repeats a device from *Honey is Sweeter than Blood*, where the two truncated heads between the rotting donkeys represent Lorca (below) and Dalí himself above. In *Little Ashes* the two heads, positioned at the edge of the landline could both be Dalí himself. They have an important function in terms of the identity of the subject and the character of what is being depicted. The head on the left, whose ears resemble so closely the Cubist drawing entitled *Self-Portrait* (1926), is asleep

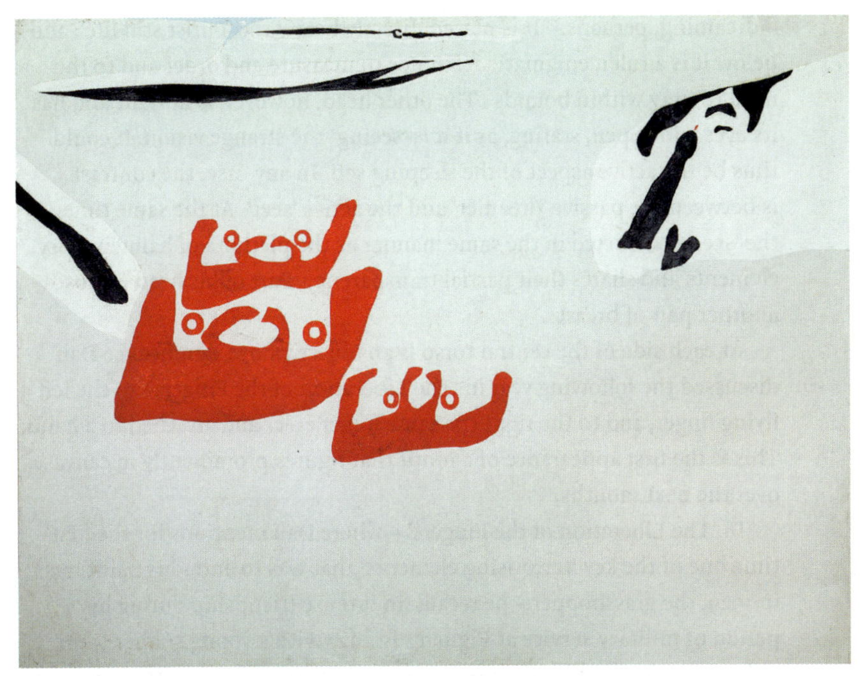

Salvador Dalí
Four Fishermen's Wives of Cadaqués, c.1928
Oil on canvas
148 × 196 cm | 58¼ × 77⅛ in

– dreaming, perhaps.[33] It is placed directly below the 'Purist still life', and below it is a ruler, enigmatic reference to measure and order and to the need to 'stay within bounds'. The other head, however, is upright and has its eyes wide open, staring, as if it is 'seeing' the strange vision. It could thus be the active aspect of the sleeping self. In any case, the contrast is between the passive 'dreamer' and the active 'seer'. At the same time, the 'seer' is depicted in the same manner as the plethora of hallucinatory elements and shares their partial transparency. Part of his head encloses another pair of breasts.

At each side of the central torso is an object whose significance Dalí discussed the following year in 'The Liberation of the Fingers': to the left a flying finger, and to the right the same finger erect and attached to a hand. This is the first appearance of a motif that figures prominently in canvases over the next months.

In 'The Liberation of the Fingers' – where Dalí mentions for the first time one of the key 'terrorising elements' that was to enter his paintings in 1929, the grasshopper – he recalls an intense friendship during his period of military service at Figueres in 1927 with a young soldier who, although able to read and write, was otherwise completely without culture. Surrealist texts Dalí showed him were probably the first literature he had ever read. He proved, nonetheless, extraordinarily responsive to Surrealist ideas, and not only 'would automatically fill sheets and sheets with incomparable suggestiveness', but also spoke with spontaneous freedom.[34] Dalí gives as example his sudden exclamation after a long silence: 'There is a flying phallus', which he then drew on the marble cafe tabletop. This particularly struck Dalí because he himself had become obsessed with the image of an isolated, floating finger, which he suggests might have originated in 'a hypnagogic image of pre-sleep', but which also was connected to the troubled surprise he sometimes experienced on seeing his own thumb isolated in the hole of his palette. Dalí comments on the 'flying phallus' that his friend could not possibly have known of the winged phallus of the ancients, to which, as he later learned, Freud had made allusion.

33 The drawing was reproduced in *L'Amic de les arts*, no.10, 31 January 1927. It is reproduced in *Salvador Dalí: The Early Years*, p.145.

34 Dalí, 'L'Alliberament dels dits', *L'Amic de les Arts*, no.31, 31 March 1929, pp.6–7. This final issue of the Sitges review, dominated by Dalí, had a new format.

There are several interesting aspects to this story. Firstly, it provides clear evidence of Dalí's involvement in Surrealist writings and ideas by the summer of 1927, long before he formally declared a commitment to them. It gives us a context for the automatic drawings and for 'Two Prose Pieces', but at the same time infers that Dalí found himself less disposed to the freedom of verbal automatism than his unlettered friend. His unease with automatism – which tended to lack the morphological hardness and clarity to which he was strongly attracted – was to be more fully spelled out in *La Femme visible* (The Visible Woman, 1930), where he contrasts the 'passivity' of automatism unfavourably with the 'active' mode of paranoia. The paintings and writings of 1927–30 witness the gradual formulation of this key idea.

Secondly, the story offers some insight into Dalí's familiarity with Freud. The fact that he says that at the point of discovery of the 'flying phallus/finger' he was as yet unaware of Freud's allusions to this phenomenon does not imply that he was totally unfamiliar with Freud's work. In *The Secret Life of Salvador Dalí* he says that he had read *The Interpretation of Dreams* (1899, which was translated into Spanish in 1923) while still a student in Madrid, and been gripped with a mania for self-interpretation. But it does reveal that between the summer of 1927 and writing 'The Liberation of the Fingers' early in 1929 he had been paying particular attention to Freud.

References to the winged phallus of the ancients are fleeting but quite frequent in Freud's writing. Both in *The Interpretation of Dreams* and, for instance, in 'Leonardo da Vinci' Freud alludes to the winged phallus in the context of dreams of flying, and 'in connection with a whole mass of connected ideas, from which we learn that in dreams the wish to be able to fly is to be understood as nothing else than a longing to be capable of sexual performance'.[35] Freud gives several examples of linguistic expressions for sexual activity drawn from birds/flying. In *The Interpretation of Dreams* it is implied that dreams of flying are gendered, in that it is 'in men (that) flying dreams usually have a grossly sensual meaning'.[36]

35 Sigmund Freud, 'Leonardo da Vinci and a Memory of his Childhood' (1910), The Pelican Freud Library, vol.14, London, 1987, p.219.

36 Freud, *The Interpretation of Dreams*, trans. James Strachey, George Allen and Unwin, London and Frome, 1954, p.594.

Thus, they are linked to the phenomenon of erection, 'around which the human imagination has constantly played... involving as it does an apparent suspension of the laws of gravity. (Cf. in this connection the winged phalli of the ancients.)'[37]

In *Little Ashes* the sky-borne erect fingers, the birds' heads and wings, and the fleshy torso (if, as I suggested, it represents Mercury) can all be read as bearing on the same set of ideas: anxiety and desire regarding sexual activity. But there is a further twist to these images in *Little Ashes,* respecting the question of sexual identity. For the most startling aspect of the 'Mercury' form is its disgendered character. Hinting at both Venus and Mercury, it bulges ambiguously, the body with the incipient breast topped with a gross phallic protruberance. Rather than desire, it is sexual anxiety that is most strongly conjured; erect fingers, and body parts disembodied and fragmented, unfocused and multiplied, at first seem to open on to a Freudian Oedipal reading, the detached finger/phallus obviously hinting at the castration complex outlined by Freud. Dalí certainly makes this one of the themes of 1929 paintings like *Dismal Sport* and *Illuminated Pleasures*. But the disturbing character of *Little Ashes* seems more forcefully to be located in the mixture of gendered elements (breasts scattered and isolated as well as the 'winged phalli') and the central torso of ambivalent gender. The very sexual identity of the presumed subject seems to be at stake.

Some of the paintings that succeeded *Little Ashes* over the next few months, such as *Composition (Torso)*, show signs of incompletion, uncertainty and changes of mind and veer between advanced abstraction and distorted figuration. Through 1928, images more explicitly sexual, though not necessarily in terms of gender, alternate with canvases of more obvious pictorial sophistication, using the body of symbols Dalí was developing. The pair of paintings that he sent in to the 1928 Autumn Salon represented precisely this division: *Thumb, Beach, Moon and Rotting Bird*, and *Two Figures on a Beach (Unsatisfied Desires).* The rejection of the latter by the owner of the salon on the grounds that it was too 'explicit' and shocking to be shown publicly marked another highpoint in Dalí's controversial career in Spain. Two paintings, *Bathers* and *Female Nude*, from

37 *Ibid.*, p.394.

the same 'series' as *Two Figures on a Beach* were reproduced by Georges Bataille in *Documents;* these concentrate the dispersed fragments of *Little Ashes* into monstrous masses of huge body/digits. *Female Nude* presents the theme of masturbation rather than a dialogue between bodies, and the autoerotic character of this canvas, in which the figure has a hugely enlarged hand but a minimal dot for a head, opens on to an interesting split in Dalí's modes of self-representation: self-portraits with truncated heads contrasted with headless or minimally stoppered bodies.

'STÉRILISER'

Dalí's motto for his exhibition in November 1929 at the Galerie Goemans in Paris, which took place with the full backing of the Surrealist movement and a catalogue preface by André Breton, was the single word 'stériliser'. In this affront to the traditional artistic language of creativity, there is still an echo of his post-machinist *Yellow Manifesto* ('...a sportsman free from artistic notions and all erudition is nearer and more suited to experience the art and the poetry of today than myopic intellectuals, burdened by negative training...'). But the proposal 'to sterilise' also evidently grows out of Dalí's preoccupation with the *putrefact.* Sterilisation is the opposite of putrefaction: it arrests decay, prevents collapse and death and, in Dalí's terminology, the contamination of the sentimental and the artistic. In the sense of preventing collapse, this idea was later to be linked to the crutches that made their appearance in Dalí's paintings in the early 1930s. These crutches prop up decadent bodies: the dying aristocratic civilisation of Europe, was the way Dalí later explained it. But at this moment in 1929, with Dalí on the threshold of his Surrealist career, it almost certainly here denotes the opposite: that is to say, the erection of a hygienic barrier between Surrealism and a bourgeois culture that is threadbare, rotten and avid for novelty.

With two exceptions,[38] all the works in Dalí's Goemans exhibition date from 1929; with one further exception, *The Sacred Heart,* (*Sometimes I Spit*

38 The only two paintings in the catalogue not from 1929 were *Apparatus and Hand* and *Les Efforts stériles*, which was probably *Little Ashes*. These were incorrectly dated 1926 in the catalogue.

with Pleasure on the Portrait of My Mother) (1929) in which Dalí takes Miró's anti-artistic word-paintings to an extreme of iconoclasm,[39] they are all in a new, deliberately dream-like, Surrealist manner. Although in some ways this is closer to the 1927 paintings like *Honey is Sweeter than Blood* and *Little Ashes* than to the more abstract works of 1928, it seems likely that the transformation that occurred also had much to do with the film that he and Buñuel made together early in 1929 in Paris, *Un Chien andalou.* Up to this point Dalí's paintings had been moving in a direction that was simultaneously anti-aesthetic and abstract. *Male and Female Figures on a Beach* (1928) was reproduced in *La Gaceta Literaria* at the beginning of February 1929, and the cork torso *Female Nude* in *Nuevo Mundo* (Madrid, 29 March 1929). The final issue of *L'Amic de les Arts,* of March 1929, dominated by Dalí and his two co-signatories on the *Yellow Manifesto,* Montanyà and Gasch, did not reproduce a single painting, but simply photographs, including the detail of the eye lifted from Moholy-Nagy's *Painting Photography Film,* a shot of a Hollywood musical, and several photographs of isolated fingers related to the 'winged phallus' theme, which are interesting forerunners of the photographs taken by Jacques-André Boiffard for Georges Bataille's notorious article on 'The Big Toe'.[40]

The Surrealist poetry of the film is achieved, just as Dalí had suggested in his earlier texts on film and photography, from its concentration on 'things themselves', juxtaposed through montage in strange sequences, shown in close-up or metamorphosing into other objects. Without underestimating the impact on Dalí of seeing such key Surrealist works in Paris as Max Ernst's *Pietà or Revolution by Night* (1923), itself susceptible to a Freudian reading, it would seem that the experience of the film certainly contributed to the return in his paintings to 'concrete' poetic images.

Un Chien andalou is Freudian in its references to childhood and repression, but above all in its exploration of desire through the linked

39 Dalí's anti-artistic attitude was to a degree inspired by Miró's 'assassinat de la peinture', and this phrase was used with reference to Dalí by Catalan critics. The work was exhibited in Paris under the title *Le sacré-coeur* (The Sacred Heart); the inscription roughly drawn in ink on the canvas, 'sometimes I spit with pleasure on the portrait of my mother', drew on Dalí his father's curse and was the cause of his banishment from the family home in Figueres. However, the intention was more probably sacrilegious than offensive to the memory of his mother.

40 Bataille, 'Le gros orteil', *Documents*, no.6, November 1929; trans. in Stoekl, *op. cit.*

themes of love and death. To see how Dalí discovered a pictorial language which could embody these obsessional ideas in terms of his long-standing interest in morphology and the qualities of hard and soft, form and formlessness, we might look in detail at *The Great Masturbator* (1929) – whose title in the 1929 exhibition was *Visage du grand masturbateur* (Face of the Great Masturbator).

Filling the foreground of *The Great Masturbator* is a swelling yellow shape which metamorphoses from a head – that of Dalí himself – lying horizontal and supported by its nose, through a delirious cluster of sexual symbols, a woman's head, and a male torso into a curving fragment of art nouveau design. The movement of transformation could be going the other way, from the piece of architecture (or furniture) towards the head. As in such sequences in *Un Chien andalou* as the images of the slit eye and the moon cut by a cloud, there is no primary term to the metaphor. What is important is not the direction of the metamorphosis between head, body and architecture, but the way it is expressed in extravagant morphological alterations, between flesh, stone, petal and hair, so that the whole mass looks like an eruption of lava, with convulsive contractions and expansions of form, flowing loosely or temporarily sucked into forms of modelled precision like the marble-flesh shoulder of the swooning woman.

The appearance of the art nouveau (*Le Style moderne,* modern style) fragment in *The Great Masturbator* bears witness to a particular stage in the complex relationship between the conflicting categories of hard and soft, and the development of Dalí's paranoiac method. In *La Femme Visible,* a collection of texts he wrote from the end of 1929 to 1930, and more extensively in 'Of the terrifying and edible beauty of Modern Style architecture',[41] Dalí argues the significance of this architecture in terms which make it clear that its fascination for him was not just a matter of flouting the current taste for modernist architecture of 'our swinish contemporary aestheticians', in favour of the unfashionably ornamental art nouveau. For Dalí, it was connected with his concept of paranoiac mental processes and the idea of 'simulacra'.

41 Dalí, 'De la beauté terrifiante et comestible de l'architecture modern style', *Minotaure,* nos.5/4, December 1955, pp.69–76.

'L'âne pourri' (The Rotting Donkey), the first of the texts in his book *La femme visible,* (The Visible Woman, 1930) was also printed in the first issue of *Le Surréalisme au service de la révolution* (1930). Here he presents for the first time his idea of the paranoiac method of double figuration. He was experimenting with this at the same time in *The Invisible Man* (1929; p.498), and in the painting he reproduced in *La Femme visible: Invisible Sleeping Woman, Horse, Lion* (1930). Paranoiac activity, for Dalí the systematic 'misreading' of objects in the external world according to an overriding idea, will, he says, 'systematise confusion and contribute to the total discrediting of the world of reality'. Paranoiac thought brings into being what Dalí calls new simulacra. These are something like symbols of a particular morphological category with psychological significance, which lie at the crossroads of his phobias, obsessions and desires and their concrete realisations. The 'three great simulacra', he writes, are 'excrement, blood and putrefaction'.[42] But, he goes on, we do not know if behind these ignominious simulacra of terror are hidden 'the longed-for "land of treasure"'.

Art nouveau buildings, 'on the margins of architecture', are a grand simulacrum, which he says could be described as *ideal:* a 'pure and troubling world of dreams', the 'true realisations of solidified desires'. The soft but frozen quality of art nouveau forms introduced a troubling confusion between internal and external, mobile and immobile, and its irrational likeness to flesh led for Dalí towards a sense of dissolution, expressed in *The Great Masturbator* as the collapse of the head into the mass of rock/ architecture.

Dalí illustrated his article with details of 'the delirious and cold buildings spread throughout Europe': Gaudí's Barcelona works and Hector Guimard's Paris Metro entrances, photographed by Brassaï and Man Ray. Beneath one of the photographs of Gaudí's Casa Batlló, Dalí added the caption 'the bones are on the outside'. This architecture, Dalí proposes, was born of a response to unconscious desires, which involve the need to ingest the desired object. Hence the caption beneath a photograph of a column of Guimard's building Castel Béranger, 'the soft base of this column seems to ask us: eat me!', and the reformulation of Breton's

42 Dalí, 'L'Âne pourri', *La Femme Visible*, Editions Surréalistes, Paris, 1930, p.18.

'Beauty will be convulsive or will cease to be' to 'Beauty will be comestible or will cease to be.'

Dalí used the horror and the pleasure of the experience of eating as a powerful analogy or simulacrum for more abstract ideas related to the interior and exterior of bodies. The first chapter of *The Secret Life of Salvador Dalí* opens with an analysis of the hard and the soft in food, which involves an inversion of the affective character of the latter. His memorable first sentence runs: 'Fortunately I am not one of those beings who when they smile are apt to expose remnants, however small, of horrible and degrading spinach clinging to their teeth... It so happens that I attach to spinach, as to everything more or less pertaining to food, essential values of a moral and aesthetic order.'[43] The opposite of spinach, he goes on, is armour, and 'that is why I like to eat armour so much, and especially the small varieties, namely, all shell-fish. By virtue of their armour, which is what their exoskeleton actually is, these are a material realisation of the highly original and intelligent idea of wearing one's bones outside rather than inside, as is the usual practice.' However, the 'soft' released from its resistant shell is a different matter from the formlessness of spinach: 'Having once overcome the obstacle by virtue of which all self-respecting food "preserves its form", nothing can be regarded as too slimy, gelatinous, quivering, indeterminate or ignominious to be desired, whether it be the sublime viscosities of a fish-eye, the slithery cerebellum of a bird, the spermatozoal marrow of a bone or the soft and swampy opulence of an oyster.'

This celebration of soft matter, simultaneously repellant and desired, is deliberately echoed in the description in the following chapter of the intrauterine paradise which Dalí claims to remember. This paradise of the womb was 'the colour of hell' (blood), but 'above all it was soft, immobile, warm, symmetrical, double, gluey'.[44] Dalí suggests that the effort to surmount the traumatic expulsion from this paradise, forgotten in our conscious life, dominates our unconscious or imaginative life: 'the whole imaginative life of man tends to reconstitute symbolically that initial paradisal state.'

The desire for love and the desire for death are not simply opposed

43 Dalí, *The Secret Life of Salvador Dalí*, *op. cit.*, p.9.
44 *Ibid.*, p.27.

to one another, but circulate in a constantly shifting dance. In 'Love', the final text in *La femme visible,* Dalí wrote:

> The relations between dream, love and the sense of annihilation that belongs to each of them, have always appeared obvious. Sleeping is a form of dying, or at least of dying towards reality, but reality dies in love as in a dream. The bloody osmoses of dream and of love completely fill the life of man... If love is dreams made flesh, let us not forget that we often dream of our own dissolution and that this, to judge by dream life, would be one of the most violent and tumultuous of man's unconscious desires... Everything that psycho-physiology has taught us of the phenomenology of the repugnant leads us to believe that desire can easily conquer unconscious symbolic representation. Repugnance would thus be a symbolic defence against the vertigo of the death wish. We experience repugnance and disgust for that which, basically, we desire to get closer to, and this is the root of an invisible attraction for the 'morbid' which is often translated as the incomprehensible curiosity for what seems to us repugnant. In love, we reign over torrents of images of auto-annihilation. Scatological simulacra, the simulacra of desire and the simulacra of terror take on the most lucid and dazzling confusion.[45]

The morphology of the head dissolving into the soft but frozen art nouveau fragment in *The Great Masturbator* reaches an even more exaggerated state in *The Profanation of the Host* (c.1930), where Dalí's heads multiply and struggle to emerge from a fantastic thicket of art nouveau forms, figured in thick, pale, viscous paint. To each head is attached a fragile and delicately painted grasshopper, the precision of its depiction, which is almost at the level of a plate in an album of natural history, contrasting strongly with the lumpy painting of the heads and the monument.

Dalí on several occasions identified the grasshopper as a 'terrorising element' like excrement; it had been an object of extreme terror for him from childhood, and the positioning of the insect in the 1929 paintings,

45 Dalí, 'L'Amour', *La Femme Visible*, *op. cit.*, p.65.

invariably attached to the mouth of the self-portrait head, is horrific. But the head itself, mouthless and with closed eyes, lacks any expression or indeed any visible signs of consciousness. If the childhood story is true, though, there must have been some strong compulsion at work to lead him to repeat a sensation of such unpleasure. Dalí first tells the story in 'The Liberation of the Fingers' early in 1929, and repeated it in *The Secret Life of Salvador Dalí.* At the age of about seven or eight, he says, he loved chasing grasshoppers and catching them to admire at close quarters the beauty of their wings. But one day on the beach at Cadaqués he caught a small fish, of the type nicknamed 'slobberer', in his hand, which he suddenly threw away in horror and screamed that it had the same face as a grasshopper. From that moment he acquired a violent terror of grasshoppers, and suffered agonies from the teasing of his schoolfellows. The incident of the fish, however, he had completely forgotten, he writes in 'The Liberation of the Fingers', until reminded of it by his father on whom the incident had made a profound impression.[46]

The re-tracing of this childhood experience strengthens the earlier suggestion that Dalí was at this moment reading Freud, and the writings of other psychologists, with renewed attention. Although he was clearly very familiar with *The Interpretation of Dreams,* it is also possible that he read one of the strangest of Freud's meta-psychological texts, 'Beyond the Pleasure Principle' (1920). Whether or not he did, this text illuminates Dalí's paintings in a remarkable way, for it discusses the complex relationship between the death instinct and the life instinct, Thanatos and Eros, and addresses the problem of the compulsion of patients under analysis to repeat even unpleasurable experiences of childhood, for the repetition was something which in itself gives pleasure. This Freud sees as the corollary to the obscure dread in people unfamiliar with analysis of rousing something better left sleeping: which he suggests is fear of 'the emergence of this compulsion with its hint of possession by some "daemonic" power'. What he believes he has discovered is the universal attribute of instincts and even of organic life itself:

46 Dalí was passionately interested in zoology as a child and kept a number of small animals. He was also interested in natural history, and mentions in letters to Lorca how disturbed he was at the illustrated plates of insects in Jean-Henri Fabre's books. An early collage in the Captain Moore Museum in Cadaqués uses a coloured engraving of a snake from a natural history album.

It seems, then, that an instinct is an urge inherent in organic life to restore an earlier state of things which the living entity has been obliged to abandon under the pressure of external disturbing forces; that is, it is a kind of organic elasticity, or, to put it another way, the expression of the inertia inherent in organic life.[47]

The first instinct, he writes, is the instinct to return to an inanimate state: 'the aim of all life is death'. Freud then makes parallels between biology and morphological theories of animate and inanimate matter and human neuroses, which, although it is impossible to consider here at length, offer remarkable resonances with Dalí's rich visual and theoretical analogies between morphologies and instinctual responses.

In 1936 Dalí published 'First law of morphology concerning hair in soft structures', in the Surrealist review *Minotaure*.[48] In images honed to achieve the maximum sensual disgust he considers the equivocal character of soft forms, and contrasts the geodesic with the formless. Rather than referring to biology and natural history, Dalí here follows the notion of the 'formless' in terms closer to those of Bataille in his 'informe', where this troubling non-defined, immeasurable state is given the task of challenging all given moral and philosophical categories.[49]

One of the remarkable aspects of the paintings of 1929 is their capacity to express alternations of sensations through what Dalí has described as 'hierarchies of forms'. In *The Great Masturbator* forms of great precision contrast with the fluid mass of the head/rock/architecture: the grasshopper, and also the cluster of shells embedded in a little hole, and another gastropod balanced between a cork and a black pebble. These shells stand, not just for the containers of soft substances, but, to recall Dalí's earlier obsession with mathematics and order, as organic forms 'peculiarly adapted to mathematical methods of investigation'.[50] The spirals in horns and shells are remarkable, retaining an unchanging form

47 Freud, *Beyond the Pleasure Principle*, trans. James Strachey, Liveright Publishing Corporation, New York, NY, 1961, p.30.

48 Dalí, 'La première loi morphologique sur les poils dans les structures molles', *Minotaure*, no.9, 1936, pp.60–61.

49 Bataille, 'Informe', *Documents*, no.7, December 1929; trans. in Stoekl, *op. cit.*

50 D'Arcy Thompson, *On Growth and Form* (1917), Cambridge University Press, Cambridge, 1961, p.172.

in spite of their asymmetrical growth, for they grow at one end only. They offer, thus, a morphology that is the exact opposite to the ambiguous mass of the head: a contrast, too, between hard and soft, which echoes his earlier preoccupations.

The First Days of Spring was one of the earliest pictures of 1929 to work with these elements, and was probably the first he painted following the completion of *Un Chien andalou.* The fish head in lurid red is centrally placed across the deep shadows cast by the steps of the wide terrace that disappear dramatically towards the horizon like railway lines. It is a kind of pictorial autobiography, with Dalí as a child in a tiny photograph in the centre, shown again with his father in the distance, a haunting pair that appear again and again in the works of the 1930s; in a scene of frenzied but displaced sexual activity at the left a man wearing moustaches masturbates beside a woman's body reduced to a sexual litany, with a sex in the place of a head, swarming with signs of putrefaction. Dalí's own head, again, is shown at the other side, almost invisible among the other scattered and more graphic forms, and again with the large and fearsomely feelered grasshopper locked to its mouth, springing from a multi-coloured parrot's head on a pedestal. Contrasting with these images, that rise like a medium's visions from the pedestal at the lower right are mini-scenarios – father and sister at right, and two men in the background engaged in a suggestive ritual, one astride the other.

Louis Aragon included this painting in his exhibition of collages of 1930, *La Peinture au défi* (Painting Challenged),[51] and noted how Dalí, instead of using collage as an element that contradicted and conflicted with the unity of the picture surface and ruptured the cohesion of the image, deliberately concealed it, and made the surface as uniform as possible, to such an extent that in reproduction it is often quite impossible to detect the pasted-on bits (and in the case of 'First Days of Spring', stencils). The painted images are licked into existence to mimic as closely as possible the photographic and the printed. Yet at the same time the principle of collage – dislocation, the shock of unlikely juxtapositions, the rejection of a single, coherent representation and the appeal to a multiplicity of connections – is crucial to the overall effect of the disintegration of the

51 Louis Aragon, *La peinture au défi*, Librairie José Corti, Paris, March 1930.

subject. The painting seems to pulsate between contradictory movements: desire and repulsion, memory and act, form and formlessness.

The illusions and deceptions of desire are perfectly matched by the confusion between the painted and the ready-made printed surfaces. In *The Accommodations of Desire* (1929), a small coloured print of a lion's head is pasted onto one of the pebbles painted on the canvas and appears to be the starting point for an unfolding sequence of images.[52] In almost all the 1929 paintings, a lion, or more usually a lion's head, appears; it forms part of the bestiary which goes to make up Dalí's iconography of sexual obsessions and fears. The more private elements of this iconography, the grasshopper, fish and drooping self-portrait are absent from *The Accommodations of Desire*, but in several paintings within this group they are combined with the lion. *The Accommodations of Desire* appears to include both explicit and symbolic ways of expressing desire and fear of sex. The sequence of lion's heads culminates in the pebble at the top right, where the lion's head in negative frames a luminous, headless, steatopygous female body whose genitals are replaced by the whole body of a lion rather than the same snarling head repeated. Perhaps the substitution of a lion's head for the female genitals was too obvious a reference to vagina dentata for Dalí. In any case, the lion could be read both as a now slightly more disguised reference to the terrorising effect of the female genitals, combined with a reference to that other source of sexual anxiety and fear, the father. Freud links the dream symbol of the lion to violence, passion and authority, all of which can constitute the paternal relation. (From 1930, Dalí introduced the figure of William Tell as a symbol of the threatening father figure – in Dalí's case, an all too real figure.) The lion's head becomes a sexually ambivalent symbol, and in so far as these paintings seem to turn on problems of gender and sexual identity, shifts its significance. In *Illuminated Pleasures*, the lion's head and jug-woman melt into one another, the teeth of both threateningly bared. However, in *The Accommodations of Desire* the same visual comparison is drawn with the mouth of the bearded man in the little group at the top of the painting. This group appears to flow from the young man holding his head in his

52 For an extended discussion of this picture, see Dawn Ades, 'The Visual Imperatives of Surrealism', in William Lieberman (ed), *Twentieth-Century Modern Masters: The Jacques and Natasha Gelman Collection*, Metropolitan Museum of Art, New York, NY, 1989.

hands, and includes a naked figure embracing the bearded man. This figure, like the statue in *Dismal Sport,* is androgynous. It is tempting to say that this figure, as well as others that appear less ambiguously to represent a young man, like the one who peers into the boxed 'picture within a picture' in *Illuminated Pleasures,* is Dalí himself.

Perhaps the pebbles in *The Accommodations of Desire* recall a game Lorca played with the children at Cadaqués during the summer of 1927, when he would improvise 'letters' and once 'read' a stone they handed him.[53] They certainly form very ingeniously a 'second level' of reality. Like the 'picture within a picture' structure of *Little Ashes*, they suggest the generative hallucinatory power of an object. The 'picture within a picture' becomes, in *Illuminated Pleasures,* a more complex and varied device, to signal interconnecting levels of experience in dream, hallucination and reality.

PARANOIA

The Surrealists invested dreams and hallucinations with a new set of values. Recognising, in Freud's wake, the ingenuity, resourcefulness, creativity and unreason of the dreaming mind, they had since the early 1920s drawn upon or tried to record the products of dreams. An important and undeniable part of the human psyche, the dreaming mind seemed to offer a privileged channel of communication to the 'hidden forces' of the unconscious mind. This 'communication' was couched in strange symbols, unreal juxtapositions, condensed and displaced events and objects. The 'hidden' meaning of dreams, their 'latent' content, provoked in Dalí a passion for interpretation, although other Surrealists were happy to let the manifest 'dream' stand in its pure fullness. Dalí often included in paintings both symbols and their interpretations. However, towards the end of 1929 Dalí began to devise a new tool, which he called 'critical paranoia', or the paranoiac method, which he distinguished from dreams and hallucinations, and which introduced a different kind of interpretation.

In his text 'L'Âne pourri' (The Rotting Donkey), Dalí introduced

53 Ian Gibson, *Federico García Lorca: A Life*, Faber and Faber, London, 1989, p.188.

paranoiac activity as an active thought process, by contrast to 'automatism and other passive states', such as hallucination and dreams. His notion of paranoia had close ties to the Surrealists' contemporary explorations and simulations of insanity, and was broadly derived, as David Lomas has proved, from recent French psychiatric sources.[54] Dalí defined paranoiac activity as a 'delirium of interpretation', basing his terminology on clinical diagnoses of a type of mental derangement characterised as *délire d'interprétation*. Psychiatrists Paul Sérieux and Joseph Capgras, for example, described the 'chronic systematised psychosis based on delusional interpretations', which was termed 'paranoia' in Emil Kraepelin's taxonomy. Paranoia, Dalí wrote, 'makes use of the external world in order to assert its obsessional idea, with the disturbing characteristic of making others accept the reality of this idea. The reality of the external world is used for illustration and proof, and so comes to serve the reality of our mind.'[55] This had for Dalí an important visual application. It was, he argued, by a 'clearly paranoiac process' that he arrived at his double images: 'the representation of an object which, without the slightest figurative or anatomical modification, is at the same time the representation of another entirely different object, the second representation being equally devoid of any deformation or abnormality which might betray some arrangement.'

Dalí was beginning at this time to work out the implications of his 'paranoiac method' pictorially, in the canvases *The Invisible Man* and *Invisible Sleeping Woman, Horse, Lion*. *The Invisible Man* was exhibited unfinished at Dalí's 1931 exhibition at the Pierre Colle Gallery, where it was dated '1929–32'. *Invisible Sleeping Woman, Horse, Lion*, of which more than one version exists, was shown in the foyer exhibition at Studio 28 at the screening of Dalí and Buñuel's second film, *L'Âge d'or* in 1930. This is the image he refers to in 'L'Âne pourri': 'an image of a horse which is at the same time an image of a woman.' A schematic drawing Dalí prepared of this image shows the process of transformation from reclining woman, through horse to lion. The technique of constructing images susceptible

54 David Lomas, *The Haunted Self: Surrealism, Psychoanalysis, Subjectivity*, Yale University Press, New Haven, CT, and London, 2000, p.150.

55 Dalí, 'L'Âne pourri', *Le Surréalisme au service de la révolution*, no.1, July 1930 p.9. This text was incorporated into his book *La Femme Visible*, *op. cit.*

of double, triple or even more numerous different readings was eventually to become highly sophisticated, whether on the minute scale of the details in *Impressions of Africa* (1938), or the huge scale of *The Hallucinogenic Toreador* (1968–70).

But it was not solely as a pictorial technique that Dalí developed his paranoiac critical method. It should be understood within the climate of Surrealism, which focused attention on madness and disturbed mental states and challenged the institutions in charge of the insane. Their long-standing interest in madness and mental illness reached a critical point in 1929, and had begun to have repercussions on a wider stage. The *First Surrealist Manifesto* (1924) had excepted children and the mad from its general condemnation of a sclerotic society, which suppressed any needs or desires not strictly linked to practical ends. Breton's attack on mental institutions in his novel *Nadja* (1928) had come to the attention of the Société médico-psychologique; he was accused in the *Annales médico-psychologiques* of inciting patients to murder, and the Surrealists' position was discussed at meetings of the society by Professors Pierre Janet and Gaëtan de Clérambault, episodes which Breton reported in the prologue to his *Second Surrealist Manifesto* when it was published as a book in 1930. The violence and intemperance of Breton's attack was one extreme point in the Surrealists' multi-faceted investigation of mental illness. They had opened a dangerous debate on fundamental issues of human rights and the right to define madness. At the same time they saw in it a form of creative energy. In the section 'The Possessions', in Breton and Éluard's *The Immaculate Conception* (1930), which has been described as lying partway 'between poetry and manifesto',[56] Breton and Éluard wrote texts in simulation of disturbed states of mind. One of these was 'Essai de simulation du délire d'interprétation' (Simulation of the Delirium of Interpretation Essayed), in which the 'obsessional idea' centres on birds. The connection with Dalí's 'L'Âne pourri' was clear and both texts were published in the Surrealist number of *This Quarter*, which had a special section on 'Surrealism and Madness'.[57] At about the same time Dalí began to write his 'psycho-analytical essay', as he called it, *The Tragic Myth of Millet's Angelus*, a paranoiac-critical interpretation of a series of 'delirious

56 Mark Polizzotti, *André Breton: Revolution of the Mind*, Bloomsbury, London, 1995, p.352.

phenomena' related to this famous devotional image.[58] It should not be surprising that the most radical young French psychologist, Jacques Lacan, formed close links with the Surrealists and, following the publication of his thesis, *De la psychose paranoïaque dans ses rapports avec la personnalité* (On paranoid psychosis and its connections with the personality) in 1932, contributed on two occasions to the Surrealist journal *Minotaure*. 'Le problème du style et la conception psychiatrique des formes paranoïaques de l'expérience' (The problem of style and the psychiatric conception of paranoiac forms of experience) appeared immediately after Dalí's first essay on the *Angelus*, 'Interprétation Paranoiaque-critique de l'image obsédante de "L'Angélus" de Millet' (Paranoiac-critical interpretation of the obsessional image of the *Angelus* of Millet), in which Dalí referred in glowing terms to the young psychologist, often paraphrasing his work. Lacan argued that the inadequacy of the classical description of the 'paranoid' psychoses was due to 'a hypertrophy of the reasoning function', and put the case that their plastic and poetic productions were of high human value.

> One could conceive of the lived paranoiac experience, and the conception of the world that it engenders, as an original syntax which helps to affirm, through those links of understanding that are special to it, the human community. The knowledge of this syntax seems to us an indispensable introduction to an understanding of the symbolic values of art, and especially to the problems of style... problems for ever insoluble for any anthropology that is not liberated from the naive realism of the object.[59]

57 *This Quarter*, with the subtitle 'Surrealist number' was guest edited by André Breton, September 1932. The essays from 'The Possessions', including 'Simulation of the Delirium of Interpretation Essayed' by Breton and Paul Éluard, were translated by Samuel Beckett.

58 The manuscript for *The Tragic Myth of Millet's Angleus* was complete by 1934, but the book was not published until 1963. See Dawn Ades, 'The experimental demonstration of critical paranoia: Salvador Dalí's 'The Tragic Myth of Millet's Angelus', Slade lecture, Oxford, 10 February 2010, and Dawn Ades and Fiona Bradley (eds), *Salvador Dalí: A Mythology*, exhibition catalogue, Tate Gallery, London, 1998.

59 Jacques Lacan, 'Le problème du style et la conception paranoiaque de l'expérience', *Minotaure*, no.1, February 1933, p.69.

Dalí had made contact with Lacan quite early in his association with the Surrealists, and both his own account of this meeting in *The Secret Life of Salvador Dalí* and the internal evidence of his writings shows that it was fruitful. Lacan's extensive research on the history of the nosology of paranoia, which formed the first part of his thesis, must have been of great interest to Dalí, though how much the latter already knew of the theories of, for instance, Sérieux and Capgras is difficult to determine. He certainly invested the concept with a broad significance, put it in his own idiosyncratic terms and interpenetrated it with morphology, so that in his paintings there was a shift from the 'interpretative' character of the use of symbols towards a 'perceptual delirium', which undermined any notion of a 'naive realism'. In his double images, there is no resolution, no recognition that there is a 'correct' reading. The disturbance that is always felt when a shape, a face, even a word is momentarily misread, but normally evaporates when the 'real' object is correctly identified and is palpably there, remains. Dalí enthusiastically embraced the idea first proposed by Breton in *Introduction to the Discourse on the Paucity of Reality* (1924), that the introduction of surrealist objects into the 'real' and utilitarian world would create confusion and help to undermine faith in the truth of realism, and saw his double images in this context. 'As a functional form of thought, the new images will come to follow the free bent of desire… and may also contribute to the destruction of reality…'[60]

Although the 'double images' of paranoia must to some degree be rooted in earlier symbolic configurations, like the fish-head/grass-hopper, they are now aspects of a 'concrete irrationality', as Dalí called his paranoiac critical method, in their own right. There is a kind of permanent instability in these images, which can produce a disturbing to-fro alternation between hard and soft, mineral and fleshy, concave and convex, solid and hollow, exacerbated by the powerful features of Dalí's imaginative morphology.

60 Dalí, 'L'Âne pourri', *op cit.* p.12.

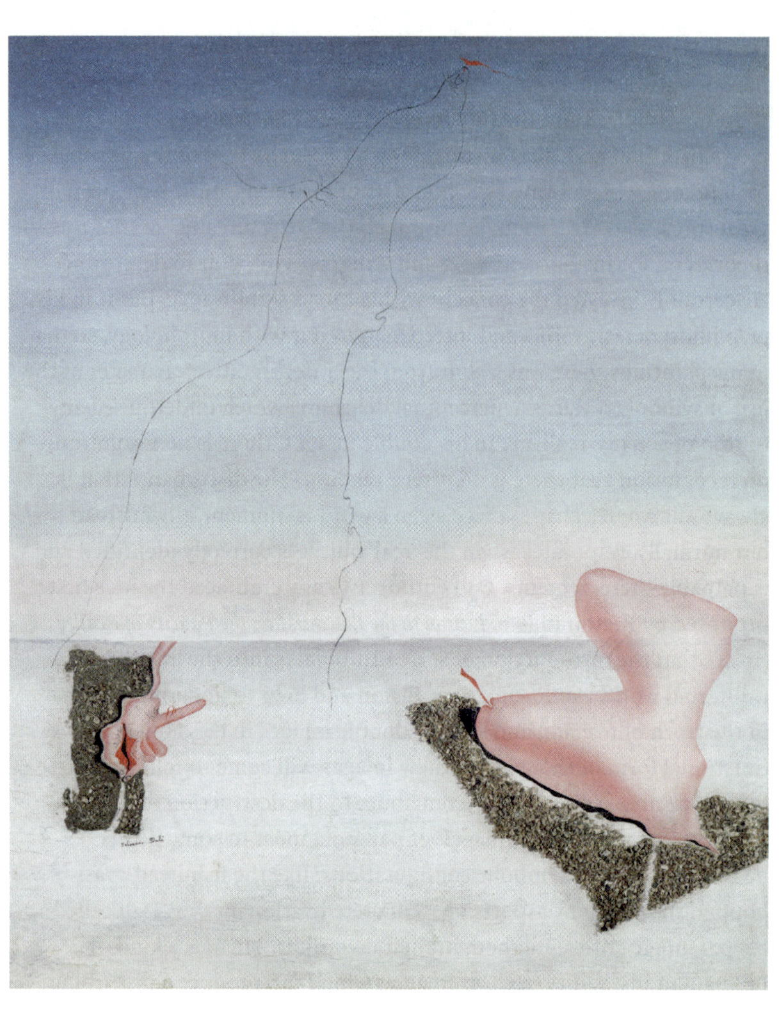

474 **Salvador Dalí**
Two Figures on a Beach (Unsatisfied Desires), 1928
Oil and sand on card
76.2 × 62.2 cm | 30 × 24½ in

Why Film?

Dalí & Film, Matthew Gale (ed), Tate Publishing, London, 2007

Salvador Dalí grew up during the great age of the silent film, when even small towns had at least one cinema and cine clubs abounded. Film absorbed the old optical amusements of the nineteenth century and changed dramatically in Dalí's lifetime, with the advent of sound and of colour, animation, experiments with stereoscopic film (the Todd-AO high-definition format, for example), wraparound sound, television and video. He kept pace with the technological advances, was closely involved in one of the earliest European talkies, and made arguably the first artist's video.[1] He never gave up the struggle to work in film, proposing documentaries, sketching out scenarios, contributing to Hollywood movies, enthusiastically exploring animation, and treading an ambiguous line between directing and starring in cinematic adventures of many kinds. The story of his affair with film is in some ways one of disappointments, over-ridden by endless optimism.

Dalí knew, however, from a very early age, that he wanted to be a painter. As a child, the images of the great painters of the past were as real to him as his actual surroundings, and as an adolescent he lived for the summers in Cadaqués, where his indulgent family rented a studio and he could devote himself to painting. We know this from his own diaries of the time because even then, despite his absolute commitment

1 See, for instance, Dawn Ades (ed), *Salvador Dalí: the Centenary Retrospective*, Palazzo Grassi, Venice, 2004, and Philadelphia Museum of Art, 2004, which included every aspect of Dalí's work; and Fèlix Fanés, *Dalí: Cultura de Masas*, exhibition catalogue, CaixaForum, Barcelona, Museo Nacional de Arte Reina Sofía, Salvador Dalí Museum, St Petersburg, FL, and (as *It's All Dalí*), Museum Boijmans Van Beuningen, Rotterdam, 2004–05.

to pigments and canvas, he also loved writing.[2] Indeed, he wrote almost as obsessively as he painted. Film, the 'Seventh Art', as it was regularly called in *La Gaceta Literaria* in the 1920s, occupies a very interesting position for Dalí in relation to image and text. Though potentially antagonistic to painting, film was a medium in which he could draw both on his visual and his verbal skills in the service of his imagination, and there is a constant triangulation formed by the flow of film, painting and text.

Was there, for Dalí, a special appeal in film? Was it an alternative to his paintings, adaptable to certain effects beyond the reach of the canvas? Was it an extension of the pictorial image, or rather of his writings? Or was it just one of the many media that he utilised to give expression to ideas that had their own dynamic?

Reviewing Dalí's multifarious cinematic projects, it is curious how few saw the light of the screen. Following the great, if controversial, successes of the collaborations with Luis Buñuel – *Un Chien andalou* (An Andalusian Dog, 1929) and *L'Âge d'or* (The Golden Age, 1930) – only the dream sequence of Alfred Hitchcock's *Spellbound* (1945), the video *Chaos and Creation* (directed by Philippe Halsman, 1960), the television film *Impressions de la Haute Mongolie – Hommage à Raymond Roussel* (Impressions of Upper Mongolia — Homage to Raymond Roussel, 1975) and the autobiographical *L'Autoportrait mou de Salvador Dalí* (Soft Self-Portrait of Salvador Dalí, 1967), directed by Jean-Christophe Averty, were realised in his lifetime. The only scenario, apart from *Un Chien andalou* and *L'Âge d'or* published in full at the time was *Babaouo*, in 1932. The footage shot for a major film, *L'Histoire prodigieuse de la dentellière et du rhinoceros* (The Prodigious Adventure of the Lacemaker and the Rhinoceros, 1954), remained unedited at his death, as did the animation for the Disney film *Destino* (Destiny, 1946 and released in 2003). But many scenarios, fragmentary sketches and ideas for films lurk among Dalí's manuscripts, 11 of the most complete of which have now been translated into Spanish in the *Obra Completa* (Complete Works, 2004).[3] These, along with his writings about as well as for film, numerous cinematic and television projects that range from collaborations with the

2 Salvador Dalí, *Un diari, 1919–1920: Les meves impressions i records intims*, Fèlix Fanés (ed), Editions 62, Barcelona, 1994.

3 Dalí, *Obra Completa, vol.III: Poesía, Prosa, Teatro y Cine*, Agustín Sánchez Vidal (ed), Destino, Barcelona, 2004.

New York avant garde to the NO-DO (Noticiarios y Documentales, News and Documentaries) news films in Franco's Spain, testify to his unbroken desire to work in this medium.

How, then, to account for the disparity between idea and realisation? The only two fully realised films in which Dalí had a major role were *Un Chien andalou* and *L'Âge d'or*, both undeniable masterpieces. The absence of a Buñuel in Dalí's subsequent projects was clearly fundamental, and there was also an increasing gap between Dalí's notion of cinema's potential to be the bearer of his ideas and the actual demands of the industry. The place of film in his thinking about art altered over time. Having enthusiastically embraced film and photography in 1927, he eventually voiced his disillusionment in the face of the massive increase in the complexity of production: 'I don't believe that cinema can ever become an artistic form. It is a secondary form because too many people are involved in its creation. The only true means of producing a work of art is painting, in which only the eye and the point of the brush are employed.'[4]

Film and photography were initially key weapons in his polemic against the old, picturesque and 'artistic', and his fervent support of modernity. This is clear from the declarations in the *Manifest groc* (Yellow Manifesto) of 1928:

> THERE IS the cinema
> THERE ARE stadia, boxing, rugby, tennis and a thousand other sports
> THERE IS the popular music of today: jazz and modern dance...
>
> THERE ARE art exhibitions of modern artists
> THERE ARE moreover, great engineering and some magnificent ocean liners...
>
> THERE IS the gramophone, which is a little machine
> THERE IS the camera, which is another little machine
>
> WE DENOUNCE young people who seek to repeat painting of the past
> WE DENOUNCE old, authentic architecture
> WE DENOUNCE decorative art, unless it is standardised.[5]

Dalí's theoretical texts between 1927 and 1929 about film and photography distinguish firmly between 'artistic' and 'anti-artistic' film, the latter, encompassing film director Mack Sennett and comics like Buster Keaton, the only kind he approves. 'The anti-artistic film... reveals... the entirely new poetic emotion of all the most humble and immediate facts, which were impossible to imagine or foresee before cinema.'[6] While not necessarily directly challenging painting, the camera reveals a different reality. 'The world of cinema and the world of painting are very different; clearly, the possibilities of photography and cinema are to be found in that unlimited imagination which is born of things themselves.'[7] In practice, Dalí continued to experiment with painting, and his article 'Film-arte, film anti-artistico' (Art Film, Anti-artistic Film, 1927) was accompanied by an illustration of a recent painting, *Honey is Sweeter than Blood* (1927), and a drawing of a head, both with the caption 'Cinematismo de Dalí' (Dalí's Cinematism). He considered his paintings 'anti-artistic', like the films he admired, and in 1929 he threatened to abandon painting altogether, choosing to illustrate the final issue of the journal *L'Amic de les Arts* only with photographs.

There are two dimensions to Dalí's theories on film and cinema. First, the simple insistence on 'things themselves', on the world of facts presented by the camera. In Dalí's own work, it was his poems and poetic texts that respond most directly to this limitless arena, and which mediate between film and painting. He questioned the traditional poetic use of image and metaphor as being anecdotal and soluble like a riddle, and prefers the pure enumeration of facts. Lists, and the profusion of 'small things', as author Haim Finkelstein has argued, were the common ground in Dalí's paintings and his poetry at this time.[8] In *Poem: to Lydia*

4 Quoted by James Bigwood, 'Cinquante ans de cinema Dalínien', in *Salvador Dalí*, exhibition catalogue, Centre Pompidou, Paris, 1979, p.353.

5 Dalí, Lluís Montanyà, Sebastià Gasch, *Manifest groc* (Yellow Manifesto, or Catalan Anti-Artistic Manifesto), Barcelona, March 1928; trans. in *Salvador Dalí: The Early Years*, exhibition catalogue, South Bank Centre, London, 1994, pp.221–22.

6 Dalí, 'Film arte, film anti-artistico', *La Gaceta Literaria*, 15 December 1927, p.8. See full translation in Haim Finkelstein (ed), *The Collected Writings of Salvador Dalí*, Cambridge University Press, Cambridge, 1998, and Matthew Gale (ed), *Dalí & Film*, Tate Publishing, London, 2007.

7 *Ibid.*

8 Finkelstein, *op. cit.*, p.16.

of Cadaqués, Dalí lists a succession of disparate objects: 'Near the cold boulder there lies an eyelash/A torn piece of flesh signalling bad weather.'[9] The accumulation of details and their scattering in an indeterminate space recalls paintings such as *Cenicitas* (Little Ashes, 1927–28) and *Honey is Sweeter than Blood.*

The second dimension to the new reality revealed for Dalí by film and photography concerns its imaginative possibilities, which are still rooted in fact. Film and photography have introduced a new way of looking:

> Knowing how to look is a way of inventing... The camera has immediate practical possibilities, for new themes where painting necessarily remains only in the experience and understanding. Photography glides with continual imagination over new events, which in the pictorial realm have only possibilities for being signs.[10]

The objectivity of the lens *is* contemporary poetry: it is the 'Glass of real poetry'.[11]

> First poet of all PICASSO
> There are no poets who write
> The best paint or make film. Buster,
> Harry Langdon.[12]

This 'photographic imagination' owes much to technical possibilities, such as the close-up and slow motion. The poetic magic of the 'film-fact' comes from its ability to transform the reality we see before our eyes. Seizing on László Moholy-Nagy's notion, in his influential Bauhaus book *Malerei Fotografie Film* (Painting Photography Film, 1925), that the camera

9 Dalí, 'Poema: a la Lydia Cadaqués', *La Gaceta Literaria*, 15 February 1928; trans. in *ibid.*, p.27.

10 Dalí, 'La fotografía, pura creacio de l'esperít', *L'Amic de les Arts*, 30 September 1927, pp.90–91; trans. as 'Photography, Pure Creation of the Mind', in *Salvador Dalí: The Early Years*, p.216.

11 *Ibid.*

12 Dalí, letter to Federico García Lorca, 15 January 1928, published in *Poesía*, 14 April 1987, p.85, and trans. in Christopher Maurer, *Sebastian's Arrows: Letter and Mementos of Salvador Dalí and Federico García Lorca*, University of Chicago Press, Chicago, IL, 2004, p.96.

13 László Moholy-Nagy, *Painting Photography Film* (1925), Lund Humphries, London, 1969, p.28.

is an extension of 'our optical instrument, the eye',[13] Dalí emphasised its transformative powers: 'A lump of sugar on the screen can *become* larger than an infinite perspective of gigantic buildings.'[14] One of the photographs in the last issue of *L'Amic de les Arts* was filched by Dalí from *Painting Photography Film*, a close-up of the eye of a marabou (mistitled by Dalí 'Ull d'elefant' – elephant's eye.) The inventive visuality of the close-up was explored in *Un Chien andalou*, for instance in the sequence magnifying the death's-head hawkmoth. It was an image that endured: one of the most striking passages in his late film *L'Histoire prodigieuse...* is the attempt to film gooseflesh close-up on a female breast.

In his text 'Photography, Pure Creation of the Mind' (1927), Dalí contrasts painting more brutally with photography and film. 'The photographic crystal can caress the cold delicacy of white lavatories, follow the sleepy slowness of aquaria. In painting on the other hand, if you want to paint a jellyfish, it is absolutely necessary to depict a guitar or a harlequin playing the clarinet.'[15] Perhaps in the reference to aquaria he has in mind the extraordinary films of Jean Painlevé, where extreme close-ups of a shrimp, for example, render it completely unrecognisable and virtually abstract.[16] Dalí's point seems to be that to rival the 'photographic marvellous' which resides in the fact, painting can only resort to fantasy, symbol and substitution.

Despite the superiority, in his own arguments, of the camera, Dalí was not prepared to abandon painting. Recognition that cinematic effects were beyond the reach of painting did not stop him experimenting, and in pictures like *Honey is Sweeter than Blood* and especially *Cenicitas* he seeks to represent the metamorphosis of form in paint; towering over the scattered fragments of bodies (torso and breasts painted with photographic realism) and 'little things' is a large pink shape that emerges from a curved guitar-torso and seems to be in the process of mutating. The swirling blue sky of *Apparatus and Hand* (1927), together with the floating objects, convey, if only distantly, an urge for mobility. After this brief tussle with the

14 Dalí, 'Film arte, film anti-artistico', *op. cit.*.

15 Dalí, 'Photography, Pure Creation of Mind', *op. cit.*, p.216.

16 Jean Painlevé, *Crabes et crevettes* (1929). For his interest in scientific films see also Dalí's 'Cinema', *L'Amic de les Arts*, no.23, 31 March 1928, p.175, republished in Fèlix Fanés (ed), *Salvador Dalí, L'Alliberament del dits: Obra catalana completa*, Quaderns Crema, Barcelona, 1995, pp.89–91.

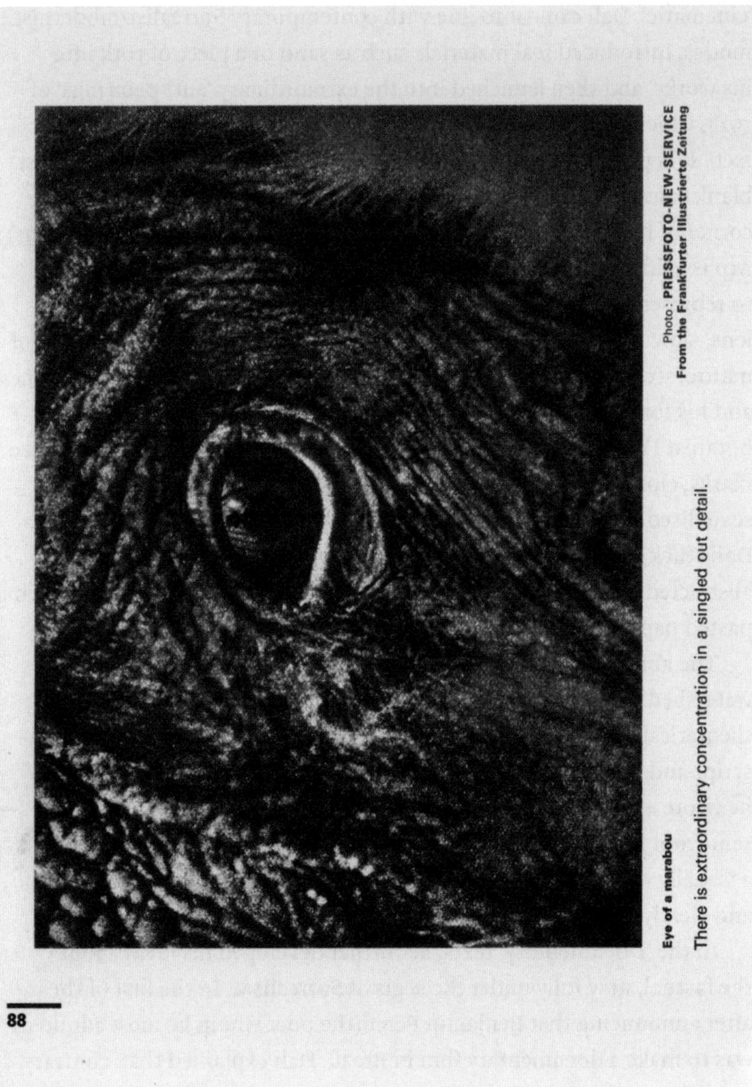
Eye of a marabou

There is extraordinary concentration in a singled out detail.

Photo: PRESSFOTO-NEW-SERVICE
From the Frankfurter Illustrierte Zeitung

88

László Moholy-Nagy
Photograph of the eye of a marabou
Page from *Painting Photography Film*, 1925

'cinematic', Dalí came into line with contemporary Surrealist/modernist modes, introduced real materials such as sand or a piece of cork into his works, and then launched into the extraordinary 'anti-paintings' of 1928, which seemed to retreat as far as possible from the 'photographic fact'. It is possible that he came to regard these large, sometimes almost blank canvases, as failed experiments since he thrust them away in the corner of his studio. Although the influence of Joan Miró and Jean (Hans) Arp is evident in the amorphous shapes, they could also be an attempt to represent forms of plant and animal life as revealed by microscopic lens, slow motion or close-ups. Dalí was himself a passionate observer of nature, studying the creatures in the shallows and rocks around Cadaqués, and his forms have a curious resemblance to the 'plant-animals' of the botanist Frederick Keeble.[17] The exaggerated blobs, spidery and crab-like marks, elongated forms like late-evening shadows are also often highly sexualised male and female body fragments. On some of these canvases Dalí stuck sand, feathers or wire, material supplements to the spare abstracted shapes – which, often thickly painted, give the illusion of being pasted paper.

The abrupt change that his paintings then underwent marks a watershed in his career, coinciding with the culmination of his intense theoretical interest in film and in his collaboration with Buñuel on the script and direction of *Un Chien andalou* in early 1929. Simultaneously, he wrote a remarkable series of short 'Documentary' texts, which he sent from Paris to the Catalan newspaper *La Publicitat*, and returned to a visually realist mode of painting, distinct from the 1927–28 paintings and clearly a response to his experience of filmmaking with Buñuel.[18]

In the 'Documentary' texts, he further developed his ideas about the factual, now fully under the aegis of Surrealism. In the first of these, after announcing that Benjamin Péret (the poet whom he most admired) was to make a documentary film in Brazil, Dalí explained that, contrary

17 Frederick Keeble, *Plant-Animals: A Study in Symbiosis*, Cambridge University Press, Cambridge, 1910.

18 See Jordana Mendelson, 'From the Banal to the Extraordinary: Dalí's Anti-artistic Documentaries', in Hank Hine, William Jeffett and Kelly Reynolds (eds), *Persistence of Memory: New Critical Perspectives on Dalí at the Centennial*, The Salvador Dalí Museum, St Petersburg, FL, and Bompiani Arte, Milan, 2004, for a discussion of the different critical uses of 'documentary' in the Catalan avant garde.

to popular opinion, there was nothing antagonistic between rigorously objective documentary and Surrealist texts, which:

> coincide from the outset in their essentially anti-artistic and more particularly anti-literary process… The documentary notes things said of the objective world anti-literarily. In parallel fashion the Surrealist text transcribes with the same rigour and as anti-literarily as documentary, the REAL free functioning of thought, of events which occur in reality in our mind, thanks to psychic automatism and to other passive states (inspiration).[19]

Promising not to write another line of theory and denouncing 'description' as 'immoral next to the marvellous means of photography and cinema', Dalí devoted himself to documenting facts. In a 20-centimetre square (like a film frame or photographic plate), drawn in the wet sand of the Luxembourg Gardens in Paris, he saw in succession: 'the heel of a man's shoe, the tip of a woman's shoe, the shadow of a wisp of smoke… a plant fibre flying slowly… two simultaneous drops of liquid, yet another drop of liquid, a small submarine pulled by a string, a fallen linden leaf.'[20] Prefacing this (and breaking his promise not to theorise) was a comment on recent research about the synchronicity of diverse phenomena; 'a lion's yawn, a bud opening on an acacia branch, a passer-by's steps, an ostrich's tracks, an insect's flight, the submersion of a jellyfish' share an algebraic proportion that established 'a certain rhythmic relation to which everything is subject'.[21]

This rhythmic relation fascinated Dalí, and he returned to the idea in later scenarios; however, when he asked Buñuel what value the latter placed on 'scenario, star, editing, rhythm, photo, lighting', Buñuel said he gave absolute importance to photography and editing, but as for rhythm, 'I don't know what that is.'[22] Although in Dalí's 1929 'Documentary' texts

19 Dalí, 'Documental – Paris 1929–1', *La Publicitat*, 26 April 1929; trans. in Robert Descharnes (ed), *Oui: Salvador Dalí – The Paranoid-Critical Revolution Writings 1927–33*, trans. Yvonne Shafir, Exact Change, Boston, MA, 1998, p.93.

20 Dalí, 'Documental – Paris 1929–6', *La Publicitat*, 28 June 1929, *ibid.*, p.106.

21 *Ibid.*

22 'Luis Buñuel', interview with Dalí, *L'Amic de les Arts*, 31 March 1929; trans. in Descharnes, *op. cit.*, p.88.

the synchronicity between these phenomena was to do with movement, formal rhythms – such as that noted by the naturalist D'Arcy Thompson in *On Growth and Form* (1917) – continued to fascinate him.[23] The equiangular or logarithmic spiral, which as Thompson notes is a mathematical law of growth manifest in horns, the florets of a sunflower, the Nautilus shell, was the morphological link between various objects in Dalí's later work that seem quite disconnected. The rhinoceros horn was one of these, and the origin of *L'Histoire prodigieuse…* lay in his 'discovery' of the same shape in Vermeer's *The Lacemaker* (1669–70).

Film and photography entered the avant-garde consciousness in the 1920s. Despite Dalí's denunciation of what he called 'artistic film', *Un Chien andalou* and his own ideas about photography and film, which centre on the capacity of the lens, of close-up and slow motion to make the 'photographic *donnée*' strange, as well as the 'gags' of comedy, owe a great deal to the experimental pioneers like Walter Ruttman, Dziga Vertov and Lászlό Moholy-Nagy. There are echoes of Ruttman's *Berlin: Symphony of a Great City* (1927), for instance, or Sergei Eisenstein's *October* (1928), in *Un Chien andalou*.

In his painting *The First Days of Spring*, which inaugurates his 'return to the image' in 1929, Dalí translated his ideas about the 'document' into a variety of modes of visual recording: actual photographs, including himself as a little boy, stencils, a readymade coloured print of a scene on board an ocean liner. Here, and even more strikingly in succeeding paintings from 1929 like *The Lugubrious Game* and *The Accommodations of Desire*, paint and photograph, or collage, are indistinguishable from one another. Sometimes, as in *The Lugubrious Game*, the photographs are unrecognisable close-ups of natural objects. In the lower left of *The First Days of Spring*, the scandalous scene of a masturbating man beside a woman with flayed face buzzing with flies appears superimposed on the illustration of deck jollities, as though it is a zoom-in on a couple from that scene. Separate pictorial incidents are scattered over the surface, and though they broadly adhere to a scale determined by the non-cinematic principle of perspective (its exaggerated return here perhaps a reassertion of an especially painterly technique), their relationship follows a rhythm

23 See D'Arcy Thompson, *On Growth and Form* (1917), Cambridge University Press, Cambridge, 1961, p.172 and further.

similar to montage sequences in *Un chien andalou.* In *The Accommodations of Desire*, the successive images of the lion's head, hair and ants imposed on the pebbles on the beach quote part of one such sequence: 'Close up of the hand full of ants crawling out of a black hole in the palm... Dissolve to the hairs on the armpit of a young woman... Dissolve to the undulating spines of a sea-urchin. Dissolve to the head of a girl seen directly from above.'[24] Such chains of images are themselves related to descriptions of the shifting perception of an object in the prose piece 'My girlfriend and the beach': 'the new-born baby was no other than my girlfriend's pink breast... it was not her breast either: it was little pieces of cigarette paper'.[25] They also contributed to the development of one of Dalí's key concepts, the 'paranoiac-critical method'.

While Dalí's notion of critical paranoia was to be one of the most significant mechanisms linking his painting to film, there are other aspects to his work of the 1930s that have a complex relationship with film. Awareness of its power to create and manipulate another reality in time is countered by an exaggerated emphasis on the particular qualities of the static pictorial image. The re-assertion of perspective, for example, was not a return to pre-Cubist realism but, in a manner not unlike Marcel Duchamp's 'rehabilitation' of perspective in *The Bride Stripped Bare by her Bachelors, Even (The Large Glass)* (1915–23), unmasked its artificiality while capitalising on its illusions. Sometimes Dalí used incompatible perspectives, as Giorgio de Chirico had done, and often exaggerated the effect of perspective on landscapes, buildings and objects, with forms dizzily receding. In *The First Days of Spring*, dramatic central receding lines mark the steps of a giant platform; they also resemble railway lines or even the rails of a tracking camera.

Often, perspective, which traditionally functioned to centre and harmonise a composition, was used to precisely the opposite purpose. In *Vertigo* (1930) and *The Bleeding Roses* (1930), the sharp side of the building, visible at the very edge of the canvas, drops terrifyingly into empty space. Suspense and sensations of awe or fear, at which film is so adept, are conjured here through the manipulation of painting techniques.

24 Dalí, '*Un Chien andalou*, scenario', *La Révolution surréaliste*, no.12, 15 December 1929, p.34.

25 Dalí, 'La meva amiga i la platja', from 'Dues Proses', *L'Amic de les Arts*, 30 November 1927, p.104; trans. in *Salvador Dalí: The Early Years*, *op. cit.*, p.218.

The impression of vast spaces and great hollow depths is emphasised by the use of shadows and violent differences in the relative size of objects. Perspective was drawn into the personal drama of such images as *The Font* (1930), or the paintings related to the 'Angelus' series, in which he plays with the sizes of figures and objects: they appear to be in miniature or loom as enormous, so that scale is disrupted and irrational. Dalí also used the trope of the screen to reflect on the relationship between film and painting. Several paintings of the early 1930s feature a suspended sheet, which functions as screen and shield. Sometimes, as in *The Old Age of William Tell* (1931), shadows from an unseen form are cast on the screen. It is plausible that he was making a reference to the scene in Raymond Roussel's book *Impressions d'Afrique* (Impressions of Africa, 1910), where a lost character is made to appear by virtue of a moving shadow cast on a white cloth, one of many games between illusion and reality in the play and a reference to pre-cinematic techniques. In Dalí's paintings, typically, associations multiply and the sheet becomes shroud or toga, hiding the body in formless drapes recalling the standing figure in the boat in Arnold Böcklin's painting *Isle of the Dead* (1880–86).

Dalí's concept of the paranoiac mechanism, 'from which is born the image of multiple figuration',[26] was to have a long and profound impact on his paintings, writings and his involvement in film. It was based, not on the common understanding of paranoia as persecution complex, but on an idea widespread in the literature of psychology and psychoanalysis at the time, of a mental condition in which the subject interprets his or her surroundings according to an over-riding obsession, in a 'delirium of interpretation' that creates an alternative virtual 'reality'. This delirium was not arbitrary but, according to Dalí's associate Jacques Lacan, rooted in unconscious and suppressed emotions or desires, hence for Dalí potentially a 'document' for interpretation.[27] Critical paranoia was a rich source for Dalí, the inspiration for one of his most powerful texts, *The Tragic Myth of Millet's Angelus* (1934/1963),[28] and for a series of paintings

26 Dalí, 'L'Âne pourri', *La Femme Visible*, Editions Surréalistes, Paris, 1930 and *Le Surréalisme au service de la révolution*, no.1, July 1930; trans. in Finkelstein, *op. cit.*, p.224.

27 See Robert Lubar, 'Dalí's ParaNONia', in Hine, Jeffett and Reynolds, *op. cit.*, 2004, pp.123–29; David Lomas, *The Haunted Self*, Yale University Press, New Haven, CT, and London, 2000.

with multiple readings like *The Endless Enigma* (1938). The moving image was potentially a particularly apt medium; he described the scenario *La Carretilla de carne* (The Wheelbarrow of Flesh, 1948–52) as 'the first paranoiac film', and *Destino* was almost entirely planned around this visual device.[29]

Dalí did not at first exploit film's potential in this context. In his documentary on Surrealism (*Cinq minutes à propos du surréalisme*, 1931–33) he proposes mobile graphics to illustrate his paranoiac method.[30] A sequence of six drawings based on his painting *Invisible Sleeping Woman, Horse, Lion* (1930), are disposed horizontally in two columns to show the successive readings of the woman as horse and then as lion. However, what he is concerned with is the 'delirious interpretation' of the single configuration: the odalisque is at the same time horse and lion. The paranoiac reading is not a progressive transformation from A to C; the odalisque becomes horse, reappears and becomes lion. Cinematic movement can therefore demonstrate the mechanism diagrammatically but is not, at this point anyway, a substitute for the pictorial image. The reversible switch, the 'duck-rabbit' effect, in which alternative readings oscillate but are not simultaneous, as in some of Dalí's most perfected paranoiac images such as *Apparition of a Face and Fruit Dish on a Beach* (1938), inheres in the static configuration of the painting.[31]

Although there is a link with the transformative imagery of earlier paintings and sequences in *Un Chien andalou*, film was not at this point for Dalí the inevitable destination of his 'critical paranoia'. The nightmare sequence that he devised for the film *Moontide* (1942) would have included a startling instance of a 'paranoiac' double image fully conceived for film, rather than the reversible pictorial image, with the needle-threatened

28 *The Tragic Myth of Millet's Angelus* was not published until 1963, but Dalí was certainly working on it in 1934 and the completed text, edited (by Breton) for publication, exists in the Fundació Gala-Salvador Dalí, Figueres. The reasons for its non-publication at the time are unknown. The text was mislaid when Dalí and Gala fled Paris in 1939, and only recovered in 1962.

29 On these projects see Agustín Sánchez Vidal, 'La Carretilla de carne', and Fèlix Fanés, 'Film as Metaphor', in Gale, *op. cit.*, 2007.

30 See Ades, 'Cinq minutes à propos du surréalisme', in Gale, *op. cit.*, 2007.

31 The 'duck-rabbit' effect was popularised by Ernst Gombrich, *Art and Illusion: A Study in the Psychology of Pictorial Representation*, Phaidon, London, 1960, p.4, drawing upon Norma V. Scheideman, *Experiments in General Psychology*, University of Chicago Press, Chicago, IL, 1930, p.67.

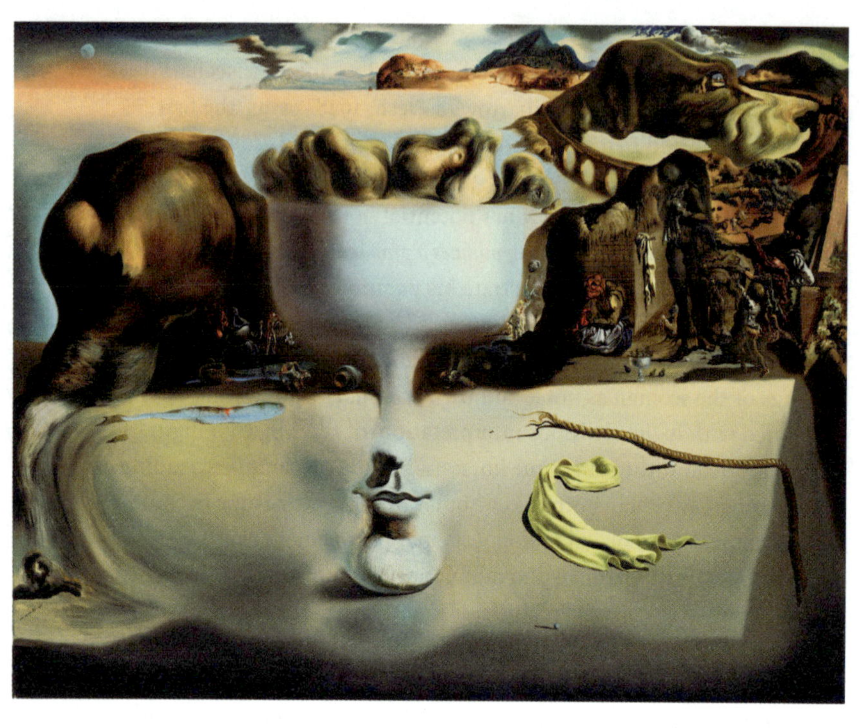

488 **Salvador Dalí**
Apparition of Face and Fruit Dish on a Beach, 1938
Oil on canvas
114.3 × 143.8 cm | 45 × 56⅝ in

eye becoming at the last moment the globe of the sun,[32] and *Destino* is a brilliant fusion of classic cartoon animation and Dalí's 'double images'. However, it was in *Impressions de la Haute Mongolie* that Dalí found an original cinematic outlet for 'delirious interpretation'. This film, made for television, united his long-term interest in close-up – to which he had also returned in *L'Histoire prodigieuse...* – with imaginary readings-in on a grand scale. Landscapes, animated scenes, figures and heads emerge into focus and mutate out of a colourful, formless mass not unlike an unusually abstract 'impressionist' landscape. It is revealed at the end that all has been constructed from the close-up filming of the metallic band round a biro, the band pitted and stained, apparently, with uric acid.[33]

Dalí's film projects, which exist in various states from full scenarios to scattered notes, addressed pretty well every potential function of the medium, including documentary, epic and the 'impossible' scenario. The latter, of which Benjamin Péret's *Pulchérie veut une auto* (Bonny wants a car, 1923) is a fine extended example, is closely related to the animated cartoon. *Pulchérie veut une auto* flies off from comic-film gags into an extraordinary fairy tale of extreme and hilarious violence.[34] As in animated cartoons, figures suffer appalling accidents or die and come blithely back to life; objects and limbs mutate and transform, all effects that were unrealisable in the physical medium of cinema proper, where even the most inventive tricks and stunt comedians 'could not fully dissolve... into the celluloid world'.[35] Some scenes in *Babaouo* resemble the 'impossible' scenario, such as the horrific accident after which Babaouo, blind, gropes for his beloved Mathilde. Touching a cushion, he thinks he has found her body, and kisses her 'head and hair', which is only the loose insides of the cushion. Crying, 'You are alive!' he embraces the embers of the cushion, which is now on fire. Horribly burned, he throws it away screaming 'Shit!'[36]

32 See Ilene Susan Fort, 'Moontide', in Gale, *op. cit.*, 2007.

33 See Elliott H. King, 'Crazy Movies that Disappear', in Gale, *op. cit.*, 2007.

34 Benjamin Péret, 'Pulchérie veut une auto: FILM', *Littérature*, no.10, May 1923; trans. 'Bonny Wants a Car', in Dawn Ades (ed), *The Dada Reader: A Critical Anthology*, Tate Publishing, London, 2006, pp.226–31.

35 Esther Leslie, *Hollywood Flatlands: Animation, Critical Theory and the Avant-garde*, Verso, London, 2002, p.15.

36 Dalí, *Babaouo, Scenario inédit, précédé d'un abrégé d'un histoire critique du cinéma, et suivi de Guillaume Tell ballet portugais*, Cahiers Libre, Paris, 1932; see William Jeffett, 'Babaouo', in Gale, *op. cit.*, 2007.

Cartoons signalled a new direction for experimental artists and film-makers in the 1920s, and many avant-garde film projects combine forms of graphic animation with photographic montage. How far Dalí was aware in the 1920s of early animated cartoons like *Felix the Cat* is unclear. The plasmic, stretching and convulsing line of cartoon drawing, form changing into formlessness and back again in the twinkling of an eye, might have melded with his passion for art nouveau or Catalan Modernista architecture to inform his melting shapes. Certainly Eisenstein, whose own drawings were 'pseudo-pods of the primal plasma-amoeba', thought that the drawings in Mickey Mouse films shared this quality with both Picasso and Dalí.[37] Later object-constructions by Dalí like *Babaouo* or *The Little Theatre* (1934) have another possible connection with the process of cartoon animation, in that the former used cut-out layers of celluloid to give the impression of depth in a landscape.[38] Dalí's dioramas similarly mimic three-dimensionality through two-dimensional layers of glass screens.

From 1930 on, many of Dalí's scripts aspired to be full-scale films, but apart from *Babaouo*, *Giraffes on Horseback Salad* (1937) and *La Carretilla de carne* (Meat Cart), often remain an unfinished mixture of ideas for a plot and isolated, but often fully conceived, scenes. These scenes or episodes were invested with a special emotional power for Dalí; minutely imagined and described events with an emphasis on actions, their closest ties are with important texts like the 1931 'Rêverie'.[39]

La Chèvre sanitaire (The Hygienic Goat, c.1930–31), 'a talking film', undated and never made, reveals this mechanism well. It is an attempt to develop the theme of the 'documentary' *Contre la famille* (Against the Family, 1932) into a narrative film. There is no coherent and consistent storyline, but, rather, general directions about themes and the effects that Dalí wanted to obtain – the gratuitous, sensations of vacuity and absence, the systematic use 'of elements that would be in sterile disaccord with the action and the scenery'. The script veers between abstract and

37 Leslie, *op. cit.*, p.223.

38 See *Il etait du fois: Walt Disney*, Galeries nationales du Grand Palais, Paris, and Musée des Beaux-Arts, Montreal, 2006, pp.134–35.

39 'Rêverie', *Le Surréalisme au service de la révolution*, no.4, 1931; trans. 'Daydream', Finkelstein, *op. cit.*, p.150. This uninhibited tale of Dalí's masturbatory fantasies drew a severe reprimand from the Parti communiste français (PCF, the French Communist Party).

general ideas, very concrete images (such as a decapitated chicken running about) and specific vividly imagined settings (a large deserted square under a twilight sky, a huge modernist house). It was to be a Surrealist film, with 'dreams and hypnagogic images', the intervention of 'chance of a surrealist order', the imagination and 'mental reality' co-existing with sensorial reality.[40] The most vividly imagined passages in the scenario are the minutely choreographed situations in which the protagonists come together in a dramatised encounter. At the heart of his film is a situation that is recognisably the same as that depicted in paintings and drawings of 1929–30, notably *The Invisible Man* (1929–32) and *The Butterfly Hunt* (1929).[41] This is a scene figuring a family grouped with intense concentration round something invisible in the painting but revealed in the drawing as a butterfly net. There is a paradoxical impression of secretive desires and open if deviant sexuality. That it evokes for Dalí the female sex and the womb (which he claimed to remember as glutinous, blood-red and formless) is suggested by a note in *Contre la famille*: '*Prologue scene of the butterfly hunt* / Intra-uterine dreams… the birth trauma of Otto Rank.'[42] The way in which Dalí imagines and describes the scene recalls his erotic 'Rêverie', and through this situation he is similarly able to indulge his fantasies. Central to his pictorial images and also to this scene in the scenario is the figure of the father, although he is not implied in the three amorous 'themes' of the narrative. The film starts with birdsong and laughter. The camera draws back and reveals the mother who cries out and catches a butterfly. The father arrives and takes her tenderly by the shoulders:

40 As 'La Cabra Sanitaria' (The Hygienic Goat), in Sánchez Vidal, *op. cit.*, 2004, p.1085. Dalí explains the phrase 'the hygienic goat' in terms of his idea of the gratuitous (see Sánchez Vidal, 'La Chèvre sanitaire', in Gale, *op. cit.*, 2007). The 'hygienic goat' thus had absolutely no connection, conscious or unconscious, with what it designated (though one might speculate that it could be the opposite to 'the rotting donkey', just as the painting title *The Invisible Man* is to the book *The Visible Woman*, and moreover contains notions of objectivity, sterilisation and precision, which for Dalí opposed the sentimental, emotional, putrid and picturesque).

41 'La Chèvre sanitaire' shares its title with the second part of Dalí's book *La Femme Visible* (1930), where the drawing is reproduced.

42 Dalí, 'Contra la familie' (Against the Family), *Obra Completa*, vol.III, *op. cit.*, p.1079.

> with an expression of compassion and a certain inevitability (the Initiation Sacrifice, introduce the concept in the spoken part). Then the children arrive, and after them the aunt. The sister places herself by her mother so that the butterfly net held by the mother is exactly at the height of her stomach. When the group is formed, there is the sensation of a very grave and solemn moment... The mother very slowly introduces her hand into the net. The aunt bites her lips... the father shows the whites of his eyes as if in a convulsion... The brother watches the scene with avid curiosity. The girl directs a look of reproach at the wife. When the mother's hand slowly reaches the bottom of the net, which is exactly at the height of the sister's sex, the latter gives a penetrating, animal shriek.[43]

The drama does not unfold as a story, though it has temporal narrative elements, but is encapsulated in a situation. This is why the reverie, dream or nightmare is Dalí's most effective cinematic model, in which, to follow Freud's ideas, people, objects or settings can be invested with multiple and even contradictory affects. Such episodes in the scenario, while echoed in figure groups in the paintings, include motions or sounds unavailable in the static media of canvas or paper and are agencies of erotic suspense. The father's eyes roll into his head like those of Gaston Modot, who plays 'The Man', in *L'Âge d'or*, the tension rises as the mother reaches into the net, the girl screams, and so on. At the same time, these filmic descriptions offer insights into the psychological dramas underlying the imagery of paintings like *The Lugubrious Game*, *The Old Age of William Tell* or *The Birth of Liquid Desires* (1932). There is a connection between Dalí's inclination for a single, psychologically loaded incident, the dream narrative and his own preferred 'rêverie'. It is not so much that they resemble the episodic cinema of his youth, but that as nuclei for an accumulation of associations to be revealed or hinted at, rather than as stages in a narrative, they use suspense and deferral within a self-contained event as an erotic device.

One can assume that Dalí envisaged close-ups, montage and intercutting in *La Chèvre sanitaire* as in *Un Chien andalou*, but he rarely

43 Dalí, 'La Cabra Sanitaria', *Obra Completa*, vol.III, *op. cit.*, pp.1095–96.

includes camera directions in his scenarios. His approach to visualising the material as film is quite different from that of Federico García Lorca. Although the poet had less experience with cinema, he created the film script *Viaje a la luna* (Trip to the Moon) while he was in New York in 1929–30. Lorca had watched a short 35-millimetre film called *777* (c.1929), by the Mexican graphic artist Emilio Amero, 'an abstract thing about shop machines'. The two started discussing contemporary movies, such as 'Salvador Dalí's surrealistic *Un Chien andalou*. Lorca saw the possibilities of doing a film of the order of *777* with the direct use of motion... The film was completely plastic, completely visual, and in it Lorca tried to describe portions of New York life as he saw it.'[44] *Trip to the Moon* is numbered shot-by-shot, with detailed camera directions:

> 51. In the street the man with the veins appears, lying with his arms outstretched.
> 52. The preceding fades into a criss-cross of a triple double exposure of fast trains.
> 53. The trains fade into a double exposure of piano keys and hands playing.[45]

It is in the genre of the short 'surrealist-experimental' and 'impossible' films, and would have been a mixture of graphics and montage, but is effectively a shooting script, fully visualised. Lorca's script interweaves death and love through momentary and disconnected shots; it is film as ephemeral and fleeting. Dalí, on the other hand, prolongs suggestive encounters or actions to build up erotic suspense.

Dalí's writings – scenarios, novel, theoretical texts, autobiography – develop a kind of modern, personal *ut pictura poesis*, a set of narratives from which breathtaking moments can be individually extracted for pictorial images or cinematic incidents. Just as Dalí constructed his personal mythologies, such as that of the vengeful patriarch, in the guise of William Tell, Abraham, Saturn and God the Father, or its maternal variant in *The Tragic Myth of Millet's Angelus*, so he began in his paintings, instinctively it seems, to adopt the classical solution to the depiction of

44 Richard Diers, 'A Filmscript by Lorca', *Windmill*, spring 1963, p.27.
45 Federico García Lorca, 'Trip to the Moon', trans. Bernice G. Duncan, *ibid.*, pp.31–37.

a grand myth – the choice of the key moment at which the preceding and subsequent elements of the story are encapsulated.

Dalí's paintings in the postwar period have a paradoxical relationship to tradition and modernity, with epic historical works that deliberately reference Velázquez, Zurbarán and many others on one hand, and on the other works positioned ambiguously *vis à vis* contemporary art like Pop art and Op art. Similarly, his film projects range from Hollywood biopics to collaborations with Andy Warhol and Jonas Mekas. Preserved among his manuscripts are plans for a film on the Spanish hero of the fifteenth-century wars of independence El Cid (subject of a 1637 play by Pierre Corneille, *Le Cid*), and for 'Une Vie de Goya' (A Life of Goya). The latter consists of a single page designed to resemble film credits: 'scenario and artistic direction by Salvador Dalí, first colour film directed by a great painter'.[46]

Dalí's idea (how far this ever reached those named is unknown) was for Jean Renoir to direct it, for Charles Laughton to play Goya and Bette Davis the Duchess of Alba. As with so many of his projects, lack of funding probably scuppered his hopes. Although technologically advanced projects like the video *Chaos and Creation* were intended to mock modernist abstraction, and he often emphasised the value of the naked eye and the brush, the documentary potentialities of film continued to attract him, not least as a supplement to his status as painter and genius. He envisaged a film of his autobiography *The Secret Life of Salvador Dalí*, which was published in New York in 1942:

> SAMUEL GOLDWYN
> Presents
> 'SECRET LIFE OF SALVADOR DALÍ'
> played by Salvador Dalí himself

This was to be '"a double parallel biography" – that of DALÍ, and that of the eminent philosopher SIGMUND FREUD. The latter, with the magic of his genius – like a modern Faustus – influences and determines, from afar, the eclosion of a half-mad individual, lost in the obscurity of a tiny

46 Dalí, 'Une vie de Goya', unpublished manuscript, n.d., Fundació Gala-Salvador Dalí, Figueres.

Spanish town.' A curious aspect of Dalí's plans was to use anamorphosis, a form of perspectival distension that rendered the image unreadable when viewed from the front. The distortion could be corrected by looking at the picture from an oblique angle. 'Dalí has conceived an original idea whereby most of the scenes will be shown on the screen in an "oblique" fashion.'[47] Presumably, the viewer would still watch the screen head on, and thus be faced with a distorted image. The idea was perhaps, as with the seventeenth-century artists who used anamorphosis to indicate a metaphysical reality beyond the apparent world, to suggest what is hidden beyond daily reality, the arena of dreams and paranoia. Dalí here transposes to film, or at least its projection, a technique to which he had recourse, or whose effects he mimics, in paintings like *Diurnal Fantasies* (1932) or *The Enigma of William Tell* (1933).

Dalí frequently used film to document his exploits. Although there are fragments in *L'Histoire prodigieuse...* showing him copying Vermeer's *The Lacemaker*, he failed to persuade Jack Warner to make a documentary of himself painting. In 1948, he wrote to Warner (whose portrait he painted in 1951, suggesting a short documentary to coincide with the publication of his book *50 Secrets of Magic Craftsmanship* (1948):

> Very dear friend, I have never wanted to take advantage of our great friendship for projects that might seem more or less problematic, but now and to mark the completion of my book... I have recognised the truly sensational cultural and pedagogic possibilities of realising a short documentary on the subject, with myself as protagonist... This film on my technique of painting would be historic in the history of cinema and of painting... Only the cinema can analyse efficiently each of the painter's movements and offer the spectator the development of the successive stages of the painting just as it would for those of a living organism in growth.[48]

This documentary, which would indeed have been invaluable, and would have stood beside the famous films of Picasso and Jackson Pollock in

47 'Samuel Godwyn presents The Secret Life of Salvador Dalí...', unpublished typescript in English, n.d., Fundació Gala-Salvador Dalí, Figueres.

48 Dalí, letter to Jack Warner, unpublished manuscript, Fundació Gala-Salvador Dalí, Figueres.

action, was never made. Film was to remain for Dalí an endlessly alluring but elusive medium, whose potential from his own changing perspective was tantalisingly appropriate to his ideas, but whose increasingly complex modes of production often placed their realisation beyond his reach.

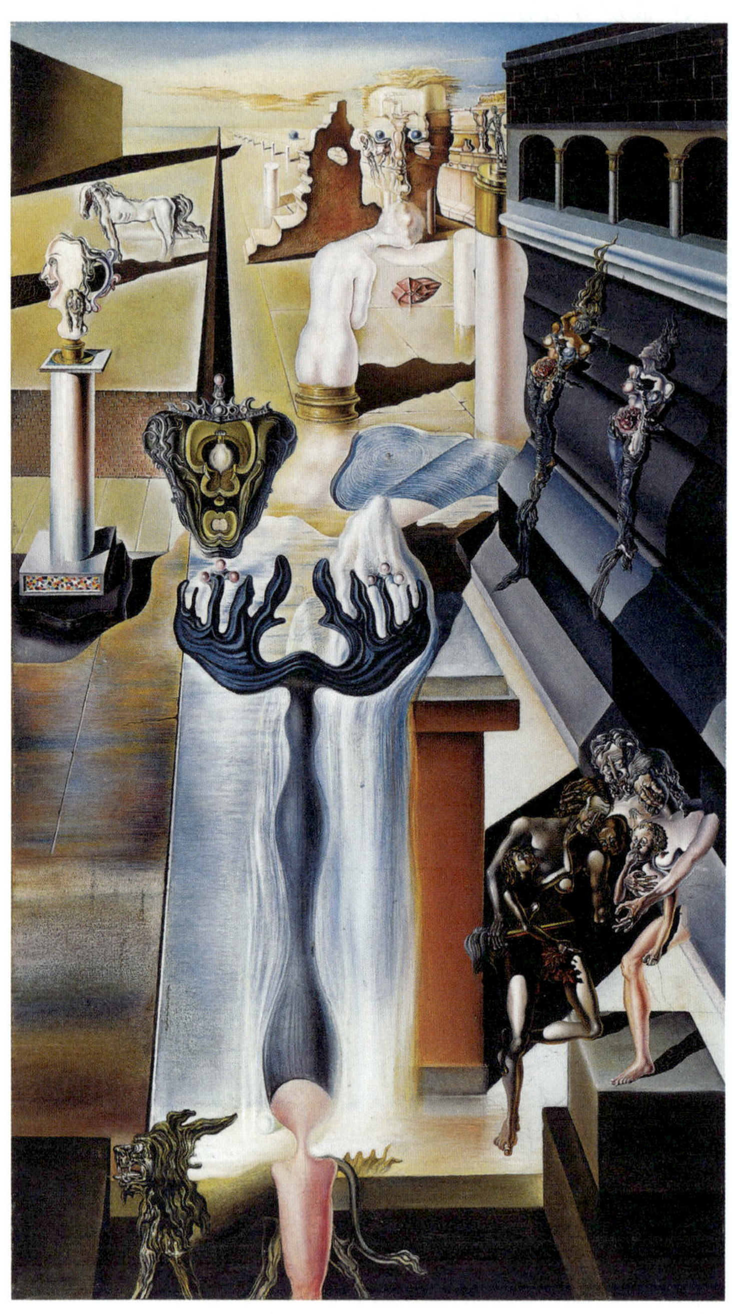

498 **Salvador Dalí**
The Invisible Man, 1929
Oil on canvas
140 × 81 cm | 55⅛ × 31⅞ in

Contre la famille

Dalí & Film, Matthew Gale (ed), Tate Publishing, London, 2007

Contre la famille (Against the Family), is a short sketch for a documentary film intended to expose the family as a historical construct and breeding ground for neuroses and psychological conflict. The preoccupations are recognisably Dalí's own, although inflected by Surrealism's larger political concerns.

The scenario can be dated to 1932. Dalí was at the time in regular correspondence with his friend the Catalan poet and journalist J.V. Foix, keeping him up to date with Surrealist activities, especially his own, and eager for their dissemination in Catalonia. On 25 February Foix published a note in his regular column 'Meridians' in the prestigious cultural section of *La Publicitat,* under the heading 'Surrealist Activism'. There he announced a new publication by Dalí: '*Vive le surréalisme!* (surrealist novel) with Gala, Dulita, André Breton, Marlene Dietrich, René Crevel, Buster Keaton, Kaergiki, surrealist objects etc. Just now he tells me he is writing a "scenario" against the family.'[1]

Contre la famille confirms not only Dalí's obsessional interest in the conflict between father and son, exemplified in the William Tell paintings from 1930, but his desire to analyse the psychological damage inflicted on the individual by the family in the light of its historical and sociopolitical

1 Rafael Santos Torroella, *Salvador Dalí: Corresponsal de J.V. Foix 1932–1936*, Editorial Mediterrània S.A., Barcelona, 1986, p.84. Unaware of the existence of this scenario, Santos Torroella made the reasonable suggestion that the reference was to Dalí's William Tell theme, especially the 'Guillame Tell: ballet portugais', which concludes the *Babaouo* scenario (for which, see William Jeffett, 'Babaouo', *Dalí & Film*, Matthew Gale (ed), Tate Publishing, London, 2007). However, what Dalí had evidently communicated to Foix was the plan for a film 'against the family'.

history. It is a remarkable attempt to unite a psychoanalytical approach with a Marxist analysis of a dominant social institution.

The short scenario could, however, just as well have been a plan for a treatise, since it almost entirely lacks any visualisation of actual scenes, and mainly consists of headings and brief notes outlining the key subjects.[2] Dalí's chief reference points are Freud and Engels, but primarily the former. The scenario treats the idea of family in terms of an individual passing through the stages of sexual development. It is in two sections: a summary of the main points (as well as a 'bibliography' of the film), which are then more fully developed under the heading 'The Film'.

The introduction begins: 'Intra-uterine dreams. Freud... The birth trauma of Otto Rank. Beginning of the pre-natal sexual life. Theory of the polymorphous perverse...' Later, in his autobiography *The Secret Life* (1942), Dalí was to devote a chapter to 'Intra-uterine memories' in which he claims that his personal memories of the womb 'corroborate on every point' Dr Rank's 'sensational book', which 'identifies the said intra-uterine period with paradise, and birth – the traumatism of birth – with the myth, so decisive in human life, of the "Lost Paradise".'[3] Rank's *Das Trauma der Geburt* (The Trauma of Birth) was published in 1924 and translated into French in 1928. The 'polymorphous perverse' is a reference to the idea, developed by Freud in *Three Essays on the Theory of Sexuality* (1905), that 'a disposition to perversions is an original and universal disposition of the human sexual instinct' and that the potential for sexual excess is innate in children.[4] Dalí later made a curious 'assisted readymade' entitled *Freud's Perverse Polymorph* (1939), depicting a child eating a rat. The prologue to the scenario continues 'Infancy, formation of the Oedipus complex, castration – Freud... Intervention of the social and economic factors, Engels's history of the family.' After mentioning 'Eumenides – Oedipus at Colonnus', it ends 'Legal prostitution of matrimony'.

2 The original manuscript, in French, is held in the Fundació Gala-Salvador Dalí, Figueres; a full publication appears (in Spanish translation) as 'Contra la familia', in Salvador Dalí, *Obra Completa, vol.III: Poesía, Prosa, Teatro y Cine*, Agustín Sánchez Vidal (ed), Destino, Barcelona, 2004, pp.1079–82.

3 Salvador Dalí, *The Secret Life of Salvador Dalí*, Dial Press, New York, 1942 and London, 1948, p.26.

4 Sigmund Freud, 'Three Essays on the Theory of Sexuality', *On Sexuality*, The Pelican Freud Library, vol.7, Harmondsworth, 1977, p.155.

Dalí starts the second section, 'The Film', with two 'scenes' but then swiftly reverts to notes. The first 'scene' is obscure but contains a telling slippage from 'husband' to 'father': 'Scene of the neurosis which explodes at the moment of the cure of the husband whom they have been treating – passage – the father deals with tomorrow, the son starts a speech about the next day.' This odd temporality is somewhat clarified further on when Dalí elides historical and evolutionary progress: 'The simple fact of his later birth situates the son on a level historically more developed in the future. Fathers, in Marx's words, should be educated by their children.' The second scene introduces an image recurrent in Dalí's paintings and drawings of the period: 'Prologue-scene of the butterfly hunt.'[5] This is not elaborated but is immediately succeeded by a reiteration of the stages of the individual's development, from intra-uterine life, the birth trauma (Rank), infancy and the 'formation of complexes – the Oedipal complex, castration complex, knowledge of death and birth of the aversion feeling'. Several drawings from 1930 entitled *La chasse aux papillons*, (The Butterfly Hunt), are nightmarish scenes, showing a family group, man and woman grotesquely sexualised, and children, gathered round a large butterfly net into which one of the women thrusts her hand.[6] There is a troubling ambiguity in the scene between loving closeness and imminent threat, with the butterfly net as a striking sexual symbol.

In a relatively discursive passage, Dalí accounts for one of the recurrent themes in *Contre la famille*: the inhibition of desire and of the faculty of the imagination. Here he makes reference to Freud's idea of repression: 'Reality principle against the pleasure principle, theory of repression – all vital human aspirations are repressed by the social conventions incarnated by the family.' Dalí plans to treat familial relationships via Freudian case studies: 'All the situations develop on the basis of registered and analysed clinical cases.' Among these, he mentions son and mother ('Oedipus complex which prevents love'), brother and sister, and again the 'Eumenides'. These are the Furies, 'avengers of crime, especially crime

5 For a detailed discussion of this theme in relation to *La Chèvre sanitaire* see Ades, 'Why Film?', pp.490–91 in present volume.

6 See, for instance, Daniel Filipacchi (ed), *Surrealism: Two Private Eyes*, Guggenheim Museum, New York, NY, 1999, vol.2, nos.384 and 385.

7 Paul Harvey, *The Oxford Companion to Classical Literature*, The Clarendon Press, Oxford, 1951.

against the ties of kinship',[7] who figure most famously in the Greek story of Orestes, who murdered his mother Clytemnestra. The Electra complex was proposed by Jung as the female equivalent to the Oedipus complex, Electra being Orestes's sister who assisted in the killing of the mother. But it is not this basic inversion of father/son to mother/daughter that Dalí invokes, but rather the more general notion of the child rebelling against the parent (potentially son against mother) and suffering for it. Dalí began, very shortly after this unresolved scenario, to explore his obsession with Millet's *Angelus* (1859), the simple devotional painting of a couple pausing to pray at the sound of the Angelus bell. His paranoiac-critical analysis of this obsession, which involves the slippage of the man in the couple from husband to son, concluded that it represented (for him) the maternal equivalent of the terrible paternal myth of the father devouring his own son. Since Dalí is always the protagonist, this is thus the mother annihilating the son.[8]

Although Dalí ignores the issue of class in the history of marriage as Engels analysed it in *The Origin of the Family: Private Property and the State* (1884), his note 'Prostitution of marriage... Evolution from maternal to paternal relationship' draws on Engels, who wrote that the 'marriage of convenience turns often into the crassest prostitution'.[9] Dalí also seems to reflect Engels's acceptance of the argument of the German social anthropologist Johann Jakob Bachofen that women had once held power under a maternal rather than paternal order:

> We have seen how right Bachofen was in regarding the advance from group marriage to individual marriage as primarily due to the women. Only the step from pairing marriage to monogamy can be put down to the credit of the men, and historically the essence of this was to make the position of women worse and the infidelities of men easier.[10]

8 *Le Mythe tragique de l'Angélus de Millet* was written 1932–34 but not published until 1963, as *Le Mythe tragique de l'Angélus de Millet: Interpretation 'paranoïaque-critique'*, Paris, 1963; trans. as *The Tragic Myth of Millet's Angelus*, The Salvador Dalí Museum, St Petersburg, FL, 1986.

9 Frederick Engels, *The Origin of the Family: Private Property and the State*, Lawrence & Wishart, London 1972, p.134. Dalí remained quite indifferent to Engels's extensive discussion of non-Western – specifically Iroquois – notions of kinship.

10 *Ibid.*, p.144.

Freud's harnessing of Greek myth to his identification of enduring human instincts and complexes had provided a model for Dalí's attempt to tell the history of the family through the individual, in which he relies on theories of ontogenesis and phylogenesis. In the final passages of the film, this guide is lacking. Dalí evidently intended to represent the psychological, social and sexual implications of the 'myths' of Christianity and of Communism. In doing so, the 'problem of woman' presents itself to him in a different light. Rather than taking familial relationships (mother, sister, wife etc.) he introduces female types. Christianity itself is relatively straightforward: 'Paternal authority. Repression of pleasure, Christian idea of the nobility of suffering', but Dalí moves immediately from this to the contrasting ideas of the *camarada* (female friend) and the 'exotic woman' – 'cases which could present themselves – Realisation of desires' and then to Communism.

Communism has 'conquered love and with it, the full liberty of the imagination'. Presumably he means that love has been released from its sordid links to property and money and perhaps this was intended to propitiate the PCF (Parti communiste français) which had recently been outraged by Dalí's erotic text 'Rêverie' (1931).[11] The scenario ends with two ideas: the son as agent of change and the condition of 'woman' in the modern era. The 'son' will 'reproduce the conflict provoking the crisis of transition, the eruption of utopian ideas heralded by the concept of total liberty of the imagination, imagination which is directly proportional to the humanity and spirituality of love'. However, Dalí's attitude to the utopia of Communism is ambivalent and he ends with notes on the unresolved condition of woman: 'Social deviation, condition of the woman as object to be made use of, opposed to the communist idea of the companion, in which erotic relations are discarded.' Neither, it would appear, is satisfactory to him.

Dalí's animus against paternal authority and its incarnation in the family was doubtless inspired by his recent experience with his own

11 'Rêverie', *Le Surréalisme au service de la révolution*, no.4, December 1931. Dalí's text was regarded by the PCF as pornographic and Breton was criticised for publishing it. Relations between Surrealism and the Communist Party deteriorated during the early 1930s, the former insisting on retaining their independence and the latter on the need to subsume personal/artistic practices to the interests of the Party.

family: in 1930, his father disowned him and threw him out of the family home, leaving Dalí and Gala homeless and penniless. *Contre la famille* provides an interesting theoretical basis for paintings such as *The Birth of Liquid Desires* (1932) or *The Enigma of William Tell* (1933), but, despite his practice in scenario writing at this moment (notably for *Babaouo*, 1932), it is hard to imagine *Contre la famille* evolving into a complete film.

The Photographic Image

The camera, photographs and film rejuvenated perception and revolutionised artistic production. The essay 'Little Things: Close-Up in Photo and Film 1839–1963' was written for the exhibition Simon Baker and I organised for Fiona Bradley at The Fruitmarket Gallery in Edinburgh in 2009. This looked at one particular aspect of the photographic image – the close-up, which Salvador Dalí described as 'the registering of an UNKNOWN REALITY'. The title of the essay comes from Dalí's 'Poema de les cosetes' (Poem of little things, 1928) and his art and writing was pivotal to our thinking about the exhibition. The close-up produces images of things in the world invisible to the naked eye, simultaneously rendering them unrecognisable and revealing the unknown. The exhibition started with microphotographs, 'The wonders of the microscope photographically revealed', as one of the early scientist-photographers put it, and then concentrated on two periods, the 1920s and 1930s when the avant garde discovered the camera, and the 1960s to the present. The latter included Simon Starling's *Inventar-Nr 8573 (Man Ray) 4m–400nm* (2006), a projection of 80 black-and-white slides which close in on a Man Ray vintage photograph to the microscopic level of the surface structure of silver particles.

Many artists shared László Moholy-Nagy's enthusiastic welcome of photography and his idea, expressed in his highly influential Bauhuas book *Painting Photography Film* (1925), that it complemented and extended 'our optical instrument, the eye', and either switched to that medium or made use of it in various ways in their painting. For Marcel Duchamp it rendered painting redundant – 'unbearable' was his word. Photographs have provided an inexhaustible, ready-made medium for constructing and deconstructing the image, in photomontages and collages, as discussed above in 'Art and Power' and 'Gender and Identity'. John Stezaker works with given photographic materials, especially film stills. He finds hidden stories in old photographs, and in his collages combines two or more disparate images to uncover uncanny likenesses. Photography has proved to be one of the most flexible mediums for artists.

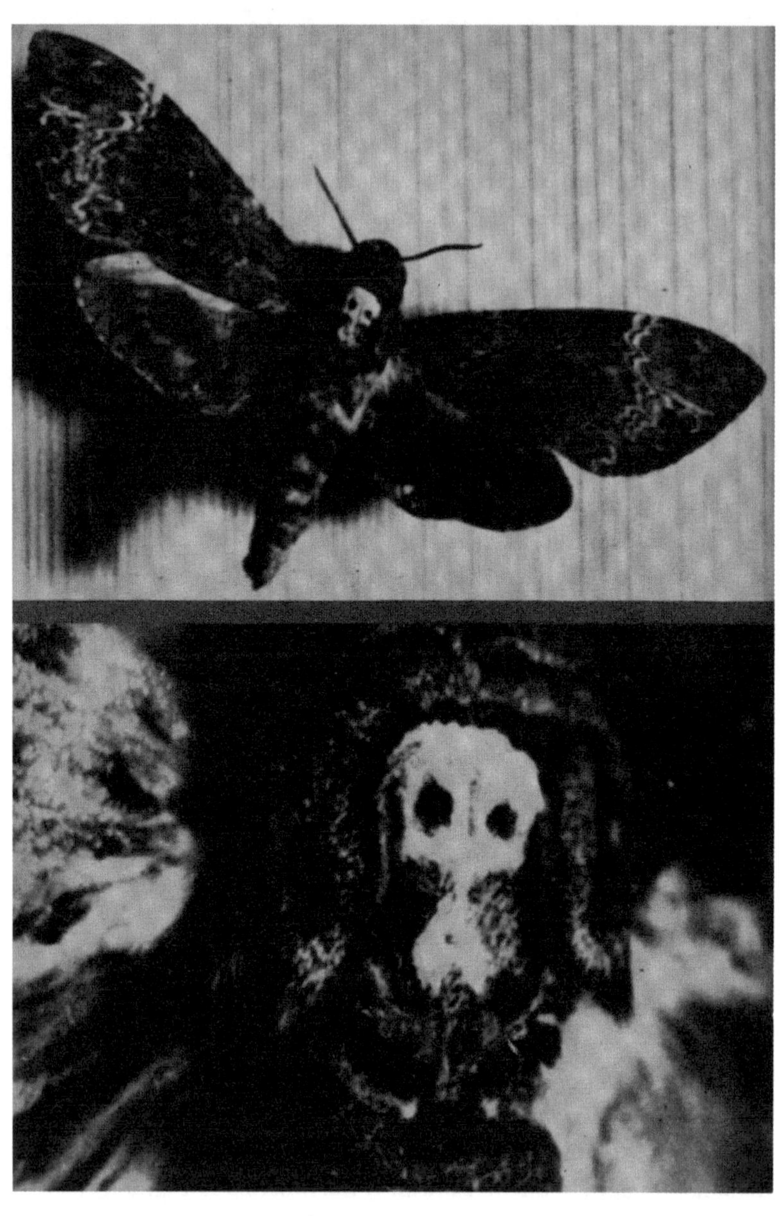

510 Luis Buñuel and Salvador Dalí
Un Chien andalou (An Andalusian Dog), 1919
Film still

Little Things: Close-up in Photo and Film 1839–1963

Close-Up: Proximity and defamiliarisation in art, film and photography,
Fiona Bradley (ed), The Fruitmarket Gallery, Edinburgh, 2009

> The young woman… carefully examines the wall where the murderer was standing a short time ago. On the centre of the wall, now bare, there is a small black spot.
> Dissolve to a close-up of the black spot – a Death's Head Hawk Moth.
> Cut back to the young woman, staring intently.
> Dissolve to a large close-up of the actual skull pattern on the moth's back. Then iris in to the skull pattern. Cut to a very large close-up of the skull pattern, which fills the shot.[1]

When the avant garde identified photography as the key to a new 'optic' after the First World War, close-up was at the core of their experiments. It appears in Dada photomontage, Surrealism, 'New Objectivity' and in film, very often in combination with montage, as in the Death's Head Hawk Moth sequence from Luis Buñuel and Salvador Dalí's 1929 film *Un Chien andalou* (An Andalusian Dog). Close-up – magnification through a lens – can reveal structures and organisms invisible to the naked eye, it can heighten the reality of the everyday object and render the familiar strange and unrecognisable. As both a technology and an epistemology it looked back to the scientific beginnings of photography in the microscopic study

1 Luis Buñuel and Salvador Dalí, *Un Chien andalou* (1929). See *L'Âge d'or* and *Un Chien andalou* (Classic Film Scripts), Simon and Schuster, London, 1968, p.113. Buñuel shot the Death's Head Hawk Moth sequence in *Un Chien andalou* himself, unlike the opening scenes of *L'Âge d'or*, which were taken from 'a splendid documentary on a scorpion that I bought' (*Le scorpion languedocien*, 1912). This is referenced in 'Letter to Charles de Noailles', Paris, 21 April 1930, in *L'Âge d'or: Correspondence Luis Buñuel–Charles de Noailles*, Centre Pompidou, Paris, 1993, p.67.

of the natural world, but also, like the later inventions of X-rays, aerial photography and slow motion in film, changed the viewer's perception of the world and challenged the primacy of the human eye as interpreter.

MICROPHOTOGRAPHY

The microscope leads me to see a world in every atom.[2]

The close-up was integral to the evolution of photography in the 1830s. The solar microscope was a development of Antonie van Leeuwenhoek's 'breakthrough in optical technology' of the seventeenth century, the microscope.[3] It enabled the projection of microscopic images on a large-scale in a darkroom and was responsible for the presence of so many 'close-up' microphotographs in early photography. The ambition accurately and lastingly to record the seen world propelled the development of photography, which emerged from the conjunction of experiments with the effects of light in fixing images on materials such as compounds of silver, with the camera obscura.

Existing devices to aid vision stimulated the desire accurately to fix the images thus obtained. The camera obscura – literally 'dark chamber' – had been known for centuries. At its most basic this is a small hole that allows light to pass into a dark room, projecting the exterior image (upside down) onto a wall. Using a lens improved the brightness, a movable screen allowed adjustment for focus and a mirror would reflect an inverted image onto a screen or other surface. The 'chamber' eventually became a box small enough to carry. The camera lucida, invented in the early nineteenth century, was of less practical use in the development of the photographic camera but famously provoked one of its pioneers, William Henry Fox Talbot, to pursue more durable ways of recording images. The camera lucida was a portable optical device with a prism, mounted on an arm, that created the illusion of an image on the paper

2 Dr Chalmers, quoted in W.H. Olley, *The Wonders of the Microscope Photographically Revealed*, W. Kent & Co., London, 1861.

3 Mimi Cazort, 'Photography's Illustrative Ancestors: The Printed Image', in Thomas, *op. cit.*, p.23.

in front of it. This is visible only from one angle and is of use only to very skilled artists. Fox Talbot, frustrated at his inability to draw with any success using the camera lucida, remarked:

> this led me to reflect on the inimitable beauty of the pictures of nature's painting which the glass lens of the Camera throws upon the paper in its focus – fairy pictures, creations of a moment, and destined as rapidly to fade away. It was during these thoughts that the idea occurred to me... how charming it would be if it were possible to cause these natural images to imprint themselves durably, and remain fixed upon the paper![4]

Optics and chemistry combined to create the conditions for the fixing of images seen through the microscope or via the camera obscura, although knowledge in these fields was still insufficient in the early days to 'give any plausible explanation of this delicate and complicated process'.[5] The story of the early pioneers and rivals in the development of the new medium, and of the chemical experiments that produced in succession the heliograph, the daguerreotype, photogenic drawings, the calotype, and the collodion wet-plate and gelatin dry-plate processes is one of rapid change, dead-ends and experimental breakthroughs. But there is no doubt that 'close-up' in the form of the extraordinary, unimaginable wonders revealed by the microscope, increasingly transmissible in faithful images, was as integral to the development of the fledgling art of photography as the images captured of faces, landscapes and buildings. Copying from 'Nature' took on wholly new significance. Nature was not just what could be observed with the naked eye – as wonderful, improbable or bizarre as the microscope's revelations were, they were still facts. In January 1839 Fox Talbot presented examples of his 'photogenic drawing' process in a special exhibition in the library of the Royal Society in London: 'among

4 William Henry Fox Talbot, 'Brief Historical Sketch of the Invention of the Art' (1844), quoted in Larry Schaaf, 'Invention and Discovery: First Images', in Ann Thomas (ed), *Beauty of Another Order: Photography in Science*, Yale University Press, New Haven, CT, and London, 1997, p.29.

5 François Jean Dominique Arago, Director of the Paris Observatory and Secretary of the Academy of Science, as quoted by Fox Talbot in 1839. See Schaaf's essay in Thomas, *op. cit.*, p.41.

them were pictures of flowers and leaves; a pattern of lace... a view of Venice copied from an engraving; some images formed by the Solar Microscope, viz. a slice of wood very highly magnified, exhibiting pores of two kinds, one set much smaller than the other, and more numerous. Another Microscopic set, exhibiting the reticulations on the wing of an insect.'[6]

Louis-Jacques-Mandé Daguerre, like Fox Talbot, produced images using his solar microscope, but following a different technique. A polished silver plate was exposed in the camera and the latent image developed using mercury. Daguerreotypes were unique objects but achieved a startling level of detail, as one can see in Andreas Ritter von Ettingshausen's *Cross-section of a clematis* (1840), which was taken in a solar microscope and anticipates the 'decorative micrography' of Laure Albin Guillot. Fox Talbot and other pioneers were aware that the consequences and applications of the new medium were unpredictable; as far as microphotography was concerned, its primary uses for the next decades were in botany, zoology, biology, entomology and palaeontology. Hitherto, drawings had been the means of transmitting the wonders of the structures and shapes of creatures, plants and animals newly visible through the microscope; in some respects it is surprising that there was such a long gap – over a century – between the invention of the microscope and of photography. But extremely detailed drawings and engravings of specimens under a compound microscope such as those of Robert Hooke's *Eyes and head of a grey drone-fly* from his endlessly amazing 1665 *Micrographia* fulfilled initial curiosity with their precision. Hooke, an unjustly neglected natural philosopher, experimental scientist and architect, introduced the term 'cell' to describe the tiniest visible organisms seen through the lens and invented the iris diaphragm, a contractile lens.[7] The need for ever-greater precision of detail as the capacity of lenses for magnification increased fed into the growing mechanisation and accuracy of microscopic recording. To some extent microphotography was just a more precise image of the structures of plants, creatures and other objects invisible to the naked

6 *Ibid.*, p.38. Fox Talbot used paper for his prints and was to invent the negative-positive process. This term, like the word 'photography' itself were due to his friend and colleague, Sir John Herschel.

7 Hooke's neglect historically is largely due to his feud with Isaac Newton.

eye already known through microscopes, and there was a long period of overlap between drawings, tracings and microphotography. However, the differences, and the advantages of the latter, were increasingly evident. Not only were the drawings dependent on memory, but there were certain phenomena that would be beyond the skill of the most accomplished artist to copy accurately, such as snow crystals. In many respects microphotography emerged from the difficulty of tracing the things seen through a microscope.

The delicate microphotographs in William Henry Olley's *The Wonders of the Microscope Photographically Revealed* (1861) are presented as the 'wonders of a world hitherto... wholly invisible' and as 'perfect transcriptions of nature'.[8] The images – a bee's sting, the tongue and cornea of a fly, a section of the membrane of a fly's wing, scales from a butterfly's wings – are strange, beautiful and, at least to a layperson, unrecognisable without their identifying titles. Each of Olley's microphotographs was individually cut out in the circular form created by the lens view and pasted into the book, which was originally published in monthly parts. The selection of objects for illustration was calculated to 'awaken popular and rational interest in the marvellous though generally little known discoveries of the microscope: The work would reveal these discoveries to the 'unassisted eye... in all their fidelity and beauty. This object, we believe, could only have been accomplished by enabling nature to delineate herself; in other words by the aid of photography.' Drawings of microscopic preparations would be, Olley says, by contrast, 'more or less defective and unnatural'. It is the mechanical eye of the camera that guarantees accuracy. Improvements in lenses, as reflected in this passage from a Chambers tract of 1872, uncovered ever-smaller organisms and particles, though it was not until the 1950s that they were powerful enough to register atoms:

> Take any drop of water from the stagnant pools around us, from our rivers, from our lakes, or from the vast ocean itself and place it under your microscope; you will find therein countless living beings... Increase the power of your glasses, and you will soon perceive, inhabiting the same drop, other animals compared to which the former

8 Preface, in Olley, *op. cit.*

> were elephantine in their dimensions. Exhaust the art of the optician, strain your eye to the utmost, until the aching sense refuses to perceive the little quivering movement that indicates the presence of life, and you will find that you have not exhausted Nature in the descending scale. Perfect as our optical instruments now are, we need not be long in convincing ourselves that there are animals around us so small, that in all probability human perseverance will fail in enabling us accurately to detect their forms, much less fully to understand their organisation.[9]

The microscope and microphotography transformed medical research and shattered some fundamental taxonomic assumptions – for instance, the categorical difference between plants and animals. A favourite subject among the scientific photographers was diatoms, unicellular organisms, which abound in any body of water and are very diverse, with estimates of the different species numbering anything from 30,000 to 100,000. They include *Epithemia,* as shown in John Redmayne's *Microphotographs from the Diatomaceae*, and *Pleurosigma,* as shown in Lt Col J.J. Woodward's plates. Woodward, an American army surgeon, developed the most precise microphotography of the latter part of the nineteenth century. He published his research in pathological histology through the 1860s and 1870s with the intention of aiding speedy diagnosis. Woodward tested his lenses to the utmost, famously resolving the final band of the 19-band test-plate devised by the German optician F.A. Norbert (57 lines ruled with a diamond on glass at an average line separation of 0.225μ).[10] The structure of *Pleurosigma Angulatum*, a species of diatom, was particularly difficult to resolve, and the successive images show the organism's diversity at increasing levels of magnification.

Lectures using lantern slides became popular forms of entertainment and instruction by the end of the nineteenth century. The revelations of microphotography were projected on a huge scale, for the audience to marvel at the infinite variety of pattern in the natural world and in hitherto unseen organisms. The horticulturalist Ellen Willmott's

9 'The Wonders of the Microscope', in *Chambers's Miscellany of Instructive and Entertaining Tracts*, no.83, W. & R. Chambers, Edinburgh, 1872, p.11.

10 G.L.E. Turner, 'Dr J.J. Woodward: Microscopist', *Proceedings of the Royal Microscopical Society*, vol.1, part 1, 1966, pp.32–39.

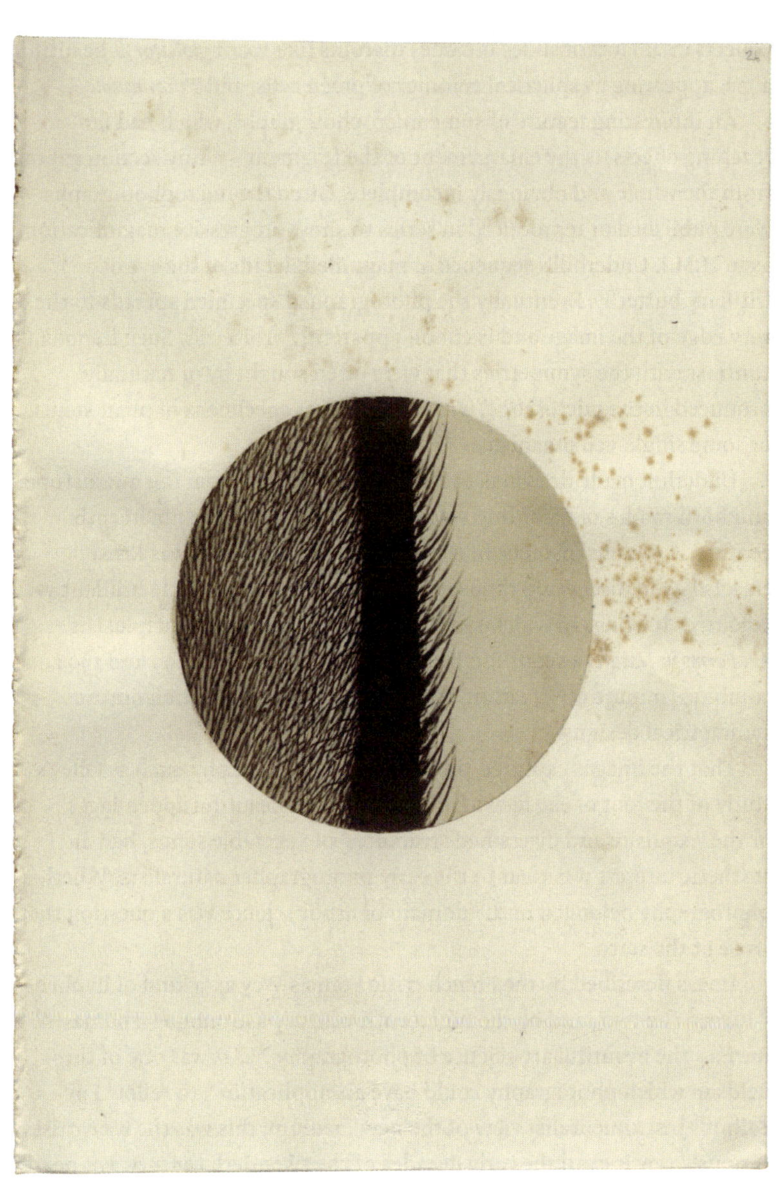

William Henry Olley
Membrane on the wing of a fly
23.3 × 16.2 cm | 9⅛ × 6⅜ in
Vintage print from *The Wonders of the Microscope*, 1861

collection of lantern slides includes diatoms like *Volvox globator*, a beautiful algae appearing as spherical colonies of green cells, and *Triceratium*.

An interesting feature of some microphotographs, which had far-reaching effects, is the enlargement of the fragment – a tiny section cut off from the whole and obviously incomplete. Often the microphotographs were published or reproduced in series to show progressive magnification, as in H.M.J. Underhill's sequence of magnified details of the eye of a fritillary butterfly. Eventually the photographed specimen spreads to the very edge of the image and is cut off apparently arbitrarily. Such fragments contrast with the symmetries that were often sought by or naturally produced in the microscope, with the segment specimens of plant stems or some single-cell organisms.

Underhill made drawings as well as photographs from the microscope, and both modes of recording were kept alive through the nineteenth century. A curious instance of the scientist-draughtsman was Ernst Haeckel, who discovered thousands of new species and made brilliantly-coloured drawings in which symmetry was the guiding principle. His *Art Forms in Nature,* a set of 100 prints published between 1899 and 1904, combines minute observation, including microscopic, with fantastic symmetrical designs.

That the images captured through microphotography, such as Olley's study of the foot of the fly with 'its curious and beautiful appendages', or the 'exquisite and diversified structures' of vegetable stems, had an aesthetic interest was clear to the early photographer naturalists. Whether photography belonged in the domain of art or science was a question that arose at the start.

It was described by the French critic Francis Wey as 'a kind of hyphen between the two', and by the nineteenth-century astronomer Thomas W. Burr as 'the beautiful art-science of photography'.[11] Art was one of the fields in which photography could have an 'application', to follow Fox Talbot's instrumentalist view of the new medium; this was the way artists variously saw it until the early decades of the twentieth century. For nearly 100 years painters were interested in photography only in so far as it could support or supplement painting as an *aide-mémoire* or a handy shortcut as

11 Thomas, 'The Search for Pattern', in Thomas, *op. cit.*, p.76.

in the old days of the camera obscura, while photographers, on the other hand, tried to imitate painting.

INSTRUMENTS OF NEW VISION

> There's something in the air called objectivity
> There's something in the air like electricity...' [12]

Modern photography emerged during the 'glorious technomania of the 1920s'.[13] Its most articulate spokesperson, László Moholy-Nagy, argued that photography was more than just a means of reproduction; it was revolutionising vision, although artists had been slow to recognise that something optically new had entered the world and changed the way we understood it. The post-First World War avant garde now embraced the camera as the instrument of a newly objective vision whose antecedents lay more in science than in photography's attempts to ape Impressionist or academic painting. Utopian as the belief in a new form of expression appropriate to a modern, technological, democratic society may have been, the photographic and filmic experiments of the 1920s and early 1930s, including close-up, revolutionised and have continued to influence artistic practice.

Two events in the mid-1920s were to define and name the new trend. In 1925 Moholy-Nagy published his hugely influential Bauhaus book *Malerei Fotografie Film* (Painting Photography Film), which was effectively a manifesto of the new vision. In 1923 an exhibition of paintings at the Kunsthalle Mannheim had introduced the term *Neue Sachlichkeit* (New Objectivity), to describe the work of artists who had 'remained unswervingly faithful to positive, palpable reality' or had returned to it.[14] (The exhibition included the cool, leftist post-Dada works of George Grosz

12 Lyrics from the theme song from Schiffer-Spoliansky revue *Es Liegt in der Luft* (1928), from John Willett, *Art and Politics in the Weimar Period: The New Sobriety, 1917–1933*, Thames & Hudson, London, 1978, p.111. See also Herbert Molderings, 'The Modernist Cause: New Vision and New Objectivity 1919–1945', in Herbert Molderings et al., *Collection Photographs*, Steidl/Centre Pompidou, Paris, 2007.

13 László Moholy-Nagy, 'The Contribution of the Arts to Social Reconstruction' (1943), in Richard Kostelanetz (ed), *Moholy-Nagy*, Praeger, New York, NY, 1970, p.21.

and Otto Dix, the neo-classicism of Picasso and the magical realism indebted to Italian metaphysical artists like Giorgio de Chirico.) The term 'New Objectivity' swiftly spread beyond its initial application to an object-based art to encompass a technological and objective approach to art, architecture, photography, film and design that valued the modern, utilitarian, documentary and non-sentimental over self-expression.

Moholy-Nagy's *Painting Photography Film* succinctly argued the case for the new vision and clearly demonstrated the tenor of the new photography and its complete break with pictorialist 'art' photography. The illustrations include scientific photographs (microphotography and X-rays), photograms, photojournalism, trick photographs, long exposures, advertisements, high-angled viewpoints, film strips, photomontages and close-ups. The range is exhilarating and powerfully demonstrates Moholy-Nagy's argument that the 'camera has offered us amazing possibilities which we are only just beginning to exploit. The visual image has been expanded and even the modern lens is no longer tied to the narrow limits of our eye.'[15]

Close-up as 'intensified seeing', in the form of microphotography, was one of 'Eight Varieties of Photographic Vision' defined by Moholy-Nagy.[16] Its scientific origins were important in a context that valued function and documentation above art, but equally significant was the emphasis on the photographic as a new means in its own right, to be experimented with and explored, and here the close-up was to appear in other and more ambiguous forms. It was in some ways the very soul of objective vision; the 'real' beyond the defective human gaze, but also mutated either towards the unrecognisable, the defamiliarised and abstracted (what is it?) or invited metaphorical or symbolic connections (what does it looks like?). Close-up was, in many ways, symptomatic of the modernist split, balanced between pure photography and representation.

In *Painting Photography Film* Moholy-Nagy redefined 'optical creation',

14 Circular letter from G.F. Hartlaub, Director of the Kunsthalle Mannheim, 18 May 1923, quoted in Fritz Schmalenbach, 'The term Neue Sachlichkeit', *The Art Bulletin*, vol.22, no.3, 1940, p.161.

15 Moholy-Nagy, *Painting Photography Film*, Bauhaus Books 8, Munich, 1925; 2nd edition, 1927: English edition published by Lund Humphries, London, 1969, p.7. The English edition replicated the typography and layout of the original as closely as possible.

16 Moholy-Nagy, 'A New Instrument of Vision' (1932), in Kostelanetz, *op. cit.*, p.52.

giving photography an independent identity equal to painting and other forms of visual expression. The technical means of photography had 'split the hitherto indivisible field of optical expression' and opened up ways of seeing no longer subject to traditional dependence on the eye.[17] *Painting Photography Film* was a manifesto for the avant garde, sidelining the issue of art altogether in the light of the new vision and a modern role for photography. Moholy-Nagy's insistence on the technical potential of film and photography contrasts interestingly with a passage from a pre-war manifesto by the Futurist Filippo Tommaso Marinetti. 'Destruction of Syntax – Imagination Without Strings – Words-in-Freedom' (1913) is a passionate argument for new forms of expression responsive to the decisive change in our psyches 'brought about by the great discoveries of science' – telegraph, telephone, phonograph, train, bicycle, motorcycle, automobile, ocean liner, dirigible, aeroplane, cinema, the great newspaper ('synthesis of a day in the world's life'). Marinetti demands the suppression of the 'obsessive *I*' of the poets and of the tendency to humanise nature. Instead:

> We should express the infinite smallness that surrounds us, the imperceptible, the invisible, the agitation of atoms, the Brownian movements, all the passionate hypotheses and all the domains explored by the high-powered microscope. To explain: I want to introduce the infinite molecular life into poetry not as a scientific document but as an intuitive element. It should mix, in the work of art, with the infinitely great spectacles and dramas, because this fusion constitutes the integral synthesis of life.[18]

Both the scientific revelations of the microscope and the principle of montage – expressed here as the mix of the 'infinitely small' and the 'infinitely great' – are vividly evoked. Although Marinetti is thinking of language, and poetry, his belief in the 'complete renewal of human sensibility', and the examples he gives of those inventions that have

17 Moholy-Nagy, *Painting Photography Film*, *op. cit.*, p.8.
18 Filippo Tommaso Marinetti, 'Destruction of Syntax – Imagination Without Strings – Words-in-Freedom' (1913), in Umbro Apollonio (ed), *Futurist Manifestos*, Thames & Hudson, London, 1973, p.100.

decisively changed it, invite a visual as much as a linguistic revolution. But the medium best able visually to realise Marinetti's ideas – photography – is lacking and cinema is mentioned only as a thing to be experienced rather than as a potential form of expression in itself. Futurist rhetoric electrified its audience and heralded modernity but Futurist artists largely remained stuck in the traditional media.

The camera, Moholy-Nagy argued, had on the whole hitherto been used only in a secondary capacity. There had been a failure to recognise that it can, '*make visible* existences which cannot be perceived or taken in by our optical instrument, the eye; *i.e. the photographic camera can either complete or supplement our optical instrument, the eye.*'[19]

This principle had 'been applied in a few scientific experiments', such as the study of movement and with the microscopic photographs produced in zoology, botany and mineralogy. But it was the opposite of a mode of seeing conditioned by pictorial conventions such as perspective, which is centred in the human eye and subject to rational and conceptual adjustment. The camera, by contrast, 'reproduces the optically true distortions, deformations and foreshortenings etc.'[20]

The idea that by accessing realities hidden to the naked eye, photography had analogies with the psychoanalytical concept of the unconscious, emerged in the early-twentieth century and was later neatly formulated in 1931 by the German cultural critic Walter Benjamin as an 'optical unconscious': 'For it is another nature that speaks to the camera than to the eye: other in the sense that a space informed by human consciousness gives way to a space informed by the unconscious... Photography, with its devices of slow motion and enlargement, reveals the secret. It is through photography that we first discover the existence of this optical unconscious.'[21]

The implication is already there in André Breton's 1921 preface to an exhibition of Max Ernst's Dada collages and overpaintings: 'The invention of photography has dealt a mortal blow to the old modes of expression, in painting as well as in poetry, where automatic writing, which appeared

19 Moholy-Nagy, *Painting Photography Film*, *op. cit.*, p.28.
20 *Ibid.*
21 Walter Benjamin, 'A Small History of Photography', in Walter Benjamin, *One-Way Street*, Verso, London, 1997, p.243.

at the end of the nineteenth century, is a true photography of thought.'[22] Breton brought both photography and film into his discussion: slow- and fast-motion cameras will accustom us to 'seeing oaks spring up and antelopes floating through the air', and soon 'the expression "as far as the eye can see" will seem to us devoid of meaning, that is we shall perceive the passage from birth to death without as much as blinking and we shall observe infinite variations.'[23] Dalí suggests even this is inadequate recognition of the camera's 'hidden optics': 'Photographic imagination, your brain waves are faster and more agile than the murky processes of the subconscious!'[24]

Crucially, there was no prescriptive aesthetic in *Painting Photography Film*. True to the Constructivist approach in which he was formed, Moholy-Nagy advocated the exploration of materials and technologies: pure colour composition in painting, light displays using a reflector and, in photography, representation – which was not identical with nature. Photography has 'amazing possibilities' which should be handled 'not traditionally, but experimentally'.[25] X-ray was probably a more significant scientific inspiration than microphotography for Moholy-Nagy himself: 'Penetration of the body with light is one of the greatest visual experiences',[26] and Moholy-Nagy related it to his experiments in cameraless photography, reproducing examples of each side by side in *Painting Photography Film*. The photogram was one way of experimenting with light, and these light-compositions were a kind of 'abstract seeing', capturing on light-sensitive paper the most delicate tonal gradations.

The close-ups favoured by the new photography were magnified images of fragments of things, rather than the microscopic, and tend to reveal the strangeness of the everyday, rather than the literally invisible of the natural world revealed through the microscope. *Painting Photography Film* included close-ups of plants and creatures, including a horrific head louse and the eye of a marabou on which Moholy-Nagy had commented:

22 André Breton, 'Max Ernst' (1921), in *Max Ernst, Beyond Painting and Other Writings By the Artist and His Friends*, Wittenborn, Schultz Inc., New York, NY, 1948, p.177.

23 *Ibid.*

24 Dalí, 'Photography: Pure Creation of the Mind', *L'Amic de les Arts*, no.18, September 1927. Reprinted in Dalí, *Oui: The Paranoid-Critical Revolution*, trans. Yvonne Shafir, Exact Change, Boston, MA, 1998, p.13.

25 Moholy-Nagy, *Painting Photography Film*, *op. cit.*, p.7.

26 *Ibid.*, p.69.

‘There is extraordinary concentration in a singled out detail.’ More redolent of the jazz age and the mechanical reproduction of music is the magnified detail of a gramophone record with the caption ‘Heightened reality of an every-day object’.

Photo-Eye (1929) – a collection of ‘76 photos of our time’ selected by Franz Roh and Jan Tschichold, with an important essay by Roh – shared the aesthetic of *Painting Photography Film*. Both publications paired images to emphasise the virtuosity of the ‘new optic’. There are startling similarities between things of vastly different sizes: the light catching the ridges of the gramophone record and lines of headlights snaking through a street at night, captured through long exposure in *Painting Photography Film*; or extreme contrasts: such as a pair of lips denatured through close-up, beside a crowd shot from above, neither ‘human’ in scale, in *Photo-Eye*. In the pages of *Painting Photography Film* and *Photo-Eye*, magnified ball bearings, camshafts and gear wheels jostle gigantic details of plants, cells, crustaceans, etc. One of the most brilliant of the ‘new photographers’, Albert Renger-Patzsch, best known for his industrial and mechanical imagery, also worked with microscopy. His *Heterotrichum macrodum* (c.1922–23) is reproduced in *Photo-Eye* beside a microphotograph of crystals, whose hard-edged asymmetry contrasts with the dynamic symmetries of the leaf forms.

One of the few early-twentieth-century photographers to explore microphotography further was Laure Albin Guillot. She based her most famous works on the microscopic slide preparations made by her husband, who was a doctor and naturalist, but the focus of interest in her work has shifted from wonder at the revelations of the natural world invisible to the human eye, as epitomised by Olley, to the study of form and structure for their own sake and as potential sources for art and design. Although their scientific credentials are impeccable, Albin Guillot’s microphotographs speak to the new arena of abstract art, to the Abstraction-Création group for example, but were also deployed for decorative purposes. In 1931 she published 20 of them under the title *Micrographie décorative* with a preface by Paul Léon, the Director General of the Beaux-Arts, who stresses a natural, as opposed to theoretical or constructed order: 'This original research invites the artist henceforth to see further than his own sight. He will wonder at the order that controls the tiniest elements. But there is no geometry, symmetry, mechanism.'[27]

Whale-bone cartilage, a drop of lemon juice, a section of a barley root, cow urine – all produce an astonishing variety of forms as different from each other as they are from their material originals.

Albin Guillot had already turned her abstract images to practical ends. Articles in *Arts et Métiers Graphiques* and in *Vu* in 1929 celebrated the transformation of the detail of a peacock's feather into a fabric design, and a microscopic organism belonging to the radiolarium species into a gold and dark brown book cover. The designs were especially popular in a sub-branch of luxury book production – endpapers.[28] Later commentators on Albin Guillot have found the use of her microphotographs as decoration problematic and incompatible with their status with art: 'To wish to reduce her micrographs to decorative images close to endpapers would be a grave error. Laure Albin Guillot seeks to enlarge our vision of the world in penetrating this microscopic world'.[29]

From this point of view the forms should be seen as pure abstract art for its own sake. Her dislike of the title *Micrographie décorative,* imposed by her publishers, rather than her preferred *Micrographie,* is quoted as evidence, and an analogy is drawn with Renger-Patzsch, whose own title for an album of photographs, *Things,* was changed by the publishers to *The World is Beautiful.* The relationship between design and pure art, the problem of how abstract art is to be seen and the fear of its contamination by the simply decorative, goes back to abstract art's beginnings, but does not seem to have been a concern for Albin Guillot herself.

The question of visual analogy and the need to control it in order to prevent simple resemblance creeping in to abstraction by the back door was debated at the time but was in a sense courted by photographers like Albin Guillot. The tendency to read known phenomena into an unknown

27 Paul Léon, Preface, in Laure Albin Guillot, *Micrographie décorative*, Paris, 1931 (edition of 305).

28 Bertrand Guégan, 'Notes sur l'histoire et la fabrication des papiers de garde', *Arts et Métiers Graphiques*, no.10, 15 March 1929, pp.633–36.

29 Christian Bouquerer, *Laure Albin Guillot ou la volonté d'art*, exhibition catalogue, Marval, Paris, 1996, p.9.

image, to misrepresent the unfamiliar, is revelled in by Henri Tracol in 'Le Microscope au service de la Décoration'.[30] The writer recounts a visit to Albin Guillot's studio, where he is initiated into the world of the microscope – the trickery of scale confuses the eye so that the radiating streets of Paris's Place de l'Étoile turn out to be an organism from the radiolarium species, and vast mountains that would astound a geographer are but crystals. A textile design based on a microphotograph of fish skin looks like flowers and sparkling jewels. To point out the value of the extension of scientific discoveries and the natural world into the fabric of our daily lives Tracol describes a curious therapeutic use of design based on microphotography. Albin Guillot was asked by an insomniac to create curtain hangings for his bedroom; after long research in her photographic archives she came up with a design based on the trichomonas organism, which apparently did the trick. But her microphotographs were certainly not solely intended for design purposes. They are extraordinary objects in their own right, products of the highest quality made according to some of the most complex and advanced photographic printing techniques of the period, whose multiple layering and tinted ground give a rich metallic effect.[31]

Like Albin Guillot, the naturalist and photographer Karl Blossfeldt – subsequently closely identified with the new photography – had his origins in nineteenth-century scientific photography and its potential uses within art and design, in his case quite directly pedagogical. From 1898 Blossfeldt taught 'Modelling from Plants' in relative obscurity at the Academy of the Royal Museum of Arts and Crafts in Berlin and started taking photographs of botanical samples to assist the study of basic design in natural forms. Over the next 31 years he amassed around 6,000 close-up images of plants, 'always utilising the same plate camera, a plain, flat background and a minimal number of variations in lighting'.[32] Fragments of plants and flowers, panicles, seeds, stems, shoots and

30 Henri Tracol, 'Le microscope au service de la décoration', *Vu*, no.52, Paris, 13 March 1929, p.197.
31 The 20 plates in *Micrographie décorative* were produced by a slightly simpler technique than the 'Fresson' charcoal ground used for her single plates, but are still magnificent objects.

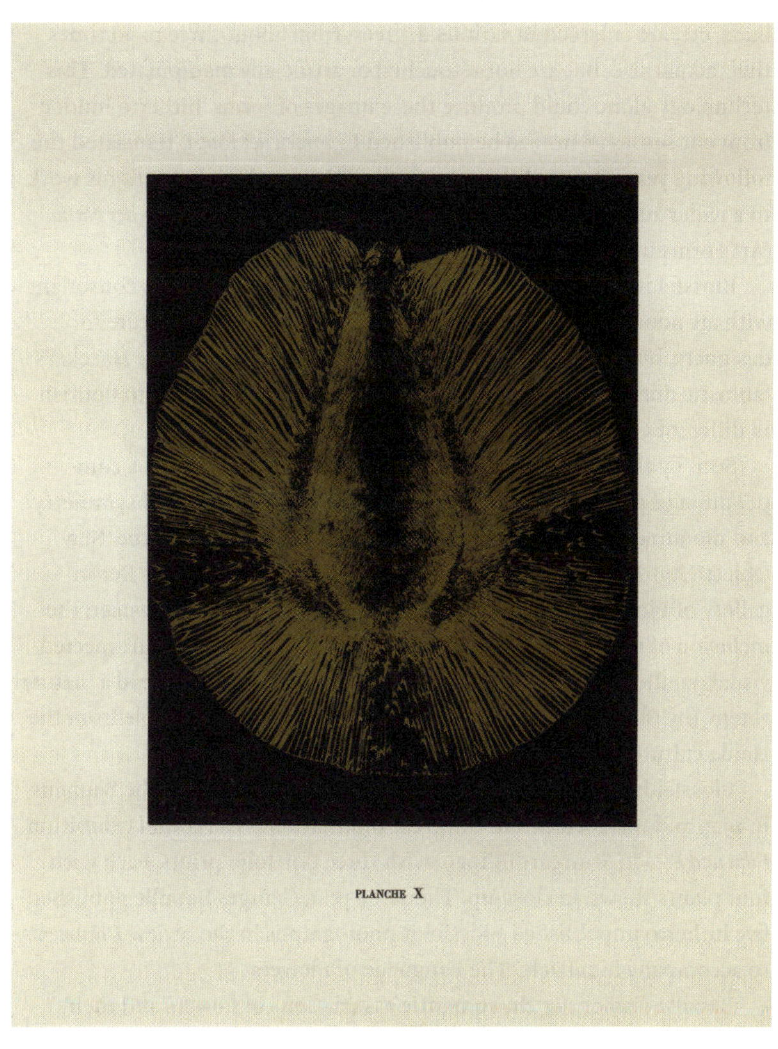

Laure Albin-Guillot
Graine (Seed)
Photogravure in gold ink on black and gold paper
Overall: 43.2 × 35.6 cm | 17⅛ × 14⅛ in
Plate X from *Micrographie décorative*, 1931

buds, etc. are enlarged in various degrees, from about three to 30 times their actual size, but are not retouched or artificially manipulated. This technology alone could produce these images of forms 'hitherto hidden from our senses'.[33] In 1928 he published *Urformen der Kunst,* translated the following year into English as *Art Forms in Nature,* which brought his work to a wider audience. Parallels with Ernst Haeckel's *Kunstformen der Natur* (Art Forms in Nature, 1899–1904), are intriguing.

Blossfeldt's original purpose can, like Haeckel's, be seen as consonant with art nouveau, to provide sources and inspiration from nature for designers, but the resulting close-up photographs have, unlike Haeckel's fantastic drawings, turned out to have a life of their own and to flourish in different contexts.

Seen by the gallery owner and collector Karl Nierendorf as a compendium of past styles, from Rococo to Gothic, their stripped symmetry and monumental impersonality also aligned Blossfeldt with the 'New Objectivity'. In 1926 Nierendorf organised an exhibition in his Berlin gallery of Blossfeldt's photographs entitled *Exotics, Cacti and Janthur*; the inclusion of sculptures from Africa and New Guinea invited unexpected visual parallels, picked up by the magazine *UHU*.[34] In one spread a 'natural totem' (by Blossfeldt) is compared with a 'primitive' totem pole from the Haida culture of the North-West coast of Canada.

Blossfeldt's fame spread and he was invited to exhibit at the Bauhaus in 1929 and was included in the great International Werkbund exhibition *Film und Foto* in Stuttgart in 1929, with three portfolio prints, each with four plants shown in close-up. The same year, Georges Bataille published five hitherto unpublished Blossfeldt photographs in the review *Documents,* to accompany his article 'The Language of Flowers'.[35]

Bataille dismantles the romantic associations of flowers and their

32 Ian Walker, 'Blossfeldt and Surrealism', *Photoresearcher*, vol.11, April 2008, p.29.

33 Karl Nierendorf, 'Introduction to Blossfeldt', in Karl Blossfeldt, *Art Forms in Nature*, London, 1929. Blossfeldt's *Urformen der Kunst* (1928) was also translated into Swedish and French (as *La Plante*).

34 *Urformen der Kunst: aus Pflanzenreich und Fremden Welten*, Karl Blossfeldt Archiv Züplich, 2004. Richard Janthur was an artist represented by Nierendorf who painted exotic jungle scenes.

35 Georges Bataille, 'Le langage des fleurs', *Documents*, no.3, Paris, June 1929, pp.160–68. Reprinted in Allan Stoekl (ed), *Georges Bataille Visions of Excess: Selected Writings, 1927–1939*, trans. Allan Stoekl, University of Minnesota Press, Minneapolis, MN, 1985, p.10.

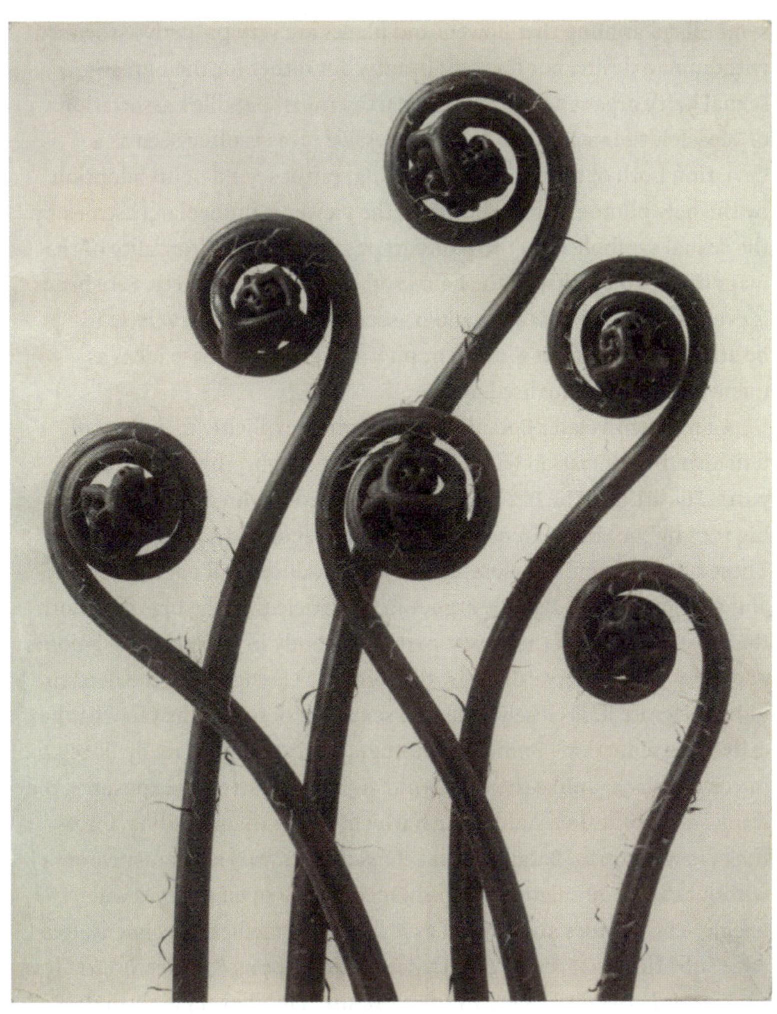

Karl Blossfeldt
Urformen der Kunst: Adiantum pedatum (American Maidenhair Fern. Young rolled-up fronds enlarged 8 times), c.1928
Gelatin silver print
29.5 × 23.6 cm | 11⅝ × 9$\frac{5}{16}$ in

symbolism, arguing that flowers and plants are very properly associated with human desire, not for their beauty, but rather for their grossly sexual hairy organs and disgusting earthy roots. Bataille's association of Blossfeldt's images with these aggressive ideas is often seen as a deviation both of the naturalist's original purpose and of his adoption by the new photographers; however, the viewer is immediately struck by the sexual symbolism of the photographs, by the erect frontality of the magnified plant parts, by the hairy, soft or wrinkled surfaces. Fetishism is everywhere, and Bataille could be seen not so much perversely to be attaching Blossfeldt's innocent photographs to his base ideas as uncovering their sexualised optic.

A few months later Bataille returned more explicitly to an idea of fetishism in association with close-up photographs, this time of body parts. His article 'The Big Toe' is accompanied by three photographs of big toes by the young French photographer Jacques-André Boiffard.[36] These hugely magnified close-ups were reproduced full page to dramatic and repellent effect. Bataille argues in his article that the big toe is both the most human and the lowest part of the body in every sense – ignoble and dirty. The anxiety caused by the foot, the classic fetish, the need to hide or elevate it, is closely linked to sexual anxiety and thus to what he calls 'base seduction'. Boiffard's photographs isolate the cruelly-lit big toe in velvety black; unlike the clear white light of Blossfeldt's exposures, they *écarquillent les yeux* in a sudden flash which, rather than blinding, forces the eyes wide open. Bataille's term *écarquiller (les yeux)* is a transitive verb without exact equivalent in English, meaning to open the eyes wide, to goggle. The big toes are labelled as if they were medical specimens: two were subtitled as *Masculine Subject, Aged 30* and one as *Feminine Subject, Aged 24*. Certainly the pitiless eye of the close-up magnifies their 'secondary deformations' such as the ill-cut and unhealthy nails. But, Bataille argues, the big toe is not inherently monstrous like the interior of the

36 Bataille, 'Le gros orteil', *Documents*, no.6, Paris, November 1929. Reprinted in Stoekl, *op. cit.*, p.20. Boiffard had interrupted his medical studies to learn photography with Man Ray; he was a member of the Communist Party and later joined the photo-cinéma section of the Association of Revolutionary Writers and Artists, exhibiting widely with fellow leftist photographers like Germaine Krull and Eli Lotar. Although he continued to be involved marginally in films, he returned to the medical profession in 1935 and became a radiologist.

mouth; hence its burlesque as well as its sacrilegious and basely seductive character is captured so accurately by Boiffard's photographs.

By contrast with Boiffard's photographs of the big toe or of the human mouth, which remain recognisable parts of the human body even if transformed through close-up, the stills from natural history films by Jean Painlevé and Eli Lotar, which were also reproduced in *Documents*, are visual puzzles. They are taken from Painlevé and Lotar's film *Crabs and Shrimps* of 1929, one of the first of Painlevé's films of marine life, made with a specially adapted underwater camera. In the film the gradual magnification of the shrimp's head anchors the identity of the image for the viewer, at least conceptually. But in the stills of the hugely magnified shrimp's head, the absence of any scale makes the reading of the image problematic and intriguing. There is an interesting difference between the still of the shrimp's head reproduced in *Documents* and the close-up, also of a shrimp's head, that was produced as a photographic print. In the former, both substance and structure are unclear, although there seems to be an eye in the upper-right corner. It falls naturally into association with Bataille's notion of the *informe,* or 'formless', a term that he mobilised in one of his 'Critical Dictionary' entries in *Documents* as a mocking tool in his challenge to philosophy: 'for academics to be happy, the universe would have to take on form. The whole of philosophy has no other goal: to provide a frock coat for what is, a mathematical frock coat. On the other hand, affirming that the universe resembles nothing and is only formless amounts to saying that the universe is something like a spider or spit.'[37] For the philosophers and scholars whose job it would be to explain and interpret the world, things need to be defined and categorised. 'Formless' is an adjective that has the job of declassifying, of suborning identity; it 'serves to bring things down in the world, generally requiring that each thing have its form. What it designates has no rights in any sense and gets itself squashed everywhere, like a spider or a worm.'[38] A number of photographs in *Documents* are touched by Bataille's anti-idealist notion of the formless. The still of the shrimp's head, like the close-up of the spider, also by Painlevé and Lotar (whose slaughterhouse photographs

37 Bataille, 'Informe', *Documents*, no.7, Paris, December 1929, p.382.
38 *Ibid.*

were reproduced in the same issue of *Documents* as the shrimp), resembles nothing but is indeed 'something'. Close-up images like these by Painlevé and Lotar relate to debates at the time about abstraction in art as well as to the long tradition of microphotography. As records, or imprints, of palpable things they bring a different dimension to abstract, or 'concrete', art – a term which more accurately captures the idea of the work that exists in its own right rather than as an imitation of or abstraction from something else; the close-ups are 'concrete' but unrecognisable facts.

The other photograph of the *Enlargement of the head of a shrimp* (1930) contrasts visually with these images of the 'formless'. It shows a section of the shrimp's feeler, a delicate spine form crossing the frame diagonally, with regular spikes and thin fern-like hairs. The photograph seems to emphasise geometry, admittedly of a picturesque kind, rather than the shapelessness of spit, but in fact is no more easily identifiable than the shrimp head film still. Here, furthermore, the destruction of scale so that one has no idea what actual size the object photographed is – at least if one ignores or is not told the degree of magnification – frustrates rather than invites the illusion of resemblances. Whereas startling likenesses were foregrounded in Blossfeldt's photographs (plants that look like skyscrapers, primitive sculptures or phalluses) and Albin Guillot's microphotographs of crystals were compared to mountains, here the spiky bone sweeping upwards and the hint of spotted skin are clearly only a fraction of the whole, and although, as with Olley's butterfly wings or fly's leg, the eye is invited to marvel at the structures revealed, invisible to the naked eye, the emphasis is rather on the potentially gigantic creature of which it is part. Fragmentary as the close-up of the *Enlargement of the head of a shrimp* is, it invites us to imagine what the thing as a whole would look like on this scale. Jacques Baron's 'Critical Dictionary' entry on 'Shell-fish' in *Documents* quoted 'a painter friend of mine' as saying that '"if a grasshopper were the size of a lion it would be the most beautiful animal in the world". How true that would be of a giant crayfish, a crab enormous as a house, and a shrimp as tall as a tree!'[39]

39 Jacques Baron, 'Crustacés', *Documents*, no.6, Paris, November 1929, p.332.

> The close-up is the soul of the cinema.[40]

The use of close-up reached a climax in silent film of the 1920s at the same moment as avant-garde artists began to exploit it in photography. The journal *Close Up* (1927–33) set out to discuss film in a spirit similar to that of Moholy-Nagy, in the sense that it was committed to it as both a technology and an epistemology whose potential was still wide open. Its choice of title indicates the critical role of close-up in, as Anne Friedberg argues:

> a wholly new visual rhetoric. To the French film-maker and theorist Jean Epstein, the close-up was an essential component of *photogénie* – it limited and directed attention, indicated emotion, magnified aesthetic import. To the Hungarian scenarist and director Béla Balázs, the close-up produced revelations of a new emotional and dramatic magnitude in showing the 'microphysiognomy' of the human face. To Walter Benjamin, the close-up supplied a new visual order, rendering 'entirely new structural formations of the subject'. Soviet film-maker and theorist Sergei Eisenstein appropriated the film technique of the close-up and deployed it as a model for a certain kind of writing about film through a 'prism of firm analysis'. The close-up provided a particularly modern optic, a new revelatory epistemology. As the title for a film journal, *Close Up* implied the conflation of technical specificity with philosophical endeavour.[41]

The journal, which Eisenstein described as 'the closest up to what cinema should be',[42] announced itself as 'the only magazine dedicated to films as art' and paid close attention as much to what was coming out of Paris and Surrealism as to Russian and German cinema. Man Ray's 1926 film

40 Epstein, 'Grossissement', *Promenoirs*, nos.1/2, February/March 1921. Reprinted in Epstein, *Ecrits sur le cinéma: Volume 1*, Seghers, Paris, 1974, p.93.

41 Anne Friedberg, 'Introduction: Reading Close Up, 1927–1933', in James Donald, Anne Friedberg, Laura Marcus (eds), *Close Up 1927–1933: Cinema and Modernism*, Princeton University Press, Princeton, NJ, 1998, p.2.

42 Sergei Eisenstein, 'Tribute to K. MacPherson (Editor)', *Close Up*, vol.IV, no.1, January 1929.

Emak-Bakia (the title taken from an old Basque expression meaning 'don't bother me') is described in the second issue of *Close Up* in 1927 as 'a series of fragments, a cinepoem with a certain optical sequence makes up a whole that still remains a fragment'.[43]

Un Chien andalou was part of the last great flowering of silent cinema before the talkies changed it forever. It scandalised, intrigued and baffled its audiences in 1929 but Dalí repudiated any connection between the film and avant-garde cinema: 'Our film, created without any aesthetic intention whatsoever, has nothing to do with any of the cinematic attempts of what is called *pure cinema*... It is about simple notation, the observation of facts.'[44] Nonetheless, *Un Chien andalou* does share techniques with other experimental filmmakers, though often subverting and exaggerating them. Moholy-Nagy's sketch for a film, *Dynamic of the Metropolis*, spells out these techniques very clearly, not least the effect intended from the close-up. As with Walter Ruttmann's *Berlin: Symphony of a Metropolis* (1927) or the films of Dziga Vertov and Eisenstein, close-up is used by Moholy-Nagy in his scenario to punctuate scenes of the city, together with other devices such as split screen, running the film backwards, slow motion and double exposure. The *Dynamic of the Metropolis* sketch includes repeated close-ups of a lion's head whose 'frequent and unexpected appearance... is meant to cause uneasiness and oppression.'[45] The lion's head is rapidly intercut with a theatre audience, police with rubber truncheons in the Potsdamer Platz and a close-up of a rubber truncheon – 'and STILL THE HEAD comes!' 'The lion's head gets bigger and bigger until at last the vast jaws fill the screen.' The rapid shift of scale enforces a Futurist-like shift of perception, from the individual-centred to the simultaneous, multifocal, dynamic and impersonal. Although Buñuel used many of the same devices in *Un Chien andalou*, the sequence of the gradual magnification of the Death's Head Hawk Moth seems to draw less from urban avant-garde filmmakers and more directly from popular scientific films of the time, or sequences of microphotographs of creatures or plant sections common in the nineteenth century. The progressive enlargement of the markings

43 Marc Allégret, *Close Up*, no.2, 1927, p.40.
44 Dalí, 'Un Chien andalou', *Mirador*, no.39, Barcelona, October 1929. Reprinted in Dalí, *op. cit.*, p.108.
45 Moholy-Nagy, *Painting Photography Film*, *op. cit.*, p.135.

builds up to a climax when we recognise a skull. Like the film as a whole, the rhythm of this sequence – the stalking, the climax, and the analogy between moth markings and a man's head – is somewhere between a natural history documentary and a dream. The Death's Head Hawk Moth sequence is one of several in which close-up combines with montage to create the 'image' in the Surrealist sense, 'the bringing together of two distant realities' and striking a spark from their contact as Breton described it.[46] Likenesses, comparisons, contrasts, fake resemblances, stretch the two terms of the metaphor; in the case of the most famous image – the shocking slitting of the woman's eye at the start of the film – the running comparison between eye and moon collapses into a brutal fact. The dissected eye spills out in a hugely magnified gooey mass, wholly un-moonlike, more like a nightmare of a biology demonstration.

Notable in Buñuel and Dalí's shooting script for *Un Chien andalou* are the directions about the expressions on the characters' faces: terror, astonishment, distress, disdain, lust. For filmmakers like Balázs, close-up was properly used to express human drama, scrutinising through the lens the manifestations of emotion on the human physiognomy. He was scornful of precisely those qualities that endeared the close-up to Buñuel and Dalí: 'Having discovered the soul of things in the close-up, the silent film undeniably overrated their importance and sometimes succumbed to the temptation of showing "the hidden little life" as an end in itself, divorced from human destinies; it strayed away from the dramatic plot and presented the "poetry of things" instead of human beings.'[47]

Un Chien andalou lingers on close-ups of things, in metaphorical montages like the head/sea urchin/underarm hair sequence, granting them the kind of attention Balázs believes properly belongs to the human face. Balancing always on the edge between horror and hilarity, there are joke close-ups like the sudden appearance of a violently agitated cocktail shaker to stand for the ringing of a doorbell. The expressions on the faces of the characters in *Un Chien andalou* are so emphatic as to be almost parodic; they certainly don't attempt the nuances of expression described by Balázs.

46 Breton, 'Max Ernst', *op. cit.*, p.177.

47 Béla Balázs, 'The Close-up', in *Theory of the Film* (English edition), Dennis Dobson, London, 1952. Reprinted in Gerald Mast and Marshall Cohen (eds), *Film Theory and Criticism: Introductory Reading*, Oxford University Press, New York, NY, 1974, p.187.

Little things, little things, little things, etc.[48]

The idea of close-up infiltrates Dalí's writings of all kinds in the late 1920s. Although influenced by Moholy-Nagy's *Painting Photography Film,* his texts on film and photography are also some of the most original of the period and show how exaggerated is the division historically enforced between Surrealism and 'New Objectivity'. Close-up for Dalí is both photographic fact – the 'anaesthetic gaze of the naked, lashless eye of Zeiss' – and stimulus for the imagination.[49] Dalí filched the *Eye of a marabou* from *Painting Photography Film* and reproduced it in the Catalan magazine *L'Amic de les Arts,* entitling it instead *Eye of an elephant.*[50] What attracted him, rather than the discovery of details of texture or shape revealed by the close-up, was the tiny image of the photographer reflected in the pupil. Although the following is not a description of this precise example it celebrates a similar effect: 'In a wide and limpid cow's eye, we see a minuscule post-machinist landscape, deformed in the spherical sense, exact to the very details of the sky where minuscule and luminous clouds are floating by.'[51]

The visual pleasure celebrated by Moholy-Nagy in the 'heightened reality' of the magnified detail differs sharply from Dalí's interest in the imaginative potential of the photographic fact, hitherto hidden or unconscious. The endless unfolding of new worlds through progressive magnification of little things, which had been the realm of the microscope and microphotography, becomes for Dalí the source of inventions. His first published text, 'Saint Sebastian' (1927), centres on a magnifying glass, which is 'concave, convex and flat at the same time' and effectively indicates the variable conditions of objective vision and aesthetic sensibility. 'Seeing' through the magnifying glass, the enlarged detail opens not onto the 'heightened reality' of the thing in itself but onto 'a succession of clear spectacles… on the bridge of a white steamer, a girl

48 Dalí, 'Poem of little things', *L'Amic de les Arts*, no.27, 31 August 1928. Reprinted in Dalí, *op. cit.*, p.55.

49 Dalí, 'Photography: Pure Creation of the Mind', *L'Amic de les Arts*, no.18, 30 September 1927. Reprinted in Dalí, *op. cit.*, p.13.

50 Dalí, *L'Amic de les Arts*, no.31, 31 March 1929, p.4.

51 Dalí, *op. cit.*, p.13.

without breasts was teaching the sailors saturated by the south wind how to dance the black bottom... When my eyes lighted on some detail or other, this detail was engorged as if in a cinematographic close-up shot.'[52]

The close-up thus stands here for the new, objective vision, although deviating from Moholy-Nagy's ideas and already seeded with the paranoiac notion of multiple interpretations or 'reading in'. Dalí was probably drawing on a poem by the eccentric writer Raymond Roussel, *La Vue* (The View, 1904), whose 2,000 lines are 'devoted to a minute photograph of a beach scene set into the lens of a souvenir pen holder', described in fanatical detail.[53] By contrast with these swollen miniatures, like views initially seen through the wrong end of a telescope, Dalí also experimented with a form of documentary recording and the enumeration of facts in his 'Documentaries', written around the time of *Un Chien andalou* in 1929.[54] His method derives from the scientific study of nature: just as naturalists chart out a defined area of vegetation/ground to record the various species within it, Dalí takes a limited area (20 square centimetres of sand in the Jardin du Luxembourg in Paris) and observes, in close-up scrutiny, what is in, passes or drops onto it over a period of five minutes – a kind of simulation of photographic exposure.

In 1933 Brassaï and Dalí collaborated on a series of experiments with the magnification of tiny objects and fragments, which the photographer annotated variously as 'automatic objects photographed with Dalí' and 'large-scale objects'. Brassaï's contact prints include different shots of various objects: paper clips, thimble, fluff, buttons, a shell, smear of toothpaste, rolled ticket. Six of the results were reproduced in the Surrealist journal *Minotaure* under the heading 'Involuntary Sculptures'.[55] In the

52 Dalí, 'Saint Sebastian', *L'Amic de les Arts*, no.16, 31 July 1927. Reprinted in Dalí, *op. cit.*, p.6.

53 See Mark Ford, *Raymond Roussel and the Republic of Dreams*, Faber and Faber, London, 2000, p.83. Ford relates that Vladimir Nabokov bought a similar pen-holder in 1909 'with a tiny peephole of crystal in its ornamental part. One held it quite close to one's eye, screwing up the other, and when one had got rid of the shimmer of one's own lashes, a miraculous photographic view of the bay and the line of cliffs ending in a lighthouse could be seen inside.' Vladimir Nabokov, *The Stories of Vladimir Nabokov*, Alfred A. Knopf, New York, NY, 1995, p.610. Roussel acquired the pen-holder in Biarritz, where his mother had built a house.

54 Dalí, 'Documentary – Paris 1929 – VI', in *La Publicidad*, Barcelona, 26 June 1929. Reprinted in Dalí, *op. cit.*, p.106.

55 'Sculptures involontaires', *Minotaure*, nos.3/4, Paris, 12 December 1933, p.68. No anchor is credited; the index lists 'Sculptures involontaires – XXX'.

collection of Brassaï's entire oeuvre in the Centre Pompidou in Paris, the six or so sheets of contact prints of 'automatic objects' or 'involuntary sculptures' immediately precede the close-ups of Paris Metro art nouveau ironwork and the photographs used by Dalí for his collage *The Phenomenon of Ecstasy* (1933). The 'involuntary sculptures' and *The Phenomenon of Ecstasy* frame Dalí's article in *Minotaure*, 'On the terrifying edible beauty of modern-style architecture', which was illustrated both with Brassaï's Metro photographs and Man Ray's images of Gaudí's modern-style buildings in Barcelona. The sequence of Brassaï's contact sheets suggests that the automatic objects were rather more than a sideline amusement for the two artists while working on the Paris Metro photographs. It's tempting to say that Dalí's essay is framed by repugnance and ecstasy. The six objects photographed in close-up are mostly unrecognisable. They are messy and repellent with captions in a mock documentary medical-psychiatric style, as though analysing symptoms: 'Bus ticket rolled "symmetrically"; very rare form of morphological automatism with evident germs of the stereotype.' The 'involuntary sculptures' chosen for *Minotaure* are ephemeral – toothpaste, soap, a bus ticket, though only one is edible. Blown up, these waste scraps embody the base materialist side of Dalí's notion of 'beyond the sculptural', which is how he describes Gaudí's modern-style architecture: 'Sculpture de tout l'extrasculptural: l'eau, la fumée...' (Sculpture of everything extra-sculptural: water, smoke...).[56] Dalí takes perverse delight in tracing in these scrumpled, torn, gluey and melting bits of matter the forms of Gaudí's modern-style architecture – sophisticated, irrational and anti-functionalist, and encrusted with 'convulsive-undulating' shapes and ecstatic heads. They are emphatically handmade, though automatic, unconscious, anonymous parodies of the artist's gestures.

The 'involuntary sculptures' exist *as* photographs, by virtue of magnification and lighting. Some of the objects cast no shadow, while the shadows in the two lowest photographs indicate that the object is suspended, presumably on glass. On the right is a tightly rolled tube of

56 Dalí, 'De la beauté terrifiante et comestible de l'architecture Modern Style', *Minotaure*, no.3, Paris, 12 December 1933, p.73.

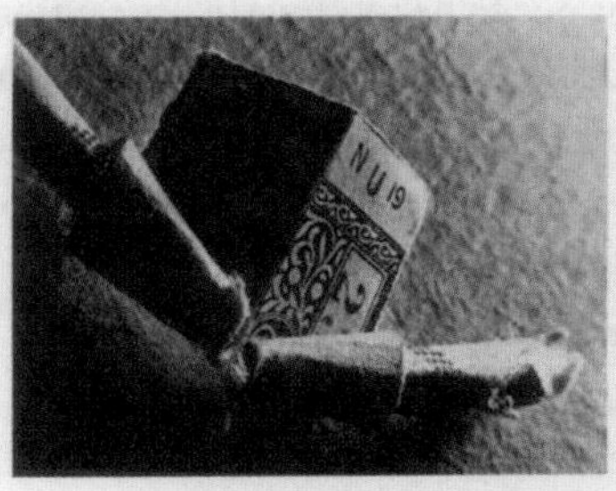

Billet d'autobus roulé "symétriquement", forme très rare d'automatisme morphologique avec germes évidents de stéréotypie.

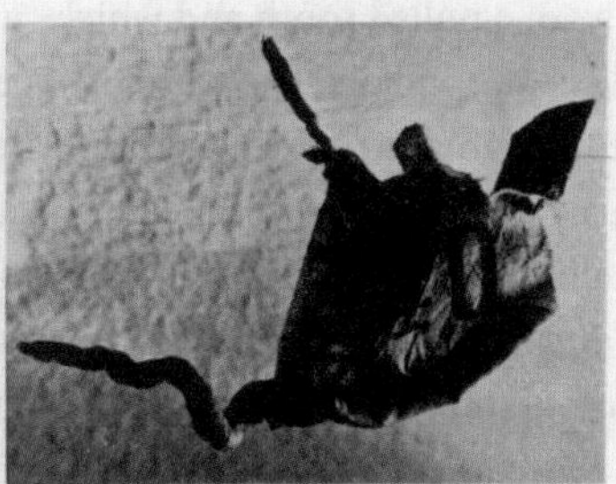

Numéro d'autobus roulé, trouvé dans la poche de veston d'un bureaucrate moyen (Crédit Lyonnais) ; caractéristiques les plus fréquentes de "modern'style".

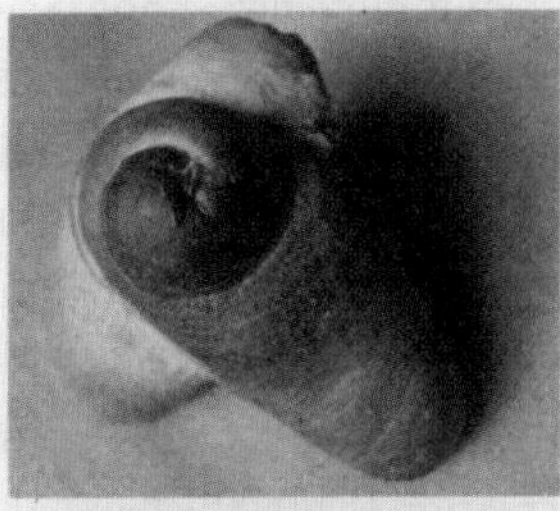

Le pain ornemental et modern'style échappe a la stéréotypie molle

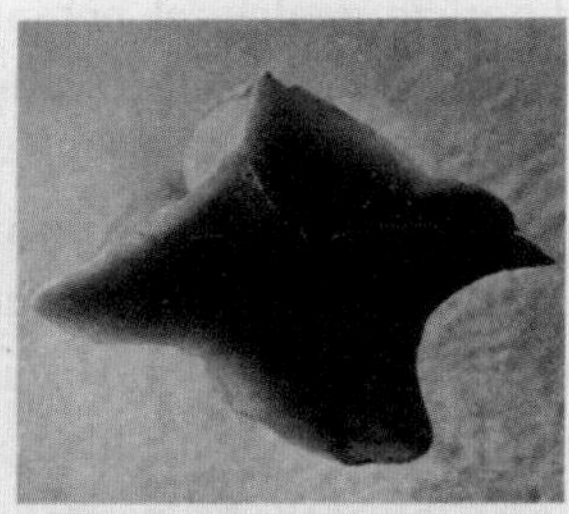

Morceau de savon présentant des formes automatiques modern'style trouvé dans un lavabo.

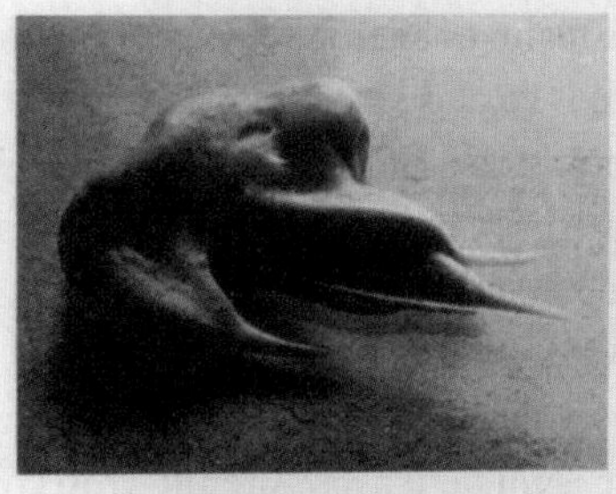

Le hasard morphologique du dentrifice répandu n'échappe pas a la stéréotypie fine et ornementale.

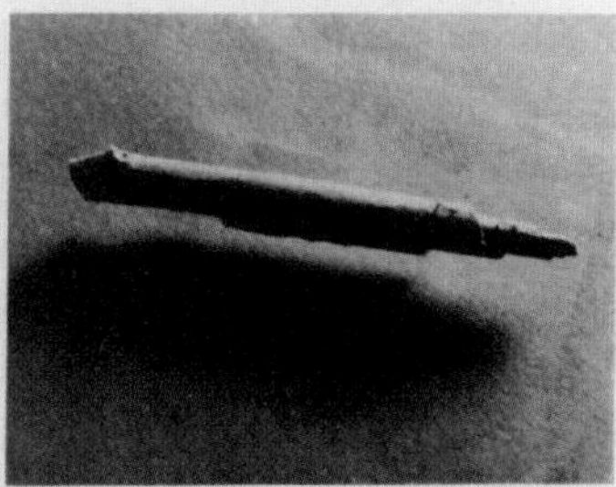

Enroulement élémentaire obtenu chez un "débile mental".

SCULPTURES INVOLONTAIRES

Brassaï
Sculptures Involontaires (Involuntary Sculptures)
Page from *Minotaure*, nos.3/4, 1933

paper; on the left an unidentifiable blob whose tendrils resemble the roots of a pulled tooth and which turns out to be toothpaste. Its caption reads: 'Morphological chance of squeezed out toothpaste does not escape the fine, ornamental stereotype.' The glass shelf on which the objects are placed is reminiscent of the glass slides used for microscopic preparation, recalling the scientific roots of close-up photography.

In *Minotaure,* the main outlet for Surrealism through the 1930s, photographs, and especially close-ups, form the most important visual evidence of Breton's idea of convulsive beauty, which in many ways is the direct opposite of Bataille's notion of formless – *informe.* Photographs of scientific origin, zoological, botanical, entomological, appear side by side throughout the journal with work by photographers associated with the Surrealist movement, especially Man Ray and Brassaï, reinforcing the Surrealists' resistance to the divorce of art from life. A page of close-up photographs of corals, crystals and minerals by Brassaï illustrates Breton's article 'Beauty will be convulsive' from *Minotaure,* no.5, in 1934. For Breton, crystals, which are hard, rigid, regular and lustrous, are the perfect expression of the spontaneous creation that is the basis of beauty in both nature and art, and is the opposite of all voluntary attempts to create formal beauty. Belonging to this realm of spontaneous creation are the coral forests, where, 'The inanimate is so close to the animate that the imagination is free to play without limit on these forms that look entirely mineral, to repeat the process of recognising a nest, or a bunch of grapes, emerging from a fountain that turns to stone.'[57]

Brassaï's close-up image of madrepore coral from 1930 is cropped in *Minotaure,* bringing its surface even closer to the eye, but also emphasising its endless mysterious extension. There is no better way, Breton wrote, of concretely enclosing for the human eye the constant process of formation and destruction, as in life itself, than 'the bridge of treasures of the Australian Great Barrier Reef'.[58]

Brassaï's *Butterfly and Candle* (c.1933) belongs to a series that was used, together with close-up photographs of moths by the entomologist Le Charles, in a photographic essay on night to accompany an extract from

57 Breton, 'La beauté sera convulsive', trans. Timothy Ades, *Minotaure*, no.5, Paris, 12 May 1934, p.13.

58 *Ibid.*

the eighteenth-century English poet Edward Young's *Night-Thoughts* (1742–45), a favourite of the Surrealists.[59] Le Charles's close-up studies of the praying mantis and the stick insect also accompanied Roger Caillois's famous article 'Mimicry and Legendary Psychasthenia' in the same issue of *Minotaure,* which was given over to the theme of night. The markings on the outspread wings in Brassaï's butterfly photograph are as clear as in those of the entomologist, though the presence of the fatal candle flame in Brassaï's image shifts the mood away from document to poetry.

In 'Beauty will be convulsive', Breton also talks about the found object and its relation to objective chance, to the idea that a chance encounter can prompt recognition of a hidden desire. He illustrates the article with some of Man Ray's photographs of found and interpreted Surrealist objects. These are composites, combinations of readymade and found materials whose conjunction arouses a frisson of recognition or surprise. While photography can enhance the effect of these Surrealist objects, the photo-objects that are created *by* photography, such as Man Ray's *Ostrich egg* (1944) or Dora Maar's *Portrait d'Ubu* (1936) – depend upon the special effects of close-up, magnification that disturbs rather than heightens reality. These are the progeny of scientific photography, but the deliberate absence of scale unsettles rather than reveals nature. The images have great physicality but uncertain identity: the titles might apparently reassure, as with *Ostrich egg,* which, however, looks uncannily like stone or ceramic; or further distort, as with Maar's *Portrait d'Ubu.* The association with the playwright Alfred Jarry's monster dictator Ubu who 'debrained' his victims, as suggested by the title, is almost too human for the eyeless, faceless, scaly form with its carapace and sharp nails, whose blindness awakens the same horror as slugs and worms. The subject of the photograph, a baby armadillo, becomes victim, too, like the term 'formless', of the fear of the unknown and uncategorisable.[60]

59 E. Young, 'Le jour est trop court', *Minotaure*, no.7, Paris, 10 June 1935, pp.23–29.
60 Note: this is an abridged version of the original essay (2015).

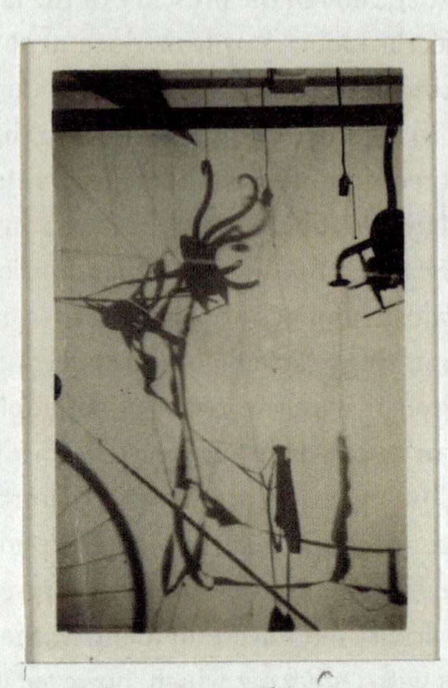

542 **Marcel Duchamp**
Ombres portées (Cast Shadows), 1917–18
Gelatin silver print on paper
Plate: 6.1 × 3.9 cm | 2⅜ × 1½ in

Camera Creation

Duchamp, Man Ray, Picabia, Jennifer Mundy (ed), Tate Publishing, London, 2008

Dear Stieglitz
Even a few words I don't feel like writing.
You know exactly what I think about photography.
I would like to see it make people despise
painting until something else will make
photography unbearable –
There we are.
Affectionately
Marcel Duchamp
17 May 1922, New York[1]

Marcel Duchamp's response to Alfred Stieglitz's questionnaire, 'Can a photograph have the significance of art?' was published, together with other replies, in the latter's periodical *MSS* in 1922. Stieglitz, the celebrated American photographer, editor of *Camera Work*, proprietor of the Little Galleries of the Photo-Secession (known as 291), was a champion of modern and experimental art, especially American, and above all, a passionate advocate of photography as fine art. His question was familiar and even now lingers on, but for Duchamp it started from the wrong premise. Having already laid open the question of what made a work 'art' with his readymades, Duchamp in his response implicitly challenges the notion that art's significance could depend upon a

1 Frances Naumann and Hector Obalk (eds), *Affectionately Marcel: The Selected Correspondence of Marcel Duchamp*, trans. Jill Taylor, Ludion, Ghent, 2000, p.109.

medium as such. He would have appreciated Walter Benjamin's later comment on 'art', in *Small History of Photography*. Benjamin cites a critic who had attacked photography as blasphemous, thundering against the very idea of mechanically produced mirror images of 'man's God-given features'. Benjamin wrote: 'Here we have the philistine notion of art in all its overweening obtuseness, a stranger to all technical considerations, which feels that its end is nigh with the alarming appearance of the new technology.'[2]

Photography belonged to a series of wider transformations, to a new world of communications: part of what we think of as modernity. In so far as art was to survive and hold a place in relation to modern experience, it could not ignore a 'new technology' that appeared to mediate in a different way the interchanges between reproduction, perception and the real world. It was precisely the technology that intrigued Duchamp. Photography was not so new by the early 1920s, but was newly discovered by the avant garde, and offered limitless possibilities; the technology itself was developing rapidly, and photographs were invading every aspect of modern life.

Photography may have rendered some of painting's functions redundant, but it was not an easy option. As Man Ray said, the camera awed painters, since it seemed to 'require devilish dexterity and great scientific knowledge'.[3] He was the only true adept of the three artists (Duchamp, Man Ray and Picabia) but all of them drew on photography, though it had a different dynamic in their respective work. For Man Ray it became for a while his chief activity and livelihood, though he never gave up painting; Picabia only occasionally used actual photographs, but drew on photography and other readymade imagery extensively in his paintings; Duchamp, after finally abandoning oil painting on canvas in 1918, experimented with this among other media, especially in so far as it pertained to optics and the moving image. The collaborations between Man Ray and Duchamp from c.1919 produced photographs that have gained in interest during recent years.

2 Walter Benjamin, 'A Small History of Photography' (1931), *One-way Street and Other Writings*, Verso, London, 1985.

3 Man Ray, *Self-Portrait* (1963), Bloomsbury, London, 1988, p.54.

Nineteen twenty-two, the date of Stieglitz's questionnaire, was a year of uncertainty, expectation, experiment and disappointment in the circles in which the three artists moved, and photography had already played a significant part in their work. It was the year in which Man Ray discovered rayographs; the year of a great scandal around Picabia's submissions to the Salon des Indépendants involving photography; the year of the experiments with hypnotic trances in the post-Dada, pre-Surrealist circles; the year the magazine *Littérature* published photographs for the first time: Man Ray's *Vue prise en aéroplane* (View Taken From an Aeroplane, later known as *Elevage de poussière* (Dust Breeding)) and a shop window by or after the photographer Eugène Atget. These two photographs, in the December 1922 issue of *Littérature* dedicated to Rrose Sélavy, are premonitory of the new life of photography within the avant garde. As far as Duchamp was concerned, painting was over. He had completed his final oil painting on canvas, *Tu m'* in 1918 and was about to terminate work on his painting on glass, *The Bride Stripped Bare by her Bachelors, Even (The Large Glass)* (1915–23). That he had abandoned painting for the camera was public knowledge. The gossip column in *The Little Review* reported in spring 1922: 'Some of the painters are going in for camera creation and new forms of cinema: Sheeler, Duchamp etc.'[4] Cinema and, more broadly, the moving image were, to judge from Duchamp's letters at the time, the main forms of visual activity in which he retained an interest, albeit a tenuous one: 'I have a movie camera and am going to start using it seriously',[5] he wrote to his former lover Yvonne Chastel, but also complained to Henri-Pierre Roché: 'I've had it up to here with being a painter or a cinematographer. The only thing that could arouse my interest right now is a wonder drug that would make me play chess *divinely.*'[6]

4 Jane Heap, 'The Art Season', *The Little Review: Picabia Number*, spring 1922, p.60.
5 Naumann and Obalk, *op. cit.*, p.119.
6 *Ibid.*, p.105.

Opinions were divided from its inception about photography's influence on and relationship with painting; in *Art and Photography* Aaron Scharf described the wide spectrum of responses to the camera, from those like Benjamin's critic who deplored the loss of the artist's hand in mechanical reproduction to those who advocated the marvellous discoveries of the lens that were of benefit as much to scientists as to artists.[7]

At a basic level, photography remained a source of imagery for paintings. Before his renunciation of painting, Duchamp had found it a fruitful source for his interest in movement and its representation. Independently of the Futurists, he discovered the chronophotographs of Étienne-Jules Marey. These, unlike the successive images of bodies in movement registered by Eadweard Muybridge, who used a battery of cameras, took imprints of movements on a single photographic plate to reproduce the actual flow of a body in motion in one image.[8] Duchamp's pictorial investigations of movement reached a logical terminus in the first readymade, *Bicycle Wheel* (1913), from static representation of movement to something that actually moved. Duchamp's interest in cinema in the early 1920s was to involve mobile constructions that can be traced back to *Bicycle Wheel.*

Picabia made use of photographs and postcards for his Impressionist and post-Impressionist landscapes in the early 1900s, and off and on continued the practice of borrowing from readymade sources, adopting mechanical motifs from scientific diagrams and illustrations in the Dada period, and culminating in the spectacular pin-up paintings of the 1940s, which are based on photographs from popular magazines.[9] As a

7 Aaron Scharf, *Art and Photography*, Pelican Books, London, 1974.

8 See Jean Clair, *Duchamp et la photographie*, Éditions Du Chêne, Paris, 1977.

9 See Sarah Wilson, *Francis Picabia: Accommodations of Desire; Transparencies 1924–1932*, Kent Gallery, Kent, 1989; Sara Cochran, 'Francis Picabia's Painting During the Second World War and His Use of Photography', in Zdenek Felix (ed), *Francis Picabia; The Late Work*, Hatje Cantz, Ostfildern-Ruit, and Museum Boijmans van Beyningen, Rotterdam, 1998; Carole Boulbès, *Picabia: Le Saint manqué*, Éditions Jean-Michel Place, Paris, 1998; Emmanuelle de l'Ecotais, 'Picabia et la photographie', in *Francis Picabia: Singulier idéal*, exhibition catalogue, Musée d'Art Moderne de la Ville de Paris, Paris, 2002.

young man, he was probably influenced by his grandfather Alphonse Davanne, amateur photographer and friend of Daguerre, who predicted that photography would kill painting. Picabia's attitude was defiant and ironic, taunting a hierarchy in which oil painting was king: a medium, however, he never abandoned. And although very close to Stieglitz at the time of *Camera Work* and 291, making frequent reference to the camera in drawings, and reproducing photo-objects in his review *391*, Picabia did not try it out for himself. But he was one of the first to exploit the influence of photography on how we see the world around us and to extrapolate this in paintings, from the transparencies of the late 1920s to the stylised erotica of the 1940s.

Did Picabia know that photographs were specifically excluded by the otherwise open and jury-free Salon des Indépendants in Paris, when he sent in *La Veuve joyeuse* (The Merry Widow) in 1922? In a statement reported in *Comoedia* (21 January 1922), the president of the Société des Artistes Indépendants, Paul Signac, justified the Salon committee's decision to reject *La Veuve joyeuse*: 'We have not judged... if that is painting or not. We are content to apply the rule. Article 12 declares that photographs cannot be accepted, and article 13, that the committee reserves rights in the matter of works which pose a question of publicity or of impropriety.'[10] The waste of canvas in *La Veuve joyeuse* scandalised the old painter, given, he said, that so many artists struggled to make a living.

The photograph by Man Ray of Picabia at the wheel of his Mercer – carefully signed and dated – and the 'drawing' beneath it, identical in size, are dwarfed by the large blank canvas. They look more like the layout for a magazine cover than a work of art. The two media, photography and drawing, on what should be the support for a third medium, oil paint, not only 'spoil' the canvas but emphasise paint's absence. Their juxtaposition evokes an aspect of debates about photography to which

10 William Camfield, *Francis Picabia: His Art, Life and Times*, Princeton University Press, Princeton, NJ, 1979, p.173. All three works submitted by Picabia were listed in the catalogue for the 1922 Salon des Indépendants: *La Veuve joyeuse* and *Le Chapeau de paille* (The Straw Hat), which bore the inscription 'M... pour celui qui regarde' and little else, were rejected, while *Danse de Saint-Guy*, consisting of an empty picture frame strung with twine, was accepted.

Man Ray later referred somewhat cavalierly in *La Photographie n'est pas l'art* (Photography Is Not an Art, 1937): it was not the fault of Leonardo or Uccello if they had to waste hours accurately limning the anatomy of bodies, horses etc., a job now done in a flash by the camera.[11] In *La Veuve joyeuse*, 'dessin' is rudimentary, and Picabia could either be underlining the way in which photography has superseded drawing as a mode of accurate representation or revelling in the freedom this brings the draughtsman.

La Veuve joyeuse also recalls Duchamp's *Fresh Widow* (1920), the first work signed by his alter ego Rrose Sélavy.[12] Both evoke the sinister nickname for the guillotine, *'la veuve'*, which in 1922 was still in use in France. Rrose Sélavy, Duchamp's alter ego, was thus among other things a 'widow' (like all too many women in Europe in the aftermath of the First World War). Her appearances in Man Ray's photographs curiously merge mourning with glamour.[13] One of the earliest, where she appears in low-browed black feather hat and heavy ruched collar, graced the label of the perfume bottle *Belle Haleine, Eau de Voilette*, and was later used for the cover of *New York Dada* of April 1921. There is a striking resemblance between this photograph of Rrose Sélavy and Man Ray's 1923 oil portrait of Duchamp, for which it clearly served as one of the models. As Man Ray said, 'I set about to do a portrait of him in oils, but, influenced by the many photographic portraits I had made of him, the work was in black and sepia, mimicking a photograph... It was neither a painting nor a photograph; the confusion pleased me.'[14]

Man Ray, in theory, kept the mediums apart, although initially taking up the camera in order to make records of his paintings. 'I had never shared the contempt shown by other painters for photography; there was no competition involved, rather the two mediums were engaged in different paths.'[15] His mastery of the apparatus and openness to experiment

11 Man Ray, *La Photographie n'est pas l'art*, Éditions GLM, Paris, 1937.

12 The double 'r' was added in 1921.

13 See Dawn Ades, 'Duchamp's Masquerades' in Graham Clarke (ed), *The Portrait in Photography*, Reaktion Books, London 1992; David Hopkins, 'Men Before the Mirror: Duchamp, Man Ray and Masculinity', *Art History*, September 1998.

14 Man Ray, *Self-Portrait*, *op. cit.*, p.187.

15 *Ibid.*, p.54.

and innovation quickly demonstrated ways in which photography could exceed or contradict its own assumed role as faithful record or document. Here, the question of 'truth to materials' that was so powerful a motive among artists in the early twentieth century becomes very interesting. Stieglitz and the Photo-Secessionists valued pure, unmanipulated and carefully composed photographs, and Man Ray was aware of transgressing their ideas. He commented that his 'solarisations', a process that produces a kind of dark halo round the image, could be criticised by the Photo-Secessionists as too close to drawing.

There are nonetheless many examples of paintings with a photographic source, most famously the close-up of his lover Kiki de Montparnasse's lips, which became *Observatory Time – The Lovers* (1932–34). 'One of these enlargements of a pair of lips haunted me like a dream remembered; I decided to paint the subject on a scale of superhuman proportions… If there had been a colour process enabling me to make a photograph of such dimensions and showing the lips floating over a landscape I would certainly have preferred to do it that way.'[16] The morphological ambiguity of the elongated lips, which resemble naked limbs, was underlined in shots of the painting with a nude lying underneath. Another instance of the metaphorical possibilities of a photographic image being picked up later in a painting concerns the image initially titled *Moving Sculpture* (1920).[17] Man Ray called the painting he based on the photograph *Flying Dutchman*, transforming the white underclothes and sheets into ghostly, ragged sails.

16 *Ibid.*, p.206. Man Ray reshaped the close-up of Kiki's lips in memory of Lee Miller's.

17 When the photograph was reproduced as the cover image for *La révolution surréaliste*, no.6, March 1926, it was titled *La France*.

> There is Man Ray, who always seems to be looking into little pieces of glass, or else, dreaming about some new-fangled sort of photographic apparatus.[18]

> Thou now livest motionless in a mirror! Everything is a mirage in thee – thine world is glass – glassy![19]

When Man Ray and Duchamp met in 1915, their respective interests in glass were poised to intersect. Man Ray was in the process of mastering the complicated business of the camera. Noting the unsatisfactory results of most photographic reproductions of paintings for catalogues and the press, he decided that the painter himself was the person best fitted to translate colour into black and white. In 1915, while preparing for his coming painting show in New York, he set about learning how to make photographs in order to reproduce his own work. He acquired the skills with ease, mastered the business of glass plates and filters, and later set up his own darkroom and 'explored the mysteries of developing'.[20]

Duchamp was starting construction in New York of his *Large Glass*, which had already been meticulously planned in a quantity of notes, diagrams and calculations. One of these notes, published in 1934 in Duchamp's *Green Box*, included an obvious photographic metaphor:

> Kind of Sub-Title
> Delay in Glass
> Use 'delay' instead of 'picture' or 'painting';
> 'picture on glass' becomes 'delay in glass'[21]

18 Ernest Hemingway, introduction, *Kiki's Memoirs*, Black Manikin Press, Paris, 1930, p.176.

19 Elsa von Freytag-Loringhoven, 'Love-Chemical Relationship', *The Little Review*, June 1918, p.59. The poem was 'a shrewd and mocking reading of Duchamp's cerebrally erotic strategies at work in the *Large Glass*', Irene Gammel, *Baroness Elsa, Gender, Dada and Everyday Modernity*, MIT Press, Cambridge, MA, and London, 2002, p.176.

20 Man Ray, *Self-Portrait*, *op. cit.*, p.55.

21 Marcel Duchamp, *The Bride Stripped Bare by her Bachelors, Even (The Green Box Notes)*, typographic version by Richard Hamilton, trans. George Heard Hamilton, Percy Lund Humphries, London, 1960, n.p.

Duchamp claimed that it was the poetic union of these words that pleased him,[22] but the idea of time-lapse 'in' glass suggests that he considered the *Large Glass* as, among other things, a 'giant photographic plate', in the words of art historian Jean Clair.[23] Perhaps by chance, Man Ray encapsulated the 'delay' in the extraordinary and justly celebrated photograph *Élevage de poussière* (Dust Breeding). Having offered to photograph the *Glass,* as practice for his commission to photograph Katherine Dreier's collection and her new museum of modern art, Man Ray set up his tripod in Duchamp's room, which had a single unshaded light bulb. 'Since it was to be a long exposure, I opened the shutter and we went out to eat something, returning about an hour later, when I closed the shutter... The negative was perfect.'[24] It was also wholly uncharacteristic of the kind of photograph usually prepared of a work of art for reproduction. Capturing only a fragment of the glass, and from a steep angle, it de-familiarises the dust and fluff and other detritus and invites us to see a desertscape. When reproduced, cropped, in *Littérature* it was titled '*Vue prise en aéroplane* par Man Ray', the close-up became an aerial view, to disorient and confuse the viewer.[25]

Among the reasons that Duchamp gave for using glass was the fact that it eliminated the need for background. The transparency of the glass meant that its emptiness was always filled with whatever its surroundings were. He also mentioned that he used a glass palette and was struck by the freshness of the colours on it. He might have seen Bavarian glass paintings during his summer in Munich in 1912, and of course there were the ubiquitous stained-glass windows. Nonetheless, photography was there at the start as one of the models that inspired the choice of glass for *The Bride Stripped Bare by her Bachelors, Even* and Duchamp briefly attempted to deploy it literally, exploring the possibility of transferring the image of the 'Bride' from the 1912 painting onto the glass photographically. Finding this impossible, he imitated it: 'The imitation of photography/make it

22 Pierre Cabanne, *Dialogues with Marcel Duchamp* (first published as *Entretiens avec Marcel Duchamp*, Paris, 1967), trans. Ron Padgett, Thames & Hudson, London, 1971, p.68.

23 Clair, 'Opticeries', *October*, summer 1978, Cambridge, MA, p.101.

24 Man Ray, *Self-Portrait*, *op. cit.*, p.79.

25 *Littérature*, no.5, October 1922, p.11. The full caption read: 'This is the domain of Rrose Sélavy: How arid it is – How fertile it is / How happy it is – How sad it is!'

noticeable in the "Pendu femelle"' – hence the Bride (hanged female) in the *Large Glass* is black and white.[26]

Duchamp's notes are littered with photographic terms and allusions, some intended for actual implementation, others experimental or notional. For instance, in a note headed 'Preface', he talks about 'extra-rapid exposure', a term common in photographic manufacturers' advertisements. Duchamp had packed the facsimiles of the notes for *The Box of 1914* in cardboard containers for photographic plates, one of which announced on its lid: 'Extra-rapid Plates'. The note on the draft pistons – the 'holes' in the Milky Way in the Bride's domain – is a good example of his typical, slightly distorted implementation of photography:

> 3 Photos of a piece of white cloth –
> pistons of the draft...
> after
> the photo, the group of marked squares
> disSymmetrically arranged, will present
> on a flat surface a conventional representation
> of the 3 draft pistons.[27]

The shapes of the 'draft pistons', the distorted squares in the Milky Way, were indeed based on photographs of squares of black gauze (like a widow's veil) blowing in the wind. Chance enters here, via photography. The camera catches the cloth square when it is not a square, when the undulating surface lifted into three dimensions alters its identity, just as dropping the metre of string did in *3 stoppages étalon* (3 Standard Stoppages).

While Duchamp played on the metaphorical connections between glass plate, reflections, transparency and painting on glass, Man Ray was experimenting with mechanical devices in his painting, extending these in one case to a work on glass. Man Ray's *Danger/Dancer* of 1920 was 'an aerograph composition of gear wheels, which had been inspired by the gyrations of a Spanish dancer I had seen in a musical play.'[28] However,

26 Duchamp, *Notes*, facsimiles of the notes, arrangement and translation Paul Matisse, Centre Pompidou, Paris, 1980, no.147.

27 Duchamp, *The Bride Stripped Bare...*, *op. cit.*, note dated May 1915.

28 Man Ray, *Self-Portrait*, *op. cit.*, p.79.

he did not emphasise the fact that the painting is on glass, and did not repeat the idea. *Danger/Dancer* brings together diagrammatic, mechanical precision in the flat, exact circular forms of the cog wheels (not dissimilar to Picabia's *Machine Turn Quickly*, c.1916–18) and the illusionistic effects of the airbrush.

PHOTOGRAPHY AND READYMADES

> ...so-called New York Dada photography cannot be thought of apart from the contemporary deployment of the readymade across the whole gamut of work devoted to it, primarily at the hands of Duchamp and Picabia.[29]

Since only two of the readymades (as distinct from the assisted ready-mades) survive physically – *Comb* (1916) and *Air de Paris* (1919) – it is through photographs that they are known to us. These are more than a record: the photographs are seldom straightforward and are interesting in their own right.

Although two of the readymades were exhibited in 1916, the public career of these works took off with a photograph.[30] The second issue of *The Blind Man*, published in May 1917, prominently reproduced 'the Exhibit refused by the Independents', *Fountain* (1917) by R. Mutt, photographed by Alfred Stieglitz. 'Stieglitz, to voice his protest, made a beautiful photograph of the bowl.'[31] The setting and lighting of this famous photograph have been exhaustively analysed.[32] Stieglitz photographed it carefully positioned in front of Marsden Hartley's painting *The Warriors* (1913), at

29 Rosalind Krauss, 'The Object Caught By the Heel', in Francis Naumann with Beth Venn (eds), *Making Mischief: Dada Invades New York*, exhibition catalogue, Whitney Museum of American Art, New York, NY, 1996, p.251.

30 Although two readymades had been exhibited in 1916, they aroused virtually no interest.

31 Man Ray, *Self-Portrait*, *op. cit.*, p.65.

32 See William Camfield, *Marcel Duchamp: Fountain*, exhibition catalogue, Menil Collection, Houston, TX, 1989, for the most complete coverage; see also Francis Naumann, 'The Blind Man: Fountain de R. Mutt, Photographiée par Stieglitz', in Jan Baetens, *New York et l'Art Moderne: Alfred Stieglitz et son cercle (1905–1930)*, exhibition catalogue, Musée d'Orsay, Paris, 2004.

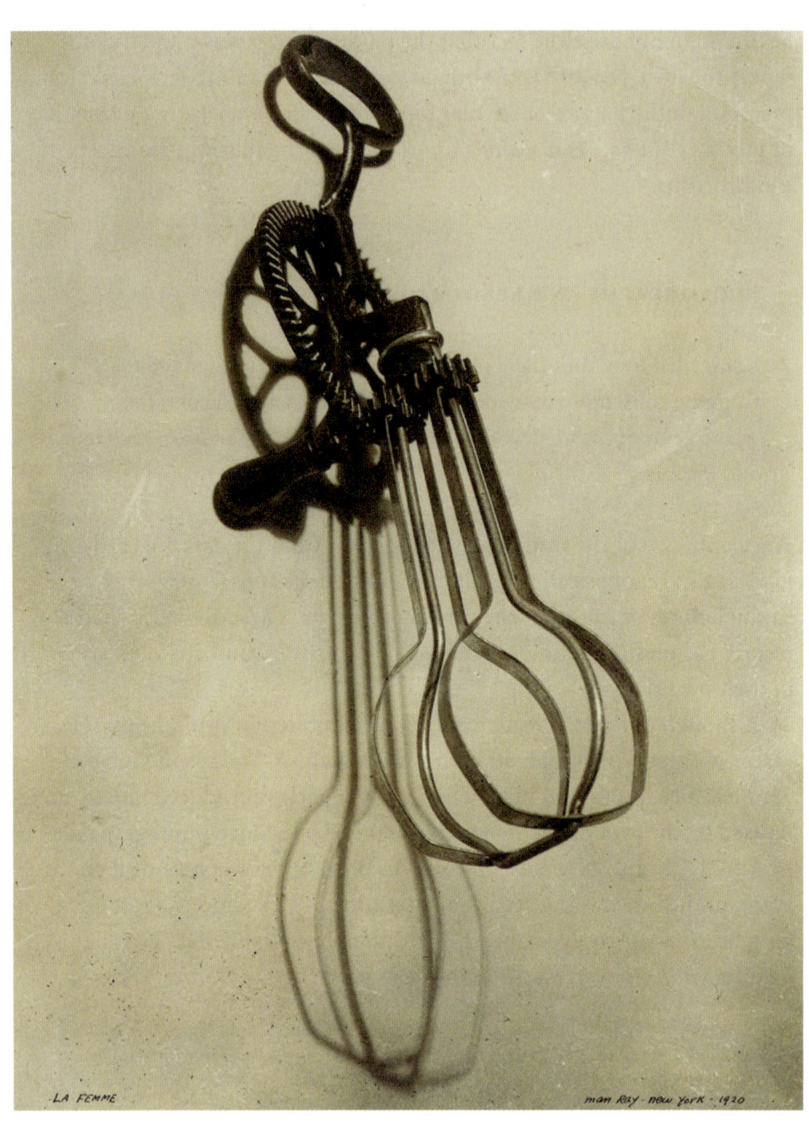

554 **Man Ray**
Man and *Woman*, 1918/1920
Gelatin silver prints
Left: 38.8 × 29.1 cm | 15¼ × 11½ in
Right: 43.7 × 33.5 cm | 17¼ × 13¼ in

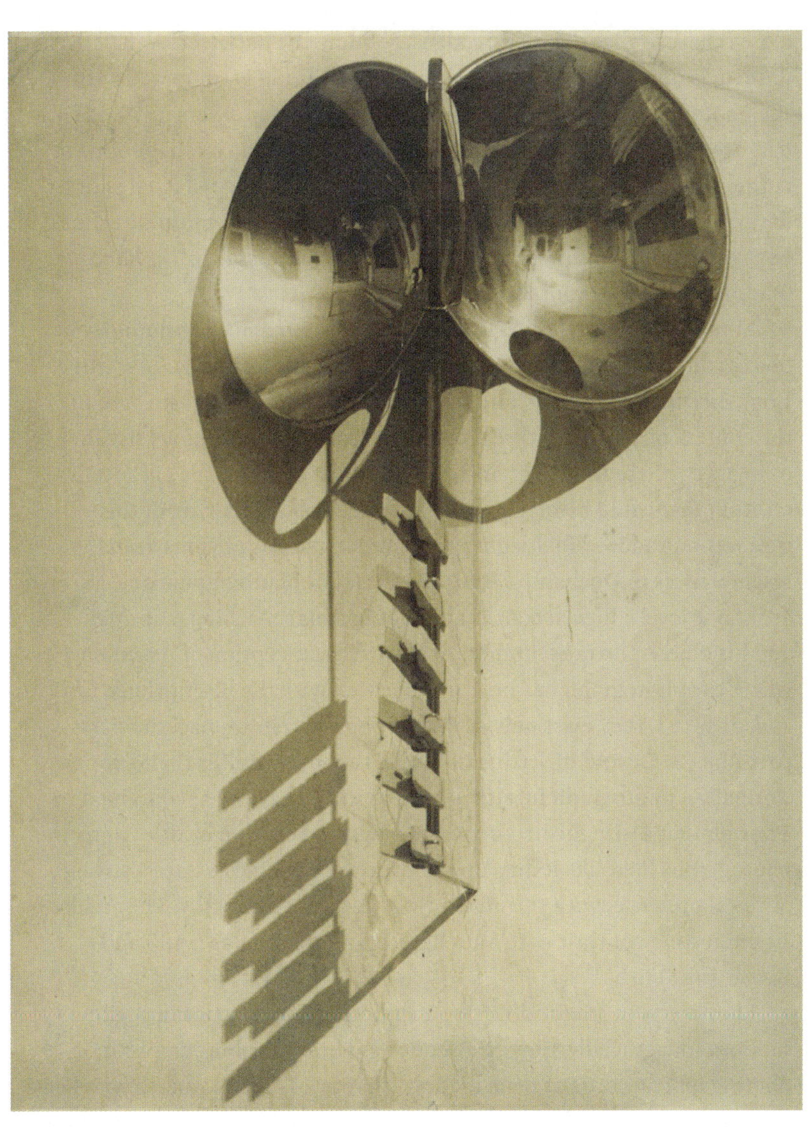

close range, so that the picture, densely filling the background, its edges unseen, is unreadable. When the complete painting is compared with the photograph, however, it is plain that Stieglitz (or others involved) had been amused to see a resemblance between *Fountain's* shape and the curious mountain form in *The Warriors.* The porcelain bowl itself is lit to dramatise highlights and shadows, producing anthropomorphic echoes both of a Buddha (as picked up in Louise Norton's essay in *The Blind Man,* 'Buddha of the Bathroom') and a Madonna.

Almost simultaneously, Picabia included a sequence of photographed objects on the covers of the New York issues of his review *391, Âne* (June 1917), *Américaine* (July 1917) and finally *Ballet mécanique* (August 1917). In the context of *391,* these three images are part of a continuous stream of imagery celebrating the 'girl born without a mother', the automatist creation that could be machine or camera. Picabia's drawing of this title was reproduced in Stieglitz's review *291* and has obvious visual resemblances to Duchamp's Bride. So these *391* photographic objects are at one level a logical continuation of Picabia's machine paintings and his object-portraits; unmodified (with the exception of *Américaine,* where the photograph has been ornamented with the inscriptions 'flirt' and 'divorce'), they exist only as cutout photographs of machine-parts, part-objects. Devoid of setting or frame, the cover itself is their support. Normally a photograph in such a context would have been contained by a border that distinguished between image and caption or title. Here, the photographs float like letters on the page, yet the objects have a strong physical presence, with the illusion of three-dimensionality. They make an interesting contrast with Man Ray's photographs *Man* (1918) and *Woman* (1918).

The objects in *Man* and *Woman* are photographed against a shallow support and, crucially, they cast shadows. These are photographs, not photographic records of readymades. Their titles, like Picabia's propeller dubbed *Âne* (Ass), anthropomorphise and satirise their subjects, but have confused them historically due to a gender switch: what was once *Man,* the whisk from the female domain of the kitchen drawer, was retitled *La Femme* (Woman) for an exhibition in 1921. Its counterpart depicts

33 Denis Hollier, 'Surrealist Precipitates', in Rosalind Krauss (ed), *October, The Second Decade 1986–1995*, Cambridge, MA, 1997, p.6.

the tools of the photographer; reflectors and a strip of glass with pegs to hold drying negatives. The closely related photograph *Integration of Shadows* (1918) shows the same object from a different angle. They trail the anti-art aura of the readymades, but are unequivocally photographs. It is the shadows that constitute their particular photographic quality. 'Cast shadows', Denis Hollier has written:

> ...are one of the rare types of sign that escape what (André) Breton calls ambiguity. They are the very exemplar of a nondisplaceable sign: rigorously contemporary with the object it doubles, it is simultaneous, nondetachable and, because of this, without exchange-value... With it the relation of the sign to the thing signified escapes the metaphor of the separation of body and soul: cast shadow is a sign that doesn't survive.[33]

Photography presents a special case: the cast shadow gains iconic autonomy. Having begun as a trace, an indexical sign, in that it is, to begin with, the shadow of a real object, in the photograph, which is itself the trace of an object, the shadow becomes independent, an integral part of the whole image.

Shortly before Man Ray made *Man* and *Woman,* Duchamp photographed his own *Sculpture de voyage* (Sculpture for Travelling, 1918), a rubber bathing cap cut into strips and stretched like a 'sort of multicoloured cobweb' across his studio. A second photograph, entitled *Ombres portées* (Cast Shadows, 1918; p.542), is the only image reproduced by Duchamp among his 'infra thin' notes,[34] a number of which are concerned with shadows and shadow-casters, which are 'represented by all the sources of light/(sun, moon, stars, candles, fire–)'.

In his notes, Duchamp toys with the idea of producing a figure from the combined shadows:

> shadows cast by Readymades
> shadow cast by 2.3.4. Readymades.
> '*brought together*'.[35]

34 Duchamp, *Notes*, *op. cit.*, no.13.

In the *Ombres portées* photograph the shadows of *Sculpture de voyage* (1918), *Bicycle Wheel, Hat Rack* (1917) and *With Hidden Noise* (1916) combine to create a configuration resembling the spidery form of the Bride in the *Large Glass*.

Wholly shadow-less, however, are the readymades in the photographs that Duchamp chose for reproduction in his *Box in a Suitcase* (1935–41). This enterprise, to reproduce as multiples and in miniature almost all his works, involved a particularly paradoxical use of photography with respect to the readymades. Four of the readymades and assisted readymades are reproduced sculpturally in miniature in the *Box in a Suitcase* and the others are represented in photographs from 1917–18.[36] The elaborate modes of photographic reproduction Duchamp employs simultaneously recognise the fundamental change that photography made to the work of art, now endlessly repeatable and thus bereft of its 'aura' of unique presence, and subtly challenges it by manipulating the photograph to isolate the readymade as an icon.

The 1917–18 photographs of the New York studio with the readymades were prepared in 1940 in as meticulous and labour-intensive a way as the *pochoir* (stencilled) reproductions of his paintings. The original photographs, one by Man Ray and the others probably by Duchamp himself, were retouched and then the readymades themselves highlighted by means of the hand-coloured *pochoir* technique, so that they stand out, detached, against the dimmed, faded background.

One of these hybrid, eerie images – a view of a room inhabited only by readymades and other objects – shows *Bicycle Wheel* (the 1916 version) and *Trébuchet* (Trap, 1917).[37] To highlight the latter, Duchamp devised a special technique. He blocked out the whole object in white, made a line drawing of it, prepared two letterpress blocks, of the room and of the drawing, then 'the line block of the ready-made was overprinted on (or "dropped into") the half-tone block of the rest of the room'.[38] Having coloured 350 copies, Duchamp curiously decided to omit the word 'ATELIER' from

35 Duchamp, *The Bride Stripped Bare…*, *op. cit.*, n.p.

36 *In Advance of the Broken Arm*, photograph by Man Ray, 1920; *Ready made*, photograph by Duchamp 1916–17; 33 West 67th photograph by Duchamp, 1917–18. All prepared 1940. See Ecke Bonk, *Marcel Duchamp: The Portable Museum*, Thames & Hudson, London, 1989, for an indispensable account of the making of *Box in a Suitcase*.

37 *Box in a Suitcase*, no.52; Bonk, *ibid.*, p.238.

38 *Ibid.*, p.238.

the captions. He cut this out and pasted just the address on the lower right-hand corner: 33 West 67th New York 1917–18 [sic]. ATELIER (studio) signifies a painter's space and would certainly have bestowed an identity not obvious from the photograph of the room, even alien to it. Inaction and disorder, on the one hand, mental activity on the other (books and papers on the table, the chess board inscribed on the wall, retouched and delicately coloured with particular care). It is surely not by chance that in the centre of the photograph is an empty easy chair.

Another photograph of the same room, with *Ready Made (Hat Rack), Fountain* and *In Advance of the Broken Arm* suspended from the ceiling, includes, amid an even greater mess, a ghostly figure of Duchamp himself. Although the photograph is attributed to Duchamp's friend Henri-Pierre Roché, given the length of time then required for photographic exposures, it is quite possible that Duchamp was simply both behind and in front of the camera. The phantom effect could have been fortuitous – in his autobiography Man Ray describes several examples of the unpredictable nature of time exposure in cameras at the time – but might also have amused Duchamp in its echo of 'spirit' photographs. A little later he wrote to Jacques and Gaby Villon, 'I know a photographer here who takes pictures of ectoplasm on a male medium: I promised I would go along to his sessions, then I couldn't be bothered, but I would find it most amusing.'[39]

STEREOSCOPY

Duchamp's interest in the relationship between eye and camera as optical instruments extended in about 1918 to a focus on the effects of monocular and binocular vision. *To Be Looked at (From the Other Side of the Glass) With One Eye, Close To, For Almost an Hour* and *Stéréoscopie à la main* (Handmade Stereopticon Slide, c.1918–19), both concerned with questions of optics and perspective, were made in Buenos Aires, where he spent some months

39 25 December 1922, Naumann and Obalk, *Selected Correspondence of Marcel Duchamp, op. cit.*, p.128. Duchamp had recently received the November issue of *Littérature*, with Breton's account of the 'seances' inspired by spirit mediums, 'L'Entrée des mediums'. Robert Desnos, one of the stars of the 'hypnotic sleeps', had also just published the puns he claimed were transmitted to him by Rrose Sélavy.

from 1918 to 1919. The title and part of the figure in the small glass *To Be Looked at (From the Other Side of the Glass) With One Eye, Close To, For Almost an Hour,* derive, as Jean Clair has shown, from Emmanuel Maignan's *Perspectiva Horaria* (1648), a treatise concerned with the triangulation of bodies in space at different times of day.[40] The gnomon or stela on which the magnifying glass is balanced rises from the spokes of an elliptical figure resembling one of the oculist witnesses in the *Large Glass,* and is intended to mark the position from which observation (with one eye) would be made.

Stereoscopy, on the other hand, is based on binocular vision. It was invented at about the same time as the Daguerrotype itself. By the end of the nineteenth century and for the first decade or two of the twentieth, stereoscopic photographs were hugely popular among the 'scientific toys' that united entertainment and instruction. Pairs of photographs taken of the same subject but with a slight shift in the camera's position (replicating that of the spectator looking at a thing first with one eye closed then the other) produced, when seen through a special viewer, the illusion of three dimensions, a 'real' scene. In *Stéréoscopie à la main* either Duchamp himself or an unknown photographer took two almost identical photographs of a seascape in which the faint image of the boat on the right is, in the right-hand slide, shifted slightly nearer the frame of the slide, as though seen with the right eye closed. Otherwise the scene is undifferentiated but, when observed through a stereoscopic viewer, the two slides would be merged so that one would see the sea stretching back in depth to the horizon.

To the original photographs in *Stéréoscopie à la main* Duchamp has added a further feature: a geometrical figure, which, like the boat, is repeated at a very slightly different point in relation to the frame, which should thus also produce a three-dimensional effect.[41] As Clair has argued, the geometrical figure is based on the diagrams in treatises on classical perspective that use rays to demonstrate both the notional field of vision of the subject and the vanishing point in the picture. The pyramid with rectangular base is lifted straight from Dubreuil's *La Perspective pratique*

40 Clair, 'Perspective', in Clair, with the collaboration of Ulf Linde et al., *Marcel Duchamp: Abécedaire. Approches critiques*, exhibition catalogue, Centre Pompidou, Paris, 1977, p.141.

41 Ecke Bonk states that the 'handmade drawing' is identical in both images, which would leave the diagram flat; Bonk, *op. cit.*, p.251.

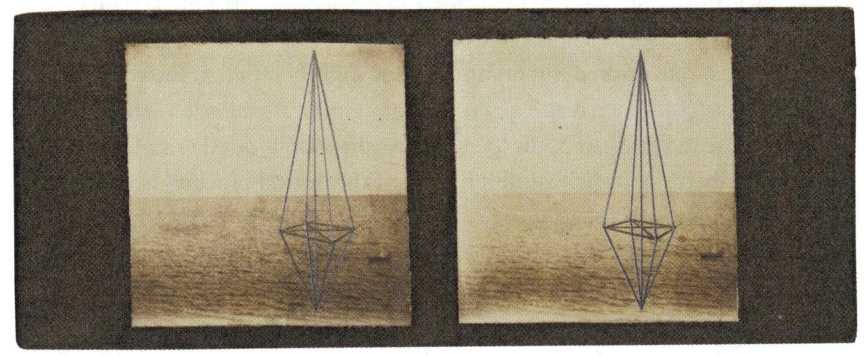

Marcel Duchamp
Stéréoscopie á la main (Handmade Stereopticon Slide), c.1918–19
Pencil on gelatin silver prints mounted
on black-paper-surfaced board
6.8 × 17.2 cm | 2⅝ × 6¾ in

nécessaire à tous les peintres (Practical Perspective For All Painters, 1649) which Duchamp then repeats, inverted.[42] His diagram, heavily drawn over the photographs in lead pencil, appears to float disconnected from the banal scene behind.

Duchamp's diagram could also be linked to an offshoot of classical stereoscopic photography called anaglyphs, and if so would belong to a slightly different system for obtaining the illusion of three-dimensionality. Duchamp knew Henri Vuibert's *Les Anaglyphes géométriques* (1912), which described the procedure whereby pairs of stereoscopic geometrical figures were printed, superimposed but slightly offset, in the complementary colours red and green.[43] Although the *Stéréoscopie à la main* does not use red and green, the 'perspective' diagram is not dissimilar to those in Vuibert's book, whose description of the optical process – sometimes slow – whereby the geometrical figures magically spring into space is revealing:

> Even with a well-constructed drawing, a good filter and strong enough lighting, one often has to wait a bit; when the adaptation is made, when the brain has united the two images, then you begin to recognise the figure. But you still need a little more patience, you need to apply yourself really to *possess* the anaglyph; a moment comes when you see it rise and plant itself in front of you; it looks as if you could touch it, grasp it, and follow its contours with your hand.[44]

The ability to 'see' the anaglyphic image was unpredictable: some *saw* faster than others, by contrast with the stereoscopic photograph, which was almost foolproof. But the point here is that Duchamp has apparently mixed two different kinds of visual illusion. By separating, rather than superimposing, the geometrical figures of the anaglyph, he has shunted them into the world of the stereoscopic photograph. So both diagram and photograph now depend on stereoscopic techniques for producing the illusion of three-dimensionality, but one in the interest of a real scene, the

42 Clair, *op. cit.*, p.132.

43 Clair, 'Opticeries' in *ibid.* A copy of Vuibert was included in an assemblage listed as a work by Schwarz 1997, no.661.

44 Quoted by Clair, *op. cit.*, p.106.

other in the interests of an ideal abstract form.

Stéréoscopie à la main is probably the first instance of Duchamp's lifelong interest in stereoscopy and anaglyphs; Duchamp 'always liked anaglyphs' and one of his last works was a drawing titled *Anaglyphic Chimney* (1968).[45] In this work, like Vuibert's anaglyphs, the outline of the chimney hood that Duchamp designed for his Cadaqués home is drawn twice, in blue and in red and superimposed with a slight gap between them. 'This hand-made anaglyph', Duchamp wrote, 'should produce a three-dimensional effect when viewed through a pair of spectacles with red and green filters.'[46] On the morning of the day of his death he was delighted that 'the red and blue coloured glasses he had been hunting for weeks to accompany the drawing' were available at the Librairie Vuibert.[47]

From stereoscopy, Duchamp moved on to optical machines and film. In a letter to his sister and brother in law, c.20 October 1920, he stated: 'I've had a "Moving Picture Camera" for six months now, but it's so expensive (the film) that I have to space out my cinematographic outpourings.'[48] Duchamp had, according to Man Ray:

> conceived an idea for making three-dimensional movies. Miss Dreier had presented him with a movie camera, and he obtained another cheap one – the idea was to join them with gears and a common axis so that a double, stereoscopic film could be made of a globe with a spiral painted on it... [A] young mechanic living in my building... managed to join the two cameras together. Duchamp decided to develop the film himself; I helped him. First, we obtained a couple of shallow garbage-can covers for tanks, a round plywood board was cut to fit, then waterproofed with paraffin. To wind the film on these,

45 Letter to Serge Stauffer, quoted by Clair, *op. cit.*, p.109.

46 Letter to Arturo Schwarz, in Schwarz, *op. cit.*, p.892.

47 Clair, *op. cit.*, p.109. Green and blue were interchangeable; red and blue was the cheapest combination of colours. Today an equal combination of blue and green in one filter and red in the other is most common. Duchamp's reference to red and green filters in his letter to Schwarz seems to be an error: Schwarz, *op. cit.*, p.892.

48 Naumann and Obalk, *op. cit.*, p.94.

> Duchamp drew radiating lines from the centers and hammered 400 nails along them. After taking 50 feet of film, we waited for nightfall and in the dark managed to wind the film onto the labyrinth of nails. I had already poured the developer into one of the trays, the fixing liquid into the other. We immersed the board into the first and timed the development, then transferred it to the fixer tank. After about twenty minutes we turned on the light. The film looked like a mass of tangled seaweed. It had swelled and was stuck together, most of it not having been acted on by the developer… Duchamp and I went out to eat. He was imperturbable; if we could save a few feet to verify his experiment, he'd be satisfied. I was depressed, after all the effort… We did save some film, two matching strips which, on examination through an old stereopticon, gave the effect of relief. To carry on the experiment, capital was needed as well as several other adjustments to make it practical for public presentation; the project was abandoned.[49]

Two frames from the ruined film survive, one red, the other green. The idea presumably would have been to view the film through anaglyphic glasses to produce the three-dimensional effect.

49 Man Ray, *Self-Portrait*, *op. cit.*, p.86. The history of the experiments with stereoscopic film/optical machines is as mangled as the film Man Ray describes. The problem with his account is that while the object he remembers filming seems to be *Rotary Demisphere (Precision Optics)* of 1924–25, which was made in Paris, the event he describes, from strong circumstantial evidence, took place in his New York studio. As Man Ray left New York in July 1921 and did not return to America for nearly 20 years, the incident must have taken place between January 1920 and June 1921 and would therefore be linked to the earlier *Precision Optics, Rotary Glass Plates* rather than the *Rotary Demisphere*. The fragment of film that survives is indeed of *Rotary Demisphere*, but it could be that there was more than one attempt at a stereoscopic film, which merged in Man Ray's memory. Significantly Duchamp mentions experiments with his 'Moving Picture Camera' immediately after describing his 'monocle': the *Rotary Glass Plates*. There are also stereoscopic photographs of the *Rotary Glass Plates* made by Man Ray in New York in 1920, which may have contributed to the confusion; see Schwarz, *op. cit.*, p.682 and p.707. Later in Paris, Man Ray recalled that Duchamp 'was working on a series of black-and-white spirals of which he wished to make a film embellished with anagrammatic phrases. On Sundays we went out in the suburbs to his brother Jacques Villon for lunch; and afterwards set up the old movie camera in the garden and filmed the spirals on an upright bicycle wheel, as it revolved slowly. He called the film *Anémic Cinéma*, a pretty anagram.' *Ibid.*, p.97. On 1 September 1921 Duchamp wrote to Florine Stettheimer: 'I'm trying to get some cinema effects with my camera.' These 'effects' are identified by Francis Naumann as the sketches of spirals fixed on the bicycle wheel; Naumann and Obalk, *op. cit.*, p.101. *Anémic Cinéma* was completed by Rrose Sélavy in 1926.

Duchamp's pursuit of the moving three-dimensional image continued, and some of the *Rotoreliefs* (1935) optical discs, also allude to anaglyphs. *Verre de bohème* (1935), for example, plays with the idea of the slightly offset red and green geometrical figures described by Vuibert, although it is by no means a pure experiment in anaglyphs, the forms deriving from a wine glass seen axonometrically. Significantly, this is the *Rotorelief* that Duchamp reproduced photographically in the *Box in a Suitcase*, next to the *Rotary Glass Plates*.

RAYOGRAPHS

> When everything that called itself art was stricken with palsy, the photographer switched on his thousand candle-power lamp and gradually the light-sensitive paper absorbed the darkness of a few everyday objects. He had discovered what could be done by a pure and sensitive flash of light that was more important than all the constellations arranged for the eye's pleasure.[50]

Man Ray's reputation, both within the avant garde and in high society fashion circles, after his move in 1921 to Paris, was established with remarkable speed. Duchamp wrote to him in the summer of 1922, 'I received your two Rayographs which, I think, are wonderful', and remarked on Man Ray's success as a portrait photographer: '*Vanity Fair* is full of portraits by you.'[51]

Man Ray appears to have chanced on the technique of rayographs independently, but the process itself was not new. Direct exposure of objects onto photosensitive paper is as old as photography itself, but was emerging again in various avant-garde contexts in the early 1920s. Christian Schad, associated with Zurich Dada, had also experimented with camera-less photography, and one of his 'schadographs' was reproduced in *Dadaphone* (Paris, March 1920). Despite its comic title ('Arp et Val Serner dans le crocrodrarium royal de Londres'), this was an abstract photogram, made using string and various folded and textured layers. By coincidence,

50 Tristan Tzara, Preface to *Champs Délicieux*, 1922, quoted in Benjamin, *op. cit.*, p.254.

51 Naumann and Obalk, *op. cit.*, p.121.

the Dadaist Tristan Tzara was the first to see Man Ray's new prints, which were, he said, 'far superior to similar attempts – simple flat textural prints in black and white – made a few years ago by Christian Schad, an early dadaist.'[52] This is a quite unfair dismissal of Schad's 'schadographs', which have considerable formal subtlety. The real difference, which Tzara must have recognised, was that they are abstract, not by chance, like the rayographs, but by conviction. Man Ray, by contrast, encountered the abstract by surprise. It happened in the middle of developing prints from his photo shoot for the fashion designer Poiret. In the process of making contact prints from the large glass negatives, an unexposed sheet of paper got into the developing tray by mistake. Without thinking, he:

> mechanically placed a small glass funnel, the graduate and the thermometer in the tray on the wetted paper. I turned on the light; before my eyes an image began to form, not quite a simple silhouette of the objects as in a straight photograph, but distorted and refracted by the glass more or less in contact with the paper and standing out against a black background, the part directly exposed to the light. I remembered when I was a boy, placing fern leaves in a printing frame with proof paper, exposing it to sunlight and obtaining a white negative of the leaves. This was the same idea, but with an added three-dimensional quality and tone graduation.[53]

The rayographs create receding spaces, the objects rendered indistinct by extreme close-up or by distance.

They were instantly hailed by the Surrealists as the true equivalents of automatic writing, visual images of great power and, apparently, free of the trammels of learned skills and conscious control. It was nonetheless quickly evident that only someone with 'devilish dexterity' and a profound understanding of the technical effects of light even in camera-less photography could produce Man Ray's album *Champs Délicieux* (Fields of Delight, 1922). Breton acknowledged as much when he wrote of Man Ray, in a text dedicated to the defence of painting:

52 Conversation reported by Man Ray in Man Ray, *Self-Portrait, op. cit.*, p.106.
53 Man Ray, *Self-Portrait, op. cit.*, p.106.

> At a time when painting, far outdistanced by photography in the pure and simple imitation of actual things, was posing to itself the problem of its reason for existence… it was necessary for someone to come forward who should be not only an accomplished technician of photography but also an outstanding painter; someone who should, on the one hand, assign to photography the exact limits of the role that it can legitimately claim to play, and on the other hand, guide it towards other ends than those for which it appears to have been created – in particular, the thorough exploration on its behalf, within the limits of its resources, of that region which painting imagined it was going to be able to keep all to itself. It was the great good fortune of Man Ray to have been that man.[54]

The region that painting imagined it could keep to itself was that of the imagination, of dream and the unconscious, of fortuitous gestures and revelations. The rayographs, in their unpredictable treatment of objects, sometimes recognisable, sometimes stripped of identity to become layers of light forms, in their creation of depths and densities of tone, in the rediscovery of shades of grey to deep black, produce an unknown world that is like a metaphor of the unconscious itself. 'When Things Dream' was the title of Tristan Tzara's text introducing the rayographs in *Photographs by Man Ray 1920–Paris 1934*. But Man Ray, in 'L'Âge de la lumière', put his own spin on Breton's ambivalence towards photography, and emphasised the need for a freedom that required some disrespect of the medium:

> For whether a painter, emphasising the importance of the idea he wishes to convey, introduces bits of readymade chromos alongside his handiwork, or whether another working directly with light and chemistry, so deforms the subject as almost to hide the identity of the original and creates a new form, the ensuing violation of the medium employed is the most perfect assurance of the author's convictions. A certain amount of contempt for the material employed to express an idea is indispensable to the purist realisation of this idea.[55]

54 André Breton, 'Le Surréalisme et la peinture', *La Révolution surréaliste*, nos.9/10, 1927, p.41, in André Breton, *Surrealism and Painting*, trans. Simon Watson-Taylor, Macdonald, London 1972, p.32.

In his autobiography, *Self-Portrait,* Man Ray gives the impression that he never reconciled himself to being one of the greatest and most innovative photographers. He frequently complains of the lack of notice friends, critics and amateurs paid to what he regarded as his primary creative activity. Lack of recognition as a painter is the leitmotif of his autobiography and was still his theme in his last years. Visitors to his studio in the rue Férou would be shown his latest decalcomanias and other paintings, and questions about the photographs were deflected.[56] But it was through photography – through his portraits of artists, celebrities and musicians, his films, rayographs, solarisations, close-ups – that he visually defined an era.

Several of Man Ray's photographs, notably *Noire et Blanche* (Black and White, 1926), have been the subject of detailed study, in which attention to the technical aspects of reproduction, the state of the negative and original treatment of the vintage prints, has been as crucial to an understanding of their historical status and the photographer's intentions as to the image's subsequent fate and interpretations.[57] But all too often, such studies remain confined to the history of photography rather than contextualised within modern art as a whole. For often quite banal reasons, such as unfamiliarity with the technology, the photographic in the histories of modern art has been overlooked; but 'camera creation' in film and photography has been as much a part of these histories as painting and sculpture. At the same time, it brought radical changes to the very idea of 'art', as Duchamp indicated in his blunt response to Stieglitz's question. Photography seemed to signal the end of the unique work of art, with its 'aura', the special value placed on the emotions of the individual creator, and the birth of a new age with an order of visuality appropriate to its secular and objective spirit. How this was explored in the first decades of the last century when the avant garde 'discovered' photography is an important strand in this exhibition, whose constellation of artists has brought photography into focus as a challenge

55 Man Ray, *Photographs by Man Ray 1920–Paris 1934*, James Thrall Soby, Hartford, CT, 1934. First published as 'L'Âge de la lumière', *Minotaure*, no.3, 1933.

56 Conversation with the author, 1969.

57 See, for example, Wendy Grossman and Steven Manford, 'Unmasking Man Ray's Noire et Blanche', *Archives of American Art Journal*, Smithsonian Institution, Washington, DC, vol.20, no.2, 2006.

and forum for experiment in relation to other mediums such as painting, objects and readymades, as well as a medium in its own right.

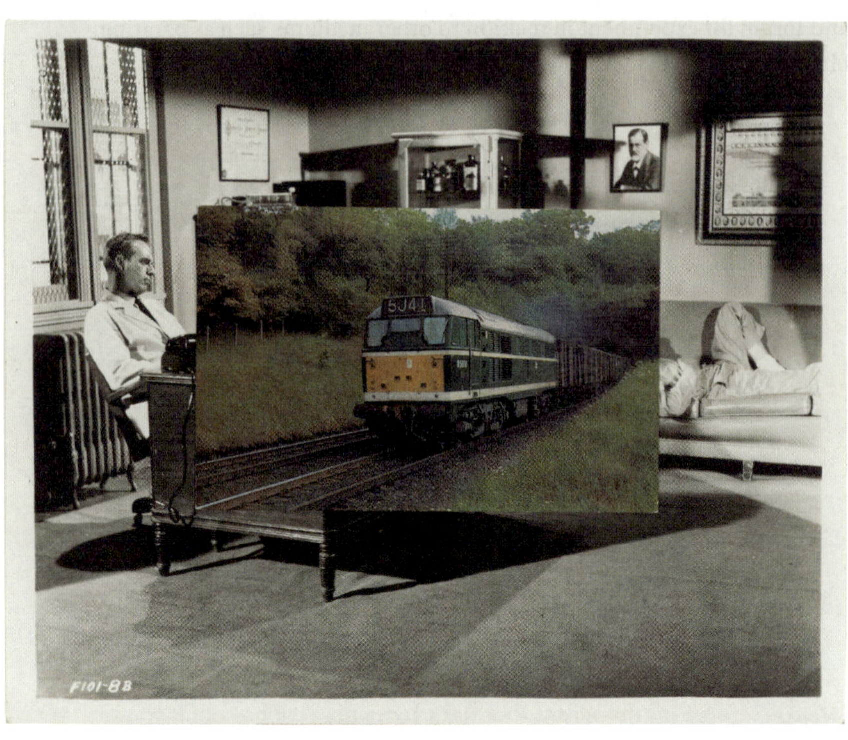

570 **John Stezaker**
Negotiable Space I, 1978
Collage
20.6 × 25.3 cm | 8⅛ × 10 in

John Stezaker, *Monteur*

John Stezaker, Ridinghouse and Whitechapel Gallery, London, 2010

Negotiable Space I, a 1978 collage, combines a film still and a colour picture postcard of a train. The postcard is placed dead centre of the rectangular black-and-white photograph. The instant shock at the disjunction is followed by recognition of the witty take on René Magritte's *Time Transfixed* (1939), in which a train, instead of a stovepipe, emerges from a fireplace. Here, the scene in the still is a psychoanalyst's consulting room, with a portrait of Freud on the wall. The train roars out from a tunnel just where the head of the figure reclining on the analyst's couch should be found. The doctor's room turns out to be more mysterious than it seemed at first, interior and exterior spaces suggesting subtle analogies for the unconscious. What is the dark cross-shape on the wall between Freud and the medicine cabinet? It seems to be cast shadows or the reflection of a window. Why is there a chart with US presidents on the wall beside Freud? Is the still from Hitchcock's *Spellbound* (1945)? Could it be related to the many out-takes of scenes that didn't make it to the final version? There are multiple associations prompted by each image and by their conjunction, and a natural curiosity about their sources. This, however, is just a by-product for John Stezaker. He often does not know where his stills come from, and doesn't directly research them; though he is pleased if, watching an old B-movie on television, he recognises a scene or the actors and can thus identify his still.

After a while, looking at this collage, something quite different arrests the attention: a visual coherence at odds with the visible clash. A very precise conjunction of lines and angles is formed by the railway track at bottom left of the postcard and the edge of the doctor's desk.

It should be, and to an extent is, a clashing of unmatched perspectives, such as one finds in paintings by Giorgio de Chirico, but there is also a sense of matching, a geometrical fitness. The dramatic perspective of the rails disappearing out into the room – our space – to the left is in effect married to the gentler perspective of the desk: the vanishing points of the desk and the train itself are identical. Thus the intersection of unrelated objects in space is achieved by purely pictorial means, and the two images meld despite their total dissimilarity.

Stezaker had already explored the perspectival use of railway tracks in his 'Lost Tracks' series of 1992. Earlier, in 1979, he wrote a series of notes that he called 'A Meeting (On the Horizon)' in connection with his work *Vanishing Point/Vantage Points.*[1] This collage consists of three frames from the flight sequence in Hitchcock's *Psycho* (1960). Here, the road stretches ahead to the horizon and backwards to another horizon reflected in the mirror. Each of the three images are lettered respectively, 'either', 'and', 'or'. In his notes, Stezaker meditates on the vanishing point in film and in the still image: 'The camera – the mobile window. Film – the dissolution of vantage point and spatial continuum into temporal continuum. The vantage point seeks its rest in the Vanishing Point. Vanishing Point = THE END.'[2] Both film and still image are flat projections, but the camera is not necessarily in the same position as the spectator. He continues, in the note entitled 'THE WINDOW':

> The blown-up intersection of vertical and horizontal in the vanishing point. The invisible become visible. The point becomes the frame. (This is the sense of space in the flat projection.) The world projects itself into sight, into frame. We learn to suppress our projection into the world by identifying with the darkness of the frame. The condition of the seeable – our presence in the scene as a kind of absence. Space achieves its objectivity in this way.

Shortly after his notes on 'A Meeting', Stezaker began to combine two images, as in *Negotiable Space I.* There, the spatial resolution through the

1 John Stezaker, 'A Meeting (On the Horizon)', *De Kunst*, Kunstmuseum Luzern, 1979, p.20.
2 *Ibid.*

aligned vanishing points has nothing to do with the spectator (who could be thought of as doubly absent) but is purely internal, something made visible from within each image, through their conjunction.

The comparison with De Chirico, whose contradictory perspectives I referred to above, could be pursued a little further, more to determine difference than similarity. While Stezaker draws out unexpected resemblances and echoes between two images that differ from one another in terms of scale and space, De Chirico presents apparently unified images in which the elements do not cohere spatially. He subverts the conventional rules of pictorial perspective by introducing divergent vanishing points for what appears to be a single scene. The walls of a street or the arcades of a city square, for instance, which seem to belong to the same cityscape, follow different perspectives and are irreconcilable in terms of pictorial spatial logic. They have been described as expressing, and even generating, agoraphobia: the fear of open spaces.

De Chirico, familiar with the fragmentation of pictorial space in Cubist painting, collages and *papiers collés*, carried it into his paintings, which are in a sense painted collages. Stezaker, by contrast, starts with the disparate, with unrelated images from the vast repertoire of film and photography, and finds unexpected connections. This is not to say that contrast, disjunction and clash are not still present, but the purpose, in collages like *Negotiable Space I*, is not so much defamiliarisation as the creation of a quite unexpected continuum, of visual rhymes and of metaphors. In some ways the interplay between the apparently disjunctive pairings are even more startling than the initial clashes.

Stezaker has talked about bringing out the possibilities in any image by linking it to another, and creating a space for contemplation. His use of collage, which is perhaps the most widespread visual mode of the last hundred years, is very distinctive. There are some interesting parallels with other artists, especially with those linked to Dada and Surrealism, and he is immensely knowledgeable about the history of collage. But he has forged a thoroughly individual route, using collage to different effects and in a variety of different ways.

Stezaker's formation as an artist in the late 1960s and early 1970s coincided with a resurgence of earlier twentieth-century avant-garde practices, such as collage and photomontage. He already had an interest in collage, but at the Slade still thought of himself as a painter who used photographs, and liked the work of Gerhard Richter and Sigmar Polke. An unfortunate incident led to the destruction of all his paintings from his student days: they were left at the school over the summer and were destroyed in a fire. He then turned his back on painting and dedicated himself to collage, to collecting and using found images from the massive picture culture of advertisements, postcards, film stills and studio portraits. Popular images had long fascinated him: the fragment from a giant postcard of the clock tower that houses Big Ben in the 1975 collage *The End* had been with him since he was a teenager and was steeped in childhood memories. With its lurid sunset colours it stood for him as the 'apocalyptic possibility of an art subsumed by popular culture'.[3] He had decided that he did not want, as an artist, to add any new images to the world, but would only recycle existing ones.

Stezaker remembers his first encounter with two works that have been long-term resources for him. On his first day at the Slade, William Coldstream showed the new students around the special collections of rare books in the library, among them Max Ernst's collage-novel *Une semaine de bonté* (1933–34) and Giovanni Battista Piranesi's *Carceri* or *Prisons* (late 1740s). Ernst's appropriation of nineteenth-century engravings to create new, complete, powerful and thoroughly disorienting images, Surrealism at its most exciting, is an example Stezaker has nourished. The book of engravings by Piranesi – an artist much admired by the Surrealists – suggested unusual space constructions. Both, of course, are sequences of images, visual books, and as such relevant to Stezaker's preference for working in series and amassing images to make an archive.

While Stezaker was a student, a political and cultural crisis exploded in the events of 1968, and his first year ended with the sit-in at the Slade. Students had been at the forefront of the *évènements* in Paris, and in the UK art schools were also seething with discontent and desire for radical

3 'The Encounter with the Real: John Stezaker in conversation with Krysztof Fijalkowski and Lynda Morris (March 2006)', *John Stezaker: Mask and Shadow*, A Palazzo Gallery, Brescia, 2008, p.26.

change. This cultural alienation found its most influential expression in the writings of Guy Debord and other Situationist International publications, which Stezaker read. Especially striking for him were the modified and re-captioned images, taken from advertisements and other kinds of capitalist promotional spectacles, based on the notion of *détournement*. Debord and Asger Jorn's book, *Fin de Copenhague* (1959), for example, was intended as

> a satirical attack on consumer and technological society, using elements from commercial culture to critique itself. You can sense their disdain when they quoted a text promising that, thanks to electronics, automation and nuclear energy 'we are entering the new Industrial Revolution which will supply our every need, easily, quickly, cheaply, abundantly'.[4]

Books like *Fin de Copenhague* and the *IS* journal used sources 'as diverse as travel brochures, novels, political tracts, and newspapers, and appropriated imagery including photographs, cartoons, maps and old book illustrations.'[5] The challenge for the art student was obvious, and as Stezaker said, the experience became quite schizophrenic; in his academic course at the Slade, he continued to do life drawing with Euan Uglow, while 'entertaining ideas from Guy Debord'.[6] A devastating Situationist analysis of a student's formation, *On the Poverty of Student Life* (1966), described the student's role in modern capitalism as the 'future specialist in a culture of general passivity', passing their time as 'conspicuous cultural consumers of corpses and "anaemic gods": "Art is dead but the student is necrophiliac".'[7] Situationist statements were sometimes obfuscatory but the message was clear: get out of the studio, take action.

The atmosphere was exciting but for the young artist the future was

4 Simon Ford, *The Situationist International: A User's Guide*, Black Dog Publishing, London, 2005, p.60.

5 *Ibid.*, p.63.

6 'Demand the Impossible and More: John Stezaker Speaks with Michael Bracewell', *John Stezaker: Rubell Family Collection*, Rubell Family Collection, Miami, FL, 2007, p.34.

7 Ford, *op. cit.*, p.114 (*De la misère en milieu Ètudiant, considérée sous ses aspects économique, politique, psychologique, sexuel et notamment intellectuel et de quelques moyens pour y remédier*, Strasbourg, 1966; first English translation 1967; quotation from new translation: *On the Poverty of Student Life*, London, 1983.)

alarmingly uncertain. Stezaker had a very brief fling with far-left politics but quickly returned to confront the big problem: 'how can you be an artist in a culture of images?' If the traditional practices like painting were no more than corpses, and readymade images flooded modern life to saturation, what room was there for an artist? In retrospect, the lessons from Uglow, who taught the importance of close scrutiny, of observation, and discussed the absorbing problems of transferring the seen world onto the flat surface, were to be of lasting significance. He must also have been helped to focus on solutions by Richard Wollheim, Professor of Philosophy at University College London, who was not only a brilliant philosopher of aesthetics but also had wide-ranging interests in the history of painting and in contemporary art. Wollheim had published an important essay, 'Minimal Art', in 1965 (in *Arts Magazine*), which addressed Marcel Duchamp and the question of the readymade. Stezaker broke the mould of the graduate art student when he was the first at the Slade to write a dissertation – on Duchamp and Wittgenstein – and has remained a highly independent thinker. He was sceptical of Conceptual art, but has always liked Duchamp, and is critical of the way in which his work and ideas are distorted by 'Duchampianism'. Stezaker was also open to Surrealism at a time when this was a total no-go area in art schools, and recognised how much the Situationists owed to Surrealism.

The Situationists had made him aware of the image culture we live in, and in 1973, the year he left the Slade, he started to recycle readymade imagery. He collected advertising photographs and drawings, often retaining the poster format, and included captions, sometimes adding curious and apparently unrelated texts, as in *Who? What? Why?* (1974), which consisted of four panels of photographs and texts.[8] Although he was working with the same kinds of material as Pop artists, it was to different ends. Rather than uncritically embracing the transient, expendable, sexy and gimmicky readily available in popular culture, he was taking a critical and thoughtful look at it.[9] The effect was subversive and ironic but not quite in the Situationist manner. As Brian Hatton wrote in 1979, Stezaker 'seems always to have been more interested [than Burgin]

8 Stezaker, Luzern, *op. cit.*, p.7.

9 See Richard Hamilton, 'Letter to the Smithsons (16 January 1957)', quoted in Gablik and Russell (eds), *Pop Art Redefined*, Thames & Hudson, London, 1969, p.33.

in the ambiguous life of the dreams in the original commercial material, and the way that they often seemed to parody and exploit the dream of the 'liberated' modern artist himself.'[10] He has not, in the end, been averse to the glamorous and witty in popular imagery, but has cut deep into what he thinks of as the collective unconscious, 'a sharded yet collective fabric of dreams, stereotypes, behavioural and social projections, all registered and mediated in the common currency of photographic reproduction.'[11]

Captions were crucial to the appropriated images in Stezaker's work between 1973 and 1976. As Walter Benjamin had argued, regarding photographs in picture magazines, 'captions have become obligatory. And it is clear that they have an altogether different character than the title of a painting.'[12] They were 'directives', assigning meaning to the photograph. The Situationists, like the Dadaists before them, confronted and tried to expose the debased rhetoric of language in a consumer society and its role in masking the fake nature of the spectacle. Debord wrote in *Society of the Spectacle* (1967): 'The entire destruction of language can here be found flatly acknowledged as an official positive value, since the task is to advertise a reconciliation with the dominant state of things, where all communication is joyously proclaimed to be absent…'[13]

But Stezaker became increasingly dissatisfied with the image's assumed dependence on language. This did not seem to him to correspond to the potential in images to register, to arrest and engage the attention, in ways that could not be fully accounted for in words. A caption gives one meaning to a photograph but closes off others. A collage of 1976, *Le Mot* (The Word), is a humorous comment in the manner of Magritte on the relationship between word and image, between painted, named and 'real' things. An obvious homage to Magritte's 'Ceci n'est pas une pipe', it has the word 'le' (the), a preposition without a noun, a conundrum without solution: 'put that in your pipe and smoke it.'

10 Brian Hatton, 'John Stezaker's Photomontage: The Image and The Cut', *John Stezaker*, 1979, p.viii.
11 *Ibid.* p.viii.
12 Walter Benjamin, 'The Work of Art in the Age of Mechanical Reproduction', *Illuminations*, Fontana, London, 1973, p.228.
13 Hatton, *op. cit.*, p.vii.

Stezaker agreed with Mircea Eliade's statement:

> If the mind makes use of images to grasp the ultimate reality of things, it is just because reality manifests itself in contradictory ways and therefore cannot be expressed in concepts... To translate an image into concrete terminology by restricting it to any one of its frames of reference is to do worse than mutilate it – it is to annihilate it, to annul it as an instrument of cognition.[14]

After 1976 Stezaker abandoned captions. The most extreme example of caption-less images, no title, no interpretation, no comment, is *The 3rd Person Archive*: small, haunting photo-fragments of unidentified figures in unnamed places. In an interview Stezaker explained that the fragments are figures cut out of topographical photographs, firstly from a pre-war *Photographic Atlas of World Geography* and later from Victorian examples.[15] Incidental to the photographer's purpose and peripheral to his vision, the figures are caught usually in motion, in streets and squares, oblivious to the camera that is usually above them. Some are so tiny as to be almost invisible. There is a disturbing combination of surveillance and anonymity; these overlooked beings seem helpless, at the mercy of forces beyond their control, while at the same time the fragment is intimate and close-by, showing often a single figure. The collages are Stezaker's, but the photo-fragments are as anonymous as the people.

Stezaker works in series, which have a habit of remaining open over a long period. The 2007 'Masks', for example, continue an investigation begun in 1982 with *Mask X*: a portrait head, perhaps of a circus trapeze artist, with a picture postcard of a bridge over a river superimposed on the head. This striking image effortlessly floats the metaphor of face/landscape: the double arches of the bridge are the eyebrows, the central stanchion the

14 *Ibid.*, p.ix.

15 'Conversation between David Lillington, John Stezaker and William Horner', *John Stezaker; Fumetti*, GAK, Bremen, and Verlag der Buchhandlung Walther König, Cologne, 2008, p.89; Stezaker began to mount the fragments into the archive in 1976.

nose, and so on. In *Sonata* (2009) the bush is a minutely accurate metaphor for the hair, the substitution suppressing the need for the notion 'like'. Metaphor, unlike simile, has no 'primary' term: the two things brought together are equal. In the background there is an awareness of Salvador Dalí's 'double images', in which a single configuration can be read in two or more ways. Stezaker owned a copy of Dalí's *Communication: Paranoiac Face* (1935), the postcard of an African hut in which Dalí had 'seen' a Cubist painting by Picasso. In the 'Pair' collages of 2007, the picturesque landscape postcards that obscure and mask the faces take on an additional symbolic value. Two of these feature rivers surrounded by high banks, which seem to indicate division, separation, and send the viewer back to the couple in the original photograph, to realise that aggression and threat as much as desire might have been the trope here. In a series of 'Masks' of 2005, the photo-portraits, this time of single figures, are covered by the postcard of a landscape feature. Here too, the 'masking' landscapes work as visual doubles of the hidden faces, the formal 'resemblances' to invisible features as striking as their symbolic value (the 'icy' beauty in *Mask XXXV*, or the 'craggy' hero in *Mask VII*). There's a dash of cruelty in the film portrait series 'Marriage' and 'Betrayal'; in the male-female gender combines, stereotypes are mercilessly exposed as well as disconcerting likenesses in supposed opposites.

Stezaker works purely with found images, which he takes out of circulation and returns, altered, in a different context. He combines, cuts, masks and repeats, using only two images, usually, very occasionally three, and sometimes, as in *The 3rd Person Archive*, only one, to reveal the latent possibilities. Inviting us to stop and look again is to work against the grain of a speeded-up and proliferating image culture. He talks about trying to arrest the flow, and in connection with this refers to Duchamp's idea of 'delay'.[16] The resistance, the *arrêt*, that appeals to Stezaker is linked not so much to the 'anti-art' aspect of Duchamp's stance as to his response to the ambiguous position of the artist in modernity, and to the marriage of idea and material in his work. Duchamp arrived, as André Breton put it, at the critical point faster than anyone else. His acknowledgement

16 Marcel Duchamp used this term to explain why the *Large Glass* was not a painting: it was a 'delay in glass'. This is one of many hints in Duchamp's *Green Box* notes, published in 1934, about the relationship between photography and the *Large Glass*.

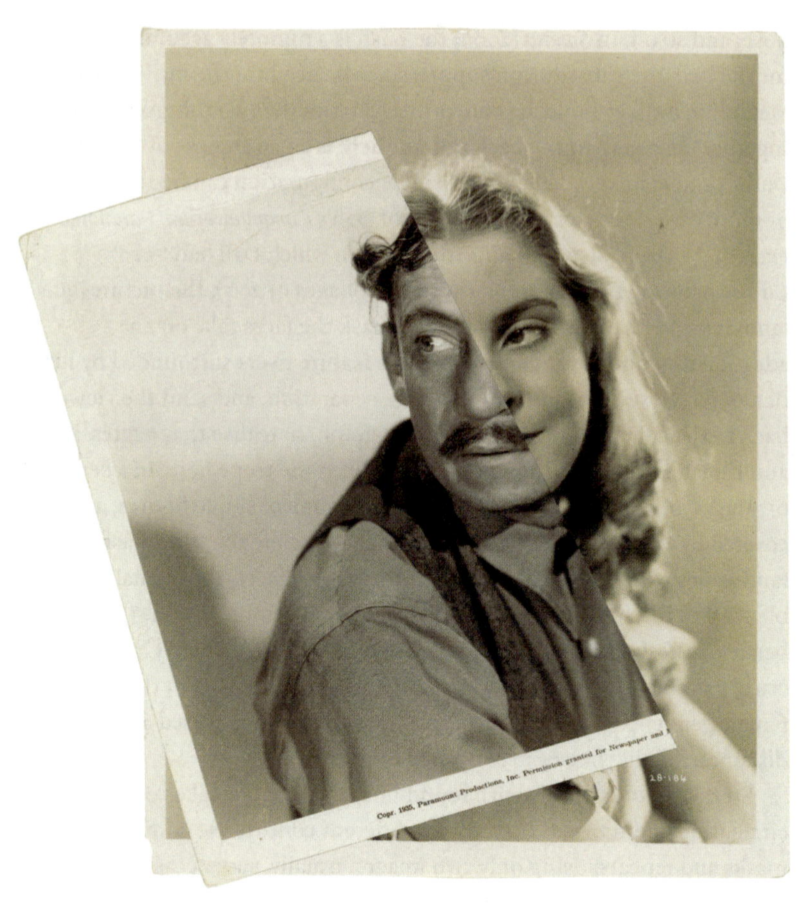

580 **John Stezaker**
Marriage (Film Portrait Collage) LVI, 2007
Collage
25.8 × 23.8 cm | 10⅛ × 9⅜ in

that the artist 'in the age of mechanical reproduction' had definitively to change was many-faceted if also minimal. He questioned the purely retinal bias of painting (which he finally abandoned in 1918), slowed work on his *Large Glass, The Bride Stripped Bare by her Bachelors, Even* (1915–23) which he described as a 'delay in glass' rather than a picture or painting, selected the odd readymade, tinkered with films, made it possible to use anything to make art, and relished experimenting with materials as well as sometimes choosing slightly out-of-date techniques, such as *pochoirs*, or stencils. Duchamp occasionally used photographs, and photography itself was a constant point of theoretical and metaphorical reference in his notes as the greatest challenge to painting: the 'delay in glass', after all, is also the timed photographic exposure in the days of the glass negative. But if the idea of the 'delay' for Duchamp was linked to the 'timing' of photography, for Stezaker, in what might be described as a post-photography as well as a post-painting era, it implies a pause, an invitation to look closely at what can be done to the material, readymade image. In a sense it is paradoxically a return to the retinal, to the exercise of the eyes, and Stezaker acknowledges that the lessons he learned with Euan Uglow have retained a precious quality for him.

Stezaker prefers the term collage to photomontage, which he dislikes. There is no cut and dried definition of either term that would easily justify his preference, though there are several possible arguments that can support it. Historically, the term photomontage is linked both to the Russian Constructivists and to Dada in Berlin, and also has associations with Sergei Eisenstein's and Lev Kuleshov's theories of montage in film. Stezaker admits he is a *monteur*, the term Georg Grosz and John Heartfield appropriated from engineering – a 'fitter', but not with its anti-art overtones. The difference between collage and photomontage cannot be defined solely through technical issues: Dada photomontages, for example, are not restricted to photographs but very often used non-photographic materials, cuttings from newspapers, etc. It was the political uses of photomontage – which have on the whole dominated its historical reception – that were alien to Stezaker, not so much because of the politics as the effect on art and the image itself. A 1925 text, *Die Kunst ist in Gefahr* (Art is in Danger) by Grosz and Wieland Herzfelde, pinpoints the situation at the time. Dada and its products, they write, had appeared to be worthless nonsense, and it was only later that they realised a system underlay the nonsense and was exposed by it. This was capitalism:

> The approaching revolution brought a gradual recognition of this system. There was no further ground for laughter. There were weightier problems than that of art. If art were to retain any meaning it must subordinate itself to these problems...[17]

For art to retain its value, they believed, it had to turn inventions like photomontage to political purpose. This is what Heartfield did, developing it in the 1930s into a pro-Communist and anti-Nazi weapon. The main reason, I think, for Stezaker's dislike of Heartfield, is the very effectiveness of his use of photographs for political propaganda, the photographic image locked forever into a specific emotional and intellectual appeal. He likes, however, another of the Berlin Dadaists, Hannah Höch, in particular her photomontage *Da-Dandy* (1919), where fragmented images of women's heads are juxtaposed in an arc, eyes and mouths appear on different scale and the whole configuration forms the silhouette of a man outlined in red. Her work is closer in spirit to Stezaker's interest in unlocking the possibilities of an image than Heartfield's airbrushed photographs, combined to simulate a 'real' scene that exposes the lies in political rhetoric, but remains dependent on its caption. The history of photomontage highlights the dilemma that dominated art in the 1920s and 1930s, and it was uniquely felt by the Surrealists, who continued against opposition from right and left to maintain the value of art, and also of laughter. From the perspective of the Surrealists, 'photomontage' came to be closely identified with the Communist Party, which they had lost faith in by the early 1930s.

Breton's preference for the work of Max Ernst, who had had little time for Berlin Dada, lay in the shared understanding of a very different

17 George Grosz and Wieland Herzfelde, *Die Kunst ist in Gefahr*, Malik, Berlin, 1925 (author's translation).

collage practice. Breton summarised it as follows: '...the marvellous faculty of attaining two widely separate realities without departing from the realm of our experience, of bringing them together and drawing a spark from their contact... of disorienting us in our own memory by depriving us of a frame of reference...'[18]. This was written about Ernst's 1919–20 collages, in which Breton recognised visual analogues of the poetic image created by the juxtaposition of the dissimilar and distant; this was to be the basis of the Surrealist image, with the proviso that such images could only be reached via automatic processes. Ernst claimed that these collages – where fragments of bodies and things cluster or float, and change identity in strange landscapes or skies – had been created without any preconceptions, but spontaneously, from the rapid flicking through illustrated books of geology, anatomy etc. Stezaker too talks about an intuitive leap in the making of his collages, which may be rationalised afterwards. Sometimes rather than emphasising transformation, difference and contrast, his collages are based on pairing, on combining 'like with like'. In this way he is closer, perhaps, to the collages of Joseph Cornell, whose 'soap box' assemblages and films such as *Rose Hobart* Stezaker also admires.

The relationship between collage and film is enormously complex. The whole history of twentieth-century art could be seen in terms of responses to, defences against and challenges to the moving image. From this point of view photography could be invoked on either side of the lines – and in some respects it is exactly in this ambiguous area that Stezaker intervenes. Film was linked to collage from the start. Dada photomontages often include a strip of celluloid, as though they are reflecting on their own connection with film in the rejection of a fixed viewpoint and temporal coherence. Breton, writing of Ernst in 1921, described his collages as 'the most captivating film in the world':

18 André Breton, 'Max Ernst', *Max Ernst Beyond Painting*, Wittenborn, Schultz, New York, NY, 1948, p.177. (Preface to the first exhibition of Ernst collages, which the artist dubbed *Fatagaga*, in Paris, 1921).

> As the use of slow motion and fast motion cameras becomes more general, as we grow accustomed to seeing oaks spring up and antelopes floating through the air, we begin to foresee... what this time-space of which people are talking may be.[19]

What Breton saw as magical, Walter Benjamin thought barbarous. Dada works were useless for 'contemplative immersion', their poems were 'word salad' containing obscenities... The same is true of their paintings, on which they mounted buttons and tickets.'[20] In achieving the destruction of the aura of their creations, Benjamin opined, their works of art 'hit the spectator like a bullet'. In doing so, they created a demand for film, the 'distracting element of which is also primarily tactile.' The 'barbarisms' of Dada anticipated film; they were characteristic of the way an impulse in art may aspire to effects the technology cannot yet satisfy, but whereby a demand is created. 'Dadaism attempted to create by pictorial – and literary – means the effects which the public today seeks in the film.' Comparing the screen with a canvas, he goes on: 'The painting invites the spectator to contemplation; before it the spectator can abandon himself to his associations. Before the movie frame he cannot do so...'[21] The projective, aggressive power of collage, like film, in Benjamin's view, destroys any possibility of thoughtful response.

Stezaker effectively reverses the relationship caricatured by Benjamin. In his collages, which encompass a huge variety of effects, he aims to restore to the image a 'provisional space of repose', to pin it down, temporarily, to attempt to 'build a place of contemplation and transcendence in this space of continuous movement.'[22] The film stills in Stezaker's collages are just that – still. At first sight, this quality is puzzling as one tries to connect it to its original cinematic narrative. In a very illuminating essay on 'The Film Still and its Double: Reflections on the "Found" Film Still', Stezaker clarifies the relationship between the still (or 'production shot') and the single film frame, or photogram, 'with which they are sometimes confused.'[23] The former are not, as is often mistakenly believed, frozen

19 *Ibid.*
20 Benjamin, *op. cit.*, p.239.
21 *Ibid.*, p.240.
22 Stezaker, *Rubell Family Collection*, *op. cit.*, p.38.

moments from the actual film, but posed shots photographed usually just after a cinematic take. The difference is crucial: the film still resembles an old-fashioned *tableau vivant* with fixed poses and exaggerated gestures, rather than a moment captured from the relative naturalism of a rolling scene. But this also raises the question of the relationship between the narrative arts of cinema and painting. Stezaker was intrigued by a study comparing the film still and cinematic close-ups with baroque realism and Dutch genre painting. The study traced iconic cinematic moments, such as the prelude to a kiss, to Dutch genre painting, and raised fascinating comparisons between painting and photography, for example the ability of painting to contain and concentrate the pregnant moment, and the treacherous indexicality of the photographic image. Film stills, he writes, 'are reminiscent of the problems of representing movement within a tradition of narrative representation that antecedes both film and photography.'[24] They resemble, in other words, paintings, or sculpture like the *Laocoön* (early first century BC), whose achievement is a 'hold on action', a kind of image synthesis of the before and after of 'now'. In the cinema, with its 'double momentum of action and viewpoint', this disappears. The stills may be failures in these terms but nonetheless are the site for 'the return of the repressed detail'. They expose the constructedness of the scene, sometimes with the corner of the studio visible, with the exaggerated expressions and stiff poses of the actors, but at the same time can reveal the origin of stereotype images such as the seduction scene, the close-up film kiss, the trial. The film still even makes possible, Stezaker suggests, a return to 'pre-photographic stillness'.

In *The Trial (The Oath)* (1978) and *The Trial* (1978), picture postcards pasted over the courtroom scenes intercede classic images of famous landmarks in the claustrophobic interiors. In *The Trial*, the postcard showing the 'mirrored calm of the River Cam as it flows under the Bridge of Sighs' echoes the stillness of the drama.[25] Cutting directly across the female witness who is the focus of the film still, the postcard also mirrors rather

23 Stezaker, 'The Film Still and its Double: Reflections on the "Found" Film Still', in David Green and Joanna Lowry (eds), *Stillness and Time: Photography and the Moving Image*, Photoforum and Photoworks, Brighton, 2006, p.114.

24 *Ibid.*, p.117.

25 Mark Coetzee, 'The Gaze Interrupted', *Rubell Family Collection*, *op. cit.*, p.14.

ironically her calm countenance – presumably in the face of vicious questioning from the counsel whose face it hides. However, the juxtaposition of the two images goes beyond the formal and the emotive, and associations multiply: this Bridge of Sighs at St John's College in Cambridge was named after the notorious bridge in Venice that led from the council chamber in the Doge's Palace across a canal to the dungeons. So one stereotyped tourist postcard pasted over a stiff film still suddenly releases associations that, regardless of the actual story of the forgotten film, arouse feelings of anxiety or sympathy normally foreign to such images.

In *The Trial (The Oath)*, another 'incident' from the same set of courtroom film stills is interrupted by a postcard of classical ruins photographed at sunset. Associations, again, abound, and the tenor of the intervention is ambivalent. On the one hand, the upright figure of the woman raising her hand to take the oath seems to be in the same spirit as the noble arcade of columns, and she even appears to be holding up this scene of ancient grandeur. On the other hand the fragment of classical architecture shows up the debased classicism of its distant descendant in the courtroom: the moulded wood panelling, the heavy curves of the balustrade on the left and the rudimentary posts and railing of the witness stand. Something about the latter echoes grimly the arcade: thoughts of bars, of frames, of enclosure bring out those of freedom, justice, hollowness and betrayal through the juxtaposition of imagery. One's attention is constantly arrested by visual comparisons, metaphors and even hints at allegories. This, though, is obviously a very personal response. My associations will not necessarily be shared by others, nor are they necessarily what the collage's maker had in mind. But this is, I would argue, part of the power of these collages. In films, at least since the dominance of Hollywood, the story takes over and determines the viewer's response. Even in films with scenes as carefully composed as those by Hitchcock there is no time to savour the image and the medium. In Stezaker's collages, the viewer neither floats off into fantasies nor is locked into a predetermined narrative, but constantly returns to the image and its visible, now static, forms and structures. As the film still itself now belongs to a distant moment in cinema culture, there is a fascinating double distancing in the collages. Obsolete, the film still has the potential to make visible the 'always in the past' cinematic experience as well as forming the basis for a new image.

Stezaker, like the Surrealists, cherishes the obsolete. He comments on Breton's interest in 'the revelatory power of obsolete objects', which he sees as linked to their loss of function. In addition to Stezaker's now massive collection of film stills, he also has a hoard of vintage studio portraits of actors and actresses. In a secondhand shop he once came across two boxes of these redundant photographs, labelled respectively 'Film Portraits' and 'Film Stills', and retained these titles for his series.[26] The 'Film Portrait' collages are brilliant and often very funny investigations of the human face. At a stroke the pampered glamour of the film stars' masks is subverted, and quite unexpected characters with a dual aspect emerge. They do, as has been suggested, bear a disconcerting resemblance to shamanic transformation, in which the animal 'other' of a human is revealed. In one Olmec statue from Pre-Columbian Mexico, for example, the face of a standing human figure is stripped away to uncover the jaguar head beneath, whose power the shaman is able to share. The mask does not necessarily hide, but may be the 'real', in this belief system. Despite the occasional, probably fortuitous, hint at the animal in the 'Film Portrait' collages, the faces are all human; some of the pairings mix gender, others combine male with male, female with female. The ambiguity of reality and masquerade is retained through the balance of the two components. The faces are not fragmented with combinations of features like eyes and nose of different scales, as in the photomontages of Höch or Richard Hamilton, but are instead chosen to align as closely as possible. Mouth, or nose, often, runs continuously from one face to the other, the two minutely matched, or married, but this then heightens the mismatch elsewhere – eyes facing in different directions, a monstrous chin, profile nose on a three-quarter face, and so on. As in *Negotiable Space I*, with which I began, the initial scrupulous, internal marriage of forms runs up against the juxtaposition of unlike images to exhilarating effect. Stezaker has succeeded in pinning down and pausing the speeded-up world of popular images as we contemplate his collages, and the longer we look, the more absorbing they become.

26 Cecilia Järdemar, 'Unspeakable Faces', *John Stezaker: Marriage,* Ridinghouse, London, 2007, p.7.

The temptation to rewrite or at least revise earlier essays probably should have been succumbed to in some cases but I have resisted it because of the potential knock-on effect. The only changes are a few corrections to glaring errors and an occasional additional footnote. There are more overlaps and repetitions than I would have wished – the enduring obsessions are all too obvious. But I hope there are advantages to the heterogeneity of a collection of essays which address a range of topics from different perspectives over time.

Art and Power

Dawn Ades, *Art in Latin America: The Modern Era, 1820–1980*, exhibition catalogue, Yale University Press, New Haven, CT, and London, 1989

Abstraction

'Making Visible: Abstract Drawing', in Richard Deacon (ed), *Abstract Drawing: Curated by Richard Deacon*, exhibition catalogue, Ridinghouse and Drawing Room, London, 2014, pp.106–17

Surrealism

Dawn Ades (ed), *Dada and Surrealism Reviewed*, Hayward Gallery, Arts Council of Great Britain, London, 1978

'Between Dada and Surrealism: Painting in the Mouvement flou', in Terry Ann R. Neff (ed), *In the Mind's Eye: Dada and Surrealism*, Museum of Contemporary Art Chicago, Chicago, IL, 1984, pp.23–41

'The Transcendental Surrealism of Joseph Cornell', in Kynaston McShine (ed), *Joseph Cornell*, exhibition catalogue, Museum of Modern Art, New York, NY, 1980, pp.14–41

Dawn Ades, *The Colour of My Dreams: The Surrealist Revolution in Art*, Vancouver Art Gallery, Vancouver, 2011

'Preface', in David Gascoyne, *A Short Survey of Surrealism* (1935), Enitharmon Press, London, 2000

'Visions de la matière: Breton, Cubisme et Surréalisme', in *Pleine Marge*, no.13, June 1991, pp.23–37

Dawn Ades and Simon Baker (eds), *Undercover Surrealism: Georges Bataille and Documents*, exhibition catalogue, Hayward Publishing, London, 2006

'Surrealism Discovers Earnshaw', in Les Cloeman (ed), *Anthony Earnshaw: The Imp of Surrealism*, Research Group for Artists Publications, Ripley, 2011

'"We who have neither church nor country": César Moro and Surrealism', in Dawn Ades, Rita Eder and Graciela Speranza (eds), *Surrealism in Latin America: Vivísimo muerto*, Getty Research Institute, Los Angeles, CA, 2012

'DYN: An Introduction', *Farewell to Surrealism: The DYN Circle in Mexico*, Annette Leddy and Donna Conwell (ed), Getty Research Institute, Los Angeles, CA, 2012

Gender and Identity

'Afterword', in José Pierre (ed), *Investigating Sex: Surrealist Discussions 1928–1932*, trans. Malcolm Imrie, Verso, London, 1992

'Introduction' in A. Brotchie (ed), *3 New York Dadas and The Blind Man*, Atlas Press, London, 2014

Dalí

Salvador Dalí, World of Art Series, Thames & Hudson, London, 1982

Dawn Ades and Fiona Bradley (eds), *Salvador Dalí: A Mythology*, exhibition catalogue, Tate Gallery, London, 1998

Dawn Ades (ed), *Dalí's Optical Illusions*, Wadsworth Atheneum Museum of Art and Yale University Press, New Haven, CT, and London, 2000

Dawn Ades (ed), *Salvador Dalí: The Centenary Retrospective*, Thames & Hudson, London, 2004

The Photographic Image

'Photography and the Surrealist Text', in Rosalind Krauss and Jane Livingston (eds), *L'Amour fou: Photography and Surrealism*, Abbeville Press, New York, NY, 1985, pp.155–92

'One Hundred Percent Photographic', in *In Wonderland: The Surrealist Adventures of Women Artists in Mexico and the United States*, Los Angeles County Museum of Art, Los Angeles, CA; Museo de Arte Moderno, Mexico City and Prestel, New York, 2012

TEXT CREDITS

Introduction from *Photomontage* by Dawn Ades. © 1976 Thames and Hudson Ltd, London. Reprinted by kind permission of Thames & Hudson: pp.35–66

Courtesy Hayward Publishing: pp.89–106, 433–73

Courtesy Abbeville Press, New York and Walker Art Center, Minneapolis: pp.113–58

The original publisher of this text is Yale University Press. © 1989 the South Bank Centre and the authors: pp.161–71

Courtesy British Council: pp.173–79

© 1985 The Trustees of the Tate Gallery and Thames & Hudson Ltd, London: pp.213–42

Courtesy Tate Publishing, London. Reprinted by kind permission of Tate Trustees: pp.213–42, 371–93, 475–504, 543–69

Courtesy The Trustees of the British Museum: pp.245–53

Courtesy Hayward Publishing, Royal Pavilion & Museums, Brighton & Hove and Lund Humphries: pp.255–79

© 2007, Marquette University, Milwaukee, Wisconsin and Haggerty Museum of Art: pp.281–97

Courtesy Moscow Kremlin Museums: pp.299–318

Courtesy Museo Thyssen-Bornemisza, Madrid: pp.321–41

'Duchamp's Masquerades', *The Portrait in Photography*, ed. Graham Clarke, Reaktion Books, London, 1992, pp.94–114. © Reaktion Books 1992: pp.347–68

Courtesy of The MIT Press, from *Mirror Images: Women, Surrealism, and Self-Representation*, ed. Whitney Chadwick, The MIT Press, Cambridge and London, 1998: pp.395–413

The publisher credits Dawn Ades 'Hannah Höch and the "New Woman"', originally published in *Hannah Höch: Works on Paper*, Whitechapel Gallery, London and Prestel Verlag, Munich, 2014: pp.415–26

Commissioned and first published by The Fruitmarket Gallery, Edinburgh: pp.511–41

Courtesy Whitechapel Gallery, London and Ridinghouse, London: pp.571–87

IMAGE CREDITS

© The Heartfield Community of Heirs/ VG Bild-Kunst, Bonn and DACS, London 2015: pp.34, 68

John Heartfield (1891–1968)/Private Collection/The Bridgeman Art Library: p.34

© ADAGP, Paris and DACS, London 2015: pp.58, 75, 85 (top and bottom), 254 (top left), 280, 288, 336–37, 380

© 2015. Digital image, The Museum of Modern Art, New York/Scala, Florence: pp.58, 112, 132, 288, 350, 353, 529, 561

Museum of Modern Art, New York. Purchase. Acc. n.: 282.1937: p.58

© Estate of George Grosz, Princeton, NJ/ DACS, 2015. Dada-Zeitschriften-Reprint, Hamburg: Edition Nautilus, 1978. Private collection: p.68

Collection: Courtesy International Dada Archive, Special Collections, University of Iowa Libraries: p.75

© DACS 2015: pp.82–85, 124, 132, 408, 414, 421

Kunstbibliothek, Staatliche Museen zu Berlin. Inventory No: WR_03522_01. Photographer: Willy Roemer. © 2015. Photo Scala, Florence/BPK, Bildagentur fuer Kunst, Kultur und Geschichte, Berlin: p.88

Archives nationales/pôle image: p.94

© Albert Harlingue/Roger-Viollet: p.98

Museum of Modern Art, New York. Arthur Drexler Fund 173.1991: p.112

Henry van de Velde (1863–1957)/Private Collection/Photo © Christie's Images/ Bridgeman Images: p.124

Museum of Modern Art, New York. 205.1968: p.132

Universal History Archive/UIG/The Bridgeman Art Library: p.137

First international exhibition of Madí Art at Réalités Nouvelles, Paris, 1948: p.160

© Gyula Kosice. © Philippe Migeat – Centre Pompidou, MNAM-CCI (diffusion RMN): p.169

© the artist; courtesy, Lisson Gallery, London: pp.172, 177

Courtesy the artist and Galerie Peter Kilchmann, Zurich: pp.180, 183, 188

Private collection. Photo: FXP, London: p.188

Photo: Prudence Cuming: p.196

The Big Toe/Jacques-André Boiffard/Photo © Centre Pompidou, MNAM-CCI, Dist. RMN-Grand Palais/Phillippe Migeat. © Mme Denise Boiffard: p.202

Collection Musée National d'Art Moderne – Centre Georges Pompidou: p.202

Francis Bacon (1909–1992). Tate, London. Presented by Eric Hall 1953. Photo © Tate, London 2015: p.212

© The Estate of Francis Bacon. All rights reserved. DACS 2015. Photo: Hugo Maertens: p.231

© Trustees of the Paolozzi Foundation, Licensed by DACS 2015: p.244

© Salvador Dalí, Fundació Gala-Salvador Dalí, DACS, 2015: pp.254 (top right), 432–74, 488, 498, 510

© Man Ray Trust/ADAGP, Paris and DACS, London 2015: pp.254 (bottom), 554–55, front cover

© Wifredo Lam Estate: pp.280, 288

Museum of Modern Art, New York. Inter-American Fund. Acc. n.:140.1945: p.288

Reproduced by permission of The Henry Moore Foundation: pp.298, 309, 316

Photo: Errol Jackson: p.309

Photo: Menor Creative Imaging: p.316

© Successió Miró/ADAGP, Paris and DACS London 2015. Metropolitan Museum of Art, New York. The Pierre and Maria-Gaetana Matisse Collection, 2002 (2002.456.5): p.320

© 2015. Image copyright The Metropolitan Museum of Art/Art Resource/Scala, Florence: pp.320, 555
Private collection: pp.336–37
© Man Ray Trust ARS-ADAGP. The J. Paul Getty Museum, Los Angeles: p.346
© Succession Marcel Duchamp/ADAGP, Paris and DACS, London 2015: pp.350, 353, 542, 561, front cover
Museum of Modern Art, New York. Gift of the Pasadena Art Museum 749.1963: p.350
Museum of Modern Art, New York. Gift of the artist. Acc. n.: 3.1939: p.353
Collection: Courtesy of the Jersey Heritage Collections: p.390
© 2015. Banco de México Diego Rivera Frida Kahlo Museums Trust, Mexico, D.F./DACS. © 2015. Photo Art Resource/Bob Schalkwijk/Scala, Florence. Collection: Fundacion Dolores Olmedo, Mexico City: p.394
NG 57/61. Photo: Jörg P. Anders. © 2015. Photo Scala, Florence/BPK, Bildagentur fuer Kunst, Kultur und Geschichte, Berlin. Collection: Nationalgalerie, Staatliche Museum, Berlin: p.414
Scottish National Gallery of Modern Art: p.421
Salvador Dalí (1904–1989)/Museo Nacional Centro de Arte Reina Sofia, Madrid, Spain/Index/The Bridgeman Art Library: p.432
Collection: Museo Nacional Centro de Arte Reina Sofia, Madrid, Spain: pp.432, 455, 498
Salvador Dalí, Dibujos de Trovador cubista y personaje, con anotación de Federico García Lorca, 1928. Collection: Fundación Federico García Lorca, Madrid: p.445
Salvador Dalí/Private Collection/Giraudon/The Bridgeman Art Library: p.474
© Hattula Moholy-Nagy/DACS 2015: p.481
© Wadsworth Atheneum Museum of Art/Art Resource. Collection: Wadsworth Atheneum Museum of Art. The Ella Gallup Sumner and Mary Catlin Sumner Collection Fund. 1939.269: p.488
Photographic Archives Museo Nacional Centro de Arte Reina Sofia: p.498
Buñuel Institute: p.510
© Museum of the History of Science, University of Oxford: p.517
Plate X from *Micrographie décorative*, plate (each): 20.6 × 21.6 cm. Collection: National Gallery of Australia, Canberra. Purchased 2005: p.527
Museum of Modern Art, New York. Thomas Walther Collection. Purchase. Acc.n.: 1626.2001: p.529
Brassaï/*Involuntary Sculptures*/© Estate Brassaï – RMN-Grand Palais. Photo © RMN-Grand Palais/Jean-Gilles Berizzi. Private collection: p.539
Staatsgalerie Stuttgart, Graphische Sammlung. © Foto: Staatsgalerie Stuttgart: p.542
La Femme/Man Ray/Photo © Centre Pompidou, MNAM-CCI, Dist. RMN-Grand Palais/Bertrand Prévost. Collection: Musée National d'Art Moderne – Centre Georges Pompidou: p.554
The Metropolitan Museum of Art, New York. Gilman Collection, Gift of The Howard Gilman Foundation, 2005 (2005.100.206): p.555
Museum of Modern Art, New York. Katherine S. Dreier Bequest. Acc. n.:152.1953: p.561
© John Stezaker, courtesy of The Approach, London: pp.570, 580
© Carla Borel: back flap

Published in 2015 by Ridinghouse
46 Lexington Street
London W1F 0LP
United Kingdom
ridinghouse.co.uk

Ridinghouse Publisher: Doro Globus
Publishing Manager: Louisa Green
Publishing Assistant: Daniel Griffiths

Distributed in the UK and Europe by
Cornerhouse Publications
c/o Home
2 Tony Wilson Place
Manchester M15 4FN
United Kingdom
cornerhousepublications.org

Distributed in the US by
RAM Publications + Distribution, Inc.
2525 Michigan Avenue Building A2
Santa Monica, CA 90404
United States
rampub.com

British Library Cataloguing-in-Publication Data
A full catalogue record of this book is available from the British Library

ISBN 978 1 905464 63 0

Edited by Doro Globus
Proofread by Eileen Daly and
Gerrie van Noord
Reprographics by Dexter Premedia

Designed by Mark Thomson
Set in Haultin and Ludwig (Fred Smeijers)
Printed in Latvia by Livonia Print

The Henry Moore
Foundation

Ridinghouse